Texts for Preaching

Year B

Also published by Westminster John Knox Press

Texts for Preaching:
A Lectionary Commentary Based on the NRSV—
Year A

by Walter Brueggemann, Charles B. Cousar,
Beverly R. Gaventa, and James D. Newsome

Texts for Preaching:
A Lectionary Commentary Based on the NRSV—
Year C

by Charles B. Cousar, Beverly R. Gaventa,
J. Clinton McCann, Jr., and James D. Newsome

TEXTS FOR PREACHING

*A Lectionary Commentary
Based on the NRSV*

YEAR B

Walter Brueggemann, Charles B. Cousar,
Beverly R. Gaventa, James D. Newsome

© 1993 Westminster John Knox Press

2014 paperback edition
Originally published in hardback in the United States
by Westminster John Knox Press in 1993
Louisville, Kentucky

14 15 16 17 18 19 20 21 22 23 — 10 9 8 7 6 5 4 3 2 1

All rights reserved. No part of this book may be reproduced or transmitted in any form or by any means, electronic or mechanical, including photocopying, recording, or by any information storage or retrieval system, without permission in writing from the publisher. For information, address Westminster John Knox Press, 100 Witherspoon Street, Louisville, Kentucky 40202–1396. Or contact us online at www.wjkbooks.com.

Acknowledgments will be found on page viii.

Book design by Drew Stevens

Library of Congress Cataloging-in-Publication Data

Texts for preaching : a lectionary commentary, based on the NRSV, Year B / Walter Brueggemann . . . [et al.].
    p.   cm.
ISBN: 0-664-21970-5

  1. Lectionary preaching. 2. Bible—Commentaries.
I. Brueggemann,Walter.
BV4235.L43T488 1993
251—dc20   93-8023
ISBN: 978-0-664-23916-9 (v. 1 paperback)
ISBN: 978-0-664-23917-6 (v. 2 paperback)
ISBN: 978-0-664-23687-8 (v. 3 paperback)

♾ This book is printed on acid-free paper that meets the American National Standards Institute Z39.48 standard.

Contents

Preface		vii
Acknowledgments		ix

First Sunday of Advent		1
Second Sunday of Advent		11
Third Sunday of Advent		21
Fourth Sunday of Advent		31

Christmas, First Proper		41
Christmas, Second Proper		50
Christmas, Third Proper		59
First Sunday After Christmas		68
Second Sunday After Christmas		78

Epiphany			87
First Sunday After Epiphany *(Baptism of the Lord)*		Ordinary Time 1	96
Second Sunday After Epiphany		Ordinary Time 2	105
Third Sunday After Epiphany		Ordinary Time 3	115
Fourth Sunday After Epiphany		Ordinary Time 4	125
Fifth Sunday After Epiphany		Ordinary Time 5	134
Sixth Sunday After Epiphany	Proper 1	Ordinary Time 6	143
Seventh Sunday After Epiphany	Proper 2	Ordinary Time 7	152
Eighth Sunday After Epiphany	Proper 3	Ordinary Time 8	162
Last Sunday After Epiphany *(Transfiguration Sunday)*			172

Ash Wednesday	182
First Sunday in Lent	191
Second Sunday in Lent	201
Third Sunday in Lent	211
Fourth Sunday in Lent	220
Fifth Sunday in Lent	230
Sixth Sunday in Lent *(Palm Sunday or Passion Sunday)*	240
Holy Thursday	250

Good Friday			259
Easter			268
Second Sunday of Easter			277
Third Sunday of Easter			287
Fourth Sunday of Easter			297
Fifth Sunday of Easter			307
Sixth Sunday of Easter			317
Ascension			327
Seventh Sunday of Easter			336
Pentecost			346
Trinity Sunday			355
Proper 4	Ordinary Time 9	May 29–June 4 *(if after Trinity)*	363
Proper 5	Ordinary Time 10	June 5–11 *(if after Trinity)*	373
Proper 6	Ordinary Time 11	June 12–18 *(if after Trinity)*	383
Proper 7	Ordinary Time 12	June 19–25 *(if after Trinity)*	392
Proper 8	Ordinary Time 13	June 26–July 2	402
Proper 9	Ordinary Time 14	July 3–9	411
Proper 10	Ordinary Time 15	July 10–16	421
Proper 11	Ordinary Time 16	July 17–23	428
Proper 12	Ordinary Time 17	July 24–30	438
Proper 13	Ordinary Time 18	July 31–August 6	448
Proper 14	Ordinary Time 19	August 7–13	457
Proper 15	Ordinary Time 20	August 14–20	465
Proper 16	Ordinary Time 21	August 21–27	474
Proper 17	Ordinary Time 22	August 28–September 3	484
Proper 18	Ordinary Time 23	September 4–10	494
Proper 19	Ordinary Time 24	September 11–17	504
Proper 20	Ordinary Time 25	September 18–24	514
Proper 21	Ordinary Time 26	September 25–October 1	522
Proper 22	Ordinary Time 27	October 2–8	532
Proper 23	Ordinary Time 28	October 9–15	541
Proper 24	Ordinary Time 29	October 16–22	549
Proper 25	Ordinary Time 30	October 23–29	557
Proper 26	Ordinary Time 31	October 30–November 5	566
Proper 27	Ordinary Time 32	November 6–12	576
Proper 28	Ordinary Time 33	November 13–19	586
Proper 29	Ordinary Time 34	November 20–26	
(Christ the King or Reign of Christ)			596
All Saints		November 1 *(or first Sunday in November)*	606

Index of Lectionary Readings   614

Preface

Standing in the pulpit each Sunday of the Christian year is a daunting responsibility. With the Syrophoenician woman, those who preach sometimes find themselves pressing Jesus for just the crumbs that fall from the table. Along with Jesus' disciples, they wonder how far the loaves and fish can be spread. Occasionally they share Moses' question to God: "Where am I to get meat to give to all this people?" (Num. 11:13).

This book reflects both our conviction about the centrality of the Bible in preaching and our respect for those who regularly face the task of bringing the text to contemporary speech. The studies that follow focus directly on the task of proclamation. We do not attempt to reproduce the discussions to be found in scholarly commentaries. Neither do we offer outlines for specific sermons. Instead, these studies consider the structure and the content of the texts with a view to preaching.

Both because of the diverse nature of the texts included in the lectionary and because of the diversity among the four writers, readers will find considerable variety in the studies that follow. Different texts demand different treatments. Some texts are approached thematically, with more attention to theological content than to verse-by-verse exposition. Other texts seem to demand a careful analysis of the movement of the argument. Still others reflect a pressing historical concern that will be discussed. Our hope is that this diversity will be enriching rather than bewildering.

From the First Sunday of Advent through Good Friday, Walter Brueggemann contributes studies of the Old Testament lessons; James Newsome, the Psalms; Charles Cousar, the Epistle lessons; and Beverly Gaventa, the Gospel lessons. For the remainder of the year, James Newsome writes on the Old Testament lessons, Walter Brueggemann on the Psalms, Beverly Gaventa on the Epistle lessons, and Charles Cousar on the Gospel lessons. The writing of the introductions is shared by all.

Just as it is true that "of making many books there is no end," it sometimes seems that even the making of one book will have no end. Encouragement for a task such as this one is highly valued, and we are grateful to pastors who reminded us of the need for our work, to colleagues who struggled along with us in its development, and to students who tolerated yet one more digression regarding "the lectionary project." We are especially grateful to Davis Perkins, Cynthia Thompson, and Harold Twiss of Westminster/John Knox Press, who eagerly accepted the proposal, gently nudged it along, and greatly improved the final product.

BEVERLY R. GAVENTA
Editor, Year B

Scripture quotations from the Revised Standard Version of the Bible are copyright 1946, 1952, © 1971, 1973 by the Division of Christian Education of the National Council of the Churches of Christ in the U.S.A. and are used by permission.

Scripture quotations from the New Revised Standard Version of the Bible are copyright © 1989 by the Division of Christian Education of the National Council of the Churches of Christ in the U.S.A. and are used by permission. In some instances "Yahweh" has been substituted for "the LORD."

Scripture quotations from the New English Bible are copyright © 1961, 1970 by The Delegates of the Oxford University Press and The Syndics of the Cambridge University Press, and are used by permission.

Scripture quotations from the Revised English Bible are copyright © 1989 by Oxford University Press and Cambridge University Press, and are used by permission.

Scripture references for the lectionary readings are from the *Revised Common Lectionary*, copyright © 1992, Consultation on Common Texts, admin. Augsburg Fortress. Reproduced by permission.

Excerpt from "St. Francis and the Sow," from *Mortal Acts, Mortal Words* by Galway Kinnell. Copyright © 1980 by Galway Kinnell and renewed 2008 by Galway Kinnell. Used by permission of Houghton Mifflin Harcourt Publishing Company. All rights reserved.

First Sunday of Advent

Contrary to the manner in which it is often celebrated in the churches, Advent begins not on a note of joy, but of despair. Humankind has reached the end of its rope. All our schemes for self-improvement, for extricating ourselves from the traps we have set for ourselves, have come to nothing. We have now realized at the deepest level of our being that we cannot save ourselves and that, apart from the intervention of God, we are totally and irretrievably lost.

Thus Advent serves a dual purpose. On the one hand, it is the culmination of the long weeks after Pentecost. For virtually half the year the church has liturgically celebrated the work of the Spirit in its own life and in the life of the world. During this time, the church has also reminded itself of its responsibility, of *our* responsibility, to do the work of the kingdom. But now comes the realization that, in spite of the intervention of the Spirit and in spite of the very best intentions of the people of God, the world has yet to be redeemed. And so the prayer of Advent is that Christ will soon come again to rule over God's creation in power and in justice.

On the other hand, Advent also takes us back to the beginning of things. Back to that time so long ago when men and women of faith yearned for the first coming of the Savior. The season thus attempts to capture that spirit of hope in the midst of hopelessness, a spirit of yearning for that which would be too good to be true: some new and unique expression of God's intention to save a world gone wrong.

Thus, Advent both anticipates God's fresh beginnings with creation in the person of Jesus Christ and, at the same time, celebrates the promise that that same Jesus Christ will return to consummate all history under his gracious rule.

The texts for this day affirm these different, yet parallel, purposes of the season. The passages from Isa. 64 and Ps. 80 express the longing of faithful people for God to break into their isolation and to shatter the gridlock of human sin. The New Testament lections in 1 Cor. 1 and Mark 13 anticipate with both awe and thanksgiving the coming of "the day of our Lord Jesus Christ."

Isaiah 64:1–9

These verses are a prayer to God by a people that is powerless and under oppression. The prayer exhibits the two main features of genuine Advent hope: on the one hand, a deep *sense of desperation* about a situation out of control is sounded. On the other hand, a *bold and confident trust* in God is voiced, addressed to a God who can intervene (if God will) to make life peaceable and joyous. Life without God is unbearable. That is the present tense. Life with God can be completely transformed. That is the urgent hope of the prayer.

The prayer begins with a petition (Isa. 64:1–4), asking God to "come down" with theophanic splendor and terror (v. 1). The imagery suggests that God is remote in the heavens and so cut off from the earth. To intervene in the earth, God must with raw power break open the "skin" of the firmament, like an animal tearing open a cage, to be released into the earth.

The intention of the coming of God is to assert a name and a sovereignty that will override and curb the destructiveness of the nations. The yearning of Israel is that Yahweh should show the nations who is in charge, for the nations have assumed that they themselves (or their gods) are in charge and can do what they want in abuse of Israel.

In v. 3, the prayer relates the hoped-for intrusion to the remembered intrusions of the past. While the reference is not explicit, the verb "come down" echoes the exodus (see Ex. 3:8), and the quaking mountain of Sinai (Ex. 19:16–18). Thus the model for this petition is God's coming (advent) in the focal memory of Exodus-Sinai, when Israel was decisively liberated and covenant was made. Advent is a hope that the fundamental events of Israel's memory will be reenacted, so that life may begin again unfettered, as it began in the days of Moses. Life can begin again only if there are "awesome deeds," acts so terrible and wondrous that they defy all explanatory categories. Verse 4 adds the doxological note, perhaps to motivate God, that the earth has since the beginning not known any other god who saves.

In v. 5, the prayer abruptly changes tone. Now the prayer lowers its voice and utters a confession of guilt. The main point of these verses is that Israel has sinned and transgressed (v. 5), is unclean and filthy (v. 6). The term "unclean" means ritually unacceptable, so that Israel is not a community in which God's presence is willing to touch down (cf. Isa. 6:4). Isaiah 64:6 offers two poignant images: a filthy cloth, so impure and contaminated no one would dare touch it, and a faded leaf, so light and vulnerable that it will be blown away into oblivion.

Whereas in vs. 1–4 Israel expects and insists on God's coming, in vs. 5–7 Israel gives ample reason why God cannot and will not come into such uncleanness. Israel's failure precludes the very intervention for which it prays so passionately. That juxtaposition between yearning and failure, however, is exactly the mode in which faith awaits "the coming." We are mixtures of expectation and defeat, of urgency and self-awareness, of insistence and the very candor that blocks our best hope.

In v. 8 there is a jarring rhetorical leap. The verse begins with a disjunctive "yet" (=nevertheless). In Hebrew, it is wĕ'attāh, "and now," which moves decisively from all that is past (vs. 1–7) to this new present-tense moment. Moreover, this shift names Yahweh (LORD) for the first time in the poem. It is as though this forceful, intimate address to Yahweh puts behind and nullifies all that has just been said and focuses on a more powerful claim that overrides all that has been said.

In its prayer, Israel now speaks its ultimate truth to Yahweh in three staggering indicatives:

> You are our Father;
> you are our potter;
> we are all the work of your hand.

In these two images of father and potter, Israel affirms, "You made us, you own us, you are responsible for us, we belong to you." We are your responsibility, your burden, your problem, your treasured possession. You have begotten us (see Num. 11:12), you formed us (see Isa. 45:10–11). This pair of images (also paired in 45:9–13) asserts that Israel has a claim upon God and needs not make its own future. It also asserts God's obligation to Israel and resists any notion that God is "off the hook" with Israel. Israel's *deep trust* in Yahweh is matched by Yahweh's *deep obligation* to Israel.

The indicatives of 64:8, which appeal to the whole of Israel's faith tradition, provide the basis for the passionate petition of v. 9, which is now more intense and poignant than the petition of v. 1. There are three imperatives: Do not be terribly angry (see v. 5), do not hold it against us forever (remember), notice (consider)—we are your people, we belong to you and you cannot disown us. We have no other source of help. The prayer for God's coming, which began in bombast, ends on a note of needful, pathos-filled intimacy. In the end, Advent focuses not on God's massive power, but on God's family sense of solidarity, the same sort of solidarity that causes parents to do irrational caring deeds for wayward, beloved children.

Psalm 80:1–7, 17–19

The church year begins with a consideration of the basic posture of human beings before God: helplessness and need. Not only are we vulnerable to those forces that may destroy our happiness—indeed, our very existence—but there is little or nothing that we, when left to ourselves, are capable of doing about our precarious state. And so the psalm text utters a simple and primal cry: O God, help!

The God whose name is invoked is a special Being, and it is on the basis of the psalmist's knowledge of the divine nature that appeal is made. This is a God of compassion who, although specific deeds go unmentioned in that part of Psalm 80 which serves as this day's lection, has a history of salvation in the life of the people (compare vs. 8–11). This God is the "Shepherd of Israel," the One who leads "Joseph like a flock." This is distinctive language not used elsewhere, although close parallels exist (compare Ezek. 34; Ps. 23), and the bold terminology heightens the freshness of the text. (References to "Joseph" in v. 1 and to "Ephraim" and "Manasseh" in v. 2 have suggested to some interpreters a Northern provenance for this psalm.) Tenderness and immediacy are the images here, for God is One who can be trusted and One who is intimately available.

God is also the being who so far transcends normal human experience that a special theophany is required in the present circumstance. Reference to the One who is "enthroned upon the cherubim" (v. 1) recalls the ecstatic experiences of Ezekiel in Ezek. 1:5–28 and 10:1–20. There, as in the present text, the cherubim suggest—at the same time—distance as well as proximity, "thereness" as well as "hereness." The person of God is so unfathomable that this One must be represented in the likeness of bizarre creatures who possess both human and animal qualities. Thus, when this transcendent God engages human life it is with devastating decisiveness.

And so the contrasting images are brought together: tender shepherd and absolute ruler of the universe. And to this paradoxical

One is flung the cry "Stir up your might, and . . . save us!" (Ps. 80:2; compare v. 3).

That the distress of the people is not caused by the indifference of God is made clear by vs. 4–6. Indeed, quite the opposite is true: God has intended, or at least permitted, the suffering of the people. Anger at their prayers (v. 4) is the nearest the entire psalm comes to identifying a cause for the present distress, which is characterized by the unusual and cryptic phrases "bread of tears" and "tears to drink" (v. 5). In language more typical of other psalm texts, the anguish of the people is further described as arising in no small part out of their social isolation (v. 6; compare Pss. 27:2; 31:13). Quite interestingly, nowhere does the psalm link the crisis of the moment to the sinfulness of the people. Perhaps that is because the psalmist felt that connection would be so obvious it did not demand notation. But more likely is the explanation that, like Job (Job 23:1–7), the psalmist viewed the pain as, in this instance at least, undeserved.

At the heart of the psalm, then, lies a cry for salvation, the urgency of which is conveyed by the repeated cadences of vs. 3, 7, and 19. In this refrain the elements of restoration and illumination are paramount, and both are present as references to salvation. "Restore us, O [Lord] God [of hosts]" employs a verb (šûb) which elsewhere carries the clear meaning of a return to an original state, in this case a state of health and wholeness (compare Ps. 23:3). Even the plea "let your face shine" is a cry for salvation, in that it recalls the presence of God at the exodus and in the wilderness, where the glory of God "lit up the night" (Ex. 14:20) and protected the Israelites from the pursuing Egyptians.

As is evident from the repeated use of the pronouns "us" and "we," this psalm speaks to a crisis involving the whole community of Yahweh's people (compare "your people's prayers" of v. 4). Individuals may (and often do) find themselves in threatening situations, either because of their own sinfulness or because of forces over which they have no control, and the Old Testament frequently gives voice to their terror (Ps. 13, as one example among many). But this day's lection is a reminder—if one were needed—that an entire community, even the community of faith, may stand in need of God's intervening love.

An appeal to the office of the king, "the one at your right hand" (v. 17), rounds out the community's petition and anticipates the church's Advent expectation of the coming Messiah, Jesus Christ. In the strength of the King is life for the people (v. 18).

As an Advent lesson, this text seems to serve the purpose of injecting an important element of realism into the new season of the church's life. There is no room here for a sentimental or romantic assessment of the human situation, even of the church's situation before God. The community of faith is not different from humankind at large in terms of our need for divine grace. The distinction is rather that the body of Christ, when it is true to its purpose, acknowledges its inadequacy—both corporately and individually—and throws itself open to the intervention of God's grace. Only when the people of Christ acknowledge their need can we claim the message of anticipation that Advent proclaims. It is only when, with Israel-of-old, the church honestly prays (as in Ps. 80),

> Restore us, O God;
>   let your face shine, that we may be saved.

that the redemptive dimensions of Advent and Christmas may become realities.

1 Corinthians 1:3-9

It is intriguing to read today's epistolary lesson in the liturgical context of the First Sunday of Advent. It is a salutation and prayer of thanksgiving, typical of the openings of most of Paul's letters, containing the conventional patterns and phrases one would expect. When the reader's attention, however, is focused on the motifs of the Advent season, the passage takes on a new depth.

First, the text affirms that *our present life is lived between advents*. Jesus has come once, and the divine generosity has been bestowed in him (1 Cor. 1:4). But the passage gives special attention to his second advent, which Christians await (the Greek verb in v. 7 carries the connotation of eager expectation). The present is an in-between time, and human existence is characterized by a certain in-betweenness, between a beginning and an end (v. 8).

The metaphors are rich. (a) We live between hiddenness and revelation (v. 7). Indistinctly and in partial glimpses we grasp Christ's presence with us now. We are not gifted with twenty-twenty vision to perceive all we would like to see, and thus we live in anticipation of a full disclosure of Christ and his purposes. The crucified figure, who is a stumbling block to some and foolishness to others (v. 23), will then become transparent. The time of his coming will be "day" and not darkness (v. 8). As Paul writes later in this letter, "Now we see in a mirror, dimly, but then we will see face to face" (13:12).

(b) We live between guilt and blamelessness (1:8). Our own failures and our participation in a social system that oppresses and destroys many of God's creatures leave us depressed. We are only too aware that we fall short of the divine intentions for us, and yet we find it difficult, if not impossible, to transcend who we are and what we continually do with ourselves. The prospect of an impending judgment leaves us helpless and exposed—except for this promise that we will be continually sustained so that we may be "blameless on the day of our Lord Jesus Christ" (v. 8). The plans God has made for us are plans for good and not evil, and the promise is not condemnation but vindication.

The time between the advents is a time of transition, full of uncertainties and ambiguity. It is likely that the original readers of this letter denied their in-betweenness and presumed that they had already reached the end of the tunnel. They had "arrived," as we say, and interpreted their giftedness as evidence of a full salvation (4:8). Paul therefore continually keeps before them the Christ who has not yet returned and concludes the letter with the *Marana tha* prayer ("Our Lord, come!" 16:22b).

For others caught in the despair of their own circumstances, however, the need is for reassurance about the future, a rehearing of God's promise of the Second Advent. They have denied their in-betweenness by denying the future. They may need to discover again that there is light at the end of the tunnel. This Sunday becomes an opportunity to let the text address either or both groups.

The second affirmation in the text is that *God's gifts are more than sufficient for the in-between times*. Paul is effusive in the way he describes the benefits lavished on the Corinthian readers: "In every way you have been enriched in him, in speech and knowledge of every kind" (1:5); "you are not lacking in any spiritual gift" (v. 7). This same audience is later addressed sharply for its many problems, but the problems are not because of a lack of gifts.

When thinking of the in-between time, the key statement is "God is faithful" (v. 9). The gifts have not been given only to be revoked because the Corinthians have not used them properly. God is not fickle, gracious one minute and wrathful the next. God has called the readers into a unique, participatory community with Jesus Christ, and with that calling comes the promise that "he will strengthen you to the end" (v. 8). God can be trusted.

Third, the text appeals to the readers that *in the between-time they should demonstrate in the community a genuine unity*. The prayer of thanksgiving takes on an added dimension when we peer over beyond the bounds of the passage to the body of the letter (vs.

10–17). The lavish spiritual gifts given the Corinthians are not merely for the personal enrichment of the ones who possess them; they are to lead to a common intent, to a unity of mind and purpose.

It becomes a fitting appeal, since the very spiritual gifts about which Paul writes have in fact led to the splits within the community, to the squabbles and bitterness. Though gifted "in speech and knowledge of every kind" (v. 5), they are reminded that the power of the gospel comes not through eloquence but through the foolishness of the cross (v. 17).

The time in between is not a time either for passivity or for selfish pursuits, but for exercising the divine gifts in the cause of the larger community. First Corinthians is the book that speaks about forgoing rights, of attending to the weaker sister or brother, of a worship that edifies the entire congregation, and of love that "does not insist on its own way" (13:5). These are the ingredients that make for unity and that characterize those "called into the fellowship of his Son, Jesus Christ our Lord" (1:9).

Mark 13:24–37

The Gospel readings for Advent begin with an extended section from the complex chapter of Mark often referred to as the "little apocalypse." In its Markan setting, the whole of ch. 13 consists of Jesus' prophecy regarding the destruction of the Jerusalem Temple and the return of the "Son of Man." Following the introductory question and declaration regarding the destruction of the Temple (vs. 1–2), the discourse opens with a description of the signs of impending crisis (vs. 3–8), instructions to the disciples (vs. 9–13), and the crisis of the "desolating sacrilege" (vs. 14–23). The lection itself consists of three distinct sections: prophecy regarding the return of the Son of Man (vs. 24–27), the lesson of the fig tree regarding the impending crisis (vs. 28–31), and the need for alertness (vs. 32–37).

Quotations from and allusions to passages from the Hebrew Bible are thick in this section of the chapter. In addition to the direct quotations identified in vs. 24, 25, and 26 (from Isaiah, Joel, and Daniel), there are allusions to Jeremiah, Deuteronomy, and Zechariah. The reason for this density of biblical references is not hard to locate: the author draws on traditional apocalyptic imagery to underscore the crisis that impends when the Son of Man returns. For example, imagery of the darkening of the sun and moon and the falling of the stars derives from Isa. 13:10, where it describes the day of the Lord. As is well known, the Son of Man prophecy itself comes from Dan. 7:13, and is repeated in Mark 14:62, in Jesus' trial before the chief priest.

Questions regarding the historicity of this passage and especially questions regarding the title "Son of Man" become exceedingly difficult and have little direct bearing on the proclamation of this passage during Advent. Whatever its history, at least one major aim of the passage in its Markan context is to urge watchfulness. The return of the Son of Man and the crises associated with that return are not events subject to human control or prediction. Disciples must be constantly on the alert for that return, or they will be caught unprepared. This note is signaled first in v. 9 with the warning about the betrayal that awaits disciples; it appears again in vs. 23 and 33 with the warning to be alert for what lies ahead; the chapter concludes with another extended warning about the need to stay alert in vs. 35–37.

Watchfulness is necessary for at least two reasons. First, there are false alarms from charlatans who do not know what the real crisis is and who do not know what time it is. They point to the wrong signs (vs. 6–8) or to themselves (vs. 21–22), and their false prophecy threatens God's people. Second, and more important, watchfulness is necessary because only God knows what time it really is. Not even the angels or the Son of God (v. 32) know when the critical moment will come, for it belongs in God's hands alone.

The significance of this passage for Mark's Gospel can hardly be overstated. Located just prior to the beginning of the Passion narrative, it stands as a commentary on what will follow. The crucifixion of Jesus is a call to watchfulness, a call the disciples in Mark's story fail to heed; even the women who find the tomb empty fail to understand the meaning of watchfulness, as they flee the tomb in fear. Mark 13 importantly reminds the church of the need to remain ever vigilant.

What lies behind the use of this passage on the First Sunday of Advent is, of course, the church's traditional connection between the first advent of Christ and the Second Advent, or the Parousia. In the season of Advent, the church always recalls the promise of the Second Advent, the promise that God's people will not be left on their own. By the same token, confidence in the Second Advent is possible only when the church recollects the fulfillment of the first advent.

Something more is at stake here, however, than the association of the two advents with each other. Advent is also a season of watching and waiting. The Markan passage importantly reminds us not only of that need but of *why* it is necessary. Watchfulness is necessary, according to Mark 13, because there are those who, intentionally or not, mislead the faithful. What time is it, anyway? Who knows what time it is? Many voices, inside and outside the church, claim to know what time it is and what crisis is at hand—a political crisis, a religious crisis, an economic crisis, an ecological crisis, a social crisis. To which voices are we to listen? Not all of them know what time it truly is or what response is appropriate.

Watchfulness is necessary, according to Mark 13, because only God knows what time it is. Only God knows what the real crisis is and how it will manifest itself. During Advent, the recollection of the waiting of Mary reminds the church that the crisis of Jesus' birth was anticipated by only a few and understood by no one. Only God knows what time approaches. As the people of God wait even now, they can anticipate only that the times are in God's hands and not their own. They know that God will not leave them alone, that God will not leave them without hope.

Second Sunday of Advent

Hopeful anticipation is the mood that characterizes the texts for the Second Sunday of Advent. God's people have understood their need and, at the same time, have come to terms with their own inability to save themselves. Missing is the note of despair that was present in the lections for the First Sunday of Advent. Instead there is the assurance that God's mercy is soon to be made evident in fresh ways.

The text from Isa. 40 addresses the matter straightaway. Jerusalem has "served her term" in bondage to sin, and a new era is about to dawn. The voice in the wilderness is bringing a message of great joy: "Here is your God!" This God is both a ruler who subdues all efforts to thwart the joy of the people, and a shepherd who tenderly cares for all the needs of the flock. There is no need to fear. There is every need to be very grateful and glad.

Psalm 85 continues the theme, as the poet expresses the thanksgiving of the people that a once-promised salvation—the exodus, perhaps—came to pass. Old sins were forgiven, and the "fortunes of Jacob" restored. But that was long ago, and there is now an urgent need for some fresh outbreak of God's initiatives. Yet, again, there is no cause for fright. Those who trust in the Lord may be at peace, for the God who intervened once in the lives of the people will surely do so again. Harmonious and responsible relationships are to dominate the hearts of the people. "Righteousness and peace will kiss each other."

Thoughts of righteousness and peace also pervade the passage from 2 Peter 3. Yet the focus here is clearly on Christ's Second Advent. He whose first coming inaugurated a new era in God's dealing with all creation is sure to come again, and for the Second Coming those who love him wait in hopeful anticipation. Will the time be long or short? No one knows. His coming will be as sudden and unannounced as that of a thief, but with far different results. The new creation that will then appear will be one in which "righteousness is at home." Therefore, the people of Christ work to be "found by him at peace" on that decisive day.

The Gospel lection focuses on the earthly ministry of Jesus and centers the attention of the reader once more on the first coming. As did the messenger described in the passage from Isa. 40, John the Baptist comes to sensitize all hearts to the advent of the one promised so long ago.

Isaiah 40:1–11

This piece of poetry is strategically placed in the book of Isaiah to mark the end of the long exile that was decreed by the prophet in 39:6–7. That is, between the threat of ch. 39 and the promise of ch. 40, there has been a two-hundred-year hiatus, during which all of royal Israel was "carried to Babylon" (39:6). Or, speaking in terms of critical scholarship, ch. 40 begins Second Isaiah in Babylon after First Isaiah in Jerusalem. One does not need a lot of critical detail to sense that these verses are new, unexpected speech after the terrible silence of suffering. God speaks a radical inexplicable assurance that is to change the lot of forlorn Judah. It is no wonder that part of this poem is quoted in all four Gospels, a text that voices the radical newness that is to be initiated in the story of Jesus (see Mark 1:2–3).

God speaks anew into the silence and desolation of exile (Isa. 40:1–2). God's first word is "comfort"; God's next words are "O comfort." God's utterance into the exile is to be a word of well-being, assurance, and solidarity. The word is not addressed to "my people," as NRSV might suggest, for the verb is a plural imperative. It is, rather, addressed to those whom God recruits to speak to Israel. It is suggested by scholars that the ones addressed by God are the other gods (angels) who surround the throne of Yahweh, messengers who wait to be dispatched by the high God, who sends decrees from God's government throughout the earth, God's proper range of administration.

Given this imagery, the new decree now to be sent to Jerusalem and to Jews in exile is that Jerusalem (and Judah) have now paid fully for their offense (see 39:6–7), and are to be released from prison (exile), and permitted a return home. The word is like the commutation of a prison sentence in which a hoped-for but unexpected release is announced. Jerusalem is indeed to be comforted and assured, addressed in such a positive way by the "God of all consolation" (2 Cor. 1:3–7) that Jerusalem can end its desolate state of abandonment.

SECOND SUNDAY OF ADVENT

The next part of the poem (Isa. 40:3-8) presents a series of speaking parts, but it is not obvious whose voices these are. The exchange may be among various members of God's entourage, or perhaps it is conversation between several messengers and God. The first voice issues an instruction to build a superhighway across the desert on which God will travel in triumph (vs. 3-5). These verses anticipate an enormous engineering project of leveling the land for a smooth road. The purpose of the new road is that Yahweh shall move in triumphal procession as a conquering God. It is assumed in such a reading that the road runs from Babylonian exile all the way to Jerusalem, and that along with this triumphant God will come all the long-exiled Jews in a glorious, victorious homecoming. All those watching along the road will be astonished to see the undiminished splendor and unrivaled majesty of Yahweh. The God who seemed to be defeated by the Babylonian gods will march in a wondrous show of unrestricted power.

The second voice issues only a brief instruction. "Cry out!" as if to urge getting on with the program of triumph (v. 6a). The third voice is an "I," but we do not know who speaks (vs. 6-7). It is a reluctant voice, perhaps the prophet, who resists the proclamation of victory because the gains for this people are fleeting, ephemeral, and unreliable. The speaker lacks confidence in the program just enunciated. This voice, however, is countered immediately by yet another speaking voice in v. 8. This voice accepts the preceding diagnosis of ephemerality concerning Israel given in vs. 6b-7, but then counters it with the last line of v. 8. While it is true that Israel is fleeting and unreliable, the process of triumphal homecoming does not depend on the constancy of Israel, but is rooted only in the word (decree) of "our God," a decree that does not wither or fade, but is utterly reliable. The new season of Jewish life in the earth, a season of well-being, is grounded in and authorized only by God's own intentionality. Thus hope in Advent is not grounded in the possibilities we can see in the human community, but in the faithfulness of God that is not conditioned by human frailty or fickleness.

Thus the negotiated quarrel or argument among these several voices is resolved. The concreteness of historical return is linked to the decree and purpose of God, which is situated beyond the vagaries of history and is a settled, sovereign resolve.

On the basis of such a resolve on God's part, a messenger is dispatched who is to speak out loud and clear (vs. 9-11). The term "herald" (*měbaśśēr, měbaśśeret,*) from *bāśar*, "proclaim") is the Hebrew equivalent of "gospeler," thus the one who speaks good news, the "evangel" of God's victory and homecoming. The gospeler is to stand high and speak loudly, announce the new decree of God, which will decisively change the history and destiny of the listening community. The word to be spoken without timidity is "Here is your God!" Here is the one in glory, who seemed to be defeated, returning in power. As a result, the Jews need no longer obey or fear the power of Babylon. The work of evangelism is to show God in God's resolve for a newness where none seemed possible.

The new rule of God is evident in a stunning procession across the desert to make a new communal beginning with power and well-being (vs. 10–11). God at the head of the great victory parade is an armed warrior with ferocious power and weapons. This God is marked by macho, and it is clear that this God is able to give good gifts of well-being as God chooses. But then, quickly, the rhetoric is reversed. The God who moves at the head of the joyous process is as gentle as a shepherd with a feeble sheep, as tender as a nursemaid who cares for the vulnerable. With these two images of macho warrior and gentle nursing carrier, the poem lets God be all in all for all. The people who had no future are indeed comforted by the powerful, gentle God. On the way home in joy, exile ends, darkness is dispelled, drought yields to springs of water, life begins anew, whole, safe, protected. Everything is new upon hearing the new decree, trusting it, and acting on it.

Psalm 85:1–2, 8–13

This day's Psalm lection celebrates the mercy and goodness of God in poetry whose imagery is expansive, yet tender. It is a declaration concerning the essential nature of God, one made—when the entire Ps. 85 is considered—in response to the petitions of vs. 1–7. Perhaps a priest, or even the psalmist, is the speaker here, delivering a healing and hopeful word to the questions raised by the worshiping and anxious congregation. Thus the setting is one of uncertainty and doubt, perhaps even fear, for although the specific threats behind the language of vs. 1–7 are unclear, the people are apparently quite unsettled. Since that is also the mood of the Psalm lection for the First Sunday of Advent (compare, for example, Pss. 80:4 and 85:5), there is somewhat the same progression from that lection to this one as exists within the entirety of Ps. 85. The people have cried out for help, and now we hear the reply.

The basis of the hope on which the people rest their expectation is identified. God, who has acted before (vs. 1–2), will "speak peace" because the listeners are "his people," "his faithful [ones]." They are "those who turn to him in their hearts," if one accepts here the NRSV translation, one that follows the Septuagint. (The marginal notation in NRSV, however, gives the literal meaning of the Hebrew. Compare REB.) Thus the implication is that those who receive God's words of peace are those who are prepared to listen for them. For them the "salvation" of Yahweh "is at hand" (v. 9a).

Then the text—with scarcely a glance to the side—refers the reader to an issue of monumental import. An effect, perhaps *the* effect, of this renewal in the life of the people is that the reality of God's presence may be declared with a fresh urgency. The saved people themselves become the evidence of the presence of God. "That his glory may dwell in our land" (v. 9b) is not as theologically striking in English as in Hebrew. Both the verb šākan ("to dwell") and the noun kābôd ("glory")—terms from the vocabulary of Israel's priests—recall the wilderness wanderings, among other experiences in Israel's life. In Ex. 40:35, for example, these words are used in the same sentence to convey the active involvement of God in the life of the people. And so the force of Ps. 85:9b is that the people themselves—delivered from their peril—"showcase" God. A terrifying thought for God's people in any age.

Verse 10 draws on an inventory of words that were close to the prophets' hearts (compare Isa. 5:7; Hos. 2:19–20), but here these attributes of God become personifications. This is surely a literary device and not, as has been suggested, divinization of these qualities. That "steadfast love," "faithfulness," "righteousness," and "peace" converge is but the psalmist's way of stressing that these are but various facets of that unitary reality: Yahweh.

The personifications continue in Ps. 85:11, and it may be that the "faithfulness" that "will spring up from the ground" is a reference to human lives lived in obedience to God, and that this obedience is answered, in turn, by the "righteousness" of God, which "will look down from the sky." But another possibility is to see these words as a transformation of Gen. 7:11, part of the Priestly account of the Flood. There the chaos waters are described as penetrating the earth both from below ("the fountains of the great deep burst forth") and from above ("the windows of the heavens were opened"). But that act of God's judgment performed so long ago is now overruled by an act of God's gracious love: "faithfulness" from below, and "righteousness" from above.

After an "aside" in Ps. 85:12, which has to do with the fertility of the land, the final personification is found in v. 13. Righteousness, like a royal messenger, "will go before him" and prepare God's way, imagery reminiscent of the Second Isaiah (Isa. 40:3–5). This appears to be a creative manner of describing the reality that God's righteousness, in the sense of moral responsibility and predictability, is integral to the nature of Israel's saving God.

Of the several elements in this text that make it an appropriate reading for the Advent season, perhaps the strongest is that of anticipation. It is clear that the God whom the psalmist describes is a Being who has intervened in the life of the people in the past to save them from forces over which they had no control (compare Ps. 85:1). This is, indeed, the basis of their trust. But new perils are present, fresh exigencies from which no power of their own is sufficient to shield them. In the urgency of this moment, fresh initiatives from God are required.

And God will surely respond to the people's need. God could not be God and do otherwise. Yet the divine help has not so far arrived; it is out there in the arena of unfulfilled promise. Hovering, brooding, like the Spirit of God at Creation (Gen. 1:2). "His salvation is at hand" (Ps. 85:9a), the psalmist confidently declares, and all eyes strain to catch a first glimpse. Soon the reality of Israel's Savior will be such that it will seem that those qualities which define the life of God will become tangible persons: steadfast love, faithfulness, righteousness, peace. It will be as if the very God has become incarnate and lived among them. Soon. Very soon.

2 Peter 3:8–15a

Second Peter is not a book from which preachers regularly draw texts. Its brevity and the issues it addresses make it a scarce commodity in the contemporary church. Yet it wrestles with one of the critical problems the early church faced—the delay of Jesus' return and the moral laxity that regularly accompanied a skeptical stance. During the Advent season, when the liturgical spotlight falls on the second as well as the first coming of Jesus, we do well to return to 2 Peter and listen to the implications of an eschatological faith. While the usual apocalyptic images appear in the text (the thief in the night, cosmic dissolution, fire, and new heavens and a new earth), the text struggles with more than a mere repetition of the old mythology, perhaps in an effort to speak to hellenized readers for whom the ancient symbols no longer held meaning.

The beginning of the chapter sets the tone for the argument and appeals that follow (3:1–4). Not unexpectedly (since they had been anticipated by the prophets and apostles), skeptics scoff at the delay of the longed-for return and live as if there will be no judgment. They cynically ask what has happened to the promise, and suggest that the created order from its very beginning has happily rocked along without any divine intrusion on God's part (v. 4).

The writer's first response is to address the issue of God and creation (vs. 5–7). God has been active not only in the establishing of the heavens and the earth but also in preserving and maintaining the present order. It would be disastrously shortsighted to assume that the world operates without God. Look at the Flood. God essentially destroyed the earth with water, and in fact is the one who has thus far kept the present world from being destroyed again by fire.

Then the writer faces head-on the matter of the delay of the Parousia. First, there is the problem of human limitations. The Ninetieth Psalm meditates on the inestimable gap between God's perspective and the time and mortality of humans, and the writer of 2 Peter in 3:8 recalls a verse from Ps. 90:4 for the skeptics who assume their own perspective is so certain. God does not reckon time the way humans reckon time. When humans grow itchy and impatient, then doubting and cynical, God remains committed to the divine promise. In fact, God's patience is a measure of divine grace. God is not eager to destroy and punish disobedient children. God wants sufficient time for all to repent.

Rather than interpreting the delay as an indication of a failed promise, the writer follows the prophets and Paul (2 Peter 3:15b; compare Rom. 2:4–5) in pointing to the divine mercy, which holds back the judgment and prolongs the time to enable true remorse. This explanation of the delay may not satisfy every question we have about the return of Christ, especially the questions of the oppressed and marginalized, who yearn for the end so as to have vindication and a relief from their predicament. But then it was not written for such a group, but for scoffers and cynics whose presumptuous perspective needs challenging. The challenge is that they live faithfully in the present and "regard the patience of our Lord as salvation" (2 Peter 3:15a).

Second, once the writer has reminded readers of God's viewpoint on history, a reaffirmation of the traditional "day of the Lord" is made (compare Amos 5:18–20; Joel 2:28–32). Two features stand out. On the one hand, the image of the thief suggests suddenness and unexpectedness. There is no need for speculation. Preparation for the final day is critical, but it does not consist of developing timetables and calculating precise moments. On the other hand, the traditional language of the dissolution of the created order with fire is not without meaning. "Fire" connotes testing, the burning of what is peripheral and the continuance of what is lasting, valuable, and worthy. This leads to the third and final movement in the passage.

The writer asks what all this means for the present lives of the readers. Given the prospects of a future dissolution of this order, they go about their business in a mood of expectancy ("waiting for and hastening the coming of the day of God," 3:12–14). In place of skepticism and cynicism, they hope for what lies beyond dissolution: new heavens and a new earth (v. 13). A proper preparation for the future consists not in speculation, but "in leading lives of holiness and godliness" (v. 11), in striving for peace (v. 14).

The new world is a place "where righteousness is *at home*" (v. 13, emphasis added). Admittedly, in the present world "the way of righteousness" (2:21) is hard to maintain, given the hostile and enticing context that threatens to overpower believers, but the future promises something better. Just as Noah, at this time of the first dissolution of the world, was "a herald of righteousness" (2:5), so now "the righteousness of our God and Savior Jesus Christ" (1:1) will prevail beyond the second dissolution into the new order, where it is "at home."

Holiness, godliness, peace, and righteousness are four ingredients characterizing the waiting mood of the Advent season. They include both personal and social dimensions, both attention to the self and attention to the broader community.

Mark 1:1–8

Familiarity with the birth narratives of Matthew and Luke and the elegant prologue of John makes the beginning of Mark's Gospel seem not only abrupt but vaguely disappointing. Here no angelic pronouncements anticipate the birth of Jesus. No word of the Christ's place in creation itself signals the importance of the narrative that is to follow. A careful reading of this passage, however, reveals that Mark also begins with detailed attention to an antecedent of Jesus, this time in the person of John the Baptist.

The first verse of Mark's Gospel teems with ambiguity: Who or what constitutes the "beginning of the good news of Jesus Christ"? Does Mark here simply identify the beginning of the story? Is the whole of what follows in Mark merely "the beginning"? Another possibility is that John himself is the beginning, or that the beginning lies in the prophecy concerning John as forerunner of Jesus. Whatever the nuances of v. 1, clearly Mark understands John as the one who prepares "the way of the Lord."

In at least four ways, Mark identifies John the Baptist as the forerunner of Jesus, the one who prepares his way. First, and perhaps most obvious, the arrival of John is itself an object of prophecy, and he in turn prophesies the advent of Jesus. The biblical quotations in vs. 2–3, taken from Mal. 3:1 and Isa. 40:3 (despite the introduction's identifying the quotation solely with Isaiah), serve in this context as prophecies of the activity of John, and the description of John's dress identifies him with the tradition of Elijah (see 2 Kings 1:8). The major activity associated with John in Mark's account, of course, is his announcement of the One who is to come.

John is not simply the forerunner of Jesus in the sense of announcing his imminent arrival, however. John and Jesus share a common location in the wilderness. Mark's insistence on the wilderness as the location of John the Baptist, probably in conformity to the quotation from Isa. 40:3, makes the description of John's activity puzzling. If John appeared in the *wilderness*, as Mark 1:4 indicates, and if John did his preaching there, how is it that people were aware of his activity or went out to hear him and be baptized by him? The location is thematic or theological rather than geographical, as is confirmed in 1:12, when Jesus is driven into the wilderness, and later in Mark, when Jesus repeatedly retreats to the wilderness (1:35, 45; 6:31, 32, 35).

A third way in which John serves as forerunner of Jesus is in the act of proclamation. The only words attributed to John in this passage are the pronouncement about the coming of Jesus, and the first words attributed to Jesus are, again, words of proclamation. The content of their preaching differs, in that John proclaims Jesus and his baptism and Jesus proclaims the nearness of the kingdom. Yet both call for repentance (1:4, 15), which again connects the two figures.

The final way in which John serves as forerunner of Jesus stands outside this immediate passage, but it nevertheless impinges on Mark's understanding of John. John becomes the forerunner of Jesus in being handed over for death. The same word (*paradidōmi*) describes John's arrest or betrayal in 1:14 and that of Jesus later in Mark's Gospel (for example, 3:19; 9:31; 14:18). More significantly, the reference to John's arrest in 1:14 comes well before the actual story of John's arrest and execution in Mark 6:14–29. One reason for that untimely reference is that it foreshadows not only *John's* death but also that of Jesus.

These parallels between Mark's presentation of John the Baptist and that of Jesus serve more than a merely decorative or mnemonic function. Mark's story invites disciples (and probably readers as well) to follow in the way of John and Jesus. Late in the Gospel story, the disciples accompany Jesus into the wilderness (the "deserted place" of 6:31). Part of their task is to engage in the proclamation of the gospel (6:12; 13:10). And, as 13:9–13 makes painfully clear, disciples will also be handed over or betrayed (*paradidōmi*). What Mark creates, then, is not a simple identification, in which disciples *become* John or Jesus or their equivalent. Instead, disciples follow in the *way* of John and Jesus, as Bartimaeus is invited to do following his healing (10:46–52).

The celebrative mood of Advent makes it easy to think only in terms of the coming of a baby who is greeted by an angel chorus, the astonishment of shepherds, and the praise of prophet and prophetess in the Temple. Even from the beginning, however, Mark's presentation of the forerunner of Jesus does not allow readers to lose sight of the fact that the "one who is coming" comes to be betrayed and to die. For that reason, scholars have often referred to the Gospel of Mark as a "passion narrative with a long introduction."

Mark's presentation of the followers of Jesus summons them to the isolation of the wilderness, the task of proclamation, and the risk of betrayal. While these are not welcome and familiar themes of Advent, they are nevertheless hinted at both in Mark and in the more congenial birth narratives of Matthew, where Herod seeks to kill the infant Jesus, and of Luke, where Simeon's oracle anticipates the resistance to Jesus that will follow.

Third Sunday of Advent

The coming of the Lord is accompanied by great joy on the part of the people. As anticipation mounts toward a climax, muted expectancy turns more and more into expressions of gladness and celebration. That which was is past and a new day has begun to dawn. There is no suppressing the consequent mood of hopeful ecstacy.

The Lord's Anointed and then the Lord are the speakers in the lection from Isa. 61. The Anointed One declares a message of liberation: the oppressed will be freed, while the brokenhearted will be restored to wholeness—and this by no other effort than that of the Lord and of the Lord's Anointed. Justice (v. 8), righteousness, and praise (v. 11) will blossom as new shoots of growth in the garden of the Lord, and all nations will be witnesses to this new life.

Psalm 126 remembers a time in the past when God's mercy broke forth in an unparalleled manner, resulting in a mood of great celebration among the people. "Laughter" and "joy" (v. 2) dominated their lives at that memorable time, and the poet now prays that these same mercies, producing these same joys, may be released in the lives of the people. Those who have sown "in tears" will then "reap with shouts of joy," and the character of the community and of the individuals who are members of it will be transformed.

The lection from 1 Thessalonians yearns for the "coming of our Lord Jesus Christ" (5:23), yet the very promise of the Second Advent has kindled great hope and gladness in the heart of the Christian community. No matter that the promise is yet unrealized. Its effect is immediate and unmistakable. Christians will "rejoice," "pray," and "give thanks" (vs. 16–18) as if that advent had already occurred. For as far as their own hearts are concerned, it has occurred indeed.

The reading from the Gospel of John also raises the issue of the mood of expectancy that characterizes the period of time between promise and fulfillment. John the Baptist has come to "make straight the way of the Lord" (v. 23), yet the Lord himself has not appeared.

Soon, very soon, the Advent will be a reality, and until that time John's baptism will stand as a sign pointing toward that wondrous moment.

More and more the despair that may be sensed in lections of the First Sunday of Advent fades away into an awareness that a gracious inbreaking of God's presence is at hand.

Isaiah 61:1–4, 8–11

This wondrously lyrical poem anticipates a massive reversal of fortunes, wrought by the power of God. Through that reversal, which will reorder social power arrangements, those who are now abused and oppressed will be given a circumstance of well-being, joy, security, and prosperity.

In Isa. 61:1–4, an unnamed and unknown speaker announces a special vocation that has been given by God, a vocation that concerns the renewal of community. Three terms ground and identify that vocation: (*a*) the work is authorized and energized by God's own Spirit; (*b*) the speaker is anointed, designated, and empowered by God; and (*c*) the work is to bring the gospel. (The verb *bāśar* is the same as in Isa. 40:9 from the reading for the Second Sunday of Advent.) The speaker of this poem asserts that the good news willed by God has been given us through an assignment to a human agent to work for transformation in the public domain.

The good news in this announcement of a specific human vocation is that the beloved city of Jerusalem, left in shambles by the Babylonians, will be rebuilt (61:4). Very much of the hope for a restored Judaism after the exile is rooted in the conviction that Jerusalem will be fully restored, both as safe home and as powerful symbol. Notice that in v. 4, the subject of rebuilding is three times "they." The work of rebuilding is not to be done by this anointed, authorized speaker, but by the "they" who are unnamed.

If we want to know who these agents of rebuilding are, we must look again at the verses that fall between the vocational affirmation of v. 1a and the promise of v. 4. In vs. 1b–3, the speaker knows where to find the workers, the expertise, the energy and passion for the rebuilding of the city. Those workers, the "they" of v. 4, are the oppressed, the brokenhearted, the captives, the prisoners, those who mourn. That is, the subjects and agents of the promised rebuilding are those who have been defeated, marginated, and rendered powerless, either by the economic pressures within the community or by the economic policies of foreign powers. Either way, "they" are the ones who have ended up in bondage and therefore impotent, because they have debts they cannot pay. The pressures of economic paralysis have led to hopelessness, powerlessness, and finally despair.

It is the work of this speaker, driven by God's Spirit and anointed by God's authority, to "gospel" these defeated folk back to power and constructive action. The gospel here is not a pious or religious act, but rather an intervention into economic life that will break the cycle of indebtedness. The phrase "proclaim liberty" (*drr*) is the term from the old Torah provision for the cancelation of debts and the rehabilitation of poor people (Lev. 25:10; compare Jer. 34:8, 15, 17). Many scholars conclude that the "year of the LORD's favor" and "the day of vengeance" refer to the jubilee year (see Lev. 25), when disadvantaged, indebted people are restored to their full common rights and power in the community. Thus the energy and resources to rebuild the shattered city have as a prerequisite the rearrangement of economic power. This tradition would entertain no "permanent underclass."

No wonder the ones rehabilitated and comforted (see Isa. 61:2) are marked by gladness and praise and take on the powerful, solid, stable quality of "oaks of righteousness" (v. 3). "They" will indeed recover the lost fortune of Jerusalem.

Now God (not the Anointed) speaks (vs. 8–9). First, Yahweh identifies that which God yearns for and despises. God "loves" the practice of justice, hates oppression (compare Amos 5:15). God hates the kind of economic oppression that has led to the sorry state of Isa. 61:1, but loves what the Anointed will do to correct that sorry state. God loves the reordering of economic power toward justice. And because of this sort of preference, God promises to do two things. First, God will "recompense," that is, give them reward for their effort (compare 40:10, with a different word). God will give them the payout that has long been denied to them. Second, God will make with them "an everlasting covenant." Remarkable! The very ones who have been rendered powerless and defeated are now the object of Yahweh's most extravagant, unconditional commitment. God will be in solidarity with and attentive to them. For all time to come, these will be the beloved and blessed of God (61:9). The contrast between the situation of v. 1 and that of v. 9 could hardly be more stark. The change of fortunes for the dispossessed and powerless occurs because of God's predilection, and because of a human agent who intervenes concretely into economic affairs. The human condition is supple and open to transformation, wherever the wind of God authorizes practical change.

In vs. 10–11 the Anointed of vs. 1–4 speaks again, expressing celebrative delight at what is about to happen. The speaker exults in his own mission, for he has been equipped with the dress of salvation and righteousness (compare Eph. 6:11–17). The speaker, emboldened by God's Spirit, is as buoyant as a bride, as exuberant as a bridegroom, eager and ready to begin action. The news (compare *bāśar* in Isa. 61:1) is that righteousness and praise are about to appear, wrought by God through this anointed speaker. All the nations will see the transformation, when the defeated become "oaks of stability," the ruins become habitation, sadness becomes joy. Everything depends on the human agent (vs. 1–4, 10–11), the One powered by God's own resolve.

This text is wondrous for Advent: (*a*) It enacts hope that a genuine, public transformation is in prospect; (*b*) it asserts that the transformation willed by God depends on a concrete, human agent; and (*c*) in Luke 4:18–19, Jesus quite specifically claims this text for his own definition and vocation. (Compare Sharon H. Ringe, *Jesus, Liberation, and the Biblical Jubilee*, Overtures to Biblical Theology; Philadelphia: Fortress Press, 1985, pp. 36–45.) He is the one who will liberate the defeated. No wonder the beneficiaries of injustice were "filled with rage" at his subversive words and his dangerous actions (Luke 4:28).

Psalm 126

(Those who wish to use Luke 1:47–55 as the Psalm lection for this Sunday are referred to the comments on this text under the Fourth Sunday of Advent.)

Psalm 126 is a cry for help on the part of the Israelite community which, in lifting its petition, remembers God's mercies of old. What God has done in the past, therefore, becomes paradigmatic of what the community now pleads for. Thus words denoting deliverance and great joy are embedded in a text that is basically a lament.

The original setting of the psalm could have been any occasion on which the well-being of the nation was imperiled, although, since v. 1 is usually interpreted as a reference to the return from Babylonian captivity, the date is probably postexilic. The initial section (vs. 1–3) recalls a supreme moment of exaltation from the nation's past, and the marginal (literal) reading of the NRSV's v. 1, "When the LORD brought back those who returned to Zion," appears to locate this happy time as 538 B.C. Here the language is effervescent. "Laughter" and "shouts of joy" (v. 2) fill the mouths of the returning exiles, while onlookers can only be amazed at the power of Israel's God.

In this respect, notice should be made of the manner in which the last line of v. 2 is repeated in the first line of v. 3. "The LORD has done great things for them," the awed comment of Israel's neighbors, becomes "The LORD has done great things for us," the no-less-astonished cry of Israel itself. To push the matter just a bit farther, perhaps the statement in v. 3 should more accurately be rendered as an English past perfect *"had* done," since the speakers of v. 3 are presumably now describing an event that took place some time before their present moment.

One other matter of linguistic interest in the section is the balance struck between similar phrases in vs. 1 and 3. Verse 1 ends, literally, "we were like dreamers," while v. 3 uses almost identical syntax to say "we were rejoicers." Both phrases attempt to capture not just the mood of the people, but something of the character of the community.

The second section of the psalm (v. 4) contains the heart of the matter, a prayer that says, in effect: Redeem us again, O Lord, as you redeemed us before. The language of the first line of the verse is evocative of the first line of v. 1 in that the same words (or their cognates) form the vocabulary, a manner by which the text emphasizes that what is being sought is a new expression of a previous act of salvation. The petitioners liken their status to the wadis of the arid south, which during much of the year are bone dry, but which with the coming of the autumnal rains overflow their banks.

And so the cry becomes not just, "Help us!" but "Help us abundantly and decisively!"

The final section (vs. 5–6) reads to many scholars as if it has been adapted from some agricultural ritual, perhaps performed by a priest at a time of planting or of harvest. Whether that be true or not, the words as they stand constitute a reminder that the tides of life are constantly shifting, that she or he who laments today may celebrate tomorrow. The reverse is also quite obviously true (as the present condition of the community stands witness), but significantly vs. 5–6 make no reference to that possibility. The movement is in a positive direction, from tears to joy, thus indicating that the basic orientation of the community is one of hope. In spite of the reality that yesterday's laughter (v. 2) may dissolve in the face of subsequent experiences, its very memory kindles the expectation that it may return.

Thus, it is the content of the community's memory that forms the basis of the psalmist's hope. In this psalm, prayer is directed to no God-without-a-story. Yahweh, the God of Israel, possessed a long and distinguished story, which, at heart and core, was a narrative of judgment transformed into redemption. And because Israel could remember that story, Israel sheltered strong hopes and expectations about both present and future, for Israel knew that its life could never be lived apart from Yahweh. It remembered its former joy, and that remembrance enabled it to see beyond its present tears.

The implications of this message for Advent are immediate, for the church has a memory too. Like Israel-of-old, the church remembers God's saving deeds, but in this instance they are memories vested in Jesus of Nazareth—in his birth, in his life, in his redemptive death and resurrection. And because we remember what God has done, we also have certain hopes and expectations concerning what God can and will do: that he who came once will come again, and that the interim is a time in which the church actualizes the living Christ to the world by means of its witness and its works of service.

The Lord has indeed done great things for us, and we have rejoiced!

1 Thessalonians 5:16–24

Each of the epistolary texts for the first three Sundays of Advent binds the expectation of the second coming of Jesus to the demand for faithful living. The text for this third Sunday, which concludes a letter particularly concerned with eschatological expectations, makes the demand a special matter through a series of short injunctions.

It may be hard to sense the urgency of the injunctions, because we do not know enough about the original readers to know how the injunctions immediately addressed their lives. We can, however, appreciate that short, pointed exhortations like these, with a certain immediacy, invite the reader to accept their message, to see what life would be like if they were followed. They indicate directions in which one moves in obedience. The demands are directly put to the reader, no ifs, ands, or buts. At the same time, the injunctions are general. They do not define the "good" that is to be sought or the "evil" to be avoided. Nor do they prescribe circumstances under which the injunctions are especially relevant. Readers are not relieved of making ethical decisions. They are faced with a new kind of discernment as they are forced to determine the particularity of the will of God in the challenges of their everyday lives.

The injunctions at the end of 1 Thessalonians concern three related matters. First, there is *the specific call to a life of worship* (5:16–18). Rejoicing, prayer, and thanksgiving are not designated

THIRD SUNDAY OF ADVENT

here as Sunday activities. They are each identified by the repeated adverbial emphasis: "always," "without ceasing," "in all circumstances."

The injunctions indicate an existence oriented to God, where believers recognize in every moment of their lives, in every decision they face, that they have to do with the reality of God. Life cannot be simply divided into the God-related and non-God-related dimensions of human activity: the latter do not exist. Writing checks, marking ballots in the voting booth, relating to family members in the home, making business decisions—as well as private and public worship—are the ways in which God seeks to be glorified.

It is intriguing that verbs for worship are used (rather than verbs like "obey," "serve," "submit to"). The manner of life imagined here is characterized by delight, by gratitude, by confidence. We may not be inclined to give thanks *for* all the circumstances of our lives, but the text envisions no situation *in the midst of which* we cannot recognize expressions of divine mercy and give God thanks. (Note that the original readers had known considerable persecution; see 2:14–16.)

Second, there is *a specific call to a life of discernment* (5:19–22). Aspects of the Christian experience are ambiguous, even frightful. The Spirit is the divine activity in human life over which we have no control. Believers can deny the Spirit's presence or fail to heed the Spirit's promptings, but believers (though they may often presume to do so) cannot ultimately manipulate the Spirit. Paul, therefore, urges readers not to quench the Spirit.

Precisely because the Spirit's activity is mysterious and often ambiguous, believers are enjoined to a life of discernment. As in Rom. 12:2, they are to test and prove the will of God; but more, they are to test and prove "everything." All of human experience—events, practices, relationships—invariably demands discrimination to determine the "good" that is to be clung to and the "evil" to be avoided. Prophets, who speak with authority and insight, are to be listened to, though not necessarily heeded. They may or they may not disclose the divine will. They, along with every source of direction, have to be tested.

The verbs throughout this passage as well as the second-person pronouns are all plural. Since the letter is also addressed to a congregation, the notion seems clear that the Christian community is the locus for this discerning and discriminating activity. It is not that the individual has to make all the weighty, burdensome ethical decisions alone. Rather the church is called to be a community of moral discernment, to test the various voices who speak the wisdom of the age to see if there is divine guidance for the confusing decisions of life.

Third, there is *a specific call to a life of holiness* (1 Thess. 5:23–24). The verb "sanctify [make holy]" may send shudders through us if we have had much experience with legalistic brands of religion that organize life around a list of do's and don'ts. We quickly counter that we want no part of such moralism. There is no question that "holy" (both in Hebrew and in Greek) does carry with it the notion of separation, but in Paul's framework it describes life oriented to the new age that has come in Jesus Christ as distinguished from the old age. It depicts a separation from the transitory, passing order, a break with the illusionary power brokers who have not heard or will not accept the radical newness God has promised.

Rather than through a list of do's and don'ts, the call to a life of holiness comes through a prayer. Only God can "sanctify" us completely. Only God can make our whole selves "sound" and keep us "blameless at the coming of our Lord Jesus Christ." At heart, sanctification is first and foremost a gift of God, not an act of human will. The faithful God guarantees a positive response to a prayer for holiness.

John 1:6–8, 19–28

Of all the Gospels, John's gives the most sustained attention to the testimony of John the Baptist, and this lection consists of two segments of that testimony. The prose of vs. 6–8 interrupts the poetry of the prologue, perhaps indicating that these verses were inserted into an existing poem (see also v. 15, which again interrupts the poetic structure). Verses 19–28 contain the first part of the Baptist's testimony, which continues through v. 34.

Despite the emphasis on the testimony of John, at first glance what is most striking about these passages is not the positive assertions John the Baptist makes concerning Jesus, but the negative assertions made about John, both by the narrator and through the direct speech of John himself. As early as v. 8, the narrator insists that "he [John] was not the light." The repeated and formal assertions in vs. 19–28 seem calculated to limit John's role: "He confessed and did not deny it, but confessed, 'I am not the Messiah.' " While John's testimony ostensibly concerns "the light," the content of vs. 19–28 has more to do with *John's* identity—or with denying certain identities to John—than with that of *Jesus*.

Historically, an explanation for these negative assertions regarding John the Baptist comes readily enough. Apparently at least some of John's followers understood him to be superior to Jesus, and a rivalry developed between the two groups. The story of Jesus' baptism by John easily lends itself to the inference that Jesus thereby yields to John's greater authority, making it important for Jesus' interpreters to explain how it is that the Christ came to be baptized by John. Although they treat the issue differently, Matthew and Luke also appear to downplay John's significance, either by having John himself resist the notion of baptizing and then having Jesus explain the reasons for his baptism (Matt. 3:13–17) or by placing John in prison at the time of Jesus' baptism (Luke 3:18–22). By negatively stating John's identity (he is *not* the light [John 1:8], nor is he the Messiah, Elijah, or the prophet [vs. 20–21]), the Fourth Gospel counters any attempt to rank John above Jesus.

Polemic against the followers of John the Baptist is not, however, the sole function of these passages. They also serve to emphasize the importance of the one about whom John gives his testimony. Indeed, John's authority (like that of all proclaimers) appears to consist of his honest denial of exalted titles for himself in favor of pointing the way to Jesus. Throughout the Fourth Gospel, characters who encounter Jesus serve largely to illuminate him in some way and, thus, the reader learns little about them as individuals. The treatment of John the Baptist is but an extreme example of that tendency.

Theologically, what the character John the Baptist does in this Gospel is to point ever away from himself and toward Jesus. The narrator explicitly gives that role, the role of witness, to John in 1:6–8, and John acts it out in the scenes that follow. John's rejection of titles for himself serves as prelude to his assertion about the One who follows him: "Among you stands one whom you do not know, the one who is coming after me; I am not worthy to untie the thong of his sandal" (vs. 26–27). Just beyond the confines of this lection, John elaborates on Jesus' identity as "Lamb of God," and concludes with the formal assertion, "I myself have seen and have testified that this is the Son of God" (v. 34), an assertion that circles back to and fulfills the vocation of John as witness (giver of testimony) in v. 7.

John the Baptist's comments about Jesus here differ from those in the Markan account of the Second Sunday of Advent, primarily in the assertion that the one who comes is "one whom you do not know." This signals an important Johannine theme. Indeed, throughout John's Gospel Jesus remains one whom people either do not know or do not understand. Nicodemus (3:4) and the Samaritan woman (4:11–12) understand his words but not their meaning. The high priest understands him only as a threat to the status quo

(11:45–53). Pilate gives him the right title, but for the wrong reasons (19:19–22). Even the disciples consistently reveal their misunderstandings.

John's proclamation of Jesus as the one who is unknown challenges the church to acknowledge its presumptuous assumption that it does know who Jesus is. Whether it portrays Jesus as innocuous infant, as dispenser of salvation (however currently understood), as revolutionary leader, as spiritual guru, or in any of a dozen other ways, the church and its people claim to understand Jesus. Each of those understandings, however, like the understandings of various characters in the Fourth Gospel, at best grasps only one facet of Jesus' identity.

As the church waits during the season of Advent, anticipating the birth of the infant Jesus, it needs to recall the startling fact that Jesus continues to make his appearance in ways that are surprising, unexpected, even unwelcome. The gentle baby of the Christmas story shortly becomes the One who challenges the religious authorities, overthrows the Temple's status quo, offers the people teachings that make little or no sense, dismisses his own family, and finally provokes the suspicion of the government.

Fourth Sunday of Advent

The deep sense of apprehension and despair voiced by texts for the First Sunday of Advent has given way over the intervening weeks to a mood of great joy and expectation. The people of God now understand that God is about to do a new and marvelous thing. The saving power of Israel's Redeemer, proclaimed by prophet and priest alike, is now about to break forth in dimensions that confound normal human understanding and that point beyond themselves to a new era in God's relationship with all creation.

The Old Testament lection from 2 Sam. 7 extols Yahweh's choice of the family of David as the extraordinary vehicle for divine salvation. The Davidic kingship has been established in perpetuity, in that David's throne "shall be made sure forever" (v. 16). Yet it is clear that no political power now remains with Israel's greatest dynasty of rulers, and so the entire promise is seen to be a mockery unless—and it is a large "unless"—God now plans to do a new and unparalleled thing in the life of humankind.

That is precisely what God has in mind, of course, and the text of the Psalm lection for this day is the Magnificat, Mary's song of wonder in Luke 1 over the news that she is to be the bearer of the "Son of the Most High" (Luke 1:32). The joy that bursts forth from Mary's heart is not centered on the fact that she has been favored above all other women (although she is astounded by that reality), but on her realization that human life will now never be the same. That which is high will be brought low, while those who cannot lift themselves will be elevated to new hopes by the power of God.

The Epistle reading is the final three verses of Rom. 16, Paul's ascription at the conclusion of his most influential letter. The apostle rejoices that, by the power of God, the times are what they are. That which was "kept secret for long ages . . . is now disclosed" (vs. 25–26), and therefore the people of God can only rejoice. The God who promised a Davidic king like no other has made that promise true, and to that God "be the glory forever! Amen."

The Gospel lection, like the Psalm lection from Luke 1, brings the sequence of readings full circle and provides a narrative that ties all the other passages together. Gabriel announces to Mary that she is to bear the "Son of God" (v. 35). Overwhelmed by both the holiness and the enormity of the moment, Mary nonetheless consents to the will of God's messenger: "Let it be with me according to your word" (v. 38).

All rejoice, for the new King is soon to appear!

2 Samuel 7:1–11, 16

This narrative text concerns the establishment of the *tribal chief*, David, to be the *founder of an enduring dynasty*. Thus it marks a decisive transition in David's status, as he is now for the first time marked by God as an enduring figure in God's long-term intention for Israel.

The narrative opens in 2 Sam. 7:1–7 with a debate about the appropriateness of a temple for Yahweh in Jerusalem. Temple building was an act of great piety (and no doubt a great gain for political propaganda) for kings in the ancient world. David proposes to do what all self-serving kings in the ancient world do (vs. 1–2).

In vs. 4–7, however, God's mind is changed. God offers a second opinion to David through Nathan. What had been a routine divine approval now becomes an occasion to assert the peculiar character of the God of the Bible. This God is a free, mobile, dynamic God who sojourns, bivouacs, and comes and goes, but never settles and becomes confined in one place. Thus, unlike every other god, this God wants no temple, needs no temple, and will approve no temple. David's pet project is rejected!

Verse 8 abruptly and decisively changes the subject of the narrative. It turns out that the question of the temple is in fact of no special interest for this narrative, but is only a preliminary device with which to surface the real subject. The decisive turn in the rhetoric is marked with the powerful Hebrew *wĕʻattāh*, "and now," the same transitional device we saw in Isa. 64:8 (First Sunday of Advent). It is as though God says, "But enough about me. Let's focus on you." What does God say to "you," (David)? Well, this: "You, David, were nobody until I came along. I am the one who made you what you are." Then follow four first-person verbs in 2 Sam. 7:8–9 (three in the usual English translation), detailing God's gracious, powerful acts on behalf of David:

> I took you . . .
> I have been with you . . .
> [I] have cut off all your enemies . . .
> I will make for you a great name.

In these four statements, the speech refers to all of David's past in which David has been blessed and prospered, and anticipates even David's future, when David will have a "great name," that is an extravagant, quite visible reputation. All of this has been and will be God's doing. David is a receiver of gifts, not an achiever, according to this rhetoric.

Moreover, God's promised fidelity for the future concerns not only David, but the whole community of David's people (vs. 10–11a). It is promised that this people Israel, which has lived at the edge of power, vulnerable in the hill country, exposed to the Philistine threat, will be utterly safe and have "rest," their territory protected and secure.

Finally, after the general promise to David (vs. 8–9) and to Israel (vs. 10–11a), the statement of God reaches its wondrous climax (v. 11b). Yahweh will make David "a house," a dynasty. The sentence plays on the term "house." In vs. 1–2, David wanted to make Yahweh a "house" (=temple), but the process is here inverted. Yahweh generously makes the house (=dynasty), and David is the passive recipient of it. The notice of dynasty is a heady one for a precarious tribal chieftain, with its implication of long-term survival and preeminence. In this promise from God, no doubt laden with propagandistic intention, the family of David takes on abiding significance for the future of Israel and for all of biblical faith. The family of David preempts (hijacks?) the future of Israel's faith.

In v. 16, which concludes this pivotal oracle of God, the rhetoric is stretched and the political-theological intention of the oracle is extended in extraordinary and unprecedented ways. What had been a personal assurance and a political authorization now is escalated into something like an ontological dimension. There is no doubt that this escalated rhetoric is court hyperbole, which wants to claim theological legitimacy for David's powerful political ambition. That is, the king is "wrapped in a flag," and the design of the flag is that of Yahweh's own divine purpose. Thus David arrives at the sort of solidarity with God that not only legitimates him for the future, but places him and his movement beyond political criticism. Read as a political act, this oracle is an act of shameless nerve.

However, in the ongoing development of "messianic faith" in ancient Israel, and certainly in the Advent practice of the church, this text is not seen as shameless political chutzpah. It is, rather, seen as a theological guarantee for the promises of God to Israel, which are to be embodied concretely in this man, this family, and this dynasty. The "house" and the "kingdom" refer to the Davidic establishment and to the "Davidic idea" that endured in and through exile, even after the political apparatus of city and Temple was destroyed. The "Davidic idea" continued for Jews to be a profound rallying point; through it Jews have been able to believe that in God's own time a new member of this promissory family would arise, and with power and authority restore this people to its proper place of dignity and security in the world of political reality. The phrases "sure forever" and "established forever" fix this hope in the imagination of Israel in ways that override the threats, defeats, and vagaries of historical experience.

The vigorous hope of Jews and Christians in God's future for human history through a human agent is rooted in this oracle of 2 Sam. 7. The hope stays on in Jewish (and Christian) hearts. In Advent, Christians dare to claim that this remembered and coming Jesus carries the promise of David for newness and well-being. No wonder John's followers asked of him, "Are you the one who is to come?" (Luke 7:19–20). Advent is for hoping; Christmas is for receiving God's unambiguous, confident Yes!

Luke 1:47–55

As is the case in the lections for the Third Sunday of Advent, the Fourth Sunday offers the worship leader a choice of "Psalm" lections. Here, however, the "Magnificat is preferable to the psalm" (in the words of the lectionary editors), because it relates so closely to the Gospel reading. It also helps to shape our understanding of the Messianic promise in the Old Testament lesson (2 Sam. 7:1–11, 16) which, if allowed to stand alone, is capable of a political interpretation.

But before dismissing the alternative Psalm reading for this day (Ps. 89:1–4, 19–26), one may wish to notice the manner in which it renders its own particular interpretation of 2 Sam. 7. Although the psalm as a whole raises some difficult literary and historical ques-

FOURTH SUNDAY OF ADVENT

tions, those verses that constitute the alternative lection for this day clearly reaffirm Nathan's prophetic words. It is clear that God's covenant with David is the central focus of this passage (see especially v. 3), but the text concludes on a note that lifts the covenant concept out of the mundane world of ancient politics and confers on it an eschatological cast. "Sea" and "rivers" of v. 25 are references to the primal waters of chaos, which God tamed at Creation (Gen. 1:6–10), but which pose an enduring threat to human life and well-being (Gen. 7:11). The pacification of this evil force by the Messianic King, who relies on the power of the supreme God (Ps. 89:26), is a statement not only concerning the present authority of the Messiah, but especially of his rule over the eschaton. Thus this note resonates to one of the important themes of Advent: that the King who has come will also "come again in glory to judge the living and the dead."

The preferred Psalm lection, Luke 1:47–55, takes us in a different direction and speaks to another dimension of Jesus' Messiahship, although one related to that emphasized in Ps. 89:1–4, 19–26. At the outset it should be stressed that to conceptualize the Magnificat as a "psalm" does no violence to the passage in either a literary or a theological sense. It is clearly hymnic in nature, as its repeated use in a musical setting in Christian worship attests.

In addition, its close theological kinship to a number of Old Testament texts indicates that its roots are firmly planted in the soil of Israel-of-old. A number of passages from the Hebrew Bible come to mind when one reads the Magnificat, including 1 Sam. 2:1–10; Ps. 72:12–14; and Isa. 42:5–9. If, never having seen it before, we had come across this text nestled snugly among other Royal psalms in the book of Psalms, we would have scarcely raised an eyebrow.

Its value as a lection on this day is at least twofold. First, as the editors of the lectionary point out, it fills out the story of the annunciation to Mary in Luke 1:26–38, the Gospel lection for the day. The emotional power of that moment is developed with great skill, so that the reader (no matter how often this familiar text is encountered) continues to be as stunned as Mary (well, almost) over the shock of Gabriel's proclamation. Mary's response in that text is muted, as if she has been rendered nearly speechless by the power of the angel's words.

At some point, Mary just *has* to say something! (Notice that in vs. 39–45, the "bridge" between the Gospel and Psalm lections, it is Elizabeth, not Mary, whose words are recorded.) And so when Mary does find her voice, the words gush forth in a torrent of wonder and praise. Verses 46–55 represent the Virgin's moment of catharsis, the venting of her most deeply held emotions. It is one of those elements within the text which endow the entire narrative of Jesus' birth with the flesh-and-blood quality it deserves.

Second, and more important, however, the value of this text lies in the manner in which it helps us to understand God's promise to David. In other words, the Magnificat portrays Messiahship in quite distinctive ways, ways that are in some tension with alternative views of what the Messiah should be and do. In this regard, the initial verses of our text (46–49) serve as a kind of introduction to the whole, and for a brief moment allow Mary to spell out her wonder over what is happening. This is, just to repeat what was noted above, they are a recognition by the text that this woman is a very real human being. How could she not express the deepest sense of awe over God's astounding grace?

The next section (vs. 50–51) emphasizes two qualities of God that are to result in the coming of the King. One of these is mercy, the other is power, qualities that elsewhere are characteristic not only of God but of the divinely anointed king (see Ps. 72:2). It is both because God cares *and* because God is able to bring it about that a new and distinctive Davidic King is soon to come. In the very final section (vs. 54–55) this mercy and power are remembered and are linked to God's promises to Israel-of-old, "to Abraham and to his descendants forever."

The heart of the passage, however, lies in the penultimate section (vs. 52–53). The work of the coming King will be, in part at least, to set the established order on its head. That which is up will be down, while that which is not up will be. The literary models for vs. 52–53 are certainly to be found in such places as 1 Sam. 2:7–8 and Isa. 42:6–7, but the precise manner by which they are here related to the birth of Jesus helps us to understand the peculiar nature of this Davidic King and, as well, helps us to understand that the implications of his messianic rule are both now and yet to come.

Romans 16:25–27

The doxology that concludes Paul's letter to the Romans seems an unlikely choice for a sermon text on a Sunday so close to Christmas. It contains nothing of the romance of the season—no angelic choirs, no weary shepherds, no seeking Magi. In fact, there is no narrative quality to the text at all, and we need stories at Christmas. Furthermore, these three verses have a disputed textual heritage. Some Greek manuscripts locate them at the end of ch. 14 or at the end of ch. 15; others omit them entirely. A number of reputable commentators will argue that the verses were probably added after Paul's time by a later editor. All these considerations may scare the preacher off, sending him or her to the more familiar words of Luke.

But the doxology should not be summarily dismissed. It provides a fitting ending to Romans, and even if added by a later editor, it picks up the themes developed throughout the complex argument of the letter and expresses them liturgically. All good theology ultimately must come to expression in worship, and what better time to express it than the Christmas season! In the context of praise, the heart of God's intentions in the sending of Jesus Christ into the world is a matter of adoration—"to the only wise God, through Jesus Christ, to whom be the glory forever!"

First, a word about liturgical language. We shall try to identify the movements in the doxology that undoubtedly led the shapers of the lectionary to select this text for this Sunday. But the words of worship always tend to be effusive rather than precise, expressions of heartfelt emotion rather than analytical argumentation. It is impossible to outline the prayers in the *Book of Common Prayer* or to diagram their sentences. So with this doxology. Critical to any interpretation must be the recognition of its liturgical quality.

We can observe three movements in the passage that distinguish this doxological expression. First, there is elaboration of Paul's gospel and the proclamation (kerygma) of Jesus Christ as *the revelation of the mystery, long kept secret but now revealed*. The gospel as disclosure has to be taken seriously. The story of Jesus Christ does not have the kind of rational basis that makes it possible for people to "think" their way into becoming believers. Without denigrating theology, it is critical to recognize that the gospel is not an intellectual exercise. The shepherds (who might be stereotyped as nonthinkers) and the Magi (who might be labeled thinkers) each got to Bethlehem by means of disclosure—the shepherds from an angel, the Magi from the scribes at Jerusalem. And so it has been ever since.

To speak of the revelation of a mystery is another way to speak of grace. The divine initiative that makes Christmas possible does not stop with the birth of Jesus, but continues in the unveiling of the meaning of the birth for generations that follow. The penny drops, the light dawns, eyes are opened in the experiences of people who are given to see beyond the trappings of Christmas the significance of the One strangely born.

A second movement in the doxology is a backward movement—to *the prophetic writings* where the mystery was hidden that is now made known *to all the Gentiles*. No specific text in the prophets is cited in the passage (though it is legitimate to think of the Old Testament reading from 2 Sam. 7 as "prophetic"). The letter to the Romans, however, is filled with citations of Old Testament texts that anticipate the revelation of the mystery. The point is that the story of Jesus, odd as it may seem (remember, Paul called it "foolishness" and "a stumbling block," 1 Cor. 1:23), is not an accident of history. The gospel is both planned ("according to the command of the eternal God") and anticipated. As said earlier in Romans, the disclosure of the mystery proves that God's faithfulness is not invalidated (3:3; 15:7–13), that God can be fully trusted (3:21–26).

What about the specific mention of the inclusion of "all the Gentiles"? It is difficult to recapture the force of such a disclosure today, when the church has become exclusively "Gentile." Yet Christmas is an appropriate time to recall that *we* are the outsiders (not the Jews), who have been drawn into the family of God and made recipients of the revealed mystery. The very mention of the word "Gentiles" reminds us of brothers and sisters in the family who during December celebrate Hanukkah.

From gospel to revealed mystery, from revealed mystery to prophetic writings—and the third move is from prophetic writings to human response, *"the obedience of faith."* The phrase serves as the interpretive brackets that begin (1:5) and end (16:26) this significant letter describing what the gospel is to evoke in the lives of those to whom the mystery is disclosed.

Though commentators do not universally agree on the grammatical analysis of the phrase "unto obedience of faith" (literally), the expression nevertheless reminds us that the two words "obedience" and "faith" are inexorably bound together, almost synonymous. An obedience not born of faith is inevitably prone to legalism and to becoming a burden too heavy to bear. Likewise, a faith that fails to obey is empty and vain, no more than mere lip service.

The text, then, confronts us with the wonder and demand of the Christian gospel, expressed in the language of worship and offered as an act of adoration to the God of Christmas.

Luke 1:26–38

The annunciation of Jesus' birth has as its focus just that fact—the advent of Jesus Christ. If modern Christians come to the text with a number of historical, biographical, even biological questions, those are not the questions Luke addresses. Gabriel's extended identification of the child who is to be born indicates where the focus lies for Luke: "You will name him Jesus . . . Son of the Most High . . . the throne of his ancestor David . . . holy . . . Son of God." First and foremost, Luke here identifies Jesus as the subject matter of his entire two-volume work.

Within this annunciation of Christ's advent, three themes take on particular importance. The first theme Gabriel states explicitly: "For nothing will be impossible with God" (1:37). Gabriel's final words to Mary sum up the birth stories both of John the Baptist and of Jesus. Although the conception of John the Baptist is highly unusual, his parents being old and his mother barren, that story nevertheless recalls similar stories from the Hebrew Bible, so that the reader knows what to anticipate. Like Sarah and Abraham, surely Zechariah and Elizabeth will find their hopes fulfilled. But if their hopes are for that which is improbable, the pregnancy of a virgin is manifestly impossible; yet it is just that impossibility which Gabriel says has been overcome.

These words from Gabriel interpret not only the annuciation of Jesus' birth but the whole sweep of Luke-Acts. If Luke's is an "orderly account" (1:3), it is also—and first—an account of the impossible things that God has in fact done. The healing of the sick, the resurrection of Jesus, the gift of the Holy Spirit, the formation of community, the release of the captive apostles—again and again Luke tells of the impossible things actually accomplished by God. The "events that have been fulfilled among us" (v. 1) are events that cannot be believed and yet *must* be believed.

A second theme in this story, and a theme too often neglected, is that of grace. Gabriel greets Mary with the words "Greetings, favored one! The Lord is with you," and assures her, "You have found favor with God." The Greek verb and noun (*charizomai* and *charis*), here translated "favor," could equally well be translated as "grace." Mary is the object of God's grace.

What is it about Mary that makes her appropriate as an object of God's grace? Startlingly, nothing in the text provides even a hint to the answer to that question. Luke identifies her simply as a young girl who was engaged to be married. More is said about Joseph (he is of the house of David) than about Mary. Even in the case of Zechariah and Elizabeth, Luke explains that they are righteous and blameless, that they kept God's commandments and prayed to God (1:6–7, 13). Yet not a single word describes the virtues or vices of Mary or explains why God might have chosen her.

That is, of course, precisely the point: God chooses because God chooses. Mary does not earn or deserve the honor of becoming the mother of Jesus any more than would any other woman. This text might profitably be read alongside Romans 9:6–29, where Paul articulates the right of God as God to make whatever choices God elects to make. The biblical story is not one of virtue rewarded—or vice punished—but of the relentlessly unmerited nature of God's grace.

What is Mary's response to this grace? The answer to that question touches on the third theme of the passage. Following Gabriel's announcement, Mary first identifies herself as "the servant of the Lord." A better translation would be "slave of the Lord" since the Greek word (*doulos*) certainly connotes the involuntary relationship of slavery, not one in which an individual has agreed to service for a wage. Mary's first response, then, recognizes that she has been selected by God and that God's choosing leaves no room for her own volition. Like others within Luke's story, most notably the apostle Paul, Mary's service comes about as a result of God's plan, not her own.

Nevertheless, with the second part of her response, Mary consents to God's plan: "Let it be with me according to your word." In the Magnificat that follows immediately upon this scene, Luke places in Mary's mouth words that powerfully interpret the birth of Jesus Christ as the triumph of God for God's people. Later still, she puzzles over events surrounding her child's birth and his behavior. Here at the beginning, however, Mary signals her "yes" to God's action, a consent that she cannot fully understand.

Contemporary Christians sometimes balk at the passivity attributed to Mary in this scene, especially in light of the fact that she is sometimes invoked as a model for all women. What needs to be recalled, however, is that Mary later does take initiative, when she interprets events in the Magnificat and when she seeks after her child in the Temple. It is also important to recall that Luke portrays most of his characters, both women and men, as the passive objects of God's intervention. Luke's is, beginning to end, a story of God's plan and God's action for the salvation of the whole people of God; given that starting point, it is little wonder that human characters appear quiescent.

CHRISTMAS, FIRST PROPER

The themes of the rule of God and of the divinely appointed monarch, so prominent in Advent texts, also figure in large measure in these lections for Christmas Eve/Day. In certain ways, these texts are predictable, in that they not only announce the coming of the King, but also project the nature of the divine rule. The two lections from the Old Testament, Isa. 9:2–7 and Ps. 96, are closely related to the political ideology of the Davidic monarch in ancient Israel and, in the view of many scholars, functioned in the life of the people in a political sense, before their transpolitical authority was understood. The Gospel lection is the engaging story from Luke 2:1–20, without a reading of which Christmas could simply not be Christmas at all.

But in other respects these texts are startling and intrusive. In Isa. 9:2–7, the new king is welcomed with all the trumpetry surrounding an important royal birth or coronation, but the text then points not to a triumph of the new king's armies (as one might expect), but to the ascendancy of "justice" and "righteousness." Psalm 96 echoes that expectation, even as it looks beyond any human king to the rule of King Yahweh. Luke 2, for all its familiarity to ears that have heard it over and over again, jolts us by its juxtaposition of the figures of King Jesus, wrapped in swaddling cloths, and the Emperor Augustus, ordering the census of the people. We who have read beyond Luke 2 know which king will truly and ultimately reign, but of that the text itself only hints. And Titus 2:11–14, while perhaps not striking the reader immediately as a royal text, outdistances the other lections for this day, in that it not only celebrates the King who has come, but him who will come again, "our great God and Savior, Jesus Christ" (v. 13).

Thus there are common threads that bind these lections together, but there is also a sense of theological "movement." And together, the texts express that which goes beyond the boundaries of any single one of them. For they urge those who read them and who hear them read not only to celebrate the coming of the King and the dawning of the special qualities of the kingdom, but to prepare for the return of Him whose rule is both "yet" and "not yet," both present and still to come.

Isaiah 9:2–7 (A B C)

This well-known oracle is apparently a public decree from the royal palace. It concerns the emergence of a new king in Jerusalem. Two scholarly hypotheses are usual concerning the oracle. First, it may be the *birth announcement* of a new heir to the Davidic throne. Second, the oracle may be a *coronation announcement* when the prince succeeds his father on the throne. In either case, the celebrative rhetoric proclaims the new heir as the fulfillment of all the long-standing hopes and expectations of the realm.

The oracle persists in its "power" voice long after any concrete reference to a specific king has been given up. The oracle has become an announcement of God's faithful gift of newness through a new ruler, in response to sore need in the community. The newness mediated by the oracle is that the realm has come under new governance. That oracle then may have had repeated use in the royal court, as each new king is thought to be at last the one who will establish a right government. Moreover, if the oracle had taken on a life of its own in the political-liturgical rhetoric of ancient Israel, then it is not surprising that the church found the oracle useful and appropriate for its announcement of Jesus.

That indeed is the role of the angels in the Bethlehem story (Luke 2:10–14). They are making an announcement (either birth or coronation) on behalf of the court. A new heir has been designated, who will faithfully inaugurate a new creation. Thus Jesus is not announced in a rhetorical vacuum, but the tradition utilizes the common royal language of newness.

The oracle begins with *a general expression of joy* at the profound transformation that is just under way (Isa. 9:1–2). The joy at the newness is characterized by two references. It is joy as in the time of a good harvest (v. 3). The joy of harvest comes when anxiety about crops is nullified and economic prosperity is assured for another year. Or it is joy as at the end of the battle, when the enemy has been routed (vs. 4–5). The poem anticipates an utter newness, which overcomes all the harsh reality of the recent past.

Future well-being depends on *defeat of the enemy* that has been threatening (vs. 4–5). These verses are commonly skipped over in church reading. They are, however, crucial to the development of the poem. They indicate that the newness is concretely related to the realities of power. The community has lived under the boot of oppression, exploitation, and humiliation. Now, however, in the form of the new king comes rescue!

The anticipated rescue will be brutal and violent. The coming "light" is powerful enough to seize all the boots of the enemy soldiers, all their uniforms, which are soaked in their blood, to burn them in a huge fire (compare Ps. 46:8–9). This is disarmament, but it is disarmament by a victor. The fire is an act of triumph and defiance that nullifies the enemy, to eliminate his threat and to destroy his myth of invincibility. No wonder the folk cheered, for the occupying enemy had generated deep and abiding hatred.

Only now do we learn the cause of the joy (Isa. 9:2–3) and the reason for victory (vs. 4–5). The turn of the future is because *there is an heir*, a son (vs. 6–7)! He will head the government, which has been desolate and irrelevant. In the announcement of birth or of coronation, the new heir is given names that assert Judah's best memories and deepest hopes. The new king will be utterly sagacious in dispensing justice ("Wonderful Counselor"), will have the power, prowess, and potency of a god ("Mighty God"), will be as reassuring and protective as a great tribal leader ("Everlasting Father"), and will be a bringer of peace and prosperity ("Prince of Peace").

The oracle ends with two theological affirmations (v. 7). First, the coming rule is marked by "justice" and "righteousness," by care for people and mercy toward the weak. The new rule is not one of self-aggrandizing power, but it will enact and embody the best hopes of the old Mosaic covenant. Jerusalem had long neglected justice and righteousness (compare 1:21–23; 5:7), but now it will be rehabilitated (compare 56:1). The king will at last do what the prophets had always hoped. Second, the newness embodied by the new heir is the work of Yahweh, wrought by the passion and faithfulness of God. This faithful king is no self-starter. Israel's daily hope is rooted in the reality of this covenant-making, world-transforming, justice-working God!

Psalm 96 (A B C)

This psalm, with its expansive mood of joy and celebration, is an exclamation of praise perfectly appropriate for Christmas Eve or Christmas Day. Like other psalms of praise, Ps. 96 reads as if it were written with an eye toward its use in public worship, the worshiping congregation (v. 7) and the temple of God (v. 6) being almost tangible objects within the poem. Whether, as some scholars argue, it was originally an enthronement psalm for ancient Judean kings or, as others propose, a song in celebration of the ark of the covenant, this psalm has been changed and spoken at festive moments in the life of the people of God over the centuries. Indeed, it is striking that it is the people who are addressed directly throughout this psalm, as Yahweh, the God of Israel, is consistently referred to in the third person.

Perhaps the initial feature of this psalm to attract the reader's attention is the triple imperative that begins the psalm: Sing! (vs. 1–2). The imperative is plural in Hebrew, a feature that, once more, underscores the psalm's interest in the worshiping congregation. Furthermore, this imperative (*šîrû*) is strengthened by the cognate noun "song" (*šîr*), which appears in the very first line of the psalm. An additional note of emphasis is the triple use of the phrase "to the LORD." In other words, the poet has used the very effective devices of repetition and similarity of sound to urge the worshiping people: "Praise the LORD!"

As is often the case in psalms of praise, Ps. 96 soon addresses the reasons for praising God. In the first part of the psalm, these are at least two in number: first, Yahweh is an actual God and not, like the deities of other nations, a nonentity (v. 5a). Second, it is Yahweh, Israel's God, who created the heavens (v. 5b) and who is encountered as a living Reality in the house of worship (v. 6). (It is interesting that 1 Chron. 16, which provides a somewhat different version of Ps. 96, reads for 96:6b, "strength and *joy* are in his [holy] place," 1 Chron. 16:27, emphasis added).

The structure of Ps. 96:1–6—the imperative to praise Yahweh followed by the reasons for doing so—is repeated in vs. 7–13. Here the imperative is "Give [NRSV: Ascribe] glory to Yahweh!" a call to worship that is linked with a very specific act of self-giving: "Bring an offering" (v. 8).

In vs. 7–13 the reason for praising Yahweh is as straightforward as it is profound: "The LORD is king!" (v. 10), and here we come to what is perhaps the central affirmation of the psalm. The kingship of God, which was revealed at creation (v. 10b), is further expressed in Yahweh's role as the administrator of justice (vs. 10c, 13). Verse 13, in fact, might be translated, instead of NRSV's "judge," as "bring justice." And v. 13 goes on to detail the means by which Yahweh's justice is to be expressed: "with righteousness" and "with his truth." Thus, as do a number of the psalms that refer to the rule of God or to that of the God-appointed Davidic monarch, the justice of Yahweh the King is linked to the divine expression of other moral values.

And because Yahweh is a king of justice, righteousness, and peace, all creation rejoices (vs. 11–12):

> the heavens,
> the earth,
> the sea and its creatures,
> the field and its creatures,
> the trees of the woods.

All join in praising the coming of the King!

And it is of great significance that the King *is coming* (or has come—the Hebrew is ambiguous). Whatever the original significance of this phrase (v. 13a) within the liturgy of ancient Israel may have been—and we cannot be sure—it deepens our understanding that the psalmist sang not of some distant God, remote and unconcerned. Rather, the God who reigns over Israel and over the world is a God who cares, who insists on justice, righteousness, and peace in the lives of the people, and who is personally present to see that these qualities mold the nature of human life. Thus, the ultimate reason for this song of joy is not simply that the God of justice reigns, but that that God is here. Now.

This is, of course, the story of Christmas: the Babe of Bethlehem and the regnant God are one. That the story is one of mystery and wonder is, of course, a part of its power. Yet the mystery and wonder are not limited to the question of the incarnation: "How in the world could God become a human being?" The mystery and wonder also extend to the prior question, "How could the Maker and Ruler of the universe care whether life is just?" We cannot fathom the answer to either question, of course. But just as the lection from Luke 2 affirms that God assumed human flesh at Bethlehem, so Ps. 96, in lyric tones, insists that God cares how men and women live. When we are seized by the joy of which the psalmist sings, we begin to understand—however dimly—the full meaning of the birth of Mary's Son.

Titus 2:11–14 (A B C)

In common with the other readings assigned for this day, Titus 2:11–14 celebrates the glorious appearance of God's grace. What distinguishes this lesson from the others is the explicit connection the writer makes between that grace and the ethical response it entails.

Warnings about appropriate behavior run throughout this letter.

Even the salutation identifies Paul's apostleship with the furtherance of "godliness" (1:1). The bulk of the first chapter concerns qualifications for Christian leadership, and dominating those qualifications is the need for moral and upright behavior. Chapter 2 continues instructions about what Titus is to teach various groups within the community regarding their Christian behavior. While specific admonitions in Titus sharply offend late twentieth-century Christians (for example, the expectation that women are to be submissive to their husbands and slaves to their masters), the need for discipline and identity within the Christian community emerges as a crucial issue in our own time.

Titus 2:11 shows that the disciplined behavior urged by the author of Titus has a profoundly theological root: "For the grace of God has appeared, bringing salvation to all." In this single verse we find an apt summary of the Christmas story. First, it is about God's grace. In common with other New Testament writings, the event of the birth, death, and resurrection of Jesus Christ is subsumed under the single title "grace."

English translations necessarily obscure the fact that the Greek verb here is *epiphainein*, from the root of which we get our English noun, epiphany. God's grace makes its appearance in Jesus Christ. Notice the way in which what we sometimes think of as an attribute of God—that is, grace—is anthropomorphized by its use with a verb.

The appearance of grace has its purpose in the salvation of all people. It is worth pondering what alternative purpose there might be for the epiphany of God's grace. Perhaps God's grace might find its purpose in self-glorification or in the sheer awe of human acknowledgment of God. The testimony of scripture, however, is that God's intent in the epiphany is to save humankind.

No qualifications limit those who are the object of God's salvation. The noun used in the Greek text, *anthrōpos*, includes both men and women, although it is often translated as "man." "All people" surely includes the well-known categories of human beings Paul uses in Gal. 3:28 (Jew and Greek, slave and free, male and female). It also includes sinner and penitent, persecutor and persecuted, "insiders" and "outsiders" of every type. God's salvific grace knows no limits.

God's grace does, however, have an impact on the way people live their lives. Following v. 11's powerful statement of the Christmas message, vs. 12–14 explain how grace "trains" or, better, "disciplines" human beings in three distinct but related ways. The first discipline of grace is stated in negative terms. Believers are to "renounce impiety and worldly passions," terms that may well reflect the Gentile origins of the writer and his audience. A Gentile who became a Christian was said to have turned away from the worship of idols, things that are not God (Gal. 4:8–9; 1 Thess. 1:9). The same claim would not, of course, be made about Jewish Christians, who had always worshiped the true and only God.

It is not enough, of course, merely to renounce things that are bad, although perhaps some early Christians, like some latter-day Christians, regarded Christian behavior simply as a list of prohibitions. The second discipline of grace consists of living "lives that are self-controlled, upright, and godly." This wording has an austere, nearly puritanical connotation that is unnecessarily harsh. To be "self-controlled" (*sōphronōs*) is to show moderation. The word has to do with being reasonable or sensible. "Upright" translates the familiar *dikaiōs*, which pertains to living justly or rightly. To live a "godly" (*eusebōs*) life pertains to devotion or awe that one addresses to God. The first word pertains to the way one deals with oneself (with control), the second to the way one deals with others (justly), and the third to the way one deals with God (with reverence).

While these first two disciplines of grace are confined to life in "this world," that is, in the present, the third discipline results in expectation. Grace teaches believers to wait for "the blessed hope and the manifestation of the glory of our great God and Savior, Jesus Christ. He it is who gave himself for us that he might redeem us from all iniquity and purify for himself a people of his own who are zealous for good deeds" (Titus 2:13–14). This summary of Christian confidence in the future reminds us that our celebration of the first advent of God's grace in Jesus Christ is a celebration of the promised Second Advent as well.

Luke 2:1–14 (15–20) (A B C)

Luke's account of the birth of Jesus appears as the Gospel lesson for both the First and Second Propers of Christmas. Since the reading for the Second Proper is limited to vs. 8–20, we shall concentrate the commentary on vs. 1–7 for the First Proper and deal with the remainder of the story under the Second Proper.

This passage, so beautifully crafted in Luke's narrative, certainly counts among the most familiar passages in the Bible. Dramatizations of the Christmas story as well as repeated readings make it a well-known text. People in North America who know little or nothing about the Christian faith know about the shepherds and the angelic chorus. For that reason, the text presents a challenge to the preacher to hear and declare a fresh word that probes the familiar and yet moves beyond it.

What immediately emerges from the early portion of this story is the political context in which the birth of Jesus is recounted. We are told that Emperor Augustus had ordered an enrollment and that Quirinius was governor of Syria. Despite the problems surrounding the historical accuracy of this beginning (dealt with in most commentaries), the narrative setting cannot be ignored. It is not against the background of the reign of Herod, the local ruler who is known for his heavy-handed and brutal ways, that the story of Jesus' birth is told (as in Matthew's Gospel), but against the background of the Roman Empire.

The emperor Octavian was a prominent figure, who solidified the somewhat divided loyalties of the various regions of the empire and ushered in the famous Pax Romana. In 27 B.C., the Roman senate gave him the title "the August One." Poets wrote of his peaceful ideals and anticipated that his reign would signal a golden age based on virtue. Ancient monuments even ascribed to him the title "savior." He represented a high and hopeful moment in Roman history.

Luke gives Octavian his familiar title and recognizes his authority by noting that "all the world" (actually the Roman Empire) is encompassed by his decree. Often in ancient times the demand for a census evoked rebellion and opposition, but Luke records a dutiful response: "All went to their own towns to be registered." The mention of Augustus not only provides an indispensable time reference to help readers date the events that are being narrated, but also enables Luke to explain how Mary and Joseph, who lived in Nazareth, had a baby born in Bethlehem.

The introduction, however, provides a much more important function than this. It sets the stage for the birth of one who is Savior, Christ the Lord. Octavian is not pictured as an evil, oppressive tyrant, a bloody beast "uttering haughty and blasphemous words" (Rev. 13:5). The Roman state in Luke's narrative simply does not represent the enemy against which Christians must fight. The backdrop for Jesus' birth is rather a relatively humane and stable structure, the best of ancient governments, which led to dreams of a peaceful era and aspirations of a new and wonderful age. The decades between the time of Jesus' birth and the time of Luke's narrative, however, exposed the failed hopes and the doused aspirations. Octavian is succeeded by caesars who turn the imperial dreams into nightmares.

Against the horizon of disillusionment, we read of the birth of another ruler, from the lineage of David, whose meager beginnings, on the surface, do not compare with the promise and hope of Augustus. All the world obeys the caesar, but Jesus' parents are rejected and relegated to a cattle stall. Yet the birth of Jesus is good news for all the people, ensuring a new and lasting promise of peace and goodwill.

The narrative does not present us with a confrontation between Augustus and Jesus, but with a contrast between vain expectations and true hope, between the disappointment that follows misplaced anticipations and the energy born of a divine promise, between the imposing but short-lived power of Caesar's rule and the humble manifestation of the eternal dominion of God, between the peace of Rome and the peace of Christ. The titles for Jesus, found later in the narrative (Luke 2:11)—Savior, Christ, and Lord—stand out starkly against the claims made for Augustus, and in the ensuing story become titles interpreted in fresh and surprising ways.

The setting for Luke's birth narrative clarifies for us the distinction between false hopes and true ones. Relatively humane, stable structures that contribute to the well-being of others often tend to promise more than they can deliver. Their very positive nature becomes seductive and generates impossible expectations. In contrast, Jesus is the anchor for reliable hope, for dependable promises, for anticipations that are more than fulfilled.

CHRISTMAS, SECOND PROPER

A variety of perspectives characterizes this collection of Christmas lections, and a variety of emotions as well, ranging from hope over what God has promised to do to joy over what God has done. The verses from Isa. 62 express the people's sense of expectation that God will complete that which God has already promised. But this expectation is couched in terms that suggest that God's people—and the hope they cherish—are vulnerable and cannot forever endure God's apparent need to be reminded of what God has promised to do. Psalm 97, on the other hand, knows nothing of vulnerability but is a straightforward celebration of the presence of God, a presence that all creation affirms and that results in righteousness and justice drawn to dimensions which are both cosmic and human.

The tender story of the visitation to the shepherds in Luke 2:8–20 is but an extension of the royal theology of Ps. 97. But what an extension! Here there are no melting mountains giving witness to the rule of God, but a chorus of angels who testify that the King of kings is to be found in a most unkingly milieu—a manger. Finally, the lection from the epistles, Titus 3:4–7, adds to this theological and emotional mix the important element of grace: the good news of God's intervention in human life is a declaration not of that which men and women deserve, but of what God has freely given.

In a significant manner, therefore, the four lections rehearse the drama of redemption, beginning with human need, moving through an acknowledgment of God's concern and power, and culminating in a declaration of God's compassion out of which issues God's saving initiative. They thereby formulate a history of salvation for women and men everywhere who have found in Jesus Christ the expression of all that God is and does.

Christmas is an acknowledgment of that history and, as any meaningful celebration must be, a rehearsal of it. But it is a rehearsal that views the history of salvation, not as chronological increments, but as a progression of events all of which happen simultaneously. Even we who rejoice over a gracious God's gift of the Son and our acceptance of this gift—the latter stages of the drama—must acknowledge that in certain ways we are still mired in the earlier stages in that we are vulnerable and must pray daily for God's presence and affirmation.

That view of Christmas, therefore, which tends to emphasize the triumphalist aspects of the occasion to the exclusion of its statements concerning human weakness and need is only partially on target. The diversity of these four lections helps us to hear the many voices with which Christmas speaks and sings.

Isaiah 62:6–12 (A B C)

This poem is set in the context of exiles who have returned to Jerusalem. They found the city to which they returned less than honored. Indeed, the city, which had been destroyed by the Babylonians, is still pitiful in its desolation, a source of embarrassment. God had promised a transformation, but has not yet worked it. The poem concerns the expectation and insistence of the faithful that God must be moved to act for the sake of the beloved city.

The problem is to compel God to act as God has promised to act. The poet does not reflect on why God has not acted; he only knows that there has been none of the saving action promised by God. For that reason, the poet devises a strategy to secure from God a rescued, restored city (vs. 6–7). "Sentinels" will be stationed on the walls around the city. They will be endlessly diligent in their work; they have only one task, a most peculiar task. They are to speak, not be silent. They are to speak incessantly. Their speech is to remind God of God's promises, to alert God to the needs of the city, to nag God, to invoke God, to move God to act.

The prayer on behalf of the city is an act of passionate hope. The hope is governed by the particle "until" (see v. 1). The city of Jerusalem waits eagerly under the influence of God's "until." The community is in expectation, waiting until God will keep God's promise. Thus the "until" of hoping faith stands between the passionate prayer of Israel and God's own faithful action. It is the conviction of the poet that God can be forced to enact that "until" by persuasive intercession. That, however, can happen only if God is endlessly reminded to be faithful.

The affirmation of these verses is that God has indeed heeded the "reminders" of vs. 6–7, has acted to restore Jerusalem; the city is assured a future of joy and well-being (vs. 10–12). Thus, vs. 6–7 have "worked," and Jerusalem has received its "until" from God.

God's spectacular presence will give the city a new name. The city had appeared to observers to be pitiful and abandoned, called "Forsaken" (see v. 4). Now the ones in the city are a holy people, believing utterly in God. They are Yahweh's redeemed, Yahweh's special project, and recipient of God's staggering care.

As anyone can see, the city is no longer "forsaken," but can be called "Sought Out," cared for, valued, treasured. Thus, what is a hope in vs. 6–7 now has become a reality. The poem asserts that the God who seemed not to care can be mobilized to act.

This poem testifies to God's faithfulness, which transforms Jerusalem. The difficult question is how to treat a Jerusalem text in terms of the rule of Jesus, as the opening of the new age.

It is most plausible to take "Jerusalem" as a metaphor, but as a metaphor for what? We may suggest three ways in which the metaphor might function in rethinking the larger impact of Jesus' birth:

1. Calvin takes "Jerusalem" to be *the church*, God's beloved community, which God shelters and for which God cares. On this reading, the text promises that the church will be healed of its disarray and will become an adequate habitat for the power and ministry of God.

2. "Jerusalem" is no doubt linked to *"creation"* in the tradition, so that "new Jerusalem" bespeaks "new creation" (compare Isa. 65:17–18; Rev. 21:1–4). On this reading, the text anticipates the renovation of a needy, distraught world.

3. "Jerusalem" functions in the Gospel narratives in relation to the notion of "kingdom." Thus the kingdom of David becomes the kingdom of Jesus, which is the kingdom of God (compare Mark 1:14–15). On this reading, "Jerusalem" is a reference to the new society, the new socioeconomic arrangement that makes human, humane life possible.

It is odd that Jerusalem is "invaded" by Jesus in ways that threaten the authorities (Luke 9:51). The same Jesus, however, weeps over and yearns for Jerusalem, waiting with this text for God's promises to be kept (Luke 13:33–35; 19:41–44). Our reading of this text must not be so freely metaphorical that we miss the actual flesh-and-blood reality of the city, a reality enmeshed in dismay, but only "until"—until God acts. When God acts, Jerusalem is "sought out," as is the church, as is every city, as is creation, as is humanity, sought out by God for love, care, healing, forgiveness, and finally newness. The preachable point is God's "until."

CHRISTMAS, SECOND PROPER

Psalm 97 (A B C)

A celebration of the kingship of God, a belief that figures prominently in the faith of ancient Israel, is at the heart of this psalm. The first half of the psalm (vs. 1–6) describes the majesty of the divine King, while the last half (vs. 7–12) raises implications for the life of the people concerning God's rule.

Yahweh's majesty is portrayed primarily by means of figures of speech associated with a thunderstorm: clouds, darkness, fire, and lightning. The presence of Yahweh is so awesome that Yahweh's enemies are reduced to ashes, and even the otherwise solid mountains melt. Hyperbole, to be sure (for similar uses of these figures, see especially Ps. 29). Yet nestled among the metaphors are straightforward statements concerning the personal qualities of Yahweh. Yahweh's rule is based on righteousness and justice (v. 2b), a moral order built into the very fabric of the universe (v. 6).

As to what the rule of God means in the lives of people, the psalm notes that idolatry inevitably leads to despair, whereas Yahweh's presence sustains and supports Yahweh's people (vs. 7–10). Light and joy await those for whom the righteousness of the King has become a personal moral order (v. 11).

The final verse of the psalm (v. 12) is a call to these righteous ones to rejoice and give thanks to the Lord!

The relevance of this text to Christmas lies, first, in its celebration of the royal presence of God. In some ways the fire and lightning of the first half of the psalm may seem out of place in the celebration of the birth of a Babe, the "gentle Jesus, meek and mild" of the familiar hymn. But the church has maintained from its earliest beginnings that the Infant of Bethlehem is but one aspect of the nature of the incarnate Son, that he who "was conceived by the Holy Spirit" and "born of the Virgin Mary" will also "come to judge the living and the dead." And thus this Psalm lection recalls for us that the God who, in the Holy Child, comes to us in vulnerability and weakness is also the One who presides over the affairs of the universe and who insists that justice be done. If the violent language of the thunderstorm seems to the modern mind an unusual means of expressing the nature of God—to say nothing of the concept of the annihilation of God's enemies (v. 3b)—it may be helpful to remember that the language of the biblical poets is often extravagant, in that they frequently used the most intense human experiences to convey the nature of a God whom ordinary words cannot contain (compare Ex. 15:3, "The LORD is a warrior").

Beyond its celebration of the presence of Yahweh the King, this Psalm lection is consistent with other Advent and Christmas texts in its declaration that the rule of God is based on righteousness and justice. The manner in which these qualities are described here makes it clear that they are not incidental to human life, but are part of the tissue that God has woven into the universe. To act unjustly or unrighteously—to be an unjust or unrighteous person or society—is to repudiate the purposes for which all life exists. And it is, of course, to repudiate God.

Thus the value of this psalm as a Christmas lection lies in its ability to project the larger dimensions of the incarnation. It is tempting on this day to be occupied with the image of the helpless child in the manger and, therefore, to orient our festival around the children in our families and around the childishness in us all. To be sure, that is an important quality to be preserved, because it helps us to come to terms with our own weakness and vulnerability. It also brings us nearer to Jesus' teaching that the kingdom of God is a kingdom of children (Mark 9:36–37 and parallels).

But a more comprehensive understanding of Christmas includes the acknowledgment that Jesus' weakness—evident not only at Bethlehem, but at Calvary as well—is complemented by his role as King and divine Lord. At the heart of Christian belief is the affirmation that the infant son of Mary and the crucified Galilean peasant is also the Sovereign of the universe, who was present at the beginning (John 1:1) and who will preside over the end (Rev. 1:4–8). His rule is one of justice, righteousness, and peace, and those who would prepare themselves to be the citizens of his kingdom will dedicate themselves to these qualities now, as they/we try to create of the present time an anticipation of the time yet to come.

To celebrate Christmas without embracing this larger meaning is to sentimentalize and trivialize the festival. Christ's presence in human life is intended to change us, to reshape our commitments and our priorities so that they reflect the values of the kingdom of God. We may meet Christ at this season as the pink and cuddly Babe who reminds us of the innocence with which life begins. But when we follow him from the manger into the harsh and struggling world, we are asked to follow him to a cross. Our Christmas joy, however, derives from our knowing that not even a cross could defeat the just and peaceable kingdom over which he will preside at the end of time.

Titus 3:4–7 (A B C)

This text appropriately stands coupled with the angelic visitation to the shepherds in Luke 2:8–20, for what Luke conveys in narrative, the epistle to Titus asserts in the form of a creed—namely, that the inbreaking of God through Jesus Christ results entirely from God's decision.

In Titus, this assertion begins with a striking contrast between human existence before and after the Christ-event. Verse 3 details a catalog of evils to which human beings are susceptible, in order to show the profound character of God's salvation. Verse 4 introduces the advent of Jesus Christ as an event of radical discontinuity ("But when...").

Here the coming of Jesus Christ, the Christmas event, is described as "the goodness and loving kindness of God our Savior." As in Titus 2:11-14 and elsewhere in the New Testament, God's action stems not from self-glorification but from God's profound love of humankind. This attribute of God "appears" in human history, and the verb used here is the same one from which we derive our term "epiphany" (see 2:11).

The verses that follow characterize the meaning of this epiphany for humankind. Titus 3:5 introduces an important contrast, which can best be seen through a somewhat literal translation:

> not from works on the basis of righteousness
> that *we* did
> but on the basis of *his* mercy
> he saved *us*.

Several pairs of opposites give emphasis to the contrast here. The first and third lines contrast the means by which salvation has been accomplished—that is, not righteousness but mercy. The second and fourth lines contrast the agents of salvation—not human beings but God alone. The pronouns underscore this contrast, and the result of the whole is a denial of any notion that the salvation of human beings results from their own virtue.

The end of v. 5 amplifies God's salvation. It comes about as a result of his mercy and "by the water of rebirth and renewal by the Holy Spirit." Probably "water" refers to the practice of baptism, which Christians early on associated with renewal and the gift of the Holy Spirit. "Rebirth" (*paliggenesia*), of course, is a concept that many religious traditions associate with conversion. In the context of Titus, rebirth refers specifically to moral rebirth. The gift of God in Jesus Christ enables human beings to turn from their former lives and to live in conformity with God's will.

At first glance, v. 6 adds little to what has already been said, but it is nevertheless a significant part of the text. First, the statement that

God "poured out [this Spirit] on us richly" characterizes God's gift as a generous one. This imagery of pouring out water rather than measuring a minimal amount sufficient for the task conveys the extravagance of God's salvation. Second, the reference to Jesus Christ as the agent of God's salvation tells in concrete terms the means by which God's salvation made its epiphany. Through a human being, God has embraced all of humankind.

Verse 7 recalls the goal of salvation in terms of justification and the eschatological hope. Having been justified by the grace of Christ, believers become heirs "to the hope of eternal life." This statement carefully avoids asserting that believers *already* possess eternal life, for that final gift stands as the culmination of God's acts of salvation. Nevertheless, believers live out of their hope, their confidence, in God's power over death itself.

The opening words of v. 8 ("The saying is sure") suggest that what precedes in vs. 4–7 is taken from an early Christian tradition which the author quotes. These opening words also reinforce the trustworthiness of the claims that have just been made. God may be relied on to complete the salvation begun in Jesus Christ.

As a reading for Christmas Day, this text reminds us of the fact that the birth of Jesus Christ takes place as sheer gift. No human act imagined it, willed it, brought it about. It results solely from the generous, even outrageous, love of God for humankind. This text, with its strong assertions about the salvation accomplished in Jesus Christ, also reminds us that the events of Christmas occur *on our behalf*. The celebration of Christmas as a wonderful story about the lowly birth of a great hero completely misses the point that the Savior who is born is born for us. Here Titus 3:4–7 announces the message of the angels: "To you is born this day in the city of David a Savior. . . ."

Luke 2:(1–7) 8–20 (A B C)

The birth of Jesus is the center of Christmas. What one learns about Jesus from the narratives that relate his birth comes, however, from the actions and words of the other characters of Christmas—in Luke, from the shepherds, the angelic messenger, the heavenly chorus, the mysterious bystanders (2:18), and Mary; in Matthew, from repeated angelic messengers, Joseph, the Wise Men, Herod, the chief priests and scribes. Nowhere is that more evident than in the Lukan story, where a bare statement of the birth of Jesus is followed by the intriguing account of the nameless shepherds. They are traced from their location in the field tending their flock through their visit to Bethlehem and back to where they originated. From their actions and their interactions with the angelic messenger and the heavenly host, we learn about the character and significance of Jesus' birth.

We first meet the shepherds doing what shepherds are supposed to be doing—tending their flocks. They no doubt remind Luke's readers of the shepherding done once in these same regions by Jesus' famous ancestor, David. The routineness of these shepherds' lives is abruptly interrupted by the appearance of the angelic messenger. Their world, circumscribed at night by the wandering of the sheep, is exploded by the awesome presence of this one who brings news of Jesus' birth. The manifestation of the divine glory, the shepherds' fright, the announcement of the messenger disrupt their order and uniformity and set them on a journey to hear and see earth-changing events.

Three things we note about the intrusive announcement of the messenger. First, the good news includes great joy for "all the people." It is not merely the shepherds' small world that is changed by the word of Jesus' birth, but it is Israel's world. While Luke sets the story of the birth in the context of the Roman Empire (2:1–2), he has a primary interest in the destiny of Israel and "the falling and the rising of many" for whom this baby is set (v. 34). Jesus' relevance for the world, in fact, begins in the city of David as the fulfillment of Jewish expectations. It includes the acceptance of Jewish traditions (vs. 21, 22–40, 41–52), and only from this very particular origin does its universal character emerge.

Second, the announcement focuses on three astounding titles this baby is to carry—Savior, Messiah, and Lord. "Savior" has meaning in the narrative because original readers would recognize that such a title the exalted Emperor Augustus had borne. Unfortunately, the eager anticipations for a brighter, more peaceful day stirred by his rule were long since dashed by the brutality and weakness of his successors. Now a true and promise-fulfilling Savior appears. "Messiah" (or "Christ") reminds us of Israel's hope for the anointed figure and God's grand design which he will inaugurate. "Lord," interestingly, occurs four times in our passage, and in the other three instances is used for God (2:9 [twice], 15). It is inescapable in such a context, then, that divine associations be attached to Jesus (in v. 11).

Third, the angelic announcement designates the sign that will assure the shepherds that they have found "a Savior, who is the Messiah, the Lord." But such a strange sign! Hardly fitting for one bearing such honored titles! The babe "wrapped in bands of cloth and lying in a manger," however, is only the beginning of the story of God's unusual ways in accomplishing the divine rule. Not by might or coercive tactics, but in submission and humbleness, Jesus fulfills his vocation.

Perhaps it is the perplexity caused by such a menial sign for such an exalted baby that evokes the immediate confirmation of the heavenly chorus, who join the angelic messenger in a doxology. God is praised for the birth of this child because the birth begins God's reign of peace on earth. The creatures of the heavenly world, in a context of praise, announce God's good plans for this world.

Having heard the heavenly witnesses, the shepherds now decide to go to Bethlehem and "see" this revelation. Like other disciples who abruptly leave fishing boats and tax tables, they go "with haste." We are not told what happened to the flocks, apparently left in the fields. The shepherds' old world has been shattered by the appearance of the messenger, and now they are in search of a new one, one centered in the event that has occurred in Bethlehem.

When the shepherds find Mary, Joseph, and Jesus, the narrator records that they report the message that had been made known to them about the baby. To whom did they give their report? To Mary and Joseph? Perhaps. Perhaps the shepherds in responding to the angelic messenger in fact become a confirmation to Mary and Joseph of the significance of this baby so unusually born. But there must have been a wider audience for the shepherds' report too, since "all who heard it" were astonished—not believing or thoughtful or adoring, just "amazed." Apparently nothing spurred them to ask questions or pursue the matter further. In contrast, Mary clings to what has happened. She continues to ponder the events and the words (the Greek word is inclusive of both) of the shepherds' visit.

Finally, the shepherds go back to where they came from, apparently back to fields and to flocks, but not back to business as usual. What was told them by the angelic messenger has been confirmed. They have heard and seen for themselves. Their old world is gone, replaced by a new world. Whatever the structure and order of life before, their world now is centered in the praise and glorifying of God. The nights in the field will never be the same.

CHRISTMAS, THIRD PROPER

Ecstasy over the Christmas miracle is the theme that binds these lections together—unrestrained joy over what God has done and over who God is. Yet it is a clearly focused, informed ecstasy, whose very power is generated by the precision with which events are viewed. The God whom these texts celebrate is a God who, in the royalist imagery of the day, reigns in strength, and whose activity on behalf of humankind is timelessly ancient, coinciding with the initial impulses of creation. Yet the eternal Monarch is not distant and remote, qualities that might be suggested by the terms of majesty in which the king is described. Rather this God is near and immediate, a participant in the human struggle for light and salvation.

The texts begin in a mode of transcendency, but move quickly to one of immediacy. As worshipers, we join in rejoicing over the coming of the messenger "who says to Zion, 'Your God reigns' " (Isa. 52:7). We also celebrate "the Lord, for he is coming to judge the earth ... with righteousness, and ... equity" (Ps. 98:9). Then the note of immediacy is struck by the focus on what God has done just now, in these "last days," in which "he has spoken to us by a Son" (Heb. 1:2). The One who was present at creation, the eternal Word, "became flesh and lived among us" (John 1:14).

In reading these texts, one is reminded again of the difficulty that all human wordsmiths—be they preachers or whoever—have in articulating the depth of emotion that accompanies Christmas. For all four of these texts are songs, which rhapsodize rather than explain that which happened at Christmas. Perhaps the one exception is the lection from Heb. 1. Yet even this text, which begins as sober prose, soon breaks into song, as if unable, when faced with the limits of simple narration, to restrain its enthusiasm and joy. Small wonder that worshipers on Christmas Day are more likely to leave the church whistling the anthem sung exuberantly by the choir than repeating to one another phrases from the minister's sermon.

Yet the preacher cannot abdicate the task of proclaiming the Christmas good news to the "musicians" who constitute the church, but must wrestle with the impossible challenge of capturing the meaning of Christ's nativity in the frailty of words. These texts are of incomparable value as she or he attempts to meet the challenge.

Isaiah 52:7–10 (A B C)

This poetic unit is the pivotal statement in "the gospel to exiles" in Isa. 40–55. The poet creates a wondrous scenario in which there are four characters in the dramatic moment of homecoming.

The first character is *"the messenger"* (v. 7). He is the one who hurries across the desert of the Fertile Crescent with news about the titanic battle between Yahweh and the powers of the empire. He has the first news—in a pre-electronic mode—of the outcome of the battle. The term "messenger" is the biblical word for gospel, so that he is the "carrier of the gospel." His way of running already signals that the news is good. Messengers with bad news do not run as well, or as lightly or buoyantly.

The poet piles up words to summarize the message he carries. He announces *"shalom."* He asserts *"good."* He declares *rescue* ("salvation"). Then finally, excited, out of breath, the messenger blurts out the outcome of the contest: "Your God has become king!" The gods have battled for control of the future. The news, the gospel, is the victory of Yahweh. This means for "Zion" a new, joyous, holy governance.

Enter the second voice, *"the sentinel"* (v. 8). On the walls of destroyed Jerusalem, in despair yet still yearning, are sentries. They watch, and they call out what they see. Over the horizon, according to this poetic scenario, they see the runner of v. 7 approaching with a message. They see how he runs. They notice how light and eager are his feet. They conclude immediately that he runs with good news, or he would not run so eagerly. The sentries watch and see only the messenger. They are able, however, to extrapolate from what they see. As they look at the runner and the horizon, they are able to translate both the messenger and the message. What they really see, in a bold act of imagination, is nothing other than victorious Yahweh.

The watchmen sing for joy. They are jubilant because Yahweh is coming. The God long held exile by the empire, the God held as captive as were the Jews, has broken free and is coming home.

The third character in this dramatic scenario is *wounded, defeated, fearful Jerusalem* (v. 9a). The poet imagines that the city, left desolate by the Babylonians, still consists of shattered walls and gates, defeated doors, broken-up streets, all disheveled, despondent, despairing (compare Neh. 1:3).

Then, however, the watchmen on the wall call down into the city. Yahweh is victorious; Yahweh is coming home. The watchmen then invite the broken, forlorn city to change its mood. It is time to sing and dance, because decisive help is on the way. The fate of the city has been broken.

This sequence of messenger (Isa. 52:7), watchmen (v. 8), broken city (v. 9a) is all stage setting for the central character of the plot. The central character, Yahweh, enters the action at this point (vs. 9b–10). There had been anticipation of Yahweh as the messenger announced Yahweh's rule (v. 7), as the sentries see Yahweh's return (v. 8).

Now the poet pays careful attention to Yahweh's dramatic entrance into the poem and into the city. Four statements characterize Yahweh in this moment of triumphal entry.

(*a*) "Yahweh has comforted Yahweh's people" (v. 9b). Since Isa. 40:1, the poet has taken "comfort" as the central yearning of the exiles. "Comfort" does not mean simply resigned consolation, but active intervention, which alters the circumstances of the community.

(*b*) "Yahweh has redeemed Jerusalem." Some texts, instead of "Jerusalem," read "Israel." Either way, Yahweh has gotten the special object of love out of hock, permitted it again to live its own life in freedom.

(*c*) Yahweh has rolled up sleeves as a powerful, strong, intimidating warrior (v. 10). The empires of the world notice Yahweh's power and back off from their dehumanizing policies. In this particular text, the poet finds it necessary to utilize a machismo metaphor to make the claim of power. (Notice elsewhere the use of maternal metaphors to make a very different point: 40:11; 49:14–15.)

(*d*) The culmination of the entire dramatic scenario concerns the salvation and homecoming wrought by Yahweh. God is indeed a God who liberates. Moreover, this is "our God," the God who is "for us," whose whole life is given over to "us." This poem is relentlessly good news for the faithful who are defeated.

Psalm 98 (A B C)

Like the Psalm lections for the first two propers of Christmas, this text is also a psalm of praise to God. Moreover, its primary images are similar to Pss. 96 and 97: God as the victorious warrior and as the creator of the world. The first image is found in vs. 1–3, where the language reminds us of the exodus narrative, especially Ex. 15. Yahweh is portrayed here as the defender of the people of God who, by means of "his right hand and his holy arm" (that is, without human aid), has achieved the people's liberation. In doing this, Yahweh has communicated a basic truth concerning the divine nature in that "he has revealed his vindication." In other words, Yahweh *is* Savior, so that not to have saved the people would have been a fundamental violation of who Yahweh is. And in achieving this liberation, Yahweh has acted in public and demonstrative ways, so that "all the ends of the earth" have witnessed these mighty deeds.

The image of God as reigning creator dominates vs. 4–8, and in the background one detects ancient Israel's memory of the old Creation myths of the ancient Near East in which a hostile primeval ocean was tamed by the power of God (compare Ps. 93:3–4). But if the "sea" once rumbled in anger as Yahweh's enemy, it and all creation (the "world" of v. 7b) now roars its praise of the majestic Lord who rules over it, and it claps its hands in joy (v. 8). Only this cosmological dimension to Israel's understanding of God's activity can account for the universal scope of the imperative in v. 4: All the earth is to sing before the Lord in joy. Israel is to join in this outpouring of praise, of course, with lyre, trumpets, horn, and—needless to say—the human voice.

In all these things, echoes of the Second Isaiah may be detected, since that prophet also compares Yahweh to a warrior and makes frequent use of the Creation as a model for God's other acts of salvation (that is, re-creation). Isaiah 42:10–13 is especially close to our psalm, the first words of Isa. 42:10 and Ps. 98:1 being identical.

But there is a third section to this psalm, and the transition into it is so subtle that it may easily be missed. The One who is Victor-Creator-King is also Judge, and the climax of the text is achieved in the proclamation that the past is but prologue to the coming of this divine Judge (v. 9). Yahweh now comes to judge both creation and those who inhabit it, and to do so by means of righteousness and equity (the Hebrew noun for "equity" is related to an adjective meaning "straight" or "upright"). Verse 9 prevents the psalm from being simply a celebration of what Yahweh *has* done, and decisively shifts the focus of the celebration to what Yahweh *is* doing now.

The relevance of this text to Christmas is obvious, for at Christmastide we reflexively look backward in time, remembering the manger, the Holy Family, the angels and shepherds, and so on. The temptation is to allow our celebration to be lodged there, in the past.

To be sure, our joy is motivated by our profession that the Infant is also the risen Christ, through whose death and resurrection we are reconciled to God. And yet, our thoughts tend to remain focused on a scene long ago and far away.

The force of this psalm is to move us away from the past into the present, into the now. And there are at least two words in the psalm that compel this redirection of our attention. The first of these is the word "new" in the first line of v. 1 (compare Ps. 96:1). The implication is that the old songs will no longer do, in that they are incapable of capturing the human response to what God is doing now. (In the mind of the psalmist these "old" songs were likely the laments over Israel's past disasters; see Ps. 74 or the book of Lamentations.) So it seems clear that the Hebrew poet intends to urge the people to adopt fresh expressions of joy commensurate with the present outbreak of Yahweh's activity. God, who is now working in original and primal ways, must be praised in songs similarly cast.

The second term that calls our attention to the contemporary nature of God's activity is the verb "to come," in v. 9. It is true that there is a certain ambiguity in the Hebrew (*bā'*), in that the perfect indicative ("he comes") and the active participle ("is coming") have the same form. But one may argue for the sense "is coming" (NRSV) because of the parallel verb "will judge" (*yišpōṭ*), which is imperfect (compare Ps. 96:13). Thus God is in the act of coming now to set things right, and God's former acts of creation and re-creation, although fascinating and wonderful, are but preliminary to what God is in the process of doing at the present moment.

Christmas, while commemorating what God did in the long ago at Bethlehem, is in reality the joyful celebration of what God is doing here and now. God is judging creation, specifically the human family, in the sense that God is at work to set things right. Therefore, the contribution of this psalm to the anthology of Christmas lections is to redirect our Christmas wonder. Our carols of great gladness are not just over what God did at Bethlehem, but over what the reigning Christ does today to straighten that which is crooked in human life and to set right that which has fallen.

Hebrews 1:1–4 (5–12) (A B C)

In these opening lines, the author of Hebrews draws upon considerable rhetorical skill to produce one of the most elegant passages in the New Testament. The first four verses, rich in alliteration and imagery, announce the major themes of the book as a whole: Christ is both the exalted Son of God and the one whose sacrifice atoned for human sin. Verses 1–2 introduce the theme of the exalted Son by contrasting him with God's messages to humanity in previous generations, and the contrast between Christ and God's angels runs throughout Heb. 1 and 2. This contrast between Christ and the prophets, or between Christ and the angels, does not cancel out the deep continuity that Hebrews affirms. The God who "spoke to our ancestors . . . by the prophets" is identical with the God who "has spoken to us by a Son." God's action in Jesus Christ is absolutely superior to God's earlier actions on behalf of humankind, but former history is in no way denied or negated, as becomes clear when Hebrews draws on Israel's scripture and history throughout.

Verse 2 identifies God's Son as both the "heir of all things" and the one through whom the world was created. Christ stands at both ends of cosmic history. As the writer of Revelation puts it, he is both Alpha and Omega (Rev. 22:13). The world has its origin and its destiny in Christ. This language bears a striking resemblance to Jewish wisdom literature, in which similar claims appear about the figure of Lady Wisdom. Its use here and elsewhere in early Christianity reflects not only the Jewish "background" to Christian thought but the perennial need to portray Christ in language that people can understand.

With its assertions about Christ reflecting God's glory and his role in purification, Heb. 1:3 introduces the dialectic that is at the heart of Christian faith. Jesus is said to be "the exact imprint" of God's nature—that is, Jesus is in every way like God. And Jesus is simultaneously the one who sacrificed himself as a human being for other human beings.

Verse 4 introduces the motif of Christ's superiority to angels, which continues in the quotations from scripture in vs. 5–12. In common with other New Testament writers, the author of Hebrews displays no concern for the original context of the passages he cites. What matters is that scripture lends itself to the claims being made about Christ. In v. 5, the quotations (Ps. 2:7 and 2 Sam. 7:14) reinforce the assertion of Heb. 1:1–2, that Jesus is indeed the Son of God. Similarly, vs. 6–7 reinforce the contrast between God's Son and God's angels (v. 4) by showing that the angels are instructed to worship God's Son.

God may make "his angels winds, and his servants flames," but the Son is destined to rule forever (v. 8). Verse 9 introduces the notion of the goodness of Christ. He exemplifies faithfulness to God by his righteousness, and thereby demonstrates his fitness for reign.

CHRISTMAS, THIRD PROPER

Verses 10–12 continue the contrast with angels by reinforcing the earlier claim that God's Son stands both at the beginning of history and at its end. Christ is God's agent in creation. Christ will always remain the same: "and your years will never end."

The primary thrust of this opening section of Hebrews appears to be doxological. God's eschatological gift of the Son merits human thanks and praise. Within this doxology, the major themes of the book are sounded, and they will be developed in the course of the text. Perhaps there is also a polemical thrust to the contrast between God's Son and God's angels. For example, it could be that some Christians are interpreting Jesus as simply one of God's messengers or that some are actually worshiping angels. Such theories are very difficult to support because of the absence of any explicit polemic.

Whatever the thrust of this text in its own day, the reading of it on Christmas presents several possibilities. With its powerful insistence on Christ as the beginning and end of all things, this text stands as a corrective to any tendency to romanticize the infant Jesus. Just as the theme of Christ's sacrifice stands in tension with his majesty (1:3), so that helplessness of the babe in a manger stands in tension with Christ as the agent and goal of all creation. While the christological language of Hebrews may sound foreign indeed to many contemporary Christians, the proclamation that God's Son stands, unchanging and unchanged, both at the beginning and at the end, may be gospel indeed to people who experience change as the only constant in their lives and who seek frantically for something that abides.

John 1:1–14 (A B C)

The prologue to John's Gospel has perhaps had more influence on the church's doctrine of the incarnation than any other passage. It affirms in carefully stated language the preexistence of the Word, who is identified with and yet distinct from God, who is the divine agent in creation and yet incarnate in the flesh. But when the congregation gathers for worship on Christmas Day, it does not want or need to hear about the precise distinctions of the church's doctrine. The mood of the season hardly calls for a didactic sermon. It is rather the time to celebrate the birth at Bethlehem and to ask about its meaning, its implications for the congregation, for the church, and for the world. Therefore, the question to ask of the Gospel reading for this service is: How does John 1:1–14 interpret Christmas? What can we learn from it about the baby born in the manger and the meaning of that birth for human life?

First and foremost, from the prologue to John's Gospel *we learn that in Jesus Christ we meet nothing less than the revelation of God.* Word (or Logos), the subject of all the verbs in vs. 1–2, has a rich and illustrious heritage in both Hellenistic and Jewish circles. What is most important, however, is the simple notion of communication. When one speaks or writes a word, one is communicating. "The word of the Lord came to the prophet"—and we through the prophet hear God's message. Now we discover that in Jesus Christ the word identified with God from the very beginning (1:1–3) has taken human form (v. 14), and Christmas is the story of the birth of God's self-communication to the world.

Rather than speaking in Johannine terms, it is perhaps more popular today to think of a "Christology from below," that is, to begin with the historical figure who walked the dusty roads of Galilee, who associated with tax collectors and sinners, who was like us in every respect, and then to speak of his special relationship to God. John's "Christology from above," however, still has its place. It provides us with the healthy reminder of God's distance, that we can only know God as God is *given* to us in an act of revelation. Not our best aspirations or fondest longings or even most sincere service can precipitate such an event. Christmas is first of all the celebration of a gracious decision on God's part to become human in the baby of Bethlehem.

Second, from John's prologue *we learn that God's revelation in Jesus Christ is not altogether obvious.* The Word came to a world that should have known him. After all, he had created the world. In particular, he came to a special people chosen from all the nations to be his own and to a land that was his heritage, but he was rejected. Jesus was not universally acclaimed as the revelation of God, nor worshiped as the one in whom we touch ultimate reality. In fact, the rest of John's Gospel relates story after story of how prominent religious people not only did not recognize Jesus but found him offensive, accused him of blasphemy, charged him with being demon-possessed. Those who confidently thought that they saw things rightly in fact turned out to be blind.

John simply will not let his readers off the hook. He confronts us with a divine self-disclosure that does not document itself with foolproof evidence. We are not provided with irrefutable grounds for faith. We are asked to believe that a particular individual, living in a buffer state in the Middle East, powerless before a Roman governor, is the One in whom we meet the Creator of heaven and earth. The fact that the genuinely religious people who should have received him in fact rejected him leaves readers even more uneasy.

But rejection is not the whole story. There are those who received Jesus, who trusted him, who found themselves by a creative act of God reborn, empowered to be children of God. On the surface they hardly seem potential candidates for the divine family—a Samaritan woman, an unnamed Roman official, a man born blind, an extravagant Mary of Bethany. They are a somewhat unlikely group to become that community called into being and nurtured by the revelation of God in Jesus. But that in itself tells us something about the character of God and God's intentions in Jesus.

Third, from John's prologue *we learn that there is continuity between God's works of creation and revelation*. It begins with language reminiscent of Gen. 1:1, recalling the ancient account of Creation. Then readers are told that the Word enfleshed at Bethlehem is the agent in creation, the one by whom all things were made. There were those in the early church (as there have been those in the modern church) who drove a wedge between nature and grace. The material world for various reasons was thought to be evil, a place from which to escape to a realm of the spirit. Redemption meant freedom from the earthly, the historical, the sensual.

The prologue will have none of this. Salvation is the fulfillment, not the negation, of creation. Jesus does not rescue God's people from a dark and dangerous world. Rather the one who was God's partner in creation has made God concretely known by becoming "flesh." Such a connection between nature and grace certainly underscores the Christian responsibility to care for the earth.

First Sunday After Christmas

Over against the deeply entrenched human desire to limit salvation to self, family, and nation, the readings for the First Sunday After Christmas relentlessly insist that God alone draws the boundary around God's salvation and that God includes all creation within it. No aspect of life remains untouched by the redemptive promise of the Christmas season.

The reading from Isaiah eloquently depicts God as the fashioner of the "garments of salvation" and as the gardener whose plantings are "righteousness and praise." God redeems Jerusalem not for the sake of Jerusalem alone, but so that her salvation will shine for all the nations to see. The pledge to vindicate Jerusalem simultaneously becomes a pledge for all people.

In the psalm, praise for God and God's salvation comes from all quarters of creation. Not human life alone, but the elements, the wild monsters of the deep, the planets themselves are enjoined to praise Israel's God. Yahweh and only Yahweh merits exaltation and glory.

Although the Epistle lesson also speaks in terms of the redemption of humankind as a whole, it attends as well to the impact of God's salvation in every person. While all the lessons remind us that the gifts of Christmas are not private possessions, and are certainly not under the control of individuals, they do result in the radical liberation of individual human beings. To cry to God as God's own child is possible only because one has experienced God's salvation.

The story of Mary and Joseph taking the infant Jesus to the temple elegantly proclaims that salvation comes through the most unlikely vehicle of a tiny Jewish babe. It comes not only as glory for Israel but as revelation for the Gentiles (Luke 2:32); that is, God's salvation is for all human beings, as all are created by God. The solemn words of Simeon's oracles anticipate that not all will see and understand God's salvation. To the burning light of a reestablished Jerusalem some will remain blind. The demand for praise of the God of creation will fall on deaf ears. Adoption will be rejected. Even as Simeon's oracles recall that God's salvation continues to cause division and pain, however, the lessons for this Sunday recall the even greater extent of God's salvation.

Isaiah 61:10–62:3

This lectionary grouping of the text seems especially peculiar, joining together Isa. 61:10–11 and 62:1–3 which, according to their rhetorical patterns, are quite distinct poetic elements.

We have considered 61:10–11 for the Third Sunday of Advent. It appears that these verses look back to 61:1–4 (5–7) and not, as the lectionary selection suggests, forward to 62:1–3. In 61:8–9, God is speaking. Since God is spoken of in v. 10 in the third person, this is not a continuation of God's speech from vs. 8–9. It seems most plausible that the speaker in these verses is the same as the speaker in vs. 1–4 (5–7).

The speaker is ready! He is dressed for the occasion. He is suited up in "garments of salvation" and a "robe of righteousness." The language may originally have referred to actual ceremonial dress, but now seems to be metaphorical (compare Eph. 6:11–17). The speaker is ready, eager as a bridegroom on a wedding day, prepared and outfitted as a bride before a wedding. The lines suggest an excited impatience, as the speaker can hardly wait to get on with the daring act of public transformation.

The new community about to be enacted through the jubilee is as unexpected, wondrous, and irresistible as new growth that shoots up out of the ground (Isa. 61:11). Thus the poem dramatically changes images from wedding (v. 10) to agriculture (v. 11). The God who "loves justice" (v. 8) will create righteousness, which means altering circumstance of the oppressed, brokenhearted, captives, and prisoners (61:1). God will reorder social reality into a viable, equitable working community. The poetry so easily joins together God's large purpose and the social specificity of the human agent of transformation.

In 62:1–3 we hear God's own voice, quite distinct from the human agent who spoke in 61:10–11. These three verses are a statement of fresh resolve on God's part. The announcement is itself an enactment, for the decree of the king is sure. But God has not spoken, has not issued a decree, has not asserted sovereignty. God has kept silent. Indeed, the sorry state of exiled Judah (for a long time, perhaps seventy years, perhaps more, depending on the dating of the poem) is regarded as a result of the abdicating silence. In the silence God is unnoticed and unheeded, so that God's very sovereignty has been effectively nullified. Where God is silent, God's people suffer at the hands of other powers.

Now, however, finally, God resolves to break the silence and to assert sovereignty. On this theme, see also two other passages. In Ps. 39:12, the petition asks of God:

> Hear my prayer, O LORD,
>   and give ear to my cry;
>   do not hold your peace at my tears.
> For I am your passing guest,
>   an alien, like all my forebears.

The speaker is dependent on God's hearing and responding. And in Isa. 42:14, God resolves:

> For a long time I have held my peace,
>   I have kept still and restrained myself;
> now I will cry out like a woman in labor,
>   I will gasp and pant.

As God breaks the silence of indifference and neglect, God moves into decisive action, because "I will not forsake them" (42:16; compare 62:12).

So now, in 62:1-3, God will break the silence and speak out. God will speak and act for the sake of and on behalf of beloved Jerusalem, home of all of Israel's best yearnings.

God's resolve to enact sovereignty is "until"—for as long as it takes (v. 1). God will remain active, engaged, and attentive until Jerusalem has vindication (ṣĕdāqāh) and salvation (yĕšûʻāh). The term "vindication" means that all is rightly ordered for life; "salvation" here means rescue from oppression. That is, God will not quit, once mobilized, until the social situation of the oppressed is altered.

The terms of Yahweh's intention nicely serve the season of Christmas, for the new well-being of Jerusalem (vindication, salvation) are imaged as shining dawn and burning torch, a light that will be visible to all the watching nations. The nations have noticed that the city of Jerusalem has been plundered and bereft, and they conclude that the God of Jerusalem is impotent and indifferent. Now, however, all of that will change as God breaks the silence. The watching nations will see Jerusalem glow in new splendor and will discern Yahweh's awesome resumption of sovereignty. Thus the rehabilitation of Jerusalem and God's resumption of authority go together.

The benefit of the new assertion of Yahweh's sovereignty will accrue precisely to Jerusalem, who will receive a new name, that is, a new status, a new identity, a new, lively possibility. (The new names are given in v. 4, which lies beyond the limit of the lectionary reading). The new name and new condition bespeak a radical reversal of the fortunes of Jerusalem. The dishonored, discarded, disregarded ruins (and all the "nonpersons" that dwell there) now become a glorious ornament at the very throne of God, a glorious crown, a wondrous diadem, a treasure and delight to God, a way of honoring God.

Psalm 148

The Psalm lection for this day is a typical psalm of praise, with the usual tripartite structure: introduction, body, and conclusion. Indeed, Ps. 148 shares an important characteristic with its neighbors on the final pages of the Psalter in that the introduction and the conclusion are the identical exclamation, "Hallelujah!" "Praise the LORD!" (compare Pss. 146; 147; 149; 150). These final five psalms, in fact, constitute the crescendo of praise that brings the "hymnbook" of Israel-of-old to an exuberant climax. Notice the manner in which each of the first four of the five "books" within the Psalter ends on an affirmation of praise (41:13; 72:18–19; 89:52; 106:48). Is it imagining too much to see in this penchant for the number five a statement concerning the theological centrality of the five books of the Torah, Genesis through Deuteronomy? There are some who point to Ps. 1 as an introduction to the Psalter and who, therefore, see the entire book of Psalms as Torah commentary.

Yet as predictable as Ps. 148 may be in terms of its structure, it is quite distinctive in content. Most of the psalm is given over to the body, that component in most psalms of praise which describes why Yahweh is to be considered praiseworthy. In this case the body (vs. 1b–14c) is divided into two sections, each of which is announced by an imperative. "Praise Yahweh from the heavens" (v. 1b) is paralleled by "Praise Yahweh from the earth" (v. 7a), and each of these commands determines the direction of the lines that follow. In other words, the heavenly dimensions of creation have reason to praise Israel's God as surely as do the earthly, and it is the clear intention of the text to explicate these reasons.

The first of the two commands is followed by a list of heavenly beings who are under orders to praise Yahweh, even heaven itself (v. 4a) and the "waters above the heavens" (v. 4b). This latter reference clearly has in mind that ancient cosmology which the Israelites shared with many of their neighbors, which conceptualized heaven as a dome resting on a flat earth, both of which were immersed in a primordial and chaotic sea. The waters of this sea are here just as surely under Yahweh's control as they were in the time of Noah, when they reinvaded the cosmos at the divine command (compare Gen. 7:11). No less under Yahweh's control are "his angels," "his host," his "sun," "moon," and "stars."

These celestial beings are to praise Yahweh (notice how Ps. 148:5a repeats the thought of v. 1b) because they owe their very existence to Yahweh's creative power. The lines 5b and 6a are very nearly parallel, except that 6a prepares the way for 6b as a way of saying that Yahweh did not simply bring the celestial world into being, but that Yahweh endowed that world with a place within the larger order of things, and that its place is forever determined. (The NRSV marginal note to v. 6b calls attention to the literal translation of that line, "he set a law that cannot pass away," which reinforces our sense of the close connection between the theology of the psalms and that of the Torah, referred to above.)

The second of the two major commands within the body of the psalm text (v. 7a) focuses on the earthly dimensions of creation. The "sea monsters and all deeps" of v. 7b echo the same chaos as that noted in v. 4b, in that the Hebrew word for "deeps" (*těhōmôt*) is the plural form of the same noun used in Gen. 1:2. The listing of the nonliving forms of earthly creation that are to praise Yahweh ("sea monsters" seem to be understood as mythical, not animal, realities, at least on the basis of their place in the hierarchy of creation) reaches a conclusion in Ps. 148:9a, and is followed by references to flora (v. 9b) and fauna (v. 10). Finally, human beings are enrolled in the praisers of Yahweh, from rulers to common folk (vs. 11–12). High and low, young and old, individuals and the community at large— all are to lift voice in adoration and worship.

Then, as in vs. 5–6, the rationale by which these creatures are to praise Yahweh is declared (vs. 13–14c). But here there is a surprise in store! It is not simply that Yahweh has made the "wild animals" and the "kings of the earth," although that affirmation is surely understood. It is, rather, that *Yahweh is who Yahweh is!* That is to say, there is no other one or no other thing like Yahweh. This God of Israel is absolutely unique; "his name alone is exalted." That alone would be reason enough to affirm "Hallelujah."

Yet there is more to it than even that. This absolutely God-like-no-other-god, who created the heavens and the earth, has also intervened in the life of the people to save them from that from which they could not save themselves. "He has raised up a horn [of salvation] for his people" (v. 14a) is reminiscent of Ps. 18:2, and reminds the community that not only are they the creation of God, but the re-creation as well; that the God who made Israel has also saved Israel (compare Isa. 42:5–9); that the One who constituted the worlds in the first place has reconstituted the people of God as an act of pure grace.

The celebration of Christmas, the sounds of which still ring in our ears and the joy of which resounds in our hearts, is an important new beginning in the life of humankind. The Babe of Bethlehem is also to become the crucified Savior and Lord, God's affirmation that that world which was brought into being so long ago will never be allowed to become irredeemably corrupted. In the spirit of that reality, this psalm celebrates the indissoluble link between creation and salvation.

Galatians 4:4–7

The Epistle reading for the First Sunday After Christmas provides a chance to step back from the pace and frenzy of the season to reflect theologically on the meaning of Jesus' coming into the world. While none of the familiar details of the Christmas narrative can be found in the passage, the text nevertheless relates a story, a story of inheritance, liberation, and adoption built around the plot of the divine decision to send the Son. The background for the story this time is not the political situation of Palestine in the first century (Herod or Caesar Augustus) but the human situation—waiting, enslaved, and homeless people.

Before tracing the plot and characters in this drama, we pause to note that Paul mingles throughout the passage three sets of images that need to be carefully distinguished, lest they cause confusion (especially in 4:7). Paul begins (vs. 1–3) with the analogy of the minor who awaits the time of adulthood when he or she can possess the family inheritance. Apparently, the time of inheritance is established by the (deceased) parent's will. Perhaps because the minor occupies such a subordinate position during the waiting period ("under guardians and trustees"), two other images emerge. One is that of the slave under the control of the elemental spirits of the universe and in need of deliverance. The other is the image of orphans, who remain homeless until they are adopted into the family as full members. Though the dominant image seems to be that of the minors who come to their full inheritance, the other two are vivid and strong. Thus the preacher faces the critical task of deciding how the images are to be exploited effectively in the sermon and yet not in a way that perplexes the congregation.

First of all, we note that the primary actor in this Christmas drama is God. It is God who waits for the right moment, takes the decisive action to send the Son, and confirms the action by sending the Spirit. The liberating plot does not unfold as a dedicated group of individuals band together to throw off the yoke of oppression, either for themselves or for their maligned neighbors. Rather, the God who is deeply involved in history and has a stake in its outcome acts quite independently to bring about a changed situation. In sharp contrast to the opposition, who are later described as "weak and beggarly" (4:9), feeble and helpless characters who can only come with their hands out seeking aid, God functions in a powerful way to free the captives and bring them into the divine family. The human situation, desperate as it seems, is not helpless before God. Thus for Paul, above all else, Christmas is a story about God.

Second, the plot of the drama is built around two moves God makes—the sending of the Son and the sending of the Spirit—both of which are critical to the final outcome of the story. The phrase "God sent his Son," while implying the preexistence and incarnation of Christ, does not argue, however, a doctrine of revelation, but relates an event of liberation and adoption. The phrase may have special relevance for the holiday season, when people think that of all the moments of the year this is the one when they *ought* to act as free, joyous, and spontaneously happy persons, but instead feel caught in their own despair and very much alone. The text affirms that Jesus came right into the strains and traps of "oughtness" to effect liberation.

The sending of the Spirit of the Son confirms the experience of adoption. Orphans brought into the home of a foster family may initially mistrust the reception they receive and may need a special gesture on the part of the parents in order to feel they are really and truly at home. The gift of the Spirit is God's special gesture to operate at a deep level ("into our hearts") to overcome our fear and timidity. Not once, but repeatedly, the Spirit enables the cry "Abba! Father!" corroborating the reality of acceptance into the divine family, a corroborating experience that addresses the intense loneliness of many at Christmas.

Finally, there are the recipients of God's gracious activity—minors given full possession of the inheritance (in this case, the inheritance promised to Abraham, 3:29); slaves who are freed; homeless children who come to enjoy the family relations. Who are these people? Strangely, the pronouns shift about from first to second person in the section from 3:23 to 4:11. It may be that when the first person occurs it denotes Jewish Christians, and when the second person appears it designates Gentile Christians. But in any case, the abrupt shifting serves to stress the inclusiveness of both. Both could be depicted as minors but now in possession of the inheritance, formerly enslaved but now free, orphaned but now adopted.

In 4:7 the pronoun shifts from plural to singular. "So you [singular] are no longer a slave but a child, and if a child then also an heir, through God." The drama is not only concerned about Jewish and Gentile Christians, but about the individual. Each reader is forced out of the role of pure spectator and is personally confronted with the remarkable drama of Christmas.

Luke 2:22–40

Luke's story of the presentation of Jesus in the Temple is far more than a simple story about the piety of Jesus' parents, although it does involve that motif. The oracles of Simeon announce themes that are central to the whole of Luke-Acts, making this a key text in Luke's two volumes.

Jesus' parents initiate the action that sets the stage for Simeon. They take the infant Jesus to the Temple for "their purification" and in order to offer the prescribed sacrifice. Here Luke apparently misunderstands Lev. 12, which requires purification for the mother rather than for the child or for mother and child ("their purification," Luke 2:22). This anomaly notwithstanding, the visit to the Temple underscores the piety of Mary and Joseph, already established in the case of Mary in 1:38, 46–55 and continued in 2:41–42. The fact that the sacrifice of Mary and Joseph consists of "a pair of turtledoves or two young pigeons," rather than the more costly sheep, signals the modest economic standing of the family. (Leviticus 12:8 specifies that the appropriate offering in this instance is a sheep, unless that is beyond the mother's means.)

Although Mary and Joseph initiate the action in this passage by taking Jesus to the Temple, their action is complemented by the "actions" of Simeon and Anna. Luke presents both of them as waiting for God's intervention and salvation of Israel, Simeon by "looking forward to the consolation of Israel," and Anna by constantly worshiping in the Temple. The association of the two, and of Jesus and his family, with the city and its Temple is underscored by the way in which references to Jerusalem bracket the story of Simeon and Anna. Luke 2:25 begins by referring to "a man in Jerusalem," when that specificity regarding place is probably gratuitous, given v. 22. Likewise, the parallel story of Anna ends with reference to the "redemption of Jerusalem." Jerusalem, and the Temple in particular, plays a significant role in Luke's story, from the annunciation to Zechariah (1:8–20) to Paul's final arrest (Acts 21:13). Even if the people of Israel and their leaders become the objects of Luke's sharp attack, Jerusalem and the Temple remain important locations of God's action and the community's life.

Both Simeon and Anna enter the story largely to focus attention on Jesus and his future. Luke lays the foundation for their statements by parading their impeccable credentials. Simeon is a "righteous and devout" person who has longed for the "consolation of Israel." In three distinct ways the Holy Spirit's inspiration of Simeon is asserted: v. 25 claims that the Holy Spirit "rested on" Simeon; then the Spirit tells him that he will not die without seeing the Messiah; then the Spirit directs him to the Temple when Jesus is presented. By the time Simeon speaks, there can be no doubt as to his reliability. While Anna's speech receives less attention (v. 38), her credentials are nevertheless clear: "She never left the temple but worshiped there with fasting and prayer night and day" (v. 37).

These two astonishing figures announce that the infant Jesus is directly connected with "the consolation of Israel" (v. 25), "the redemption of Jerusalem." That much is clear already in v. 30, when Simeon proclaims that he has witnessed God's salvation. Whatever else is said about Jesus, already the reader knows that Jesus *is* God's salvation.

Verse 32 makes two claims about this salvation, claims that echo the language of Isaiah (Isa. 40:5; 42:6; 46:13; 49:6) and will echo throughout Luke-Acts. This salvation is to be "a light for revelation to the Gentiles" and "glory to your people Israel." The Lukan Gospel and the early chapters of Acts primarily concern themselves with Jesus in relation to Israel, for whom he is the fulfillment, if also the reinterpretation, of long-cherished hopes. With the second half of Acts, and especially the Pauline mission, the proclamation of Jesus becomes "light for revelation to the Gentiles" (see Acts 26:19–23).

The story of Luke-Acts plainly reveals that neither all of Israel nor all of the Gentiles agreed with Simeon's assessment. Many saw in Jesus anything but salvation! Does that fact make Simeon's oracle a false one? His second oracle, Luke 2:34–35, suggests that the answer to that question is no. If Jesus is God's salvation "in the presence of all peoples," he nevertheless creates division. Up to this point, Luke has played only themes of joy and triumph. Jesus is to inherit the throne of David (1:32), he comes as the fulfillment of God's promise (1:55), he is the Savior (2:11), he is glory for Israel (2:32). Here a more somber theme is sounded for the first time: Jesus will prompt division. Many will oppose him. The relentless theme of rejection and resistance cannot wait even for the infancy narrative to come to an end.

Like several other scenes in the Lukan infancy narrative, this one ends with a note that the characters involved went to their homes (1:23; 1:56; 2:51) or went away (1:38; 2:20). Continuing the parallels with the birth of John the Baptist, Jesus is described as growing in strength and in wisdom and as having God's favor upon him (compare 1:80; 2:52; also 1 Sam. 2:21, 26). The note regarding the boy Jesus not only provides information about him of the sort that popular tradition will later elaborate, but also reinforces the seamless movement between the infant Jesus and the adult who emerges in Luke 3.

Second Sunday After Christmas

With a variety of striking images, the readings for the Second Sunday After Christmas invoke praise and thanksgiving to God for God's outrageous generosity in the gift of Jesus Christ. The first three readings all contrast that generosity with the situation of humanity apart from God's intervention. Jeremiah 31:7–14 portrays for us a people in exile, a people for whom despair and grief seem to be the only option. The apparent eternity of winter's grasp dominates Ps. 147:12–20, with its picture of God sending "snow like wool" and "frost like ashes." John's prologue conjures up the hopelessness of life lived out in a dark world, a powerful place in which humans cannot even see how to proceed for themselves.

Common to all these texts is not only the assertion of human helplessness and hopelessness apart from God, but also the proclamation that God has already invaded the world and caused a new world to come into being. God invades and overturns the exile, replacing mourning with exuberant joy. God's gift of spring occurs even without our request for aid, simply because God is one who rescues. The incarnation of Jesus Christ powerfully breaks in as God's Light triumphs over against all darkness. Ephesians 1 asserts the soteriological consequences of God's invasion and proclaims those consequences to have been part of God's will even from the beginning. The gospel is not God's afterthought in response to a problem: it is deeply rooted in God's nature to act on behalf of creation.

Another element common to these texts is their assertion of praise and thanksgiving to God. In response to this proclamation of the gospel, the only right action for human beings is to sing the doxology.

Jeremiah 31:7–14 (A B C)

The exile of Israel smells of defeat, despair, and abandonment. Moreover, it is a place of deadly silence. All the voices of possibility have been crushed and nullified. Our capacity to make this text available depends on making two daring connections.

1. The *deadliness of exile* is the context into which *Jesus is born* and in which Christmas is celebrated. Christmas is an act against exile.

2. The *deadliness of exile* continues to be a metaphor through which to understand *our own social, cultural situation* of defeat, dehumanization, and despair.

Thus all three settings, in the exile of Jer. 31, in the New Testament, and in our time, are closely parallel in their silent hopelessness. Into all three scenes, the gospel flings this strident speech of God.

In the first part of our text, God addresses the exilic community and invites it to a new reality, which is rooted only in God's faithful resolve (vs. 7–9).

1. God issues an invitation to Israel in exile filled with glad imperatives (v. 7). In characteristic hymnic fashion, Israel is invited to sing aloud, raise shouts, proclaim, praise, say. These are all acts of joyous assertion which muted Israel thought it could never voice. The reason for the rejoicing is in the substance of the saying, which might be paraphrased: "Yahweh has *saved* the covenant partner!" God intervenes to liberate and new life begins, new life that was not at all expected. The reason for singing is that the deathly grip of Babylon is broken!

2. Verses 8–9 give the reason for the singing. The introductory "see" invites Israel to notice something utterly new. Now God speaks in the first person. Moreover, God is the willing subject of active verbs that will transform the life of Israel: "I am going to bring, I will gather, I will lead, I will let them walk." The poet conjures a great pilgrimage of people headed home, the ones who thought they would never have a home. In that pilgrimage are included the ones who are vulnerable and dependent, the blind, the lame, the pregnant women. These are the ones who are always at risk. Now, however, that risk is ended; they are safe, kept, and guarded on the way.

Now God addresses the nations (vs. 10–14).

1. The speech of God puts the nations on notice (vs. 10–11). They will have to yield to God's deep resolve. They will have to release their hostages and forgo their supply of cheap labor. God will be the

faithful shepherd who values every sheep, even the lost, even the ones in exile. The nations can do nothing to stop God from this daring resolve.

2. The poet then conjures for us what new life will be like when the exiles come home and the power of fear and death is broken (vs. 12–14).

(*a*) Creation will flourish; there will be extravagant material goods (v. 12). In an arid climate that has only marginal supplies of water, to be by reliable "brooks of water" (see v. 9) is a powerful image of material well-being. Death is fended off.

(*b*) Social life will resume (v. 13a). Young people can have their loud, boisterous parties. No one will mind; older people will join in, because such noise is a song of confidence, stability, freedom, and well-being.

(*c*) Restored creation (v. 12) and restored community (v. 13a) are rooted in God's transformative power. It is God, only God, but surely God, who transforms mourning to joy, exile to homecoming, death to life, sorrow to gladness (v. 13b; compare John 16:20).

(*d*) An ordained religious community will live in utter well-being (v. 14). People will prosper, priests will prosper. Priests and people together will live in well-being, where blessings abound.

In every season, including ours, the oracle of God breaks the dread of exile. Exiles are those who live in resignation, believing no newness is possible. That gripping hopelessness is not explained by the psychology of modernity, but is a deep theological crisis. The only ground for newness is God. Here God speaks unambiguously, against all our presumed death. It is by the power and faithfulness of God that life begins again.

Psalm 147:12–20 (A B C)

The ability of this lection to stand independently of the rest of the psalm of which it is a part is illustrated by the fact that in the Septuagint it is a distinct psalm, Ps. 147 in the Septuagint enumeration (vs. 1–11 of this psalm constituting the Septuagint's Ps. 146). It consists of two basic parts, of which the first is vs. 12–14. These lines urge the people to praise God (v. 12) because God has endowed the nation with peace (the first lines of vs. 13 and 14, respectively) and prosperity (the second lines of these same verses).

The second part of the psalm, vs. 15–20, celebrates the power of God's word. This theme is announced in v. 15, where the Hebrew wordplay goes undetected in most English translations. The Hebrew behind "his command" (NRSV, REB) is *'imĕrātô*, and literally means something like "his utterance," since it is related to the root *'āmar*, "to utter" or "to say." This term is paralleled by "word" (*dĕbārô*) of v. 15b, and the effect of the whole verse is to remind the reader that God is in an ongoing conversation with creation. The action verbs "send out" and "run swiftly" imply incessant dialogue (not monologue, as we shall note below) between God and the people of God (compare v. 19), a continuing hum of communication.

The nature of God's word—that part of the dialogue which originates with the Deity—is described metaphorically in vs. 16–18. It is perhaps coincidental that this description of the wintry blast in ancient Israel is appointed to be read in North American churches at the coldest time of year in the northern temperate zone, and the articulation of these verses will be strengthened in those congregations whose houses of worship lie under blankets of snow on this day. NRSV's "Who can stand before his cold?" in v. 17b is an accurate translation of the Masoretic Text as it stands, but a slight change in the Hebrew letters yields "before his cold the waters stand still," that is, "freeze," perhaps a preferred rendering (see REB).

If vs. 16–17 portray God's deep freeze, v. 18 describes God's thaw. Here is found another wordplay. "Word" of 18a echoes the same term (*dĕbārô*) in 15b, but here it is paralleled not by *'imĕrātô*, but by *rûḥô*, which may mean either "his wind" (NRSV), "his breath," or "his Spirit." The ambiguity is probably not accidental, for another Hebrew poet has written an extended play on this very word in Ezek. 37:1–14, an ingenious creation in which the power of language to speak on several levels at once is remarkably demonstrated. Psalm 147:18 seems to be an intriguing way of saying, "As the warm spring winds blow to melt the ice and snow of winter, so the Spirit of God melts all that is frozen in human life."

As noted above, the statement in v. 15 concerning the presence of God in human life is balanced by a similar statement in v. 19, a pair of "brackets" around the metaphor of vs. 16–18. Yet in v. 19 the application to human life of God's word is given a sharper focus than in v. 15, for here it is applied in a special way to Israel, a thought that is extended into the first two lines of v. 20.

The entire text is climaxed by a final *halĕlû-yāh*, which not only echoes similar imperatives in v. 12, but balances the psalm's opening *halĕlû-yāh*, in v. 1.

The heart of this text is, of course, the metaphor of winter and spring. It limits the power of this passage to see it as a simple statement of God's power over the world of nature, although it does make such a statement. But beyond that it portrays God's role in the movement of the individual person (or human community) from death to life, from desolation to hope, from meaninglessness to purpose. Verses 16–17 may be compared to many of the psalms of lament and of thanksgiving, which describe the human condition of alienation and estrangement in the language of imagery. Psalm 30:9, for example, complains that if the psalmist (or reader of the psalm) is allowed to die, God will be the loser, since the dead are incapable of praise. But "death" is no more the final word in Ps. 30 than is "winter" in Ps. 147:12–20. In vs. 11–12 of Ps. 30 God responds to the human plea for help by restoring the helpless one to life:

> You have turned my mourning into dancing; . . .
> so that my soul may praise you and not be silent.

Yet it is significant that in this lection God intervenes to restore the helpless even though there is no stated plea for help. The warm winds of spring do not thaw the frozen water because of human intercession, but simply because it is God's nature to restore and redeem. The same God who rebukes the ice and snow also rebukes sin and evil, because that's the kind of being God is. Men and women may cry to God for help, but it is God's nature to help whether or not men and women cry.

This reality brings forth the human response of praise, that part of the divine-human dialogue referred to above that originates with men and women. The God of Israel is the Lord of both freezing and thawing, of both death and life, of both alienation and fellowship. And because this God is always at work moving life from the one to the other, the community of faith sings in joyful response: Hallelujah!

Ephesians 1:3–14 (A B C)

Paul customarily opens his letters with an expression of thanksgiving for God's action in the lives of the congregation he addresses. Ephesians, which was probably written by a disciple of Paul rather than by Paul himself, not only continues that practice but expands it. Virtually the whole of chs. 1–3 is taken up with expressions of praise and thanksgiving. Ephesians 1:3 introduces this dominant mood of doxology with an ascription of praise to God for God's gifts to humankind. Since the word "blessing" in Greek can refer both to an act of thanksgiving or praise and to an act of bestowing some gift on another, the play on the word in this verse sets the tone for what follows: God is to be blessed for God's blessings. The extent of these blessings comes to expression in the phrase "every spiritual blessing in the heavenly places." God's goodness takes every conceivable form.

Verses 4–14 detail the form of God's blessings and focus on God's choosing of the elect. First, the author points to the agelessness of God's election: "He chose us in Christ before the foundation of the world." This bit of eloquence need not be turned into a literal proposition about God's act of election. Instead, the author asserts that God's choosing has no beginning. Just as it is impossible to identify the beginning of God's Christ (John 1:1), so it is impossible to conceive of a time when God did not choose on behalf of humankind.

God's election creates a people who are "holy and blameless before him." Verse 5 elaborates this characterization of God's people. They become God's children through Jesus Christ, but always what happens is "according to the good pleasure of his will." Everything that has occurred comes as a result of God's will and results in "the praise of his glorious grace that he freely bestowed on us in the Beloved." In the face of God's eternal choice on behalf of humankind, in the face of God's revelation of his Son, Jesus Christ, in the face of God's grace, the only appropriate response is one of praise (v. 6).

Verses 7–14 continue the exposition of God's gifts to humankind—redemption, forgiveness, wisdom, faith. The exposition culminates with repeated references to the inheritance believers receive through Christ (vs. 11, 14). That inheritance carries with it the responsibility already articulated in v. 6, which is to praise God's glory. Primary among the Christian's responsibilities is the giving of praise to God. With v. 15, the writer moves from this general expression of thanksgiving for God's actions on behalf of humankind to particular expressions of thanks relevant to his context. He constantly keeps the Ephesians in his prayers, asking for them "a spirit of wisdom and of revelation as you come to know him" (v. 17). The prayer continues in v. 18 with the petition that believers might be enlightened so that they know the hope to which they have been called and the riches that are part of God's inheritance. This mood of doxology continues throughout chapter 2 and most of chapter 3, as the author celebrates the nature of God's action in Christ Jesus.

For Christians in the West, particularly for those in North America, these words may have an alien and perhaps even an exotic tone. They run counter to at least two of our most deeply held values. First, these verses insist over and over again that humankind is utterly dependent on God. To assert that God creates, God destines, God wills, God reveals, God accomplishes God's own plan means that human beings, in and of themselves, accomplish nothing. This assault on the Western sense of independence and autonomy poses not only a challenge, but also a significant opportunity for preaching.

The second way in which this text cuts against the grain of Christianity in a North American context derives from its insistence on the obligation to praise God. Our thoroughgoing pragmatism inclines us to respond to the claim that God has acted on our behalf with the question, "What are we to *do*?" If we stand in God's debt, then we understand ourselves to be obliged to pay back the amount owed. The text, however, stipulates no repayment, for the debt can never be paid. Instead, the exhortation is to give God thanks and praise. To our way of thinking, this is no response at all, and yet it is fundamental to our existence as God's creatures. The reading of Ephesians should prompt us to recall the words of the Westminster Larger Catechism, that the chief end of human life is "to glorify God, and fully to enjoy him forever."

John 1:(1–9) 10–18 (A B C)

A portion of the prologue to the Fourth Gospel appeared as the Gospel reading for the Third Proper of Christmas, and the commentary on that lesson focused on Jesus as the revelation of God. Beyond the sentimentality and romance of Christmas, we encounter in the baby born at Bethlehem, so the passage tells us, nothing less than God's decision to become human. The full prologue (if one chooses) now occurs as the reading for the Second Sunday After Christmas, and provides us with the opportunity to reflect on further dimensions of God's incarnation as they emerge from the text.

One notable feature of the prologue is the prominence of visual language (a particularly relevant feature for the Epiphany season). "Light" and "glory" are terms associated with the Word, and "seeing" (alongside "receiving" and "believing") is the verb used for the perception of faith. Even before a statement of the incarnation, we read that the life found in the Word illuminates human experience, that the light continually shines in the darkness, and that the darkness has neither understood nor succeeded in extinguishing the light. (The Greek verb in 1:5 translated in the NRSV as "overcome" has a double meaning: "comprehend" and "seize with hostile intent." Perhaps an appropriate English word retaining the ambiguity would be "grasp," or "apprehend.")

The mention of John the Baptist, who is a kind of lesser luminary or reflected light (5:35) and is contrasted with the true light, signals the movement from a preincarnate lumination to the historic advent of the light in Jesus. It is in this context that we understand that the coming of the light into the world "enlightens everyone" (1:9). This universal reference has sometimes been taken to refer to the ancient notion that every individual possesses a spark of the divine, a measure of a universal conscience. The function of religion (any religion?) is to nurture the inextinguishable spark until it glows with understanding, so the argument goes. But such a reading hardly coheres with the evangelist's use of the image of light throughout the gospel. Jesus claims in a specific way to be the light of the world (8:12), without whom people grope in the darkness (12:35). The coming of the light entails judgment, because it discloses that people prefer darkness to light (3:19). What seems to be implied in the prologue is that all people, whether they believe it or not, live in a world illuminated by the light just as they live in a world created by the Word. What they are called to do is to trust the light, to walk in it, and thereby to become children of light (12:36).

Whether as a bolt of lightning in a dark sky, or as a distant beam toward which one moves, or as the dawn that chases the night, what light does is to push back darkness. The prologue, however, gives no hint that the light has totally banished the darkness, that life now is a perpetual day. In fact, the story John tells reiterates the powerful opposition of the darkness in the ministry of Jesus and beyond. But the promise of the prologue is that the darkness, despite its best efforts, including even a crucifixion, has not put out the light.

The last paragraph of the prologue has to be understood in terms of the many references to the book of Exodus, which it reflects. In a sense its background is the statement that "no one has ever seen God" (1:18). Though in fact there are places in the Hebrew Bible where people "see" God (for example, Ex. 24:9–11; Isa. 6:1), the statement seems to recall the occasion where Moses, eager to behold the divine glory, is not allowed to view the face of God, only God's backside (Ex. 33:23). In contrast, now God is seen in "the only Son."

Furthermore, the seeing of the divine glory is made possible by the incarnation of the Word, who "tabernacled among us." The Greek verb translated in the NRSV (John 1:14) as "lived" more specifically means "tented" or "tabernacled," and recalls the theme of God's dwelling with Israel, in the tabernacle of the wilderness wanderings and the Temple at Jerusalem. In the humanity of Jesus, the Christian community has beheld the very divine glory Moses wished to see, that unique and specific presence of God that hovered over the tabernacle as a cloud by day and a fire by night.

Terms like "light" and "glory" tend toward abstractions and become very difficult to communicate in concrete language to a contemporary congregation. What, then, does it mean to "see" God, to behold the divine glory? Two other words repeated in the prologue help in the translation: grace and truth. To behold God is to be a recipient of wave after wave of the divine generosity (grace) and to experience God's faithfulness to the ancient promises (truth). "Seeing" includes but goes beyond mere sense perception; it has to do with becoming children of God, with discovering the divine benevolence and reliability. Revelation in the Fourth Gospel has a strongly soteriological cast (17:3).

EPIPHANY

As the reading of Isa. 60:1–6 in the context of the celebration of Epiphany recalls, the coming of God into the world is often understood as the coming of a brilliant light. That light, the gift of God, carries with it the power to transform Israel so that Israel is restored and also those outside Israel are inevitably drawn to the light seen in Israel. While the social context differs dramatically, Eph. 3:1–12 makes a similar point: part of the mystery of the Epiphany is the mysterious inclusion of Gentiles among God's people. Submission to God's gift of light carries with it the obligation to accept and proclaim the inclusion of all outsiders within this mystery.

Psalm 72:1–7, 10–14 and Matt. 2:1–12 draw on imagery of the king and his enthronement, rather than the appearance of light. For the psalmist, the king's power and longevity must serve the purpose of the people's good. Prominent among the king's obligations is his responsibility to protect and liberate those who are not able to protect and liberate themselves. Ironically, Matt. 2:1–12 concerns the birth of an infant king whose power and longevity are severely threatened by another king, who acts only to protect himself. The Magi, outsiders drawn by the light that marks the infant king's birth, mark the beginning of the procession of those outsiders who see in the gospel the mystery of salvation. The juxtaposition of the enthronement psalm and the story of the infant Jesus, already King, dramatically poses the question of where authentic power lies and what constitutes genuine kingship.

Isaiah 60:1–6 (A B C)

Israel has had a long season of darkness (the despair of exile). Now comes its season of light. The light is not self-generated by Israel. It is a gift given by Yahweh. In the liturgical life of Israel,

God's powerful coming is often presented as the coming of light, though the word used for such light is "glory." God's glory "shines." And when God's glory (powerful, magisterial presence) "shines," Israel lives in the glow, and is itself a presence of light in the world. Thus the text that moves Israel from darkness to light is a dramatic move from absence to presence, from despair to hope, from dismay to well-being.

God's coming will decisively transform Israel's circumstance of despondency (Isa. 60:1–2). Israel is addressed with an imperative: "Arise." The imperative, however, is in fact an invitation. The imperative is not a burden, but good news. The imperative is an invitation for Israel to return to the land of the living.

The ground for the imperative is introduced by "for" (= because). Israel can arise because "your light has come." The words are wondrously and deliberately ambiguous. "Your light" is in fact Yahweh, who is Israel's only source of hope and possibility. At the same time, however, "your light" refers to Israel's own "glow," which is a gift from Yahweh that changes the very character of Israel. Thus "your light" is both *intrusion from Yahweh* and *restored Israel*.

These poetic lines are constructed so that an affirmation of "God's glory" is stated in v. 1b and reiterated in v. 2d. Between these two affirmations is a statement about darkness and thick darkness, gloom and despair. Thus the "glory" brackets and comprehends, contains and overwhelms, the darkness.

The poet waxes eloquent and extravagant about the magnet of Jerusalem among the nations (vs. 4–7). Something new is happening that Israel could not have expected or believed. When Israel finally lifts its eyes from its despair, it will not believe what it sees! There is a huge procession from all over the known world. Jerusalem had thought itself abandoned; now all the others are making the journey to be in Jerusalem.

On the one hand, "your sons" and "your daughters" will come, cared for, protected, valued (v. 4). These are the exiles that have been scattered far from Jerusalem. They had remained scattered long after the "official return," either because they were restrained by their "hosts" from coming home, or because they had lost their will and desire and resolve to come home. The light ends the exile. The poet imagines a world in which the abused and nearly forgotten now are drawn back to their proper habitat among God's beloved people.

On the other hand, the procession also includes more than the scattered Jewish exiles. It also includes the "wealth of the nations" (v. 5). Israel was rarely if ever one of the affluent nations. Most often Israel, in its disadvantage, stood in awe of its more powerful, prosperous neighbors. The poet plays on Israel's long-established sense of disadvantage, of being a rather second-rate people. Now, in this scenario, realities are reversed. The exotic material of the nations, long coveted from a distance, is given to Israel, who is the locus of the light in the world. The exiles are not coming home empty-handed. The exiles bring all that the nations can offer—camels, gold, frankincense, and flocks. Damaged Jerusalem has become the pivot and possibility for a new world.

The rhetoric of the poem is double-focused, in a quite careful way. On the one hand, there is no doubt that Israel gains as a political, economic power and is assured security and prosperity. On the other hand, that assurance is passionately theological. The exiles bring this much wealth, not to prosper Jerusalem, but to worship Yahweh (v. 7). The passage begins in God's glory (vs. 1–2) and ends in God's glory (v. 7). Israel's new reality of prosperity exists exactly in the envelope of God's glory.

Whenever the nations bring such exotic gifts, they are in fact submitting themselves to God's new future. That is what is happening with the bringing of "gold, frankincense, and myrrh" (Matt. 2:11). When God is thus worshiped, Israel prospers, Jerusalem glows, the nations come to their proper existence, all bask in the glow of God's well-being. God's presence creates newness for the entire world. In this poem, all—Jerusalem, the exiles, the nations—receive the gift of life.

Psalm 72:1–7, 10–14 (A B C)

A widely held scholarly view sees this psalm as a hymn sung at the time of the enthronement of the Davidic king, or if ancient Israel possessed an annual ceremony of reenthronement, as did ancient Babylon, a hymn devoted to that occasion. In either event, there is a sense in which the king is entering (or reentering) the public life of the nation, and the psalm expresses the hopes that the people have vested in this monarch, who is also the representative of God. Therefore it is an appropriate text for the Epiphany observance, a celebration of the entrance of the messianic ruler, Jesus Christ, into the life of humankind.

The opening (vs. 1–4) constitutes a prayer to God that the king will establish a right social order. Prominent in these lines are terms that were often found on the lips of the prophets: righteousness (vs. 1, 2, 3), justice (vs. 1, 2), and peace (v. 3: in NRSV, "prosperity"). They are also found in certain of the psalms of praise, where they refer not only to qualities characteristic of God, but to the nature of human life before God (Pss. 97:2; 98:9). For the author of Ps. 72, these qualities are not abstractions, but are moral ideals which have become incarnate in the Davidic king. Those qualities which began with God (*"your* justice, . . . *your* righteousness," v. 1, emphasis added) have become the standards by which the human king is to rule. His role is to help those who cannot help themselves (v. 4).

The following section (vs. 5–7) begins as a prayer for the king's long life, the kind of ritualistic formula that has been a part of coronation ceremonies ancient and modern ("Long live the king!"). Yet it is of the nature of this psalm that it will not dwell on the king's good health, but returns to the larger question of the health of the community. As in the first section, "righteousness" and "peace" (v. 7) are the standards by which the well-being of the people is judged, and it is they, not just the heartbeat of the king, that must be preserved past the end of the moon (v. 7, compare v. 5).

The discourse soon turns to the urgent affairs of the society: the well-being (šālôm of vs. 3, 7) of the poorest, most helpless citizens. Notice the verbs: "delivers" (v. 12), "has pity" (v. 13), "saves" (v. 13), "redeems" (v. 14). Clearly God's king is to bring the same energies to bear on the quality of the nation's domestic life as on foreign affairs. And—if the literary form means anything—since the king's concern for domestic matters is placed in a climactic position within the psalm, this aspect of his duties is to weigh more heavily upon him than his military adventures.

This lection ends with an affirmation of the value of human life in the king's eyes: "Precious is their blood in his sight" (v. 14).

The most often remarked emphasis of Epiphany is on the appearance of the messianic king, Jesus Christ, and it is in this connection that other lections for this day emphasize light (Isa. 60:1; Matt. 2:2) and the ability of men and women to see God's work (Isa. 60:2; Eph. 1:9, 18). But this Psalm lection contributes an added dimension to the Epiphany observance by celebrating not only the appearance of the king, but the nature of the king's rule as the liberator of those who are unable to liberate themselves. To be sure, the same note is struck in other texts that describe the birth and infancy of Jesus (notably Luke 1:52–53), but few texts draw so tightly the connection between God's act of sending a king and the responsibilities of the king as protector of the poor and the weak.

There is an irony in this theme when it is applied to Epiphany, for Epiphany is the celebration of the visit of the Magi, bearers of precious gifts to the boy-king Jesus. The description of wealth in the traditional Gospel lection for Epiphany (Matt. 2:1–12) is to be found in the gold, frankincense, and myrrh, the treasures of the Magi. In that narrative the messianic King is a weak and vulnerable child, under threat from the tyrannical Herod. His one kingly act is a passive one of receiving the tokens of royalty bestowed by others.

But in the Epiphany Psalm lection, all of that is turned around. Here the royal office itself is that which has been bestowed, not just its tokens. And the giver is not some earthly seer or potentate, but the one true King, Israel's God. As for the theme of wealth in the psalm, while there is some traditional language of empire, the real wealth consists in šālôm (vs. 3, 7). This is more than "peace" in the sense of an absence of warfare. It is also more than "prosperity," as the NRSV—with some justification—has it (v. 3). Šālôm in this case is the total well-being of the people (compare NEB's "peace and prosperity"), their ability to live free from "oppression and violence" imposed by others (v. 14) and free from the devastating effects of poverty.

Thus the Epiphany celebration is the joyous proclamation of a kingdom like no other. It is the joyous acceptance of a King who has come to set us free.

Ephesians 3:1–12 (A B C)

Following the first two chapters of Ephesians, with their extensive thanksgiving to God, in 3:1 the author takes up Paul's ministry in the context of God's mystery. Verses 1–3 characterize Paul's calling as his "commission." Verses 4–6 elaborate on the nature of God's mystery that is now revealed, and this section provides the most obvious entrance into a discussion of the Epiphany. In vs. 7–9, the focus is once again on Paul's ministry concerning that mystery, and in vs. 10–12 it is on the ministry of the church as a whole.

The opening statement breaks off awkwardly after the identification of Paul as "a prisoner for Christ Jesus for the sake of you Gentiles." Verse 2 verifies Paul's calling as prisoner on behalf of the Gentiles by referring to the gift of God's grace which bestowed on him a "commission" on behalf of Gentiles. Verse 3 makes specific the nature of this gift of grace, in that the mystery became known to Paul through revelation. In common with all believers, Paul's knowledge of God's action comes to him solely through God's own free gift.

Verse 4 returns to the term "mystery," which is initially described only as a "mystery of Christ." The newness of the revelation of this mystery emerges in v. 5, which emphasizes that only in the present time has the mystery been revealed. This assertion stands in tension with statements elsewhere in the Pauline corpus regarding the witness of the prophets to God's action in Jesus Christ (for example, Rom. 1:2; 16:26). What the author celebrates is the present revelation of God's mystery, and the contrast with the past helps to emphasize that fact but should not become a critique or rejection of past generations. Similarly, the second part of v. 5 identifies the "holy apostles and prophets" as recipients of revelation, not because revelation confines itself to those individuals but because of their central role in proclamation.

Verse 6 identifies the "mystery of Christ": "the Gentiles have become fellow heirs, members of the same body, and sharers in the promise in Christ Jesus through the gospel." Given the previous few verses, we might anticipate that the "mystery" refers to the mystery of Jesus' advent. For this letter, however, the "mystery of Christ" has a very specific connotation, namely, the inclusion of the Gentiles. Each word identifying the Gentiles in v. 6 begins with the prefix *syn*, "together," emphasizing the oneness created through the mystery. We might convey this phrase in English as "heirs together, a body together, sharers together." For the writer of Ephesians, central to the "mystery of Christ" is the oneness of Jew and Gentile.

The emphasis here on the social dimension of the gospel, the unification of human beings, needs specific attention. Certainly Ephesians does not limit the mystery to its social component, as if the only characteristic of the gospel is its impact on human relations. The extensive praise of God and of Jesus Christ in chs. 1 and 2 prevents us from reductionism. Nevertheless, here the radical oneness of Jew and Gentile who become one new humanity (2:15) becomes a necessary ingredient in the larger reconciliation of humankind to God (2:16). Any separation between "vertical" and "horizontal" dimensions of faith here stands exposed as inadequate.

Verses 7–9 return us to Paul's role with respect to the gospel. He, despite his own standing as "the very least of all the saints," receives the gift of preaching among the Gentiles and, indeed, among all people (v. 9). Proclamation of the gospel comes not from Paul and his fellow apostles alone, however. Verse 10 identifies the role of the whole church in proclamation. The church, both through its verbal proclamation and through its actions, makes known God's wisdom. Here that wisdom is addressed to "the rulers and authorities in the heavenly places." The gospel addresses not only human beings but all of God's creation.

Verses 11–12 affirm once again the purpose of God in the proclamation of Paul and of the church. God's purpose has its final goal in Christ Jesus our Lord, "in whom we have access to God in boldness and confidence through faith in him." These last terms connote more in Greek than the English translations can convey. To speak "boldly" (*parrēsia*) is to speak without regard for the consequences, and to have "access" (*prosagōgē*) is to have, through Jesus Christ, a means of drawing near to God. In other words, the revelation, or epiphany, of Jesus Christ carries with it both the obligation of proclaiming the gospel and the strength needed for carrying out that obligation.

Matthew 2:1-12 (A B C)

The story of the Magi coming from the East to bring gifts to the infant Jesus is associated in the minds of most churchgoers with Christmas. It is a piece of the scene usually enacted at the Christmas service or pageant. The story, however, with its strong connections with the Hebrew scriptures and its prominent depiction of these non-Jewish worshipers, fits more appropriately the celebration of Epiphany. It telegraphs for the reader of Matthew's narrative the opening of the gospel beyond Jewish boundaries and the reminder of the worldwide mission of the church.

We shall examine the passage in terms of its three primary characters. First are the Magi. The Greek term *magoi* suggests that the "wise men" were priestly sages from Persia, who were experts in astrology and the interpretation of dreams. What distinguishes them in the narrative is *their sincere and persistent search* for the baby "born king of the Jews." While one might suppose them to have been veteran, sophisticated travelers, what is striking is their candor and openness. Almost naive, they seem to anticipate no difficulty in inquiring of Herod the king about the birth of a rival king. Their inquisitiveness forces a troubled Herod to seek help from the chief priests and scribes, who, though aligned with Herod, ironically produce the decisive clue that finally leads to Bethlehem.

Throughout their journeys, the Magi are *patently guided by God*. It is, first, a star in the East and then a text from Micah that lead them to their goal. When the time comes for them to leave Bethlehem, they are warned in a dream to take a different route home to avoid Herod. These strange outsiders do not stumble onto the Messiah as if by accident. They search with purpose and are directed each step of the way by a divine hand.

The Magi's stay in Bethlehem is *marked by great joy, by the worship of the infant Jesus, and by the giving of gifts*. They come prepared and seem to know what to do when they arrive. The narrative is specific about the gifts—gold, frankincense, and myrrh—expensive gifts suitable for royalty. We are not given any clues about the motivations of the Magi, why they came and why they worshiped. The narrator only seems interested in the response they made, the proper response to the King of Israel.

Now the remarkable fact that undergirds the entire portrait of the Magi—their searching, their guidance, their worship—is its character as the fulfillment of scripture. Isaiah 60:1–6 and Ps. 72:1–7, 10–14, two other texts for Epiphany, speak of the time of restoration when

> the wealth of the nations shall come to you. . . .
> They shall bring gold and frankincense,
> and shall proclaim the praise of the Lord.
> (Isa. 60:5–6)

The arrival of the non-Jews at Bethlehem turns out to be a part of the divine plan, an accomplishment of the promises made long ago. The Magi, as representatives of all non-Jews, belong here in the company of those worshiping the infant Messiah. In a sense they pave the way for the command the risen Christ gives to the eleven at the end of Matthew's narrative: make disciples of all the nations.

A second key figure in our text is Herod the king. He also plays a prominent role in the latter half of Matt. 2, a passage that serves as the Gospel reading for the First Sunday After Christmas in the A cycle. Suffice it here to say that the scheming of the troubled and cruel Herod turns out to be no match for the guileless Magi, guided by the hand of God. Herod's plot to have the Magi search out and identify his rival for him backfires when they are directed in a dream to go home a different way. If the Magi represent the presence of non-Jews who appropriately worship Jesus, Herod represents the imperial powers, imposing and conspiring but threatened and ultimately frustrated by King Jesus.

Third, we turn to the figure of Jesus, who in this narrative says and does nothing, but nevertheless is the chief protagonist. The entire plot revolves around the affirmation that Jesus is King of Israel. The text from Micah that the chief priests and scribes uncover identifies him as "a ruler who is to shepherd my people Israel" (2:6). The Greek verb translated as "shepherd" actually depicts what shepherds do with their flocks—tend, protect, guide, nurture. Jesus' rule is distinguished from Herod's rule by his gentle guardianship, his compassionate care for his people. But it is just this shepherd-king who is finally rejected and mocked by the same chief priests and scribes who, at the crucifixion, say, "He is the King of Israel; let him come down from the cross now" (27:42).

The account of the Magi's visit to Bethlehem and their worship of the King of the Jews becomes a critical episode in the larger story of God's redemptive plan for humankind. Salvation comes through Jesus the Jew, the fulfillment of the prophetic dreams, but it reaches far beyond to strangers from the East, to a Roman centurion, and to a Canaanite woman. At the end of the story it is no longer a matter of non-Jews coming to Bethlehem, but of Jewish disciples going out to all the nations.

First Sunday After Epiphany

(BAPTISM OF THE LORD)
Ordinary Time 1

It is rather unusual to find four texts assigned for a given Sunday in the lectionary cycle that demonstrate as much commonality as do the texts for this Sunday. Any combination from among the four would be appropriate and would lend itself to reflection about the sacrament of baptism, about new beginnings, about the power of God in the human arena, about divine revelation.

Water is an obvious and prominent symbol in the four passages, and yet it functions in different ways. In both of the Old Testament texts (Gen. 1:1–5 and Ps. 29), water represents the surging chaos out which God brings order, the stormy deeps over which Yahweh rules. In the New Testament passages (Acts 19:1–7 and Mark 1:4–11), however, the symbolism has changed, and water is linked to baptism. It represents the utterly new beginning that comes with the gift of the Spirit.

More consistent in the texts is the presence and reality of the Spirit/wind, demonstrating the surprising, uncontrollable power of God. Not like a gentle breeze, but like a mighty gale, the Spirit tames the formless void (parallel in Ps. 29 to "the voice of the LORD") and pushes back the destructive waters. Likewise in Paul's baptism of the Ephesian believers in Acts 19, the Spirit intrudes, controls, and re-creates. Those who receive the Spirit are led to a profound worship and a powerful proclamation, unlike anything they have known before.

In the account of Jesus' baptism, the Spirit accompanies the violent rending of the heavens and the sound of a voice, identifying Jesus as the beloved Son. It is the same voice of the Lord about which the psalmist sings. It is a moment of revelation for Jesus—and for us who read the story.

Genesis 1:1-5

The first and most familiar words of the Bible announce the themes that recur in this set of lections: new *beginnings, water,* and *spirit.* This reading itself is surprisingly truncated in the lection, but it is extended enough to exhibit these themes with enormous power. The scope of our reading is "the first day," the day when life begins out of the ominous dark.

The first two verses of Genesis present a difficult grammatical problem which turns on the first word of the Hebrew text. How the first word is read determines the relation between the first two verses. There are two important alternatives in reading that first word.

On the one hand, the more conventional and familiar translation is "In the beginning, God created . . . ." This rendering makes v. 1 an independent and absolute statement, introduced by a temporal phrase. The upshot is that Creation is an absolute new beginning. As a result, v. 2, which speaks of a chaotic deep, is quite subordinate, though it is difficult to understand from whence came the ominous deep of v. 2 if v. 1 witnesses to an absolute beginning.

On the other hand, in a reading offered in NRSV (marginal reading) and preferred by a great number of scholars, the first word of the Hebrew text is taken as a temporal, dependent clause: "When God began to create. . . ." The result is to make v. 1 dependent and to make v. 2 the main clause. Consequently, God's creation activity is not an absolute beginning point, but God began the work of creation by operating on the already existing ominous material of chaos. This suggests that creation is not ex nihilo, but consists in the magisterial ordering of chaos that is there from the beginning. (The text, on this reading, is not curious about the origin of the extant chaos; the chaos is simply there as a given.)

In any case, the beginning of the world's story features three elements. There is the dark, formless, disordered watery chaos that is ominous, threatening, rebellious, and destructive. The imagery is that of surging waters. Any contact with the wild, relentless force of an ocean tide lets us know about the unbridled power of "many waters," a power that cannot be managed, channeled, domesticated, or resisted.

The second feature in this tale of beginnings is the God who is the subject of this awesome, magisterial word "create." This God, so the text suggests, has no point of origin, no antecedents, but is simply there at the outset, undertaking the inexplicable activity (which only God can undertake) of ordering, forming, shaping, willing, decreeing, and summoning an ordered potential life-space. There is no anxiety or precariousness about this God, who proceeds deliberately to fashion a context for viable life.

The third factor is the wind, God's active instrument for ordering the watery materials of life. The older, more familiar rendering of the Hebrew term is "spirit," that is, God's life-force, God's principle of vitality, which sweeps over the waters. More recent renderings, however, including NRSV, take the term *rûah* as "wind," thus permitting a more graphic, concrete picture of the wind given by God, which blows over the waters and blows them back, making life-space dry and safe. The term *rûah* as "wind/spirit" thus permits on the one hand a graphic notion of the waters being restrained by physical force, and on the other hand a direct link between this powerful, palpable life-force and the holy, inscrutable purpose of God.

These first two verses testify that a safe, dry space for life depends on the life-force of God, for none of us has the power or resource to command or master the waters (compare Jer. 5:22; Mark 4:35–41). This life-space is never a creaturely achievement, but is always a free gift of the creator God. One of the lessons from this text is to see that "the spirit of God," so crucial in the other readings for the day, needs to be understood as the intrusive power for life that only God can command. The wind that blows at baptism or at Pentecost is the same wind as in our text, in each case making new life wondrously and inexplicably possible.

In Gen. 1:3–5 God now speaks for the first time, for God has not yet spoken in vs. 1–2. God speaks in a bold, confident, sovereign voice. This is the voice of a ruler on a throne who will be obeyed, who will be obeyed even by those creatures who exist only when addressed. The light, not heretofore mentioned, exists and functions only at the behest of this sovereign voice. This is the God who "calls into existence the things that do not exist" (Rom. 4:17). It is the light that is prized and is the new gift of God wrought to counter the deep of Gen. 1:2 (compare John 1:1–5).

The darkness, however, is not condemned or rejected. It also is named and valued. This God is not simply on the side of light against the dark; this God values and administers both light and dark. Both are named, both are given statutory legitimacy. Both belong to the ordered world of God, both prized, neither scorned. The day of astonishing beginning anticipates the balanced, ordered, reliable world of "seedtime and harvest, cold and heat, summer and winter, day and night" that will make a viable, guaranteed home for all God's creatures (Gen. 8:22).

The new beginning is not worked in threat and conflict, but in buoyant ordering (compare Ps. 139:11–12). Our world, that is, God's world, begins in assurance, summoned by God to a balanced, life-permitting order.

Psalm 29

One of the most forceful of all the hymns of praise in the Psalter, Ps. 29 has been the subject of much scholarly investigation, especially with regard to its possible connections with Ugaritic literature and with the beginning of the autumn rains. However all of that may be, in the form that we have received it this psalm presents Yahweh, the God of Israel, as the Lord of the storm and therefore as the Lord of all of life.

As is typical of many psalms of praise, Ps. 29 is composed of three parts: introduction, body, and conclusion. The introduction (vs. 1–2) calls on the members of the heavenly council, the "heavenly beings" of NRSV, to give glory to the Lord, "glory and strength," "the glory of his name." Since the term "glory" (*kābôd*) is often found in Priestly literature within the Old Testament, where it refers to the theophany of Yahweh (for example, Ex. 16:7; 24:16; compare Ezek. 1:28), the repeated use of the term here emphasizes that this psalm is describing not a God who is a distant abstraction, but a God who has appeared in the life of the people.

The second section, the body (vs. 3–10), describes the manner of the Lord's appearing. Here the language, some of the most vivid in the Psalter, evokes images of a violent storm. Especially noteworthy is the repeated phrase "the voice of the LORD," which begins each verse except 6 and 10. At one level this would seem to be a reference to the claps of thunder that accompany the storm, as in Ex. 19:16, but at a deeper level the "voice of the LORD" is synonymous with the "word of God," that is, God's self-revelation.

This section lists various aspects of the natural world over which the Lord's glory presides. First, there are the "waters," the "mighty waters," of v. 3. We are not told just which waters the psalmist has in mind (that becomes clearer in a moment), but the presumption of the reader at this point is that these waters are both seas and rivers, as well as lakes and pools. That is to say, all waters are under the rule of the Lord of the storm, the Lord who brings the rains. Next, the forests that grace the land are brought into view (vs. 5–6). The violence of the storm bends and breaks the trees, so that even the solid mountains ("Lebanon" and "Sirion"—the latter meaning Mt. Hermon) appear to skip like frolicking young animals. The lightning and thunder even rattle the uninhabited spaces.

The final verse of this section (v. 10) forms a climax to the body of the psalm and brings us back to the "waters" of v. 3. The "flood" here is nothing other than the waters of chaos that God pushed back at Creation, making place for heaven and earth (Gen. 1:7). These are the same waters, the flood, which invaded creation in the time of Noah (Gen. 7:11), but which God then expelled and over which God promised to rule forever (Gen. 9:11). Now we understand the "waters" of Ps. 29:3 and all the other images of this psalm: God is the ruler of all of life. Every aspect of our existence is subject to the divine sovereignty. "The LORD sits enthroned as king forever."

The third section of the psalm (v. 11) is a prayer that expresses the hope that God will bless the people with strength and peace.

There are at least three elements in the psalm that make it appropriate for use on the Sunday which, in many churches, is observed as a festival to commemorate Jesus' baptism (compare the Gospel lection for this week). The first is the element of water. The psalm assumes that the reader is aware of the old stories, known by both Hebrews and other ancient peoples, which describe God's conquest of the unruly waters at Creation. In the story of Jesus' baptism, not only is the water peaceful and calm, but—by the power and love of God—it has become a medium for the revelation of God's love. It symbolizes the washing away of human sinfulness, God's forgiveness of the dark side of our nature. It also symbolizes a sinless Jesus' identification with this sinful humankind.

A second element in the psalm that makes it appropriate for this day is that of theophany, that is, God's self-manifestation. The recurring use of the word "glory" (vs. 1, 2, 3, 9) reminds the reader of God's continual indwelling in human life in order to lead and save the people. And the almost incessant "voice of the LORD" points to God's nature as One who communicates with the people for their instruction and redemption. This anticipates the voice "from heaven" of Mark 1:11, which announces to a sinful humankind the Sonship and Kingship of Jesus.

The kingly nature of Jesus connects with a third element within Ps. 29 that renders it appropriate for this day. That is the majestic (v. 4), regal (v. 10) nature of the God of the theophany, the Appearing One. This is the Lord of the Universe, who rules with strength (v. 1), who bestows strength on the people (v. 11) in order that they may live in safety and peace. Strength is thus seen as one of the qualities of the Son, King Jesus, and his baptism therefore becomes not only a moment of his identification with sinful humankind, but also a moment of his anointing as the Lord and Ruler of life.

Acts 19:1–7

The story of Paul's initial encounter with the "disciples" at Ephesus, though containing several perplexing details, provides an occasion for the church to raise questions with itself about its own theological deficiencies. I deliberately use the expression "raise questions," because that it is precisely Paul's way of dealing with the Ephesians. He does not berate them for their failures, nor does he chide them because they have apparently departed from their roots in John the Baptist. He merely asks a relevant theological question, followed by another, and then by instruction. Their ignorance or regression into syncretism is not an occasion for blame or even harsh confrontation, but for patient probing that leads to an empowerment for mission.

Who were these "disciples" (also called "believers")? The preceding story relates the preaching at Ephesus of Apollos, an eloquent interpreter of the scripture and one who "taught accurately the things concerning Jesus" but who "knew only the baptism of John." It was Priscilla and Aquila, Paul's friends, who took Apollos aside and privately tutored him in a fuller understanding of the faith (Acts 18:24–26). Apparently, "some disciples" (19:1) still adhered to the message of the early Apollos, which they received prior to his instruction by Priscilla and Aquila, and they were the group Paul found when he arrived at Ephesus. They knew about Jesus; they had received John's baptism; but they did not know or had forgotten that John was a voice announcing that Jesus would baptize with the Spirit. The point is that their faith was deficient at a critical point, not yet what it could or should be, and Paul's perceptive queries became the means for growth.

What do we learn from Paul's instruction of the Ephesian "disciples"? First, we learn that the Spirit comes through the message and baptism of Jesus Christ. What was lacking in the theology and experience of these people could not be remedied by a gimmick or by an urging, but only through hearing and a sacramental act. The dialogue between Paul and the "disciples" is remarkably sparse—pointed questions and simple answers. Could the narrator by the sparseness mean to convey that the absence of the Spirit is not due to complex social problems that have to be engaged or mysterious theological questions that have to be answered? What the Ephesians needed was simple—a clear statement of the witness to Jesus and Christian baptism. (The narrator is inconsistent about whether the sacrament precedes or follows the gift of the Spirit. The order was apparently not an issue. See Acts 10:44–48.)

The narrative may be especially instructive in a day when people struggle for meaning in life and for a new depth of spirituality. Individuals long for something more real than what can be found in a frantic, impersonal, and materialistic world. The very word "Spirit" becomes an attraction by suggesting an animating force, a reality giving ardor, vitality, and warmth of feeling. The quest for spirituality, however, is open to distortion, to the search for strategies and methods that seek to force God's hand and that neglect the divine freedom. God is free to act where and how God wills. The promise to be claimed from our text is that the Spirit is to be sought in the word preached and the sacrament enacted.

Second, we learn from Paul's encounter with the Ephesians that the Spirit generates a profound worship and an active mission. The immediate reaction to Christian baptism and the commissioning by the laying on of hands was twofold: speaking in tongues and prophesying. The former is to be distinguished from the experience of the church in Jerusalem at Pentecost, where foreign languages were spoken and understood (Acts 2:4). Here the phenomenon is that of profound worship for which words are inadequate (Acts 10:45–46) and for which in some places the church came to demand an interpretation so that other worshipers could be edified (1 Cor. 14:27–28). The lively Spirit of God produces lively worship.

The other result of the Spirit's presence is prophesying (fulfilling the wish expressed in Num. 11:29, "Would that all the Lord's people were prophets, and that the Lord would put his spirit on them!"). In the New Testament church, prophesying is an activity nearly synonymous with preaching, with the intelligible speaking of the word of God. Prophesying has to do with the edification and growth of the church. Outsiders are reproved by it and are led themselves to the worship of God (as in 1 Cor. 14:24–25). An integral piece of spirituality, then, is the declaration of the faith, clearly and intelligibly.

It is possible (though perhaps risky) in preaching from Acts 19:1–7 for the modern-day preacher to assume the role of Paul and to be the instructor for a congregation with a deficient theology. It may be better for the minister to identify with the Ephesian disciples, needing instruction, and, along with the congregation, to be led by Paul to a deeper spirituality and discipleship.

Mark 1:4–11

By contrast with the other evangelists, Mark's treatment of John the Baptist and the baptism of Jesus is exceedingly lean. While Mark understands John as the forerunner of Jesus, he conveys that portrait with his customary frugality (see the discussion of Mark 1:1–8 earlier, under Second Sunday of Advent). Mark shows no interest in explaining the content of John's preaching (compare Matt. 3:7–12; Luke 3:7–17) or in having John distinguish his identity from that of Jesus (John 1:19–27).

In the same way, Mark narrates the baptism of Jesus without concern for the questions that event raises about the authority of Jesus. If John baptizes Jesus, does that action suggest that John was somehow superior to Jesus in godliness, in power, in understanding? The other Gospels carefully construct stories of Jesus' baptism that will acknowledge the event without giving too much over to John and his followers, but Mark appears not to recognize the potential for confusion.

For Mark, what is important in the baptism is less the relationship between John and Jesus than the revelation of vs. 10–11. The baptism of Jesus provides the occasion for the revelation of his identity in vs. 10–11, which in turn prompts Jesus' journey into the wilderness and the beginning of his ministry. The baptism becomes the setting in which the revelation occurs, not its cause.

Jesus' baptism signals both his continuity with Israel's history and his discontinuity from that history. By virtue of his baptism at the hands of John, one clearly identified in terms of Israel's prophetic history (vs. 2–6), Jesus appears to be one more stage in the long procession of God's actions on behalf of Israel. The revelation in vs. 10–11, on the other hand, marks Jesus as something far greater than any of Israel's prophets.

The details of vs. 10–11 signal the scene's importance as far beyond that of a mere postscript to the baptism itself. The opening of the heavens, no mere mechanical device by which the Spirit descends, indicates that divine revelation is at hand (as in Ezek. 1:1; Acts 7:56; 10:11; Rev. 19:11). Whatever Mark understands by the Spirit, he clearly understands it to be connected with the very presence of God. Hearing the heavenly voice, of course, becomes the climactic point of the scene.

Questions about what it is Jesus saw and what those present saw and understood will prove unavoidable but also utterly fruitless. To ask how the Spirit looks is to misunderstand the story's insistence that Jesus somehow experienced the Spirit. Saying that the Spirit appeared "like a dove" does not mean that the Spirit *is* a dove, but that the Spirit could somehow be seen. What others saw and understood is of no interest here (by contrast with Mark 9:2–8), for the reader is the one who becomes the bystander who sees, hears, and puzzles over what is said.

What the voice declares is that Jesus is "my Son, the Beloved; with you I am well pleased" (see Ps. 2:7). At the outset of the Gospel, then, the audience knows who Jesus is. At crucial points in the story, Mark reinforces this identification: at the transfiguration, when a voice from the clouds again declares Jesus "my Son, the Beloved" (9:7); at Jesus' trial, when Jesus affirmatively answers the high priest's question, "Are you the Messiah, the Son of the Blessed One?" (14:61–62); and most importantly, at the cross, when the Roman centurion declares "Truly this man was God's Son!" Mark openly announces that Jesus is God's Son.

Yet the baptismal declaration also conceals who Jesus is, even as it reveals him. What does it mean to be "my Son, the Beloved"? Throughout Mark's story, characters struggle to understand what Jesus' words and actions mean. Whose power stands behind Jesus' healings? What do his enigmatic teachings in the parables mean? How can he be the Messiah and also undergo suffering and even crucifixion? "My Son, the Beloved" remains concealed even as he is revealed.

Mark's story of Jesus' baptism, with its emphasis on revealing the unique identity of Jesus as Son of God, scarcely serves as a prototype for Christian baptism. And yet John the Baptist's earlier saying ("He will baptize you with the Holy Spirit," 1:8) provides a connection between Jesus' baptism and Christian practice. Jesus' bringing of the Spirit enables persons to be baptized into the community called into being by that Spirit. The Christian's baptism becomes that of Jesus in that believers are called to live out Jesus' path of proclamation and of servanthood (see 10:38–40).

SECOND SUNDAY AFTER EPIPHANY

Ordinary Time 2

Two narratives, a song of praise, and a pastoral directive to a struggling congregation of believers present us with a diverse offering of forms for this Sunday, but with texts linked by their common confession of the sovereign God and the appropriate response of total obedience. At the heart of the series is the remarkable and personal confession of the psalmist, who sees his life encompassed behind and before by the inescapable presence of God (Ps. 139). The awareness of such a God prompts words of astonishment and ultimately of submission (as in Ps. 139:23–24).

The familiar story of the boy Samuel being disturbed in the night by the intrusive word of God contains also the poignant figure of Eli, the mentor of Samuel, sensitive to the voice of God and submissive to the divine word, even when the word comes as terrifying judgment on him and his priestly descendants. Samuel as God's chosen voice for the future stands in sharp contrast to the disobedient and disdainful sons of Eli, for whom Eli must bear responsibility (1 Sam. 3:1–20).

The calls of the disciples in John (1:43–51), so different from the calls depicted in the Synoptic tradition, highlight the confession of Jesus as the heart of discipleship. The movement of Nathanael from skepticism to faith culminates in the amazing acknowledgment of Jesus as Son of God, King of Israel.

Finally, Paul reminds us that the obedience that marks true discipleship expresses itself in the way believers conduct their lives in the world. The whole self, body as well as spirit, redeemed by Christ is the whole self that glorifies God in all its relationships.

1 Samuel 3:1–10 (11–20)

This text is best taken to include vs. 11–20, which the lectionary makes optional. If one treats only 1 Sam. 3:1–10 without vs. 11–20, one has only an idyllic narrative about an innocent young boy called into the service of God. With vs. 11–20, however, the primary thrust of the passage changes decisively. The narrative then is an assertion of God's overthrow of the old order of reality represented by the priest, an overthrow evoked because of the failure of the priestly family, which has been greedy and disobedient.

The narrative concerns the rise of the boy Samuel into an adult figure central to the life and politics of Israel. The introductory verse, matched by the conclusion of vs. 19–21, concerns the "word of the LORD," the assertion of God's concrete will and specific purpose voiced by human agents.

In vs. 2–9, the two characters in this narrative exchange are the old priest Eli and the young boy Samuel. Eli is portrayed as a feeble old man, emblem of a failed priestly order that has exhausted its authority and its credibility. Samuel is situated in this narrative as an apprentice to Eli. But he learns quickly and is shown to be more discerning and more responsive to God than is the family of Eli. Samuel is indeed the wave of God's future.

The third character in this narrative is Yahweh, who appears as a voice in the drama, who is treated as an imposing, intruding, but not unexpected figure in the story. The narrative accents the persistence of Yahweh, the dullness of Eli, and the guileless responsiveness of Samuel. In v. 4, Yahweh addresses Samuel directly, and Samuel answers. Samuel, however, is undiscerning in this first occasion as to who it is that addresses him and intrudes upon his sleep. A second time Yahweh addresses Samuel directly. Again Samuel misperceives (v. 6). A third time Yahweh addresses Samuel, and yet a third time Samuel misunderstands (v. 8). In this third case, finally, Eli sorts out the confusion and rightly interprets for the boy what is in fact happening. Eli is not so old or so distracted that he cannot recognize the holy voice that intrudes where least expected. It comes as no great surprise to Eli that Yahweh speaks.

A fourth time Yahweh calls; Samuel, instructed by Eli, is now ready to listen (v. 10). So Yahweh voices a quite extended speech (vs. 11–12). Samuel is warned that Yahweh is about to issue an ominous verdict that will be deeply disturbing, causing the tingling of ears. (See 2 Kings 21:12; Jer. 19:3 for other uses of the imagery of v. 11, again in a context of a deeply negative pronouncement.) Verses 12–13 allude to the oracle of 2:30–32, which is a savage sentence against the priestly house of Eli, promising that it will be terminated because of Eli's disobedient sons (see 2:12–17). After the general threat of 3:11 and the allusion back in vs. 12–13, finally in v. 14 Yahweh utters a climactic "therefore," indicating that the house of Eli is lost beyond any ritual rescue. This is a moment of deep dread in the narrative, for the divine assertion marks the delegitimation of the dominant priestly family, and with it, the delegitimation of the entire symbol system on which Israel has relied.

The boy Samuel has the terrible message in hand: he knows that Israel's power arrangements are about to be drastically altered. No wonder the boy is afraid to tell the old man (v. 15). Nonetheless, Eli insists on knowing the whole message. While the text is not explicit, it may be that Eli anticipates the harsh word. The old priest demands that he know all, even threatening the boy if he withholds anything (v. 17).

Finally, under such a threat from Eli, Samuel blurts out the truth (v. 18). The actual message is not reiterated as we might expect, but reference is made back to the verdict of vs. 12–14. Even if the message is not repeated, the point is inescapable. The old priest is told directly to his face that his order and his house are to be terminated and he is to be expelled from the priesthood. No wonder the boy is frightened; the news is not good. Eli might respond in anger or in disbelief, or even in violence. We are not prepared, however, for Eli's response, which is marked by deep faith with the grace of nobility: "It is Yahweh" (v. 18). Eli is immediately submissive and accepting, in no way questioning or resisting the verdict given by the boy, which he accepts as the truth of Yahweh.

The concluding verses (vs. 19–24) look back to v. 1 and focus on the larger issue of Samuel's rise to power and authority. As in v. 1, these verses concern the "word of the LORD," which is carried by the boy, who by now has become a formidable man.

The long chapter begins with and ends with Samuel and the word. In between, the chapter offers a concrete instance of the word, which effects a change in power and the deposition of Eli and his house. The focus of this text would seem to be on the power of God's initiative, both in the rise of Samuel and in the loss to Eli. The boy Samuel is a model of one who is completely responsive and obedient to the word. It surprises us, however, that Eli emerges as the model character who submits to the word of Yahweh, even though that word means his own death (see 4:18). It is that word, a purpose that stands outside every human strategy, which causes the rise and fall of those in power. The boy Samuel is a marvelous, innocent vehicle for that word. What matters finally, however, is this overriding, transcendent but concrete, purpose of God to which all must submit, where that purpose works good and even where it works ill.

Psalm 139:1–6, 13–18

Since one of the burning questions of human existence concerns how a woman or a man may find a place in an often hostile universe, the enthusiasm with which readers over the generations have responded to Ps. 139 is understandable. For this wonderful hymn of Israel-of-old sings not just of a God who cares, but of a God whose being is so intimately connected with our own that that being (and that Being) forms part of the fabric of the person each of us is. As do other of the day's lections, Ps. 139 also describes a God who assumes the initiative in claiming each individual, so that our knowledge of God derives not from some superior skill of our own, but from God's knowledge of and care for us.

Verses 1–6 are the words of one who knows that each of us stands completely naked before God, that there is no aspect of our lives—even of our most secret impulses—that is concealed from God. At first blush this may not appear to be good news, for a God who invades our deepest privacy may also intimidate and tyrannize us. A young child reports being frightened by a large sign advertising the Main Street location of an optometrist. The sign is a huge eye, which can be seen for blocks and which to the child appears as a sinister presence, taking notice of his every move. The God who knows "when I sit down and when I rise up" (v. 2) may not be for everyone a welcomed guest.

However, there is no suggestion in these lines of judgment. Although the psalmist surely does not consider that God's moral commitments have been abandoned, the God who is portrayed here is not a tyrant who comes to condemn. Rather God is so intimately involved with creation that God engages it at its deepest levels. Yet the involvement is not just with creation in general, but with the human being, that part of creation with which God has a special relationship. And not just with any human being, but with me!

A substantial part of this psalm's power lies in the elaborate deployment of parts of speech in the first person singular. "O LORD, you have searched *me* and known *me*. / You know when *I* sit down and when *I* rise up" (emphasis added). In the translation of the NRSV (which accurately reflects the Hebrew text) there is not a single verse of this section in which "I," "me," or "my" does not appear at least once, usually several times. It is this feature which reinforces the sense that this is no abstract philosophical discussion about a distant deity, but is a statement about me and my God—me, of course, being the reader who over the centuries has engaged this psalm. It is this skillful use of language that has made this psalm so deeply personal.

The climax in this section of the psalm is attained in v. 6. The consequence of the encounter with this God is not some kind of union with or mastery over God. God may know me more intimately than I know myself, but the reverse is not true. My posture before God is one of awe and wonder. This is a God who cannot be fully known or grasped by mere mortals. In a sense it is curious that there is no direct mention in the entire psalm of God's love either for the individual or for God's partner-in-the-covenant, Israel. But that characteristic surely arises out of the context in which the psalm was first used, a culture in which the idols of the nations were subject to manipulation and human control. The God of Israel is not such a god. The God of Israel far outreaches all human efforts at containment and contrivance.

The marvel is that this God seeks us, or, more pointedly, this God seeks me! And in the act of God's seeking me and finding me, I discover my own identity as God's beloved creature. (If there exist in the mind of the reader of this psalm any doubts that God's basic attitude is one of love, the tender lines of v. 10—which are not in the lection—should dispel them.)

Verses 13-18 constitute the second section of the lection, and they carry forward and amplify the themes laid out in vs. 1-6. The psalmist wishes to make clear that God's involvement in the life of each person is not an ad hoc relationship or the result of an afterthought. "You knit me together in my mother's womb" (v. 13) stresses God's involvement in the creation of the individual, while v. 16 not only credits the person's total life span to God, but speaks of God's premeditation in bringing the individual into existence and in shaping his or her life.

And, as in the case of vs. 1-6, the result of all this is a sense of joyful astonishment on the part of the psalmist. Verses 17-18 declare the same wonder and awe as that projected by v. 6. (The proper translation of the second line of v. 18 is somewhat unclear. The literal rendering, "I awake, I am still with you," has been interpreted by some as a reference to resurrection. While that may be so, it is unlikely, given the paucity of references to resurrection elsewhere in the Old Testament. But the verse almost certainly has the consummation of the individual's life in mind, as v. 13 has his or her conception and birth.) Alpha and Omega is the God of Israel (Rev. 21:6)! The first and the last (Isa. 44:6)! The God who presided over my beginning stands present at my life's fulfillment! This God

whom I cannot understand understands me and loves me and provides for me.
Astonishing!
Hallelujah!

1 Corinthians 6:12–20

The epistolary readings for the next eight Sundays (until the beginning of Lent), as well as Ash Wednesday, come from the two letters to the Corinthians. Very distinctly they show Paul as one whose theology does not hang in the air as an unrelated intellectual exercise, but comes to expression in addressing critical pastoral issues. As a pastoral theologian, Paul brings responses to the problems in the Corinthian community dictated neither by expediency nor by timidity. Both his rhetoric and his theology take seriously the human situation on the one hand and the mandate of the gospel on the other hand.

Since 1 Cor. 6:12–20 contains several complicated expressions, we shall first make four exegetical comments about structure and details and then conclude with two observations about directions that may be taken in preaching the passage. First, the people addressed by Paul's message are described in vs. 9–11. Some of them have come from the seamier side of life, but they have all experienced divine forgiveness (forcefully stated with three passive-voice verbs: washed, sanctified, justified). The ensuing injunctions to refrain from prostitution and glorify God, then, are explicitly directed to the Christian community. It is not the larger, social problem of prostitution that is being addressed (which may demand a different response), but the behavior of believers.

Second, Paul apparently speaks to two slogans being used together in the Corinthian community to justify the involvement with prostitution. The first ("All things are lawful for me") is a distorted statement of Christian freedom and vulnerable to a libertine interpretation. The second ("Food is meant for the stomach and the stomach for food," probably also including "God will destroy both one and the other") shows a complete disregard for the significance of the physical dimension of life. Bodily drives are pretty much the same, so the logic goes—hunger for food and hunger for sex. God is eventually going to destroy such drives, and so why not gratify one of them by becoming involved with prostitutes?

Third, Paul answers the Corinthian slogans by making five

theological affirmations about the body. "The body is . . . for the Lord, and the Lord for the body"; "God raised the Lord and will also raise us"; "Your bodies are members of Christ"; "Your body is a temple of the Holy Spirit"; and "You are not your own," but "were bought with a price." The bodily dimension of human existence simply cannot be relegated to an inferior position, subordinate to the human spirit. It is important to God, who has not only created it but also redeemed it. Rather than being destroyed, the body is destined for resurrection.

Fourth, the rhetorical impact of the passage is heightened by the repeated use of questions, which force the readers to reflect on the basics of the Christian life ("Do you not know . . .?" vs. 15, 16, 19). The theology being affirmed is part of the ABC's of the experience of forgiven people, something the readers should have known but obviously have forgotten.

What direction does one take when preaching on a passage like this? First, there is the clear statement that fornication is destructive of the individual's relationship to God. In the midst of sexual mores that are more and more permissive, the sounding of the prohibition is certainly not inappropriate. (It is significant to recognize that in Paul's day there was both male and female prostitution.)

What may be more important than the prohibition itself is the underlying reasoning that led the Corinthians astray. They could easily follow the logic of their slogans and become involved with prostitutes because they espoused a distorted spirituality that placed little or no value on the material order. The sanctity of the body was ignored.

What the text affirms, then, is the parity of body and spirit in obedience to God. Christian spirituality by its very nature has to struggle constantly against a dualism that either punishes the body because it is thought to be innately sinful or indulges the body because it is ultimately of little value. A full-bodied spirituality, however, does not retreat into mystical experiences, nor does it deem the body a mere prison house for the spirit. Creation and redemption involve the whole self.

Second, in preaching one needs to be clear that what is implied in the text is different from a fetish about exercise, diet, and a healthy life-style, that bodily faithfulness goes beyond ceasing to smoke, drink, or engage in sex outside of marriage. As Ernst Käsemann noted, for Paul the body is "the piece of the world which we ourselves are and for which we bear responsibility" (*New Testament Questions of Today;* Philadelphia: Fortress Press, 1969, p. 13).

It is not reduced to the individual, but encompasses the whole network of relationships that make us what we are. To "glorify God in your body" is to accept the world as the arena for discipleship. It is to acknowledge the marketplace, the home, the voting booth, the classroom as places where the worldly worship of God takes place. While Paul deals with a specific problem of fornication, the affirmations he makes have wide repercussions.

John 1:43–51

Much happens in this brief and elusive text: the calling of Philip, Philip's invitation to Nathanael, the conversation between Philip and Nathanael, the longer conversation between Jesus and Nathanael. At one level, at least, the second part of the lection appears to be little more than an amusing anecdote. Nathanael, whose skepticism prompts him to doubt that anything good can come from Nazareth, meets Jesus, who abruptly declares him to be free from deceit. Of course, in the Fourth Gospel stories often take place at more than one level simultaneously, and this story conforms to that pattern.

The story opens in a way that connects it firmly with the narrative about John the Baptist in John 1:19–42. The introduction and call of Philip connects back to the previous scene in which Andrew and Simon Peter are called. Philip's identification of Jesus in v. 45 similarly recalls Andrew's claim about Jesus in v. 41. The assertion that Jesus is "him about whom Moses in the law and also the prophets wrote" (v. 45) generalizes John the Baptist's earlier assertions about his own role as forerunner of Jesus (v. 23).

In this story, however, Philip's proclamation of Jesus' identity is greeted with skepticism. Nathanael's rejoinder, "Can anything good come out of Nazareth?" may reflect some local rivalries or a well-known proverb, but it also provides the Gospel's first fulfillment of 1:10–11 ("his own people did not accept him"). Nathanael does not initially respond to the proclamation about Jesus. Late in the Gospel, of course, another moment of skepticism accompanies the appearance of the risen Jesus to his disciples, when Thomas refuses to believe without seeing and touching Jesus himself (20:24–25).

The meeting between Jesus and Nathanael has given rise to much speculation about what it is that prompts Jesus to declare Nathanael "an Israelite in whom there is no deceit!" The answer to that question, which will almost certainly remain hidden, is far less significant than the function of the question in the narrative. Nathanael asks how it is that Jesus knows him, and Jesus responds with another perplexing statement: "I saw you under the fig tree before Philip called you." In the Fourth Gospel, Jesus often knows things not yet known by others (for example, 2:24; 6:6), things normally inaccessible to human beings. This particular instance is paralleled in the story of the Samaritan woman, who finds that Jesus mysteriously knows her marital history. Jesus discloses things that have remained concealed, just as Jesus discloses his own identity and the identity of his Father.

In response to this disclosure, Nathanael declares, "Rabbi, you are the Son of God! You are the King of Israel!" Ironically, what Nathanael now confesses is far more specific and far more grandiose than the proclamation of Philip that he had previously dismissed out of hand. Nathanael, as it turns out, does not remain with those who will not "know" or "accept" Jesus; instead, he joins those who receive him (1:10–13).

This theme of accepting or rejecting Jesus occupies a place of significance in the Gospel of John, where the people Jesus encounters are provoked to make a judgment about him. They must decide for him or against him. John has little tolerance for refusal or unwillingness to make a decision. For example, Nicodemus comes to Jesus "by night," hiding his inquiry from the eyes of his peers and colleagues, and is called upon to be "born from above" (3:1–10). Pilate attempts to find a way to release Jesus without acknowledging who he is, only to find that Jesus will not accept this sort of "compromise" (18:28–19:16). Nathanael's move from skeptical rejection to affirmation of faith separates him from those who wish to occupy some nonexistent middle ground.

Following Nathanael's confession, Jesus offers two promises to him: "You will see greater things than these" and "You will see heaven opened and the angels of God ascending and descending upon the Son of Man" (vs. 50–51). The first promise Jesus fulfills almost immediately in Cana, where the narrator declares that in his miraculous changing of water into wine he "revealed his glory" (2:11). The other miracles that follow also serve to complete this promise.

The second promise is more perplexing. Certainly the promise is not fulfilled in any literal way. Similar statements in the Synoptic Gospels refer to the parousia of Jesus (see Matt. 16:27–28 and 26:64), but a reference to the parousia seems out of place here. Since the opening of heaven often signals revelation (see, for example, Acts 7:56; 10:11), the ascent and descent of the angels may identify Jesus as the one who comes and goes between heaven and earth. That understanding of Jesus is certainly consistent with the treatment of him elsewhere in the Fourth Gospel as the one who descends from and returns to the Heavenly Father (see, for example, 3:31).

This reading is the bridge from the testimony of John the Baptist to the narrative of Jesus' ministry. In the stories that follow, the evangelist depicts "greater things than these" and draws attention to the One who does move from heaven to earth and again from earth to heaven. The challenge to John's readers, of course, is whether they will see Jesus with Nathanael's initial skepticism or with Nathanael's eyes of faith.

Third Sunday After Epiphany

Ordinary Time 3

The Epiphany season concerns nothing less than the disclosure of God's power and purpose in the midst of our daily world. There is something inexpressible and irrational about this disclosure, for God's coming is a disruptive incursion that is unwelcome and ill-fitting in what was our comfortably ordered world. Where our "reality" is "invaded," by the "really Real" of God, all other reality must submit, yield, and be changed.

The two New Testament readings explicate two sides of this transformative intrusion. The Gospel reading, on the one hand, presents to us an immediate, present-tense summons to the new rule of God, whereby discipleship entails a prompt reorientation of life, occupational and economic. On the other hand, the Epistle reading reflects on social relations that seem quite conventional. Paul's "eschatological proviso," however, brings even such social conventions under the rule of God, so that life in all its dailiness is shattered and opened, for the sake of a deep reordering. Paul is subtle as he sees that even in social relations that persist and are not subject to change, even there things are qualitatively modified.

This reordering depends on God's reliability, to which the psalm attests. God's offer of a new ordering of life means, in Jonah, that even hated Nineveh can live its life differently. Thus the readings converge. This is "the news" in the readings: *all things new*—in social relations, in vocation, in public power! All made new by the rule of God.

Jonah 3:1–5, 10

The tale of Jonah is a study in God's capacity for judgment and God's freedom in forgiveness. The city of Nineveh is taken up as a case study of a great concentration of human power (superpower), which finally must come to terms with the purposes of God. In these verses, Jonah plays only a minimal role, as a device for reflection on God's word.

The first exchange in this brief portion of text is between Yahweh and Jonah (3:1–3). Yahweh here speaks to Jonah for the second time, only to allude back to the first address of 1:2. This first address of 1:2 is the driving force of the entire Jonah narrative. Jonah's mission, which he consistently resists, is to "cry out against" Nineveh. After the interruption of 1:3–2:10, which concerns the reaction and behavior of Jonah, our text resumes the main story line from 1:2.

In Yahweh's second address to Jonah (3:2), the message is reiterated, but only by reference to 1:2. This time, unlike the response of 1:3, Jonah is obedient. He goes to Nineveh as commanded.

In vs. 4–5, the now obedient Jonah goes to Nineveh and "cries out against it." The actual wording of Jonah's message is new and has not previously been given by Yahweh or sounded by Jonah. As 1:2 implies, the message is one of unqualified threat. But only here is the destiny of the city made explicit: Nineveh will be "overthrown." The verb *hpk* is the same as used in Gen. 19:25, 29 for the earthquake that will destroy Sodom. The announcement is terse, ominous, and decisive. The city is doomed. Nowhere in the narrative have we been led to expect any escape for wicked Nineveh.

Thus we are scarcely prepared for the response of the people of "that great city." They "believed God"! The text does not say they believed the prophet or his message, but God. The verb "believe" here does not seem to suggest any faith in Yahweh, but only that they accepted the threat as a true and valid one. They believed that Yahweh meant what was said. Because the city took the threat of "overthrow" seriously, the city repented of its wickedness in a predictable and familiar ritual of fasting and sackcloth. There is an odd and remarkable slippage between the threat of Jonah 3:4 and the response of v. 5, for the message of Jonah does not invite this response or any response at all. Thus the city is daring, imaginative, and inventive in moving beyond the prophetic word itself to fashion an uninvited response of repentance.

It is unfortunate that the lectionary reading skips over vs. 6–9, for they fill out and enrich the drama of the decision made by the city. To be sure, the main story line can move directly from v. 5 to v. 10, as the lectionary reading proposes. Since narrative lives in detail and by its power and suggestiveness, however, the detail of vs. 6–9 is important. These intervening verses do two things. First, they detail the public procedure of repentance (vs. 6–8). They show the active engagement of the king and his intense concern, and they chronicle the extreme seriousness of the city in its fasting. The "cry" of Nineveh is one of repentance and remorse. Moreover, these verses identify the great sin of Nineveh for which it is in jeopardy, the sin of "violence" (*ḥāmās*). Such "violence" in the Old Testament is characteristically abusive exploitation that the strong work against the weak.

Second and more important, v. 9 shows the reflective capacity of the king of Nineveh and the reason v. 5 follows disjunctively after v. 4. The king of Nineveh is unwilling to accept the ominous message of Jonah in v. 4 as God's last word. In his extreme situation, the king is willing to entertain and introduce into the narrative a theological possibility that neither Jonah nor Yahweh has surfaced. In his desperation, the king anticipates that Yahweh might relent (*šûb*) and change (*nḥm*) the plan for punishment, and turn (*šûb*) away from anger. The king of Nineveh entertains the daring theological option that human action can impinge on God and cause God to alter the terrible decree, that God has freedom to act in an alternative way. The king of the awesome Gentile city of Nineveh proposes that Yahweh is not a closed principle of fate, an uncaring tyrant, or an automaton, but a live subject who can and will engage in freedom as Yahweh's partner in judgment (Nineveh) repents and changes. This remarkable capacity of Yahweh, anticipated by the king, is exactly the responsive freedom of Yahweh to which Jonah will so vehemently object (4:1–3).

The concluding verse (v. 10) indicates that the proposal of the king of Nineveh was correct. The king is a good Yahwistic theologian. The king had rightly discerned the character of Yahweh, who is able and willing to act in freedom, even in the face of Yahweh's own hard-nosed verdict. This concluding statement reiterates a word from the anticipation of the king: God changed (*nḥm*) God's mind, and was not the prisoner of God's own previous decree. It is this freedom on God's part that lets God be responsively gracious, thus avoiding the terrible judgment of "overthrow" that had been announced.

God's freedom and responsiveness create important possibilities for God's partners. The king of Nineveh, with great daring, is able to live out the "as though" of the Pauline epistle (compare 1 Cor. 7:29–31). Counting on God's free responsiveness, the king lives "as though" God could and would change. The Gentile city maximizes the possibility of God's generous freedom, much to the chagrin of this indignant prophet who would prefer that God were flat, unchanging, and predictable.

Psalm 62:5–12

The theme of this lection is that of trust in God, a calm assurance that, in spite of turmoil all around, God is the protection of the believer. Forces of disorder and hostility may claw at one's well-being (vs. 3–4), but God is faithful and will deliver the person who seeks salvation.

The lection begins (vs. 5–6) with a pair of verses (a pair of lines in the Hebrew) which are very similar to the verses (1–2) that begin the entire psalm. These words thus form a kind of refrain, which sums up the essential declaration of the poem. The imperative verb in v. 5 reflects a strength in the Hebrew that is missing in some English translations: "Be silent, my soul, for God; for my hope is from him" (author's translation). The suggestion here is that patience in the face of adversity does not come easily, even for the woman or man who is confident of God's compassionate strength. The psalmist must thus wrestle not only with the forces of evil, but with his or her own fears.

In v. 8 there is an interesting grammatical change, in that the verbs now become plural. The people are exhorted to "trust" God (v. 8), to "put no confidence in extortion" and robbery, and to refrain from the search for material wealth (v. 10). If we knew more about the use of the psalms in ancient Israelite worship, we might have a clearer understanding of what such a linguistic shift might mean. One possibility is that the individual has now turned to exhort the other members of the worshiping congregation.

In any event, the theological motif is similar to that in vs. 5–6 (actually 5–7, since v. 7 continues the thought of vs. 5–6, but has no direct parallel following v. 2). This theme is pointedly stated in v. 8: "Trust in him at all times, O people," and is followed by a contrasting set of images, false objects of devotion—wealth, power—which entice people, but which prove to be of little help (vs. 9–10). The Hebrew of v. 9 contains two phrases (*běnê 'ādām* and *běnê 'îš*) that simply mean "human beings" and which are linked to two adjectives (*hebel*, "breath" and *kāzāb*, "delusion") that point to the weakness of humans. The last line of v. 9 emphasizes the impotence of human beings when it says that, if a person were to sit on a balance scale, even a puff of air (again, *hebel*) would prove to be more weighty.

In the final two verses (vs. 11–12) the poet affirms two aspects of God's person: power and constant love. Each of these is crucial, for power without love is tyranny, while love without power lapses into sentimentalism. But God is both, and in this compassionately powerful One, men and women of faith find refuge. It is not to be overlooked that in these verses another shift of language has occurred in that God, heretofore referred to in the third person, is now addressed directly: "Steadfast love belongs to you, O Lord." Thus the lection, which to this point has been couched in the language of confession, now becomes a prayer.

A large part of the ability of this psalm to communicate with people in all ages lies in the manner in which it bespeaks both confidence in the power of God and a lack of confidence in the psalmist's own ability to persevere. The references to human frailty are obvious (v. 9), but it requires close attention to understand that the poet includes himself in the category of those who are *hebel*. He must command his soul to be patient (v. 5), and his final words are stated in a mode not so much of affirmation, as of supplication (v. 12). Apart from God's strength, the psalmist cannot be sure of anything about himself except his own weakness.

It is therefore on the power of God that the writer focuses. Notice the string of epithets for God in vs. 5–7: God is

my hope
my rock
my salvation
my fortress
my deliverance
my honor
my mighty rock
my refuge.

This list is followed by other descriptive terms:

a refuge (v. 8)
power (v. 11)
steadfast love (v. 12).

The superscription of the psalm contains the name of David, and, while there is nothing within the text of the poem to reflect directly upon David's life, the stories in the Old Testament of Israel's greatest king are illustrative of those meanings which the psalm intends to convey. One remembers David's fear before Saul (1 Sam. 21:10), yet his unwillingness to lay his hand on the Lord's anointed (24:6). Or again, David's fear for the life of his child, but his continued trust in God after the child's death (2 Sam. 12:15–23). There is a sense in which David is Everyman/Everywoman—or at least, every man and woman who is open to an encounter with God—exhibiting weakness and self-doubt on the one hand, but confidence in God on the other. Such is the life of the person of faith.

1 Corinthians 7:29–31

The seventh chapter of 1 Corinthians is hardly anyone's favorite passage. It is loaded with problems that cry for explanation, and the explanations do not come easily. Is the only reason for marriage simply a sexual one, to handle one's otherwise uncontrollable sexual drives (7:9)? What about Paul's quietism regarding slavery and the opportunities for freedom (vs. 22–24)? Is the unmarried person really a more attentive servant of the Lord than the married person (vs. 32–35)? We admit to a certain ignorance about the problems in Corinth to which this chapter is addressed, which certainly shape the advice Paul gives, and yet it remains a difficult text and a treacherous one to tackle in a sermon.

The key to the chapter, we are told, is vs. 29–31, where Paul tells us about his eschatological anticipations. This helps to put the comments about marriage, slavery, and celibacy in a different light. If Paul expects the end to be just around the corner, then we can understand why he said some of the things he said in this chapter. What constitutes Christian responsibility in the short run may not be the same as what constitutes Christian responsibility over the long haul.

Nevertheless, we are still left with a big problem. If the nearness of the end conditioned Paul's advice about marriage, slavery, and celibacy, what do *we* do? We cannot thrust ourselves back into the eschatological intensity of the first-century church and expect to recapture the urgency the early Christians felt about the return of Christ. The ensuing two millennia make a difference. What we can do, however, is to seek to understand the implications of Paul's eschatological vision, the relationships indicated by his expectations, the style of life signified.

At this point Paul becomes instructive, even to a modern context that no longer expects the end momentarily. Underlying all of Paul's counsel is the clear affirmation about the state of the world. Its present form is passing away (v. 31). The eschatological perspective provides enough of a crack in the door for Paul to perceive that the world's institutions, its structures, its social arrangements are ephemeral. They have no ultimate future. The current powers that exercise control and demand allegiances are lame-duck. Those powers and their myriad of servants may think they are permanently ensconced in the driver's seat. They obviously have things arranged to suit their own liking, but the eschatological truth is that their days are numbered.

Paul's vision closely coheres with Jesus' message in Mark 1:15. To announce that the reign of God has come near is but the positive side of what Paul perceives to be the demise of the present form of the world. While the implications of the eschatological perspective in Mark's text are repentance and faith, for Paul the issue is how Christians are to live within the continuing but transitory structures of society.

Paul sketches five scenarios of Christians' relations with the world (1 Cor. 7:29b–31a). The problem is that, when taken literally, they contradict what he has written elsewhere (even in this same chapter) or they make no sense. Is one to have a celibate marriage (what some of the Corinthians apparently were already doing), or suppress grief and joy, or play the role of a poverty-stricken business person who ignores the very people with whom he or she does business? Of course not.

The scenarios are highly rhetorical—and highly effective. They portray a stance of detached involvement, of people who have not withdrawn from the social structures of the world and in fact use them, but nevertheless recognize their provisional character. Realistically the scenarios acknowledge that life goes on, that people need and ought to marry and need and ought to earn a living, that people will continue to rejoice and grieve. Yet the recognition that the present form of the world is passing away creates a freedom from getting trapped by the world's structures and institutions. The repeated phrase is "as though" (or "as if").

This may sound a lot like stoicism—an inner freedom and an aloofness from the world. What makes this text different, however, is its eschatological perspective. Stoicism is focused on the self, which can transcend the ups and downs of life. Paul focuses on God's intent to bring about a new order. The passing of the current structures is not a cause for anguish, because there is much more to be expected. So 1 Corinthians ends with the joyous prayer *Marana tha* ("Our Lord, come!" 16:22).

Perhaps Paul's scenario regarding possessions is the most relevant one. The eschatological perspective does not demand that Christians rid themselves of all valuable commodities. It only poses the penetrating question of our attachment to those commodities. Do they dictate the nature and quality of our life? What do we have invested in them? Do we realize their provisional value? Buying and selling are critical to our existence, but can we resist being controlled by them and being co-opted by their promises and system of values?

Paul's eschatological perspective, rather than being dated and irrelevant, raises for modern Christians some acute and painful questions about our life in the world.

Mark 1:14–20

"The kingdom of God has come near." With these words, Jesus points away from himself and toward God. It is God's kingdom, God's reign, that Jesus announces. The good news has its origin in God, who here reclaims human lives and demands repentance and faith. Like the prophets before him, Jesus' task is to proclaim God's action in the world, not his own.

Yet Jesus is not simply one more in the procession of Israel's prophets. Mark 1:14–15 ought not be separated from the first thirteen verses of Mark, tied together as the two sections are by reference to John the Baptist, Jesus, and the proclamation of repentance. Mark 1:1–13 introduces Jesus as the one more powerful than John, the one who will baptize with the Holy Spirit, the Son of God. Verses 14–15 round off that introduction by connecting Jesus firmly with the proclamation of God's kingdom. Indeed, the coming of Jesus itself becomes a sign of the kingdom and its nearness.

The tension between these two strands in Mark's introduction reflects the truth of Rudolf Bultmann's famous dictum that "the proclaimer becomes the proclaimed." Jesus himself comes as the proclaimer of God's kingdom. At the same time, Jesus is part of what is proclaimed. In the very fact of telling the story, Mark (along with the early church) proclaims Jesus as Jesus proclaims God's kingdom.

With the initial call of disciples in vs. 16–20 the story moves from introducing Jesus to introducing his ministry. Mark 1:16–20 actually contains two brief call accounts, one of Simon and Andrew (vs. 16–18) and the other of James and John (vs. 19–20). Given the lean and spare story Mark usually tells, he might have been expected to combine these into one scene. The fact that he leaves them separate calls attention to the importance of the event.

As is the case with most Gospel stories, Mark says nothing about the motivation of either Jesus or the disciples. Why does Jesus call this particular foursome? What leads them to respond to him? Nothing in

THIRD SUNDAY AFTER EPIPHANY

the text provides an answer to either question; indeed, nothing indicates that they have any prior knowledge of one another.

These observations about what is "missing" from this passage lead to other observations about what is present here. First, Jesus issues a call that is authoritative. Unlike contemporary teachers or philosophers who compete to attract students, Jesus is presented here as one who issues a summons that is not refused. The starkness of that invitation contrasts ironically with our own consumer society, in which everything, even including faith, is thought to be a commodity to be packaged and marketed. Jesus does not play by the rules of a consumer society.

Second, the call Jesus issues is responded to without hesitation. Why is that the case? Here is the most perplexing feature of this text: Why do the fishermen "immediately" leave their business and follow Jesus? We might suppose that they see being Jesus' disciples as a substantial promotion, a step to bigger and better things. Nothing in the text, however, indicates that the disciples received any reward for their discipleship. Indeed, when James and John later approach Jesus with a request about sitting near him in glory, they are sharply rebuked (10:35–40). What disciples are promised, in fact, is persecution and conflict (13:9–13).

Perhaps the disciples anticipate that fishing for people will be more satisfying somehow than the fishing to which they are accustomed. This text is occasionally read as a contrast between the "worldly" occupation of catching fish and the "spiritual" occupation of fishing for people. Again, nothing in the story has prepared those being called to understand and respond to that contrast. From the point of view of the fishermen, in fact, they are giving up an occupation with a secure market for one that is ill-defined at best.

Is it even clear that the fishermen respond out of faith? They are not said to believe in Jesus or to understand his mission. As the story unfolds, these important characters persistently misunderstand Jesus, and they disappear entirely when he is crucified. Whatever they understand or believe at this point in Mark's story, they eventually forget.

Nothing in vs. 16–20 tells us why the fishermen do what they do, why they leave their nets and the hired workers and follow Jesus. Somehow they are compelled to follow him, a man whom they cannot understand, on a journey that will perplex and confuse them, to a destination as yet unspecified. The fishermen, now disciples, act in faith—not a faith that understands, takes only calculated risks, or seeks after reward, but a faith that responds to a call from outside, a call that must remain unclear and even frightening.

The journey of faith begins with this step, as does the ministry of Jesus. Responding to Jesus provides the disciples with no answers for their life struggles, but only questions. It provides them with no security, but rather with rejection and even danger. The identity of the One who calls remains concealed and misapprehended, even by them. Nevertheless, they respond and "follow him."

Fourth Sunday After Epiphany

Ordinary Time 4

The Epiphany season is a time when the church reflects on the authority of God, God's command, God's purpose, and God's promise. The notion of God's authorizing activity strikes us as odd in a privatized world where autonomous human agents seem to be the elemental unit of reality. Epiphany, against such a deep social propensity, is a time when we think precisely and with daring against autonomy, paying primal attention to the wonder and assurance given by this holy authority who stands outside us and wills us good.

That authorizing power of God is most dramatically present (in these readings) in the Gospel narrative, where Jesus overmatches the debilitating power of evil. That same authorizing power is present very differently in the Old Testament reading, where God's will for communal life is embodied in the person and office of Moses. The two readings together invite reflection on the "new world" of the gospel, in which healing possibility and urgent moral requirement are given, before us and outside of us. The new realities are not matters on which we may vote.

The authorizing power of God is evidenced in the psalm as being faithful and beneficent, providing all that is needed for healthy, joyous living. The Epistle reading considers in detail what a community that comes under this rule looks like. Every detail of life is reordered to make genuine community possible. This theme of epiphany (God's authorizing activity) counters the isolation, coercion, and despair that drives a world in which each must be against all. Because God is "for us," each becomes neighbor to the other.

Deuteronomy 18:15–20

This text occurs in the "Torah of Moses," in a section of Deuteronomy wherein Moses authorizes a series of leadership roles, judges, king, and priests, as well as prophets. All these leadership roles are to guide and guard Israel when it comes into the land, so that the community of faith may maintain its peculiar identity and vocation as Yahweh's people, even in the fact of powerful cultural seduction. Thus the twin themes arise—of *valid authorization* and *seductive idolatry* as a threat.

Verse 15 lays out the programmatic intent of the entire section, which extends through v. 22. There will be a prophet "like me," that is, like Moses. This authorized prophet for the future is unspecified. Because of the close connection between Deuteronomy and the book of Jeremiah, it might be supposed (in retrospect) that this promise turned out to be an anticipatory reference to Jeremiah. More programmatically, the tradition of Deuteronomy tends to think (against historical reality) that there was an intentional, identifiable series of prophets, each of whom in turn, in subsequent generations, occupied the role of Moses (compare 2 Kings 17:13; Zech. 1:3–6). That role of Moses is to maintain, through teaching, the distinctive character of Israel embodied through obedience.

Deuteronomy 18:16 briefly looks back to the meeting at Horeb (Mt. Sinai). In that awesome meeting at the mountain, God spoke directly to Israel only the Ten Commandments (Ex. 20:1–17). Immediately, the Israelites sensed that such direct speech from God is an enormous threat to their well-being. In order to preclude such direct meeting in time to come, the Israelites authorized Moses to serve as a mediator to transmit the word of Yahweh. It is plausible that this act of authorization in Ex. 20:18–21 pertains not only to the person of Moses, but to all those who exercise the mediatorial role and function of Moses in all time to come.

The primary interest of Deut. 18:17–20, however, is not in a backward glance to Sinai, from whence comes authorization, but forward to the prophets, who will come later into the life of Israel. The prophet is to be the bearer and speaker of God's own word (v. 17). This is a most peculiar institutional provision. Even though we may take the authorization for granted in ancient Israel, we should notice how extraordinary it in fact is. Israel claims to be authorized and led by the *transcendent purpose of God*. Here, however, provision is made for *a human agent*, who will make concretely available the transcendent purpose of God.

This means that a prophetic voice in Israel is not an accident, an intrusion, or an extra in the life of this community. Rather a prophetic voice, demanding and discomforting as it may be, is constitutive for Israel. This community, by its very character and destiny, is mandated to host and to heed the prophet. While such a prophet may seem disruptive elsewhere, a prophet who will speak a word beyond all political conventions is, in Israel, normal.

To this act of instituting the practice of the prophetic, this teaching of Moses then adds two important provisos. On the one hand, this prophet bears profound authority, and so must be taken seriously and honored. (This links our passage to the Gospel reading and the authority of Jesus.) As it turns out, the prophets are regularly an unwelcome voice in Israel. They are commonly not heeded, but are disregarded, ignored, and treated with hostility (compare Matt. 5:11–17). That is, Israel is unable to accept the demanding terms upon which its very life is constituted by God. (More generally, the inability to host a prophet is reflected in the resistance of every technological society to the disturbing voice of the poet.)

On the other hand, as the people are warned if they do not heed (Deut. 18:19), so the prophet to come is also warned (v. 20). The prophet is mandated to stick to Mosaic faith claims, to witness to the God of the exodus, the covenant, commands, and promises of Sinai. This covenantal ethic given at Sinai is precisely what makes Israel's life odd and demanding. And because it is so odd and demanding, those in prophetic authority are sore tempted to tone down the word, which in effect is to compromise Yahweh and to scuttle Yahweh's covenant.

That is, the counterpart to the *resistance by the people* is the *seduction of the prophet*. This seduction may yield a false message, but the taproot of such seduction is the witness to other gods, gods more palatable and less demanding. Thus an errant prophet becomes witness to idols who betray the faith of Moses. (This theme connects our passage to the Epistle reading. The classic case of such an idolatrous prophet is Hananiah in Jer. 27–28.)

The twin themes of authority and idolatry together suggest urgent ecclesiological reflection. That is, the issue here is not the nature of the prophet, but the nature of the community to whom the prophet speaks. The nature of the church is that it must host the prophetic-Mosaic word in all its terror. That word is often a hard one, and so both people and prophet may wish for a lesser, more palatable word. Such a temptation to tone down the word or to distort or to silence the speaker risks the whole glorious enterprise of Israel, and jeopardizes the possibility of a covenantal ethic in the world.

Psalm 111

This psalm is a celebration of the activity of God in human life, especially in the life of Israel. It is also a celebration of the nature of

God, who is proclaimed to be righteous and just, merciful, gracious, and awesome. The setting is clearly a worship service, where an individual (a priest?) speaks on behalf of the entire congregation (v. 1). That the psalm is a polished literary product, rather than an extemporaneous outburst of faith, is revealed by its form, for it is an alphabetic acrostic in which each of the twenty-two short lines (after the initial *halĕlû yāh*) begins with a letter of the alphabet, each in the appropriate order.

After the opening affirmation, which states the purpose of the psalm (v. 1), there is an extended body (vs. 2–9) in which both God and the works of God are praised. There is little logical progression in these lines, since attention is given to both God's nature and God's activity in somewhat random fashion. The works of God, which are described as "great" (v. 2), "full of honor and majesty" (v. 3), and "wonderful" (v. 4), include the following:

the provision of food (v. 5)
the giving to Israel of the possessions of their neighbors (v. 6)
the acceptance of Israel into a covenant relationship (vs. 5, 9)

God's works are such that they cannot be forgotten (vs. 4 and 8).

As for God's nature, it may be observed in the works of God, yet the latter are dependent on the former, not the other way around. The terms used to describe God's person are frequently found elsewhere in the Old Testament, including the psalms. God is not only righteous today, but righteousness is a permanent condition (v. 3). The Lord is "gracious and merciful" (v. 4), God's name is "holy and awesome" (v. 9). The connection between God's works and God's nature is this: because the worshiping community has learned to trust the activity of God, they/we may also trust God's teaching (v. 6).

The conclusion of the psalm is couched in the language of the wisdom tradition, and echoes texts found in Proverbs (1:7; 9:10; 15:33) and elsewhere (Job 28:28; Eccl. 12:13). It was an integral part of Ps. 111 from the beginning and not a later appendix, a fact determined from the inclusion of v. 10 in the alphabetic progression of the lines.

Perhaps the most important point of contact between this psalm and the Epiphany season lies in the text's dual emphasis on God's nature and God's activity in human life. For the psalmist, the two were intimately related in that the works of God constituted a "window" through which the very being of God could be glimpsed, a medium of revelation that could be comprehended by men and women who chose to do so. It is for this reason that "the works of the LORD" are "studied by all who delight in them" (v. 2). And it is because the works of God point to the nature of God that the two subjects are discussed almost simultaneously, concentration on one flowing smoothly into concentration on the other (v. 3).

This is a view of reality that was, of course, very much at home in wisdom circles in ancient Israel. That is, one may discover who God is by examining what God has done. When the author of Ecclesiastes protests that, although women and men have studied God's world, "yet they cannot find out what God has done from the beginning to the end" (Eccl. 3:11), he is simply complaining against the predominant theology of the schools of wisdom teachers. But our psalm is either ignorant of this kind of protest or chooses to ignore it, for it boldly affirms the value that observation of the world (including our knowledge of the history of Israel) leads to an understanding of God. It is only out of an assurance that the world (including Israel's experience) is a mirror of God's nature that one may confidently affirm that, since one may trust what God has *done* in human life, one may also trust what God (instructs) about human life—that is to say, one may trust who God is (v. 7).

The Epiphany season affirms that the old linkage between the deeds of God and the being of God is true. To be sure, we would want to agree with Ecclesiastes at least to the extent that our observation of what God has done leads to an imperfect understanding of who God is. This is because the world, including the world of human experience, is too filled with enigmas (to say nothing of evil) to permit us to say that it is a complete reflection of God's nature. Yet, at the heart of the Christian affirmation is the belief that God has not remained hidden, the Deus absconditus of some theologians of a bygone day, but has stepped forth from the shadows, shaping and reshaping our world so that we may see the divine face.

The Epiphany season marks the journey from Christmas to Good Friday and Easter, those most decisive moments in human history in which this self-revelation of God has occurred. In the incarnation and in the crucifixion and resurrection, God peeled back layers of our ignorance and revealed a Deity whose concern for human life and whose involvement in human life—while proclaimed by Israel's teachers of old—achieved a new level of intimacy and immediacy. With the wonder of this concern and this involvement in our minds, we join the ancient chorus (in v. 4) with all the vigor that our joy incites:

> He has gained renown by his wonderful deeds;
> the Lord is gracious and merciful.

1 Corinthians 8:1-13

Many moral issues raised and dealt with in the New Testament seem terribly irrelevant today. They do not appear to touch the burning problems that currently confront the church, and even to talk about them looks like a diversionary tactic. Why deal with peccadilloes when Rome is burning? The issue of whether to eat food associated with the pagan cultic worship in Corinth (and elsewhere) resembles one of these trivial matters that might well be avoided—until one recognizes that there is much to be learned here about dealing with controversy in the church, about attitudes to be encouraged when Christians have honest differences among themselves, about the critical matter of individualism versus community.

The eighth chapter of 1 Corinthians itself contains several controversial matters of exegesis, and the interpreter is urged to consult a good critical commentary for help in answering (or at least shedding light on) them. For example, is the question being addressed here "concerning food sacrificed to idols" (8:1) whether at private dinner parties to eat food that had been purchased in the marketplace and previously consecrated to an idol (as in 10:23—11:1), or whether to eat food while in attendance at the pagan temples (as in 10:14-22)? Probably the former, though it is dangerous to be dogmatic. Fortunately, a reading of Paul's instructions does not rest on certainty about historical circumstances.

Notice first that *within the Christian community love is to take precedence over the exercise of individual freedoms.* Paul understands the theology of those who see no problem in eating the food that has been associated with the worship of idols, and to a point agrees with it. Idols do not really exist, and "for us there is one God . . . and one Lord, Jesus Christ" (8:6). But there is the matter of those who have not yet integrated that theology into their psyches, whose heads might agree but whose hearts are still worried about idols. They cannot be ignored or run over. Love demands that their feelings, no matter how dated, be taken seriously, lest they too join in the meals and end up violating their own consciences.

The Pauline ethic is not without principles, but always love for the particular family member within the body of Christ takes precedence over principles. The ethic is other-directed. In reflecting on a projected action, Christians cannot stop with how they feel about themselves or how they think about the action in and of itself. They have to take account of the people directly or adjacently involved. As Paul puts it later in this letter, love "does not insist on its own way" (13:5). Knowledge and freedom are not to be despised, but what determines Christian behavior is love for those within the community of faith.

This means of course that *the health of the Christian community becomes a priority*. The text does not raise the question of what impact eating the food might have on outsiders, what sort of "witness" is born to non-Christians. The decisive factor concerns the insiders, those who, for whatever reason, cannot shake the notion that idols somehow exist and that eating food associated with idols is a sin. For Paul, who identifies himself with the those who discount idols, the fundamental sin is in injuring members of the family, in leading them to act against their conscience. It is a "sin against Christ" (8:12).

To put it another way, the diversity of the church is to be carefully and deliberately maintained. "Love builds up" (8:1). It keeps the various segments of the community from splintering into warring factions. It provides the adhesive that enables Jew and Greek, bond and free, male and female in reality to be one in Christ. Love puts limits on rampant individualism. It reflects the divine compassion that enables very different people to experience genuine community in Christ.

Notice that in advising some members of the church to refrain from using their liberty as "a stumbling block to the weak" (8:9), Paul's effort is to protect the weak not from being offended, but from imitating the behavior of others to their own hurt. Fear of offending others unfortunately has often made some church people tiptoe through life. They have catered to the whims of every moralist or legalist who raised a voice. They have kept silent in the face of injustices and enjoyed their freedom only in private. They have not wanted to cause offense. In doing so, they have missed the point of 1 Cor. 8.

The text never hints that conflict is to be avoided, that discussion of the issue of eating of food offered to idols should be skirted. Paul's letters, in fact, consistently argue for the church as the forum for moral discourse. The scenario from 1 Cor. 8 simply asks that every member of the community be taken seriously (even those without "knowledge") as a person for whom Christ died, and that one's actions reflect a compassionate and even restraining consideration for fellow members of the body of Christ.

Mark 1:21–28

When contemporary Christians read the stories of Jesus healing people of disease or exorcising demons, the tendency is to see these actions as signs of Jesus' compassion for the afflicted or as proofs that Jesus is God's Son. Occasionally the Gospels support these interpretations, as when Jesus is said to act out of strong emotion (for example, Mark 1:41). The designation of Jesus' miracles as "signs" in the Fourth Gospel does support the notion that they demonstrate his divinity (for example, John 2:11). On the whole, however, the Gospel writers treat Jesus' miracles as acts that raise questions about who he is and whose power he employs.

This lection, the first miracle in the Gospel of Mark, provides an excellent illustration of this understanding of miracle. The man who is afflicted with the unclean spirit is, to say the least, not the focus of the story. Indeed, he comes "onstage" only as the carrier of the unclean spirit. Nothing is said about the man himself, his background, his faith or lack thereof. Jesus' conversation is with the spirit, and Jesus' action is on the spirit. After the exorcism, the man is not even mentioned. While Gospel miracles often treat the healed person more as a prop than as a character, this story carries that custom to an extreme degree.

Not only does the man who is afflicted and then healed receive little attention, but the exorcism itself is treated with haste. Jesus is teaching, he casts out the unclean spirit that presents itself, and the final report returns to the issue of Jesus' authoritative teaching. For Mark, then, what makes this event important stems from the teaching of Jesus and the issue of authority rather than from the exorcism alone.

When the story opens, Jesus enters the synagogue in Capernaum, where his teaching amazes people because he teaches "as one having authority, and not as the scribes" (1:22). The contrast between Jesus and the scribes is noteworthy, since the scribes were regarded as important and knowledgeable teachers in the Jewish community. When Mark says that Jesus' teaching has "authority," then, he may mean something other than its credibility or reliability. Exactly what "authority" means here remains to be seen.

The unclean spirit bursts into the synagogue and confronts Jesus with a challenge ("Have you come to destroy us?" or another translation that is equally possible, "You have come to destroy us!") and with a title ("the Holy One of God"). As elsewhere in Mark, unclean spirits and others who are outside the religious power structure recognize who Jesus is, while those who might be expected to know Jesus do not. Despite this display of knowledge on the spirit's part, it obeys Jesus' rebuke. (See Acts 19:11–20; unclean spirits did not acquiesce to the demands of every would-be exorcist!)

Most miracle stories, including exorcisms, conclude with a demonstration of the effectiveness of the cure and the response of those who have observed it. Here the demonstration drops out altogether and the response that comes from bystanders is a curious one: "What is this? A new teaching—with authority! He commands even the unclean spirits, and they obey him." Jesus' power over the unclean spirits reinforces the earlier judgment that his teaching is authoritative.

Again, based on a contemporary understanding of healing as an act of compassion, we might anticipate that Jesus' exorcism would prompt bystanders to rejoicing and celebration. Jesus brings gifts that we imagine ourselves receiving with outstretched arms, but nothing in this story indicates that he was so received. Instead, the story concludes with "At once his fame began to spread," but the word translated as "fame" can also be rendered "report." It signifies only that word went out regarding this event, but not how it was received.

The story culminates, then, in a kind of question. The earlier question, "What is this?" calls up another, more profound question: "Who is this?" If the "who" question is not asked here explicitly, it surely lies just below the surface. Who is this man? What is the source of his power? What do these events mean? If the reader of Mark's Gospel knows who Jesus is because of 1:11, and if the unclean spirit knows because it recognizes superior power, and if the disciples at least know the authority of the Master who has called them, those standing by do not know what is at hand. The answer is not obvious, and in fact the question will continue through most of Mark.

What makes the question raised by Jesus' exorcism the more intriguing is that so many contemporary Christians believe that miraculous events, if ever witnessed firsthand, would produce unerring and unwavering faith. The Gospel writers know otherwise. They know that miracles demonstrate power, but power can come from a variety of sources, both good and evil. The Gospel writers also know that understanding who Jesus is and what his mission entails involves far more that simply witnessing a miracle. As with every aspect of Jesus' ministry, the miracles and the teaching raise as many questions as they provide answers.

Fifth Sunday After Epiphany

Ordinary Time 5

Epiphany, the disclosure of God in the world, invites the church to reflect upon God, God's goodness and greatness. It takes God not as a means toward something else, but as a wondrous end in God's own person. An epiphany-focused church might well be dazzled by God and intoxicated by God, so that its whole life is an exuberant doxology: "How great thou art!" The Isaiah text and the psalm for today are unfettered praise, contrasting this powerful God with would-be alternatives that are anemic and dysfunctional.

Yet the reality of God, in the biblical tradition, never permits doxology that stays remote from lived reality. The Gospel reading shows how the power of God plunges Jesus (and the company of Jesus) into the midst of human need. It is in the midst of such need that the kingdom, that is, the sovereign purpose of God for healing, is asserted and enacted. Paul's self-disclosure offers us a person of faith who is deeply smitten with this new gospel reality. His life is gospel-driven, in compulsion that makes Paul courageous, and in freedom that makes Paul joyous. Folk cannot stay long around the doxology-evoking reality of God without redeciding about their own future. God's transformative healing power displaces people, and requires redeployment of our selves and our common life, to be deployed now in liberated obedience.

Isaiah 40:21–31

This rich and complex text exhibits Yahweh in all of God's glorious splendor and power as the creator and giver of life. Israel in exile perceived itself to be abandoned by God (Isa. 40:27). This lyrical poem is designed to refute the charge of God's faithlessness, and to provide hope for Israel in its dismay.

The first section of the longer poem we will look at (vs. 21–24) begins with four rhetorical questions, which have the tone of a reprimand (v. 21). How stupid and unaware can you be not to notice, because it is perfectly obvious! The rhetorical questions serve to set up the answer of vs. 22–23, a sweeping claim for Yahweh as the powerful creator. The answer to the rhetorical questions is a series of five verbs governed by the participial form. That verbal form reports actions that are characteristic of the subject and ongoing, not one-time acts. Thus this God characteristically, all the time, "sits," "stretches," "spreads," "brings," and "makes." These are God's regular powerful, sovereign, magisterial acts, removing any ground for Israel's doubt or self-pity.

The picture of God proposed here is of a God who sits atop the vault of heaven, that is, on top of the earth, in regal splendor, so high and lifted up, so elevated and exalted, that the human inhabitants of the earth are seen only at a distance, as small as insects. In this exalted position Yahweh engages in creation activity, forming and shaping the heavens, which exist only through God's enormous power. The God who governs the heavens is also the one who intrudes on the political process, especially to delegitimate political authorities of which Yahweh no longer approves. Thus as Yahweh can summon the heavens, so this same God can dispatch the nations of the earth. In this way the text moves quickly from cosmic concerns to the specific political issues of the exiles. Kings are established, but when God rejects and destabilizes, powers are dislodged and rulers are helpless. No ruler can withstand the force of God's delegitimating wind. Some God! For that reason the closed-down, seemingly hopeless situation of exile is not for perpetuity, for the oppressor powers serve only until Yahweh begins to blow a transformative wind.

Verses 25–26 reiterate the rhetorical pattern of vs. 21–23, in which a question is asked that the poem promptly answers. Here the question is twofold (v. 25): Who is like "me" (Yahweh) in power? The implied answer of course is "no one, no other god." The answer in v. 26, like the answer in vs. 22–23, appeals to Yahweh's power as creator. The question in v. 26, again in a rhetorical ploy, "Who created these?" refers to the stars. Who made the stars? They are creatures that are authorized by Yahweh, and so are by nature responsive and obedient to the will of Yahweh. It is Yahweh who creates the stars, makes them, names them, knows them, possesses them. They are a measure of Yahweh's enormous royal power. It is because of Yahweh's strength, power, and authority that all the stars are in their places. None is absent, none is displaced, all are in order.

Yet a third time the general pattern of question-answer is reiterated (vs. 27–31). The question of v. 27 is of a different sort from the preceding questions. It is, in fact, a chiding of the exiles for having dared to accuse Yahweh and complain. The complaint is based on ignorance and poor information. For that reason, the pattern of questioning is resumed in v. 28 with a double inquiry. If exilic Israel does not know and has not heard about God's newness, then exilic Israel is the only one who does not know!

The answer, that is—what exilic Israel should have known and heard because it is perfectly obvious—is expressed in the doxology of vs. 28–31. Like vs. 22 and 26, v. 28b moves in the sphere of creation and makes a sweeping claim for Yahweh, dismissing any competing claim for any Babylonian god. Yahweh is for all time ("everlasting" = '*ôlām*); Yahweh is in all places, the "ends of the earth." Yahweh claims and preempts everything, and leaves no room for either doubt or rival.

Verse 28c moves away from creation, closer to the actual political situation that concerns the exiles. This God is tireless, never faint or weak, never lacking in energy or vitality. In vs. 28c–30, the poem reiterates the word "faint" (*y'p*) three times, and the word "weary" (*yg'*) twice. The nonfainting God ministers to fainting creation. The nonweary God gives life to weary creatures. Thus the words are used in order to establish a contrast between God and the exiles (and all of creation). The exiles are indeed faint, weary, powerless, exhausted. But Yahweh is none of these. Quite the opposite: Yahweh has the power to stand in contradiction to and over against, in order to counteract that languishing, dying condition of creation. Yahweh is indeed exactly what exiles need. Thus the best and only hope of the exiles is to stay close to Yahweh, who can do for them what is needed that they cannot do for themselves.

The faint, weary, powerless, exhausted exiles are to wait (*qûh*), that is, to hope and expect, to remain silent and passive, and let Yahweh take the initiative for a liberated future. The waiting is an act of confident faith, a willingness to accept the authority, buoyancy, and advocacy of this other. Those who wait so vibrantly have their life transformed, for the creator God will do for exiles what has been done for creation. This God will give life where there was none.

Psalm 147:1–11, 20c

Psalm 147 is one of the several psalms of praise that form an enthusiastic doxology to the entire Psalter. In typical fashion, the psalm begins and ends with the imperative *halĕlû-yāh*: Praise the LORD! (compare Ps. 146; 148; 149; 150). Although the present lection

FIFTH SUNDAY AFTER EPIPHANY 137

comprises only part of Ps. 147, v. 20c has been included in the reading in order to retain the final affirmation of praise.

Primary themes in the text are those of power and weakness: God's power and, of course, human weakness. The manner in which images representing both of these themes are juxtaposed upon one another may initially appear random, even haphazard, to the reader of this text. Yet in both parts of the lection (vs. 1–6, and 7–11) the movement is unmistakably from a statement of Yahweh's strength to a recognition of the dependence of frail humans on that strength. Yahweh's extension of grace is understood as an expression of Yahweh's compassion; man's/woman's acceptance of that grace is portrayed as an act of faith.

Psalms of praise are often concerned to identify reasons for the worship and adoration of God, and this text is no different. After the initial *halĕlû-yāh*, the psalmist invites (in reality, commands) the community to praise God and explains that this is the proper activity of God's people (v. 1).

Why? Because Israel's Lord builds the city and sets the stars, on the one hand, and, on the other, saves those who are incapable of saving themselves (vs. 2–4). The splendid conjoining of motifs that portray God's cosmic majesty with those of God's personal intimacy is striking and is one of the sources of the psalm's power. It is not enough to acknowledge that Yahweh put the stars in their places; the psalmist goes on to declare that "he gives to all of them their names" (compare Isa. 40:26). In other words, since the bestowal of a name on a subject implied power over that subject, the stars that Yahweh brought into being in the first instance continue to exist under Yahweh's control. (It may be that v. 4 contains a veiled polemic against the worship of astral deities, a common practice among some of Israel's neighbors.) But this same God "gathers the outcasts of Israel" (v. 2) and "lifts up the downtrodden," even as "he casts the wicked to the ground" (v. 6). The God who created the world also rules over creation in justice and in love. Hallelujah!

(Notice should be given in passing to v. 5 which, in the language of ancient Israelite Wisdom, summarizes the power of God so movingly described in the rest of the section, vs. 1–6.)

Verses 7–11 mirror the progression of thought in vs. 1–6, but with important differences. Verse 7 repeats the imperative of v. 1 in that it summons the people to praise Yahweh. And, as in vs. 2–6, the psalmist then undertakes an explanation as to the praiseworthiness of Israel's God. Here the emphasis is not on original creation, but on that day-to-day sustenance of creation without which it would be devoid of life. It is probably not accidental that the language of vs. 8–9 is similar to that with which Baal was sometimes described in the Canaanite literature, and the psalmist appears to be stating a case that it is Yahweh, not Baal, who is the bringer of the rains and who is therefore the Lord of life. (Compare the manner in which the prophet Hosea often applies the language of Baal worship to his statements about Yahweh, as in Hos. 14:8.)

Again, the declaration of Yahweh's power is quickly translated into an admission of creation's weakness, that is, of creation's dependence on Israel's God. Not only the "animals" and "the young ravens" (v. 9) receive their strength from God, but—more to the point—so do women and men (vs. 10–11). And here the climax of our text is reached. In measured, balanced cadences (notice the parallelism of lines in vs. 10 and 11), the psalmist once more draws on the language of the Israelite Wisdom tradition and drives home the essential point. When human beings rely on their own strength they are preparing themselves for failure. True human empowerment emerges from a "fear" of the Lord (compare Prov. 1:7) and from a "hope" in God's unflagging commitment to humankind and, indeed, to all of creation.

Hallelujah!

Power and weakness! It may be observed that the story of humankind is, in large measure, the pursuit of the former and the avoidance of the latter. The person who has no power is one who exercises no control over his or her life. To be disempowered in any significant sense is to lose part of life's essential meaning. Thus the history of the race is filled with tales of struggles for power; indeed, the cynic may observe that history is little else.

Into this terrible arena the psalmist issues a different understanding of the nature of power and weakness and of the relation between the two. There is but a single Power; all other power is illusory and transient. To participate in this Power is to admit one's own weakness, one's own dependence on the Creator and Sustainer of life. And paradoxically, it is only in the admission of one's own finitude and impotence that there emerges hope and joy. For the Power that set the stars and brings the rains is irrevocably committed to the cause of justice and compassion. The Power behind the cosmos has revealed a face. And it is a face of love.

Hallelujah!

1 Corinthians 9:16–23

One of the reasons the apostle Paul is not a favorite figure with many Christians is because he is difficult to understand (and in many cases is misunderstood). Another reason for his unpopularity, however, is because he is all too readily understood. His message comes through loud and clear and, in doing so, annoys and disturbs the patterns of life and thought to which we have become accustomed. He repeatedly nudges the comfortable accommodations we have made with the surrounding culture. Though Paul, of all the New Testament witnesses, is the theologian of grace, he refuses to let his readers rest easy with the gospel as if it were a take-or-leave-it matter, or as if it were a reality to be tacked onto the rest of our concerns, another charity to be supported. Paul constantly confronts us with the life-orienting character of the gospel, its absolute centrality.

The matter of Christian identity is at the heart of the reading assigned for this Sunday. The two issues that occupy Paul in connection with the passage are: eating food associated with the worship of idols (1 Cor. 8 and 10:23–33) and the right of an apostle to receive monetary support from the people being served (9:1–15). Neither issue seems all that momentous, and neither is likely to disturb or annoy modern readers, except that Paul describes his own behavior regarding each issue in terms of the mandate of the gospel. His way of defending himself (since he was probably being criticized in each case) tells us a great deal about what really matters.

First, for Paul there is *the compulsion of the gospel.* "An obligation is laid on me, and woe to me if I do not proclaim the gospel!"(9:16). The compulsion spoken of here does not refer to an irresistible impulse of the psyche, an irrational drive that coerces him into preaching against his better judgment. The compulsion derives from the nature of the gospel and from Paul's sense of his own place in the economy of God. The gospel is not intended only to be heard and enjoyed; it is to be lived and preached. By its very nature, it is a story that demands retelling. And that surely goes for all "garden-variety Christians" as well as for apostles.

The critical importance of retelling the story emerges in the way Paul justifies his decision not to accept financial support from the Corinthians. He recognizes that support is a "right" due an apostle (and his readers no doubt agree). In fact, "the Lord commanded that those who proclaim the gospel should get their living by the gospel" (v. 14). But in his circumstances (and we are not clear what they were) the urgency of proclamation causes him to forgo his "rights." The life-and-death character of the gospel dictates that no unnecessary hindrance should stand in the way of retelling the story. Even what is justly due is waived if the situation seems to warrant it. The compulsion of the gospel determines the exercise or nonexercise of rights—a novel idea!

The text also speaks of *the freedom of the gospel*. From the stance Paul takes on the matter of eating food consecrated to idols one could get the impression (and undoubtedly some in Corinth did) that Paul was wishy-washy, that this "play it either way" attitude masked a lack of principle.

Paul reaffirms his position by saying he can become like a Jew when with Jews or like a Gentile when with Gentiles. His "right" to eat marketplace food that has been sacralized in the pagan cult can be exercised or not exercised as the situation warrants. It is a clear statement of Christian freedom with regard to moral issues.

Each particular decision is made, however, not according to one's personal whims but in order to "win" Jews or Gentiles: "I do it all for the sake of the gospel" (v. 23). Christian freedom is not unrestricted autonomy. In fact, Paul in characteristic fashion juxtaposes the terms "free" and "slave" (v. 19). Submitting to the freedom of the gospel means making oneself a slave to Jews and Gentiles alike, letting their real needs dictate behavior. The two statements put in parentheses in the NRSV show the paradox of Paul's position: "I myself am not under the law" (v. 20); "I am not free from God's law but am under Christ's law" (v. 21).

To put the matter in a less paradoxical way, the text confronts readers with the gospel as the controlling reality in Christian identity. The sensitivities, intuitions, and discernment of the church and individuals within the church are shaped and informed by the Christian story. As moral issues arise, they are confronted by people who know about the compulsion and freedom of the gospel. Such people may respond to a given crisis in one situation one way and to the same crisis in another situation in a different way (as Paul does), but their responses always emanate from the central identity.

The decisive issue, then, comes with the shaping of identity, with the question of who we really are, with what controlling role the gospel plays in molding us. That often becomes an unpopular question to raise.

Mark 1:29–39

A first reading of this passage could send the preacher scurrying after another passage, for this one appears to lack direction or even coherence. Three distinct scenes comprise the passage: the first a terse miracle story (Mark 1:29–31), the second a summary of Jesus' activity as healer (vs. 32–34), the third a mild conflict between Simon and Jesus over what should be Jesus' next action (vs. 35–39). Little is

FIFTH SUNDAY AFTER EPIPHANY

said that holds the three scenes together, and no one of them offers an obvious starting point for preaching.

Mark has tightly connected these three with one another, however, despite the initial impression of disjointedness. The healing of Simon's mother-in-law occurs on the Sabbath, probably in the afternoon (see v. 21). It is a private event, witnessed presumably by only a few. The second scene takes place that same evening (see v. 32), and contrasts with the first in that it is public ("the whole city," v. 33). The third scene occurs the following morning and implicitly refers back to the second (vs. 35, 37). These careful links among the three scenes press us to look again at what each accomplishes and how the three interpret one another.

Although Mark tells of the healing of Simon's mother-in-law with notable brevity, all the customary features of a miracle story are included: the description of the illness, the healing itself, and the demonstration of the healing. This last feature takes place when the woman "began to serve them," proving that she was sufficiently recovered to resume her daily routine. (Ironically, her behavior is exactly that called for in Jesus' later teaching on discipleship, teaching elicited by the request for power by James and John, who are present in Simon's house but who do not understand the importance of the mother-in-law's action. See Mark 10:35–45.)

In the second scene, the healing powers of Jesus have become a matter of public knowledge. People bring to Jesus "all who were sick or possessed with demons," and "the whole city" gathers in the doorway (1:32–33). Such claims, surely exaggerated, serve notice to the reader that Jesus is now a public figure. His real identity as Son of God remains concealed, however, for the demons (and presumably only the demons) know who he is, and he forbids them to speak. (On possible reasons for this prohibition, see the commentary on Mark 1:40–45, the Sixth Sunday After Epiphany.) In other words, Jesus is sought for his power to heal, but his teaching is not acknowledged, nor is his real identity.

The third scene confirms that Jesus is misunderstood, even by Simon and other disciples. Jesus seeks a deserted place for prayer and is "hunted" by them, with the demand that Jesus return, a demand implicit in the words, "Everyone is searching for you." But Jesus rejects the demand. He does not return to Capernaum, but moves instead toward other towns in Galilee so that he may resume his task of proclamation.

Why does Jesus reject the request for more miracles, the demand even of those who are closest to him? There appear to be at least two reasons, one negative and one positive. First, what Jesus rejects seems to be a response to himself that focuses exclusively on his miracles. While the miracles demonstrate his power and force questions about his identity, they do not reveal who he is. This theme becomes more prominent later in the Gospel, but it emerges even here.

Second, Jesus appears to reject the request because he understands his vocation to lie elsewhere: "I may proclaim the message there also; for that is what I came out to do" (v. 38). Jesus came to preach the gospel (vs. 14–15) and to challenge the power of Satan (vs. 13, 39). However good and pleasant and popular it may be for him to heal large numbers of people, he understands that his real vocation lies elsewhere. The miracles do not in and of themselves conflict with that vocation, but the uncomprehending response of people to the miracles does conflict with that vocation.

Since we customarily read the Gospels with the expectation that every move of Jesus should be accepted as right and proper, we may well miss the cutting edge of this text. A contemporary analogy might be useful. Imagine that a pastor is a powerful counselor, so gifted that her office overflows day and night with those seeking insight and understanding. She, however, firmly believes that her vocation lies in a ministry of teaching, and decides to cut back on counseling in order to fulfill that vocation. The complaints would quickly emerge: "She has no time for people" . . . "What happened to her compassion?" . . . "Why doesn't she care for the needs of people the way she did earlier?"

The analogy is admittedly limited, but it illustrates what is at stake in this lection. Jesus subordinates his power for healing and exorcism to the greater need for proclamation of the kingdom of God. He does so because that is his primary task. He also does so because proclamation of the kingdom is the only context in which the power of healing gains its true meaning.

Sixth Sunday After Epiphany

Proper 1
Ordinary Time 6

Nobody knows how transformative healing happens, even with all our scientific discernment. Such healing remains hidden, inscrutable, and coded. Nonetheless, the biblical community treasures tales of specific transformative healings that have been wrought—we confess—by the power and mercy of God. The Old Testament reading and the Gospel reading here are parallel stories. Both tell of a dreadful, concrete need. Both tell of inexplicable power offered through an individual human agent. Both culminate in a rehabilitated person who has done for him what he cannot do for himself. The church's treasuring of and witnessing to these marvels is not diagnostic or explanatory. It is only testimony of what has been seen and heard—and we trust the witness!

The first and most appropriate response to such transformation is gratitude. Gratitude is an unlikely gesture in a society governed, as ours is, by quid-pro-quo self-sufficiency. Thus the psalm may be a model whereby needful, healed, grateful folk can learn to live appropriately in a new world that they neither understand nor manage. They can only yield in grateful trust.

The Epistle reading is a bit of an odd fit here. Paul himself is on the side of the healed. He knows about the healing. His response, no doubt saturated with gratitude, is a practice of discipline and freedom. Healed, grateful people are not slovenly or indifferent. They resolve to live a very different life. Such different lives (which may take many shapes) are the outcome of the disclosure and enactment of God's healing power.

2 Kings 5:1–14

This narrative is in the lectionary reading as a counterpoint to the Gospel reading on the healing of a leper. The narrative in 2 Kings contains the standard elements of a healing narrative: it begins with the *problem,* leprosy (5:1). It ends in a *resolution,* healing (v. 14). Between the problem and the resolution is an extended *narrative transaction.* The account of the healing points beyond itself to the prophet (v. 8), and finally to the God of the prophet (vs. 14–15).

The narrative, like good journalism, quickly gives us in v. 1 all the pertinent data about the key character, Naaman. We learn three important facts about him: he is a non-Israelite, a Syrian who must find healing outside his own territory; he is a highly successful military officer, greatly respected by his king; but—he has leprosy, which makes him socially dangerous and rejected, and which makes him ritually unclean and unacceptable. This little fact contradicts and completely undermines his claim to be a "great man," for he is by leprosy rendered socially marginal and politically irrelevant. He is, then, in an emergency, and is likely to try any possible resolution to his ailment, no matter how outrageous it seems.

The narrative resolution of the commander's problem is developed in three episodes, each of which builds on and intensifies the previous one (vs. 2–5a, 5b–7, 8–13). In his first episode, the key character is a young girl, an Israelite prisoner of war. It is she who alerts the Syrian general that "the prophet" could heal. The episode consists of understated irony, for it is this quite powerless, insignificant Israelite young woman who has the saving information that the great man needs and does not possess. The commander and his Syrian king promptly disregard the girl, however, and turn to the Israelite king. After all, powerful people gravitate only to their own counterparts, who also possess all the trappings of power, even if none of the real power.

In the second episode (vs. 5b–7), the needy general arrives in Samaria to consult with his counterpart, the king. He does not come as a "charity case"; he is not asking for a favor. He brings money and enough equipment to arrive in something like regal splendor. But there has been a terrible slip of communication. The young girl referred to *"the prophet,"* but the general comes to *the king* (who is also unnamed). The king, of course, is helpless in the face of leprosy, and is dumbfounded at the request for healing. Here there is a reversal of the earlier irony. In vs. 2–5a, the irony is the authority of the insignificant young girl. Here the irony is the complete inability of the king, who has no power to effect a healing. The king, certainly no healer, imagines that the coming of Naaman is a military-political trap.

Finally, only now, Elisha the prophet, who is in Samaria, appears in the narrative (vs. 8–13). He chides his own king for misunderstanding the confrontation with the general. He invites the needy commander to come his way, and explicitly seizes the opportunity of leprosy to establish his own authority. The general arrives at the house of Elisha. There is here a characteristic mismatch, which the narrator likes so much. There is the plain and simple prophet; his visitor is a great man who arrives in a great procession of limousines with police escort.

The prophet specifies the process for healing. It is all so odd and primitive. The general had expected healing by fiat, the way the general himself was able to work. After all, he is a commander and believes that things happen by magisterial command. He is not prepared to engage in the seedy performance of quasi-magical acts. It is beneath him, and he refuses. He refuses the sort of healing that belongs to this "faith healer" and would rather continue as a leper than humiliate himself and make a public spectacle of himself by washing in the Jordan seven times. He has better rivers, and will not submit (vs. 11–12).

The commander almost forfeits his odd chance for healing. The chance is salvaged only by the deferential urging of one of his aides. The unnamed aide functions as a counterpart in the narrative to the young girl of vs. 2–5a. The aide is unnamed and uncredentialed, but talks common sense to the great man who is too worried about his public image. The aide, like the girl, turns out to be an ally of Elisha, for he urges that the instruction to wash is neither demanding nor humiliating, and it is not costly for Naaman to submit. The girl, the aide, and the prophet form a conspiracy together against the obdurate commander, whose only ally is the Israelite king who also understands nothing of real healing power.

The story ends in an act of submissive obedience of the commander to the plan of the prophet (v. 14). The commander acts "according to the word of the man of God" and engages in ritual washing, which is beneath his station. The result is the one he had hoped for but doubted possible! He is made whole! He is made clean! He is made ritually acceptable. He is restored to full social acceptance, given back his humanity.

The narrative stands as odd testimony that power for life is indeed offered and available. That power for life is not given in expected or even socially approved forms. It comes in primitive ways that live close to the gifts of the earth. Thus all the pretense of the Syrian leader with his entourage, his goods brought for gifts (for bribery or negotiation), turn out to be irrelevant. Healing is an offer that is free, but only through the word and acts of this uncredentialed prophet.

Psalm 30

In spite of its superscription, Ps. 30 is a prayer of thanksgiving of one who has been saved from a serious crisis, perhaps a crisis involving a terrible sickness. (It is this aspect of the psalm which makes it an appropriate "companion" to the Old Testament lection for this day.) In thanking God for the restoration of health, the psalmist recites a personal story that involves a movement from life to death and back to life again. Hubris, or false pride, is understood to be as much a threat to human well-being as illness or death, and so the progression of the poet who crafted this psalm is portrayed not only in physical terms, but also in terms of his or her self-understanding before God.

(The superscription, incidentally, seems to refer to the purification of the Temple about 165 B.C. by the forces of Judas Maccabeus, and thus suggests a use of this psalm at the festival of Hanukkah. See 1 Macc. 4:41–59; 2 Macc. 10:1–8.)

The initial section (vs. 1–3) introduces the theme of the psalm and states the psalm's essential meaning (v. 2). The psalmist credits God with the great deliverance that has occurred, an act of saving grace which was set in motion by the psalmist's own sense of helplessness and need. Different metaphors are used for the distress in which the author has found him- or herself: "foes" of v. 1 and "Sheol" or "Pit" of v. 3. Whatever their original points of reference, these terms are suggestive of a wide range of human crises and, because they are applicable to many situations, they provide a large part of the psalm's power.

The thought of v. 1 is repeated in v. 4, but with a difference. Here the entire congregation is addressed, as if the priest at this point in the liturgical recitation of the psalm looks beyond the rescued individual and urges the larger worshiping community to join in the praise. There is a didactic quality to this section of the psalm, which has reminded some commentators of the wisdom tradition. However that may be, the words suggest that the priest (or is it the poet him- or herself?) is using the occasion of the psalmist's giving of thanks to instruct the faithful in the meaning of the ritual of which they are witnesses and also to remind them of important realities within their own lives.

The use of the first person in v. 6 brings the focus of attention back to the individual and to a remarkable confession of false pride. When all was well the psalmist gave no thought to the prosperity and/or health that characterized life at the moment. Since life was sweet, there was no reason to suspect that it would ever be any other way. But what the author failed to realize was that health and happiness are signs of God's compassionate presence, and it was not until God changed the conditions of life ("you hid your face") that the psalmist understood the full meaning of human mortality. Verses 6–7 not only are a confession of the sin of hubris, but are also an admission of human impotence. Only in the face of misfortune did the psalmist understand the full meaning of his or her own life.

When the very bottom of human experience loomed into view, the psalmist turned to the only resource available: God. "To you, O LORD, I cried" (v. 8) marks a pivotal moment in the life of the pray-er, for the powerless one has now begun to tap the ultimate source of power. The remarkable lines of v. 9 are capable of at least two different interpretations. Either the psalmist is saying, "Why should I continue to contribute to my own annihilation by feeding my false pride?" or the psalmist is reminding God that in the divine-human encounter the continuing viability of the human partner in the dialogue is essential. The first of these possible readings of v. 9 may be the more likely, but the second should not be dismissed, in spite of its somewhat shocking implication that even God is diminished by the death of a human being. If God truly loves human individuals—perhaps the psalmist is arguing—why should God not be touched by the death of one of God's own persons? Is this not close to what Jesus was later to teach about the God who knows the sparrows and who has counted the hairs of the human head (Matt. 10:29–30)?

The entire psalm concludes (vs. 11–12) on a note of the most ecstatic rejoicing. The contrasts that express this utter gaiety are striking: mourning has now become dancing, sackcloth has been transformed into joy. In the face of such marvels the human being cannot remain mute. The speech and song of celebration fill the being of the psalmist and resound in the air. And not just today, but throughout the life of the psalmist: "O LORD my God, I will give thanks to you forever."

In a sense, then, the journey is complete. The psalmist has now been restored to a state of wholeness, but in the process he or she has been permanently changed. There is a new appreciation of divine power and of human weakness. More important, there is now a new understanding of God's love and of the dependence of men and women on it.

1 Corinthians 9:24–27

For some time now the prevailing ethos of our culture has been self-fulfillment. Particularly, those in the segment of the population labeled the baby-boomers have operated on the notion that life is basically good and meant to be enjoyed. Notions of delaying gratification or denying self, characteristic of previous generations, have lost their credibility. Even in the therapeutic realm, love and meaning are defined simply as the fulfillment of the individual's emotional requirements, with little thought of subordinating one's needs to the needs of others or of giving oneself to someone or some cause beyond the self.

Members of our congregations for the most part welcome help in dealing with Christian notions of self-denial, discipline, and self-control, notions that seem very much out of step with the prevailing ethos. Almost every church member, consciously or not, feels the tension and seeks counsel. The Epistle reading for today provides an apt text for such a reflection.

But discipline and self-control are tough topics to tackle in a sermon. The problem is not their unpopularity, but the realization that members of the congregation react to the notions in differing and often opposite ways. For one member there is the remembrance of an authoritarian father, who ran a tight ship and whose own emotions were kept under such wraps that he never lost his cool or risked any tenderness. Just the mention of self-control conjures up bad recollections of a performance-oriented childhood, without the reassurance of unconditional love. Another member, however, carries on a constant struggle with an alcohol problem (or lives with a spouse who wages such a battle). Self-control may be exactly what is needed, but it looms like an insurmountable barrier, and frequent efforts to scale it have come to naught. What is said from the pulpit has to be carefully crafted in light of the current and past experiences of the congregation.

What is said from the pulpit needs also to reflect faithfully the circumstances of the text (1 Cor. 9:24–27). Paul is not presenting in these verses an isolated essay on the critical nature of self-discipline for an unrestrained culture. Taken out of context, the section could be used to promote a rigorous asceticism or a competitive spirit that sets Christians against one another, alternatives no more satisfactory than the culture already has. In fact, the verses serve as an appropriate transition between a discussion about identification with both Jews and Gentiles (9:19–23) and a warning about idolatry and attendance at pagan temples (10:1–22).

On the one hand, the incredible freedom of the gospel, which demands such unusual flexibility (9:19–23), is not to be mistaken for license. Even when engaged in mission, the one preaching the gospel may not be up to the test, and like a runner in a race or a boxer in the ring is subject to disqualification (9:27). Discipline and self-control are essential to prevent exclusion from the very salvation one is advocating.

On the other hand, the divine grace demonstrated in the gospel often leads to presumptuousness and to the grave possibility of idolatry (10:12, 14). Israel's privileges did not protect its people from the divine disfavor on their indulgences (10:1-5), and neither are baptism and the Lord's Supper to be thought of as magical rites that guarantee immunity from judgment. Readers are to exercise self-control regarding attendance at the pagan temples.

Two observations about the rich metaphors found in the text—the runner and boxer. First, the notion of competition is inherent in the image of a race, and yet for Paul it is clearly secondary. The stress falls, rather, on the prize, the imperishable wreath. Unlike the prize given to winners in a track event, this one is worth it. It is the future of God's rule, the fulfillment of the divine promises. Since eschatological talk is so pervasive in the letter, Paul does not pause here to spell out the specifics; nevertheless, the unquestionable value of the prize makes the effort and struggle worthwhile.

This leads to a second observation, namely, that the prize gives purpose to the training. The runner does not run "aimlessly," that is, without a goal in view. Neither does a boxer fight as if he had no opponent to hit. Each has an objective; each is oriented toward a goal.

This means that discipline and self-control are not ends in themselves. If they were, then the Christian experience would quickly become burdensome. It would result in more authoritarian fathers who cannot show affection and more alcoholics who find self-control far too difficult. Purposeless training has no virtue. In the pursuit of the gospel and in the sharing of its blessings (9:23), however, discipline and self-control take their appropriate places. They have their meaning and purpose in the larger perspective of God's purposes for the present and the future.

Mark 1:40-45

Healing stories in the New Testament have as their unrelenting focus the person and power of Jesus. As a result, few details are given about the nature of the diseases involved except to underscore their severity and the difficulty of the healing. For the most part, then, the disease itself is of little interest. An important exception to this general state of affairs is that of leprosy, for leprosy involves not only disease, but ritual purity laws and theological understandings as well.

As the explanatory note at Mark 1:40 of the NRSV indicates, "leprosy" in the Bible includes a broad range of skin ailments. The regulations regarding leprosy in Lev. 13–14 clearly cover a variety of diseases. Those regulations also demonstrate that leprosy, whatever its form, involves a violation of ritual purity laws. Since ritual purity laws often come into play because something is thought to be abnormal or out of place, various diseases of the skin probably were regarded as violations of ritual purity simply because they looked unusual or strange. The consequences of this violation were serious, in that persons with skin diseases would be separated from much that constituted normal society. (As always, it is difficult to determine how precisely the Levitical code was observed in day-to-day life.) Complicating matters even further for the individual so afflicted, leprosy was often interpreted as punishment for sin and healing from leprosy as an act of God (see, for example, Num. 12:10–15; Deut. 24:8–9; 28:27, 35; 2 Kings 5:19–27; 2 Chron. 26:16–21).

The person who approaches Jesus in Mark 1:40, then, may not have been stricken with a grave physical disease, but his situation was nevertheless a severe one. His words to Jesus convey complete confidence in Jesus' ability to heal him, but they also reveal a question about whether Jesus will wish to heal him: "If you choose, you can make me clean." Given that the leper was probably understood to be a sinner and an outcast, the question in his approach to Jesus is more than polite. He knows that many would not heal him even if they could.

Jesus' response emphatically rejects the walls erected between this man and himself. First, the narrator describes Jesus as being "moved with pity" or "moved with anger" (NRSV margin). A difficult text-critical problem creates the divergent translations here, and a number of scholars think the better reading is "moved with anger." Even if that reading is rejected, "moved with pity" translates a strong Greek verb (*splagchnizomai*) that literally refers to having one's intestines turn. The feeling described is more than a superficial kind of sympathy—Jesus is deeply moved. Second, he touches the man. Healings often involve touch, of course, but touching a person with a skin disease identifies Jesus with that person, making him outcast as well. (Although the situations differ in many ways, the contemporary hysteria about touching persons afflicted with AIDS offers some telling parallels.) Third, Jesus' response, "I do choose," emphatically connects him with the leper's plight.

The healing itself accomplished, Jesus gives the man two instruc-

SIXTH SUNDAY AFTER EPIPHANY

tions, instructions that almost of necessity conflict with each other. He directs the former leper to show himself to the priest and make the offering required of him. This command places Jesus in conformity with Lev. 14, which specifies the procedure and the offerings appropriate for various persons, depending on their economic standing. That this action is said to be "a testimony to them" (Mark 1:44) may mean that Jesus is hereby vindicated from charges of being hostile or indifferent to Mosaic law. In view of the various conflict stories in 2:1–3:6, however, it could also mean that Jesus challenges the authorities to acknowledge his powerful act of healing.

The first instruction Jesus gives the former leper ("Say nothing to anyone") is more difficult to understand. How could this man return to his home without explaining the origin of his cure? Surely the priest who examined him would immediately ask how he came to be healed. The man in question apparently thinks nothing of violating this injunction, since the story closes with a report about his proclamation of the event and its impact on Jesus. Several such instructions in Mark (for example, 5:43; 8:26; 8:30), customarily identified as the Messianic Secret, prompt much perplexity on the part of students of this Gospel. The injunctions to silence appear to be connected with Mark's understanding of the place of miracle in identifying Jesus. Jesus' miracles evidence his power, but they do not adequately explain who he is or what his mission is, for that explanation comes only in light of the cross (see, for example, 8:27–31; 9:9).

Whatever the explanation for the command to silence, the end of the story finds Jesus once more besieged. Earlier he fled Capernaum because "the whole city" was at his doorstep. Now no town offers him refuge, and he must stay in the country (literally, "deserted places"). The question of what the miracles mean is once again eclipsed by the people's hunger for the power itself.

SEVENTH SUNDAY AFTER EPIPHANY

Proper 2
Ordinary Time 7

The imperiled nature of human existence and the power of God to save and restore are themes that find various forms of expression in the lections for this day.

The Second Isaiah was certainly as aware as anyone of the threats posed by the sinfulness of God's people, a sinfulness that the prophet understood not just to consist of the accumulated wrongful acts in his nation's past, but more particularly to be constituted of the warped nature of the people's hearts. Against this dangerous and self-destructive state of the nation's soul, however, the prophet offers assurance that Yahweh intends to redeem the people even from their own worst follies.

As is often the case, the psalmist writes in less corporate, more individual terms, although the most seemingly individualistic of the psalms have profound corporate implications. This poet has suffered some tragic turn of events that involves not only social alienation, but deep psychic anguish. All friends have failed, and there is no one else left to appeal to but Yahweh. But at the heart of this desperation lies the faith (and thus the hope!) that the God of Israel will meet this and every human need.

The lection from 2 Corinthians reveals Paul to be in a somewhat awkward position. The suspicion on the part of some of the Corinthian believers that he is unreliable carries the implied suspicion that the gospel that he preaches is therefore unreliable. Nothing could be farther from the truth! God's promises are always "Yes." The experience of the believing community is always "Amen! It is so!" The work of the Spirit comprises the continuing evidence of the faithfulness of God and of God's ability to do what God has promised.

Mark's story of the crippled man lowered through the roof into the presence of Jesus by his four friends is a statement, in the form of a brief drama, analogous to the poetic and epistolary lections for this

Sunday. The physical condition of the man is portrayed as emblematic of his spiritual condition (although not caused by it!). And the example of Jesus' power to restore the individual's ability to walk is presented as a paradigm of God's intention to restore him and us, the readers, to a state of wholeness in our relationship to God and to one another.

Isaiah 43:18–25

The wonder of Epiphany is the sense of God's capacity to intrude upon our world, to break up old patterns of reality, to permit us to begin again from a new place. This text addressed to exiles asserts that the displacement caused by God's hostility (that is, the exile) is now ended. God will act anew to give the exiles a homecoming (Isa. 43:18–21). There is, however, also a reflection upon the unresolved issues of exile: what caused it, and who is responsible for it (vs. 22–28)? The announcement of newness is thus coupled with a defense of God's previous actions toward Jerusalem. Thus, in the end, the poem offers a theodicy.

Verses 18–21 act as a pivot for Israel's self-understanding, marking a sharp break between past and future. Indeed, Gerhard von Rad has taken these verses as an organizing theme for relating Israel *under judgment* (in the monarchy) to Israel *under promise* (in and after the exile).

God's "new thing" is an active intervention, which will transform the circumstance of Jews. The "new thing" is a miracle whereby judgment becomes promise, exile becomes homecoming, abrasion becomes reconciliation, and death becomes life. The exilic Jews had been preoccupied either with the old saving events of Moses or with the recent punishments wrought by God (the interpretive point is in dispute). Now all that is past is to be scuttled and forgotten, as Israel is overwhelmed by God's generous, gracious, decisive newness, which opens the way for the future.

The poet describes in lyrical fashion the transformation of the exilic condition (vs. 19c–21). The dry, parched land, which can hardly sustain life, will become a well-watered, life-giving territory. This is for exiles who must make their way across the desert en route home. There are all sorts of wild animals in the desert that are hard put to survive the drought, animals such as jackals and ostriches. Now, in the newness, all will have ample water, and all will join the doxology of this water-giving, life-sustaining God. The poet, in an arid climate, has seized on the image of water as a sign and measure of God's capacity and resolve to transform the world of the exiles.

For all the talk of newness, however, God still has unfinished business with Israel about "former things" (vs. 22–24). Even though God promises newness, adversarial Israel did not trust ("call upon") God. These verses make a play on two words, "weary" (vs. 22–24) and "burdened" (vs. 23–24).

God has not been a demanding God, did not make heavy cultic requirements of Israel, and did not tire Israel with religious issues. It is possible that the two phrases "you have not brought me" (v. 23) and "you have not bought me" (v. 24) are a reprimand for a failure to bring offerings to God. More likely, however, they are the recognition that Yahweh did not ask for such conventional religious practice, so that Israel's religion is not demanding or exhausting. Yahweh has not wearied or burdened Israel with requirements, but nonetheless Israel has been "weary of me," that is, tired of the relationship.

The zinger, however, is not that Israel is weary of God (v. 22), but that Yahweh is weary of Israel, tired out by Israel's sins and iniquities (v. 24). Thus this subtle play on terms is an indictment of Israel as the one who has distorted the relationship. Or, conversely, these verses assert the innocence of Yahweh. Yahweh has made no hard demands, so Yahweh cannot be the reason Israel is weary of God. Rather Israel is weary of Yahweh just because it got tired out by fidelity and acted in destructive ways. It is remarkable that even though Israel is invited not to remember the past, Yahweh is preoccupied with that past and revisits it in order to establish Yahweh's own innocence.

In vs. 25–28 (the poem continues beyond the lectionary verses), one more time, Yahweh asserts Yahweh's own power and innocence. In v. 25, Yahweh asserts the capacity and willingness to forgive "for my own sake," because forgiveness belongs quintessentially to Yahweh's own character. That is who Yahweh is, and what Yahweh will do! Because Yahweh will forgive, all that has been distorted in the past (Israel's sin) will not be remembered. Thus as Israel is urged not to remember (v. 18), so Yahweh also pledges not to remember (v. 25). There must and can be a liberating forgetting on both sides!

So much for v. 25. It is, however, as though Yahweh cannot quite forget. Or perhaps Yahweh knows that Israel does not forget. From the words of Yahweh, we infer what Israel must have been saying or thinking. That implied thought is that Israel continues to accuse Yahweh of having unjustly punished Jerusalem and caused the exile.

In response to that inferred but unspoken accusation, Yahweh makes one more self-defense (vs. 26–28).

These verses are cast as a courtroom contest to adjudicate the guilt and/or innocence of Yahweh and Israel. Verse 26 is God's defiant challenge to Israel: "Sue me! Go to court, bring your charges." Verse 27 is a defense of Yahweh made by asserting that Israel's past is filled with sinners who caused this just punishment of exile. The "first ancestor" and "your interpreters" refer to the generation of Moses and the "crooked generation" of distorters who followed. From the beginning Israel has been in the wrong and deserves exile. Then, for that reason ("therefore"), the exile has come (v. 28). The punishment is not because Yahweh is unjust, but because Israel has been characteristically unfaithful.

Psalm 41

There are few sadder realities than the fact that, whereas "winners" possess friends in abundance, "losers" (either real or imagined) are among the loneliest people in the world. Job knew this and complained bitterly of it (Job 19:13–22), and even Jesus looked down from the cross to find the most staunchly loyal of his followers looking on from some distance (Mark 15:40–41 and parallels). It is an often-told tale that, when misfortune occurs, friends are scarcely to be found.

The author of Ps. 41 knew this to be true, and in desperation turned to the only possible source of support: the God of Israel, who cares even for the downcast and abandoned!

The psalm, which is largely devoted to a cry for help and justice, begins in a most surprising manner: "Happy are those . . . ." Either there has been some kind of textual dislocation, and words (vs. 1–3) from a psalm of a different genre have found their way into this psalm of lament, or the inspired poet begins on a note of mockery, as if to say, "Some may be happy, but in my case . . ." That the latter is the preferred interpretation is suggested by the opening of v. 4 ("As for me . . ."), which appears to contrast the blessedness of those who have been favored by God with the psalmist's own sorry condition. Given this mood on the part of the writer, vs. 1–3 appear to be a kind of ideal state to which the suffering psalmist hopes to be elevated. Those who care about the well-being of others will be vindicated by God in that they will be protected from sickness and deceit. "I am such a person," the poet seems to insist, "and I therefore have a claim on the mercy of God."

The reasons for the psalmist's need for God are made apparent in the main body of the text, vs. 4–10. Initially, there is a confession of sin (v. 4), yet somehow this seems to serve a liturgical purpose more than some deeply felt spiritual need. There is no elaboration. No details are given of the transgressions (compare the different language of Ps. 51), so that the confession seems almost perfunctory. And one will remember that sin and suffering were bound tightly together in the minds of some Israelites (as in Prov. 10:3 and elsewhere). In fact, the NRSV translation seems to suggest, rather than a fresh confession, some *past* confession which God has apparently ignored. In other words: "I have confessed my sin, but I am still in great distress. Where are you, O Lord?"

For an alternative manner of considering the text, however, compare the "old" RSV, where a sense of dialogue is more evident: "I said," of Ps. 41:4, is contrasted with "My enemies say" of v. 5. In fact, RSV more than NRSV captures the wordplay of the Hebrew, and thus the artistry by which the point is made: My words (that is, the psalmist's) are true and just in that I have confessed my sin; but the words of my enemies are filled with malice (v. 5), with emptiness (v. 6), and with hatred (v. 7, where the words are now "whispered"). In this section (v. 5–6) the psalmist's familiarity with human nature is made evident, for the enemies wonder when the psalmist will die and his or her memory become extinct, a terrible fate among a people with no finely developed understanding of life beyond death (v. 7). They seem to be offering consolation to the sufferer, but in reality mischief is in their hearts, and they mock the sufferer by gossiping about the person when they are outside the house of pain (v. 6). One can almost see them gathered, perhaps just beyond the sufferer's door, where they carry on with one another in hushed tones (v. 7).

It is clear that the false friends of the psalmist have concluded the worst. This poor person will never survive! This is the final episode in his or her life (v. 8)! But what is most mischievous of all is that even the psalmist's best friend is among the "enemies," the one who "ate of my bread" (v. 9). Treachery on the part of one's acquaintances is terrible enough, but from one's "bosom friend"? That is terrible, indeed.

Yet in the midst of this anguish the writer knows that there is one Friend who can be relied on. And so: "You, O Yahweh, be gracious to me,/ and raise me up" (v. 10). Why should Yahweh do that? The reason seems at first glance to be self-serving (the "self" being that of the psalmist): "that I may repay them." Yet there is more involved than immediately meets the eye, for the verb used here, *šālēm*, is a cognate of the well-known noun *šālôm*, meaning "peace" or "health" or "wholeness." And while the NRSV's "repay" is not incorrect, the root meaning of the verb is "to return to a state of wholeness or completeness." Thus, if one reads the passage theologically and not juridically, the meaning becomes "that they may return to a state of moral and theological wholeness from which they have strayed." Or, to paraphrase v. 10, "Restore me to wellness, O Lord, in order that my physical and emotional restoration may cause the moral restoration of my enemies."

The psalm ends on a note of hope. Yahweh's mercy is evident in the preservation of the psalmist (v. 11), who, during this entire ordeal, has not rejected God (v. 12). Thus the writer's integrity and Yahweh's mercy (v. 4) have conspired to save the psalmist and, by extension, to save all who demonstrate the same faithfulness before God.

(Verse 13 is not, properly speaking, a part of this psalm, in that it constitutes the benediction to Book I of the Psalter.)

2 Corinthians 1:18–22

Paul's relationship with the church at Corinth was not always a happy one. Misunderstanding and conflict characterized it almost from the beginning. Paul speaks of postponing a visit to Corinth so as to avoid the pain that had marked a previous visit, and he describes writing a letter "out of much distress and anguish of heart and with many tears" (2 Cor. 2:4). And yet, ironically, this context of conflict evokes one of the most positive affirmations of the Christian faith and its meaning for human life that we have in the New Testament.

Such is the epistolary assignment for this Sunday—2 Cor. 1:18–22. Paul canceled a promised visit to Corinth and apparently was sharply criticized by some in the community for doing so. Not carrying through with his plans exposed him as an unreliable messenger of the gospel, a figure the Corinthians could not count on. On the surface, such a criticism hardly seems worth responding to, except that it likely eroded confidence in the gospel preached. An undependable messenger means an undependable message.

Paul's reply is twofold. On the one hand, he defends his decision not to come by saying he did not want to make another trip that would create more pain for himself and for the Corinthians (1:23–2:5). He wants them to know that he has not been talking out of both sides of his mouth at the same time, as some evidently accuse him of doing. On the other hand, Paul calls attention to the gospel he has preached to them, a gospel at whose heart is not a vacillating, unreliable word, but the full "Yes" of God. It is this positive affirmation of the gospel that warrants our special reflection.

Three observations about Paul's positive thinking are in order. First, he speaks of the faithful God who can be counted on to fulfill all the divine promises. The advent of Jesus Christ reveals that God is trustworthy. In Christ "every one of God's promises is a 'Yes' " (1:20). In the liturgy the worshiping community can say "Amen" because they can trust God.

Paul's strategy here is not to cite a single Old Testament passage and argue that Jesus has fulfilled it, but rather to make a blanket affirmation about "every one of God's promises." The issue is bigger than this or that text. The long and involved story of God's engagement in human history finds its climax in Jesus Christ, the one preached by Paul, Silvanus, and Timothy.

Now this turns out to be a critical word for an age like ours, which sets a high value on positive thinking—in business, athletics, education, and even the church. Christians have their reasons for optimism about the course of human history and even about their own personal lives, but not because they trust in the indomitable human spirit or the infinite capacity of human achievement, not because they have learned to psych themselves up to perform outstanding feats or to endure excruciating pain. Christian hope emerges from a confidence in the reliability of God, who in Jesus Christ proves to be utterly dependable—both in human history and in our personal lives.

Second, the faithful God establishes people in community (1:21). We note with interest Paul's strategy here with his initial readers: the community God establishes is composed of "us" and "you." Some in Corinth may criticize Paul for his change of plans, but they need to know that what binds them together is not his behavior or their response, but God's action.

Beyond the rhetorical move Paul makes, we can observe the remarkable intention of God—to create a single people composed of such diversity and conflict as represented by Paul and his readers. Despite all the tensions between Paul and the Corinthians and among the Corinthians themselves, God's plans have not changed, and these plans include the creation of a community in Christ. Amid the pressures and pluralism of the contemporary church, whether local or global, Paul's positive words to Corinth offer reassurance.

Third, Paul's optimism includes the confirming activity of God's Spirit. The language of 1:21–22 suggests that the notion of baptism may not be far from Paul's mind, but his emphasis lies on experience ("in our hearts"). The dependable presence of God is not limited to one moment in history, but continues in the lives of the people God has established in community.

The phrase in v. 22 translated in the NRSV as "first installment" (in the RSV as "guarantee") has particular significance in a passage that concentrates on the promises of God. It represents the down payment, or pledge, that pays part of the purchase price in advance and obligates the contracting party to the remaining payments. The experience of the Spirit in human lives functions like this.

Often the Christian community finds itself with what seem like good reasons to conclude that God has abandoned the divine promises. The vicious presence of evil in the world, the constant conflict within the church, the struggle with inexplicable tragedies would lead any reasonable person to infer that God has taken a long holiday or drastically changed the script—except for the persistent rumblings of the Spirit "in our hearts," rumblings that remind us of God's commitment to complete the story.

The gospel of Jesus Christ, the reality of the Christian community, the experience of the Spirit are grounds for positive thinking of a Pauline sort.

Mark 2:1–12

After the brief and straightforward miracle stories of Mark 1:29–31 and 40–45, this story of the healing of a paralyzed man comes as a surprise. Its setting elaborately details the effort required to bring the man into the presence of Jesus. Jesus' comments concerning the forgiveness of sins introduce some confusion about what the relationship is between forgiveness and healing. Little has prepared readers to anticipate the serious conflict between Jesus and the scribes. These features of the text reflect the fact that it forms a bridge between the miracle stories that run from 1:21 through 2:12 and the controversy stories that run from 2:1 through 3:6.

While this story, like all Gospel miracle stories, has Jesus rather than any other character as its focus, the actions of the people who bring the paralyzed man to Jesus catch our attention because of the detail Mark lavishes on them. The setting in 2:1–2 makes clear that simply getting near Jesus is a challenge. He has returned to Capernaum, the town he earlier left because of the crowds (1:21, 32–34, 38–39). Now the number of those gathered makes it impossible even to get near the door to hear him (compare 1:33). Despite these difficulties, a paralyzed man is carried to Jesus. Mark's awkward introduction of this event already draws attention to the effort required: "Then some people came, bringing to him a paralyzed man, carried by four of them." The picture Mark evokes is a comic one; a sea of people, over which four individuals are carrying the man who is paralyzed. When they cannot enter through the door, they expend the additional effort required to make a hole in the roof and lower him to Jesus.

The result of this effort Mark describes with the simple phrase, "Jesus saw their faith." In other Markan miracle stories as well, faith is ascribed to the action involved in coming to Jesus for healing (5:34; 10:52). No affirmation about the person of Jesus or the nature of God accompanies these actions; the actions themselves speak of confidence in Jesus' ability. Equally important, these faithful or trusting actions precede healing rather than coming as the result of healing.

Another prominent feature of this story is the relationship between forgiveness and healing. In response to the faith of those who bring the paralyzed man to him, the expectation is that Jesus will tell the man to walk or pronounce him healed. Instead, Jesus announces, "Son, your sins are forgiven." This, of course, prompts the controversy that follows, as a result of which Jesus then claims for himself the authority to forgive sins and then effects the cure. What is the relationship between these two actions, forgiveness and healing?

As in other biblical texts, the assumption at work is that illness or affliction comes about as the result of sin (for example, Ps. 103:3; John 5:14; 9:2; James 5:15–16). Because that connection has often been twisted to inflict needless guilt on persons, it is important to consider carefully what is said here. Jesus' statement that the man's sins are forgiven may indeed suggest that his paralysis results from sin, but the man does not rise and walk when he is forgiven. More important, Jesus' initial proclamation in 1:14–15 and the tenor of the Gospel as a whole also suggest that everyone stands in need of repentance. There are no exemptions from that category. The paralyzed man simply becomes a specific instance where two major features of Jesus' ministry, forgiveness and healing, come together. To put it another way, this remains a story about Jesus, not a story about the origin of disability.

In this particular story, where bystanders challenge Jesus' authority to make the claim that sins have been forgiven, the healing becomes Jesus' way of demonstrating that he does have this authority. The question, "Which is easier?" points to the fact that, unlike forgiveness, healing is verifiable. When healing is accomplished, Jesus' power cannot be denied, as is clear in the people's amazement at the story's conclusion.

The relationship between forgiveness and healing provides the pretext for the emergence of controversy surrounding Jesus. Even in the first healing story, the comparison between Jesus and the scribes raises eyebrows (1:21–28), and questions about Jesus' authority begin early (1:27). Here accusations come to the surface of the story, and the specific accusation of blasphemy is extremely serious, as blasphemy carried with it the death penalty (Lev. 24:15–16). If Jesus' statement, "Your sins are forgiven," is a "divine passive," a circumlocution that avoids the more direct "God forgives you," then the scribes correctly challenge Jesus' claim. His response, which takes the customary form of a question and then the act that demonstrates his authority, tosses the controversy back into the faces of his opponents.

Despite the seriousness of the charge against Jesus in this passage, it is worth recalling that the scribes do not yet speak out against him. Mark carefully says that Jesus perceives what the scribes are thinking ("questioning in their hearts"). The section that follows will bring these controversies into the open, as Pharisees begin to challenge particular actions of Jesus. The section as a whole culminates in 3:6 with the conspiracy to bring about Jesus' death.

Eighth Sunday After Epiphany

Proper 3
Ordinary Time 8

The love of God for sinful, wayward people—even for people who treat God as a faithless spouse callously treats a partner in marriage—is the haunting subject of Hosea's prophecy. But Hosea is not concerned just to describe the pain of a broken relationship and subsequent divorce. The prophet then goes on, employing language that suggests a personal experience of deep suffering, to propose reconciliation. As God has loved Israel to the point of a broken heart, so God's love for Israel is so great that God, like a brokenhearted husband, woos back his bride. The Old Testament lection for this day describes Hosea's vision of the reconsecrated marriage between God and Israel.

The verses from Ps. 103 are jubilant in their celebration of the mercy of God. Israel's God is one whose acts of creation stand as symbol of the grace and compassion that characterize God's nature. Israel may sin and may even stand in danger of forgetting the One who has called the nation into existence. But God neither forgets nor changes character. God saves and redeems the people. Therefore the people express their commitment to God and to their community with one another through praise. "Bless the LORD, O my soul."

In 2 Corinthians, Paul expresses his concern over the nature of Christian ministry. That the ministry of the individual takes place in the context of the larger ministry of the church, that the ministry of the church receives its energies from the presence of God, and that the work of the church is the living out of God's fresh initiatives in Jesus Christ—all these propositions are affirmed by Paul, as is his emphatic belief that the ongoing life of the church is sustained and directed by the living Spirit of God. The result is new life and freedom for those who, like himself, minister in Christ's name.

The series of Markan lections, which included the story of the healing of the paralyzed man last week, now moves us along into the controversy into which this and other miracles have drawn Jesus.

EIGHTH SUNDAY AFTER EPIPHANY

The call of Levi is the context for an outbreak of disquieting murmurings which, in turn, give way to a public challenge to Jesus' disciples over the Master's attitudes and practices. The tension between the old and the new, between Jesus' opponents and himself, is then addressed directly by Jesus in words that, while eschatological in their implications, also contain important truths for life in the kingdom here and now.

Hosea 2:14–20

The text of Hosea has just completed a long, harsh poem of divorce, in which Yahweh, the husband, casts out the fickle wife, Israel (2:2–13). (In its harshness, the imagery is brutalizing in a sexist, patriarchal fashion, but the completed metaphor of vs. 14–20 requires that we stay with the metaphor.) In our verses, the rhetorical field is reversed. Whereas vs. 2–13 concern the harshness of divorce, vs. 14–20 witness to the action of God, who reloves Israel in a resumed marriage.

Just before v. 14, the denunciation of the wife by the husband ends in v. 13. There is then a long rhetorical pause after v. 13 and before v. 14. During that pause, it may be that God reflects upon what has just been said and decides to change the mood and tone of the speech. Certainly there has been an abrupt change in tone, though we do not know why. Perhaps Yahweh discerned, amid the ringing echoes of vs. 1–13, that in the end God loves Israel more than God has known heretofore, and God wills an intimate relationship with Israel, its infidelity notwithstanding.

When God speaks again, the poem is filled with gentleness and yearning. Twice (vs. 6, 9), the poem used "therefore" to sound a threat. With "therefore" in v. 14, we expect an escalation of threat. The term here, however, performs a rhetorical trick, for now it introduces a new, positive resolve on God's part. In vs. 14–15, God utters a new intention in five positive verbs: "I will allure . . ., I will bring . . ., I will speak . . ., I will give . . ., I will make." The language is that of an eager suitor who intends to intervene in the life of the beloved in caring, transformative ways. What had been a threat of exile now becomes an invitation to an intimate rendezvous in the wilderness, where God will speak intimately and caringly to this sought-after partner (v. 14). After such an intense wooing, God will take this beloved from the jeopardy of wilderness (where there are no guaranteed life-supports) and bring her into the good land of productive vineyards (v. 15). The place of reentry into the land had been the "Valley of Achor," which in Josh. 7–8 is the Valley of Trouble, where wayward Israel had suffered a humiliating defeat. Now, however, that same access point to the Promised Land is to be renamed and recharacterized. What had been a "valley of trouble" will be a "door of hope." What had been a vexatious distortion will now be a buoyant, safe, life-giving place. This is Israel's reentry, in effect, "second coming," now under the miraculous aegis of Yahweh's reaffirmed love. God's new love now permits Israel to have a wholly new life.

New life in the land leads to new relations and to new circumstances (vs. 16–18). On the one hand, Israel is now restored and reconstituted to have a very different relationship with God. Now Yahweh will be "my husband" (vs. 16–17). That is, this will be a convenantal marriage of intimacy, affection, respect, trust, and delight, each for the other. That innocent, healthy relationship will replace a relationship in which Yahweh was "my Baal," the one who made the land to be productive. That is, Yahweh was a means toward an end (fertile land), but now Yahweh will be a cherished and treasured end, for the relationship now will exist for its own sake. God is enjoyed, but not used for extraneous purposes.

On the other hand, this reconstituted relationship will be accompanied by God's new relation to the created order (v. 18a). (Thus God's new self-giving in Epiphany concerns not only personal or ecclesial dimensions, but also the ecosystem of all creation.) In a direct allusion to Gen. 1, God will reorder the relationship between Israel and the beasts/birds/creeping things of the earth. Israel will be restored to its rightful place as an integral part of a covenanted creation, no longer distorted by abusive infidelity. The remaking of covenant where love drives out infidelity permits the whole earth to be healed and restored.

One result of this covenant is the abolition of war, the nullification of all its weapons, and a consequent condition of safety, well-being, and confidence (v. 18b). The third action of God in these verses ("I will remove . . . I will make . . . I will abolish") suggests a radical reorientation of all of life, so that the rule and purpose of God displace the pursuit of all self-securing. All these actions of God, however, are preliminary to the newness now asserted, which is rooted only in God's faithful love.

Verses 19–20 are cast as a wedding vow: "I, Yahweh, take you, Israel, to be my wife forever." They form a sharp contrast to and counteract the divorce proceedings of vs. 2–13. In these two verses, God unconditionally and unilaterally enters into a new lifelong relation of solidarity with and fidelity toward Israel. The oath of loyalty taken by God asserts five basic terms of Israel's covenant faith: righteousness, justice, steadfast love, mercy, and faithfulness. This crucial vocabulary of covenant offers five terms that belong to the general affirmation of fidelity, in which God commits to the well-being of Israel. These five terms culminate in the formula, "You shall know Yahweh." The verb "know" perhaps bespeaks intimacy, but also acknowledgment and recognition that Yahweh is the covenant partner who gives life and new identity to Israel, who must be honored, taken seriously, and obeyed.

The entire passage portrays God overriding the deep infidelity of Israel, not by fiat or by coercion or by reprimand, but by God's risky action which works a genuine newness, which dramatically reorients a world of infidelity, estrangement, and hostility. Newness is possible and available because of God's irrepressible desire to live with this covenant partner.

Psalm 103:1–13, 22

"Unrestrained praise" might be the phrase that characterizes this psalm. It conforms to the basic structure of that genre designated by many scholars as hymns or psalms of praise, in that it consists of an introduction (vs. 1–2), a main body (vs. 3–18), and a conclusion (vs. 19–22). (Actually, the main body of Ps. 103 may be subdivided into two sections, vs. 3–5 and 6–18). Also, like many psalms of praise, Ps. 103 begins and ends with the same imperative, in this case "Bless Yahweh, O my soul" (compare Pss. 146–150 with their familiar "Hallelujah" or "Praise Yahweh," and Ps. 104:1 and 35). In other words, the psalm is a poem of classic Hebrew construction. In the passage identified by the lectionary, only the introduction and part of the main body are included, although the final "Bless Yahweh, O my soul" (v. 22) is included in order to achieve a balanced conclusion.

The word "bless," which has a variety of meanings, contains—in this context—the imperative that both the individual (vs. 3–5) and the entire community of faithful people (vs. 6–13) should worship Yahweh. Indeed, one of the features of this psalm is its universal focus of concern. Individual persons and the worshiping congregation as a whole are alike under consideration here. The dangers from which Yahweh has protected the people include all three forms of distress traditionally found in psalms of lament and psalms of thanksgiving: the distress caused by sin (vs. 3a, 10), that which results from illness and the threat of death (vs. 3b, 4a), and that brought about by unjust oppression imposed by other people (v. 6). The Lord has intervened in order to save the people from these and all torments. Therefore: "Bless the Lord!"

Yet it is clear from v. 2b that to "bless" involves more than simple adoration. It also involves the memory, the lodging in the consciousness of the individual and of the community, the record of God's saving deeds. If anything characterizes the teaching of the Old Testament, it is that traditionalizing is a key element in the propagation of the faith. Each generation teaches the next and, in that manner, the community's ownership of its past encounters with God is perpetuated and made available to individuals for their participation. In the great exhortation to remember contained in Deut. 6:4–9, no words are more penetrating than the injunction to "recite [the elements of your faith-memory] to your children and talk about them when you are at home and when you are away, when you lie down and when you rise" (v. 7). That the introduction to Ps. 103, which begins with the admonition to worship, should end on the admonition to remember should come as no surprise to the reader. To forget would be to lose one's way entirely. It would be to lose one's self and one's God.

The initial section within the main body (vs. 3–5), where the emphasis seems to be placed on the relationship between God and the individual, actually consists of a string of participial phrases that endeavor (as well as human words may do so) to sketch a portrait of the living Yahweh. Yahweh is "the forgiving one," "the healing one," "the redeeming one," and so on. Perhaps it does not put too fine a point on the matter to observe that there is more power in the Hebrew expressions than in the English, in that the Hebrew comes nearer to equating God's being with God's doing. This stands as another reminder, if one were needed, that ancient Israel's understanding of its God was not couched in the abstract nouns and adjectives of the philosopher, but in concrete verbs, that is, in terms of action.

Verses 6–13 reflect on the nation's past and on Yahweh's saving activity in that history. The key to this section, in fact, the essence of the entire psalm, is found here, in vs. 6 and 8. Yahweh deserves the central place in Israel's worship and in its memory because it is Yahweh who, like no other, works for justice in human life, all the while pouring out mercy and compassion on the people. Justice and compassion are but two sides of the same coin, as the Old Testament affirms over and over again. The earlier call to remember is actualized here in the reference to Moses (v. 7) and to the people of Israel of earlier generations. The manner in which the appeal to memory is once more struck and is placed between the two verses that contain the psalm's ultimate expressions about God is but one more means of emphasizing the power and importance of tradition in the life of faith.

To go beyond such statements about God as those in vs. 6 and 8 is difficult, but the psalmist attempts to amplify these by means of two time-tested rhetorical devices, negation and analogy. Yahweh is one who will *"not* always accuse," will *not* "keep his anger forever," "does *not* deal with us" as our sins would suggest we be dealt with (vs. 9–10). Moreover, Yahweh's love is as great "as the heavens are high," Yahweh distances our sins from us "as far as the east is from the west"—all because Yahweh loves the people "as a father has compassion for his children" (vs. 11–13). All these efforts boil down to the affirmation that, in coming to terms with God, logic fails and language proves ultimately impotent.

What is left is praise. And so, "Bless the LORD, O my soul!"

2 Corinthians 3:1–6

From time to time it is appropriate for the church to stop and reflect on its ministry—who it is and how its life and activities are mandated by the gospel. Individual Christians have particular careers and contexts (such as home, workplace, school, voting booth) where they respond to the call of God and live out their vocations, but the church also has a corporate vocation and ministry, which from time to time need reaffirmation. The reading for this Sunday from 2 Corinthians provides such an opportunity.

While the assigned lesson includes only 2 Cor. 3:1–6, the nature of Paul's argument forces the interpreter to include the preceding section, reaching back to 2:14, where the reflection on the ministry of the new covenant really begins. Paul speaks about his own apostolic vocation, no doubt in the face of detractors who advocate a spiritual leadership contrary to his own, and yet the consistent use of the plural "we" enables us to find a word here for the church. What Paul says about the ministry he exercises together with his colleagues is appropriate for the ministry of every Christian community. The rich images of the text—a victory parade, fragrance, huckstering, and letters of recommendation—offer vivid pictures to spur the reflection.

First, the church has a critical role to play. Its ministry has a decisive (and even divisive) function. It gives forth a "fragrance that comes from knowing [Christ]," which turns out to be life for some but death for others (2:14–16). That may not be a welcome word, since we all like to be accepted and naturally shrink from the prospect of a rejected ministry. No one wants to be "a fragrance from death to death." The truth of the matter, however, is that the church is the bearer of a message that does not command universal acknowledgment. Some find the gospel of the crucified Christ to be foolish or offensive; for others it is the wisdom and power of God (see 1 Cor. 1:18–2:5).

Perhaps it is just at this point that the church is most at risk. It faces the temptation of hucksterism, of being "peddlers of God's word," of the cheapening of its ministry for its own gain, of the subtle accommodating of the message to make it more palatable. The church inevitably struggles with modifications that might remove the gospel's scandal and enable a more widely successful ministry. How it responds determines whether it retains its decisive role.

Paul knows of such temptations and goes on, in the second place, to speak of the ministry of the church as oriented to and receiving its sufficiency from God. In fact, the God-language throughout the passage is arresting. "We are the aroma of Christ to God" (2:15); "we speak . . . as persons sent from God and standing in his presence" (v. 17); "our competence is from God" (3:5). God represents not only the source of the church's energy, but also is the One to whom it is ultimately accountable.

On the one hand, an awareness of such an accountability helps to set priorities, to expose some activities as trivial and others as essential. What keeps the church honest is its sensitivity to the divine Presence. Transparency before God results in "persons of sincerity" (2:17), a community candid with itself, guileless, open.

On the other hand, an awareness of God as the source of its capabilities in turn energizes the church, frees it from a constant measuring of its own resources or lack thereof, and empowers it for the life it has to live. As it finds itself confronted by a host of imposing forces, the church is bound to join with Paul in asking, "Who is sufficient for these things?" (2:16). It can also share in his affirmation, "Our competence is from God" (3:5).

Finally, the ministry of the church is the ministry of the new covenant (3:6). To be sure, there is in the Pauline letters an acknowledgment of the continuity between the old and the new, between Moses and Christ, between the Jewish scriptures and the New Testament. But here the stress falls on the discontinuity, on the radically new world inaugurated in the gospel, on the life-giving presence of the Spirit.

The church is not a community that has arrived. Its struggles are not over, nor have its efforts to minister to the gospel in an indifferent or hostile world become easy. But it does live out of the future. It lives in the confidence that the Spirit is the foretaste of what God ultimately has in view. More than once the contrast is drawn between the letter that kills and the Spirit that gives life. One is a power that enslaves, the other a power that liberates. It is that liberating, life-giving Presence that buoys the church, enables it to resist the pressure to accommodate the gospel, and frees it to be "a fragrance from life to life."

Mark 2:13-22

In Mark 2:1–3:6, conflict between Jesus and the Pharisees moves increasingly into the open. The scribes' "questioning in their hearts" (2:6) gives way to public questioning and finally to conspiracy. This lection, which consists of three brief scenes (2:13-14, 15-17, 18-20) and two attached sayings (2:21-22), both characterizes Mark's understanding of the opposition to Jesus and portrays concerns close to the heart of Jesus' message.

A crucial problem for preaching this or any other controversy passage is how to speak about the opponents of Jesus, frequently the Pharisees. Too often the temptation is to purchase an enhanced portrait of Jesus by depicting his opponents in unrelentingly negative terms. The assumption that Pharisees were petty, legalistic, and hypocritical reinforces current severe problems in relations between Christians and Jews. While a sermon is not the right time for a lecture about the "historical Pharisees," silence about the Pharisees allows deeply entrenched stereotypes about first-century Judaism (and, indeed, contemporary Judaism) to go unchallenged.

One way to deal with this problem without overemphasizing it is to note that these stories center very much on the nature of Jesus' practice and his interpretation of that practice. They are about Jesus rather than about the Pharisees. The Pharisees come into the stories almost entirely as foils for Jesus, which means that reading the stories as accurate descriptions of the Pharisees is a little like inviting a political candidate to write a promotional piece for her opponent—what will follow will surely be jaundiced. When the Pharisees ask why Jesus eats with "tax collectors and sinners," they are in essence asking why he does not follow their practice. Similarly, when the question arises why Jesus' disciples do not fast, the answer is obvious: Jesus' disciples are not Pharisees! The questions are raised in order that Jesus' teaching can become the centerpiece.

Perhaps Jesus' answers, like his practice, would have offended Pharisees and other Jews as well, but those same answers will also offend many Christians! The call of Levi and the dinner that follows show Jesus deliberately including those who are outside the boundaries of the "good" community—tax collectors and sinners. And Jesus issues both invitations without asking those people to repent! Despite the general call to repentance in 1:15, Jesus does not demand repentance of Levi or set conditions on those with whom he shares table fellowship. Sinners are included qua sinners.

Does this mean, as one reading of 2:17 might suggest, that Jesus does *not* come for the healthy or the righteous, that they are actually excluded? That seems highly unlikely; the force of those sayings is on including those who are in need (the sick, the sinners), not on excluding those who might be regarded as healthy. On the other hand, the context in which these sayings appear gives them an ironic tone. Those who are healthy, those who are righteous, have no need of being included by Jesus, for they already stand included. Who exactly are these healthy, righteous people? Are they the Pharisees, the scribes, the religious establishment? The sayings become a mirror placed before those who understand themselves to be righteous, a mirror that reveals something other than the image anticipated. (A side-glance at Ps. 14 and Rom. 3 might be in order.)

Immediately following these stories regarding the call of tax collectors and sinners come Jesus' sayings about fasting, the bridegroom, patches, and wineskins. Each of these sayings has a strongly eschatological flavor to it. John the Baptist's disciples fast in anticipation of the arrival of the Messiah, but Jesus' disciples do not fast because they understand that the Messiah is at hand. In the same way, the bridegroom's friends do not fast during the brief period in which he is with them.

The two pieces of proverbial wisdom in 2:21–22 move in the same direction. A new patch and an old garment are incompatible. New wine and old wineskins are incompatible. Neither of these sayings reflects negatively on the old garment or the old wineskins. What is at stake is not so much a qualitative comparison as an assertion of the radical incompatibility of the kingdom of God and the world's "game" as played by the usual rules.

By placing stories about the inclusion of sinners *next to* sayings about the eschatological character of Jesus' ministry, Mark interprets each in light of the other. The radical inclusion of sinners is a sign of the nearness of the kingdom. The kingdom itself is characterized by the inclusion of those who have remained on the outside.

Another theme plays quietly in 2:18–22, an ominous theme

signaling the passion of Jesus. "When the bridegroom is taken away" points ahead to the crucifixion, when Jesus is taken away from the disciples. Similarly, the tear in the garment and the bursting of the wineskins foreshadow not only Jesus' death but the rift that will ensue. The first explicit reference to plots to destroy Jesus follows shortly, in 3:6. The theme of Jesus' passion soon dominates Mark's story, but it is not silent even here.

Last Sunday After Epiphany

(Transfiguration Sunday)

The Transfiguration of the Lord, although celebrated in the season after Pentecost (August 6) in the Roman Catholic and Episcopal traditions, is observed on the last Sunday before the beginning of Lent by many Protestants. In this manner it serves as a point of transition from Epiphany (and the celebration of Christ's self-disclosure to the world) to Lent (and the commemoration of our Lord's passion). It is an occasion of wonder and awe over the revelation of the person of God in Jesus Christ.

The lection from 2 Kings, which is the account of Elijah's transfiguration and assumption, is drenched with light. The terror of the moment, occasioned both by the translation of Elijah and by Elisha's fear of an uncertain future, is balanced by a sensation of great joy. The God who works so mightily cannot be one who does wrong. Therefore both Elisha and the company of the prophets marvel over what their eyes see and what their hearts are barely bold enough to believe.

Psalm 50 sings of a God who "shines forth" and who is "a devouring fire." It is not clear what great event in Israel's life has called forth this powerful poem—some deliverance in battle, perhaps, or from a natural catastrophe. But the event itself takes a back seat to the God whose impulses have been seen and felt so strongly in the life of the people. This is no ordinary god, but "Yahweh, the God of gods." And Israel is no ordinary people, but God's "faithful ones," who are bound to their partner in covenant by absolutely indissoluble bonds.

Paul also writes of light and glory in the passage appointed from 2 Corinthians. Christ has shone "out of darkness" and "in our hearts." In the face of Jesus Christ is found "the light of the knowledge of the glory of God." In other words, that which the ancient prophet and psalmist experienced in the life of Israel-of-old has now been given new and unparalleled expression in Jesus Christ. The world will resist this new light from God, for there are those whose minds are "blinded." But nothing will extinguish this "light of the gospel of the glory of Christ."

The Gospel lection is, of course, Mark's account of Jesus' transfiguration, that polar text around which the other texts for this day revolve. The terror and the joy of this unique moment in Jesus' life, and in that of the disciples, pulses through the Markan narrative, with its strong implications for the life that the Christian individual is to live on this and every day.

2 Kings 2:1-12

Elijah is a larger-than-life figure in the lore of Israel. He stands alongside Moses as the preeminent theological figure in Israel's memory. His life is so laden with numinous power that he is regarded not only as a dominating figure from the past, but as a carrier of Israel's faith and life into the future (see Mal. 4:5-6; Mark 8:28; Luke 1:17).

The crisis of the narrative is the transfer of leadership from one generation to the next, when the great man dies and his disciple is to continue his work. There is enormous anxiety about the "successor." Can he function in a comparable way? Will he have authority? Will he have power? How is this power to be transmitted from the leader, so manifestly powerful, to the successor, who as yet has none of the signs of power?

The narrative account of the transfer of power and authority is cast as an epiphany, as a transcendent, visionary presentation of transformation that is filled with sublime power and numinality.

In the preliminary scene (2 Kings 2:1-8), the narrative portrays the close connection between Elijah and Elisha, and the utter, unqualified devotion the disciple has to his master.

The primary transaction is the exchange between the two of them. Three times the master commands the disciple to remain behind (vs. 2, 4, 6), and three times the disciple refuses. In these three responses, Elisha uses the term "leave" ('*zb*), that is, abandon. It is as though "abandonment" is on the mind of Elisha, so that he clings dependently to Elijah. While he denies his upcoming abandonment of Elijah, perhaps he himself fears his own abandonment when Elijah departs. The dialogue moves in three stages from Bethel, to Jericho, to the Jordan, that is, in progressive stages down to the wilderness. The wilderness is the untamed place where odd, wondrous events may occur, because life has not yet been regimented by human control (see Luke 3:2; 4:1).

The departure becomes a context for passionate solidarity. It is as though Elisha is reconciled to the loss of his master but wants to delay that loss as long as possible. Finally, the departure is signaled by the crossing of the Jordan by the two of them "on dry ground"! No wonder Luke 9:31 (in the Greek), in portraying the transfiguration of Jesus, refers to the event as "exodus," for this is a departure echoing the one of the leaving from Egypt. Thus the phrase "dry ground" clearly means to allude to that ancient miracle of the exodus, which now is replicated.

Only now do we come to the final good-bye (vs. 9–12). Elijah must discern how anxious and fearful Elisha is. So he asks, in effect, "Is there anything I can give you to reassure you?" Elisha has a response ready at hand. He knows exactly what is needed. He does not ask for a mantle or for any other material object, even for any insignia of power or authority. He asks rather for "two times your spirit." The narratives of Elijah have shown the prophet to be a man visited by God's *rûaḥ*, filled with dangerous, undomesticated power and authority. That "spirit"—no maudlin or sentimental religious property—gave him the power to intervene in situations of death to bring life (1 Kings 17:17–24), to confront kings and destabilize established power (1 Kings 21:1–24), to engage rival gods in order to enact the truth of the God of Israel (1 Kings 18–19). Indeed, it is the *rûaḥ* of Yahweh that makes Elijah a larger-than-life character, able to stalk the earth in transformative ways, with no hint of self-serving advancement. And now Elisha, who has seen this uncommon capacity in Elijah, asks for such unconventional power for himself, that he may continue this odd way in the world, a way that concretely and daringly enacts the reality of God in the world of royal power.

Elijah responds with as much assurance as he can give (v. 10). His capacity to reassure, however, is limited. The *rûaḥ* is not his to assign or guarantee. The most Elijah can do is to offer a chance for the spirit, and a test of it.

Finally, the "taking" of Elijah is enacted (v. 11; see vs. 1, 3, 5). It is an event of wonder unrivaled in the Bible, though see Gen. 5:24 on Enoch. The "ascension" is not explored by the narrator or commented on. It is a "whirlwind" (*sĕʿārāh*; see Job 38:1), that is, an inexplicable, inscrutable event freighted with power and meaning. Elisha watches this strange event and cries out (v. 12). His cry is one of bereavement, now facing the abandonment he has tried so hard to avoid. But his cry is also one of devotion and celebration, acknowledging that Elijah has been and continues to be the power of Israel, the one who stands outside all forms of power and yet possesses

LAST SUNDAY AFTER EPIPHANY

power for life. Elisha's loss is great. His affirmation about Elijah is even greater.

Elisha is left alone, without his "father," Elijah (v. 12). Elisha is in dismay, so poignantly that he tears his garments in grief at his loss. He is left alone, and now he has become the point man for Yahweh. He is now required to work transformative deeds and to stand boldly against entrenched power, as is evident in the narratives that follow.

The text says, "He could no longer see him" (v. 12). The phrasing "no longer" (*'ôd*) suggests that he has indeed seen! Elijah had made seeing him the criterion for being granted twice Elijah's spirit (v. 10). Because Elisha has seen, we know he has received a double measure of prophetic *rûah*. This is indeed a tale of power, of transformation, of transfiguration. The dependent one is now authorized. The fearful one is now emboldened.

Psalm 50:1–6

There are certain moments in life that cannot be replicated in any predictable manner, occasions of unusual emotional or intellectual content which, because of their singularity, invariably surprise us. An experience of sudden and unexpected liberation is an example, or a flash of insight into some complex and heretofore unfathomed set of issues. Sadly, these moments are not always positive in nature, and even dark events may suddenly intrude to shock and numb us. Yet those unprogrammed concurrences of emotional and mental trajectories are essentially affirmative; because of their power to change our lives for the better, they are treasured in our memories, to be savored over and again. And, since we do not know when such an experience will recur, if ever, we systematize our memories, according special significance to certain times at which we recall with joy the extraordinary event that is lodged in our past.

The transfiguration of our Lord is such a time: irregular, unpredicted, not programmable. Yet our memories cherish the moment and appoint a special time for celebration.

Ancient Israel enjoyed similar experiences, and there are scholars who believe that Ps. 50 was written for use in Israel's worship on some occasion that recalled an irregular inbreaking of God's mercy into the life of the nation. One suggestion is that the occasion was one appointed for the purpose of remembering the bestowal of a covenant relationship upon Israel by Yahweh. If so, vs. 3 and 6 may be references to the theophany that accompanied the giving of the commandments to Moses on Mt. Sinai (Ex. 19). Another possibility is that this poem comes out of some liturgy involving the enthronement or reenthronement of Israel's (or Judah's) king, evidence for which may be the regal and judicial language that describes Israel's God (vs. 1, 6). However those things may be, although the body of the psalm (vs. 7-21) rings to the utterances of Israel's prophets, the introduction to the whole (vs. 1-6) clearly describes a theophany, an encounter with the living God that shocks and dazzles Israel.

The mood of the text is set in v. 1. Another manner of translating the opening line is "Yahweh, the God of gods, speaks . . . ," and this God-like-no-other commands the universe to its outermost boundaries. There is no word for "universe" in ancient Hebrew (the nearest equivalent is "heaven and earth"), but clearly Old Testament writers understood that Yahweh was the Lord of all creation. Had they but known how vast and how filled with mystery the universe is, how much greater would have been their awe. This God, who is the master of the sun and of light itself, shines in a special way "out of Zion," that is, from within the life of Israel (v. 2).

The God who comes is not a retiring deity (v. 3). In the book of Deuteronomy, Yahweh is termed "a devouring fire" when Moses recalls his own disobedience and warns Israel against the temptations of idolatry (4:24), and again when Israel is assured of protection against all its enemies in the Land of Promise (9:3). The sense of v. 3b, then, is that Yahweh is a God who brooks no evil. Verse 3c, however, seems to suggest that the very presence of Yahweh is enough to cause nature to tremble, as in Ps. 29:

> The voice of Yahweh is over the waters; . . .
> The voice of Yahweh breaks the cedars; . . .
> The voice of Yahweh flashes forth flames of fire.
> (Vs. 3, 5, 7)

Yet, as full of the sounds of fury as it is, the voice of Yahweh calls forth for a purpose, and that is to "judge his people" (v. 4). Again the universe is appealed to, in that all the elements of creation are summoned to stand as witness to the character of Yahweh. "The heavens above" and "the earth" testify that Yahweh's role in the life of Israel is that of judge. It is Yahweh who is appearing, and by means of that appearance distinction will be made between good and evil, between truth and falsehood, between right and wrong.

Yahweh the judge speaks in v. 5, and it becomes clear—if there were any doubts beforehand—that the special people of God are those who are bound to God by covenant. It is they who, because of their special relationship to God, bear special obligations of service and obedience (compare Amos 3:2). It is they, in particular, and by extension all of humankind, who stand before the coming King and Judge.

The section concludes as v. 6 repeats the thought of v. 4.

God has come into the life of the people. In a singular and perhaps never-to-be-repeated manner, God has stood with the people. And God's coming is remembered in liturgy and in song. In that which is regular and predictable, the cult, that which is irregular and astonishing is remembered. By this means even our ordinary days are transformed, because they are infused with the quality of the extraordinary. Since we cannot control or even predict that which has a will of its own, we treasure its memory and we anticipate its coming again. And by means of memory the old power flames forth again, to cleanse and to redeem.

2 Corinthians 4:3–6

Lay persons as well as preachers at times suffer from ecclesiastical burnout. The boredom of endless meetings, the routine of the same old faces and the same old conversations, the feeling of not being needed (or of being too heavily depended on), the changing configuration of their families, and a weariness with years of struggling push parishioners into sabbatical leaves. Often out of fatigue they take vacations from the church and its demands, without any intention of abandoning the faith. They just need a rest, they say.

What better time to address such a feeling of ecclesiastical burnout than Transfiguration Sunday, when the assigned texts speak of the majestic glory of God? And what better text to select than 2 Cor. 4:3–6, where Paul as a lay missionary speaks of the critical ministry placed in the hands of the church? Admittedly, Paul is not the writer to turn to if one is looking for a spiritual pat on the back, for a quick and easy word of affirmation. Affirmation is there, but only amid an honest admission of the difficulties in being a Christian in the world.

From as early as 2:14 the letter of 2 Corinthians roots the ministry of the church in the action of God. Such rootage enables one not to lose heart (3:4–6; 4:1, 7, 16) but to act with boldness (3:12). The antidote Paul offers to burnout is the divine mercy that engages persons in the activity of the gospel and leads to a guileless, open ministry (4:1–3).

The designated lection (4:3–6) provides a rationale for hope and confidence. But *first the text, with eyes wide open, lays out a realistic assessment of the church's mission.* The church faces real opposition, and the opposition is not some penny-ante group whose values are slightly skewed and who need only a new program to convince them to become believers. Using the language of apocalyptic conflict, the text indicts "the god of this world," who blinds the minds of people to prevent their seeing the splendor of Christ and to inhibit their response to the gospel.

It would be foolhardy to try to boost morale in the church by underestimating the force of the opposition. The gospel thrusts the church into a struggle of apocalyptic proportions. The battle may not always make the morning headlines or be carried on the evening news. Sometimes it amounts to only a side skirmish here and there. But the conflict is real. God has initiated the momentous encounter by striking the decisive blow in Jesus Christ, but the powers of this age have by no means capitulated, and their methods of response are cunning. They find clever ways to divert the minds of potential believers.

The realistic assessment of the mission is then followed by *a reaffirmation of the church's message and believers' place in it.* What the god of this age objects to is the declaration of Jesus' Lordship. It is a subversive declaration that challenges all other commitments and questions all other loyalties. More than simply a stereotypical confession of the liturgy, it gets to the heart of things, to the way time and money are budgeted, to how family life is ordered, to the social and political orientations one embraces. To preach "Jesus is Lord" is to move beyond the safe confines of religious talk and to confront the very deities that blind the minds of "those who are perishing."

Where are "we" in all this? "Ourselves as your slaves for Jesus' sake." It is somewhat surprising that the text does not read "ourselves as *Jesus'* slaves," which might logically follow from the confession. Instead, Paul's statement commits the church to being servants of one another and of the world, hardly an easy role to play. Confessing the Lordship of Jesus implicates one in a serving relationship to one's neighbors. In Paul's case, this meant conflicted and misguided Corinthians, many of whom stood in opposition to the very message he was preaching.

Finally, *the rationale for hope is brought to the level of personal experience.* The creator God, whose word pushed back the darkness and caused light to shine, has not retreated in the face of opposition, nor has God knuckled under to the blinding activity of the god of this age. Instead, God has shone "in our hearts" so that the veils are torn apart and the light of the divine glory is seen in Jesus Christ.

Verse 6 begins with a causative "for" (*hoti*), taking the reader behind the preaching and the service to the reason for engaging in the ministry in the first place. The face of Jesus mirrors the divine glory that now marks the new creation (in contrast to the fading glory of the old covenant, 3:13).

It is precisely in the midst of life, at times routine and at times fragile, that the divine splendor is known. The light shines—sometimes like the revolving beacon from the lighthouse, persistently searching the dark; at other times like the gradually strengthening rays at early dawn; sometimes no brighter than a flickering candle, at other times overwhelming in its brilliance. The same dazzling presence that Peter, James, and John experienced on the mountain (Mark 9:2–9) now illuminates human hearts, sustaining fatigued Christians and keeping them faithful.

Mark 9:2–9

The story of the transfiguration allows both the disciples and Mark's audience a glimpse of the true glory of Jesus. The divine voice at the baptism seems a distant memory, a memory dimmed by controversies and difficult teachings. Although words about future glory have been uttered (8:38–9:1), the persecution, passion, and death of Jesus lie close at hand. This moment of glory allows Mark's audience to recall the baptism and anticipate the final triumph of God's Son.

Glory aptly describes this scene, in which numerous features work together to dramatize the identification of Jesus with God's own majesty. Location itself provides the first clue that some special revelation is at hand, for a "high mountain" recalls the commission of Moses on Mt. Horeb and the giving of the Torah on Sinai. The sudden and unexplained brightness of Jesus' clothing signals the presence of God or God's agent, as in Dan. 7:9, where the Ancient One is depicted in clothing "white as snow," or in the accounts of Jesus' resurrection and ascension (see Matt. 28:3; Mark 16:5; Luke 24:4; John 20:12; Acts 1:10). Whiteness here connotes a light not accessible to human beings. The appearance of Moses and Elijah not only exceeds the limits of what is usually thought possible but also connects Jesus with two of Israel's major prophetic figures. The overshadowing cloud recalls the divine presence in the cloud of the exodus and at Sinai (Ex. 24:15–18). Anyone with even the faintest knowledge of Israel's history would recognize the divine glory being ascribed here to Jesus of Nazareth.

Despite the literally dazzling character of this story, nothing in it should be particularly new or shocking for Mark's audience. Those who have read or heard from the beginning know already that Jesus is God's Son, they recall the descent of the Spirit and the heavenly voice at his baptism, they have read of his miracles and his teaching. The transfiguration may intensify their understanding, but it does not radically challenge it.

If Mark's readers learn nothing especially new here, the same cannot be said of Peter, James, and John, who did not witness the baptism. As often, Peter serves as the spokesman for the other disciples with his proposal to Jesus that we "make three dwellings, one for you, one for Moses, and one for Elijah." Lest we miss the ludicrous nature of the remark, the narrator explains that Peter "did not know what to say." Peter's attempt to commemorate the occasion, however well intended, reduces the event to a photo opportunity. It also contrasts sharply with his earlier rejection of Jesus' prediction about his own passion (8:31-33). Peter rejects the suffering that lies ahead, but he is all too eager to welcome the glory!

At precisely this point, the heavenly voice speaks words similar to those at the baptism, but with a significant difference. Earlier, the voice had announced, "You are my Son, the Beloved; with you I am well pleased," addressing Jesus and focusing on God's pleasure in and with him. Here, however, the voice announces, "This is my Son, the Beloved; listen to him!" The voice identifies Jesus directly to the disciples and commands that the disciples listen.

The importance of listening becomes clear by contrast with the scene that has preceded it, in which everything is visual. The disciples *see* the transfiguration of Jesus, the whiteness of his clothing, the appearance of Elijah and Moses alongside him, the cloud that overshadows them. After the voice speaks, they look around and *see* only Jesus. Nothing is wrong with what the disciples have witnessed, except that they have not yet listened and heard what Jesus has said to them, so they are not ready to understand what they have seen.

Jesus' transfiguration not only recalls the heavenly voice at his baptism and anticipates his triumphant Parousia; it calls the disciples to listen to Jesus as well as watch his deeds. The need to listen emerges at least as early as the parable of the sower in ch. 4, which admonishes "anyone with ears to hear" to listen (vs. 9, 23), and which urges the disciples to "pay attention to what you hear" (v. 24). Because they did not hear, they could not understand the first Passion prediction (8:31). Neither will they understand the second (9:31) or third (10:33-34), as their responses plainly indicate.

What the disciples (and Mark's audience) need to understand is that Jesus is both the Son of God, powerful agent of healing and subject of dazzling glory, and the Son of Man, who will be betrayed and persecuted and crucified. The disciples, in common with many Christians throughout the church's life, want to have the glory that they can see without the message that they must hear, but the two cannot be separated. Over and over Mark lifts up both aspects of Jesus' identity, relentlessly recalling that the suffering will yield to triumph, but that the triumph cannot be had without the price of the cross. Mark's telling of that story once again at the transfiguration has an almost comic tinge to it, as Peter proposes to erect commemorative buildings, but the combination of glory and suffering lies at the heart of Mark's Gospel.

Ash Wednesday

In ancient Israel the symbolism of ashes was understood to be a forceful reminder of the pervasiveness of human sin and of the inevitability of human death. Ashes represented that which, in the human experience, was burned out and wasted, that which once was but is no more. This traditional emblem of grief and mourning has been adopted by the Christian church as a signal of our own sinful mortality; it has also been embraced as a muted trumpet to warn us of the coming dark days in Jesus' life: his passion and death.

The texts for this day are true to the ominous quality the observance is intended to convey. Yet they also point forward—again, in keeping with the character of Ash Wednesday—to the redemptive power of God's grace.

The Joel lection is an alarm bell in the darkness of the night. The crisis is not specified nor is it described in any type of detail, but there is no mistaking its urgency. Those who are caught in this terrible moment cannot hope to save themselves, for they are basically powerless to do anything on their own behalf. They are powerless to do anything, that is, except to repent and to open themselves to God's intervening mercy.

Psalm 51 is a classic (some might say *the* classic) piece of literature that captures the faithful man or woman of God in the act of throwing him- or herself open to God's mercy. The poet is convinced of the personal and profound manner in which he or she has offended God and shattered a relationship that God intended to be warmly intimate. In casting him- or herself on God's grace, the poet not only acknowledges God's role as the unique savior of faithful people, but acknowledges as well the inevitable result of God's intervention: a changed and redirected life.

Paul is acutely aware of the dark power of sin and mortality, as he writes to the Corinthian Christians. Yet the apostle understands that God shares the concern of faithful people over these issues, and he takes pains to point out that it is God, not we, who has taken the initiative to set matters right. Jesus Christ is the one who, by the mercy of God, has been appointed the agent of our reconciliation with God. This present moment is the *kairos* time. "Now is the day of salvation."

The lection from Matthew's record of the Sermon on the Mount is, on its surface, an extended warning against false and manipulative piety. But, at a deeper level, the passage is a declaration that God responds in mercy to the faithfulness of those who attempt to do God's will. Just how the faithful will "receive their reward" is not described, but the strong implication is that a large part of their fulfillment is bound up in their sense of engagement with the ongoing purposes of God.

Joel 2:1–2, 12–17 (A B C)

This text plunges the listener into a crisis. We know almost nothing about the historical setting of Joel. For that reason, it is impossible to identify the historical allusions of the poetry. It is enough to see that this text is a *summons to emergency* that is visible, public, and close at hand. The text is organized around two summonses to "Blow the trumpet in Zion." The first of these identifies the crisis (v. 1). The second requires a response to the crisis (v. 15).

The crisis is announced as urgent (vs. 1–2). The imperative at the beginning invites the sentry to sound a general alarm in Jerusalem. Read theologically, the trouble approaching the city is the "day of Yahweh," which comes as awesome, dreadful, irresistible threat. The crisis is that God has become an enemy attacker against God's own city and God's own people. Read militarily, the attack is a "great and powerful army" (v. 2). That is, the poem describes a military invasion.

We are not told, on the one hand, why God is attacking. On the other hand, we are not told who this great and powerful people is, or why they come. What matters for our reading of the text is that the hostility of God and the reality of human threat are spoken of in the same breath, that is, they are identical. This is not mere human politics, and it is not supernaturalist "scare theology." It is a genuinely human and immediate threat, rooted in and authorized by the will of God.

The poem is an invitation to imagine the city under deep assault. The poem intends to awaken a complacent, unnoticing citizenry to its actual situation, to evoke in it an intentional and urgent response.

The poem drives the listener to ask, "What then shall we do?" (compare Luke 3:10; Acts 2:37). That is the central question of concerned people in the midst of a crisis.

The answer to this implicit question is given: "Blow the trumpet in Zion" (v. 15). This trumpet, unlike that of v. 1, is not a warning. It is, rather, the signal for a response of profound, serious religion: authorize a fast, provide a meeting. The response urged to the military crisis wrought by God is an act of deep religious intentionality, an act of disciplining what is left from a shattered complacency, an act of obedience that breaks off all easy indifference. The community must come to its senses and honestly embrace its true situation. And that can be done only in a meeting that counters all "business as usual."

The "revision of reality" (repentance) urged by the poem is not a set of religious exercises. It is, rather, a deliberate act of re-presenting one's self vis-à-vis God, the same God who is invading the city. The summons to "return" and to "rend" (vs. 12–13) suggests that Jerusalem has forgotten who God is. When God is forgotten or distorted, society is inevitably, commensurately distorted and disordered. Thus the beginning point for rescue is to rediscern God. The rediscernment of God in v. 13 quotes one of Israel's oldest creeds, which voices the distinctiveness of Israel's God (Ex. 34:6–7).

Clearly Jerusalem has forgotten God's utter fidelity. When God's fidelity is jettisoned, human relations become unfaithful and society disintegrates. Thus the purpose of religious discipline is to remember who God really is, what is promised by God, and what is required for God.

This is an odd and suggestive text for Lent. This text plunges Lent (and us) into dangerous public reality. The text does not require dramatic overstatement of crisis, nor "hellfire and damnation."

It is clear to any observer, nonetheless, that our old, trusted, known world is under deep assault. AIDS and "crack" are only surface symptoms of a deathly sickness common to us all. That deep illness may be our counterpart to the invasion pictured in the text.

The "returning" and "rending" to which we are invited is the hard work of rediscerning God, and then making the responses—theological, socioeconomic, political, and personal—that are congruent with God's character. Lent is the reflective occasion out of which fresh discernments of reality may come. When we do not emulate God's mercy and faithfulness in the world, we are invaded by the power of death, which may take many forms. Either we turn in order to live, or we resist the choice and we die. Ash Wednesday is for renoticing our true situation, in the world and before God.

Psalm 51:1–17 (A B C)

Psalm 51 is the classic statement of repentance from the Old Testament Psalter, and so deeply has it shaped the language of confession in both Jewish and Christian communities that its very cadences often echo in synagogue and in church when worshipers address in a corporate fashion their sinfulness before God. The psalm is no less powerful a vehicle for expressing the individual's sense of sin as one makes private confession. Thus its inclusion as an Ash Wednesday lection seems almost mandatory.

The superscription relates the psalm to the terrible incident in which David seduces or rapes (the text is ambiguous) Bathsheba, the wife of Uriah the Hittite, only to be rebuked by the prophet Nathan (2 Sam. 11–12). Yet the text of the psalm itself is lacking any detail that would reinforce that claim. In fact, it is the very universality of the psalm's language about sin that has allowed it to speak to the widest possible variety of human experiences.

The language of the psalm suggests that its author was a priest, well rehearsed in the cultic vocabulary. For example, when the poet prays, "Cleanse me from my sin" (v. 2), the verb that is chosen (*ṭāhēr*) is one that frequently appears in the Priestly literature of the Old Testament to describe cultic or liturgical activity (Lev. 12:7, 8; 14:20). Another example: the reference to hyssop (v. 7) recalls other Old Testament texts in which this plant was used as a liturgical purgative (Lev. 14:4; Num. 19:6). Yet, amazingly, the cultic acts of confession and absolution do not lie at the core of the psalmist's concern, as Ps. 51:15–17 take great pains to point out. What is of greatest importance is the transformation of the worshiper. A "clean heart," a "right spirit" (v. 10), and a "contrite heart" (v. 17) are qualities most closely associated with God's salvation. What happens to the person is infinitely more important than what happens in the cult.

Psalm 51:1–12 exhibits many of the characteristics common to psalms of individual lament. Verses 1–2 constitute a kind of salutation in which the object of the petition is named ("O God" of v. 1), yet the most urgent phrases are those in which the psalmist pleads for redemption. Notice the four imperatives: "Have mercy," "blot out," "wash me thoroughly," and "cleanse me" (vs. 1–2). The basis on which the psalmist is so bold as to claim God's forgiveness is specifically mentioned: God's "steadfast love" (*ḥesed*) and "mercy" (v. 1).

Having set the agenda, the psalmist lays bare his soul in the subsequent section (vs. 3–5), confessing his sin with profound honesty. Several characteristics of the poet's sinfulness are made evident: (1) The poet's sense of sin is haunting in that he cannot escape it (v. 3). (2) Whatever damage the author's sinful deeds may have done to other human beings, the primary offense is against God (v. 4). Although NRSV correctly reflects the Hebrew text here, "you alone" should not be read as intending to imply that humans do not sin against one another, for there are a number of Old Testament texts that state clearly that they do (see 1 Sam. 26:21). The statement apparently means that, even when other people suffer because of human wrongdoing, all sin is basically an affront to God. (3) Sin is a universal and deeply rooted part of human nature (Ps. 51:5).

In the third section (vs. 6–12), the psalmist returns to the plea for God's redeeming presence that characterized vs. 1–2. (Verse 6 offers special problems in translation and interpretation, for it is not entirely clear to what "inward being" [the Hebrew word is a very rare term—*tuhôt*—apparently related to a verb meaning "to spread over"] and "secret heart" [Hebrew, "that which has been closed"] refer.) Although, as mentioned above, some of the language here is cultic, the primary focus is on the change that takes place within the individual as a result of God's redemptive activity. "Joy and gladness" (vs. 8, 12) characterize the outlook of the forgiven sinner, as do a "clean heart" and a "willing spirit" (vs. 10, 12) and an awareness of God's immediacy (v. 11).

A final section (vs. 13–17) brings the sequence of confession and restoration to an important climax, in that here the promise is made that salvation results in a changed and renewed individual. The psalm is insistent that to be forgiven is not to return to some status quo ante, to some level of consciousness where we resided before our experience of grace. Rather, to be forgiven is to be changed. It is to slough off the old and put on the new—to exchange the heart of despair for a heart of service of God. The climax to our psalm is vs. 13–14, which proclaim, in so many words: "When you have come into my life, O God, that life will never again be the same."

The distinctive place that this psalm has found in the literature of confession is the result not only of its beauty, but also of the relevance of its language, which enables it to speak to and for all varieties of sin-oppressed persons. What is more, it has claimed a home in so many hearts because it recognizes a crucial reality about the task of coming to terms with our sin, and that is, that apart from the grace of God we are absolutely incapable of dealing with the pervasiveness of human evil. It is not until we recognize our own finitude and corruption before God (v. 17) that we receive empowerment from the One who forgives and redeems.

2 Corinthians 5:20b–6:10 (A B C)

Contemporary Christians sometimes look back to the early days in the church's life with rose-tinted glasses. That period seems to have been inhabited by believers who were filled with zeal, who knew the necessity of evangelism, who had the advantages of a new and innocent faith. Read with care, Paul's letters reveal another side to the story, one in which there are conflicts, struggles, and misunderstandings. In the present passage, Paul pleads with baptized Christians, people whom he elsewhere characterizes as being "in Christ" and belonging to the "body of Christ," to become reconciled to God. The need for reconciliation is inherent in the Christian faith—it is not a symptom of degeneracy in the latter days of the church's life.

Set against the other texts assigned for Ash Wednesday (for example, Ps. 51) and other reflections on the need for reconciliation between God and humankind, 2 Cor. 5 sounds a distinctive note. Here human beings do not cry out to God for forgiveness and reconciliation, for it is God who seeks reconciliation. In the sending of Jesus Christ, God acts to reconcile the world to God (5:20a). Paul characterizes the gospel itself as God's making an appeal to human beings to be reconciled to God (5:20; 6:1). Consistent with Paul's comments elsewhere (Rom. 1:18–32), the point he makes here is that it is not God who must be appeased because of human actions; but human beings, who have turned away from God in rebellion, must accept God's appeal and be reconciled. Even in the face of the intransigence of human sin, it is God who takes the initiative to correct the situation; human beings have only to receive God's appeal.

The urgency of the appeal for this reception comes to the fore in 6:1–2. Without accepting God's reconciliation, the Corinthians will have accepted "the grace of God in vain." Moreover, the right time for this reconciliation is now: "Now is the acceptable time; see, now is the day of salvation!" This comment about time lays before the Corinthians the eschatological claim of the gospel. As in 5:16 ("from now on"), Paul insists that the Christ-event makes this appeal urgent. There is also, however, a very specific urgency that affects the Corinthian community. It is time—or past time—for them to lay aside their differences and hear in full the reconciling plea of God made through the apostles. Time is "at hand," (NRSV, near) both for the created order as a whole and for the Corinthians in particular.

Throughout the text, Paul asserts that it is God who brings about this reconciliation, but he also points to the role of Christ. God reconciles the world "in Christ," that is, by means of Christ. Specifically, God "made him to be sin who knew no sin" (5:21). To say that

Christ "knew no sin," consistent with Paul's understanding of sin as a state of rebelliousness against God, means that Christ was obedient to God, that Christ submitted to God's will. That God "made him to be sin" suggests, in keeping with Rom. 8:3 and Gal. 3:13, that Christ's death on the cross had redemptive significance. Through it human beings are enabled to "become the righteousness of God" (2 Cor. 5:21b); in Christ's death the reconciling act of God becomes concrete.

Paul's eloquent plea for reconciliation stands connected to comments on the ministry that he and his co-workers are exercising among the Corinthians. Throughout this entire portion of the letter (1:1–7:16), in fact, the focus is on both the nature of the gospel and the nature of the Christian ministry. That dual focus exists not simply because Paul is once more defending himself against his critics (although he certainly is defending himself!), but because the ministry can only be understood rightly where the gospel itself is understood rightly. Paul's ministry, like his gospel, has to do with reconciling human beings to God. In 6:3–10 he expands on that role, insisting that he and his colleagues have taken every measure that might enhance the faith and growth of believers in Corinth. Ironically, he begins his itemization of the things that commend him with a list of things that would certainly not impress many readers of a résumé or letter of recommendation—afflictions, hardships, calamities, beatings, imprisonments. . . . For those who see the gospel as a means of being delivered *from* difficulties rather than *into* difficulties, Paul's commendation of the ministry will have a very negative sound. As earlier in the letter, he insists on the contrast between how the apostles are viewed by the world and how they stand before God. If the world, with its standards of measure, regards them as impostors, unknown, dying, punished, those assessments matter not at all. Before God, the apostles know that they are in fact true, well known, alive, and rejoicing.

This aspect of the passage makes powerful grist for reflection for those engaged in Christian ministry today, but it is equally relevant for all Christians, especially on Ash Wednesday. The reconciliation God brings about in Jesus Christ obliges not only ordained ministers but all Christians to proclaim the outrageous, universal, reconciling love of God.

Matthew 6:1–6, 16–21 (A B C)

The Gospel text for Ash Wednesday provides a formidable context for the self-reflection and piety characteristic of the Lenten season. The text focuses not so much on what Christians should pray for or what acts of service they should perform, as on the manner in which they are to do them. The introductory verse (Matt. 6:1) in a sense says it all, and yet the repetitive parallelism of the three examples cited (almsgiving, prayer, and fasting) carries a powerful effect beyond what a single verse can convey. The language in which the examples are described serves not only to reinforce the point, but to jar the reader a bit, to open the possibility for self-reflection about a matter like hypocrisy, which otherwise could easily be dismissed.

The passage *warns against a manipulative piety that, in effect if not by conscious design, is carried out for an audience other than God.* No one in his or her right mind sets out to be a hypocrite. It is not a planned activity. People are simply drawn into situations or habits whereby their practice of religion is meant to have an impact on others—on children, on fellow church members, on the broader community—until the need for human approval subtly becomes the idol to which worship is offered. The practice often becomes so conventional that the guilty would be surprised by the charge of hypocrisy. Part of the difficulty is this blindness to what is taking place and the fact that the religious establishment tends to thrive on the social pressures that nurture such piety.

The literary structure of the passage and its hyperbolic language, as the commentators note, serve to get the reader's attention. The three examples are given in a parallel pattern, and in each case an antithesis is set up: either sounding a trumpet when giving alms or not letting the left hand know what the right hand is doing; either praying on the street corners or in the closet at home; either parading the fact that one is fasting or disguising it. No doubt most readers would judge their own intentions and actions to be somewhere in between the extremes, but the very sharply stated polarities serve as a lens through which to clarify the ambiguities. The obscure and provisional areas are brought into focus. The alternatives present the opportunity to view one's existence afresh and to detect the dangerous tendency toward hypocrisy.

It is critical that the interpreter recognize the hyperbolic character of the language and not turn the examples into new laws. The passages do not outlaw public prayer or pledging to congregational appeals. Neither do they sanction one's boasting about praying only in the closet. Instead, they function to warn Christians about the natural tendency to use religious exercises for ulterior purposes, to engage in a piety that for whatever reason seeks social approval.

But there is a positive side to the examples cited. They *speak of God's responsiveness to a single-minded piety.* It is intriguing how frequently the notion of "reward" appears in the text. In the introductory verse (6:1), those who practice their piety to be seen by others have no reward from the Father. In the description of the three examples of ostentatious piety, it is conceded that they have a kind of reward, perhaps just the reward they are looking for, namely, that they are seen by others. In the antitheses, however, those engaged in acts of piety with integrity and wholeheartedness, oriented completely to God, will encounter a responsive Father. Three times the statement occurs, ". . . and your Father who sees in secret will reward you" (vs. 4, 6, 18).

We are not told about the nature of the divine reward. From other passages in Matthew one could speculate that the reward is the joy of the presence of God (25:21, 23), but here the issue is simply that God sees the piety practiced "in secret" and responds, in contrast to ignoring the piety done for show. The desperate need for engagement with God is satisfied when God is sought in candor and simplicity.

The concluding verses of the lesson (6:19–21) in a sense initiate a new section of the Sermon on the Mount, a section dealing with one's attitude toward material possessions (vs. 19–34). The antithetical parallelism of vs. 19–20, however, prolongs the sharp either/or choice that so dominates the previous section (vs. 1–6, 16–18). What are we to make of this uncompromising attitude toward money, over against the importance of saving a little for the rainy days? The extreme character of the antithesis leaves the church feeling a bit disquieted with the usual ways wealth is valued and turns a searchlight on the practice of how people earn and spend their money. No concrete answers are offered. The text seems more interested in where the heart is: Is it bound up with a search for security vulnerable to various forms of decay, or is it engaged in a pursuit of God's will?

First Sunday in Lent

None of the readings for the First Sunday in Lent has a direct connection with the penitential themes of the season; nevertheless, each takes on a particular coloration when read in the context of preparation for Good Friday and Easter.

God's covenant with Noah and his family reaffirms God's faithfulness to all creatures, in that God promises never again to "destroy all flesh" because of its sinfulness. Human repentance and contrition occur within the framework of that covenant. That is to say, when the penitence of women and men takes place, they can be confident of their ongoing relationship with God. Whatever the consequence of human sin, it cannot result in their final rejection, because God's word is sure.

Although the passage from Ps. 25 reflects a general sense of alienation, reading it during Lent connects it with the specific shame involved in the human rejection of God's Son and the specific need to understand the truth and salvation of God reflected in Jesus of Nazareth. The psalmist's prayer for forgiveness finds its most eloquent answer in the cross. And the psalmist's confidence in God's own righteousness finds its most powerful justification in Jesus.

First Peter reminds Christians that Christ's suffering has not only a salvific but also a paradigmatic function. Just as Christ himself suffered for the doing of right, so believers must understand that their Christian faith may well lead to suffering. In common with other New Testament writings, 1 Peter does not affirm suffering as a good in and of itself or celebrate suffering, but the letter does recognize the inevitability of suffering, because Christians inevitably find themselves at odds with the world around them.

The Markan story of Jesus' wilderness sojourn also summons up the perils of discipleship. Jesus himself, whose powers over Satan and over nature Mark depicts in graphic terms later in the Gospel, is here subjected to the dangers of Satan and the wild beasts. If Mark does not make the explicit link between Jesus' sojourn and that of believers that 1 Peter makes between Jesus' suffering and that of believers, Mark nevertheless evokes in readers a powerful sense of identification with Jesus' wilderness period.

Genesis 9:8–17

The Old Testament readings for Lent are a series of texts that concern covenant. These texts are not in any special way related to one another, and a pattern must not be imposed on them. Nonetheless, the theme of covenant means that all these texts raise issues of fidelity, mutuality, and obedience.

The reading from Gen. 9:8–17 is an oracle in God's mouth, a decree about God's intention. The oracular text is situated just at the end of the Flood narrative, when Noah and his family have been rescued from destruction by the faithful sovereignty of God. The wonder of our text is that God's faithfulness to the family of Noah is not disrupted, even by the flood, which is the quintessential disruption of the Old Testament. Critical scholarship assigns this text to what is likely a sixth-century source (P), so that the context for the original hearing of this text was the exile, the quintessential disruption in the life of ancient Israel. Thus it is plausible to see that the exile is the historical experience of chaos narrated through the Flood account. (On the connection between *flood* and *exile*, see Isa. 54:9–10.)

God's initial utterance (vs. 8–10) focuses intensely on God's person and God's resolve: "As for me . . ." What is to follow is God's own peculiar, intentional, unilateral act. God claims complete initiative for the relationship. What God proposes to do is to "establish" a covenant. The verb *qûm* means to "raise up." Noah has no part in this new covenant, no role to play, and no obligation. The usual verb for covenant-making is "cut" (*krt*), but here there is no mutuality or reciprocity as there is in the verb "cut." The covenant is all God's doing, an act of amazing graciousness, the very self-giving of God.

The unilaterally established covenant is not only with the human community (now narrowly embodied in this family, the only earthly survivors), but also with all the creatures of the earth saved from the flood via the ark. This is the voice of the creator God, who enacts a bonding of loyalty with creation. Thus the speech of God suggests "new creation."

The most sweeping promise of the whole passage is v. 11, asserting that the flood will not be reenacted. The double use of "never again" (*lô' . . . 'ôd*) marks this promise as a fresh resolve on

God's part. That is, the speech admits that there has indeed been a massive destruction. It is, of course, possible to engage in casuistry about God's oath; for example, that God will not cause a flood, but God may cause other forms of destruction. Such a reading, however, would miss the point of the oracle. The assurance from God is not only about another flood. It is, rather, a pledge to creation by the Creator, a pledge of fidelity which will keep the world safe from every jeopardy. The rhetoric of this sweeping, unconditional promise is paralleled in Isa. 54:9–10 with the same "never again." The promise to exiles in Isa. 54 is a positive promise of steadfast love and covenant of peace, phrasing that expresses God's complete and unqualified solidarity with the community of exile. In this decree, the world has become a safe place, as the promise of Isa. 54 has made Israel a safe community.

The comprehensive promise of vs. 8–11 is briefly put. The larger part of our text concerns the supportive, interpretative "sign" of the rainbow. This section of the text is bracketed in vs. 12 and 17 by parallel statements that assert the comprehensiveness of the oath. The phrases "every living creature" in v. 12 and "all flesh" in v. 17 we may take as close synonyms. The scope of God's fidelity is as large as creation.

Between these bracketing verses, the "sign" that will witness to the reality of God's fidelity is the "bow." The "bow" is likely to be understood not in romantic ways, nor with an accent on political pluralism. Rather it likely refers to God's bow (and arrows) as a weapon of war, hostility, and destructiveness. That the bow is suspended in the sky means that God has made a gesture of disarmament, has hung up the primary weapon, and now has no intention of being an aggressor or adversary. That is, the demobilized weapon of God is a gesture of peace and reconciliation. God intends to be "at peace" with God's world, recalcitrant though it has been.

The bow as a suspended weapon is itself a significant gain. But it is even more important as a reminder to God. Twice God pauses to see it and remember (vs. 14, 16). The bow is not a message to humanity; it is rather an elemental reminder to God to be faithful and everlasting, as God has promised to be. This odd usage suggests two things about God. First, God has a propensity to forget the promises and needs to be reminded. This is consistent with the petitions of the psalms that God should remember and not forget (Ps. 9:12; 13:1; 25:6–7; 42:9; 74:2, 18–23; 77:9; 98:3; 106:4, 45). Moreover, several narrative texts indicate that when God remembers, gracious things happen in the world (see Gen. 19:29; 30:22; Ex. 2:24).

Second, when God forgets, God is likely to be negative and destructive, and only by the counterforce of mercy does God restrain the destructive inclination, in order to be conciliatory. Thus, the bow is not simply decorative. It is crucial in getting God to act on the basis of God's best self, pledged as God is to covenant.

When Israel sees the rainbow, Israel can reflect on God's response to it. It is this "sign" that causes God to have new generosity and new graciousness. The bow reminds exiles and survivors of many floods that the world is not under threat, because God's promise is as sure as the bow is visible. The bow is an invitation to "basic trust," for the world as God's creation is an utterly safe place.

Psalm 25:1–10

Heartache and alienation are such universal human experiences that many psalms from the liturgies of ancient Israel appear to have been composed, not for any specific occasion, but for use by any worshiper who felt himself or herself to be out of touch with God in "general," or for no particular reason whatsoever. Psalm 25 seems to be such a prayer for any season of distress, in that there are no concrete references of any sort to relate this petition to a particular crisis of the spirit, other than the psalmist's sense of human sinfulness (v. 7; compare v. 11).

And why should there not be such hymns and prayers? Just as the people of God have felt the need to speak in self-revealing ways about their individual faults and offenses, so there is the need to speak of those ways by which each of us is joined to the other members of the human race through our shared sinfulness. Psalm 25 recognizes this need and provides the necessary words that permit the pray-er to acknowledge his or her sense of estrangement from God through the universal experience of human sin.

In a manner typical of a classic lament, the psalm begins with a statement that, at the same time, identifies the object of the prayer—Yahweh—and affirms that because the psalmist trusts Yahweh, there are grounds for hope (vs. 1, 2a). Although the configuration of the Hebrew is somewhat different, the manner in which the NRSV lays out the subsequent fourfold petition (vs. 2b–3) as four lines of poetry has considerable logic, in that it emphasizes the forcefulness of the petitioner's plea:

O my God, in you I trust;
  Do not let me be put to shame;

FIRST SUNDAY IN LENT

> Do not let my enemies exult over me.
> Do not let those who wait for you be put to shame;
> [But do] let them be ashamed who are wantonly treacherous.

This is nothing less than a plea for justice; it is nothing less than the cry, "Let what ought to be, be!"

A second cluster of petitions is framed in vs. 4–5, where the poet acknowledges a need for Yahweh's instruction. It is not entirely clear that the Torah is in mind here, but that is likely, since both "ways" and "paths" are elsewhere used as synonyms for Torah (Pss. 18:21; 119:15—translated "ways" in both instances in NRSV). But what is quite clear is that "ways" and "paths" are metaphors for "truth,"— "your truth," to be precise—and the centrality of the noun is rendered all the more obvious in that it is the focus of two verbs, "lead me" and "teach me." And in a manner that faithfully reflects the pattern in the Hebrew Bible, the NRSV positions the two verbs so that they lie one to each side of the noun, as if "truth" is bracketed by the need for sinful men and women to be brought to it. The truth of Yahweh is so compellingly important that "for you I wait all day long." (It should be observed, in passing, that this line may be a gloss, in that it disturbs the alphabetical order of the initial letters of the lines.)

Justice, then, and truth are the agenda of the psalmist, and to these are now added mercy and steadfast love. Verses 6 and 7 highlight these qualities, and, in a somewhat bold statement, Yahweh is admonished not to forget that these are qualities that characterize Yahweh's own life. "They have been from of old" does not mean that these qualities have some existence apart from Yahweh, but they have been reflected in Yahweh's deeds from the very beginning (compare NEB's translation here, "shown from ages past"). It is because Yahweh is merciful and constant in love that the psalmist claims the right of appeal, in cadences that echo Ps. 51:1.

Finally (for that part of the psalm that constitutes the lectionary text), the basic goodness and moral rectitude of Yahweh are affirmed, and because Yahweh is the kind of God Yahweh is, people of God are taught to be "good and upright" themselves (vs. 8–10). If there has been any doubt that vs. 4–5 have the Torah in mind, that doubt is lifted here, for the Hebrew verb "instructs," which is linked to "way" in v. 8, is *yôreh*, a cognate of *tôrāh*. And this connection is demonstrated again in the final line of v. 10, where "his covenant" and "his decrees" surely mean "his Torah" (compare Ps. 19:7). As the paths of Yahweh are steadfast love and faithfulness, so should they be the same "for those who keep his covenant and his decrees."

The bringing together in this passage of so many qualities by which Yahweh is known, as a means of making an important statement about the faith and moral commitment of the people of God, is reminiscent of the prophets. Indeed, the vocabulary of the psalmist here is profoundly reminiscent of Amos, Hosea, and others in the prophetic tradition who also emphasized justice, truth, steadfast love, faithfulness, and righteousness, and who, like Ps. 25:1–10, went to great pains to point out that the life of God's people is most appropriately lived when these qualities prevail. Hosea 2:18–20 comes to mind:

> I will make for you a covenant on that day. . . . I will take you for my wife in righteousness and in justice, in steadfast love, and in mercy. I will take you for my wife in faithfulness; and you shall know the LORD.

God's "ways" will ultimately prevail. Of that the psalmist is convinced, and for that the psalmist prays.

1 Peter 3:18–22

The letter of 1 Peter presents a hard message, often at cross-purposes with our contemporary ethos. It calls for a manner of life that puts Christians against the stream, swimming counter to the strong currents of the broader society. The creators of the lectionary have softened the hardness of the letter a bit for us by designating only a portion of a paragraph as the epistolary lection for this Sunday. But we cannot avoid the broader context in which the lection occurs, lest we totally miss the force of the passage.

The readers for whom the letter is intended are new converts, who have left behind a "Gentile" style of life for the new life in Christ. They find themselves now as cultural nonconformists, something of an aggravation to their former friends (4:1–4). The section prior to the lection encourages the readers to do what is good in spite of the pressure to the contrary—to honor Christ as Lord and, when questioned, to provide a reason for their newfound hopefulness (3:15). They are to be both courageous (3:14) and guileless (3:16) in their actions. It is interesting that the readers are not encouraged to withdraw from their social surroundings or to pass judgment on those who malign and persecute them. It may be that their sincere, faithful manner of life well be the occasion for a change of heart in their detractors (2:12).

Doing what is good inevitably makes one an alien and vulnerable. The opposition is prone to interpret the goodness as evil, and therefore the prospects of persecution and suffering cannot be ignored. It is clear, however, that the suffering mentioned in the text is not the meaningless anguish that comes to victims of accidents and natural disasters, to sufferers from birth defects and cancerous cells, unavoidable tragedies against which there is no immunity. The suffering here is caused by the specific reaction of others to one's doing what is good. It is the suffering one could avoid by choosing not to swim against the stream. Furthermore, it is to be distinguished from the just suffering that is the punishment for doing wrong (3:17).

The assigned lesson (3:18–22) provides the rationale for Christian nonconformity. Two links are drawn to the activity of Christ. First, Christ's suffering becomes the example for Christians (see also 2:21–25; 4:1). Followers of the Jesus of Good Friday should not expect anything less than the opposition of a hostile culture. Their own lives are to be marked by gentleness and reverence (3:16), and thus they do not search for persecution or go out of their way to provoke it, but neither should it come as a surprise.

This dimension of discipleship sounds strange in a North American environment that is relatively tolerant of religion, and where only fanatics tend to evoke angry opposition, an environment, nevertheless, in which the rough edges of Christian commitment are easily smoothed and made palatable. The text pushes the church to think again about what it means to be "resident aliens," whose Model for living refused accommodation.

But Christ is more than an example for Christians. The second link speaks of his unique activity, suffering "for sins once for all, the righteous for the unrighteous," dying, preaching to the spirits in prison, being raised from the dead, ascending to heaven, and being in control of angels, authorities, and powers. What enables nonconformist Christians not to fear what the Gentiles fear, and not to be intimidated in the face of opposition (3:14), is the redemptive journey of Jesus through suffering to exaltation, a journey that brings people to God (v. 18). Being grounded in the gospel not only makes one vulnerable to suffering; it also sustains the disciplined community in living "in reverent fear during the time of [its] exile" (1:17). It means conformity to the One who sits in the seat of ultimate authority, and before whom all demonic and angelic powers are subject.

The redemptive journey of Christ includes a time of preaching to the spirits in prison (3:19–20), a notoriously difficult statement, which has long vexed the commentators. In context, the passage seems to affirm that Christ's redemptive work is not irrelevant for those who died before the coming of Christ (see also 4:6). Even a generation as disobedient as Noah's, for whom a flood had to be sent as an act of judgment, are not cut off from the saving character of the gospel.

While 1 Peter realistically faces the prospects of potential or actual opposition to a faithful community, it nevertheless maintains an optimistic stance about the world. Persons who object are not depicted in apocalyptic terms as antichrists; only Satan gets such drastic treatment (5:8). Just as there is hope for Noah's generation, there is also hope for change in the opposition, hope that somehow the quality of life among the resident aliens will make a difference (2:12; 3:1–2, 16; 4:6).

Mark 1:9–15

Of the three brief scenes that come together in this lectionary reading, the baptism of Jesus and his initial preaching appear earlier in Year B (see the discussions under Baptism of the Lord [First Sunday After Epiphany] and the Third Sunday After Epiphany). However, the temptation of Jesus, or better, the wilderness sojourn of Jesus, plays a significant role in Mark's Gospel. Because of its associations with testing, it is also especially appropriate for the season of Lent.

Four separate statements make up 1:12–13, each of which begins with the conjunction "and," although the NRSV obscures the conjunction at the beginning of v. 13:

And the Spirit immediately drove him out into the wilderness.
[And] He was in the wilderness forty days, tempted by Satan;
and he was with the wild beasts;
and the angels waited on him.

Each of these statements either explicitly or implicitly involves wilderness themes, suggesting that it is the wilderness setting rather than the temptation as such that interests Mark.

The first statement comes as a surprise. It dramatically depicts the Spirit, who has just descended on Jesus as a dove (1:10), now driving Jesus out into the wilderness. Translators and commentators sometimes attempt to soften this picture, but the verb used here is the same one later used of Jesus casting out demons, suggesting that real force is involved (as, for example, 1:34, 39; 3:15; 6:13). Of course, reading a later, Trinitarian viewpoint into this statement raises questions about how it is that the third Person of the Trinity makes decisions for Jesus, but Mark does not work with those categories. His concern is for the necessity of Jesus' going into the wilderness. Already the wilderness has served as an important location for John the Baptist, and Jesus himself must also go there.

The second statement combines the reference to forty days with Jesus' temptation by Satan. The number forty, of course, calls to mind several important biblical stories, such as the duration of the flood (Gen. 7:4, 12, 17), the wilderness years of Israel (Ex. 16:35; Deut. 2:7), and the flight of Elijah (1 Kings 19:4–8), in all of which stories the preservation of life in the midst of danger is a crucial issue. Satan's presence emphasizes the threat to life implicit in being in the wilderness for forty days. Because Matthew and Luke provide elaborate stories of Jesus' temptations, the natural tendency is to focus on this statement to the exclusion of the other three, and to read specific temptations into this account as well. Mark, by contrast, seems content with suggesting rather than itemizing those temptations. That Jesus is not overthrown by Satan is obvious from the narrative that follows.

The wild beasts of the third statement, of course, call to mind various biblical passages that promise God's protection from wild beasts, such as Job 5:22–23; Ps. 91:13; Isa. 11:6–9. That Jesus is "with the wild beasts" and emerges unscathed indicates the divine protection afforded him. Indirect reference to that divine protection comes in the fourth statement, "and the angels waited on him." The verb used here, *diakonoun,* is that used elsewhere for serving or ministering (for example, Mark 1:31; 10:45; 15:41).

As a whole, this scene concisely portrays both the danger of the wilderness and the protection of Jesus as God's son. The period of forty days, with its obvious peril to physical life, and the temptation of Satan, threaten Jesus. That he dwells safely with wild animals and is waited on by angels conveys that he will emerge safely from this danger. In 1:3–4, the wilderness was the location of revelation. Here the wilderness becomes the location of danger. Later in Mark, the wilderness, having been tamed, becomes Jesus' place of retreat from the crowds and from the misunderstandings that press upon him (1:35, 45; 6:31–32, 35).

Having focused on this particular portion of the reading, it is also important to ask how the wilderness sojourn functions in the introduction to Mark's Gospel. Jesus' initial preaching would have followed easily on the baptism and announcement of his identity, but this scene makes the transition awkward. Why include a story that suggests Jesus is, even momentarily, at risk? One reason is that the wilderness location of Jesus identifies him with the location of John the Baptist (see the commentary on Mark 1:1–8, Second Sunday of Advent). More important, however, the very identity of Jesus in this Gospel always puts him in peril. Early in his ministry, Jesus finds himself in a conflict that will culminate in the cross, and the wilderness sojourn anticipates that very danger.

The wilderness sojourn prevents readers from assuming that Jesus' ministry will be one of exaltation and glory. Already the careful reader will recognize that all is not to be heavenly voices and powerful proclamation. Danger lurks at every turn. At the same time, the reader may also understand that the dangers that wait for Jesus will not ultimately defeat him. The one who journeys safely with wild beasts and whom angels feed will finally triumph.

Mark does not encourage his readers to an easy identification with Jesus, for Jesus is both Son of God and Son of Man, and, as such, is far distinct from the lives of ordinary folk. Mark much more readily invites readers to identify with Jesus' disciples, the women around Jesus, or the religious leaders of the day. Jesus' sojourn in the wilderness may prove the exception to that generalization, as readers see in Jesus' peril an experience that seems vivid and close to their own.

SECOND SUNDAY IN LENT

God's beneficence and God's promises for future generations dominate the first three readings for this Sunday. In Genesis 17 the covenant God makes with Abraham is just that—a covenant *God* initiates and directs. God's promise of offspring for Abraham, offspring with whom the covenant will continue, signals God's intention to sustain the covenant into the distant future. The final lines of this passage, the announcement that the covenant will be made through a child born to Abraham and the barren Sarah, reveal that God fulfills God's promises in God's own way. What is thought to be impossible or absurd may prove to be precisely God's plan.

Psalm 22:23–31 does not make particular reference to the story of Abraham and Sarah, but the thematic connections between the two readings are close ones. The psalmist calls forth praise of God for God's dominion over all people. All peoples, like all the offspring of Abraham and Sarah, are to join in serving God. God's promise to future generations is here celebrated as the promise of deliverance even for those "yet unborn."

In Rom. 4, Paul argues that those "yet unborn" now include not only those who are physically the offspring of Abraham but those who have faith like that of Abraham. If Paul often makes use of Old Testament passages in ways that seem convoluted, here he appears to be following the main lines of the Genesis account; Abraham is a prime example of God's faithful and yet mysterious ways with humankind. God calls into existence, God keeps promises, and God does so in ways not subject to the prediction or control of human beings.

The Gospel lesson, the Markan account of Peter's confrontation with Jesus over the prediction of Jesus' suffering and death, does not fit neatly into the themes established by the first three lessons. Read in the context of those lessons, however, Mark 8:31–38 calls yet again for women and men to acknowledge that God alone determines what things are "divine." Peter can no more dictate to Jesus the terms of Jesus' Messiahship than Abraham can dictate to God the terms of the covenant or the possibilities for Abraham's offspring.

Genesis 17:1–7, 15–16

God's announcement of covenant is more than an assurance of friendship and solidarity. It is a way of providing protection and resources for an open future. Thus the promise in Gen. 9 (First Sunday in Lent) was a means whereby the world was to be assured a safe future, without an overwhelming threat of chaos.

The promise given by God to Abraham and Sarah in our reading is likewise a guarantee of an open, assured future. The narrative concerning Sarah and Abraham (since Gen. 12) is preoccupied with having a son and heir who can keep their glorious promise alive, who can receive the land that has been promised them by God.

The first speech element clashes up against that factual statement of "99" (ninety-nine years old). In a massive *self-announcement*, God throws the awesome, inscrutable divine identity in the face of "ninety-nine": "I am God Almighty." Enough said. There is nothing more elemental than God's good self, God's name, God's identity. It is enough to override the body-given despair of this old couple. In the utterance, God prevails over "the human condition." The name itself is an enigma, perhaps contributing to the awe of the speech. The name of God is in any case well beyond human capacity and human limitation.

The second element of God's decree is a *summons* to Abraham: "Walk before me, and be blameless." The phrase "Walk before me" may mean "Worship me" or, more likely, "Present yourself before me like a servant presenting himself before a terrible sovereign." "Be available to me on my terms." The second imperative, "Be blameless" (perfect, complete), does not refer to moral purity, but rather to being completely devoted, in unqualified loyalty. The term may come from ritual procedure, meaning to be completely acceptable and without disqualifying mark. No specific Torah commandments are given to Abraham, but Abraham's whole life is to be given over to Yahweh in unqualified devotion.

The third element of this decree is a large, unconventional *promise,* the one Abraham most wanted to hear. God will unilaterally "give [make]" (*ntn*) a covenant, the substance of which is that the family of Abraham will "be exceedingly numerous." The verb ("be numerous") is the same verb used in the Creation account, anticipating that the creation will be teeming with living things (Gen. 1:22, 28). In parallel fashion, it is promised that in the context of covenant the family of Abraham and Sarah will teem with children, heirs, descendants, all to receive the promise (see Ex. 1:7). Moreover, the verb is twice modified by the adverb "exceedingly," so that the term "numerous" is twice intensified. And all of this to a man of "ninety-nine years" with a barren ninety-year-old wife. Three aspects of God's way in the world are utilized to override the hopelessness: God's self-disclosing name, God's summons to total obedience, and God's intense promise.

Abraham submits himself bodily in a deep bow of deference (v. 3). He falls to the ground, perhaps terrified, perhaps grateful, surely overwhelmed. The speech of God is so powerful that it does not even require (or permit) assent.

Yahweh speaks again (vs. 3–7). This speech only intensifies and explicates the earlier comment of God. The initial ejaculation, "As for me," is not unlike the initial statement of God in Gen. 9:8 (see last Sunday). In both cases, it is God's staggering speech that changes everything. Now in a magisterial moment Abraham's name is changed, thereby signifying that Abraham now receives his life and his future only from the hand of God. The etymology for the name suggested in NRSV, "ancestor of a multitude," is probable, but by no means certain. In context, in any case, Abraham's identity and destiny have been decisively altered, so that the desperate one without an heir now receives a wondrous, limitless future of power and well-being.

Three aspects of this new future for Abraham are to be noted. First, the future is royal: "Kings shall come from you." If this text, as seems likely, is exilic, this is a staggering promise in a context where the royal dynasty is ended. This is a hope for power in the future, precisely in a context of powerlessness. And, of course, the royal rhetoric has served Christians well, as the text is later taken to refer to King Jesus. Second, this covenant of faithfulness is everlasting (see Gen. 9:16). Nothing can disrupt it. It is striking that these texts asserting an everlasting covenant (see also 9:8–17) are uttered precisely in exile, the crisis of deepest discontinuity. Third (in v. 8, omitted in the assigned reading), the powerful promise is for land. The desperate family that is always "on the way" will have a safe, good place in which to be "at home" (see Heb. 11:8–10).

Verses 15 and 16 serve, albeit belatedly, to include Sarah in the good future with Abraham. She also has her name changed, as she becomes "Princess." She is to carry a blessing and to bear kings to a royal future.

The text enacts a transformation in which subsequent hearers participate. Those barren at the beginning are fruitful at the end. Those abandoned have become cared for. Those displaced have become royal. Those alone have come to covenant. The text enacts a wholly new future, unutterable and impossible at the outset. The text gives, at each hearing, a future from God that this family could never devise for itself.

Psalm 22:23–31

When the human experience is laid out in all its splendor and tragedy, when philosophers and seekers-after-the-truth have distilled life down to its essential reality, the enduring word is this: God's mercy and compassion prevail! This would appear to be the thesis of the Psalm lection for this day, and the manner in which this affirmation is made tells us much about faithfulness (God's) and hope (ours).

Verses 1–22 of Ps. 22 project a mood of lamentation, and the sharp redirection of thought that occurs at v. 23 is signaled in NRSV by means of a colon at the conclusion of v. 22. This punctuation mark is pregnant with meaning, for it suggests that the psalmist ("I" and "me" of the psalm), who has now experienced the redemption so passionately requested, now turns to speak to others of what God has done. Verses 23–31 constitute that important testimony to God's love and power. If, as some scholars suggest, vs. 23–31 were originally an independent literary unit, the power of Ps. 22 in its present form is by no means diminished. (See the Psalter reading for the Fifth Sunday of Easter for additional comment.)

(Another area of scholarly attention has been the state of the Hebrew text of vs. 23–31. NRSV marginal notations indicate a number of points at which the English has departed from the Hebrew, often at the suggestion of the Septuagint, in order to produce a smoother and more logical translation. Further information about these areas of textual difficulty may be found in a good critical commentary.)

The movement in vs. 23–31 is clearly from the present to the future, yet in all of this progression of thought the emphasis is on what has passed. Initially (vs. 23–24), the psalmist invites all the members of the family of faith to join in worship and praise. Three times—a symbol of urgency—the call is issued: those who "fear Yahweh," the "offspring of Jacob/Israel" are to "praise," "glorify," and "stand in awe of him" (v. 23). The reason: Yahweh has heard the cry of one miserable sufferer and has responded in grace and compassion (v. 24). The psalmist, who was convinced that God had abandoned him or her (v. 1), now knows that that could never have been the case.

A new level of insight is achieved in the section composed of vs. 25–26. It is not enough that the psalmist should now take this newly acquired appreciation of God's ways and simply internalize it. It must be celebrated, and in the most public manner possible: in the presence of the "great congregation," the presence of "those who fear him" (compare v. 23). Some commentators have seen in this section a reference to a community meal, one oriented around the psalmist's sacrifice (for example, Deut. 14:22–29), to which other members of the worshiping community were invited, especially the dispossessed and the powerless. This would mean that the first line of v. 26 should be read quite literally and that, as an expression of his or her acceptance of Yahweh's love, the psalmist is sharing with others in the community, especially those who stand in the greatest need. The final line of v. 26, "May your hearts live forever!" sounds eschatological in the NRSV translation, and REB's "May you always be in good heart!" may be preferable. The latter rendering would suggest that the joy and merriment of the present moment will live on in the hearts of the participants in the banquet of salvation. As if to say, "The food and drink of the present occasion will soon be exhausted, but God's mercy endures!"

An additional level of insight is achieved in vs. 27–28. If the focus so far has been on the experience of the individual psalmist, shared with others in the family of faith (vs. 25–26), the scope of concern is now broadened to include all peoples everywhere. It is not unusual in the psalms of the Old Testament to find references to all humankind, but often those references are for the purpose of exalting Israel or Israel's king (note Ps. 2). But here the larger human family is addressed in order to bring it under the umbrella of Yahweh's loving care. Since Yahweh is the Lord of all peoples everywhere (v. 28), nations and races to "the ends of the earth" will acknowledge Yahweh's benevolent rule. It is this thought, in particular, which makes of this text an appropriate companion to the Old Testament lection for this day, Gen. 17:1–7, 15–16.

A final summit is achieved (vs. 29–31) in the extension of God's mercy to those who are dead and to those who are yet unborn! Verse 29 is extremely interesting, if the NRSV translation is followed, in that it is one of the few places in the Old Testament where the dead are portrayed as having communion with God. A more frequent portrayal is that of Ps. 28:1, which seems to understand that Sheol is a place where not even Yahweh ventures. (Compare REB for an alternative way of reading v. 29). Be that as it may, vs. 30–31 unambiguously point to the future. Those human generations yet to be born will experience Yahweh's mercy and, because of that, they will prepare peoples even more chronologically distant to expect God's saving grace in their own lives.

Such is the nature of Israel's God: to save! And such is the nature of Yahweh's people: to hope and to pass on the torch of faith!

Romans 4:13–25

The bottom line of so much of our human struggle is the question of God, not so much whether there is a God, but what kind of God there is. Is the one at the heart of the universe a reliable God, a God of compassion in whom we dare to trust? Or are we at the mercy of chance ("the way the ball bounces"), left with no grounds for asking of life questions of meaning and purpose? Or is God primarily an impersonal force who started things off but then let history run its own course, or an impervious deity whose ears are deaf to human cries and whose hands are helplessly and eternally tied? Sometimes the question of God seems to be the only question.

Paul struggles with the theodicy issue in different terms from the way we do, but the bottom line for him too is the character of God. Throughout the letter to the Romans, Paul wrestles with how God can act the way God does—how God can be a moral deity and at the same time justify ungodly people. Can one discern integrity and reliability in the ways of God? In Rom. 4, Abraham moves to the center of the argument, an important figure because with Abraham, God sets a precedent by which the divine character can be judged.

The epistolary reading for this Sunday makes three critical affirmations about God. First, *God is the one "who gives life to the dead and calls into existence the things that do not exist"* (4:17). From every perspective the barrenness of Abraham and Sarah makes laughable the promise of their having a long and rich line of descendants. Nothing whatsoever in the circumstances of these two senior citizens warrants the anticipation of their being progenitors of a great nation—except the presence of the miracle-working God (Gen. 17:1–7, 15–16). In fact, the history of God's relationship with Israel can be thought of as one long series of miracle stories—from the birth of Isaac to the birth of Jesus. Time and again, God creates something new and unheard of, ex nihilo, out of nothing.

Faith, then, means giving space to the surprising power of God, refusing to settle for what is possible or what is reasonable. Believers, like Abraham and Sarah, turn out to be unrealistic and even a bit mad, because their worldview includes the activity of the God of creation, who continues to bring "into existence the things that do not exist." It is not their "faith" that works miracles, but the One in whom they trust.

But if God can do anything, does that mean that I can count on God to heal my stricken child when medical science declares there is no conceivable prospect? The second affirmation about God in the text clarifies the issue further: *God does what God has promised* (Rom. 4:21). The all-powerful God is not turned into a genie who redirects the course of bullets and guarantees that all our crises will have happy endings. (Perhaps it is fortunate that we do not always have to live out our own fantasies about what constitutes a happy ending.) Rather, the context for our reflection about God's activity in the world and in our lives is the divine promise.

For Abraham and Sarah, faith in the divine promise meant living between the impossible word, that they would parent an entire nation, and its ultimate realization. Their believing was not an arbitrary claim that God would do exactly what they wished in every circumstance, but a trust in God to honor commitments made.

For us, the particular promise of Rom. 4 that shapes our faith in God's miracle-working presence is the pledge that God justifies the ungodly, that what sustains us in the day of reckoning is not an account of deeds done or not done but the certain mercy of a forgiving Judge (vs. 4–5, 16). We live between the incredible promise that God will redeem the world (including us), about which there seems little ground for hope, and its ultimate realization.

The third affirmation made about God designates him as *the one "who raised Jesus our Lord from the dead"* (v. 24). In fact the passive voice verbs in v. 25 ("was handed over," "was raised") imply that God is the primary actor in the entire Christ-event. God the creator and God the promise keeper find their fullest expression in God the redeemer. What has been promise becomes gospel in Jesus' death and resurrection. The One in whom both Abraham and Paul trusted has given a more complete self-revelation, has brought forgiveness of sins, and has set things right.

This "Christianizing" of the Abraham story at the end of Rom. 4 serves to prevent our "heroizing" Abraham as a model of steadfastness to be emulated: If you are unwavering in your faith as Abraham was, who believed against insurmountable odds, then your faith too will be reckoned as righteousness. When the story is read this way, then Abraham is turned into a hero, and the stress falls on the persistence of the human response (works?) and not on the divine promise, on Abraham and not on God. But the mention of what God has done in Christ lifts the story above mere exhortation. God's character as worthy of human trust is most convincingly depicted in the tremendous display of grace in "Jesus our Lord." The question of theodicy mysteriously finds its resolution in the crucifixion and resurrection.

Mark 8:31-38

Contemporary preachers need not be embarrassed if they find this to be a challenging text for preaching. When Matthew narrates this story, he softens the edges a bit by assigning reasonable words to Peter ("God forbid it, Lord! This must never happen to you," Matt. 16:22). Luke omits Peter's outburst altogether. Apparently the evangelists (like many other Christians) found it shocking that Peter, who has just confessed Jesus to be the Messiah, should not turn and rebuke him.

Despite the difficulties of the text, it clearly occupies a crucial place in Mark's understanding of the gospel. Three times in 8:27–10:45 Jesus predicts his suffering, death, and resurrection (8:31; 9:31; 10:33-34). Each time that prediction is followed directly by an incident in which disciples demonstrate with painful clarity their persistent inability to understand Jesus' comment (8:32-33; 9:33-34; 10:35-37). And each time the disciples' misunderstanding prompts a statement from Jesus about the true nature of discipleship (8:34-38; 9:35-37; 10:38-45). Since repetition in a narrative reflects the importance attached to a theme or event (and that assumption is particularly important when the narrative will likely be heard rather than read), the careful repetition of these sayings reveals something significant about Mark's Gospel. For this reason alone, it is useful that later lectionary readings in Year B afford the opportunity to return to these sayings in the center of Mark.

For Mark's reader, the statement of Jesus in 8:31 should not come as a complete surprise. Even the initial parallels between Jesus and John the Baptist hint at such a future for Jesus (1:1-15; 6:14-29). While those hints might be overlooked, the open hostility of the religious authorities and their plot to kill Jesus can scarcely have been overlooked (2:1-3:6), so that predictions of Jesus' death will be anticipated. What is startling is the response of Peter, and more startling still is Jesus' reaction to that response!

Mark does not directly reveal the content of Peter's rebuke or its motivation, but Jesus' comments provide an interpretation: "Get behind me, Satan! For you are setting your mind not on divine things but on human things" (8:33). Whatever Peter has said, he has somehow rejected Jesus' prediction, and for that action he receives the strongest possible condemnation, association with the figure of Satan.

The second of Jesus' comments, while not as sharp, may have proved equally puzzling to Peter. Jesus accuses him of thinking about "human things" rather than "divine things," but surely Peter would object that the opposite is the case! Peter has been thinking divine things, things about Jesus' power and his authority and even about his status as Messiah. It is Jesus who has introduced human things into the conversation with his insistence on talking about his future suffering and execution.

The conflict here, of course, has little to do with who knows the future and everything to do with perception. Which person, Jesus or Peter, knows what things are "human things" and what things are "divine things"? A side glance at 1 Cor. 1:18–25 would be helpful, for there Paul articulates a similar understanding of the cross. By the standards of wisdom that belong to human beings, the cross appears to be foolishness, but by God's standards it is wisdom. Peter's repudiation of Jesus' prediction reveals that he operates entirely on those same human standards and has not yet understood what it means to say that Jesus is the Messiah. The remainder of the Gospel will reinforce this portrait of Peter, who continually fails to grasp the necessity of Jesus' death. The remainder of the Gospel also reinforces Mark's understanding of the Messiahship as including the necessity of suffering and death.

Jesus' comment to Peter, "Get *behind me*, Satan!" (emphasis added) or more literally, "Depart *behind me*," contrasts sharply with his original call to discipleship in 1:17: "Follow me and I will make you fish for people," or literally, "Come *behind me*." That language appears again in the invitation of 8:34: "If any want to become my followers, let them deny themselves and take up their cross and follow me." Literally, this statement begins, "If anyone wishes to follow *behind me*."

Peter has not yet understood either Jesus' role or what it means to follow after him. In 8:34–37, Jesus implicitly links the two together (as he does quite explicitly in 10:41–45). Those who wish to be followers of Jesus must conform their lives to his, denying themselves, being prepared to lose their lives, taking up the cross.

These discipleship statements stand at the center of Mark's

message, and they need to stand at the center of the church's proclamation. At the same time, some care is required in interpreting them, as marginalized persons within and outside the church have too often heard them as applying only to themselves or as being forced only on them. True discipleship does involve denial of self, but that can occur only where there *is* a self to deny.

Third Sunday in Lent

The Old Testament lections for the Third Sunday in Lent recall the giving of the law to Israel and praise that law as a gift that enlivens and enlightens humankind. For Christians, particularly Protestant Christians familiar with Luther's polemic against the law, the language of Ps. 19 will seem strange. How can the law be described as "reviving the soul" (Ps. 19:7) or as more desirable than "much fine gold" (v. 10)? It is especially difficult to reconcile Western notions of freedom and individualism with early Jewish texts that depict studying and observing the law as among the reasons for life itself.

What the Decalogue presupposes and the psalmist celebrates is the conviction that freedom is never absolute. Human beings invariably find themselves in a state of servitude; the telling question, then, is what or whom one serves. The primary demand of Ex. 20 is that God be the one served; no other gods, whatever their form, are appropriate as masters of humankind. For the psalmist, this servitude of God in and of itself brings wisdom, revival, rejoicing, and enlightenment.

The irony inherent in the notion of freely serving God comes to the foreground in 1 Cor. 1:18–25, and the early Christian conflict over observance of the Mosaic law should not obscure this point. What appears to be folly in the world's eyes, whether a crucified Messiah or a freely chosen slavery, turns out to be wisdom because only God determines what is truly wise and what is truly foolish.

John 2:13–22 has little in common with the other passages for this day. In its narrative setting, the passage concerns claims about the identity of Jesus and the varying responses to those claims. Even if Jesus' disciples do not completely understand who he is, they nevertheless connect him with the fulfillment of scripture. In the face of the same evidence, others fail to understand and eventually oppose him. When read alongside the other passages and their celebration of the law, what stands out here, of course, is the inevitable human attempt to corrupt the law and derive from it a profit.

Exodus 20:1–17

Our reading is the third in a series of covenants (Gen. 9:8–17; 17:1–7, 15–16). The Commandments are not simply a list of rules, but a strategy whereby God enunciates the terms for an enduring relation with Israel. The Commandments belong in a covenant context.

Because of that context, we are helped by looking at the context of these verses in the book of Exodus. Just before these verses, Moses and Israel have, with enormous trepidation, come near the holy mountain of Sinai, and have entered the danger zone of God, which is marked by trembling, fire, thunder, smoke, and lightning.

Just after the end of the commands, because the people were frightened, Moses was asked to speak the commands of God to Israel (20:18–21). Thus, for the rest of the Old Testament, Moses is the speaker of God's law, after this moment. God never speaks the commands directly, after these verses. Thus, in these verses (vs. 1–17), the tradition presents the commands as *the only time* in which God gives commands directly in order to specify the terms of covenant. These words are of peculiar and unrivaled importance.

This peculiar and magisterial disclosure of God's self and God's purpose begins with the assertion of God's name (vs. 1–2). That name is intimately and inextricably linked to the exodus event. God's identity and purpose are forever situated in this saving event and this narrative. This is a covenantal relation that is organized against every exploitation or oppression. The God of the commands is one who intends freedom and well-being in communion.

The commands in vs. 3–7 characterize how Israel is to regard and relate to God. They insist that God is the subject and not an object, a "Thou" and not an "it," a personal agent who must be honored, taken seriously, responded to. Life at its core is interpersonal, and the Torah commands are the guarantees that keep this relationship honest, healthy, and functioning.

God insists on exclusive, total, uncompromising loyalty. In this early declaration, the God of Israel sets the tone that eventually issues in monotheism. But this is not yet a full monotheistic claim. It is not argued that there is only one God. Exactly the opposite! It is conceded that there are other gods, competing, rival, conflicting gods. Israel, however, is not to have anything to do with them. The other gods, in modern costume, may include the destructive "isms" that are all around us—racism, sexism, ageism, nationalism, consumerism, militarism—all attempts to organize life apart from the revolutionary purposes of God's freedom.

The commands of vs. 4–7 are an affirmation that God is "not

useful," has no utilitarian value, and must not be harnessed to or exploited for any purpose outside God's own distinctive purpose. To reduce God to a "form" is an attempt to capture or domesticate God, to "package" God's power and so to make God into a means rather than an end.

The command on wrongful use of the name is not about vulgar or obscene language (v. 7). It is, rather, about making the inscrutable name of God into a slogan or a formula whereby matters extraneous to God are blessed or "baptized," so that God becomes a useful support for other agendas. This is a peculiar church temptation, wanting to claim God's "endorsement" for all sorts of moral, charitable, or institutional purposes. But God in not so manipulable as to become a patron for our "good projects."

The command in vs. 8–11 stands at the very center of the Decalogue, promising "rest," both to God and to the human community. The Sabbath is a primal concern of the book of Exodus (see 16:25–30; 23:12–13; 31:12–17; 34:21; 35:2). The Sabbath is a concrete act whereby these erstwhile slaves distance themselves from the abusive production schedules of the empire. In a consumer economy like ours, moreover, covenant with Yahweh requires the breaking with the vicious cycles of consumption as well as of production. In this "rest," which is ordained into the very fabric of creation, we recover our sense of creatureliness and resist the pressure to be frantic consumers who find our joy and destiny in commodities.

Verses 12–17 address social relations, that is, the practices of the human community concerning persons and property. They necessarily derive from the first commands, for Moses teaches that when life with God is rightly ordered, life in human community can be healthy. As God refuses to be "useful," so our human counterparts are not objects and commodities to be used, but are full partners in covenant to be treated with dignity, respect, and justice.

It is clear that in this self-disclosure at Sinai, God has in mind a human covenantal community quite unlike every conventional community of abuse, leverage, and exploitation.

Psalm 19

> I shall walk at liberty,
> for I have sought your precepts.

These words from the longest psalm in the Old Testament (Ps. 119:45) strike some as containing a basic, fatal contradiction. How can freedom be enshrined in the law? If I, as an individual, submit to some outside authority (in this case God), do I not thereby forfeit my right to think and do as I please?

Ancient Israel embraced a distinctive view of God's law, the Torah, and Ps. 19 is one of those elemental texts in the Old Testament which remind us of the power of Torah to bring joy and purpose to human life. The psalm's train of thought leads us into a world that, at first, seems to have little to do with Torah and with ordinary human concerns related to daily living. It is little wonder that some scholars view vs. 1–6 as a fragment of a hymn to God the creator, the essential meaning of which is that a silent creation sings with thunderous voice of the power of the One behind the universe. Music lovers who yield to the urge to play a recording of Haydn's *The Creation* experience the majesty of vs. 1–4b in an art form that, while more at home in the eighteenth century than in our own, transcends narrow stylistic concerns and speaks with great emotion to all generations.

Verses 4c–6 may be, as some commentators point out, a snatch of poetry whose original intent was to praise Shamash, the god of the sun who was worshiped by a number of ancient Near Eastern peoples. There may be some connection between Shamash's conventional role as the giver of the law and the ultimate concern of our psalm: the beauty and power of Torah. (Note, for example, how Shamash is portrayed at the head of the famous copy of the Hammurabi Code in the Louvre as the one who instructs the Babylonian king in the content of the law.)

It is not until the reader reaches v. 7 that the actual purpose of Ps. 19 is realized, and the declaration that is made in vs. 7–9 is as remarkable for its conciseness as for its power. Matters of syntax do not always produce insight into the meaning of a text, but in this case they do. There is a polished symmetry structured into the cadences of vs. 7–9, a characteristic that is often identified with the Priestly literature of the Old Testament (compare Gen. 1:1–2:4a) and one that is surely a result of a great deal of theological deliberation and literary engineering. In the Hebrew, each of the first five lines (out of a total of six) in vs. 7–9 reveals the same syntactical pattern.

Each line begins with a noun, modified by a prepositional phrase (to use a term of English grammar), that designates Torah as the subject of the psalm. It is as if the poet was intent upon devising as many synonyms for Torah as possible. And so we have "The Torah of Yahweh," "the decrees . . . ," "the precepts . . . ," "the commandment . . . ," "the fear . . . ," and "the ordinances . . . ." Each of these phrases is followed by an adjective that describes some aspect of the power of the instruction of Yahweh. The Torah of Yahweh is . . .

perfect,
sure,
right,
clear,
pure,
true.

Then—and this is a point at which the power of the Hebrew is difficult to render into English—each of these simple predicative declarations is embellished by a participial phrase. The Torah of Yahweh is . . .

soul-reviving,
wise-making,
heart-rejoicing,
eye-enlightening,
forever enduring.

Only in the final line of this section (v. 9b) is the string of participial phrases broken by a finite verb: The Torah of Yahweh is "righteous altogether." (Behind the English adjective of NRSV is the Hebrew verb *ṣdq*, "to be in the right.") The "surprise" ending presents itself as a way of announcing: "This pithy, axiomatic treatise on Torah is now concluded."

The balance of the psalm (vs. 10–13) is devoted to a kind of denouement, a winding down of the thoughts and feelings of the reader, through a series of reflections—many from the wisdom tradition—on the validity of Torah. A final prayer (v. 14) concludes the psalm.

The astonishing manner in which these elements have been juxtaposed casts a decisive message: Of all God's good gifts at Creation, none is more precious than Torah, which can only be compared to the sun in glory. The Torah is God's perfect gift, a perfection reflected in the perfect balance of vs. 7–9. The Torah is God's gracious bestowal on the faith-community of a means whereby life may be joyously lived. The Torah is an endowment from God, which provides the family of God with an avenue through which it may express its acceptance of God's gift of covenantal love. Of all God's good gifts, there is none greater than Torah. There is none that introduces into life more hope and freedom.

Because of these qualities the New Testament claims that Jesus Christ, far from being the annulment of the Torah, is its fulfillment

(Matt. 5:17–20). If the Torah was "put in charge of us until Christ should come" (Gal. 3:24, REB), it was the Torah that provided us with the means to recognize and respond to the life of faith.

1 Corinthians 1:18–25

The question "How do we know God?" does not sound like a very important matter in the broader scheme of things. It may hold interest for the professional theologians, whose business it is to think through abstract problems, but what relevance could it possibly have for ordinary believers trying to live faithfully from one day to the next? As a matter of fact, however, such grass-roots Christians are constantly raising the question, usually in terms of the struggle to find meaning in the routine of their daily schedules, or in the effort to discern God's presence (or absence) in the chaos of their family life, or in the even more ambiguous confusion of world events. Particularly in the dark, tragic moments, what reason is there to expect God to be involved?

In its context the Epistle lection for this Sunday does not seem at first blush to be addressing these basic issues. The problem presented is the partisan conflicts in the Corinthian congregation, which have led to bickering and division (1 Cor. 1:10–17). Paul then launches into a lengthy discussion pitting human wisdom and power against divine wisdom and power, apparently because the Corinthians were boasting about the wisdom of their self-chosen leaders and, by association, their own wisdom (3:18–23). Yet there is more at stake in the text than the immediate debate over leadership.

Paul clearly does not attempt a strategy of conflict management in an effort to resolve the Paul-Apollos-Cephas-Christ discord. What is demanded of the Corinthians is something more radical, a thoroughly different way of viewing God, which, later in the letter, leads to a thoroughly different way of viewing themselves. Their attention is focused on the message of the crucified Christ, which discloses the character of God, and they are challenged to discover from it an alternative set of criteria for discerning the divine activity in their midst.

The difficulty in discovering the presence of God is the preconceived expectations of who God is and how God ought to behave. Sign-seeking Jews and wisdom-desiring Gentiles denounce the gospel because it does not meet their norms for godliness, norms that turn out to be inadequate and, ironically, result in a not-knowing. On the other hand, the gospel claims that Christ crucified is the ultimate revelation of God's wisdom and power. This offensive symbol of defeat displays God's true character and in turn provides bold criteria for perceiving the divine presence in human life.

The text urges that our thinking about God begin not with the assured canons of the academic world nor with the common sense of the person off the street, but with the word of the cross. When one begins there, the God revealed turns out paradoxically to be *radically free* and *radically engaged*. On the one hand, God is in no way bound by human categories or expectations. The first commandment of the Decalogue (Ex. 20:3) makes that unmistakable in its warning about idolatry. God turns out to be unavailable whenever sought as the patron or matron deity of a particular ideology, whether liberal or conservative, Marxist or capitalist. God simply eludes our cherished expectations and remains sovereign, undomesticated, and surprising.

On the other hand, the message of the cross also discloses that God is deeply and lovingly involved with humanity and humanity's predicament. God's freedom turns out to be something very different from aloofness and autonomy. What, in fact, makes God so utterly "different" is precisely the depth of suffering love manifested in the crucified Christ, all for the purpose of saving those who believe (1 Cor. 1:18, 21). God refuses to be banished from life's distortions and injustices, but in strange ways reverses the plight of the foolish, the weak, the low and despised in the world (vs. 27–28).

The text also probes and challenges our understanding of power. Rather than becoming mired in the assumption that power has to do with domination, coercion, and control and thrives in a context of rivalry and competition, readers are invited to discover in the message of the cross a different expression of power. God's decisive invasion of the world in Christ, accompanied as it was by humiliation and scandal, provides a brand new definition (v. 18). Such a discovery in turn relativizes the struggles of competing factions (like those in Corinth). Power belongs to the whole church, and especially to those heretofore excluded from it.

Finally, we note the ironic nature of the passage and the striking way it functions with respect to the readers. On the one hand, the text exposes, even mocks, the self-confident pretensions of the wise ("Where is the one who is wise? Where is the scribe? Where is the debater of this age?" v. 20). The "foolishness" of God is wiser and the "weakness" of God stronger than the best humans can muster. On the other hand, the irony also functions to nurture a group of readers who perceive what is going on. It creates a community of kindred souls who get the point and are drawn together by their agreement with the text. At least some of the audience are numbered among the "us" of v. 18, who share in the saving power of the gospel.

The irony of the text is still operative today. Consistent with the character of the gospel itself, it offends some and nurtures others as it presents a new lens through which God and God's community can be understood.

John 2:13–22

The elaborate discourses in the later chapters of John's Gospel incline readers to think of the Johannine Jesus as constantly engaged in verbal instruction and challenge. It may come as a surprise to realize that Jesus says little at all in the opening scenes. That is to be expected, of course, in the initial appearance of Jesus, during John's testimony about him, and perhaps even when the disciples first meet Jesus (as also in the Synoptic Gospels; see, for example, Mark 1:16–20). At the wedding in Cana and in the cleansing of the Temple, however, Jesus continues to say little, and what he does say is elusive in the extreme. His actions constitute his teaching in these areas, and his actions provoke strong responses.

At Cana, Jesus provides an extravagant quantity of wine for a wedding celebration. That story abounds with symbolism that signifies many things, not least of which is the status of Jesus as the bringer of unimaginably extravagant gifts to human beings. In response to this action, the disciples are said to believe in Jesus (2:11). The Temple scene depicts Jesus taking a very different kind of action, but here again the issue of the response to Jesus' action forms a central part of the story.

As in the parallel accounts in the Synoptic Gospels, Jesus finds in the Temple precincts those who sell animals that may be used for sacrifice and those who exchange coins engraved with human likenesses for coins that may be used for the half-shekel Temple tax. He drives out "all of them." Interpreting this action stand the words, "Take these things out of here! Stop making my Father's house a marketplace!" These words clearly identify Jesus' action with the prophetic protest against the exploitation both of the Temple and of the people of Israel. Even if John does not insert the quotation from Jer. 7:11 found in Mark and Matthew, the critique is clear; these practices constitute an abuse (see Zech. 14:21).

In John's account, however, what comes to the foreground is as much the question of Jesus' identity, and especially his authority, as the prophetic motif itself. His disciples react to the event by recalling the words of Ps. 69:9, "Zeal for your house will consume me." The quotation identifies Jesus' action as righteous zeal, but it also identifies Jesus with the speaker in the psalm. While the disciples identify Jesus positively, the enemies of Jesus, whom John regularly terms "the Jews," question Jesus' action, prompting him to make claims about raising up the "temple" in three days. For all the parties concerned, then, the question of the actual violation of the Temple and its practice recedes in the face of more pressing questions about Jesus as the agent challenging those violations.

Questions about Jesus' identity and authority invariably call for response. Particularly in John's Gospel is this the case, for Jesus' presence and actions challenge those around him to make a decision about him. In this scene, Jesus' assault on the abuse of the Temple elicits from his disciples further insight about him. When the disciples connect Jesus' actions with the psalm, the faith ascribed to them in 2:11 is enhanced. In addition, Jesus' assertion about raising up "the temple of his body" elicits understanding from the disciples about his crucifixion and resurrection. Although that insight comes only *after* the resurrection, the narrator's insertion of it here contributes to the reader's awareness that the disciples' decision about Jesus will be a decision for faith.

By contrast, the group John refers to as "the Jews" demonstrate their lack of understanding. Immediately following the disciples' perception about Jesus' zeal, "the Jews" ask a question that reveals their lack of perception: "What sign can you show us for doing this?" (v. 18). In addition, they greet Jesus' claim about raising the Temple with a pedestrian remark about the time required for building the Temple. Even if their comment is understandable from the point of view of the "real world," it is just the kind of "realistic" reaction to Jesus that John finds intolerable (see Nicodemus's response in 3:4 and that of the Samaritan woman in 4:11). The choice that "the Jews" or the world itself will make about Jesus becomes painfully clear in this story.

While all four Gospel writers include this story, John alone places it at the outset of Jesus' ministry. In the Synoptics, of course, it stands just before the Passion narratives and is explicitly linked with the authorities and their plot against Jesus (Mark 11:18; Luke 19:47). The location of the story in John, however, in no way reduces the element of danger. Just prior to this incident, Jesus makes his first reference to the "hour" that is to come (John 2:4). Here he demonstrates what will bring about that "hour": his own challenge to the world as it is and the world's abiding inability and unwillingness to hear and respond to his challenge.

Fourth Sunday in Lent

The Bible is a cloth of many colors and textures that resists easy generalizations, however relentlessly teachers and preachers find themselves making those generalizations. Each of this Sunday's lessons is profoundly connected with the workings of human sin and divine salvation, yet their diversity of scope and approach prevents one from interpreting their meanings as synonymous.

Numbers 21:4–9, drawn from the story of Israel's wilderness wanderings, depicts yet another incident in which the people of Israel become their own enemy by rebelling against God. With their complaints against God and against Moses, they succeed in provoking God to punishment. When they repent of their behavior, God in turn provides them with the means for escaping the consequences of their own deeds. The details of the story strike modern readers as odd, but the dynamics should be familiar: God's mercy delivers those who turn to God.

What the Numbers passage narrates in particular, the psalmist celebrates in general. Human sin has consequences, and those consequences include pain and affliction. Nevertheless, the "cure" lies ready to hand, as those who seek God's help find that their salvation comes from God. In elegant language, the psalmist evokes the goodness of God's mercy and calls for thanksgiving for God's numerous acts of salvation.

The language of affliction and physical suffering becomes the language of spiritual death in Eph. 2. Salvation here involves not simply rescue from distress, but something far more radical; salvation constitutes an analogy to Jesus' resurrection from the dead. Both here and in the Gospel reading, of course, salvation comes in the person of Jesus Christ, whom God lifts up just as God caused the serpent to be lifted up in the wilderness.

The forcefulness with which these passages recall God's actions for human salvation evokes the question, "Why?" Why does God

FOURTH SUNDAY IN LENT

persist in saving humankind, when humankind will itself persist in rebellion and sin? The answer comes in the familiar language of John 3:16: God acts again and again for the benefit of human beings because God loves the world in spite of itself. Even as the world resists and opposes God's Son, God persists in loving the world.

Numbers 21:4–9

This odd narrative, scarcely known among us, is included in the readings because there is an allusion to it in the Gospel narrative. In the end, we shall see that the narrative about the "serpent" becomes a "type" for the saving power of the Crucified One. Before turning the narrative into such a Christological "type," however, we may consider the narrative on its own terms.

The presenting problem of the narrative (Num. 21:4–6) is a characteristic one for the "wilderness tradition." Israel had to leave the "fleshpots" of Egypt in order to secure the new land. The farther Israel moved away from Egypt, the more romantically it engaged in nostalgia for the old brick-demanding empire. The erstwhile slaves did not remember the burden of abuse in the empire (see. Ex. 5:10–14), but only the guaranteed food supply that the empire always gives to cheap labor. That romanticized memory of course contrasted with the present circumstances of sparse supplies, dependence, and jeopardy in the wilderness. The Israelites become "impatient," that is, quarrelsome and recalcitrant (Num. 21:4).

Characteristically, in this unhappy situation, reinforced by the romanticized memory of how good it used to be, they quarreled, accused God of infidelity, and accused Moses of poor, failed leadership. (That is what people do when the economy fails.) Israel's relationship with Yahweh, reflected in many psalms, is one of abrasive candor. Very often the accusatory protest produces good results from God. Yahweh can be impacted by complaint, and so responds with good gifts; but not this time (v. 6)! We are not told why God does not respond with help. This time Yahweh is harsh and uncooperative. Yahweh gives no good gifts in response to need and complaint, but instead fashions a devastating punishment for the complainers. The wilderness is peopled by snakes, serpents, and creeping things, some surely poisonous. These are now dispatched by God in a ruthless, lethal response to complaint.

At v. 7, the narrative does a complete about-face. Now the people who complained are submissive and repentant. Commensurate with the change on the part of the people, the God who dispatched death now turns and provides a way of health. Whereas vs. 4–6 portray failed, abrasive circumstances, vs. 7–9 in contrast offer a picture of submission and corresponding generosity on God's part.

Now, in v. 7, by the show of God's devastating power, those who were "impatient" have realized they must come to terms with God's sovereign rule and that protest against that rule is not only futile, but self-destructive. Israel submits, even though the terrible, life-threatening circumstances of the wilderness persist unchanged. Moses, who in v. 5 had been a target of their accusation, now exercises his intercessory function on behalf of the people. And, as is characteristic with Mosaic prayer addressed to Yahweh, the intercession is effective.

God's response to the petition of Moses is, as in v. 6, exactly commensurate with the people's initiative. When they accuse, God responds negatively. When they submit, God responds positively. Both transactions are evidences of God's uncompromising, unaccommodating majesty, which can be either to give life or to cause death (see Deut. 32:39; Isa. 45:7). Now Yahweh, with enormous inventiveness, provides a bronze replica of the destructive serpent of Num. 21:6. (In both v. 6 and v. 8, the adjective "poisonous" is not clear in the text, for the Hebrew word seems to be "fiery" or "burning." The disputed reading "poisonous," for which there is modest textual support, however, seems required by the context.) In this gracious action, Yahweh takes the "serpent" of v. 6, a real live creature of the wilderness, and transforms it into a stable, enduring, reliable cultic object (a form of transubstantiation?). The "serpent" is now a piece of statuary set up to be visible to Israel. It functions in a cultic (magical?) way, as an antidote to poisonous serpents.

At a surface level, this is an odd, quasi-magical solution to a breakdown in a covenantal relation. Because Israel was rebellious, God sent real, destructive snakes. When Israel was penitent, God sent a "saving snake," one enshrined in the cult. Not only is this cultic image a symbol of God's generous, faithful capacity to save and to let Israel live, but the cultic image is understood in the narrative to have real, effective, salvific power. That is, Israel could "look . . . and live" (v. 9).

We may doubt the claim made for such a cultic image, because it seems to smack of magical primitivism. I suspect we cannot penetrate into the religious world of such a claim, given our scientific rationality. Two responses, however, can be made. First, the serpent of bronze is surely to be understood sacramentally. Its claim and function are not *in principle* different from the evangelical claim that "bread and wine" mediate the "body and blood" in saving ways. Of course, our sacramental claim also violates scientific rationality and leads us into a world of prescientific religious receptivity. Both the Mosaic image and our sacramental life remind us that God's life-giving power is given in ways not contained or understood by our technological reasonableness. Second, the Gospel reading of John 3:14 understands the lifted-up bronze serpent to be an anticipation (type) of the "lifted up" (crucified) Jesus. Of course, it is equally beyond our usual reason to understand how a crucified (lifted-up) Jesus can have saving power over time in the world. Odd as that claim is, this lifted-up One stands at the center of a redefined existence. The narrative invites us to be "recentered" around that gift of new life.

Psalm 107:1–3, 17–22

Among other things, Lent is the season in which the church comes to terms with suffering, especially that suffering which is the result of human sin. It is in the context of their suffering that women and men often encounter most seriously their need for God. And it is in a narrative of great suffering, that of Christ's passion, that God's response to human need becomes clear. Yet the matter of suffering is never, within the Lenten perspective, an issue for its own sake. Suffering—both Christ's and ours—is always recognized as an occasion for God's mercy. The Friday before Easter is always Good. The appeal to our own suffering is always so that we may seek God's redemption or give thanks for redemption already experienced.

The present lection is a case in point, for although the text goes to great pains to portray human distress, the beginning and ending are rooted in professions of praise. That view which sees Ps. 107 as the song of pilgrims who, after great and dangerous struggles, have reached the Holy City may be correct. But in a fashion typical of many psalms, the poem far transcends its original life setting and speaks to a wide variety of human conditions. The pilgrim is Everyman/Everywoman, the destination any worthwhile or God-sanctioned endeavor.

The lines that introduce the entirety of Ps. 107 (vs. 1–3) are by no means less gripping because of their formulaic nature. Psalm 136 has elevated the words of our v. 1 to an art form in order to provide a liturgical response to some or any now-resolved crisis (note also Ps. 118:1–4). But if the message of these words is familiar, it is still fundamental. The family of God has but one truly persistent reason to give thanks, but what a reason it is: Yahweh's "steadfast love endures forever." One can almost hear the continually recurring theme lifted by the worshiping congregation (again with Pss. 118 and 136 as models):

> His steadfast love endures forever . . .
> His steadfast love endures forever.

The very repetition has become emblematic of the constantly recurring evidence of Yahweh's covenant love. Present in good times and in bad. Present when the people deserve it and when they do not. Like a returning bass note in a mighty organ chorale: "His steadfast love endures forever. . . ."

Those who have come from all points of the compass may report similar experiences of this redeemer God, Yahweh. For this is the God who has stepped forward in the moment of "trouble" (v. 2) to fulfill the role traditionally assigned to the "redeemer" in ancient Israelite society: to prevent the falling away of that which is in mortal danger. Like Jeremiah's purchase of the field near Anathoth (Jer. 32). Like Boaz's tender mercy toward Ruth (Ruth 4). Each of those who come from east and west, from north and south, may tell in his or her own words similar tales of this merciful Yahweh.

> His steadfast love endures forever . . .

Psalm 107:17–20 traces a dramatic cycle familiar to the faith-community. Men and women sin and inevitably experience the consequences of their sin: great suffering (vs. 17–18). Out of their misery and desperation they cry to Yahweh for deliverance (v. 19a). And as a result of their petition Yahweh responds in mercy by intervening, so that the cycle of sin and judgment is broken (vs. 19b–20): "he saved them from their distress." The pages of the Bible are replete with lives whose stories have been told according to this formula. And modern cities and villages are filled with lives whose stories, if told, would provide new and equally marvelous examples of this ancient progression. Again, as is true in the case of the formulaic nature of vs. 1–3, the stylized language of vs. 17–20 does not detract from the reality it communicates; such language only serves to reinforce the reality it represents.

Because the worshiping congregation is in the presence of such an enduring narrative of salvation—indeed, is in the presence of such an enduring Redeemer—its people are summoned to give thanks (vs. 21–22). Some of the language of these lines is conventional. The people are to offer "sacrifices." They are to celebrate their salvation "with songs of joy," such as the present psalm, of course. But the presence of the word "humankind" (literally, "children of Adam") lifts the universe of discourse above the parochial and mechanically cultic. *All* women and men are the objects of Yahweh's redemptive ways.

> His steadfast love endures forever. . . .

And so the story of human suffering is placed within a redemptive perspective. Sometimes women and men suffer because of factors completely beyond their control. But often we suffer because of our hubris and sin. The final word, however, is not our suffering, but God's mercy. This critical reality is that to which the Lenten season points. It is, indeed, the verity of Calvary and Easter. We would destroy ourselves, but the God of mercy steps forward to prevent that. And so the "redeemed of the LORD" testify that "he is good."

> His steadfast love endures forever.

Ephesians 2:1–10

"Salvation" is not a term heard very much in sermons these days. It may conjure up too many recollections of old-time revivals, when people "got saved," if only for a short spell. Apparently a moratorium of sorts has fallen on the use of the term, at least in mainline churches. But "salvation" is a prominent biblical term, at the heart of the Christian gospel, and it surfaces in each of the readings for this Sunday in Lent. It may be time to dust it off and have another look. The people in our congregations know only too well the experience of lostness, and they may welcome a word of clarification about its opposite—being saved.

Ephesians 2:1–10 is a classic text about God's saving activity in Christ. It has movement and tells the story in language and images that overflow with various connotations. In fact, there is a certain lyrical quality to this passage. Words and phrases are piled on top of one another; expressions are repeated. The first nine verses in the Greek text are a single sentence and virtually impossible to diagram. The mood is praise and gratitude, the stuff of liturgy. The prayer of intercession that closes the first chapter (1:15–23) celebrates the exaltation of Christ. Chapter 2 draws out the salvific implications of such an exaltation for the people of God, both Gentiles and Jews.

The passage neatly divides into three parts.

1. Ephesians 2:1–3 depicts what the readers are saved from. Three images vividly depict humanity's hopeless state: the corpse ("dead through the trespasses and sins," v. 1); the slave ("following the course of this world, following the ruler of the power of the air," v. 2); and the condemned prisoner ("children of wrath," v. 3). Each in its own way portrays a devastating predicament, which "you" and "we" are powerless to change. A sense of helplessness pervades vs. 1–3.

And yet the section avoids accusation, because the grammatical structure is clearly aimed at vs. 4–5, where the main subject and verb of this convoluted sentence are found. The point of vs. 1–3 is not to arouse guilt, but to remind readers of the past from which they have come in order to appreciate their inclusion in the marvelous story of salvation.

2. The next section (vs. 4–7) announces God's initiative in remedying the human situation, in giving life to lifeless bodies and in elevating them to a place of security ("in the heavenly places in Christ Jesus") beyond the reach of Satan's still-powerful activity. The exuberant language to describe God in v. 4 ("rich in mercy, out of the great love with which he loved us") and in v. 7 ("the immeasurable riches of his grace in kindness") highlights the joyous mood of praise that permeates the passage. Unlike the delight of the father who rejoices at the return of the prodigal son, these verses celebrate the aggressive, liberating God who initiates and completes the rescue of entrapped people.

Of course the key word for salvation here is "life," a vitality, vibrancy, and vulnerability essential to the doing of the "good works." We dare not reduce it to a single feeling or activity. It is the mystery of Christian existence, which is as big as sharing in "the life of God" (4:18). The prominence of the preposition "with" in the passage ("with Christ," "with him") demands a corporate reading, an understanding of "life" as being with others in the company of Christ.

3. The third and perhaps most familiar section of the passage (2:8–10) turns the spotlight on the self-awareness and activity of those who are saved. They are marked by two distinctive features: a sense of grace and a doing of good works.

On the one hand, they know that "life" is a gift of God, the result of divine and not human activity. The repeated use of the perfect tense for the verb "save" in v. 5 and v. 8 (coupled in both cases with the phrase "by grace") indicates that gratitude is the appropriate human response, not merely for the beginning of one's experience of salvation, but for all one's days ("by grace you were and are being saved"). With the dominant stress on grace in this text, one could conclude that the way of forfeiting salvation is ingratitude, a self-confidence that presumes that one's accomplishments, whether material or spiritual, are one's own—what the text means by "boasting."

On the other hand, salvation also means doing what we were created to do—"good works." As the NRSV interestingly puts it, this is "to be our way of life" (v. 10). Gratitude is not to be equated with passivity, but is in fact characterized by activity. But how are the "good works" of v. 10 different from the "works" of v. 9? Apparently they may look alike; that is, they may be the same in form and substance—speaking the truth with neighbors (4:25), working so as to have something to share with the needy (4:28), acting with kindness and forgiveness (4:32). What differentiates them is their grounds: gratitude, or anticipated reward. To put it another way, the works that are "good" are the works that the doer recognizes are themselves the gift of God.

Any reading of this passage, with all its good theology, must not neglect its lyrical quality. Ultimately, salvation is not so much a reality to be analyzed and dissected, as one to be celebrated and praised. Worship is the appropriate mood.

John 3:14–21

The visit of Nicodemus to Jesus prompts Jesus to break the near-silence of John 1 and 2 in his first short discourse (see the discussion of John 2:13–22 for the Third Sunday in Lent). As Jesus elaborates on the new birth necessary for seeing the kingdom of God, he announces three themes close to the center of the Johannine Gospel: the "lifting up" of the Son of man, the sending of the Son as a manifestation of God's love, and the consequences of those actions for humankind.

Jesus explicitly connects the "lifting up" of the Son of man with the story of Moses raising up the serpent in Num. 21, another of the lections for this Sunday. Obviously, the connection is not to be located in close parallels between the two incidents; it would be difficult to imagine how Jesus resembles the "serpent of bronze" made by Moses and set on a pole! Instead, what connects the two instances of "lifting up" is that both function to save God's people. The bronze serpent saves those who look on it after having been bitten by a poisonous serpent; and Jesus likewise saves human beings by virtue of being lifted up (John 3:15).

At this point in John's story, little is said to reveal what exactly is meant by Jesus' being lifted up. Surely first readers of John would assume that "lifting up" has to do with the elevation and exaltation of Jesus at his resurrection. And it does. At the same time, however, John understands the elevation of Jesus to begin at his crucifixion. In 8:28, for example, "When you have lifted up the Son of Man" surely refers to the human act of crucifying Jesus. In 12:32–33, another of Jesus' statements about being lifted up is followed by an explanation of the narrator that Jesus was indicating the manner in which he would die.

Even in the present context, Jesus' "lifting up" is implicitly connected with his death by v. 16, which explains Jesus' exaltation as God's gift of his Son. Memorized by countless Sunday school students and, more recently, placarded at innumerable athletic events, John 3:16 takes on the character of background noise: we hear it so often that we don't listen to it at all. Like most biblical statements about salvation, it is first of all a statement about God's actions and only quite secondarily a statement about the consequences of those actions for human beings. In this passage, the central theological assertion being made is that God "loved the world." Verses 17–21 elaborate on that claim with references to God's sending of the Son "into the world" to save it and the coming of the light into the world. God acts in order to save the world, to send it light, to rescue it from itself! Those statements become the more remarkable since John's Gospel generally operates with a negative view of the world, not because the world is inherently evil, but because the world rejects Jesus. Indeed, the world stands in opposition to Jesus and to his followers (see, for example, 16:20; 17:14). That God loves the world, then—the unrepentant and even hostile world—deserves to be recited in Sunday school and even paraded at baseball games!

When Jesus speaks of the consequences of this act of love for human beings, he employs the dualistic language found often in John as well as in the rest of the New Testament and other literature of the period. Contrasts between the children of light and children of darkness or lovers of light and lovers of darkness sound an odd and alien note to the contemporary ear, but such dualistic thinking persists in political, social, and religious struggles, even if the language refers more prosaically to "us" and "them."

In John 3:16, Jesus describes those who believe as receiving "eternal life" by virtue of God's love. The immediate context as well as the rest of the Gospel make it clear that "eternal life" refers not simply to the quantity of life but to its character. "Eternal life" does indeed refer to length of life, as John 6:58 indicates; on the other hand, "eternal life" is also something quite other than a solution to the human fear of death. Eternal life somehow exists in the present (6:54–55) and comes through the action of God in Jesus Christ, who has life in himself (5:26).

God's action is simultaneously an action of salvation and an action of judgment, but the language about judgment here warrants careful reading. Jesus says that those who do not believe "are condemned already." Condemnation does not simply wait out in the future to punish those who have turned their backs to God; it exists in the present—they "are condemned already." Condemnation is evident from the fact that people "loved darkness rather than light." Just as life in the present can be said to reflect the salvation of God in Jesus Christ, so life in the present can also reflect judgment. This observation, of course, is not to be manipulated as if it were a diagnostic tool that privileges some to discern those who are already saved and others who are already condemned. Instead, it reflects a larger truth about eternal life and about judgment; both exist in the present in the lives people lead and in the deeds toward which they are drawn.

Fifth Sunday in Lent

With Jer. 31:31–34 as the frame, a story unfolds in the four texts designated for this Sunday, a story of God's gracious activity for the chosen people. It begins with Ps. 119, where the merits of the Torah are extolled, where the young (and the old as well) are promised a pathway to lead them through and around the pitfalls of life. Treasuring the words of the Torah in the heart is the antidote to sin. It is not a laborious burden to be borne, but creates delight and joy. The Torah is a critical ingredient in God's covenant relationship with Israel.

But the Jeremiah text recognizes that something else is needed. It declares to Israel in exile that God is to take unilateral action to establish a new covenant with them, a covenant that entails a renewed commitment on God's part ("I will be their God, and they shall be my people") and a renewed commitment on Israel's part ("I will put my law within them"). The Torah is not to be jettisoned in this new covenant. What will distinguish it is the gracious, forgiving word of God, who chooses to forget Israel's sins.

The third chapter in the story comes with the reading from Hebrews, which focuses on Jesus, the high priest of the promised new covenant. He can be compared to Aaron, the priest of the old covenant, but is also radically different from Aaron, more along the lines of the mysterious Melchizedek. Jesus is depicted as a praying, anguishing figure, who learns obedience through what he suffers and thereby becomes more than a priest—"the source of eternal salvation for all who obey him" (Heb. 5:9).

Unlike the previous three passages, the story of the Greeks who seek Jesus in John 12 includes no mention of covenant, Torah, or priest. And yet it depicts Jesus as one who must die, and whose dying and exaltation "will draw all people" to himself (12:32)—not Gentiles without Jews, nor Jews without Gentiles. What characterizes the people of the new covenant is their following of this One who must die, their own losing of life in order to find it.

Jeremiah 31:31-34

The Old Testament readings for Lent continue with this text on the theme of covenant. Indeed, here we have the most extreme and most wondrous text in the Old Testament concerning covenant. This promissory covenant from God's mouth is situated in Jer. 30–31, called by scholars "The Book of Comfort." The two chapters are a collection of promises from God addressed to exiles in their despair.

On the face of it, the new covenant is massively contrasted with the old. When the matter is made explicit, however, the new covenant stands with the old in the sense that it continues to feature the old Torah. Thus the new covenant is not *absolutely* new, but permits the thought that this is the old covenant drastically *renewed*. We face the characteristic issue in biblical faith of discontinuity and continuity. In New Testament usages of this passage (Heb. 8:8-12; 10:16-17), the accent is on the discontinuity, but there is a powerful aspect of continuity that is also crucial for this passage.

In any case, the primary matter is that the old covenant of Sinai has been broken, broken so decisively as to be nullified, but this new (renewed?) covenant will be "keepable." The assertion of a new, "keepable" covenant in the place of one nullified and broken makes a claim for God's own resolve and deep yearning for a covenant that overrides the painful truth of nullification. Thus, the decree of a new (renewed) covenant is an act of God's inexplicable mercy and graciousness. God wills an enduring relationship precisely with this recalcitrant, unresponsive people.

Jeremiah 31:33 and 34 now characterize and specify the newness that will be established "after those days." We may divide this characterization into four distinct motifs:

1. The Torah, that is, the commands, will be central and authoritative (as at Sinai), but now they will be intensely embraced (unlike the Sinai economy of covenant). This image of being written "on their hearts" does not permit excessive psychological speculation. The image is likely appropriated from something like Prov. 6:20-22, wherein the child in the family is to bind the family commandments "upon your heart," "around your neck," close at hand, intimately familiar with, readily embraced. The contrast in the text is not so much external/internal, as it is that the commandments are no longer a resisted imposition by an authoritarian God, but a readily embraced shape for a relationship that the "wearers of commandments" really want and are eager to enact.

2. The relationship is marked by a standard covenant formula of mutuality (Jer. 31:32). The formula, "I will be their God, and they

shall be my people" is much used in Jeremiah (11:4; 24:7; 32:38) and Ezekiel (11:20; 14:11; 36:28; 37:23, 27). This covenant formula is forcibly asserted as an act of deep fidelity on God's part in the exile, when covenantal bonding seemed not to work.

3. The newly formed community of Israel will be full of the knowledge of God (Jer. 31:34a). Two features of this formula interest us. First, the phrase "know the LORD" is a rich, open phrase. It means (*a*) deep, trustful intimacy, (*b*) acknowledgment of a sovereign authority over all of life, and (*c*) obedience that is congruent with the will and character of Yahweh. On this last motif, see Jer. 22:15–16, where knowing God consists of caring for "the poor and needy." Taken all together, knowing God means ceding over all of one's life to the claims and insistences of God as the truth of our own life.

Second, this "knowing" overcomes all social stratifications. There will be no elitism, no experts, no dominant, powerful people. This communion-in-obedience is a stunningly egalitarian affair (on which see Gal. 3:28).

4. The culminating feature of the new/renewed covenant is made possible not by repentance or conversion on the part of Israel, but by the unilateral action of God, who will "forgive and forget." Israel's future will be unburdened of all the resistance and recalcitrance that has exhausted the old relationship.

Christian preaching of this enormous promise must guard against three characteristic Christian temptations:

1. The new covenant is with the *houses* of Israel and Judah. One must take care to avoid presenting the covenant as the emergence of "individualism." On the basis of Jer. 31:29–30 (just prior to our passage), it is often asserted that Jeremiah "discovers the individual." But God makes covenant *with the community*, to which individuals have access only as members.

2. This announced covenant is "new" or "renewed." Because "new covenant" became in Latin new *testamentum*, there has been with this passage a danger of supersessionism, the claim that God's new covenant with the church, through Jesus, has superseded God's covenant with the Jews. Such a notion completely misreads the text. The issue in the text is not "Jew/Christian," but as the Gospel reading for this Sunday has it, any newness worked through discontinuity (death), so that both Jews and Christians face the nullification of what is old for the sake of the newness of God.

3. As a subpoint to item 2, there is a temptation that displaces the covenant at Sinai, to present the new covenant as antinomian, that is, without commandments. This, however, is clearly precluded in

FIFTH SUNDAY IN LENT

v. 33. The new covenant is one of radical obedience to God's commands, which have long been available in ancient Israel.

Psalm 51:1-12 or Psalm 119:9-16

(As Ps. 51:1-17 is the Psalm lection for Ash Wednesday in Years A, B, and C, those who wish to use 51:1-12 as the text for this day are referred to comments on this psalm in the Ash Wednesday section of this commentary.)

Psalm 119 is one of the three great Torah psalms in the Old Testament (the others being Ps. 1 and Ps. 19, the latter constituting the text appointed for the Third Sunday in Lent, Year B). Of these, Ps. 119 is the most elaborately detailed, in that it is an alphabetic acrostic in which each line, or verse, of an eight-line section begins with the same letter, each section progressing in alphabetic sequence. Thus, each line (verse) of the section vs. 1-8 begins with *aleph*, vs. 9-16 with *beth*, and so on. The mathematical precision with which this psalm was crafted is demonstrated in another manner, namely, by the use, in each section (with minor exceptions), of the same eight Hebrew terms representing Torah, or the instruction of God.

Because of these formulaic constraints, the ability of the poet to express a variety of ideas or concepts is quite limited, and little may be identified within the psalm by way of progression of thought or by way of thematic unity, other than that unity imposed by the recurring references to Torah. If, however, any kind of theological "movement" may be discovered in vs. 9-16, it seems to be related to the issue of the spiritual formation of the rising generation. The question is posed at the outset, in language reminiscent of the wisdom tradition: "How can young people keep their way pure?" (v. 9a). The balance of the section is an attempt to provide the answer.

The short form of the answer is, in fact, immediately forthcoming in v. 9b: A young person may keep his or her way by "guarding it according to your word." If "word" here is understood as the entirety of God's revealed will for human life, the thought here seems to be that God's instruction provides a kind of buffer, which protects the person just coming into maturity against those forces in human life that would injure or distort his or her well-being. Proverbs 2:6-8 affirms:

> Yahweh gives wisdom;
> . . . .
> he is a shield to those who walk blamelessly,
> guarding the paths of justice.

But the translation of the NRSV is problematic, and the Septuagint may have it better when it renders v. 9b: "by keeping your word." That is to say, the Torah of Yahweh is a pathway across a treacherous terrain, a landscape strewn with dangers both hidden and obvious. Only in following the lead of Yahweh's instruction may the young person be assured of safe arrival at the journey's end. The book of Proverbs also provides support for this understanding of 9b: "Therefore walk in the way of the good, and keep to the paths of the just" (2:20). In any event, these two renderings of v. 9b are not contradictory, and perhaps the psalmist is endeavoring to frame both realities at the same time.

Although the balance of the text is governed by the pronoun "I," the reader should not suppose that the poet has now left behind the original question and answer and has moved on to other things, namely, his or her own constellation of commitments, his or her own exalted righteousness. Rather vs. 10–16 are probably best read as commentary on the question and answer posed in v. 9. If the poet now personalizes the issue, that is not because the poet is attempting, in some prideful fashion, to set himself or herself up as the epitome of the righteous youth (now turned into an adult). Rather, the abundant use of the first-person pronoun should be read as stylized language in which the speaker/author assumes the role of any faithful Israelite. What is being suggested here is not that the poet has "arrived," but that he or she is now speaking in the name of any person who trusts in God but realizes the enormity of his or her need before God (note the psalmist's weakness and vulnerability in vs. 81–82).

And so, having answered the initial question of 9a by the response of 9b, the psalmist acknowledges the further implied question, "And just how is it that one guards one's way according to your word?" (Or, ". . . keeps your word?") The reply:

By seeking you wholeheartedly (v. 10a)
By not wandering from your commandments (v. 10b)
By treasuring your word in one's inmost being (v. 11a)
By speaking with one's own mouth all the teachings of your mouth (v. 13)
By delighting in the path you have decreed (v. 14a)
By fastening one's mind on your teachings (v. 15a)
By gluing one's eyes on the path where you lead (v. 15b)
By finding great joy in your instructions (v. 16a)
By remembering your word (v. 16b)

We who live in days when education is often described as "in crisis" may not have to be reminded of the recurring need in each generation to shape—according to important moral and spiritual values—the lives of those who will follow. But our text not only recalls for us that the "traditioning" of tomorrow's adults has always been a pressing issue, it also provides us with important tools for accomplishing that crucial task. And, as it always does, the text points us beyond ourselves—not to our agenda for life, but to the agenda of the One who gave us life in the first place.

Hebrews 5:5–10

Of all the Christological roles in the New Testament—Son of God, Son of man, servant, prophet—none should be more immediately relevant to the human situation than high priest. The notion of a figure who knows the pains and tragedies of life firsthand and becomes an intercessor, pleading the human cause before God, is an image to which we can relate. We like being represented by an ambassador, approved by God, who has fully identified himself with our situation and on whom we can utterly rely. Since we do not bump into high priests every day, a sermon on the high-priestly Christology of Hebrews may require a certain teaching dimension to get listeners aboard, but the force and clarity of the image are powerful. (Since Heb. 4:14–5:10 is popular with the lectionary makers, comments on the passage can be found in other places in this volume, such as on Good Friday and at Proper 24.)

Hebrews 5:1–10 is a tight unit. The first four verses describe the distinguishing characteristics of the Aaronic high priest—offering to God sacrifices for sins, empathizing with the weaknesses of the people, and exhibiting humility in light of one's appointment by God. Then in the next six verses these same characteristics are applied, in reverse order, to Jesus as high priest, with the significant addition that he becomes "the source of eternal salvation" (v. 9). The section vs. 1–3 introduces and supplies an explanatory mirror for seeing Christ in vs. 5–10.

First, Christ is not a self-appointed priest, but the one designated by God (5:5–6, 10). The citation of two appointment formulas, Ps. 2:7 and Ps. 110:4, links the title Son with that of high priest in a striking way. Son is a relational title, which always entails obedience and intimacy, and in this context softens somewhat the notion of the unique priest, who stands in the line of the mysterious Melchizedek.

In any case, the One who pleads our case before God is bound to have God's ear. He is not our elected representative nor is he self-designated, but is God's own choice.

Second, Christ has fully identified with human weaknesses (5:7–8). The text details this identification in two ways. The first connection is that the prayers, marked by "loud cries and tears" in the face of death, meet the qualifications of vs. 2–4. Whether the reference is to Gethsemane and Golgotha or to the tradition of righteous sufferers in the Old Testament, Jesus nevertheless comes face to face with his own mortality. His being heard by God does not mean that he escapes the fears of death or bypasses the agony of the cross. He shares fully in the finitude of human existence.

Jesus cried and "he was heard" (v. 7). Nothing more or less is promised. No release from the anxiety, no easing of the pain, no rescue from death, no assurance of happiness—only dialogue with God. Commentators point to the parallel with Job, who in his misery begs for communication with God. "I cry to you and you do not answer me; I stand, and you merely look at me" (Job 30:20). Job's redemption comes when God, having heard, speaks. The dialogue is critical because it banishes the loneliness and bridges the alienation.

Jesus identified with human weakness also as he "learned obedience through what he suffered" (Heb. 5:8). That one should learn from suffering is not surprising. In fact, there is in the Greek language a play on words—"he learned" (*emathen*); "he suffered" (*epathen*)—which may reflect a familiar Hellenistic proverb. That this is said, however, of God's Son, God's chosen, is arresting. The divine high priest is not immune to suffering (as some have thought God must be), but learns from it. It becomes his tutor.

Suffering is not depicted here as an evil to be fought against or overcome, but as a necessary ingredient in faithfulness to God. The readers also suffer (10:32–34), and they are exhorted to be instructed by their trials to learn discipline (12:3–11). They are encouraged because in Jesus their high priest they find a companion who thoroughly empathizes with their pain and prevents their sufferings from leading to despair.

Third, the high priest becomes "the source of eternal salvation for all who obey him" (5:9). On the one hand, this sets Jesus in a unique role. Throughout Hebrews the comparison is drawn between the old covenant and the new, between the old cultic sacrifices and the sacrifice of Christ, between the old sanctuary and the perfect tent not made with hands. The new always surpasses the old. So also here, with the comparison between the Aaronic priesthood and Christ as high priest. The latter through his participation in human weakness—facing mortality and learning obedience in what he suffered—is validated by God ("made perfect") and becomes what the Aaronic priesthood could never be, the source of ultimate redemption.

On the other hand, Jesus becomes a model for the readers. Just as he engaged in dialogue with God as the Son obedient to his Father, so those who receive the eternal salvation are called to obey him. His example of reliance on God amid his identification with human weakness establishes a firm basis for Christian decision. In some sense, the letter to the Hebrews reaches its climax in the last chapter, when it exhorts its readers to take on the priestly mantle themselves, to suffer outside the gate, as Jesus did, and continually to offer sacrifices of praise to God (13:12–15).

John 12:20–33

"The hour has come for the Son of Man to be glorified." References to the "hour" of Jesus in the first eleven chapters of John point forward. "My hour has not yet come," Jesus announces to his mother in 2:4. When Jesus' teaching astonishes Jerusalem, the leaders attempt to arrest him, but fail "because his hour had not yet come" (7:30). Again in 8:20 the narrator explains that Jesus could not be arrested because his hour "had not yet come." Abruptly, in 12:23, the situation changes, and Jesus announces that the "hour" has now come.

What prompts Jesus to make this pronouncement about his crucifixion? Two sets of clues appear in the story just preceding this lesson, clues that seem to stand in some tension with each other. The raising of Lazarus elicits belief from many (11:45), and that very belief in turn brings about the opposition of the Pharisees and leaders of the Jewish community. "From that day on," the narrator says, "they planned to put him to death" (v. 53). Indeed, the reaction to the miracle of Lazarus is so great that the authorities plot Lazarus's death as well as that of Jesus (12:10–11). One conclusion drawn from the context would be that the "hour" comes because of opposition to Jesus.

A second set of clues centers not on opposition to Jesus but on adulation of him. Several times the narrator comments that large numbers of people believed in Jesus because of the raising of Lazarus. That motif culminates in the comment of the Pharisees in 12:19: "You see, you can do nothing. Look, the world has gone after him!" Surely there is a note of irony in this statement, since John elsewhere views the "world" as hostile to Jesus (see the comments on John 3:14–21, Fourth Sunday in Lent).

An illustration of the fact that "the world" has gone after Jesus is enacted in the awkward scene, 12:20–22. First the narrator introduces the presence of certain Greeks, who are presumably proselytes in view of their having come to Jerusalem for Passover. The Greeks present themselves to the Galilean Philip with the declaration, "Sir, we wish to see Jesus." Philip presents their request to Andrew, and the two of them in turn present the request to Jesus. Strikingly absent from this elaborate scene-setting is any clear indication that the Greeks in question actually do see Jesus or that they come to faith. Nevertheless, the elaborate stage-setting highlights their quest. In other words, what makes them important emerges in Jesus' comment in v. 23 that the "hour" has come; that is, the arrival of "the world" in the persons of these Greeks indicates that Jesus' death is imminent.

The "hour" arrives because opposition to Jesus reaches its inevitable outcome: the officials will seek his death. But the "hour" also arrives because of Jesus' very "success" with the world. Here the world seeks after Jesus, but the world is fickle, seeking tomorrow after another who might do more astonishing signs or offer more soothing advice. The world is finally not able to believe that Jesus is from God and to follow after him. The popularity of Jesus in this passage quickly fades and turns into the hostility that confronts Pilate and demands Jesus' crucifixion (18:28–19:16). The world is a thoroughly unreliable place; neither its hostility nor its adoration can be trusted.

Perhaps because the world's favor is such a fickle commodity, the Johannine Jesus understands the "hour" itself as a time of confrontation with the world: "Now is the judgment of this world; now the ruler of this world will be driven out" (12:31). And that triumph over the "ruler of this world" is coupled with the claim that, in Jesus' "hour," he lifts all persons to himself. If we find a hint of universalism in this promise, we surely read into the text concerns distant from it, especially since this passage must be read alongside the highly dualistic language of ch. 17. Nevertheless, by drawing "all people" to himself, Jesus anticipates the eventual overcoming of the world's opposition and opens the door for hope that "all people" will indeed be drawn to him.

Jesus' "hour" does not belong to him alone, nor is its significance captured by the salvific implications of drawing "all people" to himself. Instead, the attitude of Jesus toward his impending death becomes a model for all believers, as is evident in 12:25–26. Because v. 25 and its Synoptic counterparts are often heard as life-denying assertions, it is important to see them in their context. Jesus does not propound some gnostic-like absolute denial of the goodness of physical life, but he does connect his own death with a certain understanding that life cannot be hoarded away; only those prepared to give up everything can receive the gift of "eternal life," both now and hereafter.

John's Gospel insists that the death of Jesus is simultaneously his exaltation; a parallel "exaltation" belongs to believers as God honors those who serve Jesus (v. 26). Both forms of honor and glory exist because, and only because, God bestows them. Believers are honored by God for their service; Jesus is exalted, but it is God's name that is glorified (v. 28). Nowhere in this schema does John make a place for believers to bring honor on themselves, but only for them to acknowledge the God who exalts Jesus, even in his death.

Sixth Sunday in Lent

(PALM SUNDAY or PASSION SUNDAY)

A first glance at the lectionary for this Sunday would suggest that the preacher must make a choice between observing the day as Palm Sunday or as Passion Sunday. On the one hand, Mark 11 tells the story of the triumphal entry into Jerusalem and quotes a verse from Ps. 118, a song of victory that describes a pilgrim approaching the gates of the Temple. The two passages appropriately go together for the commemoration of the day of hosannas sung and palm branches strewn in the path of Jesus.

On the other hand, Isa. 50 and Phil. 2:5–11 both include the more somber notes of opposition and rejection. The former is one of the so-called Suffering Servant songs, in which God's chosen messenger in seeking to sustain the weary becomes the target of abuse and insult. The latter recounts the faithful obedience of Jesus, including even death, and the promised exaltation. The connection of the two passages is obvious.

But the two sets of texts, the ones for Palm Sunday and the others for Passion Sunday, may not be so far apart. Psalm 118 and Mark 11, though focusing on praise and worship, carry a whiff of impending trouble. In the midst of the psalm are the words repeated several times in the New Testament: "The stone that the builders rejected has become the chief cornerstone" (118:22). And the entry into Jerusalem is made in light of the threefold prediction in the narrative that Jesus would be rejected and killed there (Mark 8:31; 9:31; 10:33–34).

Furthermore, the two texts naturally associated with the Passion theme (Isa. 50:4–9a and Phil. 2:5–11) both have liturgical features. They are pieces of poetry with rhythm and meter. The Christ-hymn in Philippians may well have been a creed or hymn used in the worship of the early church and cited by Paul as a paradigm of the attitude of the Christian community. It concludes with confession and praise. All four passages acknowledge and recite a confidence in the divine mercy of God.

Isaiah 50:4–9a (A B C)

This rather enigmatic statement is in the mouth of an unidentified believer who voices profound trust and confidence in God. In the high days of historical criticism, this poem was reckoned as the third "Servant Song," thus referring to an especially designated servant of God. Such a notion, however, is of almost no help in understanding the text. It is enough to see that this poem models profound faith in a situation of exposure and vulnerability. It is striking that the poem four times uses the phrase "Lord GOD." With this phrase it makes one of the strongest and most daring assertions in the tradition concerning the One upon whom utter reliance is placed. We may organize our comment around that fourfold usage.

The speaker places himself in a position of a learner and a listener (v. 4). (The text correction on the NRSV is unwarranted and unnecessary.) It is "the Lord GOD" who is the instructor to whom the speaker gladly and completely submits. The speaker describes his own position as one fully devoted and responsive to the instruction of God. He has learned to be a willing listener, that is, one addressed with words that give not only instruction, but identity. This speaker is fully God's person. The lesson learned is how to give hope and life to the weary, perhaps in this context the exiles. (On "weary," see Isa. 40:28–31.)

The first line of 50:5–6 continues the thought of v. 4. This is one with "open ears," fully instructed, fully committed to the Yahweh perspective on reality. Verses 5b–6, however, take a curious turn. It is clear that being taught by God how to listen, and then how to sustain with a word, is an unpopular and risky enterprise. We do not know why the learner's task is so dangerous and inflammatory. It is indeed a ministry "against the grain." It may be that comfort to exiles gives the exiles a sense of their identity and vocation, making them restless and assertive and therefore less than submissive to their imperial overlords. That much is conjecture, but it is the sort of outcome that occurs whenever a submissive population is instructed in "the Lord GOD."

Whatever may be the cause, this speaker is subjected to enormous abuse. What he has been taught by Yahweh is not popular. Verses 5b–6 are in fact a rather conventional prayer of complaint, which details the trouble of persecution (in a highly stylized way) and, in the end, serves as a statement of innocence. In spite of abuse, intimidation, and pressure, the speaker has not caved in or given up, but has boldly withstood the terrible pressure in order to keep teaching.

The speaker has known he is not alone or abandoned in his jeopardy (vs. 7–8). The same "Lord GOD" who gave the initial instruction that provoked the trouble is the "Lord GOD" who now "helps," intervening with active and powerful support. That is, God stands by the one whom God has dispatched into conflict, trouble, and abuse.

These verses announce a determined, almost defiant confidence in Yahweh. The language of v. 8 is juridical. That is, the speaker is being taken to court, perhaps to be accused of treason against the (unnamed) overlords, or as a subversive to the good order of the community. The speaker, however, is completely fearless and unintimidated, because he knows that God vindicates (sdq), declares innocent, and so he has no fear of court proceedings.

Verse 9, with the fourth use of our formula "the Lord GOD," completes the thought of vs. 7–8. Again the decisive verb is "help." This time the language is negative. The Lord God will condemn ($rš'$), declare guilty. This term is the negative counterpart of "vindicate" in v. 8. The word pair "vindicate, condemn" (sdq, $rš'$) constitute the two options in a court of law (see Rom. 8:33–34). And because God has already enacted the first verb of vindication, the purveyors of the second, negative action, condemnation, have their chance in court already preempted. They are helpless to do anything that can injure the defendant, and are in fact irrelevant. Indeed, they will use up all their energy in a hopeless court case, and will be exhausted like an old garment helplessly consumed by a moth.

This is an exceedingly difficult text, because we have almost no contextual clues for its interpretation. In its lectionary grouping, of course, it is heard to refer to Jesus in his passion, as he reaches his great showdown with the authorities. Jesus is the fully faithful one who becomes fully obedient, "even [to] death on a cross." As the song of Phil. 2:5–11 asserts, the obedient one at risk becomes the fully honored one by the action of God. The drama of risky obedience and powerful vindication is closely paralleled in our text and in that early hymn of the church. This poem is the voice of one so sure of his vocation that he will not be talked out of his witness. We may ponder that having the capacity to "sustain the weary with a word" is a highly subversive activity, which will get one in trouble with the authorities. The speaker, however, knows that much trouble with the authorities can be withstood, precisely because "GOD helps."

Psalm 118:1-2, 19-29 (A B C)

Palm Sunday is a juncture at which two conflicting emotions collide. On the one hand, there is the festal jubilation over the entry of the King into his royal city, a procession of majesty that dwarfs all other such ceremonial entrances, as this King dwarfs all other kings. This note of celebration is struck, in the Gospel account, by the shouts of the crowd:

> Hosanna!
> Blessed is the one who comes in the name of the Lord!
> Blessed is the coming kingdom of our ancestor David!
> (Mark 11:9-10)

On the other hand, however, there is a strong sense of foreboding, which tempers the joy of the moment. All perceptive persons who come to the Palm Sunday festival (including modern worshipers) are aware that the exaltation of the King which is shortly to occur, and of which the Palm Sunday entrance is the prelude, will be deeply scarred by pain and death.

This amalgam of sensations—anticipation, thanksgiving, supplication—is evidenced in the Psalm lection, where the various emotions are juxtaposed so strikingly that one must raise questions about the psalm's logical coherence. After the initial formulaic thanksgiving (vs. 1-2), the psalmist's song of gratitude over having been saved by Yahweh's power (v. 21) is soon matched by his petition to Yahweh for action (v. 25). The psalmist speaks now to the gatekeepers (v. 19), then to Yahweh (v. 21), and ultimately to the people (v. 29). Yet through the whole there is a consistent motif: we, the people, have arrived to celebrate God's wonderful presence. Fling open the gates that we may enter!

Thus, of the two principal moods of Palm Sunday, Ps. 118:1-2, 19-29 is clearly weighted in favor of joyous celebration. Yet even here the shadow of the cross cannot be blotted out entirely. The stone that Yahweh has chosen as the "chief cornerstone" has been rejected by others, and all who have read the story through to its conclusion know that these evil forces still lurk nearby in their attempt to make this rejection permanent.

In its entirety, Ps. 118 is a psalm of thanksgiving sung by one who has been to the edge of the abyss and who has been delivered by God (see especially vs. 10–14). But only in the verses that form this day's lection do we encounter the theme of pilgrimage to the Holy Place. In its original setting, this was most likely Jerusalem at a time of special significance—the autumn festival, perhaps—the "day that Yahweh has made" (v. 24). In that setting, the "gate of Yahweh" (v. 20) is the gate of the city or of the Temple. "The one who comes in the name of Yahweh" (v. 26) is the pious pilgrim.

In its Palm Sunday application, however, much of this meaning is transformed. The procession is not that of a band of devout worshipers, but of a king and his court. (Some scholars would insist that this "reading" of the text is consistent with its original setting, in that the hymnic literature of ancient Israel's autumn festival, including this psalm, celebrated the reenthronement of the Davidic monarch. If that much-debated interpretation is correct, the Davidic king, or King, is the subject of the psalm both in its Old Testament and its New Testament understandings.) The "blessed . . . one" is no representative pilgrim, but the King of kings. The "day that Yahweh has made" (v. 24) is not an annually repeated occasion, but a once-and-for-all moment leading up to the humiliation and exaltation of this Messiah-King.

Striking in its singularity in this text is v. 22, which juts quite unexpectedly above the surrounding context. Nothing has been said to this point in the entire psalm about a building stone, nor is the matter broached again. The thought appears as an exclamation mark in the middle of a sentence:

> The stone that the builders rejected
> has become the chief cornerstone.

And the question naturally arises: To what or whom is the psalmist referring? To declare that this is some preexisting proverb which has been incorporated into the psalm may be quite true, for the lines do have a certain axiomatic ring to them. But what flow of logic within the mind of the psalmist called forth their use, and of what building has this rejected stone become the chief corner? Various answers have been proposed, but one thing seems perfectly clear. The writers of the New Testament could think of no one to whom these lines applied more appropriately than the about-to-be-rejected Jesus, who becomes the adored and reigning risen Christ (Mark 12:10 and elsewhere).

SIXTH SUNDAY IN LENT

> This is the LORD's doing;
> it is marvelous in our eyes.
> (Ps. 118:23)

Indeed, it is the power of God in the events of Christ's passion and resurrection that Christians celebrate when we use this text as a Palm Sunday lection. The power of God is at the text's heart and core. For that which occurred at Calvary and the open tomb shattered all human expectations, even those—especially those—of the men and women who were eyewitnesses of the events. More than logic or "nature" were on display here. The One who entered the city as a ridiculous-looking, donkey-riding King destroyed the bonds of sin and death. And he did so by the strength of a loving and redeeming God.

Thus the climax of the lection, which in v. 1 appears to be an overly familiar refrain (compare Pss. 107:1; 136), here becomes a surge of thanksgiving from hearts that have been touched by a God whose saving love extends to the grave and beyond.

> O give thanks to the LORD, for he is good,
> for his steadfast love endures forever.
> (Ps. 118:29)

Philippians 2:5-11 (A B C)

While some of the assigned readings for Palm/Passion Sunday change in each of the three years of the lectionary cycle, the Old Testament and epistolary lessons remain the same. Furthermore, this is the only occasion in the cycle when the remarkable Christ-hymn from Philippians appears. Unfortunately, it is often bypassed as the choice for a sermon text because of the traditional observance on this Sunday of Jesus' triumphal entry into Jerusalem. Whether on Palm Sunday or on some other occasion within the season of Lent, Phil. 2:5–11 warrants attention because of its powerful narration of the Christ-event and its subtle manner of drawing implications from the story for the attitude and life of the community.

First of all, *the passage tells (sings?) the story of Christ's humiliation and exaltation*. In the initial movement (2:6–8), Christ is the decision maker, who chooses not to cling to his divine prerogative but enters into the enslaved human predicament. He never flinches, but obediently follows the divine will, even to his crucifixion. The second movement (vs. 9–11) relates God's responding activity, making Jesus' name exalted above all others and the confession of him as Lord a universal one.

It is not unimportant that the passage is a piece of liturgical poetry, perhaps a hymn or a creed. Scholars may debate its conceptual background, its authorship, and its exact metric flow, but there is no questioning its rhythmic quality. The NRSV helpfully prints the text in a plausible poetic structure. Its original context is that of worship, where all good theology ultimately belongs. The intent is to praise God, to invite the congregation to join in the genuflecting and in the confession of Jesus' Lordship.

The last two verses are, of course, a promise. A Philippian audience that was suffering for the sake of the gospel (1:29–30) knew only too well that all knees had not yet bent in obeisance, nor had all lips yet confessed Jesus as Lord. They, like Jesus, were living in a violent world and were facing opposition without and tensions within. But liturgy shapes life and molds expectations. Sunday after Sunday the congregation could rehearse the promise and by it be nurtured in its vocation in the world. Jesus' scandalous death, which also characterized both Paul's life and the readers' lives, was not the end. The future was in the hands of the servant Lord.

But, in context, *the hymn also calls readers to conform to Christ and adopt the same self-giving attitude in their relations to one another.* However 2:5 is translated (and it is notoriously difficult), it exhorts a style of life patterned after the self-chosen humiliation of Jesus. (The NEB reads, "Let your bearing towards one another arise out of your life in Christ Jesus.") The direction of 2:1–4, with its insistence on a common mind and attention to the interests of others, makes sense in light of the example of Christ. Or, to put it another way, the character of Jesus' life provides content for the obedience to which Jesus' followers are called.

The context emphasizes not so much specific actions as attitudes. The verb "think" (*phronein*) found in 2:5 appears an inordinate number of times in this letter (ten times). Its range of meanings includes not only the activity of the intellect, but the direction of the will—"to be intent on," "to be disposed toward," "to set the mind on." This or that kindly deed does not exhaust the obligation believers have to one another. Their entire identity—their intuitions, sensitivities, imaginations—is to be shaped by the self-giving activity of Christ.

Perhaps a word is needed on the way in which Jesus' so-called humiliation becomes a model for Christian thinking and action. Humility is often misinterpreted in our culture, leaving people with the notion that meekness equals weakness. Yet, in this context, humility differs radically from both self-deprecation and false modesty. Either putting oneself down or playing a charade that one is really not so gifted as others mocks the intent of the text. Readers are not invited to think ill of themselves or to engage in some self-degrading practice.

The model is Christ, whose self-emptying was in fact a fulfilling of his true vocation. He attended to the needs of an enslaved humanity. He "humbled himself" by resisting the temptation to follow an easier calling, which would have denied his authentic self. There is no hint at all of self-deprecation. In fact, the implication of Christ's self-giving, drawn prior to the citing of the hymn (vs. 3–4), does not forbid taking an interest in one's own affairs. It simply condemns a selfish preoccupation that ignores or prevents interest in the life of others. Readers are urged to rejoice in the good in fellow Christians.

Mark 11:1–11

Mark's account of the entry into Jerusalem is a major turning point in the Gospel and introduces the events that lead up to Jesus' death and resurrection. Here the location of the action changes, as Jerusalem and its environs occupy center stage from now on in Mark's story (by contrast with Luke, whose story begins in Jerusalem). At this point Jesus begins to make predictions about events that will occur in the immediate future (such as the finding of the colt and the response of those who see the disciples take it), and the fulfillment of those predictions reinforces the reliability of his predictions about his own death and the return of the Son of Man (8:31; 9:31; 10:33–34; 14:62). By virtue of his own action in sending for the colt and riding into Jerusalem on it, Jesus enters the public arena in a way that directly contradicts his earlier pattern of commanding silence following his miracles (for example, 1:44; 7:36; 9:9).

In addition to these new directions in Mark's story, the entry into Jerusalem continues the thread of anticipations of Jesus' crucifixion, a thread that extends back into the opening scene of the Gospel. Mention of the "Mount of Olives" in v. 1, the location of Jesus' arrest, points ahead to the real outcome of this "triumphal entry" (see Zech. 14:4). The crowd's greeting of Jesus as the "coming kingdom of our ancestor David" anticipates his response to the high priest in 14:62. His brief look at the Temple itself introduces the conflict that will follow.

Precisely because this text is a turning point in the Markan story, it teems with irony. The conflict between the apparent triumph and the impending arrest and crucifixion creates a situation in which readers are sensitive to that irony. Conventionally, the irony that stands out to readers turns on the role of the crowds. Here they welcome Jesus with their coats and with palms and with shouts of greeting, like some victorious warrior (see 1 Macc. 13:51) or latter-day sports celebrity. All too soon, the crowds, presumably the same crowds, will demand the release of a common criminal and the death of "the one who comes in the name of the Lord!" The didactic and homiletic significance of that well-known irony makes its way into many Palm Sunday sermons, and for good reason.

Another irony also has its beginning in this passage, and that irony has Jesus himself as its focus. Whatever else lurks in Mark 11:1–11, it is a story in which a guest receives gracious and generous welcome. Several prophetic passages echo through the story, in addition to the explicit quotation of Ps. 118 in v. 9. It is not at all clear that these passages were already connected with whatever messianic expectations Jesus' contemporaries may have had, as those historical questions are notoriously difficult to answer. It is clear, of course, that Mark interprets Jesus in light of these passages; that is, Mark reads them messianically and uses them to depict the welcome Jesus receives. At the very least, Jesus enters Jerusalem as a pilgrim of special standing, one the people see as a messenger of God. His arrival will surely bring with it blessings to Jerusalem and to its inhabitants, and he in turn will be blessed by the association with this holy place.

Nothing could be farther removed, of course, from the events that actually ensue. When Jesus reenters Jerusalem in 11:15, it is to disrupt Temple practice and indict those associated with it. In his "conversations" with the authorities, he undermines their authority and teaching. The parable of the wicked tenants (12:1–12) blatantly threatens the inhabitants of Jerusalem. He accuses the Sadducees of ignorance of both the scriptures and God's power (12:18–27). Finally, he predicts the destruction of the Temple itself (13:2).

Jesus turns out to be a very testy visitor. Like the house guest who seems pleasant enough at a distance but whose long-anticipated stay finds nothing that pleases, nothing that even remotely satisfies, Jesus quickly wears out his welcome. Christian readers, accustomed to reading the Gospels with antipathy toward the crowds and especially toward the authorities, might consider whether they are not due some measure of sympathy. They roll out the red carpet, only to discover that Jesus has come into town to attack all that they prize.

The irony, of course, stems from the fact that the Jesus whom the crowds welcome and want is not the Jesus they in fact get. They desire the genial guest, the teacher who will say what they want to hear and in ways that are pretty and soothing. The "kingdom" they prepare to receive in 11:10 is not a kingdom for which they are prepared.

This contradiction runs throughout Mark's narrative. Peter confesses that Jesus is the Messiah, but his understanding of that title conflicts with the Messiah who stands before him. Other disciples engage in the same misunderstanding when they want Jesus to grant them seats adjacent to his own in the kingdom. Here that misunderstanding extends to the many in Jerusalem, who welcome the kingdom of David but do not perceive what that kingdom means. As misunderstanding turns to rejection, the betrayal, arrest, and crucifixion of Jesus must inevitably follow.

Holy Thursday

With its multiple historical connections—the betrayal and arrest of Jesus, the Last Supper, the Passover—Maundy Thursday becomes an occasion on which Christians recall these important events in the life of Jesus and the history of Israel. But merely remembering does not do justice to these events, which have ongoing, present significance for believers. The passages assigned for Maundy Thursday press beyond recollection of what happened to re-presenting (in the sense of presenting again) them to Christians today.

The notion of re-presenting Passover comes to expression in the text's instructions to Israel. Elaborate instructions regarding the celebration of Passover serve not simply to remind Israel of a past event but to present, even to create, that event afresh in each generation. In that sense, the exodus is not a faint memory of something that happened to distant relations, but an experience that is shared by each new generation.

Paul's instructions regarding the Lord's Supper urge a similar connection between present community and past event. As Paul saw it, the Corinthians ate the Lord's Supper in a way that failed to acknowledge its connection with the death of Jesus, but the meal itself was a proclamation of that death. In the meal, believers stand between the death of Jesus and his parousia, living with the reality of both those events.

Although the Fourth Gospel's story of Jesus washing the feet of his disciples finds scant place in the church's liturgy, it too urges re-presentation rather than mere recollection. Not a simple tale about Jesus' humility and service, the story foreshadows the death of Jesus and thus re-presents his ultimate act of servanthood. By virtue of his service to his disciples and the service of his death, Jesus radically challenges conventional, hierarchical notions about leaders and followers. Small wonder that the story of Jesus' betrayal immediately follows this disturbing scene.

In one sense, the psalm stands apart from these stories or instructions about specific events in the life of Israel or the church. The psalmist's gratitude, however, expresses itself in a public way, "in the presence of all his people." By virtue of this public display of thanksgiving, and indeed by means of the psalm itself, the psalmist presents again to believers of every age the present need for thanksgiving and praise.

Exodus 12:1–4 (5–10) 11–14 (A B C)

Jesus' last supper with his disciples before his death is linked to the celebration of the Passover. For that reason, the Old Testament reading concerns Israel's provision for Passover. The Passover regularly needs to be understood on its own terms as a commonality shared by Christians while a genuinely Jewish practice. When understood on its own Jewish terms, it is then possible, as a second interpretative move, to incorporate into this festival the story of Jesus. Obviously such a Christian appropriation of the story and the festival must take care not to intrude on the intrinsically Jewish character of the festival.

The larger part of this text is a Priestly instruction for the careful liturgical management of the festival (Ex. 12:1–10). Liturgical rites, especially those which are precious and crucial, take on a life of their own. As a result, some of the detailed observances continue to be honored and taken seriously even though the original reasons for them may have been lost. These verses may be understood as analogous to a manual of instruction for Christian priests in a high sacramental tradition, concerning the particular gestures of celebrating the Eucharist. Every gesture counts and must be performed with precision.

This festival marks a beginning point in Israel's life (v. 2). It is as though life begins again in this moment of remembering and reenactment. The focus is the lamb. The lamb is both good food and costly commodity. A whole lamb may be too much meat and too much expense for a small household (v. 4). Careful attention is paid to the economic factors in the festival requirement. The lamb must be a good one, not a cull, for it must be worthy of its holy function (v. 5). The lamb provides blood as a sign on the doorposts and roasted meat for the meal. Israel's religious act consists in replicating a memory of eating together.

After the actual guidelines for proper celebration, we are offered theological interpretation of the act (v. 11). The meal with the lamb could be simply a meal. In the community of memory, however, the meal takes on peculiar signification. This is not an ordinary meal, and it must not be eaten in an ordinary way. Israel is to dress for the occasion in its travel clothes, with shoes (sandals) and weapons on (girded loins), with a staff in the hand, ready for leave-taking. The meal must be eaten quickly, with a sense of urgency. This "street theater" will be reenacted as though it were the moment before the exodus departure. In each new generation, the boys and girls participate in the drama of leave-taking from Egypt. They gulp the food, lean toward the door, watch in eagerness, and wait in anxiety, for they are at the brink of dangerous freedom. At the edge of freedom, nobody wants to linger with Pharaoh. This is a quick meal, not fancy or decorous, just provision for the long, hard trek to newness.

The passage concludes with a more formidable connection to the exodus memory (vs. 12–14). The term "Passover" now becomes a routinized festival, originated (so Israel remembers) in an awesome, dread-filled political act of violence wrought by God. The meal refers, as Israel tells it, to a powerfully partisan act. God acts against the Egyptian empire, on behalf of the shamelessly abused slaves who became Israel.

The text is a liturgical memory, but it is cast as a present-tense happening. God is the key actor: "I will pass through. . . . I will strike down. . . . I will execute judgments." The act of justice (judgment) that God performs is to crush the oppressive power of the empire. In that act of justice, it is clear that "our story" revolves around Yahweh, the God of freedom and justice.

Psalm 116:1–2, 12–19 (A B C)

Psalm 116 is, in its entirety, a song of thanksgiving on the part of one who has been delivered by God from some distress, probably physical illness. As is typical of both psalms of thanksgiving and psalms of lament, attention is here given to the psalmist's vow to Yahweh. While such an element may seem to modern readers an offensive sentiment, in that it smacks of an attempt to bribe God, the interest of the poet lay in quite a different direction. The vow was an effort to say, in essence, "In response to your saving love in my life, O Yahweh, I confess that I will never again be the same person that I was before." Psalm 51, a model psalm of confession, contains this realization by the psalmist:

> [In response to your love, O Yahweh,]
> ... I will teach transgressors your ways,
>   and sinners will return to you.
> [When you have delivered me, O God,]
>   O God of my salvation,
> ... my tongue will sing aloud of your deliverance.
> (Ps. 51:13–14)

The Psalm lection for Holy Thursday, after an introduction that affirms the grace of Yahweh (Ps. 116:1–2), turns to that part of the psalm which comprises the vow. Having thanked Yahweh for saving him, the poet now describes the change this salvation has brought to his life.

Structurally, this passage is composed of two quite similar parts, vs. 12–14 and vs. 16–19, separated by a verse (15) which, because it seems to break the logical flow of the text, may be a later insertion.

The first section, and thus the entire lection, is introduced by a question in v. 12 that reminds one of Micah 6:6. Yet the concern here is not, "How may I please God?" but, "How may my life more adequately express the redemptive power of God within me?" The response (Ps. 116:13) is in terms of drinking the cup of salvation and of openness to the reality ("the name") of God. The brief section closes (v. 14) with a promise, the major theme of the passage: "I will pay my vows to Yahweh."

The second section (vs. 16–19) is closely parallel to the first except in two respects. In place of the question of v. 12, v. 16 insists on the low status of the pray-er. The description of the psalmist as the child of a serving girl may suggest to Christian readers the figure of Jesus Christ, son of Mary, but to ancient readers the phrase would have been evocative of Ishmael, the son of Abraham's (Sarah's) servant Hagar (Gen. 16). Although a son of the patriarch Abraham, Ishmael was cut off from the promise because of his mother's inferior status. And so the psalmist is calling attention to his own weakness and alienation at the same time that he celebrates God's intervention, which has overruled these realities. The force of Ps. 116:16 is strikingly captured by the REB:

> Indeed, LORD, I am your slave,
> I am your slave, your slave-girl's son;
> you have loosed my bonds.

The other important manner in which the second section differs from the first is in the substitution of v. 17a for 13a, identifying a "thanksgiving sacrifice" as an appropriate vehicle for expressing God's redemptive presence instead of "the cup of salvation."

The balance of the second section replicates the first, in that vs. 17b–18 are identical of vs. 13b–14. Verse 19, which has no precise equivalent in the first section, is merely a poetic extension of v. 18b (14b).

The result of viewing the lection as two parallel sections, divided by the "foreign" (?) v. 15, is that we may identify three specific acts as the psalmist's means of expressing the reality of what God has done in his life:

1. Because of the goodness of Yahweh (vs. 1–2), I will lift the cup of salvation (v. 13a).
2. [I will] call on the name of Yahweh (v. 13b).
3. I will offer to [Yahweh] a thanksgiving sacrifice (v. 17a).

The relevance of this lection to the Last Supper and to Maundy Thursday observances through the ages may be found in all three of the psalmist's affirmations. (It is not entirely clear what the psalmist had in mind by the phrase "the cup of salvation," although a liturgical setting is likely, as in Num. 28:7.) Not only are these themes present in the narrative descriptions of Jesus' final meal with the disciples before the crucifixion (see Mark 14:22–25), but they permeate all celebrations of the Christian Eucharist. And by one of those hermeneutical "leaps" that transform many Old Testament texts, the subject of the psalm, the one who prays it and who experiences that which the text describes, is not just any human being, but Jesus Christ, that quintessential human being who is also God's representative to humankind. It is Jesus Christ who both lifts the cup of salvation and who, through his shed blood, fills that cup. It is Jesus Christ who not only calls on the name of the Lord, but provides us with that unique name by which we approach God. It is Jesus Christ who not only offers a thanksgiving sacrifice, but himself becomes that sacrifice.

Even the "intruding" (?) v. 15 of Ps. 116 assumes new meaning when this text is read christologically.

> Precious in the sight of the LORD
> is the death of his faithful ones.

Of all the Lord's faithful ones, who was more faithful than He? Of all the deaths, whose is more precious than His?

1 Corinthians 11:23–26 (A B C)

These lines concerning the sharing of bread and wine are so familiar to most Christian ministers that the act of reading the text may seem superfluous. As the "words of institution" they are known by heart and can be recited verbatim. And, indeed, that intimate knowledge of this passage is consistent with the way in which Paul introduces it. When he writes, "For I received from the Lord what I also handed on to you," he uses technical language for the transmission of tradition, and the church's intimate knowledge of this passage continues that understanding of it.

The tradition itself contains the simple and direct words that connect the ordinary sharing of bread and wine with the death of Jesus and its significance for humankind. The bread signifies the body of Jesus, broken in death. The cup signifies the blood of Jesus, poured out in death. Through that death comes a new covenant, and through participation in the meal comes the remembrance of Jesus. The word remembrance (*anamnēsis*) appears in both the statement regarding the bread and the statement regarding the wine, suggesting that the Lord's Supper is vitally connected with the church's memory of Jesus. What the exact nature of that remembrance is becomes clearer in 1 Cor. 11:26.

With v. 26 Paul no longer cites the traditional words of Jesus, but offers his own interpretation of the Supper: "For as often as you eat this bread and drink the cup, you proclaim the Lord's death until he comes." Two crucial points emerge here. First, Paul asserts that the very act of the meal *is* an act of proclamation. In the celebration of the Lord's Supper itself, the church engages in the preaching of the gospel. Protestant exegetes, uncomfortable with the omission of the verbal act of proclamation in this passage, long rejected this point by attempting to argue that Paul means that preaching *accompanies* every celebration of the Supper. If understood that way, however, the verse simply tells the Corinthians what they already know (preaching accompanies the meal) and adds nothing at all to the passage. Verse 26, in fact, culminates Paul's discussion of the meal by explaining its significance. The Lord's Supper is not just another meal, the eating of which is a matter of indifference; this celebration is itself a proclamation of the gospel of Jesus Christ.

The second point Paul makes in this verse comes in the final words, "You proclaim the Lord's death until he comes." The Lord's Supper is a very particular kind of proclamation—a proclamation of

Jesus' death. A different kind of celebration, perhaps a celebration of Jesus' miracle of multiplying the bread and the fish, might proclaim Jesus' life and teaching. Even the Lord's Supper might be understood as a celebration of the person of Jesus as a divine messenger. Building on the words of institution with their emphasis on the coming death of Jesus, Paul forcefully articulates his view that the Lord's Supper proclaims Jesus' death. Unless the final phrase, "until he comes," merely denotes the time at which celebration of the Lord's Supper will come to an end ("you keep proclaiming in this way until Jesus returns"), what it does is to convey the eschatological context in which the church lives and works. The church proclaims Jesus' *death* within the context of a confident expectation that he will come again in God's final triumph.

In this passage Paul has a very sharp point to make with Christians at Corinth, who are preoccupied with factions, with competing claims about the gospel, and with what appear to be class struggles. Paul's comments about their celebration of the Lord's Supper do not make the situation entirely clear to us, but it appears that they have followed the customs of the day, according to which the hosts of the meal served the choicer foods to their social peers and the less desirable foods to Christians of lower social or economic status. The activity of eating and drinking, and the struggle over that activity, has dominated the celebration of the meal. Paul's response to that situation is to recall forcefully the nature of the Lord's Supper. This is not another social occasion. It is *in and of itself* the proclamation of Jesus' death. Because it is a proclamation, Christians must treat it as such. Whatever conflicts there are about eating and drinking, they belong outside and apart from this occasion.

As earlier in the letter, Paul emphasizes the proclamation of Jesus' death as central to the gospel itself (see 1 Cor. 1:18–25; 2:1–2). Over against the Corinthians' apparent conviction of their own triumph over death, their own accomplishments and spiritual power, Paul asserts the weakness of Jesus, whose faithfulness to God led to his death, and Paul insists that the church lives in the tension between that death and the ultimate triumph of the resurrection.

In the context of the church's observance of Maundy Thursday, this passage recalls again the death of Jesus. That recollection is no mere commemoration, as occurs with the recollection of an anniversary or a birthday. The remembrance, especially in the Lord's Supper, serves to proclaim the death of Jesus Christ once again, as the church continues to live between that death and God's final triumph.

John 13:1–17, 31b–35 (A B C)

Thursday of Holy Week is often a time for congregations to celebrate the Lord's Supper. The four texts listed in the lectionary for the day in varying ways provide interpretations appropriate to the observance. Of the four, the reading from John's Gospel is unique. Jesus' washing of the disciples' feet is found in no other Gospel, and in the Johannine narrative it takes the place of the institution of the Supper. In doing so, it provides an interpretation of Jesus' death, just as the traditional words of institution in the Synoptic Gospels and in the Pauline letters do.

Before considering the foot washing as an example of service given to the disciples, we must first see it as *a dramatic commentary on Jesus' death*. The introductory verses (13:1–3) set an unusual context for the action Jesus performs—he knows that the time for departure has come; he loves his disciples to the uttermost; he anticipates a return to the Father. Before Jesus takes the towel and the basin, we the readers are reminded of what is immediately to occur beyond the incident. Further, the language that says he "took off his outer robe," "tied a towel around himself" (v. 4), and "put on his robe" again (v. 12) is reminiscent of the good shepherd who lays down his life in order to take it again (10:17–18).

The dialogue with Peter occupies most of the story and provides the essential explanation of Jesus' action (13:6–10). Peter is not chided for his misunderstanding, but is told, "You do not know now what I am doing, but later you will understand." After Jesus' death and resurrection, Peter will be in a position to grasp what has happened to him. When Peter vehemently resists, Jesus warns him, "Unless I wash you, you have no share with me." The only way to belong to Jesus is to receive his cleansing service, to let him do what he came to do. Peter apparently prefers a different kind of Savior, one whose journey to God takes him by another route than the cross. He might have been happier washing Jesus' feet than letting Jesus wash his. The thought of Jesus on his hands and knees at Peter's feet is too threatening. Only with great reluctance does he yield to a serving Lord.

The shorter reading of 13:10 (see the margins of RSV and NRSV) is probably to be preferred over the longer reading ("except for the feet"). "One who has bathed" *is* the one whose feet have been washed. Nothing further is needed. The humiliating death of Jesus is sufficient to provide thorough cleansing.

After seeing in Jesus' washing of feet an interpretation of his serving, saving death, the reader is in a position to view the washing as *a drama of what Jesus' followers are to be and do*. He has given "an example" which the disciples are to emulate, and what a radical example it is! More than simply kindly deeds to the neighbor, more than a cherry pie in a time of crisis, more than money donated to a worthy cause.

The precise wording of the challenge in vs. 13–14 is critical. It is "your Lord and Teacher" who washes feet. While it might not have been so unusual for the pupil to wash the feet of the teacher, in this incident the roles are reversed. The One who had come from God and was going to God performs the menial chore for reluctant disciples. The action of Jesus subverts the regular hierarchical structure. The accepted patterns of authority are undermined, or, better said, authority is redefined in new and vivid images—a towel and a basin.

Following Jesus' example ("You also ought to wash one another's feet") means creating a community of equals, where the status of superior/inferior is reversed in the act of service. The world demands a pecking order in which everyone knows his or her place and in which power is carefully protected. Jesus' deed and his subsequent challenge to the disciples reject such a structure in favor of a new kind of parity. The Lord takes on the role of the slave. When people have a share with Jesus and respond to his cleansing death, they constitute a community where such reversal of roles is the norm and not the exception. The church is "blessed" when it follows Jesus' example (v. 17).

It is instructive that at two points in the narrative there is mention of the presence among the disciples of one who will betray Jesus (vs. 10b–11, 18–19). The church should not be surprised that it is a mixed body, that it includes both the faithful and the unfaithful, both the washers of feet and the betrayers. Yet Judas is not mentioned by name. He is not singled out. The other disciples do not know who the guilty one is until after the fact. They are not told to wash only the feet of those they think are faithful and to ignore the rest. In fact, they expect to serve the betrayer in their midst—just as Jesus does.

The incident provides real depth for understanding the new commandment Jesus gives (vs. 34–35). Love is defined as more than feelings, more than liking, more than compassion-from-a-distance. "Just as I have loved you, you also should love one another."

Good Friday

The Gospel writers often frustrate modern readers, whose preoccupation with human emotion wishes to know not just what happened and why, but how those involved *felt* about things. Readers of the stories of Jesus' passion and death may wonder why the Gospels give so little detail about the crucifixion itself, especially about the emotional state of those present. John, the only Gospel writer who includes Jesus' mother among those present at the cross, ascribes to her not a single thought or word. Perhaps the utter shame of crucifixion prompted the evangelists to move with some dispatch through this scene. More likely, the horrors of crucifixion were too well known to require rehearsal for a contemporary audience.

In the Synoptic Gospels, the dominant emotional tone of the story stems from the dying Jesus, who cries out his despair and forsakenness. This connection between Jesus' death and his sense of being abandoned by God probably stems from the reading of Ps. 22 and, in turn, prompts Christians to see in this psalm, as in Isa. 52:13–53:12, reflections of the abandonment of Jesus. The passage from Heb. 4 and 5 likewise emphasizes Jesus' suffering, a suffering that makes him fully human.

At the same time, it is not appropriate to conclude that God disappears at the cross and only emerges again in the event of Easter. Christian proclamation of the cross begins with the understanding that *even* in Jesus' utter abandonment, God was nevertheless present. John's narrative displays that presence through the sign that proclaims Jesus "King of the Jews" and through Jesus' own declaration that all is fulfilled (19:30). The revelation to Mark's centurion, who proclaims Jesus to be "God's Son" when Jesus breathes his last breath, likewise shows God's presence in and through the cross.

The passages from Isaiah and from the Psalms continue to aid Christians who struggle to articulate the profound mystery of this event. It displays the profound despair of God's Son. It prompts human despair at the utterly corrupt ways of a world in which the innocent suffer, too often alone. And yet it simultaneously asserts God's presence, even within that final aloneness. If the promise of God's final triumph reveals itself only in Easter, it nevertheless presses to be seen even in the noon hour of Good Friday, for even there God does not abandon the world.

Isaiah 52:13–53:12 (A B C)

This well-known text is notoriously elusive and elliptical. The text is far from clear, and the historical reference is completely obscure. Indeed, David Clines (*I, He, We, & They: A Literary Approach to Isaiah 53*; Sheffield: JSOT Press, 1976) has urged that the poem deliberately avoids concrete historical reference. That poetic strategy, among other things, has permitted the church to hear in "my servant" an allusion to the suffering and death of Jesus as a saving event willed by God.

The poem (the part chosen for today's lection) begins with a resounding, triumphant assertion (Isa. 52:13). This nearly defiant enunciation becomes more astonishing as we hear the subsequent poem, which reads like a contradiction of this buoyant verse. Thus, from the outset, the poem voices a remarkable dissonance. This one who "had no form or majesty," this one "despised and rejected . . . held [to be] of no account . . . struck down . . . wounded . . . oppressed . . . afflicted," this one will prosper. We know from the beginning what the abusers of the servant never discern. The servant will be "lifted up . . . very high."

The servant may prosper. For now, however, the servant is lowly, unattractive, and without commanding presence (52:14–53:3). We are not told his precise condition; it is enough that he is "marred." His condition "startles." He has the sort of defect that causes people to look away in repulsion and yet to look glancingly back in fascination. He is a loser, an outsider from whom no one expects anything. He reminds nobody of authority, or of the power to transform or save.

Nonetheless, the servant carries in his body the capacity to heal and restore (53:4–9)! Verses 4–6 make some of the most remarkable statements in all of scripture. These claims are so familiar to us that we almost miss their power and daring. This unattractive loser has embraced and appropriated "our" griefs, sorrows, transgressions, and iniquities. It is *his* suffering embrace that has caused *us* to be healed, forgiven, and restored.

We are here at the central mystery of the gospel, and the miracle voiced by this poem. We are face to face with the deepest issue of biblical faith: How can one in suffering appropriate the hurt and guilt of another? This is not a question that is ever resolved by conventional logic. It rests only on a poetic affirmation that lives very close to honest human experience. It is the case, for example, that the suffering of a parent does indeed transform a child. It is the case that a "wounded healer" can profoundly heal. Here that same inscrutable power of transformation (which defies conventional logic) is embraced by the servant with overwhelming force. This servant gives self over to the hurts and guilts that he could have shunned. He does not shun, but embraces. And "we" are made whole, that is, "given shalom."

The appropriation of hurt and guilt could not happen boisterously, aggressively, or violently. It is done, rather, silently, peacefully, with no violence, with not even an outcry (vs. 7–9). The servant acts vulnerably, in the only way hurt can be healed or sin assuaged. Thus the poem not only witnesses to the agent, it radically asserts the only kind of act that can heal and make whole. In his staggering appearance and in his more staggering action, the servant has indeed changed the world, tilting it (and us) toward wholeness and well-being.

Now the promise of 52:13 will be kept (53:10–12). We return to the word "prosper" (see 52:13). This utterly obedient one will have long life and prosperity. The one who gave his life will receive back an abundant life. He will be exalted and lifted up, because he carried the burdens that were unbearable for the others.

On this holy day, the poem helps the church in rediscerning what Jesus has done and is doing. Jesus' entry into the hurt and guilt of the world has indeed changed the world toward wholeness. We must not exult and expostulate too much. The poem, and its evangelical enactment in the cross, do not warrant loud claims. They call rather for stunned, awed silence in the face of a mystery too deep for speculation or explanation. The miracle here characterized calls for a long, quiet, grateful pause. We watch while God acts vulnerably to do what could only be done vulnerably, caringly, at enormous risk, hurt, and pain. We watch while a healed world is birthed out of the wretchedness.

Psalm 22 (A B C)

The power of Ps. 22 lies in the fact that it is a statement by one who has felt utterly cut off from both God and the human community, yet who, in the end, achieves a remarkable level of peace and lifts to God moving affirmations of thanksgiving and praise. The manner in which the poet initially (vs. 1–21) alternates between expressions of despair and self-reminders of God's goodness in the past strengthens the forcefulness of the text, as if to portray the emotions of one who is utterly at the end of life's rope. The text thus becomes the vehicle for expressing the hopelessness of anyone who feels cut off from all the sources of support so necessary for happiness and well-being. And because of later echoes of this psalm in the narratives of Jesus' passion (especially vs. 1, 7–8, 18), it has a particular relevance for the Good Friday observance.

The "movement" in vs. 1–21 is that of one who tries without success to raise his head, only to sink again into despair and frustration. After having complained to God that God is not to be found in spite of all the poet's efforts (vs. 1–2), the thought of the poor mortal turns to the history of God's people (vs. 3–5). Yet the promises of old,

> To you [our ancestors] cried, and were saved;
> in you they trusted, and were not put to shame,

become a bitter mockery to the psalmist for the very reason that God's saving activity of yesteryear seems not to be available here and now.

Again the cycle is repeated, but this time the psalmist complains of total alienation from the human community. With the bitterness of one who has taken life's social relationships for granted, only to discover how vital they are now that they are gone, the poet laments the loneliness of isolation. Those other human beings who should be sources of comfort and strength have turned their backs, so that in v. 6 the very humanity of the psalmist is brought into question:

> I am a worm, and not human.

Once more a remembrance of the past goodness of God is raised by the poet (vs. 9–11), with special emphasis on one of the strongest of all human bonds, that of the mother and the child. But in despair, the poet must acknowledge that the God who created and sustained him is now nowhere to be found.

Having vainly tried twice to lift his spirits through references to the past goodness of God, the psalmist now attempts to describe his total desolation (vs. 12–21). Most of the metaphors employed here have counterparts elsewhere in the Psalter (compare Pss. 31:9–10;

GOOD FRIDAY

32:3-4), but the manner in which they are piled on one another imparts an unusually heavy mood of melancholy and resignation.

In a general sense, vs. 1-21 give tongue to the unutterable despair felt by one whom circumstance has cast completely adrift from all the reference points of life and from all other persons who lend joy and hope. There is no glimmer of divine grace, except that which the memory can borrow from the past. Only the act of prayer itself, which implies that someone must be listening, betrays any hope on the part of the poet. God is gone, and God's only presence is a distant flame, whose glimmer can be seen faintly across the years. The entire substance of vs. 1-21 is summed up in v. 1.

Yet there are two features that prevent these stanzas from becoming, like Ps. 88, an almost completely negative statement. The first is that vs. 1-21 are balanced by vs. 22-31, where the saving deeds of God are celebrated with thanksgiving and joy. (For comments on vs. 22-31, see the Second Sunday in Lent, Year B.) The other—and far more important—feature of this text is to be found in its association with the sufferings of Jesus Christ. As noted above, this includes direct connections with the passion narratives in the New Testament, but it is an association that extends beyond these verbal links. For whoever the original psalmist may have been or whatever human figure that inspired writer may have had in mind, Christians have understood that this psalm describes in a special way that human being who, because of the weight of sin attached to his suffering and death, stood in greatest isolation from God—Jesus Christ!

Thus, one cannot read v. 1 as an expression of one's own sense of apartness from God without remembering the utter despair with which these same words fell from the lips of the Crucified (Mark 15:34). One cannot consider vs. 7-8 as relevant to whatever betrayal and isolation one has experienced from those who were supposed to be friends without remembering the betrayal and mockery of Jesus (John 18). And one cannot find in v. 18 a statement concerning injustice suffered at the hands of others without recalling the terrible miscarriage of justice at Calvary (John 19:23-24).

But if despair, betrayal, and injustice had been the only realities at Calvary, we would today remember the execution of the Galilean peasant in a very different way, if we remembered it at all. However, in the end, despair was overturned by hope, betrayal gave way to trust, and injustice was conquered by the righteousness of God. For Good Friday was subordinated to Easter, and joy returned: the God who seemed to have forsaken Jesus raised him from the dead. And in Jesus' place, God crucified the despair of those who were convinced that they could never find God again.

Hebrews 4:14–16; 5:7–9 (A B C)

In its opening chapters, the Christology of Hebrews strikes a tone of exaltation. Jesus is the "heir of all things" (1:2), an agent of creation (v. 2), superior even to the angels (vs. 5–14). Even if the subjection of Jesus to the weakness of human life is mentioned (for example, 2:14–18), that subjection pales in comparison with the language that celebrates the "apostle and high priest of our confession" (3:1). In its characterization of Jesus as the "great high priest who has passed through the heavens" (4:14) and as "without sin" (v. 15), the passage assigned for Good Friday continues this theme of the exaltation of Jesus. Alongside the exaltation of Jesus, however, this passage sounds a different note. Jesus is able to "sympathize with our weaknesses" (4:15), and Jesus "offered up prayers and supplications, with loud cries and tears" (5:7). Like human beings who serve as priests, Jesus' priesthood results from God's will, rather than his own (5:1–6).

At the heart of the passage is a comparison of Jesus' priesthood with that of human beings. This comparison allows the author of Hebrews to say something important about Jesus and, at the same time, to offer comfort and encouragement to the audience. In 5:1–4, Hebrews describes three aspects of the priesthood of human beings. Human priests have a particular function (they are "put in charge of things pertaining to God"); they have certain personal characteristics (they are themselves "subject to weakness" and "must offer sacrifice" for their sins); and they are designated by God ("And one does not presume to take this honor, but takes it only when called by God").

Hebrews 5:5–10 demonstrates that the priesthood of Jesus shares in these same three aspects, taking the three in an order that is the reverse of vs. 1–4. First Jesus, like human priests, serves at the appointment of God (vs. 5–6). Second, again like human priests, Jesus has the characteristic of being subject to weakness. Jesus' weakness is not sin—a statement that seems unimaginable to Hebrews (4:15)—but nevertheless Jesus participates in the human vulnerability of feelings and needs. As evidence of Jesus' human feelings, the author refers to Jesus' act of offering "prayers and supplications, with loud cries and tears" (5:7). Read in the context of Good Friday, these "loud cries and tears" appear to refer to the agony of Jesus on the cross. In the context of Hebrews, however, where Jesus' supplication addresses "the one who was able to save him from death," Jesus' cries seem to be a plea for deliverance from *out of death.* That is, the author envisions the already crucified and dead Jesus calling to God for deliverance from death. The overarching point, however, remains that Jesus' priesthood is one characterized by sympathy with human anguish. Third, like human priests, Jesus' priesthood has a function. He learned obedience through his suffering (5:8), and he initiated not just forgiveness of sins but eternal salvation for humankind (vs. 8–9). In v. 10, the author places Jesus within the priestly order of Melchizedek, essentially repeating the opening verse of the passage with its designation of Jesus as the "great high priest."

In an attempt to make real the familiar story of Jesus' death as a criminal, Christian preachers and teachers sometimes emphasize the details of physical and emotional suffering produced by crucifixion. And, indeed, the cruelty and shame attached to this particular form of execution, reserved largely for the outcasts of society, can serve to counter the romanticism signified by the wearing of the cross as jewelry. Sometimes, however, rehearsal of the horrifying details of crucifixion has the effect of suggesting that the significance of Jesus' death arises from the extent of his suffering; that is, Jesus suffered extreme physical pain and, as a result, brought about a glorious form of salvation for humankind. The flaw in this way of thinking about the crucifixion can be seen when other deaths, arguably even more cruel and inhumane, enter the conversation. Many of those who died in the Holocaust, with no shred of human respect or decency, as a result of an unbelievable process of cruelty and torture, surely endured more sheer physical pain and emotional grief than did Jesus or other victims of crucifixion. Does that mean that their deaths are somehow salvific or that their pain purchased the eternal life of others? In common with other New Testament writers, the author of Hebrews would answer that question negatively. Hebrews does not elaborate the details of Jesus' pain because that pain is not itself salvific. Jesus' priesthood derives, not from the quantity of his suffering, but from God and from Jesus' own obedience. It is God's sacrifice of Jesus, God's Son, that makes Jesus appropriate as "great high priest."

This reflection on the priesthood of Jesus, here as elsewhere in Hebrews, has a pastoral thrust to it. *Because* of Jesus' priesthood, believers may and should "hold fast" to their confession (4:14), confident that what they say together about God is reliable. Believers may and should "approach the throne of grace with boldness" (4:16), for Jesus has taught them that God hears their prayers. Believers need not be afraid of God, who wants them to approach and who intends to help them.

John 18:1–19:42 (A B C)

John's narrative of Jesus' arrest, trials, crucifixion, and burial is made up of numerous individual scenes, each of which is appropriate for a Good Friday sermon. And yet the two chapters are themselves a literary gem, relating the events with sophistication and subtlety. The preacher's task is to isolate a piece of the broader story for preaching, but at the same time (as with all the Johannine narratives) not to lose sight of the whole and the powerful impact it makes on the careful reader. The skillfully fashioned narrative presents a portrait of Jesus as King of the Jews, who is in complete charge of his own destiny, in the presence of religious authorities who lose faith and governmental officials who lose power.

In reading the narrative, it is critical to notice the strategy of staging that gives individual scenes enormous force. Two examples (though there are many): (a) Jesus is questioned before Annas and Caiaphas in scenes that in themselves carry little significance (18:12–14, 19–24, 28). The scenes serve, however, an important purpose in that the narrator interrupts the questioning to tell about the denials of Peter (vs. 15–18, 25–27) happening simultaneously. The readers are faced then with two trials, one in which Jesus affirms his consistent testimony and is punished with a slap on the face by a guard and another in which Peter rejects his real relationships and goes free. (b) When Jesus is brought to Pilate, we are told that the Jewish authorities do not enter the praetorium, so as to maintain their ritual purity (v. 28). Pilate moves back and forth from talking to the Jews on the outside to talking to Jesus on the inside. The careful staging highlights the ludicrous behavior of the religious people, preoccupied with eating the Passover lamb, but all the while preparing for the death of the Lamb of God. A universal hazard of religious people!

Almost every scene in the narrative exhibits at least some element of irony, incongruities that expose the true nature of Jesus and the feeble, often pretentious schemes of other characters. For example, before Jesus is sentenced Pilate has him flogged by the soldiers, who turn the scene into a mock coronation of the King of the Jews (19:1–3). Interestingly, the narrator never uses the word "mock" (as do the Synoptic accounts), nor is it suggested that this is a charade. The soldiers see and speak the truth when they say, "Hail, King of the Jews!" He is in fact a rejected, maligned King.

Perhaps the most telling irony in the story occurs when Pilate brings Jesus outside the praetorium face to face with the Jews and announces him as "your King." When the people persist in demanding that Jesus be crucified, they justify their actions to Pilate by declaring, "We have no king but the emperor" (19:13–15). Within hours they would recite in their Passover liturgy that their only king is God, but here, in order to reject Jesus, they have to reject God. They unwittingly testify to the fact that Jesus and the Father are one.

Pilate is a key player in the narrative, occupying center stage with Jesus from 18:28 to 19:22. From early on, the reader gets the clear impression that Pilate, representing the power of political authority, is on trial, not Jesus. Jesus asks the pertinent question (18:34) and points out that Pilate inadvertently acknowledges his kingship (v. 37). "Do you not know that I have power to release you, and power to crucify you?" Pilate asks rhetorically (19:10), but as the trial progresses it becomes increasingly clear that Pilate has no power at all. The religious authorities play the stronger hand. Where once Pilate offered the authorities the choice of Jesus or Barabbas, now the tables are turned, and the authorities offer Pilate the choice of Jesus or Caesar (v. 12). Inside the praetorium Pilate is impressed with Jesus, but outside he is at the mercy of his subjects.

But ultimately it is neither Pilate nor the religious authorities who hold the power at the trial and crucifixion. The narrator includes three fulfillment scenes (vs. 23–24, 28, 36–37), whereby details of the story are viewed in light of the Hebrew scriptures, as the fulfillment of divine predictions. The effect is to remind the reader that what is happening is part of the greater plan of God. Jesus confronts Pilate's pretense of power: "You would have no power over me unless it had been given you from above" (v. 11). At his death Jesus utters a word not of distress or God-forsakenness, but of completion: "It is finished" (v. 30). The purpose of God has been fulfilled.

EASTER

Perhaps on no other Sunday of the Christian year are the lections so nicely focused as they are for Easter Day. The common themes of the reality of death, the powerful intrusion of the delivering God, and the manifold responses to resurrection run prominently through the texts—themes needing to be rehearsed in every congregation.

The readings from Ps. 118 and from John 20 honestly face *the reality of death*. In the former, as the psalmist rejoices at an occasion of divine deliverance, death is remembered as the threat, the power opposed to God, from whose clutches God has provided rescue. In the latter, Mary acknowledges the devastation of death and begins to come to grips in a reasonable way with her grief and consternation. In neither case is there any covering over of the fierce and destructive fashion in which death separates and threatens the vitality of life.

All four texts announce *God's deliverance from death*, the divine "power play" that brings life not only for "the one ordained by God as judge of the living and the dead" (Acts 10:42), but also for God's people (1 Cor. 15). The resurrection of Jesus is more than a miracle; it is an eschatological event that makes possible a radical style of new life. Closed worlds are broken open, and old perceptions of what is plausible and possible are shattered. The future becomes a promise of sharing in the resurrection (1 Cor. 15).

Finally, in varying ways, the Easter texts enumerate *several responses to God's deliverance*. The psalmist offers a prayer of thanksgiving for the Lord, "my strength and my might," who "has become my salvation" (118:14). Mary becomes a witness to declare, "I have seen the Lord" (John 20:18). The text of Peter's sermon alludes to eucharistic fellowship and puts the hearers under a mandate to preach and testify to the risen Jesus (Acts 10:41–42). First Corinthians 15 reports on varied groups to whom appearances happen, even to one who has persecuted God's people and for whom the appearance brings a radical transformation. In both worship and everyday human relationships, responses are made to the gracious word of the empty tomb, the word of divine deliverance.

Acts 10:34–43 (A B C)

The Easter celebration is the central event of the Christian year, the center around which all else revolves. In recognition of its special character, the lectionary provides during the entire Easter season (including Pentecost) a reading from Acts as a first lesson. The emphasis in these texts is on the kerygmatic proclamation of the early church and on the work of the Holy Spirit in the response of women and men to that proclamation. The death and resurrection of Christ are viewed by these texts as God's acts of grace, by which women and men are saved and reconciled to God and to one another. In certain respects, many of these texts are the gospel *in nuce*, and that is certainly the case with the passage at hand.

Acts 10:34–43 is one of several sermons by Peter reported in Acts, this one directed to a godly Roman centurion, Cornelius. It is evident to the reader of this text that the presence of the Roman is not incidental to the narrative, inasmuch as the author of Acts wishes to use this occasion to stress the universality of the gospel. Not only has the Spirit spoken to the Roman in a dream commanding him to seek out the preached word (10:1–8, 30–33), but Peter has likewise received a special visitation, which declares, in effect, God's inclusion of Gentiles in the church (vs. 9–16). Yet, even though we have been prepared by these elements for the inclusive nature of Peter's sermon, the force of Peter's universalism is as refreshing as it is energetic. Twice in a single breath the inclusiveness of the gospel is stressed: "In every nation anyone who fears [God] and does what is right is acceptable to him" (v. 35) and "Jesus Christ—he is Lord of all" (v. 36). No matter that the first of these assertions lays emphasis on the oneness of the human family before God, while the second is primarily focused on the unlimited nature of Christ's dominion. In the final analysis, they boil down to a basic affirmation: neither race nor any other quality that marks some as different from others may separate a person from the love of Christ. Neither ought these qualities to separate persons from one another.

Then Peter turns to the Word itself (notice how the declaration of "the message"—or, "the word" [NRSV]—in v. 36 is repeated in v. 37 and made the focus of the balance of the passage). Verses 37–42 recount the events that, in greater detail, are recorded by the four evangelists. Jesus, who had been empowered by God from the beginning (v. 38a), lived a life of remarkable good works, which were intended to thwart the power of the devil (v. 38b) and which were experienced by many people (v. 39a). (Notice that no mention is here made of what Jesus taught.) The outcome of this good life was Jesus' execution (v. 39b). But God did not allow this evil to carry the day, for God both raised Jesus from the dead on the third day and demonstrated his resurrection to those whom God chose as witnesses (vs. 40–41a). These witnesses joined Jesus in eating and drinking—a remark (v. 41b) with clear eucharistic overtones—and they have been charged with the responsibility of spreading the word about the risen Christ (v. 42). Then, almost as an afterthought, the role of the Old Testament prophets is recalled (v. 43).

Two considerations. The first is that this passage, which began by striking such a strong chord of inclusiveness, defines the human family more narrowly only at one point: those who were/are witnesses to the resurrection of Jesus do not include everyone, only those "chosen by God" (v. 41). At first blush this seems a contradiction of the bright note of universalism with which the lection opens. If God "shows no partiality" (v. 34), why are only some chosen? If Jesus Christ is "Lord of all" (v. 36), why are not all persons his witnesses?

The text has, of course, confronted one of those imponderable paradoxes of the gospel. Although the arms of the risen Christ are stretched wide to receive all persons, only some exhibit evidence of the work of the Spirit within them. And since their testimony is that it is not they, but God, who has initiated this saving relationship, we cannot help but wonder about others. Yet of one thing we may be sure: God has not abandoned them or ceased to yearn for them. But the limits of human understanding prevent us from saying more.

A second consideration: the unambiguous turning point in the text is v. 40. All that goes before and all that comes after hinges on the resurrection of Christ. It is the resurrection that demonstrates in a unique manner God's vindication of Jesus and that overturns the work of those who plotted evil. (Notice how, in the text, the murderers of Jesus are not singled out for God's wrath. These people are simply referred to by the innocuous pronoun "they" in v. 39b.) It is also the resurrection that makes it possible for those "chosen by God" to be witnesses to the risen Christ, to eat and drink with him, and to preach and to testify that God raised him from the dead.

In its spare and economic language, Acts 10:34–43 reminds us of that central affirmation of the Christian faith that is repeated in countless ways on Easter Day: "Jesus Christ is risen today. Alleluia!" Let us keep the feast!

Psalm 118:1–2, 14–24 (A B C)

(See Palm Sunday for vs. 1–2, 19–24.) The speaker of these verses (14–24) has just been rescued by God from the assaulting nations (vs. 10–13). A seemingly hopeless situation has been transformed by the radical intrusion of God: "The Lord helped me" (v. 13). For that reason, the speaker gives thanks to God. In the context of Easter, the church reads this psalm as the voice of Jesus, who has been beset by the powers of death. It is only by the greater power of God that the life of Jesus is wrenched out of the grip of death. For that reason, thanksgiving is an appropriate tone and posture for Easter.

Our reading begins with a powerful asseveration (v. 14). "[Yahweh] is my strength . . . my might . . . my salvation." The psalm echoes the language of Moses, who celebrates God's massive defeat of the Egyptian empire (Ex. 15:1–3). This verdict is, on the one hand, a conclusion in the psalm, derived from the recent rescue. On the other hand, it is a premise for what follows in the psalm. God's recent rescue of the speaker becomes the ground for the hope and buoyancy that follow.

The voice of the psalm is one of grateful righteousness (Ps. 118:15–20). The "righteous" are not necessarily the good or the obedient or the pious. They are, rather, the ones who are rescued and vindicated by God. The text speaks of the "tents of the righteous," where the rescued live (v. 15), the "gates of righteousness" through which the obedient enter to worship (v. 19), and the entry of the righteous, the willingness of Yahweh's rescued to come to worship (v. 20). This community consists of those who have known God's massive action on their behalf and who live their lives in glad response to that action. While there is a moral dimension to righteousness, this psalm concerns those who are glad benefactors of God's powerful love. They are righteous not because of what they have done, but because of what they have received from God.

The righteous are not self-congratulatory. Rather, they are exuberantly grateful. They shift all attention away from themselves to the rescuing power of God. Thus the grateful rescued sing three times, "The right hand . . . the right hand . . . the right hand" (vs. 15–16), an allusion to God's powerful, continuing purpose and presence. The church knows at Easter, as this psalm knows, that

Easter would not have happened, and new life would not have been given, except by God's powerful intrusion.

It is because of that "right hand" of power that the speaker draws the conclusion, "I shall not die" (vs. 17-19). I was about to; I could have, but I did not, because God moved against death. Death is a formidable power, which wants to take control; but God will not let it happen. Thus death is not simply a state of negativity, but is an active force for evil. Evil, however, is no match for the power and resolve of God, and so singing is appropriate. Note well that the entire structure of these verses depends on understanding death as an active force, which cannot withstand the authority of God. Neither this text nor the claim of Easter makes sense unless God and the power of death are seen to be in profound conflict.

The utterance of the word "death" is decisive for this psalm. In the world of modernity, it is exceedingly difficult to voice "death" as a hostile power that threatens to undo our lives. That, however, is what the psalm is about. And that is what Jesus knows between Friday and Sunday. Jesus is being undone by the power of death, and the world is being undone with him. But Yahweh "did not give me over to [the power of] death" (v. 18), because God has kept me for the power and prospect of life.

The reading ends in boundless gratitude (vs. 21-24). God has answered. God has heard the need. God has rushed to intervene. God has changed death to life. God has overpowered Friday for the sake of Sunday. The rejected one, left for dead, is the valued one (v. 22).

What a day (v. 24)! The day of rescue is a day for joy. What a day—Easter Day—life day—new day—beginning day. It is a special day. For those saturated with the claims of this psalm, every day is a day of new life. This is the day of God's power for life, and therefore our day of singing and gratitude. On this day, God's people are at a beginning, not an ending.

1 Corinthians 15:1-11

Paul is strangely out of fashion these days. From psychoanalysis to literary criticism to theology to preaching, narrative and reflection on narrative occupy center stage. Hearing and telling stories of faith just seems more interesting than reading long, convoluted argumentation about a particular theological point. The Pauline letters, with their lengthy and not always coherent arguments, seem strained and abstract. Perhaps Paul is nowhere more out of step with the times than in 1 Cor. 15, where he turns the dramatic story of Jesus' resurrection into an extended, even bewildering, argument, beginning with a bare list of those who were witnesses to the resurrection.

The point Paul argues removes him even farther from contemporary experience, for Paul insists that Christians *must* believe that Jesus was raised from the dead. Here he violates contemporary expectations of tolerance and norms of diversity among believing communities, making of his own convictions a kind of litmus test. What difference does it make, after all, whether Christians believe in resurrection? Assuming that Paul is right in his belief, those who do not agree will eventually learn of their error; meanwhile, what harm is done by their skepticism?

A careful rereading of 1 Cor. 15 reveals that Paul believes nothing less than the power of God is called into question when Christians deny the resurrection of Jesus. And, although Paul does not tell stories of resurrection appearances by Jesus, 1 Cor. 15 does directly impinge on the impending story of God's final triumph.

In vs. 1–11, the portion of ch. 15 assigned for Easter, the argument begins with an appeal to tradition. What the Corinthians had previously believed was what Paul preached at Corinth, and what Paul preached was what he himself had received: Christ was raised from the dead. The list in vs. 5–7 apparently consists of bits of tradition about appearances, rather than a straightforward list of those who saw the risen Lord, since the categories clearly overlap (for example, "the twelve" in v. 5 and "all the apostles" in v. 7). At the end of the list stands Paul himself, who understands his own calling to be an experience of the risen Lord.

The last line of this lesson may seem to serve merely as a way of rounding off the discussion: "Whether then it was I or they, so we proclaim and so you have come to believe." Here Paul moves away from his own experience of the resurrection and back to the topic at hand, belief in the resurrection. What Paul says in v. 11 is, however, crucial to his argument. The Corinthians must understand that belief in the resurrection is not a private whim of Paul's, an optional item in his teaching that might have been avoided had some other Christian instructor wandered into Corinth in his stead. No matter who preaches the gospel, the same thing will be said: Christ was raised from the dead. Here Paul puts confidence in the entire Christian community on the line. To deny that Jesus was raised from the dead is to deny the credibility of the community of faith and proclamation.

Is this argument, then, nothing more than a defense of Paul and his fellow apostles? Does Paul's energy for this point come mainly from self-interest, the desire to protect his own authority and that of his colleagues? Taken out of context, this lesson might be read in that way; if read in the larger context of the entire chapter, however, such a conclusion becomes absurd.

In vs. 12–19 (beyond this lection), Paul moves to connect the resurrection of Jesus with resurrection in general. As Ernst Käsemann observed, Paul always writes of Christ's resurrection as the first stage of the general resurrection of the dead. The resurrection of Jesus is not, for Paul, simply the rectification of the human mistake of crucifying Jesus or even God's way of "proving" Jesus' identity. It is, instead, the beginning of the general resurrection.

Reading farther in the chapter takes the argument yet another step: the resurrection of Jesus is the beginning of the resurrection of the dead, which is the beginning of God's final triumph over all God's enemies, even death itself. Finally the primary issue comes to the foreground. Raising Jesus from the dead is a power play on God's part. It signals the beginning of the final apocalyptic drama, in which God will rule over all God's enemies.

Nothing less than the power of God itself is the central topic in this argument. It is for that reason, and that reason alone, that Paul insists so uncharacteristically that the Corinthians must believe in the resurrection of Jesus. To deny the resurrection of Jesus is to deny the power of God, both in this particular deed of the past and in the future consummation of God's plan. The argument is relentless, driving, and driven, for everything is at stake.

Paul does not tell stories about the resurrection of Jesus Christ, at least not in his letters. What he does say, however, identifies Jesus firmly as the first chapter of the ultimate story, in which God ransoms not only all of humankind but all of creation from the powers to which they have been subjected. To affirm that Jesus is raised from the dead is to believe that God is able to do as God has promised. Small wonder, then, that Paul regarded this belief as essential.

John 20:1–18 (A B C)

At the heart of the Gospel reading for Easter is the resurrection appearance of Jesus to Mary Magdalene, leading to her confession, "I have seen the Lord." The narrative tells a wonderful story of a seeking woman, who is surprised by what she finds, or better, by the One who finds her. Hearing her name spoken by Jesus' familiar voice brings a transformation of her grief and the opening of a new world. A number of exegetical puzzles in the text remain to be solved, but, fortunately, they do not hinder our grasp of the basic story.

The actual encounter between Mary and Jesus occupies only four of the eighteen verses. We need, therefore, to pay special attention to what occurs prior to the encounter, in order to be able to understand what is at stake in Jesus' disclosure to Mary, and we need to take note of the brief account of Mary's response to Jesus in the closing verse.

Mary's participation in the story is marked by three parallel statements she makes—to the two disciples (John 20:2), to the two angels at the tomb (v. 13), and to Jesus, alias the gardener (v. 15). Her preoccupation is with the body of Jesus. The empty tomb does not prod her to faith, but rather makes her worry about what has become of the corpse. Who might the "they" be who "have taken the Lord out of the tomb" (v. 2)? The Jews? Joseph of Arimathea and Nicodemus? Grave robbers? The gardener?

Mary's anxiety and consternation are natural. She comes to the tomb early, perhaps for a time of private grieving, for beginning the slow, painful process of coming to grips with the absence of one she deeply loves. Her tears are right on the surface. The cemetery is an appropriate place to grieve. But the removal of the stone and the empty tomb disrupt what she is about and only create fear and frustration. Her mind moves logically to the conclusion that someone has taken Jesus' body. What other possibility might there be?

When faced with the open tomb, Mary functions as a reasonable, sane character. Her grief does not cloud her rational faculties. She arrives at the only conclusion a person in her (and our) right mind can arrive at. Dead bodies do not simply "disappear." Someone has to move them. In a world of cause and effect, of established rules as to what can happen and how, in a closed structure that allows only for the old and familiar to recur, Mary's logic is right on target. Find the body, wherever it has been taken, and get on with grieving.

Apparently, the two disciples (at least, "the other disciple") share Mary's predicament. On hearing the news of the empty tomb, they go to the site and confirm things for themselves. The grave clothes are there, all neatly folded. The text reports that "the other disciple . . . saw and believed" (v. 8). But believed what? Clearly *not* that Jesus was risen from the dead, since the text goes on to explain that the disciples did not yet understand the scripture and that they "returned to their homes." Their experience of the resurrected Jesus comes later (vs. 19–29). For now, what "the other disciple" believed was evidently Mary's report that the tomb was empty. His investigations confirm her statement. He sees no more than she sees, but he is less inquisitive.

Mary's closed world (and ours) is broken open when Jesus calls her name. Something illogical, impossible, and unnatural takes place. The One who was certified as dead (19:33) greets Mary. The established rules as to what can happen and how are overthrown. The old plausibility structure is left in shambles. It is a new day.

The part of the dialogue between Mary and Jesus, though not entirely transparent, is critical. Mary says to the gardener, "Tell me where you have laid him, and *I will take him away*" (20:15, emphasis added). Mary wants the body of Jesus; she wants to do for him what is conventional and proper. She cannot accept the prospect that the corpse has been stolen or hidden. He deserves a decent burial. Jesus responds, *"Do not hold on to me,* because I have not yet ascended to the Father" (20:17, emphasis added). The risen Jesus cannot be controlled, even by Mary's loving concern for him. Her logical and kindly pursuit of his deceased body simply does not leave room for the miracle that has happened, for resurrection, for ascension. The voice of Jesus calling her name shatters her customary world, reasonable though it may be, and opens up a brand-new future. What she is to do is to grieve no longer, but to go to the disciples with the word of Jesus' impending ascension.

Mary's reaction includes an obedient response to Jesus' command and an amazing statement, "I have seen the Lord" (v. 18). Her preoccupation with the corpse is made irrelevant by her encounter with the risen Jesus. Her logical language of cause and effect is replaced by the language of confession. It is a confession to sustain her in the new era without the historical Jesus, an era, nonetheless, in which Jesus' God and Father is the God and Father of the church (the *yours* of v. 17 are plural).

SECOND SUNDAY OF EASTER

The resurrection of Jesus is a community-evoking, community-forming, community-authorizing event. These readings invite a reflection, not upon the miracle of the resurrection itself, but upon the community that is the astonishing outcome of that miracle.

The Gospel reading shows Jesus now come unexpectedly into the company of the bewildered, fearful disciples. In that moment of fear, they are no community. They have lost every dimension of community—except their shared sense of fear, which is no basis for community. It is the intrusion of Jesus into their life that regathers and reconstitutes this community. Three times the newly alive Jesus says, "Peace." It turns out that his word is not only greeting, but assurance, and in the end summons to a new life of "belief," a life of faithful, obedient living.

The psalm and the reading from Acts are affirmations of the joy, power, and well-being that this community receives when freed from fear according to the good gifts of God. In the psalm, these gifts take the form of extravagant materiality. Notice that in that extravagant materiality there is no greed or hoarding, and so no threat or fear. This same communal trust is enacted in the Acts reading. This portrayal of community is part of the church's story of wondrous power, energy, and generosity given by the living God.

The Epistle reading does not so easily ally with the other readings, perhaps because it is cast in such peculiar, Johannine rhetoric. Nonetheless, here also the Easter church is a new "fellowship" enjoying communion with God, and whose members have communion with one another. While the community in its very existence is an evangelical sign and statement, this reading pushes in an ethical direction. This community is not an amorphous assembly, but is marked by "light," "truth," and "righteousness," with the need of the world in its horizon.

This community is an odd and crucial presence in a culture of competition, conflict, isolation, and brutality. Easter makes a very different way of life possible.

Acts 4:32–35

The resurrection of Jesus Christ has cast all human life into new perspective. Of that the book of Acts leaves no doubt, yet these new dimensions are not confined to the relationship between persons and God, nor exclusively oriented toward some moment beyond history. They deeply impinge on the relationships that persons have with one another and on the relationships between individuals and society. And these immediate reverberations of the gospel message occupy the present lection.

The context in which our passage is placed is of some importance, for it offers a moving contrast between the attitudes of the authorities (and the larger world over which they preside) and those of the earliest Christians. Peter and John, having healed a cripple, are detained by the Temple officials when they attempt to interpret their restorative power as an expression of the living presence of the crucified Christ (3:1–4:4). Upon their release, the two disciples worship with their friends and praise God, while praying for strength for their tasks (4:23–30). As a result, they witness new initiatives from God: "They were all filled with the Holy Spirit and spoke the word of God with boldness" (v. 31).

What happens next must be understood as a result of the work of that same Spirit who gave the disciples the power of articulate speech (v. 29). They now begin to share with one another and to care for those in need with a boldness that corresponds to that of their new language.

The experiment in communal living is remarkable, and must not be read against the background of more recent political movements that have attempted similar goals. For the rationale for this activity on the part of the early Christians was not political, but theological and humanitarian, and arose out of their conviction that in Jesus Christ they were one people. Like the members of the sectarian community at Qumran somewhat earlier, they abandoned normal modes of life because, in their view, life itself had been transformed. The kingdom of God was at hand; of that the resurrection of Jesus and the sending of the Holy Spirit were the sure signs. So they committed themselves to live as if that which had been experienced in a provisional manner were actually a present reality. The kingdom of God was soon to come, yet the kingdom of God had already come, and life must reflect the tension between the "already" and the "not yet." In this conviction they were "of one heart and soul" (v. 32), and everything they owned was held in common.

But there was also an important humanitarian dimension to their unusual economy. Beyond being a simple expression of their unity in Jesus Christ, and their anticipation and celebration of the kingdom, their commonality of goods was designed to ensure that "there was not a needy person among them" (v. 34). One remembers that many of the early Christians were people of ordinary means, which, in the ancient world, meant being especially vulnerable to changes in economic fortune. In Israel-of-old, the family had usually been the protector of the individual who, because of sickness or ill fortune, found him- or herself in dire straits. Jeremiah's purchase of the field from his cousin Hanamel (Jer. 32) is likely a case in point, as Hanamel's ability to earn a living by farming had probably been ruined by the Babylonian invasion. But the new cosmopolitanism of the Greco-Roman world had resulted in a more mobile society, one in which individuals—both Jewish and Gentile—were often separated from the family and its protection.

In Jesus Christ, however, there was now a new family: the church. It was to the fellowship of other Christians that the men and women of the resurrected Lord submitted their goods for the well-being of all, and it was to that fellowship that they looked for support in time of need. The implications of this new theology and humanitarianism are not difficult to trace. Societies may change, as may the structures of economics and finance, but the needs of people for support and strengthening do not change. Thus the spirit of Christian unity, in addition to being a proclamation of the Lordship of Jesus Christ, must work to sustain and empower men and women in the myriad ways in which sustenance and empowerment are required—even in a day of insurance policies and government benefits!

Yet, lest the reader of this lection miss its primary interest, right in the midst of this celebration of Christian unity and caring our attention is drawn back to an element that formed part of the larger context of this story. Above and beyond the proclamation of a new social and economic reality, the resurrection of Jesus Christ was (and is!) the proclamation of a new understanding of God's activity in human life.

> With great power the apostles gave their testimony to the resurrection of the Lord Jesus, and great grace was upon them all. (Acts 4:33)

Not only in deed but in word these early Christians lived their witness to the renewing power of Jesus Christ. And lives were touched and transformed.

Psalm 133

This brief psalm is now placed in a larger group of "Songs of Ascents" (Pss. 120–134), presumably grouped together to be used in pilgrimage toward the Jerusalem Temple. The entire group tends to be buoyant and somewhat celebrative, the kind of songs we might expect in a group of joyous, exuberant pilgrims on their way to Jerusalem. Such a literary-liturgical context, however, does not tell us much about Psalm 133 itself.

The theme of the psalm is clear and succinct in the first verse. To have members of an extended family (tribe) living together in harmony and unity is a wondrous thing, "good and pleasant." The alternative, which this poem wants to reject, is that a family should be at cross-purposes, quarrelsome, inclined to hostility, and, in the case of a tribe, given to internecine vengeance. Thus the poem affirms and celebrates a community that functions in a healthy, reconciling way.

This vision of communal harmony may be rooted in a quite concrete social experience. The imagery of vs. 2–3a suggests that this may be a specific agricultural community, one most likely to dispute over land and property (see Luke 12:13). That concrete, local reference, however, may be extended to offer a larger vision of ecumenical humanity. On the one hand, the reading in Acts takes the image of a reconciled community quite concretely, referring to shared property, which by its sharing had overcome need and poverty. On the other hand, the Epistle reading takes the notion of communal fellowship in a much more theological-christological direction. The image of a reconciling community itself is wondrously open in several directions of interpretation. What is clear is that animosity in a human community is inimical to the practice of gospel faith.

Verses 2 and 3a, focused in two metaphors, are subservient to the theme of v. 1. The poet characterizes the goodness and loveliness of communal harmony in two ways. First, such communal harmony is like precious oil, in which a community may luxuriate when it is festive, secure, and prosperous. Oil was a scarce and precious commodity in a local community, and was to be used only for the essentials of life, such as light and heat. But on festive occasions oil might be "wasted" in extravagance, when one could be showered with it as a sign of peculiar well-being. One can imagine a community without any surplus of riches on occasion permitting itself extravagance that is economically wasteful—life is so good that it must be marked by luxury (see Mark 14:3–9). Communal harmony is as good as extravagant oil, overflowing in joy and delight, turning life into a celebration of well-being that is unguarded, careless, and generous. A community at peace is one with more than enough.

Second, communal harmony is like mountain dew. This image may be peculiarly poignant in an arid climate, where any hint of moisture is a special gift and a cause for joy. The two images of oil and dew reinforce each other, and together present a picture of extravagant well-being—that is what harmony is like!

The incidental reference to Zion in v. 3a permits what appears to be the add-on line of v. 3b. This line seems to have no direct relation to the rest of the poem. Indeed, it has been suggested that the "Songs of Ascents" have been systemically transformed by additional reference to Zion. This could be the case if older songs have been reused by pilgrims to Jerusalem. In any case, the incidental reference to Zion in v. 3a in the next line is taken as the main subject. Now Zion is "there." Jerusalem is the place wherein the blessing of God, life forever, is located. But even if this line is somewhat extraneous to the poem, the motif of "blessing" nicely returns to the images of oil and dew, for "blessing" refers to all that enhances and affirms life. It is worth noting that in the epistle, in 1 John 1:1–4, the double accent is on life and joy, exactly the accent of our psalm. Moreover, the threefold announcement of the risen Christ in the Gospel reading concerns "peace," exactly that which is celebrated in the psalm.

The bold affirmation of our psalm is that shared human community is itself an experience of the life that God intends. Such an equation of shared community with life is a warning against religious individualism, which imagines one can have gospel blessings all alone, one at a time, and against a religious community that may be serious about faith, but is contentious and fractious, thereby contradicting its very reason for being. This equation of shared community and life is most poignantly asserted in 1 John 3:14: "We know that we have passed from death to life because we love one another. Whoever does not love abides in death."

In quite concrete and practical ways, our psalm anticipates the Johannine transposition of resurrection into genuine community.

1 John 1:1–2:2

This lesson introduces six epistolary readings drawn from 1 John, a letter that replays several prominent themes from the Gospel of John, although in a slightly different key. Earlier language about fellowship with God and among believers now comes into play to protect the community's boundaries from those who have separated themselves from the community (see 1 John 2:18–19). Love of God here takes on explicit ethical connotations, for one cannot love God and neglect God's other children (see 3:17). The details of the community's situation remain hidden, but clearly there are threats to the community's social and ethical cohesiveness.

One commentator wryly notes that the opening of this letter is "more remarkable for energy than for lucidity." If a quick first reading of 1:1–4 generates the impression that the writer wants to make an important and solemn pronouncement, additional readings may cause one to wonder whether the needle has been stuck at one spot in the record. Four times the writer invokes what has been seen, twice what was heard; three times a solemn declaration is initiated regarding what the writer and others ("we") have experienced.

All this energetic insistence points back to "what was from the beginning," an elegant reference both to the Johannine prologue's language about beginnings *and* to the beginnings of the Johannine community. Although the word "tradition" does not enter the text, the appeal to tradition is evident. Because "we" have witnessed Jesus Christ with eyes and ears and hands, "we" are able to guarantee the reliability of that tradition and to provide the needed connection between the beginnings and the present community.

This insistence on tradition does not venerate tradition as an end in itself or isolate it as something to be preserved. Instead, tradition exists "so that you also may have fellowship" (v. 3), fellowship with other Christians, fellowship with God, and fellowship with Jesus Christ. Since, as noted above, later parts of the letter provide clear indications that the community has experienced a rupture, the prominence of fellowship language here at the beginning of the letter may serve to reinforce community boundaries that have frayed. Tradition connects believers not only with the origins of the Gospel story, but also with one another.

Just as tradition does not exist as an end in itself, fellowship also does not exist as an end in itself. In the context of the gospel, fellowship is always more than social interaction alone. Verse 5 locates the center of fellowship in belief, particularly in the belief that

"God is light." Because passages about light and darkness have sometimes served to reinforce racist assumptions, it is worth noting again that "light" and "darkness" here do not refer to skin color. They reflect the light of day and the darkness of night. In societies without access to artificial illumination, the dark of night was a total darkness. Imagery about light breaking into the darkness or about light overcoming darkness conveys the powerful sense of God's presence.

The formal introduction to the assertion that God is light ("This is the message...") indicates its importance for the author's argument, but nothing in the letter suggests that a dispute has arisen about *whether* God is light. One can scarcely imagine a voice from the back of the congregation insisting, "Well, I think God surely has some darkness deep within!"

Rather than serving to answer a ludicrous charge, the declaration that "God is light" leads to an ethical conclusion in vs. 6–7. Those who believe that God is indeed light and who live in fellowship with God cannot possibly also live in darkness. Their actions, in other words, must be consistent with the assertion that God is light. Unlike Paul, who seems to have been unable to imagine a distinction between belief and action, but in common with the writer of James, who knows attempts to separate the two, the author of 1 John struggles to articulate the interrelatedness of the two. If fellowship has its center in the common affirmation that "God is light," that affirmation must be one of action as well as intellect. "God is light" is not a theoretical claim, but a profoundly practical one.

In the next breath, however, the author acknowledges the profound reality of human sin: "If we say that we have no sin, we deceive ourselves, and the truth is not in us." First John reflects a carefully nuanced understanding of sin. Those who are in fellowship with God and Jesus Christ belong to the light and not to sin; at the same time, however, sin is utterly inescapable. The one who claims to have escaped sin has made a liar of God (v. 10). The fellowship of Christians, then, is not a fellowship of those who do not sin, but a fellowship of those who know that they have Jesus as their "advocate" when they do sin (2:1–2).

The last words of this lection stand in curious tension with the tenor of the letter as a whole. Because of the perceived threat posed to the community of believers, 1 John often sounds an exclusivistic note. God's love appears to be reserved for those on the inside of the community, and those who have departed from it are regarded with something close to scorn. With the words "for the sins of the whole world," the writer leaves the door slightly ajar for the outside. God's mercy not only falls on those who stand within the walls, but extends beyond them.

John 20:19–31

John 20 brings to the fore a number of significant motifs, some of which have been touched on throughout the Gospel. Jesus clearly emerges as the primary actor, who comes and goes and reveals himself in surprising ways. His appearance to the disciples gathered behind locked doors depicts the birth of the church and its reason for being (20:19–23). The varying responses to the risen Jesus by the beloved disciple (see v. 2), Mary, the other disciples, and Thomas focus on the relation between seeing and believing, culminating in Jesus' blessing on the ones who have not seen and yet believe (v. 29) and leading to the statement of the Gospel's purpose (vs. 30–31). The chapter offers an abundance of food for thought.

While the assigned reading encompasses only the last half of the chapter (vs. 19–31), it hardly makes sense apart from the first half (vs. 1–18). There the experiences of Mary Magdalene, Simon Peter, and the beloved disciple prepare the way for Jesus' appearance to the gathered disciples and to Thomas.

First, we note that the whole narrative centers around Jesus. He seems eager to be known, to break through the incredulous astonishment on the part of each of the other characters. The mention three times of the scars he bears (vs. 20, 25, 27) becomes confirming evidence not only to the disciples and to Thomas but also to the readers of the Gospel that the Jesus who is risen is the same one who was crucified. The mysterious event of the resurrection has not erased the marks of rejection and death nor transformed Jesus into someone other than who he has been throughout his ministry. The stress on continuity is marked.

Furthermore, Jesus is not passive. He is busy bringing peace to frightened followers and charging them to be bearers of the same peace. His appearances do more than simply attest that he is risen; they evoke a transformation among the disciples and confront them with an unparalleled commission. Something absolutely new and unheard-of has happened—not only resurrection, but also empowerment for the future.

Second, we note that while vs. 19–23 function to prepare the way for Jesus' encounter with Thomas, they form a piece of the narrative with its own integrity. The locked doors underscore the trauma and fright of the disciples, who have good reason to think that they may be the next victims. In the midst of their fear comes Jesus, with his reassuring words. After he speaks and displays his wounds, the disciples rejoice. The presence of the Lord is transforming.

The repeated greeting is now joined to a powerful commission. As God's special agent, Jesus deputizes the disciples to be agents, to be engaged in the same peace-declaring activity he has carried on. The great commission of this Gospel takes on further concreteness at v. 23, where the disciples are given the heavy responsibility of declaring or refusing to declare forgiveness of sins. Through them, as the nucleus of the church, the benefits of Christ are made available to the world.

Along with the mission comes the gift of the Spirit. John has no need to wait until Pentecost, as do Luke and Acts. Rather, on the first Easter evening, the church receives the promised Paraclete (14:15–17, 25–26; 15:26; 16:7–11, 12–16), who brings both an agenda and a promise. Thus in the brief space of five verses (20:19–23) the narrator describes the beginning of the church, authorized by the risen Jesus to declare the good news of peace and forgiveness and empowered by the Holy Spirit.

Finally, the various responses to Jesus in this chapter present an interesting set of vignettes on how faith emerges. The beloved disciple sees the empty tomb and the burial wrappings to one side and believes Mary's report (v. 8), in contrast to Peter, who views the same evidence and apparently remains skeptical. Mary Magdalene sees the stone rolled away from the tomb but continues in her grief until the unrecognized Jesus calls her name. She then declares to the others, "I have seen the Lord" (vs. 1, 11–18). The disciples also must see in order to believe (v. 20). Though Thomas is really no different from the other disciples, he seems to become the celebrated case of one who remains unconvinced until he sees (vs. 25, 27–28). In each case, faith comes from sight, though what is seen may vary from discarded grave clothes to Jesus himself.

Later generations, of course, cannot see the same evidence that these four saw—no empty tomb, no voice speaking, no presence of Jesus with visible wounds. The text clearly addresses their situation and the possible feeling that the gap of years has made faith less valuable or more difficult. The nostalgic notion that says, "Oh, I wish that I could have been there" is answered by the special benediction of Jesus. "Blessed are those who have not seen and yet have come to believe" (v. 29). For them the Gospel itself is the evidence. This is why it is written (vs. 30–31). Faith is born from the word, from the witness of those who did see and whose witness remains. Thomas's triumphant confession, which comes only after seeing Jesus for himself, becomes the powerful testimony to later readers to embrace the same faith.

Third Sunday of Easter

The Easter event is an inscrutable experience in the life of the church. Out of that inscrutability, however, comes real and concrete newness. The Gospel reading shows that the risen Lord is mysterious but real. He is real in the church, because he cooks and they eat, he is present and they touch; nonetheless the narrative includes enough of an enigma that the church does not finally "grasp" this Jesus. The church clearly "pondered" and was terrified by his presence, but it did not seek to "explain." It was enough to "witness," to tell the story of what happened.

Out of that strange (recurring) encounter, the early church becomes a community that witnesses (by word and by its very life) to a real chance for new life. Whereas the old life was marked by failure, shame, doubt, and defeat, the new life is one of confidence and joy. The psalm is the voice of one in deep shame who breaks the power of shame by knowledge of and trust in Yahweh. The listeners to the sermon of Peter in the Acts reading must reflect upon their brutalizing failure, but they hear in this astonishing sermon that through this same God their sin is overcome; they may begin again. The Epistle reading reflects upon the complete transformation that is wrought by the righteousness of Jesus, which empowers the community to its own righteousness, expressed in an alternative ethic.

These texts assert the news that life can begin anew, that the community can be reorganized and individual members regenerated. In our jaded, habitual faith, we most often do not expect change—for ourselves. Or we fear a kind of privatist individualism if we talk about change. These texts cringe neither from the notion of personal newness, nor from the larger truth that Easter can disrupt all that is old and failed. The entry of the One who is touchable and who nourishes may indeed reorder life for all of us who are untouched, unfazed, and endlessly wanting better nourishment.

Acts 3:12-19

The present lection is the second in a series of three texts that are set within the immediate post-Pentecost period ("one day" of Acts 3:1) and that describe events associated with Peter and John's healing of a crippled man who begged for alms at one of the entrances to the Temple complex. In this case, the passage for the day arises out of the reaction of the crowd that witnessed the miracle, but who were at an absolute loss to comprehend what they had seen. (They were "utterly astonished," 3:11.) More specifically, the text consists of part of Peter's words to them and contains elements both of condemnation and of hope.

The first and most obvious observation regarding the text is that Peter's judgment on the bystanders (vs. 12-15) is not to be translated into some kind of anti-Jewish bias. The reality is that *all* present at Jesus' trial and crucifixion, even those closest to him, bore some measure of blame, even if their acquiescence was only passive (as in Mark 14:66-72). Jews and Romans, high officials and ordinary people, those who feared the God of Israel and those who did not—all were culpable. It was not "they" (however "they" might be identified) who killed Jesus, but "we," that is, humankind. The immediate situation that the present text reflects is that, since the events related in Acts 3-4 transpired in a Jewish holy season, Jews were present in the Temple area, and it is they who are alternately condemned and urged to new frontiers of faith—by other Jews! If there was any sense at all in which the Jewish community had a special obligation to honor Jesus rather than participate in his execution, it was that they were the heirs of a special tradition (note v. 13).

The actual import of vs. 12-16 is that that which sinful human beings perpetrated—the death of Jesus—became by the power of God a miracle of life and resurrection:

> You killed the Author of life . . .
> God raised [him] from the dead.

Three polar opposites are linked in the kind of parallelism so dear to the heart of a Hebrew poet: you/God; killed/raised; life/dead. That which sinful men and women attempted was set on its ear by a loving God, who overruled and put right that which people attempted wrongfully to do.

But that's only part of the kerygma, according to Peter. What is more is that the same power that brought to life the crucified Jesus has now empowered the impotent feet and legs of the unnamed cripple. In other words, the resurrection of Jesus was not the final climax to God's mighty deeds in the life of the people, but was an event that marked a new beginning, a fresh unleashing of the Spirit. "His name itself has made this man strong" and "has given him this perfect health in the presence of all of you" (v. 16).

Thus vs. 12–16 may perhaps be summarized as follows: That which began as a word of judgment is now not judgment at all, but a proclamation of the healing, empowering love of God, a love that not even the plots of evil men and women can frustrate.

The configuration of the second section (vs. 17–19) is somewhat unusual in that it—and the entire lection—ends in midsentence. But more about that in a moment. The initial thing to notice here is the tone of absolution in v. 17, a theme that flows logically out of the judgment-become-good news of vs. 12–16. God not only overruled the evil and ignorant intentions of human beings, but now stands ready to forgive them. In a perverse way, those who crucified Jesus were actually and unwittingly working toward the fulfillment of what God had promised: a suffering Messiah (v. 18). Without intending to do so, these persons had accomplished the will of God by plotting evil and, in so doing, had participated in one of the grand mysteries of the life of faith. As Joseph observed so long before, when musing over the failed efforts of his brothers, "Even though you intended to do harm to me, God intended it for good" (Gen. 50:20). Even our evil can be made good in the hands of God.

In Acts 3:19–20 Peter's message of hope turns from the past ("Repent therefore, and turn to God in order that your sins may be wiped out") to the future ("and that [God] may send the Messiah appointed for you"). It is perhaps understandable that in the present context of the immediate post-Easter celebration the emphasis in worship should be on the near-term implications of the Gospel message. Yet the preacher should consider extending the text to include the entirety of the grammatical unit, that is, through v. 21. The second coming of our Lord may seem a more fitting theme for Advent than for Easter, but it may occur to some that the manner in which the lectionary divides what the text itself brings together is forced and artificial. In the text, taken as a whole, the eventual return of Christ is understood to be the hope toward which the present miraculous moment (the lame man's present miraculous moment, that is) points with joy and anticipation.

Psalm 4

Psalm 4 shows Israel at passionate prayer. As we shall see, the prayer holds candor about trouble together with great faith and deep hope. This is a prayer that looks trouble full in the face, but does not let the trouble diminish confidence in God.

The prayer begins abruptly, as prayers do when we are in desperate straits. There is no time for flattering God, and nice words are driven out by urgency. The first words issue an imperative, summoning God to be present in the trouble. The imperative is reinforced by the first reference to God. The God addressed is "God of my right" (ṣedeq), that is, the one who is to defend my cause. The second line of the prayer briefly alludes to times past, when God has acted decisively to liberate from a tight place, that is, from "distress." The third line, however, returns to the petitionary urgency of the first line. This is a voice of deep need, but a voice that fully expects God to come and be transformatively present in the trouble.

The second verse is a complaint, but it is not addressed to God. Rather, it is an assault against the adversaries of the speaker. The speaker clearly lives in a "shame society" and protests that his "honor" has been trashed, and he has been reduced to shame. Whereas shame will most often reduce one to embarrassed silence, it is astonishing that this speaker can still find a shrill, insistent voice of protest, so that the shame has not yet undermined self-confidence. The speaker has been maltreated by "vain words," perhaps slanderous gossip, perhaps court perjury.

Only in v. 3 are we able to see why it is that the shamed speaker is not yet silenced. The self-confidence exhibited in these lines is rooted in a deeper confidence in God. This verse is not addressed to God, but to the taunting adversaries. The speaker is glad to bear witness to the powerful reality of God, which refuses to succumb to the power of shame. Right into the middle of the trouble, the speaker establishes an evangelical base line that permits buoyancy: Yahweh has "set apart" the covenant keepers. God takes special notice of the faithful. The practical result of that action on God's part is that God is peculiarly attentive and particularly responsive to the prayers of the faithful. That deep confidence in God overrides and neutralizes the assaults of the adversary.

It is telling to permit v. 1a and v. 3b to touch each other. Verse 1a is a plea addressed to God, a plea that is uttered but not yet answered. By contrast, v. 3b is a bold refutation addressed to human adversaries. In v. 3b the speaker may be even more bold and confident than the unanswered prayer of v. 1a warrants. But that is how faith works. Thus the extreme trouble of this speaker does not fall outside live faith. That live faith lets trouble be contextualized. The speaker knows that the faithful power of God will indeed be mobilized, and so the trouble itself is not an ultimate fact of life. It is, to be sure, a serious, demanding fact of life, but not finally decisive, for God's powerful, answering fidelity is the ultimate truth, which overrides all troubles.

Verses 4–6 are something of an interlude in the confident petition of vs. 1–3. Verses 4 and 5 have something of a didactic tone to them, as though the speaker steps outside the sphere of complaint in order to offer advice to others who are agitated over trouble in their lives. Oddly enough, the counsel given to those who may be agitated is to ponder in silence, to offer sacrifices, and to trust Yahweh. The oddity is that this urging to silence contradicts the very practice of vs. 1 and 3 which consist of out loud, imperative petition to Yahweh. It is here suggested that in the midst of trouble one can keep silent because one has deep confidence in God's reliability, thus reiterating the theme of v. 3.

Verse 6 is enigmatic, because we cannot determine the mood in which it is uttered. We cannot tell if the statement in v. 6 is sarcastic in tone, thus criticizing those who "say" when they ought to be silent in confidence, or if the speaker of the psalm is to be counted among the "many who say." If the statement is without irony, then the verse in fact utters a petition asking for God's power and presence as a way to override the shame of v. 2 and the destruction of v. 4.

Verses 7 and 8 are in any case a resolution of the petition of vs. 1a, 1c, and 3, and a confirmation of the trust voiced in vs. 1b, 3, and 5. Thus vs. 7 and 8 bring the petition and imperative at the first of the psalm to a positive closure. We are led to believe that God has heard the prayer of need and has satisfied true longing, and therefore the urgent petition is transposed into a glad statement of trust and confidence. Verse 7 acknowledges that God has brought gladness where there was urgent need, a gladness even greater than the unbridled joy in harvesttime. Life has indeed been healed and transformed.

The final verse of the psalm bespeaks quiet and complete trust. The speaker who was so anxious and agitated is now prepared to be completely at rest and at peace, to be as vulnerable as sleep. The final statement is a direct address to God, culminating in the powerful word "safety" (*bṭḥ*), echoing the same word in v. 5, which could here be rendered "confident security." Life is totally resolved by truth in Yahweh alone.

This prayer is the prayer of one in the "right" (see 1 John 3:7). The prayer does not ask for mercy or forgiveness, but only the protection properly due to the righteous. This speaker lies down in "peace," the sure protection of God, the same peace declared in the greeting of the risen Christ (Luke 24:36). The speaker may be severely troubled, but all the trouble is confidently contained in the scope of a functioning, working, trustworthy relation to God. Even severe trouble is held within the deep awareness that comes with a life utterly devoted to the purpose of God.

1 John 3:1–7

As it stands, this lesson consists of positive and negative assertions: that believers are children of God who do what is right (1 John 3:1–3), and that those who sin are lawless people who do not "abide" in God (vs. 4–7). If these assertions are read in light of the larger context (2:29–3:10), however, the contrast becomes both sharper and more refined. It is because believers are begotten by God that they are able to do what is right (2:29). And it is because they are children of the devil that nonbelievers are unable to do what is right (3:8–10). (The reason for defining the passage as the lectionary does is easy to understand: beginning with 3:1 gives the reading a more positive tone, and ending at v. 7 omits the very harsh language of vs. 8–10.)

Viewed in the context of the larger argument being made, the first section of the reading (3:1–3) becomes something of a digression, a reminder of what it means to be "born of him" (2:29). The Old Testament often portrays the people of Israel as adopted children of God, and closely connects this adoption with the covenant and the demand that Israel *live* as God's children. Both the Synoptics and Paul pick up aspects of this language (see, for example, Matt. 5:9, Rom. 8:18–25).

Modern readers who are accustomed to the language of scripture may miss something of the power of this imagery. In a world organized around the patriarchal household, where the human father was the central organizing focus, to be termed a "child of God" offered an alternative way of understanding oneself and one's loyalties. Something like Paul's use of the language of heavenly citizenship in Phil. 3:20, the notion of being God's children appropriates ordinary experience to convey the very extraordinary event of the gospel.

The writer immediately follows this assertion about being God's children with what appears to be an aside: "The reason the world does not know us is that it did not know him" (1 John 3:1b). What this comment does is to connect Christ more closely with believers. They have the common experience of being unrecognized by "the world," those outside the household of faith. But the comment also indicates that believers are known to be children of God *precisely because they are rejected*. Nothing of glory or power or beauty sets the children of God apart. Instead, they are set apart because they share with Jesus the fact that the outside rejects them.

Verse 2 delicately balances the relationship between the present and the future. Those within the believing community are already, at present, rightly called children of God. That has already occurred and does not need to be earned. Nevertheless, the future will bring some changes in those children, changes that cannot be predicted or analyzed. Given the thoroughly eschatological context of this statement, these changes are not ethical changes earned by believers. They do not "become" something else by dint of their labor. Indeed, the second part of the verse makes it clear that it is God's eschatological revelation that brings about the change in them.

The second part of the reading, with its harsh comments about sin and sinners, seems to contradict common Christian experience. Can it really be said that "no one who abides in him sins" (3:6), when the evidence offered every day is that Christians do continue to sin? Earlier the author insists that everyone has sinned and that Christ is an advocate for sinners, a position that runs contrary to what is said here.

In order to understand these statements, the community setting of 1 John needs to be recalled. This Christian community had experienced some severe schism (see 2:19), and apparently one thing that separated the two groups was conflict over the relationship between faith and action. Those who have left the community to which 1 John is addressed believed that faith in itself secured salvation. Perhaps taking quite literally certain themes from the Gospel of John (for example, John 1:29), they insisted that those who belonged within the flock were saved and could not again be threatened by evil. Actions were a matter of indifference. If that is the background of this and other passages in 1 John, then the strident tones of the author become more understandable.

Quite apart from any controversy within the Christian community, the early church emerged in a culture in which religion did not necessarily include matters of behavior or ethics. For Jews, of course, that division was unthinkable, but in the larger Greco-Roman world, religion largely had to do with paying homage to the gods so that the gods would protect and enhance one's life. Morality was a matter for philosophers, not for priests. Many early converts probably saw Christianity as yet another way of approaching the gods, of securing safety and prosperity for themselves. For such people, living a certain kind of life was simply not a part of what constituted religious practice.

Christians in the twentieth century may not articulate such a perspective, but it nevertheless lies just beneath the surface. Particularly in some movements that emphasize individual spiritual experience and downplay moral responsibility, latter-day Christianity confronts a situation not far removed from that of 1 John.

Luke 24:36–48

How does one preach on the resurrection of Jesus two weeks after Easter? The anticipation generated throughout the Lenten season is gone, making it well-nigh impossible to reconstruct the same excitement and expectation. The attention of the congregation is turned elsewhere. Even announcing that every Sunday is a celebration of the resurrection does not turn back the calendar. And yet the Gospel lesson for this Sunday (Luke 24:36–48) relates an appearance of the risen Jesus to the disciples, one that will include the transformation of their startled incredulity into worship. How can one honestly deal with the text and not simply struggle to re-create Easter?

While the story records the astonishment, fright, joy, and disbelief of the disciples, reactions that might be more easily dealt with on Easter Day, it is also a narrative that addresses theological questions that thoughtful people often ask when the chords of the "Hallelujah Chorus" have faded. What was the risen Jesus like? What is the meaning of resurrection? How is this Jesus present now? The narrator describes the various initiatives Jesus takes in confronting his followers' skepticism in such a way as to pique our interest and to remind us that these theological questions are not peculiarly ours. Furthermore, these are questions that might be helpfully dealt with in a sermon two weeks after Easter.

How can one speak of the presence of one who has died? What was the risen Jesus like? First, in response to the disciples' terror that they were seeing a ghost, Jesus does two things. He offers his hands and feet (no mention of scars or wounds as in John 20:20, 27) to be carefully examined by the disciples, and he eats a piece of fish in their presence. The two actions are clearly intended to dispel any notion that the risen Jesus is a figment of the disciples' imagination ("A ghost does not have flesh and bones, as you see that I have"). Whatever else one is to say about Jesus' risen presence, it is not an apparition.

One might mistakenly derive from the narrative the notion of a physical resurrection, except that the picture here has to be balanced with Luke's earlier story of the appearance to the disciples going to Emmaus. There Jesus comes as an unrecognized stranger and is known only in the breaking of the bread (24:13–32). The two stories taken together indicate that Jesus' presence is mysterious but real. It eludes human perception, and yet is no human fabrication. It is continuous with the earthly Jesus ("It is I myself"), and yet different. The event is more than a resuscitation of the flesh; it is a resurrection. Beyond these boundaries of the narrative, there is little more to say.

The examination of Jesus' hands and feet and the observation of his eating apparently do not erase all the doubts that linger in the minds of the disciples. The experience remains unclear. Thus Jesus takes a second initiative. He recalls the words spoken during his ministry, of how everything written about him in the scriptures had to be fulfilled; and then he interprets the scriptures so that the disciples can understand.

The narrative is clear that the meaning of Jesus' death and resurrection comes only through the study of the scriptures. No historical "proof" can convince anyone that in the final analysis death and resurrection are the way God's promises are fulfilled. For Luke, the cross and the empty tomb are no more than astonishing stories apart from the larger biblical framework that leads to and explicates what they signify. What is critical about Jesus' resurrection is not that it is a miracle, but that it brings to fruition God's plans and purposes.

At the same time, the crucified and risen Jesus becomes the clue for understanding the scriptures. While they provide the context for understanding him, he provides the key for unlocking their mysteries. The two belong together. The verb "opened" in 24:45 is the same Greek word used earlier in the chapter when the eyes of the two walking to Emmaus "were opened" (v. 31) and when Jesus, in turn, "opened" the scriptures to them (v. 32).

The third initiative Jesus makes in the text is to spell out the mission that lies ahead for the disciples. All the ingredients are here: the preaching of repentance and the forgiveness of sins, the move from Jerusalem to all the nations, the disciples as witnesses, the promise of divine power. Verses 47–49 read like the table of contents to the book of Acts.

Perhaps to the surprise of those of us who live on this side of the Enlightenment, the meaning of the resurrection of Jesus is inextricably linked not only to the study of scripture but also to engagement in mission. On the road between Jerusalem and "all the nations" the disciples discovered the presence of the risen Lord, and no longer needed to ask in what form he would be present. Any effort to understand the resurrection fails if the investigator assumes a neutral posture and supposes that it reveals its meaning through scientific scrutiny. Historical research does not take one very far. But involvement in the message of repentance and forgiveness does. Just as resurrection and scripture belong together, so resurrection and mission belong together.

FOURTH SUNDAY OF EASTER

This Friday-Sunday shape of the life of Jesus is a stunning alternative in a world where we seek always to "keep" our life, keep it from danger and keep it from neighbor. The news is that Jesus did not keep his own life, either from danger or from neighbor. He "laid it down," that is, he put himself at risk for those he loved. Both the Gospel reading and the psalm reflect upon "the shepherd" who is put at risk for the sake of the sheep.

In the Easter season, our focus is not on the willing act of self-giving by Jesus (crucifixion), but on the subsequent act of power (resurrection), whereby the self-giving Jesus has been raised to new life, and so has the power to raise and heal others. It is this stunning new gift of power that controverts the "rulers" in the Acts reading. It is this risen Jesus who is the "power" that they neither understand nor control, a power for new life in the world.

The whole life of Jesus—with his death and his resurrection—is an evidence and enactment of self-giving love. The Epistle lection turns the "message" of self-giving love into a summons for the community of Jesus itself to become just such a practice of self-giving love. Thus, Easter issues not simply in euphoric joy, but in a transformed life of shared caring.

Notice that such an ethic, grounded in God's self-risk, would be regarded as an impossible foolishness by the "rulers" of our age, as of that ancient age. We are so committed to "self-possessing" that screens us from the neighbor, that we can scarcely entertain the thought of self-giving for the neighbor. Easter not only assures us that the risk can be taken; in addition to that "cognitive" assurance, Easter authorizes and empowers. Easter issues not in some new knowledge about new life, but in concrete power for that life. Such new life at risk for the neighbor is indeed "to dwell in the house of the Lord my whole life long."

Acts 4:5–12

As do the Acts lections for the two preceding Sundays, the present text describes events set in motion by Peter and John's healing of the lame man at the Beautiful Gate of the Temple (Acts 3:1–10). In the passage before us, members of the Jewish religious and political establishment, having imprisoned Peter and John overnight because of their insistence on Jesus' resurrection (4:1–4), bring them into a tribunal of justice. Although no specific charge is leveled against Peter and John by these Saducean authorities, the implied crime is that of blasphemy, in that resurrection from the dead is credited to Jesus. It is true that the rulers would have been offended by *any* statement in support of resurrection, as their animosity toward the Pharisees (who did believe in resurrection) makes clear. But the present outrage was, in their eyes, that Peter and John testified to *Jesus'* resurrection, and—if one reads v. 2 closely—that the disciples also testified that Jesus had made resurrection available to others.

Yet the question, as it is put to Peter and John, is one of authority. "By what power or by what name did you do this?" (v. 7). The foolish question, which reminds one of the equally vacuous query put to Jesus by perhaps some of these same authorities (Matt. 21:23), is subtly ambiguous. "By whose authority do you heal the lame man?" is the surface issue, but the Sadducees' hidden agenda is the challenge, "By whose authority do you proclaim that in Jesus there is resurrection of the dead?"

Peter, who frequently speaks before his colleagues in the circle of disciples are able to collect their thoughts, replies in words inspired by the Spirit (v. 8). He speaks first to the ostensible issue, the healing of the lame man, but with an agenda only slightly less concealed than that of the Sadducees. "How absurd," Peter seems to be saying, "that we should be clapped into prison for doing something that was, by any measure, a good thing. If you rulers are so callous as to question what is clearly good, how can you be considered anything but evil?"

But if the rulers are to insist on an answer to their insipid question, here it is—thus Peter's train of thought continues—let everyone take note, both you who ask the question, and all Jews everywhere: "This man is standing before you in good health by the name of Jesus Christ of Nazareth" (v. 10). There you have it! It is not by magic or by healing potions. It is not a restoration brought about by the special skills of the disciples, or even by accident. The lame man's legs have been restored to strength through "the name of Jesus Christ of Nazareth."

But now to the real issue. The authorities could not care less about the formerly disabled man. Their pretended concern for him is a smoke screen behind which they conceal their true anxiety. And so to the point. The authority by which we proclaim that in Jesus Christ there is resurrection, asserts Peter, is simply this: The one "whom you crucified" is also the one "whom God raised from the dead" (v. 10). The evidence that resurrection is a genuine reality in human life is to be found in Jesus' own resurrection.

And so—if there were any doubts about the matter before—the resurrection of Jesus emerges as the undisputed focus of the text. The scandal is not that Peter and John restored strength to a pair of disabled legs. The scandal is that the Man of Nazareth was dead, but is now alive! That reality, which has terrorized the authorities, has placed new powers at the disposal of Peter, John, and other women and men who trust in Jesus and in the power of God.

Nor is the element of irony lost on Peter and John—or on Luke, who crafted this text. (Nor was the irony lost on other New Testament writers; see Mark 12:10; 1 Peter 2:7.) A paradigm of what God has accomplished in the resurrection of Jesus is the Davidic king in a situation of urgent distress (Ps. 118:5), surrounded by the enemies of goodness and the enemies of God, who come at him like a swarm of angry bees, causing him to be all but given up for lost (vs. 10–13). But God intervenes so that the king, while deeply wounded, will live to rule in righteousness (vs. 17–19), to the great rejoicing of the people. And the image from the construction of a great building is drawn:

> The stone that the builders rejected
> has become the chief cornerstone.
> (Acts 4:11; Ps. 118:22)

The message of the open tomb permeates this text and reminds all who read it that the resurrection of Jesus lies at the heart of the Christian faith. That reality directs and reorients our lives, in that they become channels for the working out of the agenda of the Spirit of God. The healing of the lame man, as significant as is that miracle both for the man himself and for all who witness it, is only a symptom of the new reality that is breaking in upon humankind as a result of Jesus' resurrection. The resurrection has destroyed old and comfortably held ways of knowing and doing, as symbolized by the intransigence of the rulers. (Beware of anti-Semitic implications in preaching from this text. Remember that all humankind is indicted in the death of Jesus.) At the same time, however, the new reality of the resurrection has released fresh energies, which have the ability to restore human life and make it new.

Psalm 23

This best-known and best-loved psalm invites us into a world of deep trust and lean desire. It is shaped around only two explicit mentions of the name of Yahweh: In Ps. 23:1, Yahweh is mentioned as *the premise* of the psalm, the "bottom line" assurance on which everything is based; in v. 6, Yahweh is mentioned as *the long-term goal*, expectation, and aspiration of the speaker.

The opening word of the psalm is the name of Yahweh, spoken abruptly and without qualification. Yahweh, with whom this speaker has a long and intimate acquaintance, is identified with a simple epithet, "shepherd." The term "shepherd" is more open and suggestive than our nomadic romanticism might suggest. It means not only herder of sheep, but in the ancient world of Israel it also refers to the king who actively intervenes to protect and secure the poor and needy who lack resources to guard their own lives. Thus the term is at once pastoral (bespeaking caring attentiveness) and political (bespeaking power).

The second phrase of the psalm is terse, "I shall not lack." The conventional translation, "I shall not want," misleadingly sounds like a future and suggests "wanting" as a desire. But the term is rather a present-tense assertion that Yahweh's protective attentiveness assures that the speaker has everything needed in order to live a full and whole life. The shepherd-king has anticipated and supplied all needs. (This is an enormous word in a consumer society of endless wants and unfulfilled desires.)

Verses 2 and 3 play out the pastoral dimension of the shepherd metaphor. Though Yahweh is not named explicitly, the series of assurances make Yahweh the subject of four decisive verbs. It is the shepherd-God who causes safe rest ("lie down"), adequate water ("still waters"), restored vitality ("restores my soul"), and safe paths ("right paths"). The trusting sheep who speaks here has everything needed for an uninterrupted life of tranquillity and safety, exactly the kind of life both sheep and shepherd intend. The shepherd is attentive to provide for every lack and to ward off every threat. All of this is done, moreover, "for his name's sake," that is, to maintain God's identity and reputation.

Read according to the pastoral image, the shepherd escorts the sheep through valley pastures that are filled with shadows, rocks, and crevices where may lurk threatening scavengers (v. 4). But the shepherd is there attentive and resolute, in order to keep the sheep safe. The image, however, may as well be political. On that reading, "rod and staff" are emblems of political power.

Whichever way the images are taken, we may notice that the double line of trust and confidence,

> I fear no evil;
> for you are with me,

is a restatement of God's own assurance voiced elsewhere. In a classic "salvation oracle" (Isa. 43:5), God announces to endangered Israel:

> Do not fear,
> for I am with you.

Now in the psalm, the trusting speaker says back to God in a prayer of great confidence exactly the words that God has first uttered. "Comfort" as the outcome of God's attentive solidarity does not mean simply solace or pastoral comfort, but active intervention that effectively transforms the situation. Thus the "God of all comfort" is one who keeps safe and heals life (see Isa. 40:1; 2 Cor. 1:3–7).

The political dimension of our metaphor becomes more certain in Ps. 23:5. Now the image concerns the "enemy." The "enemy" is no doubt an actual political adversary who threatens and diminishes life. But this powerful shepherd-king will not permit the "enemy" to threaten. The shepherd-king, by way of countering the threat, provides food, the oil of well-being and safety, and a cup abundantly filled with wine. The trusted shepherd-king simply refuses any diminishment of life and satisfies the beloved object with abundance, an abundance that is unexpected in an ominous wilderness situation. But then, God's overpowering generosity is often incongruous with our perceived situation, for God overrides our assumed circumstance. (On Israel's experience of such care in the wilderness, see Ps. 78:19, 23–24.)

The concluding verse of Ps. 23, growing out of the concrete and unexpected experiences of well-being recited above, anticipates a long-term future of happy, safe communion with God. After all, this speaker has known or needed nothing other than communion with God (and all the abundance God gives) for the fullness of life.

The verse begins with a powerful ejaculatory particle, "surely" or "indeed." The psalmist now draws the only conclusion possible from these past experiences with Yahweh. The verse is in two contrasting forms. In the first, the speaker is passive. The subject of the verb is "goodness and loyalty" (ḥesed). Based on the recited experience of vs. 1–5, the speaker concludes that the goodness and fidelity of God will actively "chase me, seek me out, hunt me down, and settle with me." The speaker is the object of God's vigorous pursuit.

As a result, in the second line, the speaker now utters the name of Yahweh for only the second time in the psalm, now utterly delighted to live the rest of life in God's good company. The speaker intends no more to risk exposure to threat or danger. The speaker now understands what a wondrous home life with God makes, and has no counter-yearning to pursue.

1 John 3:16–24

The epistolary readings for the Second and Third Sundays of Easter come from passages in 1 John that warn against sin (see the preceding discussions). In this passage, those general negative admonitions about avoiding sin become constructive assertions. The discussion actually begins in 1 John 3:11 with the admonition that "we should love one another." The example of Cain follows as a warning about the power sin and hate have to produce death. With v. 16, the topic of love returns.

"We know love by this, that he laid down his life for us." The simplicity and drama of this statement warrant attention. Love itself is taught by Christ's act. Here the writer does not say that Christ loved humankind and therefore gave himself, but that the *action in and of itself* enables humans to know what love is. A more literal translation of the second part of the sentence reveals much of its emphasis: "that one on behalf of us his life put aside." The conjunction of "that one" and "on behalf of us" draws attention to the goal of Christ's "putting aside" his life.

With the third statement of v. 16 the writer moves from Christ as an object lesson to the appropriation of that lesson for the Christian community: "We ought to lay down our lives for one another." The profound connection between Jesus and believers that the Johannine tradition everywhere asserts comes to expression again here. Jesus' laying down of his life demands that believers themselves enact that same love, not simply for Jesus, but for one another.

In other historical contexts, the giving of life itself has been necessary. For the Johannine community, that extreme act of love is apparently not required (that is, external persecution seems not to be a problem). What is required becomes clear in v. 17, where the writer admonishes Christians to help other believers who are in need.

When translated a bit more literally than in the NRSV, the language of v. 17 graphically depicts the question being raised:

> Whoever has the goods of the world
> and sees a brother [or sister] who has need,
> and shuts up compassion in such a case ...
> how does the love of God endure in that person?

Related indictments are familiar from the Old Testament (for example, Deut. 15:7) as well as from other early Christian writings (for example, James 2:15–16). Here the question is particularly acute, for it concerns not just the withholding of material goods from the needy but the withholding even of compassion. Can God's love be said to remain in one who can spare for fellow believers not even the gift of human concern?

First John 3:18 moves from this poignant question to an admonition ("Let us love, not in word or speech, but in truth and action") based on the lesson of Christ's love in v. 16. Love is not a matter of word or speech, a kind of theoretical commodity cut loose from any behavior. Love is, instead, action that embodies the truth. The issue here is not hypocrisy so much as it is *how one sees love*. For 1 John, love can be seen only in bodily form, never simply in words.

Verses 19–22 are notoriously difficult, full of translation problems that render even their most basic meaning highly elusive. Many commentators have concluded that this passage has about it the air of judgment; that is, because God is "greater than our hearts," God will condemn human beings if they do not sufficiently correct and condemn themselves. Others have taken an approach that is diametrically opposed, seeing here a statement about God's mercy being "greater than our hearts." In light of the Johannine tradition as a whole, with its emphasis on God's care for God's own people, the latter interpretation seems preferable. What the author appeals to here is the very greatness of God, who continues to love even the disobedient among God's children.

The passage culminates in v. 23 in a summary of the teaching about the integrity of faith and life. God's commandment is belief "in the name of his Son Jesus Christ" and love of "one another." At first glance, this statement is startling, for what is demanded is not the love of God but faith in God's Son (compare, for example, Mark 12:28–31). For a tradition so convinced of the primary relationship between Jesus and God, however, faith in the Son necessarily implies faith in and, indeed, love of God. To believe that Jesus is God's Son requires not simply belief in God but love of God, because of God's action in the sending of Jesus.

First John 3:24 returns to a central issue in this letter, namely, the integral place action has in the life of faith. Those steeped in the Pauline letters will probably find this element in 1 John difficult, for it raises the specter of understanding action ("works") as a means to salvation. What 1 John says, however, is that action is part of faith, and that both come about as a gift of the "Spirit that he has given us" (v. 24). The obedient behavior that testifies to faith, that is a necessary part of faith, comes not from one's own volition or accomplishment, but because the Spirit of God has granted it.

John 10:11–18

Shepherd and sheep are not common sights for most urbanites of North America. The pastoral scenes of the Scottish highlands or the eastern regions of New Zealand seem fairly remote. And yet the images of shepherd and sheep still carry immense force, as they did for ancient Israel. Psalm 23 undoubtedly remains the favorite and most familiar Bible passage for churchgoing people, often evoking strong feelings of security and comfort.

Jesus' words about being the good shepherd in John 10 also offer comfort, but not without first depicting the cost at which the comfort is purchased. Any encasing of the imagery in sentimentality is shattered by reading how the original audience reacted—with division (vs. 19–21) and violence (v. 31). The words are hardly maudlin, since the Jesus who speaks them finally is murdered by the very ones who listen.

The passage turns out to be a meditation on the death and resurrection of Jesus, with three foci. First, Jesus as the good shepherd is contrasted with the hired hand, who has no notion of putting his life at risk for the flock. Who is the hired hand? Well, there may be a subtle judgment here on false leaders who use the sheep for their own gain, an echo of Ezek. 34, where the faithless shepherds of Israel feed themselves instead of the flock. These types are plentiful in every age and location.

But the uninvolved hired hand primarily serves as a foil for the self-giving shepherd. His flight in the face of danger sharpens the picture of one whose care for the sheep proves costly. The language "lays down his life for the sheep" in John 10:11 must, in light of vs. 15, 17–18, reflect the terminology of the crucifixion, otherwise such a sacrifice would seem senseless, resulting only in an utterly defenseless flock.

What distinguishes the behavior of the shepherd from that of the hired hand is his care for the sheep. They belong to him. Tending the flock is not just a job to keep groceries on the table: it is his reason for being—and for dying. It is the vocation given by the Father, than which there can be no greater (v. 29).

This caring of the shepherd for the sheep leads to the second focus. "I know my own and my own know me" (v. 14). An intimate relation binds together shepherd and sheep in an inexplicable way. It is rooted in the intimate relationship between the Father and the Son, one so intimate that Jesus can later say that "the Father and I are one" (v. 30). That means there are no strangers in the flock, none who should feel that he or she is unrecognized. Each knows and is known.

But more than recognition, the knowing includes a deep involvement in the life of the other, a self-giving, evidenced in the crucifixion (v. 15). It is an interesting picture to juxtapose with many modern communities where neighbors scarcely know the names of those living next door, and where many in fact seek anonymity.

Such mutual knowing and intimacy could be construed as a form of exclusivism, a kind of coziness that has turned inward, except for the reminder that Jesus has "other sheep that do not belong to this fold." Who are they? Are they other Jewish Christian communities who were persecuted like John's community, but are part of the old flock? Are they Gentiles who will be included as part of the outreach to the broader world? Are they later generations "who have not seen and yet have come to believe" (20:29)? It is hard to tell. Each has some warrant. But in any case, the flock is not yet finally fixed. It is open-ended. There are always others who recognize the shepherd's voice and enter the fold.

The third focus of the meditation on Jesus' death and resurrection is something of a paradox. Jesus in laying down his life for the sheep is both thoroughly free and at the same time obedient to the Father's command (10:17–18). On the one hand, his life is not taken from him as if his death were an accident or a punishment imposed, but he lays it down of his own accord. Jesus is clearly not a reluctant victim of scheming opposition.

Likewise, in somewhat surprising language, Jesus has "the power to take up [his life] again." We expect from other New Testament passages to discover God as the author of the resurrection rather than Jesus. Is the text implying that the resurrection is not simply God's reward for heroic action or God's rescue of a victimized Son? Does it bind death and resurrection closely together to suggest that the power of resurrection comes only from a free self-giving, that self-surrender is the way to life?

On the other hand, Jesus' freedom is found in his filial obedience. "I have received this command from my Father" (v. 18). Freedom does not entail an arbitrary self-choosing, but is rooted in the divine will. And what is true for Jesus is also true for Jesus' followers. As he put it elsewhere, "If you continue in my word, you are truly my disciples; and you will know the truth, and the truth will make you free" (8:31–32).

Fifth Sunday of Easter

The text for this day from Acts 8 appears to capture a theme that, to some degree, is pervasive of all four lections: Christ's mandate to the people of God to witness to the truth of God's love, especially as that love has been declared through the Christ-event itself.

The figure of the Ethiopian eunuch may be an elusive one, in that he appears nowhere else in the New Testament. But there is nothing questionable concerning the essential meaning of the text that describes his conversion: Jesus is the one in whom the ancient vision of the prophet (Isa. 53) has been realized. The suffering and death of Jesus have become the basis for the "good news" that Philip now shares with the eunuch. That the man responds in faith is made evident by his subsequent baptism at the hands of Philip.

The Psalm lection contains a passage that is illustrative of the response of a faithful person to an experience of God's saving love. Although Ps. 22 begins by expressing a deep sense of alienation from God, a turning point is reached in the psalmist's life in which he or she is reconnected with God's saving ways. The result of this is a determination on the writer's part to involve the larger community in the power of God's love by sharing the saving event of his or her own life.

The series of epistolary texts from 1 John continues with a passage that reminds the reader that God's love lies at the heart of the life of faith, indeed, that it lies at the heart of all of life. There is an important sense in which 1 John 4:7–21 may serve as a kind of theological reflection piece upon the very human dynamic of the lection from Ps. 22. That is to say, because God is love, men and women are now free to reflect God's love in their own love of both God and their neighbor.

The passage from John 15 is one of those too-clear-to-be-misunderstood images so characteristic of the Fourth Gospel. Yet behind the familiarity of Jesus' words in which he identifies himself as the vine, there lie implications regarding our life in Christ that are easily overlooked. Yet these implications are of great significance as both the church and individuals within it attempt to be faithful to Christ's call.

Acts 8:26–40

In one of the more colorful narratives in Acts we are told of the conversion of "an Ethiopian eunuch." Precisely who this man was has been the subject of some discussion, but that he was a proselyte to Judaism is made clear by the stated purpose of his visit to Jerusalem, that is, "to worship" (v. 27). Thus the story may have been recorded in its present form in order to underscore the fulfillment of a promise found in Isa. 56:3–5, that is, that in the time of the consummation of the will of God foreigners as well as eunuchs—persons normally considered unclean—would be welcomed into the house of the Lord. The man whom Philip meets on the road to Gaza is representative of not one, but both these classes of marginalized people. Thus the pericope may be a subtle but significant means by which Luke declares the coming of a new age—and the consummation of an old one.

(It should be noted that this is the Philip first mentioned in Acts 6:5 as one of those chosen to minister to needs of the growing church, and is presumably the same Philip referred to as "the evangelist" in Acts 21:8. At the beginning of the present lection he is in Samaria, where he has fled to escape the persecutions in Jerusalem, 8:1–5.)

But if the passage contains echoes of Isa. 56 (other Old Testament influences have also been identified, as, for example, Zeph. 2:4 in v. 26 and 1 Kings 18:12 in v. 39), clearly the centerpiece of the narrative in this regard is Isa. 53:7–8. The crucified Jesus is described as the Suffering Servant of the Lord, the lamb unjustly slain. That Acts 8:33 is somewhat different from Isa. 53:8 is undoubtedly related to the fact that reliance here is on the Septuagint translation instead of on the original Hebrew. Yet it is interesting that Luke (or Luke's source) chose to highlight vs. 7–8 of Isa. 53 instead of, say, vs. 4–6, with their emphasis on the substitutionary purpose of the death of the Servant. In any event, the point is forcefully made that the death of Jesus not only was consistent with the will of God, but also was anticipated by the prophet long before.

There is no denying that the early church embraced the view that Jesus fulfilled the role of Messiah by means of his suffering and death, as, for example, Matt. 16:21–23 illustrates. But whether this view was also shared by Jesus himself is a question that has aroused passionate debate, some scholars insisting that only a post–Good Friday retrospective would raise such a connection. But evidence from Qumran suggests that the concept of a suffering Messiah may already have been in the theological inventory of at least some in the Jewish community by the first century A.D., and it thus may not be legitimately denied as an aspect of Jesus' self-understanding. Even if the bringing together of the roles of Suffering Servant and Messiah had not been accomplished before Jesus' time, Jesus' own theological originality in formulating such a concept may not be dismissed out of hand.

The quotation from Isa. 53 is bracketed by two questions posed by the eunuch: "How can I [understand what I have been reading], unless someone guides me?" (Acts 8:31) and "About whom ... does the prophet say this, about himself or about someone else?" (v. 34). The searching, receptive attitude of the eunuch not only leads him to a reading of the Isaiah text in the first place, but also to an openness without which Philip's interpretation would have been meaningless.

It is in Philip's response to the eunuch's searching that his (Philip's) own witness to the "good news about Jesus" (v. 35) is given expression. One may assume that the content of the evangelist's message, which is only hinted at in v. 35, was similar to other kerygmatic declarations found in greater detail elsewhere in Acts, such as the sermon of Peter in 2:14–36. That Philip's skills as a bearer of the good news had been previously used to great effectiveness is made clear by 8:5–8.

More important than the role of Philip in the story about the eunuch is the role of the Spirit of God. At three key points in the narrative the activity of God in leading the eunuch to the truth is described. First, "an angel of the Lord" provides the impulse that drives Philip from Samaria down to the Gaza road (v. 26). Second, when he catches sight of the eunuch it is the "Spirit" who directs the evangelist to approach the man (v. 29). And third, when the eunuch emerges from the water of baptism, the "Spirit of the Lord snatched Philip away" (v. 39), the apparent reason being that the Spirit had other urgent business for him elsewhere, and that his great evangelistic successes in Samaria would now be repeated all along the Mediterranean coast from the land of the ancient Philistines (Azotus was the former Philistine city of Ashdod) to the Roman provincial capital of Caesarea Maritima (v. 40). Thus, while the story is a further demonstration of the evangelist's effectiveness, beyond that it is a statement concerning the reliance of even the most persuasive proclaimers of the good news on the activity of God's Spirit. What is not stated in the text, but may be assumed, is that even the receptive attitude of the eunuch was the work of God's Spirit. Thus, without the Spirit's support and leadership not even so warming an evangelist as Philip is capable of doing the work of the Lord.

Psalm 22:25-31

This psalm, Ps. 22, is familiar to us only because v. 1 is in the mouth of Jesus on the cross (Mark 15:34). The psalm, however, does not stay with the sense of God-abandonment voiced in v. 1. The psalm features a decisive rhetorical turn, either between v. 21a and v. 21b, or between v. 21 and v. 22, depending on how one translates. At this break point, something transformative has been wrought by God which decisively changes the mood and circumstance of the speaker. We do not know if that change is liturgical, or if it refers to some action that is politically and publicly effective. Either way, the psalm moves (in the language of Claus Westermann) from "plea" to "praise." Our verses in the lectionary come in the second half of the psalm, in which the speaker expresses delight that the sense of abandonment in vs. 1–21 has been overcome by the goodness and power of God. (See the Psalter reading for the Second Sunday in Lent for additional comment.)

This powerful voice of praise moves in three concentric circles, from family (vs. 22–24), to congregation (vs. 25–26), to all the "ends of the earth" (vs. 27–31), thus in ever-widening circles. The speaker of this psalm has much to celebrate and wants to mobilize the whole world to join in the celebration of God.

Verses 25 and 26 portray a scene of exultant, celebrative, festive doxological life in the congregation. The initial complaint of vs. 1–21 was quite intense and personal, in the first person singular. These verses show the way in which the entire community of faith can enter into the joy of an individual member (see 1 Cor. 12:26).

The speaker is willing to "stand and be counted" in the congregation, that is, in the assembly of all the faithful. The speaker is willing to be on the spot, having lost all sense of intimidation and embarrassment, being so smitten with the powerful goodness of God that joy and gratitude override any social pressure to be otherwise. This would seem to be a moment of "testimony," in which the speaker tells others how good and powerful God has been. Such "praise" is matched by a more disciplined act of paying a vow. Such a payment is a conventional element in thanksgiving;

presumably the speaker, while still in the troubles of Ps. 22:1–21, had pledged that if delivered by God, certain offerings would be given in gratitude and acknowledgment of God. And now the speaker remembers the pledge, and gratefully and generously pays up.

Verse 26, if it follows from v. 25, may suggest that the payment of vow was "in kind," agricultural produce that provides the makings of a feast. Thus the produce of gratitude is transposed into a great festival meal, which is then shared especially with the poor and humble, who themselves may lack wherewithal for such a meal. We are given an image of an exuberant extravagance, in which grateful generosity surpasses economic discipline and calculation, and all members of the community of faith are to delight in the extravagance that is gratitude to God. The last line of v. 26 sounds like a generalized wish, perhaps a toast from a reveler a little bit intoxicated with wine and gratitude.

In vs. 27 and 28, the circle of gratitude is widened beyond the community of faith. It is now as large in scope as all of creation. This unrestrained speaker has a vision of all of creation being so moved by his testimony that all the ends of the earth will come to grateful delight in Yahweh, and all the families of the nations will share in the faith and allegiance of Israel. The phrase "all the families of the nations" is reminiscent of God's promises to Abraham (Gen. 12:3), and perhaps the psalmist understands this wondrous moment as the time when those ancient promises finally come to fruition. It is generosity, goodness, and fidelity experienced by this psalmist that lead to this large, visionary affirmation about Yahweh's sovereignty.

The largest circle of praise and allegiance is expressed in vs. 29–31, as the psalmist grows more comprehensively lyrical. Verse 29 refers to all those who have lived in the past and are now dead, that is, "sleep in the earth . . . down to the dust." This verse emphasizes that all those now dead shall declare allegiance to this surpassing God. The poetry is completely elliptical, and nothing is explained. There is nothing explicit here about life after death or resurrection, only the unspecified thought of the limitless claim of Yahweh.

This claim for those alive in the past is matched in vs. 30–31 with anticipation for those still to come, "posterity . . . future generations . . . people yet unborn." The reference to the future is as unspecified as is the past in v. 29. The speaker has no one in particular in mind. The psalm simply envisions all of humanity, all the past of humanity, all the future of humanity, gathered in loyalty and allegiance and delight. This is "the communion of saints," all sharing in a glad obedience that overrides the distinctions of time and place.

The single topic of this exhibit of limitless loyalty is God's "deliverance" (v. 31). "Deliverance" refers to God's active intervention into a situation of distortion in order to make life right, whole, and joyous, as it was not until God intervened. If we ask about the "active intervention" to which reference is made, I suggest it is the specific intervention in the life of the psalmist in v. 21, whereby the psalm has changed direction. Thus all of the faithful in the world, past and future as well as present, pivot on this concrete, modest datum of new life.

1 John 4:7–21

As is evident in the Gospel lesson for this day as well as in earlier lessons from 1 John, divine love and the correlative demand for love among human beings is an important theme in the Johannine tradition. Perhaps because the experience of the Johannine community demonstrated the difficulties of living with Jesus' admonitions to love, the writer of this letter labors to articulate how love comes into being and how God's love inevitably leads into human love.

How do people learn the nature of love? How do people learn *how* to love? Many contemporary Western Christians would probably answer those questions in psychological terms, appealing to the family as the primary setting in which love is experienced, modeled, nurtured (even if all too often families fail to accomplish this task adequately). Other Christians might address the questions by looking at the larger society as the crucible in which attitudes toward love are shaped and lessons learned. The answer 1 John offers is neither psychological nor social but theological, and the answer is quite clear: Love comes from God.

The Johannine tradition elsewhere claims that God's love is seen in the sending of the Son, as in John 3:16 (see 1 John 3:16, where Jesus' gift of his own life is said to teach love). What distinguishes this particular reference to the Christ-event as revelatory of God's love is the earlier assertion that "God is love" (1 John 4:8). Reversing this statement will not work; to say that "God is love" is not to say that "love is God." As the appeal to the giving of the Son makes clear, the statement describes the very person of God. It is not an abstract definition of love or even a theoretical proposition about God, but an appeal to the experience of God's love in the incarnation itself. The writer of the Odes of Solomon puts it this way:

> For I should not have known how to love the Lord,
> If He had not continuously loved me.
>
> (*Odes of Sol.* 3:3)

God's love of human beings evokes reciprocal love by human beings—with a twist. The reciprocal form of God's love for humans is human love for other humans. That is not to exclude the possibility of loving God, but to explain how loving God expresses itself in the context of the human community.

Several aspects of the way 1 John discusses the loving of other human beings warrant attention. First, the author grants this aspect of Christian life the status of a commandment, and does so both at the beginning (4:7) and at the end (v. 21) of the lesson. Admittedly, "Let us love one another" (v. 7) is a subjunctive rather than an imperative, but an imperative would have been "You love one another," thereby excluding the writer from the obligation to love. If a rupture has occurred within the Johannine community, as seems evident in 2:19, the author may find it necessary to place this particular commandment very close to home. Second, if people love others because of God's love, they do not claim for themselves credit for loving (it comes from God), nor do they love only those who are lovable. Love is God's gift, not a human achievement. The third aspect of this discussion that calls for attention is the statement that "those who do not love a brother or sister whom they have seen, cannot love God whom they have not seen" (4:20). This statement is more than a contrast between seeing and not seeing, or between loving humans and loving God. Those who do not love their sisters and brothers are simply unable to love God, because it is God's love that introduces and teaches and enables all other love.

Among the more elusive aspects of this passage is the discussion of fear. What does it mean to say that there "is no fear in love, but perfect love casts out fear" (4:18)? Certainly the love of human beings for one another contains much fear—fear of loss, fear of betrayal, fear of mistaken trust. What 1 John has in view, however, is not fear in the context of human love but fear of God. One strand of scripture does perceive fear to be an appropriate response to God, in that humans should approach God with awe and trembling. The healings of Jesus and the resurrection narratives, for example, attribute fear to those who witness them (for example, Mark 4:41; 16:8). Here, by contrast, fear occurs in an eschatological context, as is clear from the reference to the "day of judgment" in 1 John 4:17. What the author presses is a confidence in God's love that precludes fear, even fear of standing before God as judge.

The statements in v. 18 also touch on the larger issue of inappropriate fear of God. A writing attributed to Plutarch, roughly a contemporary of the writer of 1 John, venomously ridicules those who are afraid of the gods, for the intent of the gods is to benefit humankind, whereas fear of the gods renders humans pitiful: "He who fears the gods fears all things, earth and sea, air and sky, darkness and light, sound and silence, and a dream" (*On Superstition* 3). The writer of 1 John would have put the same judgment somewhat differently, perhaps as follows: Those who fear God fail to understand God's love, which intends only love and life for God's children.

John 15:1–8

Familiar texts with clear imagery, like the Gospel reading for this Sunday, are often the most difficult to preach from. Congregations have listened to so many clichés and worn-out explanations that they are weary with the usual, and the task of preaching becomes that of allowing the imagery to speak in subtle and engaging ways. The problem with John 15 is that the imagery itself is not elusive but up-front and repetitious, and even listeners who do not themselves garden can hardly miss the point.

Yet there are still dimensions of the text that warrant exploration. For starters, the context is critical. John 13 and 14 set the scene for a farewell conversation between Jesus and the disciples. He is going where they cannot come, at least for now, and thus his words take on the character of urgent instruction for what life is like without his physical presence.

The ending of ch. 14 ("Rise, let us be on our way") provokes all manner of suggestions from the commentators about literary relocation and setting, but in the narrative Jesus' words are a call to get moving. The talk about the indwelling between Jesus and the disciples is not meant for a community at rest that has settled in for business as usual, but for a community engaged in service, a community whose distinctiveness from the world evokes the world's distrust and hatred (15:18–19). In any context other than mission, the marvelous imagery of vine and branches loses its relevance.

A second observation. The historical character of the imagery must not be lost. The Old Testament is full of texts where Israel is referred to as God's special vine, often texts of admonition because of Israel's failure to fulfill its calling. Isaiah 5 is a love song to a vineyard that has produced bloodshed instead of justice. The imagery is being repeated in John 15 to an Israel now including Gentiles.

The point is that the imagery carries the notion of corporateness. The command to "abide" in the first instance is directed to the church, whose communal life and ministries of social justice are no more than branches to be tossed into the fire, apart from the indwelling Christ. Those in the Johannine community, for which this Gospel was originally written, may well have found in the process of pruning an analogy to illuminate their own corporate experience. They counted among their numbers many who, like the blind man of John 9, had experienced the harsh excommunication from the synagogue and with it separation from family and friends. Though painful, pruning has a positive intent—more fruitfulness. Our natural proclivity to read the imagery in an individualistic sense must not blind us to its natural communal orientation.

A third observation. The imagery demands an open-endedness with our congregations. We are inclined to seek specific explanations for each metaphor: What is meant by "abiding"? by "pruning"? by "bearing fruit"? The text itself offers partial answers, but is by no means meant to close off others. Abiding, for instance, includes letting Jesus' words abide in us (15:7). I take that to mean reading, meditating on, and obeying the text of scripture. In a succeeding section (vs. 9–13) and in the epistolary lesson from 1 John 4:7–21, love is highlighted. But the image of the branches abiding in the vine may helpfully connote many other notions not specifically mentioned in the text—connectedness, permanency, vitality.

Likewise, the fruit that results from the abiding and the pruning need not be defined in too limited a fashion. Prayer (John 15:7), becoming disciples (v. 8), and glorifying the Father (v. 8) are associated in the text with bearing fruit, but the very image may suggest other associations such as growth, usefulness, and nourishment. The larger context of the Gospel can serve to limit any wild associations we might want to make.

A final observation. The mutuality between Jesus and the disciples spoken of here is both a gift and a task. The passage intermingles indicatives with imperatives. It declares that the readers *are* branches (v. 5) and that the divine Gardener *is* at work to make the branches more productive: "You have already been cleansed by the word that I have spoken to you" (v. 3).

At the same time, readers are summoned to "abide" in Jesus, which certainly entails a constantly renewed commitment. The mutuality and fruitfulness do not occur automatically, apart from the participation of the disciples. The text cajoles and even threatens readers a bit with the announcement that the branches that fail to abide are worthless and fit for nothing more than firewood. But the prospect of such an outcome need not be paralyzing, since the abiding is two-sided—the disciples in Christ and Christ in the disciples. The demands are surrounded on every side with grace.

Sixth Sunday of Easter

The power of the Spirit of God to give new life is the theme of the lection from Acts 10. In these verses, which form a sequel to the Acts text for Easter Day (Peter's preaching to Cornelius, his relatives, and his friends), the mission to the Gentiles is clearly still in focus as Peter's kerygmatic proclamation results in the baptism of those who have listened to his message. Even Peter's closest associates are astounded at the audacity and freshness of the Spirit's work. Yet any terror over the unpredictability of the Spirit's initiatives is muted by the realization that the motivating energy behind the Spirit is God's love for humankind.

Psalm 98 is one of the most exuberant hymns in the scriptures, for it declares in quite extravagant language the joy that women and men experience when they come to terms with God's creative and re-creative initiatives. The psalm is characterized as a "new song," one befitting a God who continually works in loving and wonderful ways in human life. The rich vocabulary of the psalm is reflective of the myriad ways in which Israel's God responds to the needs of creation. Even the world of nature joins in praising this Sovereign, who not only judges the world, but renews it as well.

The series of readings from 1 John moves on to a text that draws ever more tightly the connections between God's love for us and our love for other persons. Although the logic of the text defies the normal categories of human reasoning, the force of the argument coheres because of the pervasive reality of God's love. Because of God's love, believers love and trust God and believers also love one another. The ultimate evidence for this transforming love of God is the death and resurrection of Jesus.

In the text from John 15 Jesus calls his disciples "friends." But this is no ordinary friendship to which Jesus summons persons; it is a friendship that he himself has initiated, and that results in commitment and trust on the part of those who identify themselves with him. It should not be assumed that friendship with Jesus signifies membership in some privileged club, for it is in reality a call to service and to loving faithfulness. This quality of the relationship with Jesus is characterized by his commandment, "that you love one another as I have loved you."

Acts 10:44–48

The present text forms a conclusion to the Acts lection appointed for Easter, Peter's declaration of the good news about Jesus to the Roman centurion Cornelius (10:34–43). While each pericope may be read as a self-contained literary and theological unit, the connections between the two should not go unnoticed. Peter's sermon to Cornelius, with "his relatives and close friends" (v. 24), is a result of the work of the Spirit, who has prepared both the Gentiles and Peter for what is about to transpire (vs. 1–33). No less the work of the Spirit is the sermon itself, incorporating, as it does, the whole scope of Christ's work of redemption and its central focus, the resurrection (v. 40). And it is the Spirit of God who determines the consequences of what Peter preaches (v. 44).

Our lection for this day, therefore, begins by affirming the life-giving power of the Spirit. Having prepared the hearts of Cornelius and the others for the hearing of the word, the Spirit now allows the power of the word to stand unleashed in those same hearts. "All who heard the word" (v. 44) were touched so that they all believed in him and received forgiveness of sins through his name (see v. 43). Had the narrative ended there, it would have been a fitting conclusion, for the Spirit had paved the way for the admission of Gentiles into the church, the point of the visions of both Cornelius (vs. 3–8) and Peter (vs. 9–16). But such an accomplishment was only a beginning. What now became just as urgent was that all the church should know of the universal love of God.

We are not sure why Peter's friends traveled with him from Joppa to Caesarea (v. 23b). Perhaps they were curious about this Cornelius, whose fame for good works had preceded him. Or perhaps they felt some unspoken fear for their companion, who was now summoned to the presence of this officer of the imperial army. Whatever their reason for accompanying Peter, they were clearly not prepared for what the Spirit was about to do. The scene is described (vs. 45–46) in terms similar to those of the Pentecost narrative of Acts 2, and the sight of these Gentiles "speaking in tongues and extolling God" leaves Peter's friends "astounded." They are not inexperienced in the surprising ways of the Spirit, since it may be assumed that some of them had been present for the Pentecost event, and all had surely heard about it. But that was an occasion on which God had stirred a powerful reaction among *Jews,* an event that, while astonishing, was not without precedent. For it had been Israelites who, during the long years of God's saving encounter with humankind, had been the focus of God's mercies. But these people who were exhibiting the endowment of the Spirit were—Gentiles!

Peter's heart had been prepared for this moment, in a manner his friends' hearts had not been. And, as was often the case with this largehearted Galilean, he was quick to follow his God-inspired insights to whatever conclusion they demanded. "Since the Holy Spirit has baptized these people, can we possibly refuse to do the same?" seems to be the essence of v. 47. This was the same Peter, one will remember, who insisted that God's laws of cleanliness and uncleanliness be strictly observed (vs. 9–16). But that was before the power of the Spirit's vision had taken hold of him. And so, under Peter's instructions, the centurion, and his family and friends as well, are baptized in the name of Jesus Christ.

It is little wonder that Peter's hosts refused to let him go until he had shared with them his full understanding of the mystery and wonder of God's saving love in Jesus Christ (v. 48b).

Much has been written on the implications for human history of the bringing of the gospel to the world of the Gentiles, and one may only speculate concerning what would have happened had the early Christian movement remained one of the several sectarian divisions within first-century Judaism. But such musings must remain within the realm of speculation, because the Spirit of God willed otherwise. And that is where the attention of our text is riveted—not on what might have been, but on the power of the Spirit.

There is a sense in which this text instills a certain terror within the reader, in spite of its familiarity. For Luke makes it clear that it is the nature of the Spirit to remain unbridled, bringing to bear the intentionality of God in the most astonishing and unexpected ways. If those who were the bearers of the gospel then were unprepared for the Spirit's fresh initiatives, how much less prepared are we? If Peter and Peter's friends could be astounded, what—we may ask—might the Spirit have in store for us?

There is yet another sense in which the text—so terrible in some ways—liberates us and sets us free from terror. For this seemingly unpredictable Spirit is in very important ways quite predictable. Although we may not be prepared for the Spirit's every expression, we may count on the Spirit to be motivated by no other concern than love for that humankind for which Christ died. So that the Spirit's seemingly astonishing movements are all quite consistent, expressing God's love for this world in ways that we, limited by our own frail powers, could never do.

And so our astonishment at the Spirit's power is accompanied by joy over the Spirit's love.

Psalm 98

This psalm pictures the people of God (and the whole of creation) at a new moment of doxology, celebrating the newness of God's triumph.

Psalm 98 celebrates the newness wrought in the earth by God (vs. 1–3). On the one hand, that celebration is distinctively a liturgical event. It is a meeting in the Temple, whereby the new power and governance of God are known and seen to be effective. Thus the congregation is invited to sing a "new song." The notion of a "new song" in the first instance likely concerns a new choir anthem, commissioned and composed for a very special liturgical moment. The notion of "new song," however, has come to mean not only freshly composed music, but an utterance that points to God's decisive action that cannot be explained, only voiced in praise. By Rev. 5:9, the phrase "new song" has become an end-time doxology, celebrating God's ultimate triumph and rule in the earth.

On the other hand, this liturgical extravagance is rooted in real-life, public events. The subject of the new song is God's "marvelous things," God's wondrous deeds of miraculous power, which decisively transform the earth and the situation of Israel.

These verses lack any specificity, so that the concrete miracles must be filled in from Israel's memory. The celebration may refer either to the cluster of miracles in the orbit of Moses and Joshua, or to the Creation miracles, whereby God had defeated the powers of chaos to make an ordered life possible. Either way, attention should be given to the rich vocabulary used for these miracles. Four terms are of interest. The term "victory" is used three times (vs. 1, 2, 3). The term is *yěšû'āh*, which might better be understood as an act of deliverance or liberation. It is a military term, an act of powerful intervention, but its intent is to rescue from an enslaving power. The second term, "vindication" (*sĕdāqāh*) refers to God's intervention to make a situation right (see Ps. 22:31 in the reading for last week). The third term, "steadfast love" (*ḥesed*), and the fourth term, "faithfulness" (*'ĕmûnāh*), refer to God's abiding promissory commitment to

Israel. All four terms, *yĕšû'āh, ṣĕdāqāh, ḥesed,* and *'ĕmûnāh,* refer to God's enduring resolve to act decisively in order to transform the circumstance of Israel into a situation of well-being, freedom, and joy. The "marvelous things" are wondrous acts of life-giving with Israel on the receiving end.

Whereas Ps. 98:1-3 focuses on the real-life, public events on Israel's historical horizon, vs. 4-6 return to the liturgical theme of "new song" in v. 1a. These verses consist of four imperatives, which summon the congregation to loud, boisterous, exuberant, unrestrained celebration that responds to the wondrous interventions of God. What else can one do in response to a visible miracle? Doxology is a prerational act of grateful commitment which matches the prerational, that is, inscrutable actions of Yahweh. Thus in the liturgical act of praise Israel gives an elemental commitment to the miracles, acknowledging them and allowing them to redefine reality.

In these verses, we may note two decisive phrases. In the beginning, the summons to praise is issued to "all the earth" (v. 4). Even though v. 2 celebrates the victory of Yahweh for Israel, "all the earth" is invited to the glad response, for non-Israelites can take these wondrous miracles as signs of God's marvelous capacity for the whole earth. At the end, for the first time in this psalm, the God here praised and celebrated is acknowledged as "the King" (v. 6), the one who rightly exercises sovereignty over all the earth. Indeed, it is Yahweh's capacity, demonstrated in the life of Israel, to do impossibilities that provide the ground and warrant for Yahweh's assertion of sovereignty over the nations. Yahweh is saluted as sovereign only because of these "qualifying events." Thus the theo-political claim for Yahweh moves from the particularity of Israel to the wholeness of the earth. The large claim is rooted in the specificity.

This psalm may reflect a liturgical event whereby Yahweh's rule over the nations is enacted, authorized, and established. In the liturgical act of praise, Yahweh is "elevated" to the office of king of the world, for which Yahweh is qualified by these events of rescue and transformation in the life of Israel. The larger claim for Yahweh is clearly freighted with socio-ideological implications, since the song is sung in the Jerusalem Temple, chapel of the Davidic kings.

The claim of Yahweh's sovereignty is made even larger in vs. 7-9. The rule of Yahweh applies not only to the nations (v. 2), but to nonhuman creatures as well. Thus the sea, the world, the floods, the hills are presented as personal participants in the great royal doxology. They, along with Israel and the nations, break out in singing and celebrative applause. They too are delighted about Yahweh's new governance. The reason for their delight is that the ordering of the earth will now, finally, become one of righteousness and equity (v. 9). The new governance implies that the waters need no longer fear pollution, the hills no longer need fear abuse and exploitation. Moreover, the "sea" and "floods" are principles of raging chaos. But they now willingly submit to their rightful liege, the one who will bring them to happy, well-ordered submission. No wonder there is a new song for a new governance! There is so much newness and goodness about which to sing—by Israel, by the nations, by the nonhuman creatures, all of whom welcome the God of fidelity as their new governor. (See additional comment under Christmas, Third Proper.)

1 John 5:1–6

The opening words of this lesson resume the theme of the reading for the Fifth Sunday of Easter, that Christians must of necessity love one another because they love God. First John 5:2, however, appears to turn the theme on its head: "By this we know that we love the children of God, when we love God." Since 4:20–21 argues in a way that is exactly opposite to this statement, readers may begin to wonder whether the writer of 1 John is thinking clearly about the topic at hand. (That question becomes even more acute in the Greek, since the grammar in this letter is notoriously ambiguous.)

What the two lessons together present is a circular argument: To love God believers must love one another, and to love one another believers must love God. What prevents this logic from being merely circular is the author's notion of the integrity of the relationships, on the one hand, between God and the believer, and, on the other hand, among believers. Separating the love believers have for God from the love they have for one another is impossible, because both forms of love stem from God and are experienced in God's gift of Jesus Christ.

The wording of 5:1 makes it clear that those to be loved are those who stand within the community of faith. However much preachers and teachers might wish otherwise, 1 John restricts the scope of this reciprocal love to those within the church. The reasons for this in the author's context probably stem from the need to define the community's boundaries and identity in a time when those are severely threatened. Of course, if Christians succeed in learning from God's love how to love one another, the task of loving those outside the church becomes easier!

The end of v. 2 continues the statement about love, with the claim that believers love God not only by their love of one another but also by their obedience to God's commandments (see the similar statements in 1 John 2:5 and 2 John 6). Despite its echo of Deut. 30:11, the assertion in 1 John 5:3 that the commandments "are not burdensome" sounds a strange note to the Protestant ear, attuned to an interpretation of certain Pauline statements in a way that suggests the opposite (for example, Gal. 3:10–14). More important for understanding this particular passage, the need to defend the reasonableness of the commandments seems out of place in the argument the author is unfolding. Perhaps in response to those who have split away from the Johannine community, who apparently deny the necessity of doing good (see, for example, 1 John 2:18–22 and the discussion for the Second Sunday of Easter), the writer affirms again not only the importance of observing the commandments but the *possibility* of doing so.

The final comment about the commandments introduces the motif of victory. The commandments are not a burden *because* they come from God, and "whatever is born of God conquers the world" (v. 4a). Faith itself conquers the world (v. 4b). Believers conquer the world (v. 5). In light of what contemporary Westerners would understand by the phrase "conquer the world," these statements are absurd. Neither the commandments, nor faith, nor believers become a quasi-military power that obliterates the opposition. On the contrary, given the Johannine tradition's understanding of "the world" as those who refuse to hear and accept the gospel, to conquer or overcome the world is to be beyond the grasp of that opposition, to be beyond the grasp of everyone and everything that is hostile to God.

Does the statement that faith itself conquers the world mean that those who believe somehow earn their standing as conquerors? Has faith here become an accomplishment? The statements on either side of v. 4b argue implicitly against that conclusion. If faith conquers the world, it is because and only because faith "is born of God" (v. 4a). And the One in whom that faith is lodged is the one who has truly conquered the world (see John 16:33) and through whom faith becomes victorious.

The final verse of the passage amplifies the statement about Jesus in v. 5 by saying that Jesus "came by water and blood." While there has been inordinate controversy over the phrase "water and blood" (and the standard commentaries will explain that debate), some reference to Jesus' birth and certainly his death is intended. The repeated references to blood indicate where the emphasis falls. It is by virtue of his death that Jesus conquers the world. The statement seems absurd, and by conventional standards of "conquering," it is absurd. But, especially in the Johannine tradition, where Jesus' crucifixion and resurrection become one continuous "lifting up" (that is, exaltation), the blood of Jesus itself signals his overcoming of the world.

At this point in particular, this lesson becomes an important one in light of its setting within Eastertide. The death and resurrection of Jesus are not, for the writer of 1 John, simply ways of addressing the problem of human sin. Instead, the death and resurrection of Jesus demonstrate that the world is bankrupt and its judgments are overturned by the God whose love alone is capable of overcoming the world.

John 15:9–17

Friendship is an all too scarce commodity in our world. Competitiveness, a mobile society, a fragmentation of life tend to isolate people and make the traditional patterns of making and sustaining friends difficult. Unfortunately, the term "friend" is often reduced to acquaintance, and the ingredients of a deep relationship, such as empathy, support, and mutual struggle, are lost.

It is striking, then, to hear Jesus lift up the language of friendship to depict his relationship with his followers. "I do not call you servants any longer. . . . I have called you friends" (John 15:15). The disciples are invited to view their soon-to-depart Lord in a new light, to accept a relationship of intimacy and reciprocity. But how can one be a friend of Jesus? Does not this negate the Lord-servant relationship? Is it not an opening to a chumminess that obscures the gap between the divine and the human? What can we learn from the text?

First, we learn that to be a friend of Jesus means to be loved and chosen. The dramatic definition of love given in 15:13 ("to lay down one's life for one's friends"), while stated in a universal way, takes its meaning from the death of Jesus (10:11, 15). The friendship is rooted in this incredible event of sacrifice, in which the Lord takes the role of servant, the Judge becomes the victim. From the very beginning, then, the disciples are deeply indebted to this One who now calls them friends.

If there is any lingering notion that this friendship results from mutual attraction, 15:16 pointedly dispels it ("You did not choose me but I chose you"). Students wishing to learn the Torah sought out a rabbi whose teaching they wanted to emulate. The choice was theirs. But Jesus reverses the order. The decision is his. He chooses his followers.

Consider three brief corollaries to v. 16. (*a*) If Jesus' loving election is the basis for the divine-human friendship, then there is no room for a consumerist attitude toward the practice of the friendship. Disciples are not in a position to dictate when and where they will act like friends or to demand this or that benefit from the relationship to satisfy their own felt needs. (*b*) The election does not warrant a sense of elitism on the part of those elected. Persons are chosen not for privilege, but for bearing lasting fruit, for an abiding productiveness in God's reign. (*c*) The choosing by Jesus provides enormous staying power when the task of bearing fruit becomes difficult. One's own fears and failures do not shake the electing hand that sustains.

Second, we learn that to be a friend of Jesus means to know what is going on. "I have called you friends, because I have made known to you everything that I have heard from my Father" (v. 15). What distinguishes servants from friends is that friends have been let in on the plans. The disciples, for instance, are told about the coming crisis and Jesus' impending departure. They are not kept in the dark about what is happening and what is going to happen.

The Gospel of John is a story of revelation, of the Word made flesh, of the restoration of sight to a man born blind. It promises the coming of the Spirit of truth, who "will teach you everything, and remind you of all that I have said to you" (14:26). What makes people friends of Jesus is their being captured by the story, following the sometimes comforting, sometimes disturbing plot that leads to the cross and the empty tomb, and finding in it the light to guide their way in the world.

Third, to be a friend of Jesus means to keep his commandments and to love as he has loved. This Gospel repeatedly speaks of love as a commandment (15:12, 17; 13:34), a notion that sounds a bit strange. The usual definition of love would forbid its being an action done or sentiment conjured up under duress. For many, to be genuine love must be spontaneous and come from within and not without.

Unlike most other New Testament writers, however, John does not use "commandment(s)" to refer to the ordinances of the Old Testament. He is never concerned about the law as a burdensome load from which Jesus brings freedom. Instead, "commandment(s)" refers either to the directives Jesus gives to the disciples (as 15:10, 12) or to the directives Jesus receives from the Father, by which his whole career in the world is guided (10:18; 12:49–50; 14:31; 15:10).

The former uses have to be seen in light of the latter. Jesus' commandments comprise the script by which he lives, and this is the same script given to guide the disciples. Verse 9 provides the chain of command: "As the Father has loved me, so I have loved you; abide in my love."

Lest talk of friendship with Jesus degenerate into maudlin sentimentality, it is salutary at least to note the section that follows the assigned reading (15:18–25). That text is realistic about the world's response to the disciples' friendship with Jesus. The dominant verb "love" gives way to "hate." One is reminded of the Greek proverb that says, "The one who has no enemies has no friends."

Ascension

The festival of the Ascension is endlessly problematic and admits of no simple or single "explanation." It is clear in these texts that the church struggled to voice a reality that ran beyond all its explanatory categories. We must take care that we do not engage in domestication that curbs the wonder and wildness of these texts.

The presenting problem is, on the one hand, the disposal of the body of Jesus, what happened to Jesus after Easter. That, however, is a small agenda. On the other hand, the continuation of the church when Jesus is no longer present is an acute issue. Thus the issue in the narrative is much more a church question than it is a Jesus question. That presenting problem, however, only provides "cover" for the larger story. That story is that this fearful, waiting community, which is anxious and bewildered, has no power of its own. It possesses none and it can generate none for itself. It has no claim and no cause for self-congratulation. And yet, oddly, power is given that causes this fragile little community to have energy, courage, imagination, and resources completely disproportionate to its size. How can one speak about this changed situation that can only be attributed to the inscrutable generosity of God? How is it that this church with no claim becomes a powerful force in the larger scheme of public life?

The church has no special language of its own through which to utter the unutterable. For that reason, it must rely on its ancient doxological tradition (in the Psalms), which breaks out beyond reasoned explanation into wonder, awe, amazement, and gratitude. Worship is the arena in which the new power given the church by God is voiced. And that lyrical worship leads to glad witness, asserting that the world is oddly open to new governance.

The preacher will profit from noticing that these stories are cast in odd modes of discourse. There is nothing here that is conventional, controlled, or predictable. The nature of the story requires a peculiar mode of utterance. The narrative lets us see in wonderment glimpses and hints, but not more. God's new rule is beyond our logic. We see only its residue and effect in a transformed community. That community is not certain what has happened, but is sure enough to affirm its identity and embrace its proper work.

Acts 1:1–11 (A B C)

In the Lukan narrative of God's saving activity in Jesus Christ (the Gospel) and in the Holy Spirit (Acts), the story of Jesus' ascension marks the end of Jesus' postresurrection appearances to his disciples and the prelude to the sending of the Spirit, thereby marking a transition point from Easter to Pentecost. In the liturgical tradition of the church, Ascension is all of that and more, for it also has become a festival of the exaltation of the risen Christ.

The Acts lection for this day consists of two main components. The first (Acts 1:1–5) serves not only as an introduction to the entire book of Acts and thus to the work of the Holy Spirit in the life of the young church, but also—in a more immediate sense—as an introduction to the Ascension miracle. The second part (vs. 6–11) is the account of the miracle itself. In both these sections, however, the primary emphasis is on the coming of the Holy Spirit.

Verses 1–5, after a brief statement of purpose (vs. 1–2) which parallels Luke 1:1–4, set forth a terse summary of the events of the forty days following Easter, a time when Jesus "presented himself alive to [the disciples] by many convincing proofs" (v. 3). It is perhaps assumed by Luke that "Theophilus" has heard of these appearances of the risen Christ, since no effort is expended to provide the details of these encounters, other than what is offered in Luke 24. Following Jesus' order to the band of his faithful followers to remain in Jerusalem (Acts 1:4), he delivers the promise of God, namely that God's Spirit is soon to be made evident in fresh ways. This coming of the Spirit is explained in baptismal terms: whereas water was the baptismal medium of old, "you will be baptized with the Holy Spirit not many days from now" (v. 5).

The second part of our text (vs. 6–11) repeats this emphasis on the coming of the Spirit, but in a different context. Here this gracious and decisive gift of God's Spirit is compared to the political hopes the disciples had vested in the Messiah. Their question about the restoration of the kingdom to Israel (v. 6) betrays that not even the events of Easter and the succeeding forty days had disabused them of a comfortable stereotype, that is, that God's Messiah would reinstitute the political fortunes of the old Davidic monarchy. Jesus deflects their question (v. 7) and refocuses their attention on the marvelous display of God's power and love that they are soon to see. It is not the restoration of the kingdom of Israel that will energize you, Jesus says in effect. Rather, "You will receive power when the Holy Spirit has come upon you" (v. 8a). Thus vs. 5 and 8 lift before the reader an announcement from God that is not to be overlooked: the age of the Spirit is about to dawn.

Then Jesus is elevated beyond the limits of their physical senses, and "two men in white robes" (compare Luke 24:4) gently chide the disciples for vacant gazing, even as they promise Jesus' Second Coming (Acts 1:9–11).

While the liturgical tradition of the church has tended to make the ascension of Jesus into a festival to his glory and power, the emphasis in the biblical tradition is elsewhere. Not only is the ascension rarely mentioned in the New Testament (compare Luke 24:51 and Mark 16:19), but the interest in Acts 1 appears to be less in what is happening to Jesus than in what is about to happen in the lives of the earliest Christians. Twice in this brief passage the declaration is made that the Holy Spirit is about to infuse the life of the church in new ways. Not that the Spirit was unknown before this. The "Spirit of God" was the phrase that from very early times had been applied to special expressions of God's guiding and redemptive presence in human life (note, for example, 1 Sam. 11:6, and compare it to 1 Sam. 16:14). But the import of Acts 1:5 and 8 is that a new dimension to the Spirit's work is about to become evident. It is as different from what has gone before as the Spirit is different from the ordinary water of baptism. It is as different from what has gone before as the transcendent kingdom of God (v. 3) is different from the political kingdom of David and his descendants.

Just how the Spirit finds expression the disciples are not told. That is a matter of suspense, which will not be resolved until Pentecost (Acts 2). In the interim, they (and the disciples in every age) are to "be my witnesses in Jerusalem, in all Judea and Samaria, and to the ends of the earth" (v. 8). It will become clear only later that in this very activity of witnessing they will provide the channels for the Spirit's power and grace.

So in the New Testament perspective, Ascension is an interim time, a period—not unlike Advent—between promise and fulfillment. The disciples of Christ are called to live faithful and obedient lives and to remember that the wonder of God's love and presence revealed so radically in the cross and the open tomb still has in store fresh surprises of joy. The disciples of Christ are called to witness, little realizing how the Spirit lurks to transform all that they do into magnificent occasions for the outpouring of God's love. In this manner Ascension points to Pentecost and to all the marvelous ways of the Holy Spirit of God.

Psalm 47 (A B C)

The festival of Ascension is not about the physical ascent of a body (the body of Jesus) into heaven. It is, rather, a liturgical celebration whereby Jesus "ascends to the throne," that is, is dramatically elevated to a position of sovereign authority. In enacting this ritual of enthronement, the church's liturgy draws heavily on the liturgy of ancient Israel, whereby Yahweh was elevated and enthroned as a powerful sovereign. Our psalm reflects such a liturgical enactment.

The initial hymnic unit celebrates the power, authority, and sovereignty of Yahweh (vs. 1–4). The hymnic summons is addressed to "all you peoples" (v. 1). The liturgy of the Jerusalem Temple dares to imagine that its worship is an act concerning all nations and peoples. This inclusive horizon is advanced by reference to Yahweh as "Most High" ('*Elyôn*, v. 2). The title is not an Israelite name for God, but is a generic name for the great god, a name to which all peoples could subscribe.

The reason for such praise is the kingship of Yahweh, the establishment of Yahweh's sovereign rule (vs. 2–4). The ground of praise is twofold. On the one hand, this God is "Elyon," the God of all peoples, who presides over all the earth, who has subdued peoples and nations and drawn them under a new aegis. On the other hand, the actual speakers in the liturgy and in the psalm are Israelites, who know this universal God by the exodus name of Yahweh, and who confess that God chose land "for us" and who loves us (v. 4). Thus the hymn holds together the sweeping notion of universal sovereignty and the concreteness of the experience of the Israelite community.

The first characterization of enthronement in this psalm is a splendid liturgical act (v. 5). "God has gone up"! The language portrays an act of coronation or enthronement whereby the candidate (like the winner of the Miss America contest) ceremoniously, magnificently, and ostentatiously ascends the throne and dramatically claims power and receives obeisance. The kingship of Yahweh is enacted and implemented liturgically, as is every political ascent to power. When we say of Jesus in the creed, "He ascended into heaven," in the first instance this is the language of ritual enthronement and coronation. What is claimed substantively, politically, and theologically is first asserted dramatically and liturgically.

The second hymnic element reiterates the main themes of the initial verses (vs. 6-7). Four times the congregation is urged to "sing praises" (*zāmar*, v. 6). The identity of Yahweh in this summons is "God," a universal title, which is matched by "our King," the governor and guarantor of the Jerusalem political-religious establishment.

The second reflective statement describes the new world situation in light of this act of coronation (vs. 8-9). We are taken into the throne room. Around the throne sit all the obedient, glad subjects (v. 9). There is among them no conflict, dispute, or challenge to the authority of Yahweh. "The princes of the peoples," that is, all the other kings and rulers whose gods have been defeated by Yahweh and who now submit to Yahweh, all are present. The wonder of our phrasing is that they are gathered together "as the people of the God of Abraham" (v. 9). This does not say that they have entered into the Mosaic covenant and have become adherents to the Torah. It is affirmed, however, that they have embraced the promises God has made to Abraham and Sarah, and have agreed to live under the power of God's promise.

This psalm invites us to understand the festival of Ascension anew. The festival is not about getting the body of Jesus off the earth, and it is therefore not marginal and incidental to the life of the church. The festival is a dramatic moment whereby the presence of Jesus in the church is converted into a large, cosmic rule. Rooted in liturgical rhetoric, this claim for God (and subsequently for Jesus) envisions important political spin-offs. All kings are indeed under God's feet (see Eph. 1:22). God's promise, we know very well, is a rule of mercy, compassion, forgiveness, and caring. The new enthronement changes the climate of the earth and the modes of power now permitted in the affairs of princes and kings. The kingship of God revamps all other forms of governance.

Ephesians 1:15-23 (A B C)

Since it separates him from his followers—at least in a physical, visible sense—the ascension of Jesus might have been recalled by the church as a time of grief and confusion. How would the straggly group of Jesus' followers continue in his absence? What meaning could his absence from them have, other than their own isolation and aimlessness?

Luke, alone among the Gospels, not only describes the ascension but portrays it as a time of empowerment. Both in the Gospel and in Acts, Jesus tells his disciples to wait for the Spirit, a Spirit that comes only after Jesus himself has departed. At the ascension itself (Luke 24:44–53; Acts 1:1–11) Jesus' final instructions immediately precede his ascension and the repeated instructions of two men in white robes. By this means, and by virtue of the narrative connection, Luke depicts the ascension of Jesus as the empowerment of the church itself.

The brief reference to the ascension in Eph. 1:15–23 stands out in contrast to the accounts in Luke and in Acts. Here we find no references to Jesus' postresurrection stay with his disciples, to his mysterious ascension, to the return to Jerusalem. Instead, the ascension functions as part of the author's general doxology about God's actions in Christ on behalf of humankind. A closer examination, however, will show that in Eph. 1, as in Luke-Acts, the ascension of Jesus signals the empowerment of the church.

While the passage is a single unit, the content of which is a prayer, it moves from thanksgiving to intercession to doxology. Verses 15–16 first recall the faith of the Ephesians and their love toward all believers. This faithfulness on their part prompts the writer to an exuberance of thanksgiving. As elsewhere in New Testament letters, the response to the gospel in itself provides a reason for gratitude to God.

That thanksgiving does not mean that the church now stands alone or can operate autonomously. The intercession of vs. 17–19 specifies that the church needs wisdom, revelation, and hope. Believers need to know God's power "for us who believe, according to the working of his great power."

At first glance, the remaining verses of the prayer appear to be only a kind of christological footnote. The content is familiar, perhaps so familiar that it slips out of the reader's awareness, dismissed as so much theological "filler" without any substantive connection to the issue at hand, the needs of the community. Several aspects of the passage, however, connect it firmly with the intercessory prayer of vs. 17–19.

Most clearly, both the intercession and the doxology revolve around the writer's confidence in the power of God. Verse 19 refers to the "immeasurable greatness" of God's power and the working of God's "great power." Verse 20, which begins the section on the ascension, begins with "God put this power to work in Christ." In Greek, vs. 19 and 20 are connected by the repetition of "working" (*energeia*) at the end of v. 19 and "put to work" (*energeō*) at the beginning of v. 20. The power already at work in the community and invoked by the author for "wisdom and revelation" is none other than the power that raised Jesus from the dead and exalted him to heavenly places.

What follows in vs. 20–23, then, serves to tie the empowerment of the community to the power of God more than it does to describe in precise detail the present whereabouts and activity of the risen Lord. The statements about Christ's ascension are nevertheless important, particularly for the way in which they underscore this notion of God's power. For the writer of Ephesians, reference to the resurrection alone does not suffice, but must be expanded by a glimpse of the further exaltation of Christ in the ascension. Christ sits at the right hand (v. 20), above every form of "rule and authority and power and dominion," and "above every name" of every age. All things are already subjected to him (v. 21).

These same motifs occur elsewhere in the New Testament, of course, but here Christ's complete triumph has already taken place. The Philippians hymn *anticipates* the exaltation of Christ above every name, but that event has not yet occurred (Phil. 2:5–11). In 1 Cor. 15, Paul confidently asserts that God will finally triumph over "every ruler and every authority and power" (15:24), but that triumph also lies in the future. The apparent conflict among these texts perhaps arises because the author of Ephesians wants to ground the power of the church in this overwhelming demonstration of the power of God. That Christ has already triumphed means that the church itself will surely be sustained by God's power.

The connection between the ascended Christ and the church becomes explicit, of course, in Eph. 1:22–23. Here the metaphor of the church as a body *in Christ*, found already in 1 Corinthians, changes so that the church itself *is the body of Christ*. In 1 Corinthians, that metaphor serves to underscore the unity necessary for the church, even within its diversity. In Ephesians, the transformed metaphor serves to ground the church itself in the power of God. The church may act with confidence, because it knows itself to *be* Christ's own body, the body of the one whose exaltation derives directly from God's own power.

Luke 24:44–53 (A B C)

In the conclusion of Luke's Gospel, the narrator draws the story to a close by sounding again several notes that the careful reader has heard in earlier chapters. They come appropriately now as the final message of the risen Jesus to his disciples and, together with the account of Jesus' departure, serve as the connecting link to the beginning of the book of Acts, Luke's second volume.

What are those repeated themes? First, the Jewish scriptures provide an understanding of the Messiah and his destiny. This concern emerges early in the chapter, as Jesus walks with the two travelers to Emmaus (Luke 24:25-27, 32). Now, as he meets with a group of disciples, he again speaks of the scriptures and their witness to him, to the gospel, and to the mission to the nations. It is not important what specific passages Jesus (or the narrator) might have had in mind. The point to be made is that what happens to Jesus and what the disciples are to do in the days ahead are consistent with God's intentions from the beginning. The suffering and resurrection of the Messiah and the mission to the nations are not accidents of history, but fulfill the divine plan. One has to look to the scriptures to discern God's strategy in inaugurating the anticipated reign of justice and peace.

While the Jewish scriptures provide an understanding of the risen Jesus, it is the risen Jesus who rightly interprets the scriptures. A veil of mystery hangs over the text, leaving it enigmatic and inscrutable, until the resurrection. "Then he opened their minds to understand the scriptures" (v. 45). Neither the intellectual acumen of the scholars nor the spiritual capacity of the mystics grasps the intent of God in the ancient writings, apart from the presence of the one to whom the writings point.

Second, the declaration is made, "You are witnesses of these things" (v. 48). What (or who) is the antecedent of "you"? At the historical level, the answer is presumably "the disciples," though one has to go all the way back to v. 33 to find a specific referent. At another level, one might answer "the Jewish community," since this commission reconstitutes the people of God and gives them the particular responsibility to begin at Jerusalem and proclaim the gospel to the non-Jewish world (see Isa. 49:6). Not surprisingly, the group returns to the Temple as the place of worship and waiting.

At still another level, the "you" is directed to a broader company of readers, ancient and modern, who at the end of the narrative are drawn in as participants in the story. They (we) are witnesses, who are not allowed to put the book down like a good novel and return to business as usual, but are mandated to proclaim the story, to call for repentance, to declare divine forgiveness. They (we), like the original hearers, are to be recipients of the power that the Father promises, an indication that God intends for the plans to be completed and the divine strategy to work.

Third, the narrative ends in a remarkable outburst of worship. Rather than being depressed that Jesus has withdrawn and left them with a heavy responsibility, the disciples are ecstatic and worship Jesus. And their joy seems more than a temporary high, since they are "continually in the temple blessing God" (Luke 24:53). Just as Jesus' entry into the world evoked songs of praise from Mary, Zechariah, Simeon, Anna, and the angelic choir, so Jesus' departure to the Father sets the community again to singing.

Worship and witness belong together. Like the bud that will not bloom without regular watering, the church's mission dries up without the renewal of worship. The singing of hymns, the prayers of thanksgiving and intercession, the reading and exposition of scripture, and the breaking of bread keep the church in touch with the promised power of the Father and make possible the glorifying and enjoying of God that is done outside the sanctuary. Worship becomes the occasion when the story that must be told and retold among the nations is heard afresh, when the witness to the world is reenvisioned. At the same time, worship divorced from witness is empty. The church merely turns in on itself, loses its reason for being, and finds its singing, praying, and reading of scripture bland and impotent.

Ascension Day is an appropriate time to reflect on the church's mission in the world, on the importance of worship as a partner to mission, and the critical role of the scriptures in providing direction.

Seventh Sunday of Easter

The issue of Christian discipleship, so prominent throughout the New Testament, receives special attention in the lection from Acts 1, which reports the process by which the early church—guided by the Spirit—selected a successor for the apostate Judas. While the details of that process are not completely disclosed by the text, two qualified candidates for membership in the apostolic council are introduced, one of whom is selected, the other of whom is passed over. Yet in an ironic twist, both are honored for their faithfulness and commitment by the story that has preserved their names.

Psalm 1 not only functions as an introduction to the entire Psalter, it also introduces the reader into the world of Jewish devotion to Torah from the (probably) late Old Testament period. One seriously misreads this passage if one interprets it in absolutist terms—that is, rules about what one must and must not do. Rather, the emphasis is on meditation and reflection of God's ways. By means of Torah, God has graciously provided humankind with a vehicle for expressing our acceptance of God's love, and to ponder God's gift is to live one's life according to the moral shape God intended for our world.

The lection from 1 John focuses on the importance of credibility. Since human experience teaches us that not all persons may be trusted, a crucial issue for us becomes the criteria by which we decide which words are and which are not true. In the case of Jesus, this matter is of the utmost urgency, since the claims made by him as well as the claims made about him are intended to generate the most important decisions a person makes. The text assures the reader that these claims are entirely trustworthy, because their source is none other than God.

The lection from John's Gospel is part of the high-priestly prayer of ch. 17. A primary concern in this text is the ongoing life of the Christian community, and Jesus prays for at least four things: that the community be protected from evil; that it be unified; that it fulfill

Jesus' joy; and that the life of the church be distinct from the life of the world. The temptation that presents itself to the commentator here is to succumb to the gnostic-like language of the text and to read Jesus' petitions in otherworldly terms. But the strong emphasis in the Fourth Gospel on the reality of Jesus' incarnation offers an important corrective to that misperception of the message of the text.

Acts 1:15–17, 21–26

Having provided "Theophilus" with an account of the ascension of Jesus, Luke then turns to the issue of Judas' successor. However one may view the role of the twelve apostles in transmitting the authority of Jesus to the church (and the matter is, of course, a controversial one within the history of Western Christianity), it is clear from this passage that membership in this group of Jesus' closest followers was an issue of some import to the earliest Christians. Judas had not only betrayed Jesus, he had also betrayed the trust of his colleagues within the apostolic circle. Even if he had not committed suicide (compare Acts 1:18 with Matt. 27:5), his place among the apostles would surely have been declared vacant. Peter, clearly the chief apostle, takes the initiative and, citing texts from the Psalms, calls for a process to be set in motion by which a new apostle may be chosen.

Peter's description (vs. 21–22) of the qualifications that the new apostle must meet are instructive. This person must have been a follower of Jesus from the very beginning, from the day of Jesus' baptism by John, and must have continued in faithfulness up to and including the moment of Jesus' ascension. Only such a person may "become a witness with us to his resurrection." It is undoubtedly the importance of this personal and immediate relation with the Lord that led Paul to express his own experience of Christ in such terms (1 Cor. 9:1–2).

By some means, the details of which are not reported, two faithful disciples are nominated, Joseph, also known as Barsabbas or Justus, and Matthias. After prayer and the casting of lots, the disciples welcome Matthias and bestow on him Judas' abandoned place of service and honor.

It is curious that Luke should have chosen to tell this story, since there is no further development in the New Testament of the theme of the apostleship of Matthias. In the memory of the church, Paul's apostolic career attracted such attention that the accomplishments of others were often forgotten. Matthias may in some manner be connected with a now-lost Gospel of Matthias, a document referred to by Origen (third century) and condemned as heretical by the Gelasian Decree (sixth century?). If this Gospel of Matthias is the same as the so-called Traditions of Matthias, mentioned by Clement of Alexandria (second to third centuries), it was a Gnostic gospel.

Only slightly less surprising is the silence of the New Testament concerning the further career of Joseph Barsabbas/Justus. Papias (c. 60–130) is reported to have said that, in fulfillment of Mark 16:18, Barsabbas drank poison and came to no harm. That may or may not be true, of course, but what is certain is that this faithful follower of Christ, who fulfilled the stringent standards laid down in Acts 1:21–22, was in the end passed over in favor of another. We can only imagine his reaction to the events related in our text, but it does not stretch the point to consider what must have been his disappointment. He must have felt so, especially since—at least on the basis of our text—no reason was identified for the selection of Matthias, no reason given for his failure to enter the select circle of the Twelve. Presuming that the prayer of vs. 24–25 was answered, all that we can say is that the matter was "God's will"!

How easy it would have been for Barsabbas to say, "If I'm not good enough to join the circle of the Twelve, I'm surely not good enough to be one of Christ's obedient ones. If the Spirit doesn't need me for the most important tasks of the kingdom, I'll just do my work elsewhere."

And perhaps Barsabbas did say just that, and then went off to tend to his wounds. We'll never know because the text does not tell us.

There is another, more likely scenario, one based on the strength of character and the quality of faithfulness that caused Barsabbas to be considered for membership in the apostolic band to begin with. If we had been told of courageous exploits of faith on the part of Matthias, while on Barsabbas's part we were greeted with an ominous silence by the text, we might suspect Barsabbas of defection. The fact is that the text is silent on the subsequent careers of both candidates for the apostolic circle, leading to the conclusion that, like so many thousands of unnamed early Christians, they spent the rest of their lives witnessing to the power of the Resurrected One. Their adventures in faithfulness did not draw the attention of the early church to the same degree as did those of Paul. But it was they, not just Paul, who won much of the Roman world to Christ, and without them there would have been no Christian community to receive and treasure Paul's letters.

The apostolic office was important—at least to some in the young church. Vastly more important were the dedication and faithfulness of Christ's women and men. In this regard both Matthias and Barsabbas were chosen, as have been untold legions in the centuries since.

Psalm 1

Belonging to God and not to the world (see the Gospel reading, John 17:6–19) yields life (see the Epistle reading, 1 John 5:11–12). Indeed, there is no way to have life protected, guarded, and kept safe except to belong to God. Psalm 1 is a didactic exploration of what it means to belong willingly to God, so that we may be safe.

It is, of course, not accidental that this psalm stands at the beginning of the Psalter. Indeed it is thought by some scholars that these verses are not in fact a psalm, but form something of a prosaic preamble to announce the governing theme of the entire collection of psalms. That theme is "Torah piety," the practice of a disciplined ethic which reflects on and gladly embraces God's intention for one's life in terms of full and complete obedience to God's will known in the Torah.

The psalm begins with a positive affirmation (vs. 1–3). The first word of the psalm is "happy." The psalm asks, what will give peaceable contentment and satisfaction in life? What will make possible a whole, safe, coherent, comfortable, anxiety-free existence? The answer is, Torah. But before that positive answer is given, the psalm issues a warning. "Happiness" of an evangelical kind will not come from those who are "emancipated" from the Torah, who imagine they are self-sufficient, and who live as though they were autonomous agents in the world. A life lived in indifference to God's intention for the world cannot end in well-being, says the psalm, but will surely end in isolation, cynicism, and destructiveness.

Yet there is an alternative to such a negative outcome (v. 2). The alternative is to take delight in the study and pondering of the Torah of Yahweh, to think incessantly about God's way in the world and God's intention for the world. There is a long-established Christian stereotype of "Jewish legalism" that pictures Jewish piety as a practice of mindless rule-keeping. Such a stereotype is fed by a flat reading of this psalm. Such a reading, however, distorts both the text and the practice, and if the preacher is not careful, a sermon on this psalm will wrongly encourage absolutist moralism among Christians. Study of the Torah is not just embracing rules; it is a playful, courageous interpretative act, whereby the community must decide about dimensions of God's commands in new circumstances that are not explicitly on the horizon of the old commands (see Matt. 5:21–48). Thus Jews who study Torah, as old rabbinic practice indicates, engage in a playful activity, for the commands are not taken flatly and obviously, but always there are many interpretative options and choices. That is why "meditating" is in order.

The outcome of a life of reflection upon and obedience to God's commands is one of rootage, solidarity, and productivity (v. 3). Notice that the psalm does not clearly and flatly promise "health, wealth, and happiness." Rather, the poet employs a metaphor to voice the outcome of Torah obedience. Torah-focused life will produce persons who are like trees in an oasis. In an arid climate, most vegetation is weak, low to the ground, and vulnerable. Only at the watering holes are larger, fruit-bearing trees available. Torah is like an oasis, which provides sustenance and deep, abiding resources.

The alternative to a Torah-oriented life is the pitiful life of the wicked—scoffers and sinners—who make light of God's command, who seek to secure their own life, and who habitually end in dismay (v. 4). This psalm firmly believes that an autonomous life is sure to end in disaster. Such a conclusion is not a heavy-handed threat, but a long-held, pathos-filled observation of too many ambitious, daring, but failed lives.

Again the poet employs a metaphor for the lot of the disobedient. The poem intends not only to make a rational, institutional appeal, but also to offer an image that can penetrate below our rationality. The metaphor here is not a counterpart to the positive image of v. 3. Here the image is of a threshing floor. In ancient practice, grain was winnowed by throwing the loosened sheaves into the air. The heavier grain dropped to the floor to be collected, but the lighter chaff simply blew away, unnoticed, unvalued, and soon forgotten. So says the poet, are the "wicked." They are not bad people. They are simply not under the discipline of Torah, do not refer their life to a norm or loyalty beyond themselves. Such self-referenced folk are ephemeral, have no staying power, will soon be "blown away" by the moral shape of reality, unnoticed, unvalued, soon forgotten, and unmourned.

Verses 5 and 6 sound as if the teacher does not quite trust the metaphors of the trees "planted by streams of water" and chaff "that the wind drives away." Thus a conclusion is drawn that is flat and without metaphorical playfulness (v. 6). There will be a time of accountability. In that time of answering, which may be quite concrete and quite final and juridical, there will be a distinction

SEVENTH SUNDAY OF EASTER

between Torah keepers and Torah mockers. The Torah mockers will be banned from the congregation, excluded from the life of the community.

The sermon invited by this text is not one of heavy-handed moralism. It is, rather, an affirmation that there is a moral shape to life in the world, a moral shape that cannot be disregarded, usurped, or negotiated away. Those who resist that moral shape (given in the Torah) will not hurt or diminish the Torah. But they will be hurt by the force of the Torah. The seemingly oversimple options given here are to "prosper" (v. 3) or to "perish" (v. 6).

1 John 5:9-13

How does one come to accept the testimony of a witness? Is it the set of the jaw, some particular look around the eyes, the steadiness of voice, a particular matter of credentials? Anyone who has served on a jury knows the difficulties of sorting through conflicting evidence, weighing the testimony of one witness over against that of another. These are matters that demand care and measured judgments. Wavering and doubt are necessary by-products of the process.

By contrast with this cautious approach, the Johannine tradition permits no room for indecision or uncertainty. Both the Gospel and the epistles castigate those who are unable to make a decision about Jesus; *not* to believe that he is Son of God is the equivalent of open rejection.

Central to the decision that must be made about Jesus is the nature of the witness offered. With the exception of those who were themselves witnesses of Jesus' teaching and ministry, of course, every Christian comes to faith by virtue of someone else's witness. Those who grow up in Christian families may never be conscious of the witness they receive, for that witness generally takes the form of example and nurture, and it occurs at such an early stage that it may not be perceived as formal witness or argumentation. The Greek word for witness, *martyrion*, from which comes the English word "martyr," suggests another form of witness. The deaths of Christians for what they believe has often served as a witness, ironically turning what was intended as the church's defeat into its growth.

When the Johannine tradition refers to witnessing, it does not speak of Christian homes as a witness or even of Christian martyrdom as a witness. The witness envisioned here is that of words—words of Jesus and words about Jesus. The Gospel of John opens with the testimony of John the Baptist about Jesus (1:6-8, 19-28) and closes by characterizing the Gospel itself as the testimony of the beloved disciple to the things Jesus did (21:24–25).

The final section of 1 John refers to several kinds of witness: "the Spirit and the water and the blood" (5:7–8), human testimony, and the testimony of God. As a review of the commentaries on this passage will amply illustrate, there is significant disagreement about what witness vs. 7–8 refer to, and whether those three are forms of the human testimony referred to in v. 9 by contrast with divine testimony. If these verses are read in light of what precedes them, it seems likely that the writer understands "the Spirit and the water and the blood" as aspects of God's testimony rather than as human testimony. The contrast, then, between divine and human testimony simply serves to emphasize the reliability of God's witness. (See John 5:31–38 for the same contrast.)

Verse 9 of 1 John 5 might be paraphrased as follows: "We accept the witness of human beings, so we ought all the more to accept this witness we have received from God." Just as God is "greater than our hearts" (3:20) and "greater than the one who is in the world" (4:4), so God's testimony is "greater." As often in attempting to speak about God, the language that comes to hand is that contrasting God's greatness with the smallness of human beings. God's testimony is better.

But *how* do we come to accept any witness? Always the deciding factor is trust. Should a person who will not look straight in the eyes of others be trusted? Can a person with a history of deceit be trusted? Can people bring themselves to trust those different from themselves? While the word "trust" does not appear in the NRSV, it might well do so. The word *pisteuein* (5:10, 13) connotes trust or confidence, just as it connotes belief. The nuances are inseparable. Those who believe in the Son of God do so because they trust in the God who sent him. Those who do not believe do not trust God.

For 1 John, the division is even more radical than trusting or not trusting. Those who do not trust God "have made him a liar" (v. 10). The language is sharp indeed, as earlier in 1:10, when the same assertion is made about those who claim they have no sin. There is no room here for second thoughts. No category allows for "undecided" votes. Anyone who does not believe God calls God a liar. The result of this trust or lack of trust appears in parallel and equally dualistic terms in v. 12: "Whoever has the Son has life; whoever does not have the Son of God does not have life."

Accustomed to the anxiety of indecision and to various abuses to which passages such as this one are put, many Christians will find this language off-putting, even offensive. How can they be reconciled with other convictions about the infinite mercy and grace of God? How can they be reconciled with experience of the inadequacy of human faith? Perhaps they cannot be, and the temptation to apologize for the text needs to be resisted. It may be that the author himself sensed the harshness of this contrast in v. 12, for it is followed by one of reassurance. Those who believe *already* have eternal life as a gift of God.

John 17:6–19

Commentators on the so-called high-priestly prayer of John 17 find themselves engaged with the gnostic-like tendencies of this chapter. Jesus is the revealer from above, who, having accomplished his mission in an alien and hostile world, is preparing to return to his pre-incarnate glory. His mission has consisted of communicating divine knowledge to these persons chosen by God. The chapter, however, cannot be read apart from its place in the larger narrative of John and the initial declaration of the incarnation, namely that the Word has become flesh (1:14). The preacher need not get caught up in the commentators' debates. At the same time, the preacher need not shy away from the radical otherworldliness of Jesus' prayer, an otherworldliness that may be a word on target for many modern Christians.

The prayer is composed of a series of reports Jesus makes to the Father about his mission now completed and a series of petitions for God's care for the community left behind. The reports and the petitions are interwoven, so that wherever the interpreter digs in he or she is not far from either.

The substance of the work God has given to Jesus, the divine Agent, is that of revelation. Just as the mysterious "I AM" is made known to Moses before beginning the task of leading Israel out of Egypt (Ex. 3), so the divine name is disclosed by Jesus to disciples in preparation for a continuing mission in the world. The words entrusted to Jesus by the Father are taught and received.

Such revelation results in the establishment of a community that receives the words, knows their truth, and believes that Jesus is sent by God (John 17:8). The community differs from an esoteric enclave in that the name that is disclosed is precisely the divine power that energizes the community for its task in the world. Neither doctrines nor structures nor programs distinguish the community, only its knowledge and belief that Jesus reveals God's name. To be "protected" in that name (v. 11) means to continue to receive its empowerment and not to be led astray by the lure of alternative powers.

Four petitions are offered by Jesus in behalf of the community. The dominant petition is that the community, which does not belong to the world, be protected from the evil one as it lives its distinctive life in the world. "World" of course signifies not the universe or the planet on which we live, but the totality of life that is at odds with God, has rejected Jesus (1:10–11), and lives in the grips of the evil one (12:31). To live in the world, then, is risky. Being identified as the unique community that clings to the name of Jesus poses a threat to all the accepted absolutes and certitudes that determine the world's values. Security and stability are not assured. Judas's capitulation to pressures around him illustrates what can happen.

Jesus specifically prays that the Christian community not be taken out of the world, but that it be guarded by a Power not known to the world. The church's radical otherworldliness (not belonging to the world) consists precisely in this: its protection by and orientation to a name not certified by the world. Whenever it neglects its otherworldliness and assumes it exists as an institution like all other institutions, it contradicts its very being.

The second petition asks that the Christian community exhibit the same oneness that exists between Jesus and the Father (17:11, though note the textual problem in this verse). The topic occurs more extensively in the latter portion of the prayer (vs. 20–26). But what is this oneness? While it has its visible expression, in context this oneness has nothing to do with institutions and bureaucratic structures, but with the mutuality that exists between Jesus and the Father. Each glorifies the other. The actions and words of the one are the actions and words of the other. Jesus asks that the church display the reciprocal "abiding" that characterizes true love.

The third petition is startling. It asks that God bring to fulfillment in the community Jesus' joy (v. 13). What a contrast it presents to the enmity of the hostile world! Obviously such joy is not to be equated with happy smiles and warm hugs. It derives from the words Jesus has spoken, words that have offended the world and evoked its hatred, but words that bring life.

The final petition is that God sanctify the church (vs. 18–19). The verb belongs to the cultic language of the Old Testament, where priests and animals were set apart for the sacrifice, and to the Holiness Code (Lev. 17–26), where the whole nation was directed to live as a special people separated for the service of a holy God.

The sanctification of the church has to do with its distinctiveness in the world. In a sense, it is a community like many other communities in society, distinguished by neither its virtues nor its moral perfection. Its separateness is the gift of God, who assigns it a special role to play and who calls it to live as a community of strangers, which, like its Lord, does not belong to the world.

PENTECOST

When the fragile circle of Jesus' earliest followers found themselves separated from him, they probably responded in a variety of ways. Some may have turned over in memory words from which some vague hope might be gleaned. Others perhaps withdrew into silence. Still others no doubt began to reconstruct their shared history with cynical interpretations about how little remained from their lofty expectations. The absence of Jesus from the community, whether immediately following the crucifixion or later after the resurrection, threatened to become the crisis that would destroy the fledgling church.

At the very same time that the church experienced such separation, however, it also experienced manifestations of Jesus' continued presence. Within a relatively short period of time, this sense of Jesus' presence within the community was interpreted in terms of the gift of the Holy Spirit. Three of the lections for Pentecost are concerned with the gift of the Spirit, and each of them interprets it somewhat differently. The first, Acts 2:1-21, dramatically depicts the coming of the Spirit as an event that breaks down the formidable barriers created by the pluralism of human languages. More important, the Spirit enables not only common language but new speech, speech through which the gospel may be heard. The second text of these three, Rom. 8:22-27, is less concerned with the enabling of speech (preaching) among human beings than with the articulation of human speech to God. In ways that remain unknown and unknowable, the Spirit conveys the needs of human hearts. In the Gospel passages, the Spirit is identified as the Advocate, the one who comes in place of Jesus and who enables testimony on Jesus' behalf.

Psalm 104, of course, does not address the issue of the Spirit as the presence of Jesus. It does, however, place the coming of the Spirit in its rightful context. The Spirit comes to us, as does every gift within life, solely by virtue of God's grace. The psalm recalls the absolute character of life as a gift from God's own hand.

Acts 2:1–21 (A B C)

New life—sudden, unmerited, irresistible new life! That is the reality the Pentecost narrative in Acts 2 broadcasts, and the text transmits the story in the most expansive way imaginable. All the stops on this great literary organ are employed: a heavenly sound like a rushing wind, descending fire, patterns of transformed speech, and the like. It is as if not even the most lavish use of human language is capable of capturing the experiences of the day, and that is undoubtedly one of the emotions the text wishes to convey.

It is not accidental, of course, that the birth of the church, this great "harvest" of souls, should occur on this important festival. The Feast of Pentecost, or Weeks, as it is known in the Old Testament, marked the end of the celebration of the spring harvest, a liturgical cycle that began at Passover and during which devout Israelite families praised God for God's grace and bounty. It also was the beginning of a period, lasting until the autumnal Festival of Booths (or Tabernacles), in which the firstfruits of the field were sacrificed to Yahweh. And among at least some Jews the Feast of Weeks was a time of covenant renewal, as the following text from the Book of Jubilees (c. 150 B.C.) makes clear:

> Therefore, it is ordained and written in the heavenly tablets that they should observe the feast of Shebuot (Weeks) in this month, once per year, in order to renew the covenant in all (respects), year by year. (*Jub.* 1:17; translated by O. S. Wintermute in James H. Charlesworth, ed., *The Old Testament Pseudepigrapha;* Garden City, N.Y.: Doubleday & Co., 1985, vol. 2, p. 67.)

Pentecost/Weeks is thus a pregnant moment in the life of the people of God and in the relationship between that people and God. Or to put the matter more graphically, but also more accurately, Pentecost is the moment when gestation ceases and birthing occurs. Thus, it is both an end and a beginning, the leaving behind of that which is past, the launching forth into that which is only now beginning to be. Pentecost therefore is not a time of completion. It is moving forward into new dimensions of being, whose basic forms are clear, but whose fulfillment has yet to be realized.

Those who follow the cycle of lectionary texts (or, for that matter, those who simply read the book of Acts) have been prepared for this moment. Twice, in connection with Jesus' ascension, the coming of the Spirit has been promised: "You will receive power when the Holy Spirit has come upon you" (Acts 1:8; compare 1:5). That promise is now realized in a manner far surpassing the expectations of even the most faithful disciples. New life for the church! New life for individuals within the church! New life through the Spirit of God! That is the meaning of Pentecost.

No one present is excluded from this display of God's grace. Unlike other important moments in the history of God's mighty acts of salvation—the transfiguration (Mark 9:2–13), for example, where only the inner few are witnesses to the work of God's Spirit—everyone is included at Pentecost. The tongues of fire rest upon "each" (Acts 2:3) of the disciples, and a moment later the crowd comes surging forward because "each one" (v. 6) has heard the disciples speaking in his or her native tongue. In order that not even the least astute reader may miss the inclusiveness of the moment, the list of place names that begins in v. 9 traces a wide sweep through the world of the Greco-Roman Diaspora. That which happens at Pentecost is thus no inner mystical experience, but an outpouring of God's energy that touches every life present.

Yet not everyone responded to the winds and fires of new life, at least not in positive ways. Some mocked (v. 13) and, in their unwillingness to believe the freshness of God's initiatives, reacted with stale words (compare 1 Sam. 1:14) as they confused Spirit-induced joy with alcohol-induced inebriation. Perhaps it was the very extravagant expression of the Spirit's presence that drove them to conclude: "This cannot be what it seems to be!" Yet what it seemed to be is precisely what it was. God's Spirit unleashed! New life—sudden, unmerited, irresistible new life! We may hope that those who mocked were among those who, on hearing Peter's sermon, were "cut to the heart" (v. 37).

Peter's sermon begins—and this day's lection ends—with a quotation (vs. 17–21) from the prophet Joel (Joel 2:28–32a), and nothing could be more symptomatic of the nature of Pentecost than the transmutation of this text. That which in the prophet's discourse appears prominently as a forecast of destruction and death has become on Peter's tongue a declaration of new life. For Joel the signs of the outpouring of the Spirit are a prelude to disaster (see especially Joel 2:32b, c), but for Peter these wonders have been fulfilled in Jesus Christ, himself the greatest of God's wonders (Acts 2:22), and their purpose, *Christ's* purpose, is nothing less than the redemption of humankind. Again the Spirit has invaded human life in ways that shatter old expectations. It is not death that is the aim of the Spirit's visitation, but new life—sudden, unmerited, irresistible new life! "Everyone who calls on the name of the Lord shall be saved" (v. 21).

Psalm 104:24-34, 35b (A B C)

The singular event of Pentecost concerns God's gift of Spirit, which gives life to a defeated church. This Psalm reading pushes our horizon of Pentecost into larger spheres of faith and reality. God's gift of Spirit concerns not only the community of faith, but the life and well-being of the whole creation. The church lives only because of the gift of God's Spirit; so also creation lives only because of the gift of God's Spirit.

The world belongs utterly to God (vs. 24–26). The first twenty-three verses of this psalm have provided a doxological inventory of creation: each part of creation is named as a product of Yahweh's inimitable power and resolve. Now, in v. 24, the psalm draws a conclusion from the long preceding recital. The psalmist speaks in astonishment and delight: How many are your creatures! We did not know there were so many creatures until we made a comprehensive list. Special attention is given to the seas, sea creatures, ships, and even Leviathan, the sea monster. In the rhetoric of ancient Israel, the sea is ominous and foreboding, a relentless threat of chaos and embodiment of evil. This psalm, however, makes the daring, massive claim that even Leviathan is a pet of Yahweh, Yahweh's "rubber duck." God utterly rules the sea; the threat of chaos is completely eliminated. All of creation is unqualifiedly and gladly Yahweh's.

All creatures are gladly dependent on Yahweh's life-giving power (vs. 27–30). These verses, closely paralleling Ps. 145:15–16, provide a wonderful "table grace." Such an incidental prayer is not casual or trivial. It is a confession of dependence on God lodged in the most elemental act of eating. All creatures depend on God's generosity and live by a ration of God's daily bread. No creature has private resources for life, and none, not even human persons, can store up power for life. Such power must be regularly and faithfully given through God's generosity, and regularly received in creaturely gratitude.

Abruptly the images shift from *food* to life-giving *presence* (104:29–30). Having made the point concretely with food, now the poem speaks more elementally about God's power for life. These verses are arranged as negative (v. 29) and positive (v. 30). The key elements are arranged chiastically: "face . . . spirit [breath] . . . spirit . . . face." In each verse, the first member of the set refers to God's life-giving presence and the second member refers to the creature's capacity to live:

v. 29 negatively: your face . . . their spirit (breath);
v. 30 positively: your spirit . . . face of the ground.

The terms "face" and "spirit" are roughly synonymous, both referring to God's life-giving presence. The negative affirmation is that the absence of God's face carries a loss of human spirit and therefore death. The positive affirmation is that God's Spirit causes newness on the face of the earth. The language is exceedingly personal and primitive. God's presence lets life live. God's absence causes life to terminate. The theological claim expressed in this language is enormous. The world is not autonomous. Creation is not a self-starter. It depends always, daily, and immediately on God's attentive self-giving.

Because the poem uses the term "spirit" twice, God's breath/world's breath, we can see that Pentecost is here writ cosmically. The world depends on God's breath and God's food for functioning viably. The text stands as a massive protest against all modernity, all mistaken autonomy, all the seductions of technical thinking that imagine we can have life on our own terms. Not any more than the church can have its life on its own terms, without reference to God's life-giving Spirit, can the world ever be self-sufficient. The "greenhouse effect," the disruption of the rain forests, and death by agricultural chemicals, all are evidence that the world cannot be made self-sufficient according to human desire, ideology, or technology. Against our powerful technological self-confidence, the primal claim of this text invites us to theological realism about our world, about the ways in which the creation finally lives from the Creator.

The psalm culminates in an exultant doxology (vs. 31–34). What else can we do in light of the preceding affirmations except praise! The doxology is a prayer that Yahweh will continue to delight in God's works, for without God's delight, the earth dies. The earth is as immediately dependent on God as is a young child on its mother. Yahweh only looks and the earth trembles (v. 32); Yahweh only touches and the mountains smoke (v. 32). Yahweh holds all the initiatives. The only adequate human response to this wonder of creation is to sing, to sing praise, to meditate, to rejoice (vs. 33–34, 35b).

Romans 8:22–27

As with much else in the Bible, Christians have demonstrated a remarkable capacity to domesticate the extravagance of Rom. 8. Instead of hearing the apocalyptist in the background, the groaning of creation is heard only as human grief. The Spirit of God becomes little more than a highly skilled messenger who conveys to God the wishes of God's people. Paul's fundamental theological assertion, in the verse following today's lection, that "all things work together for good" reemerges as a demand that people find the good in everything.

Such domestication of this particular passage appears all the more remarkable in light of its literary and theological connections with Jewish apocalyptic thought, for here Paul paints on a well-established canvas that is cosmic in scope. Like other apocalyptic thinkers, he understands the cosmos itself to be in crisis, its demise imminent. Also in common with other apocalyptic thinkers, he looks to God, and to God alone, for the renewal of the cosmos.

If Paul does not turn this expectation into a narrative about the future of creation as is done in the visions of Revelation, he nevertheless employs imagery that would have been familiar to many in the ancient world. The use of personification to speak of creation is well established in the Hebrew Bible. Job 31:38 talks of the land crying out and its furrows weeping, and Isa. 24:4 of the world languishing. In a remarkable passage, 2 Esdras depicts a conversation between the seer and a woman who weeps over the death of her son. The seer chastises her for failing to understand the insignificance of her mourning over against that of earth: "From the beginning all have been born of her, and others will come; and, lo, almost all go to perdition, and a multitude of them will come to doom" (2 Esdras 10:10).

As in this passage from 2 Esdras, Paul understands creation itself to be groaning together, to be in labor together. Verse 22, when translated somewhat more literally than in the NRSV, reads: "For we know that all creation groans together and is in labor pangs together until now." The emphasis on "together" (by means of *syn* prefixes to the Greek verbs) highlights the personification of creation. Birth imagery here suggests not merely that creation gives birth to more creation (as in the 2 Esdras passage above) but that creation *now* waits for the birth of something utterly new (see the similar use of birth imagery in, for example, Isa. 13:8; 26:17–18; Jer. 4:31; Micah 4:9–10; and see Paul's application of this imagery to himself in Gal. 4:19).

Whether "the whole creation" (*pasa hē ktisis*) includes humankind is a much-disputed question, but with v. 23 Paul makes it clear that believers also groan along with creation: "And not only the creation, but we ourselves . . . groan inwardly." The phrases that follow specify what believers already have, even as they groan toward the future. They have "the first fruits of the Spirit" (v. 23), and they also have hope or confidence in that future (vs. 24–25).

What is the relationship between these present realities (the Spirit and hope) and the groaning of believers? The text allows two very different interpretations. Verse 23 may be read causally, that is, *since* believers have the Spirit, they groan along with creation. In this sense, the gift of the Spirit enables Christians to know what time it really is and, as a result, to groan. Verse 23 may also be read concessively, the implication being that even the presence of the Spirit and the presence of hope do not prevent Christians from groaning toward the future. Either interpretation accurately translates the Greek. In light of the very positive interpretation Paul gives to the groaning, the reaching out toward the final triumph of God (see v. 18), the causal reading may be best. It is *because* Christians have the Spirit and have confidence in God that they long toward the future. (In this sense, Paul's comment here recalls the various Gospel stories that praise those who are ready for the future to break in and lament those who prepare only for the present life.)

This apocalyptic expectation importantly frames Paul's references to the Spirit. While those references can scarcely be translated into some doctrine of the third Person of the Trinity, several features of Paul's understanding do come to light.

First, as noted earlier, the Spirit enables believers to know what time it is, to know that the "redemption" lies close at hand.

Second, believers receive the Spirit itself *as* the "first fruits" of that redemption. Even more forcefully than in the quotation from Joel in Acts 2:17–21, the Spirit signals that the "last days" are at hand. As the "first fruits," it provides that inspiring glimmer of the harvest that lies ahead. Because it is the "first fruits," the Spirit carries with it the gift of hope, that confident expectation that makes for patience even in the present distress (Rom. 8:25). Even as the resurrection of Christ is the "first fruits" of God's final triumph (1 Cor. 15:20), the Spirit is the "first fruits" of the appropriation of that triumph by believers.

Third, the Spirit becomes intercessor for believers. The exact mechanics operative in vs. 26–27 remain obscure, but not so the underlying conviction about the role of the Spirit. It both knows the prayers of human beings and is known by God. Because of that dual knowledge, the Spirit somehow intercedes, turning both toward God and toward needy humankind.

John 15:26–27; 16:4b–15

The Gospel selection for Pentecost appropriately includes three of the five so-called Paraclete sayings that are found in Jesus' farewell discourse in the Gospel of John (14:16–17, 26; 15:26; 16:7–11, 13–14). They are distinguished by their use of the Greek term *paraklētos* for the Spirit who comes on Easter evening. Many translations prefer Counselor, Comforter, or Helper for the Greek word; however, the NRSV has chosen consistently to use Advocate.

The context of John 14–17 cannot be ignored. The conversation between Jesus and the disciples revolves around his coming departure and the confusion this creates among the disciples. He describes the immediate future as a time of mission and discipleship (15:16) and repeatedly warns his followers that they will be hated and persecuted by the world and excommunicated from the synagogue (15:18–25; 16:1–4a). He recognizes the disciples' "sorrow" (16:6), a sorrow born of the fact that they do not understand what is happening nor do they have any inkling of Jesus' ultimate destiny; and he promises the coming Advocate as an "advantage" for the perilous times (16:7).

Three functions of the Advocate in these sayings warrant special attention. First, the Advocate will testify on Jesus' behalf. The testimony of the Advocate is linked to but precedes the testimony the disciples are to bear (15:26–27). This linking of the witnesses is critical for the church, whose testimony (whether understood as proclamation or as a suffering life) always remains fragile and inadequate, constantly in need of divine support. Without the Spirit, the church becomes a voiceless, irrelevant institution.

But the sequence of the witnesses is striking. The Spirit is not a subsidiary of the disciples' witness, assuring its success. Rather, the disciples are a subsidiary of the Spirit's witness. The "you also are to testify" of 15:27 sets a clear priority. It leaves the church with little cause for bravado or flag-waving, as if its missionary endeavors were guaranteed faithfulness and could count on success. The church remains a servant body, constantly seeking to discern and live and speak in line with the Spirit's witness.

The second function regards the Spirit's exposure of the world.

The Spirit "will prove the world wrong about sin and righteousness and judgment" (16:8). The critical Greek verb in the sentence (*elegchein*) was translated too strongly in the RSV by "convince," as if promising a conversion of the world, and has in the NRSV been rendered in its legal connotation, "will prove wrong," that is, expose and convict.

The world has its own definitions of sin, justice, and judgment. It constantly rewards those who measure up to its standards and norms and punishes those who transgress them. Its symbols of security are enticing, and its means of enforcement are brutal. Jesus defied the reigning structures and ended up as one of those punished. The destiny of his loyal followers will be no different (15:18–19).

What the text in fact promises is that the Spirit will expose the world's way of doing things. The Spirit will pull back the curtain on the world's unbelief and show its leadership to be no longer powerful but condemned. Exactly how all this is to be accomplished is not specified, but it apparently has to do with the church's witness (15:27), with its message that the exalted Christ assures the defeat of Satan (16:10–11). The Spirit may not be limited to the proclamation and life of the church, but the Spirit nevertheless works through it as its powerful Advocate.

The mention of the third function of the Spirit may be especially directed to those who are a generation (or generations) removed from the historical Jesus. They are in no way disadvantaged by the distance of time, since the Spirit "will guide you into all the truth" (16:13). While they do not live with personal recollections of Jesus—conversations and incidents remembered—later generations still are promised an entrée into this tradition which comes from the Father to and about Jesus. History does not exclude them from the truth once disclosed.

The extravagance of the language in the text ("will guide you into all the truth," "will declare to you the things that are to come") needs to be treated with care. Those blessed by the Spirit are not guaranteed infallibility, nor are they given special tools to unlock all the eschatological mysteries. The phrase "the things that are to come" likely refers to the future life of the readers' community, about which Jesus has specifically spoken. Rather, the text promises that the Spirit will make available again and again to the church no more and no less than the same transforming reality known in the Jesus of history.

TRINITY SUNDAY

None of the texts assigned for Trinity Sunday can properly be thought of as texts *about* the Trinity, a doctrine that emerges from reflection on biblical witness and Christian experience, rather than within scripture itself. Nevertheless, each of these texts is associated with Christian reflection on the Trinity, and each also reveals something about human speech in relation to the Trinity.

In the Gospel account of Jesus' conversation with Nicodemus, human speech fumbles and falters. Nicodemus comes to Jesus asserting his belief that Jesus must be from God, only to find himself instructed about being born "from above." Understandably confusing that statement with a call for rebirth, he asks an innocent question to which Jesus provides an answer that is no answer at all. When he finally exclaims, "How can these things be?" Jesus chastises him for failing to understand. As good as are his intentions, Nicodemus speaks in ways that reveal his lack of understanding.

The passage from Rom. 8 concerns a different kind of speech, the cry of believers who can say only, "Abba! Father!" That cry, of course, emerges because Christians have confidence that they may turn to God as a child to a loving parent, but the cry also reveals the inadequacy of human speech to convey what must be said. The eager expectation, the longing, the hope of humankind come to expression with the inarticulate cry of an infant.

Human speech sometimes exceeds these limits, as the reading from Isa. 6 dramatically recalls. The cleansing of the prophet's lips enables him to speak to Israel, but only because that cleansing comes from God and only because God directs Isaiah's speech. Prophetic speech comes about not by human insight and intelligence, but as sheer gift (and demand!) from God.

Psalm 29 calls forth speech of praise addressed to God. It also contrasts with the other readings in that the psalm praises the very voice of God, a voice that thunders "over mighty waters," that "breaks the cedars" of Lebanon, that "flashes forth flames of fire," that "shakes the wilderness" and "causes the oaks to whirl."

Standing together in the context of Trinity Sunday, these four very different passages evoke the majesty and mystery of the God who is revealed to the world in three Persons. These passages also remind that world of the inadequacy of its speech before and about God.

Isaiah 6:1-8

Having celebrated fresh initiatives of the Spirit on Pentecost, the church now responds to its call to mission, a risky endeavor which it undertakes in the name of the risen and ascended Christ. That which God did by means of the earthly ministry of Jesus now lies in the past—at least in a liturgical sense—and the community of Christ's faithful people now understands that it has become a principal avenue for the expression of God's redemptive presence in human life.

There is an important sense in which the present text from Isa. 6 is so familiar a paradigm of God's call to faithful people that it may fail to speak with the freshness of some other texts. Yet it is a key passage in this regard, and deserves repeated use, for it transmits quintessential elements in the ongoing story of God's imperatives directed to people of faith.

The purpose for dating the prophet's experience of call to the final year of Judean King Uzziah (742 B.C.) is not clear (v. 1). Perhaps this is intended to be a chronological reference and no more, similar to those found in the Deuteronomistic history (note, for example, 2 Kings 15:1, among other places). But such language is rare in prophetic discourse, and the suspicion is raised that it is somehow as *a result of* the king's death that the prophet is roused to activity by the Spirit of God. The passing of Uzziah, one of Judah's last truly powerful monarchs, may have been a signal to perceptive persons that changes in the fortunes of the nation were on their way and that, in significant ways, Judah would stand in special need of God's grace in the years ahead. If so, the opening lines of this pericope stand as a reminder that the Spirit of God often works through the events of our days to draw our attention to God's will for human life.

If one word were to be employed to express the mood of our text it would be "awe." A "holy" God has taken the initiative to address a weak and sinful mortal, and the prophet—quite rightly so!—is almost paralyzed with a sense of God's power and his own inadequacy. This response to God's nature permeates the outlook not only of Isaiah of Jerusalem, whose work is recalled in chs. 1–39, but of others who lived at a later time and who spoke or wrote in the tradition of Isaiah (note Isa. 41:20 and 57:15). It is clear from this text that the sense of mission on the part of God's people flows directly out of an understanding of who God is—both in and of God's self and in relation to God's world. The seraphim must shield their faces before God's awful majesty (v. 2) and, when they sing, their words are of God's otherness, or holiness (v. 3). Only the live coal (v. 6), symbol of the justice and compassion of God, can serve to purify the prophet and render him fit for service to this King of majesty.

This "otherness" of God, that which sets God apart from the created world, operates both in a theological and in a moral context. Theologically, God's holiness implies that, while creation is dependent on its Creator, the reverse is far from true. God is holy in the sense that God is external to creation and presides in sovereignty over it.

The moral sense of holiness is affirmed in our text also. That is to say, a moral God is One who—unlike the gods of the human imagination—is consistent and reliable in dealing with humankind. This is a God of justice and love, who is characterized by these qualities day in and day out, in good times and in bad. What is more, this holy God summons the people of God to live lives characterized by the same persistent principles. This view is not that of Isaiah alone (compare, for example, Lev. 22:32), but it certainly lies at the heart of the prophet's proclamation. Thus it is that Isaiah feels inadequate until the application of the live coal to his lips by one of the seraphs (literally, "burning ones").

Central to the reality projected by this text is not only that which pertains to the nature of God, but also that which has to do with the transforming power of God's presence. Notice should be given to the interesting interplay in vs. 7–8 among words that refer to the power of speech: "mouth," "lips," "voice," "saying," and "said" (twice). The act of cleansing not only restores the condition of wholeness to a sinful person (in this case the prophet), but also releases that person's power to hear God's speech and, in turn, to speak God's words to a sinful people. Often, when we read the final verses of this text, our attention is focused on the act of *going forth* in the name of God (the etymological basis of the word "mission" is, after all, a Latin word meaning "to send out"). "Whom shall I send?" is answered by "Here am I; send me!"

However, this emphasis on motion should not be allowed to obscure an equal emphasis on speech. The prophet has been released not just to go, but to go as the bearer of God's word. And part of the message of Trinity Sunday is that, in like manner, so has the church.

Psalm 29

A full exposition of this psalm is given for the First Sunday After Epiphany, the Baptism of the Lord. The psalm traces the way in which Yahweh moves to become king of the gods. The accent on the governance of Yahweh befits Trinity Sunday, when the peculiar and magisterial character of God is affirmed. This psalm is congruent with the vision of Isa. 6, wherein the prophet sees the "real" king.

The new rule of the newly crowned king of the gods is reflected in v. 11, which stresses "peace." The shape of the new life of the world given by this king of the gods is articulated in both the Gospel and Epistle readings. Thus this psalm on the new governance of God provides a context for the other readings also concerned with the new governance.

Romans 8:12-17

The "So then" with which this passage begins indicates that reading should move backward from v. 12 before it can move forward. From the beginning of this chapter, Paul has addressed the contrast between life "according to the flesh" and life "according to the Spirit," insisting that Christian faith entails life in the Spirit and freedom from the control of the flesh's desires. Although vs. 12-17 opens with that same contrast ("we are debtors, not to the flesh, to live according to the flesh"), it soon yields to a positive statement of the meaning of life in the Spirit.

This transition is apparent even in Paul's choice of words. In the early part of ch. 8, references to "flesh" and "Spirit" are interspersed in almost every line. After the opening of v. 13, however, the word "flesh" simply drops out of the argument. It reappears in the early part of ch. 9, but there in a different sense, for it refers to the biological connection of Paul and of Christ with the people of Israel (see 9:3, 5, 8). That shift in vocabulary reinforces the move here from a negative description of life apart from the Spirit to a positive description of life in the Spirit.

Central to this positive statement about life in the Spirit is the powerful claim of v. 14 that we are children of God. It enters the discussion just where readers might anticipate some assertion that believers are "debtors of the Spirit." Verse 12 claims that they are not debtors of the flesh, and v. 13 expands by explaining what that means. Paul is not elsewhere reluctant to identify the debt believers owe because of God's action in Jesus Christ, but here the central organizing motif is that of believers as God's children.

The language that describes this particular childhood escalates throughout the passage. First, God's children are not debtors of the flesh, and they are not slaves: "For you did not receive a spirit of slavery to fall back into fear." In Galatians, of course, Paul employs the notion of slavery to the law or to the pagan world (4:1–7), and he uses the slave Hagar to extend his argument about freedom from the law (4:21–5:1). This imagery contains multiple resonances from biblical tradition, not only because of Hagar, but because it calls up the powerful motif of Israel's liberation from Egypt. Paul's correspondents would also necessarily hear this reference with ears attuned to the present situation. Since the economies of both Greece and Rome depended on the slave system, it was an everyday reality in the lives of Christians at Rome. Possessing a "spirit of slavery," or being freed from a "spirit of slavery," would sound powerfully there and throughout the world of early Christianity.

As forceful as this imagery is, being God's child does not consist only in freedom from slavery. In v. 15, Paul contrasts the slavery of life in the flesh with the adopted status of those who have life in the Spirit. In other words, Christians are not merely "freedmen," the technical term for those who had once been enslaved and achieved freedom from that slavery. Christians have become God's children by means of their adoption. Again, the language Paul uses calls to mind several passages in the Hebrew Bible regarding adoption (Ex. 2:10; 2 Sam. 7:14; 1 Chron. 28:6; Esth. 2:7). Like the reference to slavery, this reference to adoption also has cultural currency, in that several forms of adoption (both legal and less formal) were widely practiced in the Roman Empire.

As the passage moves to a close in vs. 15–17, the term "adoption" gives way to more intimate expressions: "When we cry, 'Abba! Father!' . . . we are children of God, and if children, then heirs." Whether or not the addressing of God as "Abba" can be traced to the practice of Jesus himself, its presence here powerfully attests to the Christian sense that God stands near at hand. To cry out to God with the language of a child is simultaneously to confess need and to claim relationship. Only those who know God's Spirit can call on God in this way. (Perhaps it should be noted that this assertion is about the workings of the Spirit of God, and not about a human achievement; thus, any attempt at making this gift into a kind of litmus test of faith fundamentally misunderstands the text.)

The multiplication of expressions for this special standing of Christians before God ("children of God, and if children then heirs, heirs of God and joint heirs with Christ") underscores its importance. In this brief passage, God's children are said to be not slaves, not merely freedmen but adopted, and both children and heirs. Finally, these children can be described as "joint heirs with Christ."

To be an heir, or course, means to claim at least a share in the parent's estate. Such standing normally conveys a measure of power and freedom and independence. All these normal expectations find themselves inverted by the final phrase of the text: "If, in fact, we suffer with him so that we may also be glorified with him." Becoming the glorified heir of God, fellow heir with Christ, means sharing in all that Christ is, and that begins with suffering.

John 3:1–17

Selections from John 3 appear in the lectionary as designated readings three times (here, the Second Sunday in Lent in the A cycle, and the Fourth Sunday in Lent in the B cycle). Comments on the passage can be found in the interpretations for those Sundays. Because this Sunday is Trinity Sunday, it is an occasion that provides a different context for the reading and hearing of John 3. We acknowledge from the outset that the text predates the christological and Trinitarian controversies of the fourth and fifth centuries and later, when the church reflected on the mysterious nature of the Trinity in the fine-hewn language of Greek philosophy. Obviously the author of the Gospel of John cannot be turned into an advocate of this or that theory of how the members of Godhead relate to one another.

Even so, interpretation is not a matter of finding out what the author meant, but of what the text means in new and different contexts. Modern readers themselves bring something to the process of interpretation—their own questions, hopes, and fears—and they usually stand in theological traditions (such as Lutheran, Catholic, Pentecostal, or liberationist) or represent ethnic biases that enable them both to see and to distort dimensions of the text. A frank acknowledgment of what one brings to a passage is often like wiping away the smudges on a pair of glasses. It makes possible clearer seeing.

Most readers of John 3 come with some awareness of a God

known in three Persons, and there is nothing wrong with posing to the text questions about the activity of the three as they function in the narrative. The answers by no means clarify the mystery of the Trinity, but they offer food for reflection on Trinity Sunday.

The narrative confronts us initially with the Spirit, the unpredictable, uncontrollable activity of God, who is compared with the wind. The evidence is there, but the phenomenon defies empirical investigation and resists any attempt at manipulation.

Two aspects of the Spirit emerge in Jesus' conversation with Nicodemus. First, the Spirit and the flesh are radically distinct, two separate realms. Such an observation prevents their being translated (accurately!) as "higher nature" and "lower nature." "Flesh" denotes creaturely existence as it operates and organizes itself apart from the presence of God, whereas Spirit denotes the divine activity "from above," which breaks into and disrupts the purely human.

The sharp separation of the two leads to the second thing affirmed of the Spirit. "Flesh can give birth only to flesh" (3:6, NEB). The only way of entering God's realm comes "from above," the action of God, the Spirit, who effects a new creation. The language of rebirth (really birth "from above") highlights the incongruity between the old and the new, between the personal and social structures of life that presume to function without God and the invasive, reorienting power of the new. Nicodemus is called to accept the unaccountable gift of the new.

While Jesus pervades the whole narrative, the most obvious insight into his activity comes in 3:13–15. The label "Son of Man" in John shares many features with the Synoptic picture, but adds a critical one. The Son of Man is the link between heaven and earth. Just as the ladder in Jacob's dream at Bethel enabled the angels of God to go back and forth between heaven and earth (Gen. 28:11–12), so the Son of Man is the ladder making possible communication from the opened heaven to earth (John 1:51; 3:13). But the Son of Man must be "lifted up" to be seen (like the serpent on the pole in Num. 21:8–9), and "lift up" carries the double meaning of exaltation and crucifixion (see John 12:32). (See the critical commentaries for the intriguing textual problem at the end of 3:13.)

The revelation of God brought by the Son of Man does not consist of theological abstractions about the character of the Deity, information about which theologians can speculate, but an action that conveys the heart of the Father—a death that is at the same time, in John's perspective, an exaltation. And what's more, the action of the Son of Man results in the offer of life, life of the age to come. The revelation is redemptive.

Having read this far, one might assume Jesus to be the hero of the story, until the last two verses (3:16–17). Then God becomes the subject, who is pictured as the one initiating the redemptive activity. God refuses to remain content with a world in the process of self-destruction, a "flesh" futilely trying to maintain itself. The divine action is love reaching out to the unlovely, and is expressed in the "gift" of the Son.

It is hard to overemphasize the character of redemption as a gift. Even here in John 3 the verb "believe" in 3:15–16 is often taken as a precondition to grace. "If you believe, God will love and save you." Faith is by no means unimportant, but however it is construed, it can never obscure the unmerited decision of God, who "loved," "gave," and "sent" for the salvation of the world.

PROPER 4

Ordinary Time 9

Sunday between May 29 and June 4 inclusive (if after Trinity Sunday)

The lection from Psalm 139 might well provide the lens through which to read the other lections for this Sunday. Here the psalmist relentlessly depicts God's knowledge of humankind. That knowledge extends back to the infant in its mother's womb and forward to the end of life itself. God's intimate, probing, compelling knowledge cannot be measured. The psalmist, in turn, knows God's presence and feels that presence inescapable. But the psalmist also knows that one's knowledge of God is infinitesimal when compared with God's knowledge of one's self.

The other readings for this Sunday might be thought of as portraying the dangerous implications of this intimate relationship. The persistent call to the young Samuel cannot be escaped. In his innocence, Samuel does not understand whose voice he hears. Eli, who no longer sees the visions of old, must explain to Samuel who it is who calls and how he needs to respond. But the voice will not let Samuel alone, will not let Samuel escape.

In 2 Cor. 4, Paul connects Christian knowledge of God's own glory with creation itself (v. 6). That knowledge brings with it an inexpressible joy, but the passage also reveals ways in which knowledge of God's glory is painful. It brings with it persecution, rejection, misunderstanding. Despite the profound confidence Paul displays in the final outcome of these struggles, the knowledge of God's glory, together with God's intimate, demanding knowledge of the apostle, nevertheless brings about suffering and humiliation.

The Gospel lesson comes from that section in Mark's Gospel that recounts conflict between Jesus and certain religious authorities. Mark employs this series of stories to convey the way in which Jesus confounds the respected leaders of the community and also to demonstrate the development of opposition to Jesus. When placed alongside the psalm text, however, these stories may provide a warning about the too-easy assumption that human beings know

God's ways as God knows those of humankind. The religious leaders assume that they know all about Sabbath observance, and that assumption reveals their hubris. They know the details of the law, but have forgotten the One who gives it.

1 Samuel 3:1–10 (11–20)

The Old Testament lection for this day is oriented in two directions. First, it continues the theme of God's call to faithful people raised in the Old Testament text for Trinity Sunday and, in a manner similar to that text, it serves as a paradigm for God's initiatives in the lives of women and men today. Second, the present lection introduces a series of readings from Samuel and Kings, which reaches a climax in the Old Testament lection for Proper 16, a passage that forms part of the narrative of the dedication of Solomon's Temple in 1 Kings 8. Thus the opportunity is offered the preacher of choosing among various thematic possibilities. Another choice lies in the decision whether to include vs. 11–20 of the present text from 1 Sam. 3. While the reading aloud of all twenty verses of this lection may stretch the patience of certain congregants or parishioners, the inclusion of vs. 11–20 offers additional homiletic possibilities, as outlined below.

Verses 1–10 may, for some, bear the same burden of overfamiliarity as that noted concerning Isa. 6:1–6 in the comments on that Trinity Sunday text. What child who regularly attends church school has not often heard the story of young Samuel and seen reproductions of the several paintings that illustrate the boy's innocence? Yet in an age in which biblical illiteracy is abundant, one should not assume that even the most appealing Old Testament narratives are widely known.

The primary subject of this pericope is, of course, young Samuel and the wondrous manner in which the Spirit of God speaks to the as yet unsuspecting lad. But immediately after introducing us to the relationship between Samuel and his mentor, Eli, the text drops an important hint about the condition of Eli and his ultimate judgment by God. This hint is contained in a wordplay between "visions" of v. 1 and the comment in v. 2 that Eli's "eyesight had begun to grow dim." The implication is that the absence of visions concerning Yahweh's will among the people does not arise out of a withholding by Yahweh of the truth, but that the people, because of the blindness of their leader, and thus of themselves, are unresponsive to Yahweh's overtures. Eli's blindness is emblematic of the blindness of the people.

Yahweh now turns to one who is not blind, or actually—since the metaphor is shifted by the author(s) of the text—to one who is not deaf to the word of God. But naive Samuel, who has been conditioned not to expect God's forthcoming since he lives with a man and among a people who have ceased their own expectation, is deaf. And the principal irony of the text lies in the fact that it is Eli, soon to be doomed because of his failure to shape the awareness of his own sons to their responsibilities before Yahweh (v. 13), who alerts his ward Samuel, a surrogate son, to the true nature of the voice that he hears (vs. 8–9). The issue of "traditioning," that is, of steeping each rising generation of the family of faith in the knowledge of God's amazing ways, is clearly present here. In the end, however, the initiative of Yahweh overcomes even the inertia of Yahweh's people, and Samuel, perhaps because of his very naïveté (compare Matt. 19:14), responds to God's voice. "Speak, for your servant is listening" (v. 10) is an obvious climax within the passage, and years of interpretations in sermons and church school lessons should not lead us to overlook or avoid that fact. Samuel's receptivity is a model for any faithful person of God.

Verses 11–20 raise different but related issues. The first part of this section of the text, vs. 11–18, has to do with the message that Samuel receives from Yahweh, namely that Eli's family line will be extinguished because of the unfaithfulness of Hophni and Phinehas (note 1 Sam. 4:15–18) and because of Eli's culpability in their blasphemy. How tragic that God's message to a newly called prophet is often one of judgment (see Isa. 6:9–13; Jer. 1:9–19, among other texts)! Jeremiah, more than other prophetic figures, seems to have expressed the terrible burden this placed on him (see Jer. 20:14–18), but others surely felt it too. It is to his credit that Samuel, in spite of his tender years, does not shrink from Yahweh's terrifying word (1 Sam. 3:8), although it is understandable that he had to be prodded to go forward.

Eli emerges as an entirely noble figure also, in spite of his history of sin and the neglect of his family. (It should be noted in passing that, as untold numbers of parents are well aware, efforts at moral and spiritual education within the family do not always produce the desired effect. It is not true that the sins of children can always be laid upon their parents, and she or he who preaches on this text will want to bear that reality in mind.) Eli, sensing that Yahweh's words to Samuel concern him, coaxes the news of God's impending judgment from the young man and, to his credit, does not fault Samuel for this terrible verdict. Lonely and tragic figure that he is, Eli bows to Yahweh's will, basing his attitude on the affirmation that, since Yahweh is good, that which Yahweh does cannot be otherwise (v. 18).

Verses 19 and 20 return the reader to vs. 1–2. Just as the people were once blind (deaf) because of the blindness (deafness) of the one who represented them before God, so now the vision (hearing) of their leader leads to their own responsiveness to Yahweh's presence in their lives (Yahweh's word). Although it is outside the limits of the lectionary text, v. 21 brings the thought of the text full circle: Yahweh, whose word was once "rare" (v. 1) now "continued to appear at Shiloh" and in the hearts of the people. (For additional commentary, see Second Sunday After Epiphany.)

Psalm 139:1–6, 13–18

This psalm remains enigmatic and defies any certain classification or interpretation. In Psalm 139, the speaker reflects upon the intimacy of communion with God, wherein God is closer to the speaker than even the speaker can imagine, closer, so to say, than the speaker is even to himself.

Verses 1–6 reflect on the ways in which the speaker is known by God (vs. 1–5) and end with an ejaculatory conclusion (v. 6). The words are addressed directly to Yahweh, who is named in these verses as an intimate, intense "you" ("Thou"). Thus the poem is not reflective theology, but is a primal religious meditation, and might become an occasion to witness to the interior life with God to which we are invited. Moreover, the intimate speech of direct communion is an end in itself. That is, the speaker seeks nothing, asks nothing, commands nothing, threatens nothing. The reality of intimate communion is itself enacted in and through this speech of intimacy.

The poem begins directly and abruptly: "Yahweh!" The address is terse and simple, no qualifiers or modifiers, no need to pile up words to ingratiate. This is not a first-time conversation for the speaker, but an exchange between partners who have had a long career of intimate communion. While there is directness, there is no suggestion of equality between the conversational partners. It is clear that the speaker defers to Yahweh and understands that Yahweh has the primary role in the relationship. This speaker knows that while one may be deferential, this contact is in fact fraught with risk.

The rhetoric is dominated by the use of the word "know" (vs. 1, 2, 4), plus the noun "knowledge" (same root, in v. 6). Moreover, the rhetoric of these verses consists in verbs addressed to Yahweh (You) that acknowledge Yahweh's full knowledge and dominance of the speaker. This is indeed the one "from whom no secrets are hid"! This God has "searched out" the speaker, probed, investigated, and deciphered. God knows everything about the speaker, every moment; God knows when the speaker gets up or sits down, what the speaker thinks, what the speaker will do or say, even before the utterance. God knows completely (v. 4)!

The continued acknowledgment of v. 5 is given a somewhat different nuance. The first verb, "hem in" renders the Hebrew *ṣûr*, which means "to enclose in a narrow place," and the hand of v. 5b sounds almost like a heavy hand that encloses, restrains, or holds down. Thus v. 5 may suggest that God, by knowledge and by power, holds the speaker nearly as a prisoner or hostage. The speaker is candid about the situation, but we cannot determine for sure if this statement is one of gratitude or one of resentment. We cannot tell if this is a description of communion or of confinement. The words "hem in" suggest some mild and subdued protest.

The conclusion of v. 6 is a response to the characterization of vs. 1–5. Verse 6 may be a doxology astounded by God's intimacy. But the line may also suggest that God's abnormal ("too wonderful") attentiveness is a burden beyond bearing. If so, however, the language is careful, deferential, and subdued. We cannot determine if communion is here deeply desired or modestly resented. The intervening verses omitted from the lection add credence to the view that God's attentiveness is a wearisome burden (vs. 7–12).

In vs. 13–18 the prayer of direct address continues. Whereas vs. 1–6 focused in the present tense, these verses are an act of recall, wherein the speaker reflects upon the miracle of personal origin. It was *you* who "formed" the secret parts, who delicately joined together the elements that make a human person (v. 13). Indeed, God was there, attentive to the speaker, even before the speaker had a self. The poem struggles for images and vocabulary to characterize the way in which God "selfed" the elements that became the speaking self. God's watchful, attentive care was present in the inchoate processes of conception, birth, and identity. In a magisterial act, God *beforehand* destined all the days of the life of the speaker. There is a powerful dimension of divine destiny in the life of the speaker. We are here at the edge of the capacity of speech to express the way in which an individual person is grounded in God's own will and life.

The memory and recall of miracle in the midst of fragility is not an explanation. This is not a biological or scientific reflection upon human origins, as though the words could serve some argument about abortion. Rather, a meditation on the wondrous origin of the human self leads to doxology (v. 14), in which the speaker understands personal life to be wrapped in mystery and majesty, facing the reality that the speaker is not at all a "self-starter" but gladly depends on God for the resources of life.

This reflection upon the origins of the human self does not lead to self-congratulations. Rather the speaker turns from self to God (vs. 17–18). God is overwhelming, large and weighty, and powerful and inescapable. God's purposes run rich and deep, beyond human comprehension. And when this frail human reckoning is finished, the central reality of life is intransigent and unchanging: "I am still with you" (v. 18)!

As in v. 6, however, we cannot determine the intent of this phrase. It might be a doxological sigh of relief, grateful that through all this tough process of formation, I am not abandoned. But the phrase may also be one of exasperation, mindful now that there cannot be an escape from God. One is destined to be endlessly monitored and supervised.

Intimacy with God may be an assurance and it may be a burden. If one is excessively alone, such intimacy is good news. If, however, one is yearning for one's own life, such intimacy may be an enormous discomfort and intrusion. In preaching, our temptation is to view God as an unmitigated good in life. Maybe . . . but maybe not. (See also Second Sunday After Epiphany.)

2 Corinthians 4:5–12

A paradox stands at the center of the gospel of Jesus Christ, particularly in the case of Paul's interpretation of that gospel. God, who has been revealed throughout Israel's history, is most fully and finally revealed in the ignominious death of God's Son on a Roman cross. The very power of God comes to visible expression in the voluntary powerlessness of Jesus Christ. That paradox stands close to the foreground of the early sections of 2 Corinthians, and it generates a division among humankind; some see the gospel in the world's terms, while others see it only as folly (see, for example, 2 Cor. 2:15–16; 3:12–18; compare 1 Cor. 1:17–25). The paradox of the gospel also generates a paradox in the Christian understanding of leadership, for those who occupy "first place" in the Christian community are not the powerful and the successful but the vulnerable and the (apparent) failures (2 Cor. 4:7–12).

This lection concerns that paradox of Christian leadership, beginning with the opening assertion, "For we do not proclaim ourselves." This negative claim will seem odd, unless read in the context of Paul's larger discussion of leadership, which begins in 3:1 (or even in 1:12–14). "We do not proclaim ourselves" apparently counters some expectation that Christian apostles ought to do just that. They should be confident enough to offer "letters of recommendation" (3:1) and to proclaim their own accomplishments (see also the later discussion in chs. 10–13).

Paul, however, goes on to admit that he does proclaim himself: "We proclaim Jesus Christ as Lord and ourselves as your slaves for Jesus' sake." Two features of this statement are striking. First, Paul refers to himself and his co-workers as slaves of the Corinthians. Although he elsewhere refers to himself as a slave of Christ (Rom. 1:1, NRSV margin), this is the only time he makes the dramatic claim to be enslaved to other human beings. Even the explanatory phrase ("for Jesus' sake") does not diminish the force of this assertion. Paul is not here the Corinthians' teacher, leader, or authority figure, but their helpless slave.

Second, this particular slavery has become part of the gospel Paul proclaims ("We proclaim . . . ourselves as your slaves"). As is evident elsewhere in this letter, the relationship between Paul and the Corinthians is inherent in the gospel itself. Paul will boast about the Corinthians on the day of the Parousia, just as they will boast of him (2 Cor. 1:14). Neither party can obtain a release from this relationship.

Verse 6 explains that the connection between Paul and the Corinthians has its origin in God. The "for" (*hoti*) at the beginning of the verse indicates that it provides the explanation for the statement that has preceded. When Paul describes God as the "God who said, 'Let light shine out of darkness,'" he implicitly insists on the continuity between the first Creation and this new creation in the Christian gospel. The very same God who acted at Creation to distinguish light from darkness is the God who now sheds light in human lives through Jesus Christ.

Interpreters sometimes suggest that Paul here refers to his own conversion experience, particularly because of the reference to "the face of Jesus Christ." Given the paucity of such references in his letters (see Gal. 1:11–17; Phil. 3:2–11; 1 Cor. 15:8), the search for additional comments about the conversion is understandable, and Paul does refer to "seeing" Christ. Nevertheless, he does not elsewhere speak of the "face" of Christ in connection with the conversion (but see the references to Moses' face in 2 Cor. 3), and the revelation alluded to here probably is that received by Christians in general. At most, Paul might be said to include his own experience here as he reflects on Christian experience as a whole. Still, the verse primarily concerns the continuity of God's loving care, both in creation and in the present.

With the very familiar words of 4:7–12, Paul returns to the nature of the apostleship. Here the paradox of the gospel becomes the paradox of Christian ministry. God's power remains God's own; even God's apostles manifest that power in their weakness rather than in displays of strength. Because this passage is familiar, the unusual character of Paul's logic may escape notice. As messengers or even ambassadors of God (see 5:20), apostles might be thought to exhibit some of the characteristics of God's own power. They do not. Their "treasure in clay jars" demonstrates that the power is God's and "does not come from us."

The verses that follow catalog the paradox of the apostle's existence: "afflicted in every way, but not crushed; perplexed, but not driven to despair. . . ." What appears to be the case to the eyes of the world (namely, the defeat and rejection of the apostles) is in fact the complete opposite of the truth. Even as they appear to be dying, the apostles make Jesus visible in their own lives.

This passage may be particularly important for those churches that were once referred to as "mainline." The frantic search for answers to declining membership and for new identity for denominations might well be set in a larger context, one that at least considers the possibility that in some sense the church's ministry cannot be defeated, despite all appearances to the contrary.

Mark 2:23–3:6

Following Pentecost and Trinity Sunday, the lectionary turns for its Gospel readings to Mark, and for eight Sundays focuses on the early portion of the book. The section provides the preacher with a rich store of narratives depicting the invasion of God's reign in human life and raising critical issues about the character of the invasion, such as the power of Jesus over the destructive forces of evil and the threat such power holds for entrenched authorities.

The reading for this Sunday (Mark 2:23–3:6) comes as the conclusion of a series of controversies between Jesus and the religious authorities. The chiastic pattern of the stories—A (2:1–12); B (2:13–17); C (2:18–22); B' (2:23–28); A' (3:1–6)—makes the middle section to be the interpretive key. Fasting is incompatible with the feasting at the messianic banquet. The bridegroom's presence signifies a decisive and joyous moment. Furthermore, the new can never be accommodated to the old structures. There is no room for compromise. Jesus, as the full expression of God's inbreaking rule, is unique, and the old patterns of religion, stultifying and unproductive, cannot contain the new dynamic. New wine demands new wineskins.

The two narratives that follow (2:23–28; 3:1–6) describe the conflict between the new and the old in terms of authority. First, there is the conflict over the Sabbath. The plucking of heads of grain was not a matter of petty legalism for the Pharisees. It was momentous, because Sabbath observance lay at the heart of their identity as faithful Jews. As a part of the Torah, it helped them resist the pressures to conform to the broader society. It was an ordering feature of their life, providing stability and an identifiable mark of holiness.

In response to the Pharisees' criticism, Jesus cites the precedent of David, an authoritative figure, and then sets himself even higher on the authority ladder by saying, "The Son of Man is lord even of the sabbath" (2:28). There is good reason in this context to take "Son of Man" not as a title, with apocalyptic overtones, but simply as a self-designation of Jesus (in line with its earlier occurrence in 2:10). The point is that Jesus cannot be reduced to what the tradition wants or needs. His claim to authority demands a rereading of the tradition. He sets the tradition in a brand-new light.

Then, as if to prove the point, the narrator relates the healing on the Sabbath of the man with the withered hand (3:1–6). Jesus is in charge from the very beginning. He takes the initiative with the man, without being asked, and then confronts the skeptics with the choice of doing good or harm, saving life or killing. Jesus demonstrates precisely what it means to be Lord of the Sabbath, what the tradition looks like when read from the vantage of the new.

In addition to the affirmation of Jesus as the decisive interpreter of the Sabbath, this text confronts us with a second issue of authority: Jesus' power over the forces of evil. Modern readers are often surprised that the stories of Jesus healing the sick do not contain more references to his compassion for the people with their maladies. Many accounts seem devoid of feeling. Clearly in the narrative the more significant feature is Jesus' authority.

Like the man with the unclean spirit (1:23–26), the leper (1:40–45), and the paralytic (2:3–12), the man with the withered hand symbolizes the control of destructive powers, powers that cripple and distort human life. Jesus' healing him is more than an act of compassion for a stunted life. It expresses the irruption of the divine power, the invasive rule, which seeks to restore and renew. Each exorcism and healing indicates that Jesus is the bearer of such power, that the forces of sickness are subject to his healing touch.

The issue is not irrelevant today, even though the ancient connection between sickness and the forces of evil is not so much a part of our way of thinking. The matter of power lies at the heart of many, if not most, of our deepest perplexities, which makes Mark's narration of Jesus' ultimate authority a timely text.

Third, the issue of authority is brought to a head in the concluding verse of the lection (3:6). Jesus' claim to be Lord of the Sabbath, and his demonstration of the claim by doing good, evoke an immediate and vicious response from the religious authorities. The inbreaking of God's rule in the person of Jesus poses a dramatic threat that ultimately leads to his crucifixion.

It is important to recognize why the religious authorities felt challenged by Jesus. The Pharisees were not inherently evil people, nor were they narrow-minded legalists who took great pleasure in quibbling over details. They were deeply religious Jews, who felt that what was needed was a legal structure that enabled all the people, not merely the priests, to take seriously ritual purity and Sabbath observance. In doing so, they could maintain their distinctive status as the special people called of God.

Jesus' claim and proof of authority make him a dangerous figure to the Pharisees. Their carefully constructed religious structure lies much at risk in his presence. Their conspiracy to violence indicates just how clearly they perceived the threat. It ever remains so when Jesus challenges other competing claims, whether they be religious, ethnic, economic, or national.

Proper 5

Ordinary Time 10

*Sunday between
June 5 and 11 inclusive
(if after Trinity Sunday)*

The world mirrored to us in the biblical text is often a world in which things are not what they seem. Abraham and Sarah, although apparently much too old to become the parents of a child, become the parents of an entire nation. Jesus, who seems to be defeated by his execution as a troublemaker, is proclaimed as resurrected and vindicated by God. A group at the margins of a marginal religion takes its new faith to the heart of the Roman Empire.

Three of the texts for Proper 5 play upon that familiar theme, although in diverse ways. Only a reader who knows nothing of Israel's subsequent history can avoid the irony in the passage from 1 Samuel. Here the people of Israel demand a king, one who will "govern us and go out before us and fight our battles" (8:20). The kings that follow do carry out that wish, of course, but the protection for which the people clamor proves far more troublesome than they can anticipate.

Psalm 138 does not deal with this contrast between the way things are and the way they appear, but the psalm does underscore the irony in 1 Sam. 8. Here the psalmist anticipates a time when God is praised by "all the kings of the earth." That subordination of human kings to the one real King undermines Israel's claim to know what is best by seeking a king for itself.

Second Corinthians often deals quite explicitly with the contrast between appearance and reality. Here the final verse of the text of this week's reading recalls that contrast. Even the finality of death is not the end for those who know that the "earthly tent" will be replaced by a "building from God, a house not made with hands, eternal in the heavens" (5:1). The new city God builds is the reality toward which God's victory is moving, and defeats along the way have only a limited kind of reality attached to them.

As so often, Mark's Gospel draws attention to the irony that those who are supposed to be "insiders" do not in fact know who Jesus is.

Here, both Jesus' own family and the religious scribes (the theologians of the day) conclude that he is in the grip of some evil power. The reader who has followed Mark's story from the beginning, however, recognizes that these "insiders" are not what they seem. They stand well outside the circle of understanding.

1 Samuel 8:4–11 (12–15) 16–20 (11:14–15)

It is one thing for a community of people to commit themselves to the leadership of the Lord and to promise themselves that every aspect of life will mirror the will of the Lord. It is quite another thing when the theocratic ideal is translated into everyday social and political models. Then human sinfulness intrudes, as does ignorance and incompetence, and those who are selected to represent God before the people often do no more than reflect the people's own corrupted ways. Every experiment in Utopia is bound to fail, and as ancient Israel discovered this harsh verity early on in its life in the land, so have many other human communities since the days of King Saul.

Samuel did not preside over the first effort in Israel's life to erect a throne for Yahweh's anointed king. At an earlier time, after Gideon devastated the bands of Midianite raiders, a grateful tribal confederacy urged him to accept a crown. But Gideon proved as wise as he was courageous, for he knew that neither he nor any other mortal could live up to such a high ideal. No one could rule Israel but Israel's God: "I will not rule over you, and my son will not rule over you; Yahweh will rule over you" (Judg. 8:23). And, as if to prove the point, Gideon's son Abimelech cruelly grasped after the crown his father had refused, only to bring tragedy on himself and many others (Judg. 9).

The present lection carefully sketches the clashing emotions generated by this renewed request for a king. Poor Samuel, who had once been called on to deliver words of judgment to his aged mentor, Eli (1 Sam. 3:11–18), now hears a similar verdict from the people. Samuel's sons are also worthless (8:3), as had been Hophni and Phinehas. In addition, Samuel himself was old and his leadership increasingly feeble—at least in the eyes of his compatriots. And to be quite frank about the matter, Samuel was not a warrior in any event. In all the stories told about Israel's last judge, there is not a single reference to Samuel's prowess in battle. On one occasion when the Philistines are routed, it is after Samuel offers not swords and spears, but sacrifices and prayers (1 Sam. 7:7–14)! It may be successfully argued that Israel needed moral and spiritual leadership more than it needed a skilled military, but that is not the way the people viewed the matter. "Give us a king to govern us—like the other nations," they demand (see 8:5–6; compare v. 20). And a lust for blood is clearly evident in their voices.

Samuel's emotions are quick to rise as well. Has it been for nothing that he has led the nation these many years? Do these who now cry out for a warrior-king not realize that, by means of his own combined offices of judge, prophet, and priest, he has secured the well-being of the people? In their craving for a monarchy, patterned not on Yahweh's will but on the countless kingdoms around them, they are simply giving in to the ancient temptation to counter the sword with the sword. It is little wonder that Samuel interprets the matter personally (vs. 6–7).

The narrator who is responsible for our text interestingly plays down the emotions of Samuel in order to emphasize those of Yahweh (vs. 7–18). Israel cannot have it both ways; either the nation must follow its God and eschew conventional devices of power, or it must abandon its commitment to Yahweh in favor of a strategy of survival by brute force. To be honest, there are few in our time who can fault Samuel's contemporaries, for the history of the world is too full of peaceful persons who have been led to the slaughter by their more powerful and aggressive neighbors. But the decision of the people of Israel now is a momentous one, and Yahweh, instead of rejecting them in return for their rejection, simply points out to them the terrible consequences of their choice. The human representative of Yahweh, the assistant king to the one great King, will bring tyranny to Israel as alien kings have brought tyranny to their own people, Israel's neighbors. In their effort to avoid oppression from without they have embraced it from within.

To be certain, the Old Testament does not speak with one voice on the issue of Israel's monarchy, and texts such as the present lection must be balanced against other passages, such as 2 Sam. 7, that praise the establishment by Yahweh of the office of the Davidic king. Yet it is in the very tension one encounters that one engages the paradox implicit in the effort to build the kingdom of God on earth. The people of God, no matter how great their dedication (and *that* is always questionable!), cannot resist the urge to take God's matters into their own hands. Nor should they! For simply to repose in the expectation that God will take care of all the hard issues of life is a thinly veiled form of escapism. We shall work for the kingdom, because we must. Yet, even as we do so, we are forced to admit that it is not we, but God, who will eventually bring the kingdom into perfect realization. Our efforts, while useful, are inevitably distorted and sinful. But as God did not abandon sinful Israel, so the true King will not abandon any who long and work for the in-breaking of the kingdom.

Psalm 138

This psalm is one of Israel's characteristic songs of thanksgiving, with subordinate elements of praise and petition.

In Ps. 138:1–3 the first-person expression of gratitude lives very close to an actual experience. Thanksgiving in ancient Israel is the counterpart to a complaint. The complaint that petitions God to act is uttered in contexts of serious trouble. A song of thanksgiving, such as this one, often recalls the initial petition and rejoices that God has answered the request. Here, v. 3 recalls the moment of petition when "I called," in a time of trouble. God answered and resolved the situation.

In any case, it is the resolution wrought by the intervention of God that evokes the song. To utter thanks (and perhaps to accompany the utterance with a sacrifice of thanksgiving) is to cede one's life over to God in deep gratitude for a specific act of transformation or rescue. Thus the thanks is full, with a whole heart.

The reason for this thanksgiving, we are told in v. 2, is God's steadfast love (*ḥesed*) and faithfulness (*'ĕmet*). This word pair is much used in Israel to express God's utter, active reliability. The word pair is likely reflected in the phrase "grace and truth" (John 1:14). The two words bespeak God's readiness to stand in solidarity with and attentiveness toward this individual petitioner. Perhaps the complaint behind Ps. 138:3 concerned a risk or danger or affliction. The petition assumed that the trouble came only because of God's absence and would not have happened had God been present (see John 11:21). In the framework of Israel's faith, it is enough to have God's "grace and truth" present in order to overcome any problem. And that is what has happened. God's reliable presence and steadfast purpose have been brought into the situation and resolved the trouble. In such an active intervention, God's name and speech have been "made great" (v. 2, Hebrew), that is, are shown to be formidable and decisive.

Verses 4–6 of Ps. 138 embody an unexpected change of mood, tone, and pattern of rhetoric. There is an abrupt move from thanksgiving to praise. While Claus Westermann believes the two are of the same form, it is clear that these verses constitute a very different kind of song. Now the subject is corporate and public, "all the kings of the earth." The royal language is now concerned not with God's fidelity, but with God's glory, exactly what we might expect from kings who are impressed with power, majesty, and appearance. It is not easy to see why the rhetorical change is undertaken in the psalm. Apparently the personal testimony (vs. 1–3) has been appropriated, encompassed, and transposed, so that vs. 4–6 generalize from the concreteness of vs. 1–3.

Verse 6 seems to be a return to the motifs of vs. 1–3. In its present placement, however, v. 6 concerns not the individual speaker of vs. 1–3, but the kings of vs. 4–5. Thus the "lowly" and the "haughty" seem to refer not to people in different social situations, but to different positions among the kings. Thus a king may be haughty and pretend autonomy, or a king may be lowly, acknowledging submissiveness to Yahweh. The praise here undertaken by kings thus is a show of lowliness before Yahweh, a willingness to submit one's own royal glory to the greater glory of Yahweh. Royal power thus is derivative and penultimate, and survives in authority only when submitted to Yahweh.

Verses 7–8 return to the rhetoric and mode of vs. 1–3. Again the speaker is an individual person, and not generalized royalty. Verse 7 is an expression of deep confidence in God, rooted in concrete experience, no doubt the experience of v. 3. The language of this verse parallels that of Ps. 23:4. In a context of trouble, vulnerability, and risk, God causes the speaker to live. The Hebrew is *ḥyh*, thus a stronger term than NRSV suggests with "preserve." God guarantees life in a context freighted with the threat of death. This strong verb is paralleled and supported by two other verbs: God will *stretch out* a protective hand—make a show of power—and God will *deliver*. The three verbs together bespeak God's power and capacity to intervene against any threat to or diminishment of life.

The doxological assertion of v. 7 is made more concrete in v. 8, which returns to the theme of v. 2. The psalmist counts heavily on God's enduring commitment. Again, it is Yahweh's *ḥesed* that is the decisive mark of the relation, a mark that defends against enemies, and makes functioning life possible in every circumstance. This speaker knows that alone we cannot live: we live only in God's protective, faithful presence.

The affirmation about God's abiding *ḥesed* in v. 8b sounds like a conclusion, and we expect the psalm to end there. We are more than a little surprised, then, to find an additional line which is a petition, the first in the entire psalm (v. 8c). This phrase might indeed be a later addendum, but it does pick up on the theme of v. 3. As the speaker called on God in the past, so he calls again. It is on the basis of God's ḥesed in vs. 2 and 8 that the speaker dares ask from God. The asking is a particular, pathos-filled plea. "The work of your hands" can variously refer to the world, to Israel, or perhaps to the speaker as a self. The verb rendered "forsake" is *rp'*, "to let fall." Thus, "do not let fall," because if God does not uphold, there will be nullification. Thus the petition is a desperate act, for the "work of your hands" is completely dependent. The desperate prayer, however, is also a confident one, counting on God's ḥesed, which is completely reliable.

2 Corinthians 4:13–5:1

Some readers may find themselves rushing past the beginning of this lection to make their way to the more familiar and, indeed, more beautiful section that begins in 2 Cor. 4:16. The opening lines of this passage are profoundly important, however, for they assume a radical continuity between the faith of Israel's past and the faith of the church's present. At the same time that these lines reflect that continuity, they also demonstrate the profound discontinuity introduced by the gospel of Jesus Christ.

Paul's assertion that "we have the same spirit of faith that is in accordance with scripture" quietly forges a connection between past and present that the Christian church has often neglected, to its detriment. Admittedly, the exact nuance of the phrase the NRSV translates "the same spirit of faith" is debatable, but the identification between past and present is not. The gift of faith that inspired the psalmist now enables the Christian preacher.

The quotation in v. 13 ("I believed, and so I spoke") comes directly from the Septuagint of Ps. 115:1 (the equivalent of Ps. 116:10), although the Greek here departs significantly from the Hebrew, so that this wording will not be found in English translations. In this particular instance, the continuity Paul finds concerns the movement from faith to speech, the way in which faith necessitates proclamation. As Paul indicates elsewhere, he does not view his preaching of the gospel as an optional activity, but as necessity (for example, 1 Cor. 9:16).

Despite this strong continuity between the psalmist and Paul (and his co-workers), 2 Cor. 4:14 recalls the radically new element that has entered the picture: "the one who raised the Lord Jesus will raise us also." The "same spirit of faith" now manifests itself in the new conviction *both* that God raised Jesus from the dead *and* that God will also raise those who belong to Jesus.

Here Paul expresses resurrection faith in a slightly different way than elsewhere. While he elsewhere expresses the conviction that the resurrection of humankind follows from that of Christ (as in Romans 6 and 1 Cor. 15), here he distinguishes between the resurrection of the apostles and that of Corinthian believers ("will bring us with you into his presence"). The future of the apostle and that of the church are intertwined so that extricating either party from the relationship is impossible. Even in the final triumph of God, apostle and congregation belong together (see 2 Cor. 1:13–14).

Verse 15 removes any impression that the final goal of Christian proclamation or of the resurrection itself is anthropological. Even if Paul grandly insists that "everything is for your sake," he takes a further step that qualifies that generalization. "Everything" exists so that grace as it extends "to more and more people, may increase thanksgiving, to the glory of God." Some interpreters of Paul have argued that he indeed understands the glory of God as something that can be enhanced objectively by human thanksgiving; human gratitude actually increases the glory of God. Whether or not that interpretation captures Paul's thought, it does draw attention to the *telos* of the gospel, which is the glorification of God.

Verse 16 employs a phrase from 4:1 to resume the topic of apostolic boldness. "We do not lose heart" refers not to the fear of death (or the absence thereof) but to the courage to proclaim even in the most adverse circumstances (4:1–12). Even as the psalmist proclaimed ("I believed, and so I spoke"), Paul will continue to speak, because of his conviction about the power of God (4:13–15).

The remainder of the passage amplifies the motivation that lies behind Paul's courage to preach. Here he speaks once again by means of contrasting that which appears to be significant now with that which will be significant always. The "momentary affliction" is visible, it is real, but it lasts only a brief while. Chapter 5:1 brings this line of reasoning to a head: "If the earthly tent we live in is destroyed, we have a building from God, a house not made with hands, eternal in the heavens." Debate flourishes as to the origin and meaning of the imagery employed in this verse, and the commentaries will provide the options. One important suggestion is that Paul draws on Jewish apocalyptic thought which anticipates a new eschatological temple in the newly restored Jerusalem (see, for example, 2 Esdras 10:40–57; 2 *Apocalypse Baruch* 4:3). A "building from God, a house not made with hands," then, would graphically depict the eschatological home of God's people. This interpretation does not rule out the implications of such a new home for individuals, but it does mean that Paul does not refer here to the resurrected body of individuals so much as to the new creation in which believers will find a home. It is because of the certainty of this new home that Christian preachers can speak and act boldly.

Because this section of 2 Corinthians pertains so directly to the nature of Christian preaching, some Christians may conclude that it has little to say to them (except as the recipients of preaching). Of course, that nearsighted reading of the text neglects the continuity between the task of the apostle and that of every believer. If the apostle (or the contemporary preacher) proclaims the gospel in one way, all believers become proclaimers by their lives as well as their words. The need for courage ("we do not lose heart") does not pertain to the preacher alone.

Mark 3:20–35

There is no question that Jesus is a figure to be reckoned with. He heals people of all manner of diseases; he teaches with such authority that listeners immediately recognize something new and different; he calls and commissions followers; crowds flock to him. What is going on with this imposing individual? Where does the power come from that enables him to perform the mighty works that he does? Is he one of those crazed characters who does extraordinary things but then just as quickly fades from view, a meteor falling out of the sky? Some expression of the suprahuman must be present in him, but what? How is he to be read? These are the questions that emerge in the intriguing text designated as the Gospel reading for this Sunday (Mark 3:20–35). They help to remind us that "being there" does not remove the ambiguity nor lessen the risk of decision.

The questions surface in a carefully constructed narrative structure, filled with suspense as well as conflict. The narrator tells us that Jesus' family is anxious about what is happening with him, and they come into a crowd-filled setting "to restrain him" (3:21). But then we are left hanging as to what they said and how Jesus responded, while the focus shifts to the charges against Jesus brought by scribes from Jerusalem. Only after the scribes have been dealt with are we brought back to the family and their attempt to bring Jesus to his senses (vs. 31–35). It is Mark's strategy of "sandwiching" one event or discussion between two parts of another, an effective device, particularly with readers who may be more curious about the family's reaction to Jesus than the predictable position of the scribes.

We begin with a look at the family. Verse 21 is rendered differently in various versions. The NRSV assumes that the family members have heard that others ("people") think Jesus is mentally deranged, and this motivates their move to restrain him. The Greek text, however, is ambiguous and open to the possibility that Jesus' relatives themselves have come to the conclusion that he is obsessed (see NIV). In either case, the family decides that it is time for an "intervention." One can only imagine their anxiety and concern for Jesus' well-being and also the family's good name. Something has to be done.

The narrator makes abundantly clear that when the family members arrive on the scene, they are really "outsiders." They do not even get in to talk to Jesus, but have to communicate from the edge of the crowd. Unlike the paralytic, whose friends tear up the roof to get into the presence of Jesus (2:1–12), his relatives have to pass the word along through the crowd that they are there to intervene. When Jesus speaks, he addresses not his relatives but the insiders, those gathered about him in the house.

Jesus' response is revolutionary. On the one hand, it relativizes the natural family connections so cherished in the Jewish context (and in our own?). It threatens to undermine the basic core of social stability, and thereby poses an enormous risk. On the other hand, it establishes a "new family," bound together not by blood but by the doing of God's will. It provides a different basis for solidarity. In the new age, real community is created by obedience.

The scribes, who come from Jerusalem and cannot deny Jesus' extraordinary deeds, charge him with being an agent of Beelzebul and himself possessed of an unclean spirit. Jesus has a double-pronged response. First, playing off of the common-sense notion that a divided kingdom/house cannot stand, he describes his vocation in terms of an invasion of the house and the binding of a strong man. The violent language, from which we are inclined to shrink, is a reminder that the exercise of God's reign in human life involves nothing less than a war. Any attempt to tame the imagery misses the serious nature of the conflict precipitated by Jesus' words and deeds.

The second portion of Jesus' response begins with the incredible scope of divine grace. Nothing less than all the sins and blasphemies humans commit will be forgiven. But then comes the caveat of 3:29.

What is this blasphemy against the Holy Spirit that results in an "eternal sin"? The natural (and sometimes very existential) questions about this saying of Jesus that arise among readers demand clear answers. Verse 30 directs the saying against people who apparently take note of Jesus and his undeniable, remarkable activity but dismiss it and the burden of believing by attributing it all to a demonic cause. Without equivocation they label the work of God as the work of the devil. Their certitude is born neither of weakness nor honest seeking. Since they leave no opening for God, they cannot conceive of being mistaken in their judgment. Thus they are to be sharply distinguished from persons who struggle with doubts and who are not able to put all the pieces of life together in a neat solution to the puzzle.

The passage presents us with the dramatic reactions to Jesus of two groups: Jesus' family and the religious scholars. Both could be thought of as rightfully belonging to the inner circle, and yet both turn out to be outsiders. One group may have meant well in its misguided effort to take charge of Jesus, while the other group aggressively accuses him. Both, however, fail to perceive the divine rule present in Jesus.

Proper 6

Ordinary Time 11

*Sunday between
June 12 and 18 inclusive
(if after Trinity Sunday)*

The issue of discernment constantly confronts the people of God. How is one to understand what is really going on in the world? How is one to discriminate and make decisions that are faithful to God? What standards can realistically be applied to evaluate this or that option? The culture clearly has answers for questions like these. It is basically a bottom-line mentality, which seeks for quantifiable results. Every venture is scrutinized and evaluated, and the discerner looks for verifiable outcomes that give proof of the success, partial success, or failure of the effort.

All four readings for today warn about judging on the basis of outward appearances and declare that the people of God are given eyes that enable them to discriminate in new and different ways. The ways are not spelled out in detail, but that is the way faith operates. It never functions without risk.

The experience of Samuel as he searches for a successor to Saul indicates how easily looks can be deceiving (1 Sam. 15:34–16:13). Jesse's eldest son, Eliab, seems the perfect prospect, until Samuel is advised that God does not judge according to outward appearances but according to the heart. Psalm 20 expresses the prayers of the people in behalf of the military ventures of the king, but remains quite clear that the obvious symbols of strength (chariots and horses) are not worthy of pride. Real hope lies only "in the name of the LORD our God" (Ps. 20:7).

Both New Testament readings sound the same note. Paul in writing to an overconfident Corinthian community enjoins them to walk by faith and not by sight. And walking by faith means that "worldly standards have ceased to count in our estimate of anyone" (2 Cor. 5:16, REB). The involvement of believers in the death of Christ includes a new standard of judgment. What better symbol for this than the mustard seed (Mark 4:30–32)? Though small and inconspicuous, it results in "the greatest of all shrubs." Especially regarding

God's presence in human history, believers are not to be content with worldly symbols and outward appearances. The cross becomes the ultimate canon for discernment.

1 Samuel 15:34–16:13

The wonderful ways of the Lord are often frustrated by human weakness and sin. That is undoubtedly the predominant theme in the stories about Saul, Israel's first king (1 Sam. 8–15), and the remarkable manner in which the ancient writers not only acknowledged this fact, but also openly spoke of Yahweh's vulnerability to human waywardness, comes across to the modern reader as shocking. It is striking enough that Samuel, having recognized the failure of Yahweh's choice of Saul, "grieved over Saul" (15:35), but more noteworthy still that Yahweh "was sorry that he had made Saul king over Israel." The portrait of Israel's God as one who is personally touched by human failure, who suffers when rejected by the people (Jer. 2:1–3) or who struggles internally over the proper response to human sin (Hos. 11:8), is not one to which the modern mind easily accommodates itself. But in spite of the dangers of anthropomorphism, such an understanding of God serves to remind men and women of faith that the God whom we meet in scripture and in Jesus Christ is a sensate and personal Being, not some benevolent celestial autocrat.

First Samuel 15:34–35, for all its insightful theology, however, functions within our lection as introduction to the principal narrative, which is the selection of David to be Israel's new and—as we are to learn—highly successful and beloved ruler. It is difficult to improve on the traditional interpretation of this text, which sees the essence of the matter contained in 16:7b. The normal standards of human judgment may have led to Israel's demand for a king in the first place, a demand to which Yahweh assents (1 Sam. 8), but Yahweh's standards now transcend the "normal." David is not the oldest nor the strongest among Jesse's sons; he is not even brought in from the pastures when Samuel comes calling on the family. But Samuel, acting as Yahweh's agent, is insistent; the issue will not be decided until all Jesse's sons have been seen. We can only guess at the mysterious means by which Yahweh's will is communicated to Samuel—the casting of lots, perhaps. But while Samuel is not quite sure for whom he is looking, he shelters no doubts that Yahweh's new anointed one will not be found among the older brothers. It is almost that, having been disappointed in Saul, both Yahweh and Samuel are determined that no mistakes are to be made this time.

"The LORD does not see as mortals see; they look on the outward appearance, but the LORD looks on the heart." The various ways in which men and women in our and every age are tempted to do just the opposite can be documented in our racism, our sexism, and our various forms of idolatry (love of money, clothing, glitzy automobiles, and the like). It is only when we learn to see beyond that which is most visible that we begin to assess people in terms of their character and their commitments.

While 16:7b may be the most compelling text in our lection, there are other elements here that deserve attention. One has to do with the initial reaction of the Bethlehemite elders to Samuel's uninvited presence (v. 4). It is not entirely clear why the villagers should be so fearful, but as this text follows closely on 15:32–33, it would be clear to them that Samuel was not a person to be trifled with. The text also strongly implies that Bethlehem lay within Saul's sphere of influence (note v. 2), so that anyone who was even suspected of being on friendly terms with the king from neighboring Benjamin might be treated roughly. Samuel's rejection by the people (1 Sam. 8:4–5) still rankled in the old priest's heart. So when Samuel says that he has come peaceably and invites the elders of Bethlehem to join him in worship, they are too relieved and perhaps too frightened to refuse. The exercise of temporal power, especially military power, on the part of leaders of the community of faith was an abuse that lasted far too long in the West (it is still an oppressive element in some parts of the world), and the separation of ecclesiastical and temporal power sets free from the corruption of blind dogma not only the community of faith, but the body politic as well. Samuel is a force for good in many important respects, but he also represents at least this one negative feature of life in Israel of the tenth century B.C. People should fear the men and women of God only when they (the people) are wedded to their sins, and there is no evidence that the citizens of Bethlehem were so corrupted.

An additional noteworthy feature within our passage is the chord that is struck at the end. "The spirit of the LORD came mightily upon David" (v. 13) reminds the reader not only of a similar statement about Saul (1 Sam. 11:6), but of other comparable phrases used in connection with Yahweh's confirmation of earlier judges (Judg. 6:34; 11:29; 14:6). It was this feature which characterized true leadership within early Israel, and the fact that it is repeated here with reference to David stands as symbol of God's repeated mercy on the people. In the continuing need of the people, God raised up generation after generation of divinely endowed persons, women and men who became the active embodiment of Yahweh's saving presence in

Israel's life. Thus the recurrence of this phrase, here applied to David, indicates that David is to be another in the long line of God's specially gifted representatives—and what a representative he was to be!

Psalm 20

With its mention of "his anointed" in v. 6, Ps. 20 is commonly taken to be a royal psalm, concerned with an occupant of the Davidic throne. Thus its theme is congruent with the Old Testament reading concerning the anointment of the young David as a future king. The psalm divides into two rhetorical parts, a series of optative verbs, which are in fact prayers (or wishes) for the well-being of the king, and a more or less didactic statement concerning the true mode of royal power. This psalm is often linked with Ps. 21, as both concern the destiny of the king in a military situation.

The NRSV translates all the verbs in vs. 1–5 as optatives, except for the first two, "answer . . . protect." In fact these two also might be translated as all the others. The verbs sound like a series of well-wishes for the king, with an intensely "patriotic" flavor. It could be that this is the orchestrated voice of the populace. It is more likely that this is a liturgy on behalf of the king in the temple, which is the king's "chapel." In that context, the series of optative verbs has the formal effect of a priestly blessing, thus giving support and theological legitimacy to the royal "war effort." The series of optative verbs intends to invoke and mobilize God's favor for the king's military venture.

In v. 3 there is some variation in the recital. In fact, this verse calls attention to the visible acts of piety on the part of the king, as the king has generously presented offerings and sacrifices. Thus it is implied that these pious acts of the king deserve a "reward" from God, and that if only God will remember and notice these acts of piety, the trade-off for the king will be the gift of military success. This verse operates on an unstated assumption of quid pro quo with God concerning personal piety and public policy.

Verses 4–5 continue the wish-prayer, anticipating a great public celebration of the king's victory. God has a decisive role to play in the outcome of battle, though the prayer thinks in terms of synergistic cooperation between God and king. The king does indeed have "plans," and does indeed voice "petitions." Those plans and petitions, however, depend on God, so that in the last instance it is God who is the decisive player in the public life of Israel.

The second part of the psalm, vs. 6–9, begins after a sharp rhetorical break introduced by *'attāh:* "Now I know." It is as though the speaker has arrived at a new certitude about God's willingness to support the king. And consequently there is also new certitude about the outcome of the battle.

In any case, the practical rhetorical effect of vs. 6–9 is to give assurance and legitimacy to the effort of the king. This assurance repeats, in v. 6, the verb "answer" from v. 1. The verb "help" in v. 6 responds to the verb "send help" in v. 2, though with a different Hebrew term. This new certitude is confident of great victories (*yš'*), reiterating the term from v. 5. Thus v. 6 gives response precisely to the wishes of vs. 1–5, as the wishes are transformed (presumably by an oracle) into official certitudes.

In vs. 7–8, we are given the theological warrant for the new confidence voiced here. A sharp contrast is drawn between reliance on chariots and horses, symbols of military power and arms, and on the powerful name of Yahweh, which is more powerful than conventional military resources. As is characteristic, the Bible does not spell out how "the name" is militarily reliable. It is enough to note that faithful people regularly confess that the purposes of God are powerful in the public, even military domain, so that victory does not always go to the technologically superior or better-armed contestant. The evangelical affirmation is that the inscrutable power of God makes a decisive difference in the public process, capable of confounding the best-known human calculations. On this odd contrast, see the bravado of young David (1 Sam. 17:45–46) in a military context, the confident contrast of Zech. 4:6, and the sapiential conclusion of Prov. 21:30–31.

God's will and power are not a surface "religious amateur," but are real factors in the conduct and outcome of public affairs. This conclusion resonates with the Pauline accent in the Epistle reading concerning "faith" and "sight." A technological society is inclined to "sight" (horses and chariots), but this community knows better.

The psalm culminates with a quite confident petition, counting on the hope of answered petition (v. 5) and the assurance that God will answer (v. 6). This brief petition, which may indeed be the point of the entire poem, reiterates a third time the verb "answer" and invokes once again the term "victory" (*yš'*), as in vs. 5–6. The petition is a pious act which suggests that the "anointed" does indeed believe that victory/liberation is given only by God and not in human strategy or posturing. The conclusion of this psalm is congruent with Karl Barth's notion of evangelical prayer: the proper position before God is one of need, and the proper speech before

God is an asking from God for that which we ourselves cannot do. The king in this poem is indeed a man of faith and not of sight, a faithful practitioner of evangelical faith, whose proper role is to ask and to receive.

2 Corinthians 5:6–10 (11–13) 14–17

For all the beauty and power of Paul's language in 2 Corinthians, the letter makes turns and twists that are often difficult to follow. Just as the reader glimpses what "tablets of stone" might be, Paul shifts to language about the veiling of Moses or about houses not made with hands. The Corinthians are Paul's letter of recommendation, but he needs no letter of recommendation. The apostles are at home in the body, but they would prefer to be at home with the Lord.

Whatever the problems in understanding these individual passages, it is clear that many of them reflect a struggle to articulate differences between the way things appear (in the world, to those who are not Christians) and the way they really are (to those who are Christians). Nothing is the way it seems to be—real letters are written where they cannot be read in the usual way, the gospel is hidden but transparent, the apostles seem to be close to death but they bear life within them.

The assigned lection begins with still more such contrasts and paradoxes. Christians seem to be at home in their bodies, in the physical world, but their real home is with the Lord, and to be in that home is their preference (vs. 6–10). Unlike others, Christians must make judgments based on what is inside persons, not on "outward appearance" (vs. 11–12). The apostles themselves appear to be crazy ("beside ourselves"), but they are the most sane of all (v. 13).

Finally, beginning in v. 14, Paul gets to the heart of the matter, identifying why it is that this conflict exists between what the world sees and what Christians know to be real. First, he explains the grasp of the gospel by reference to a bit of Christian tradition. With the words "one has died for all" Paul cites a creed he uses elsewhere in a somewhat different form (see, for example, 1 Cor. 15:3; Gal. 2:20; 1 Thess. 5:10). These words are too compact to associate them with any particular theory of the atonement. Whatever it means to say that Christ's death is "for all," that death also involves the death of all (v. 14) and, more important, that death claims the lives of all.

That Christ's death was "for all" means somehow that believers are bound up in that death. For Paul, Christians do not watch the cross as if it were a scene "out there" or "back there" somewhere, displayed for them now so that they can understand the historical ramifications of this event. Nor is the cross connected with believers only by virtue of some influence it has with God, so that the cross persuades God to forgive human sin. The death of Christ on the cross involves believers directly, in that they die in it and now have lives that are not their own but belong to Christ.

With vs. 16–17 Paul undertakes to state the implications of the cross for the present course of human lives: "We regard no one from a human point of view." Now all the language about conflicting perceptions comes back into view. Because of the cross, Christians see things differently. They simply do not think, perceive, assess, judge in the way they did before. The crucial case for this change of perception comes in v. 16b: even if they once viewed Christ "from a human point of view" (as a common criminal, or perhaps a fool), they no longer see him in that way. Here it becomes clear why Christians look to the heart rather than the face, and even why they see the cross itself differently (see 1 Cor. 1:18, 24).

Particularly given the stress on the individual in American Christianity, the question might arise whether Paul here refers to some private experience that the individual savors. Is this, to put it crudely, an early Christian form of New Age thought, in which what is valued is the individual's personal growth and enriching experience? The final verse in the lection should silence any such responses. To say that there is a "new creation," that "everything old has passed away," that "everything has become new" is to locate the individual's experience in a context as large as the cosmos itself.

The verses that follow further locate this experience of changed perceptions, even new creation, in the action of God: "All this is from God, who reconciled us to himself through Christ." God's action of sending Christ, thereby reconciling human beings to himself, is the objective act that results in a change in human perception.

Christians experience a radical change in their way of thinking, a change tantamount to a "new creation." When Paul makes this observation, he certainly acknowledges a personal, subjective experience. That comment about experience, however, stands between two unequivocal statements about the origin of this new experience. If Christians have new eyes, it is because and only because of the death of Christ on the cross, a death that includes them and simultaneously grants them new life (5:14–15). If Christians have new eyes, it is because God has reached out to them, initiating reconciliation, sending Christ as the agent of that reconciliation, and establishing ambassadors of that reconciliation. The new vision comes because the eyes are a gift.

Mark 4:26-34

The parables of Jesus are tricky texts for sermons. On the one hand, they offer the most vivid stories and the most luxurious metaphors to be found in the Bible, an inexhaustible resource to be exploited for preaching. On the other hand, the parables are open to multiple interpretations, and the preacher has to be careful in moving in one or another interpretative direction not to constrict the meaning of the parable or to suggest that there is a "correct" reading that closes off all other readings. As modern commentators note, a parable often demonstrates a certain teasing quality that spurs the imagination and evokes varying responses dependent on what the particular reader brings to the text.

Nowhere is this more obvious than in the two parables included in the lectionary reading for this Sunday—the seed growing secretly and the mustard seed (Mark 4:26-34). The history of the interpretation of these two parables serves as a fascinating window into the struggles of the interpreter and the church at the time of interpretation. For example, classical liberalism at the end of the nineteenth and in the early twentieth centuries tended to stress the inevitability of growth, the progressive development of the reign of God. Like a steady, upward line on a graph, life was improving, and human efforts were marshaled for the building of the kingdom on earthly soil. (What did the liberals do with the farmer in vs. 26-27?) The interpretation reflected the optimistic mood of the times.

The interpretation proposed here (with the clear acknowledgment that there are other plausible interpretations) also finds in the two parables cause for optimism, but of a different sort from that of liberal interpreters.

The two stories certainly belong together and also need to be read in light of the third parable of growth found in the chapter, that of the sower and the seed (4:3-9). An interpretation is provided for the sower and the seed (vs. 13-20) that consoles the struggling Christian community, discouraged about the inauspicious role it has to play in the broader society. Some hear the gospel and for various reasons do not persist in their responsiveness; but be assured, the text affirms, that on the proper soil the word bears abundant fruit, even beyond one's wildest imaginations. Since a sevenfold yield was about average, a thirty- or sixty- or hundredfold yield was stupendous.

The parable of the mustard seed (vs. 30-32) provides further grounds for optimism. The contrast is established between "the smallest of all the seeds on earth" and "the greatest of all shrubs."

The prospect of God's rule of earth may not appear reassuring. The newspapers in the Roman Empire hardly carried banner headlines trumpeting the success of Christianity, its overthrow of slavery, or its winning converts in high places. The promise nevertheless is there. Inconspicuous beginnings will lead to a vast conclusion. God's rule will not be thwarted.

It is critical to observe that the promise does not have to do with the immediate success of the church (membership, budgets, and so on) or with the prosperity of individual believers, but with the ultimate triumph of the reign of God ("With what can we compare the kingdom of God?" v. 30). That reign is always shrouded in mystery, not sketched as a blueprint for the course of history but talked about in stories, compared to planting and harvesting. It certainly "happens" in the context of churches and in the lives of individuals, but it also irrupts in the most unlikely places, like the slums of Calcutta or the corners of hospital emergency rooms, whenever the power of God overcomes the destructive forces of evil.

The parable of the seed growing secretly (vs. 26–29) adds a new dimension to the optimism about God's rule encouraged by the parables of the sower and the seed and the mustard seed. The farmer, once having planted the seed, contributes nothing to its growth ("The earth produces of itself") and apparently does not understand how it matures. He simply waits for the moment of harvest, when he gathers the results. The cause for optimism is still there; the harvest surely comes.

The role of the farmer is intriguing. It is probably inaccurate to speak of his inactivity, since he both plants and harvests. But rather than mentioning his plowing or weeding or irrigating, the parable speaks simply of his sleeping and rising. The mystery of growth belongs to the earth and the seed, and not to the farmer. His activity neither hastens nor deters the time of harvest.

The figure of the farmer represents a wholesome reminder that the consummation of God's reign is not dependent on our best efforts, whether in social ministries or pastoral care or evangelistic activity. We are freed from the burden of determining the harvest, of assuming that our successes or failures hasten or deter God's plans. What a liberating thought! The fortunes of the kingdom do not rise or fall with programs that succeed or fail. The basis for optimism about the future rests in God, the giver of growth and the sole determiner of the time for harvest.

PROPER 7

Ordinary Time 12

*Sunday between
June 19 and 25 inclusive
(if after Trinity Sunday)*

In the readings for this Sunday the lectionary offers two dramatic narratives depicting God's powerful intrusion into the human arena to overcome the forces of injustice and chaos (1 Sam. 17 and Mark 4); one song of thanksgiving that praises God as "a stronghold for the oppressed" and the trustworthy executor of judgment on the wicked (Ps. 9); and an urgent appeal to a congregation that it not ignore God's gracious intrusion or take lightly the implications of what has been done in their behalf (2 Cor. 6).

The narrative of David's defeat of Goliath turns out to be much more than a fairy tale of a young lad surprising a mean giant. Lurking behind the encounter is the God who refuses to tolerate continued oppression, and whose unconventional weapons of warfare (a boy too small for the appropriate outfit for battle, stones, and a sling) signify the odd ways by which God wars against and overcomes injustice.

Likewise, the plight of the disciples caught in a threatening storm and Jesus' action in bringing calm dramatize the redemptive work of God, who rebukes chaotic forces and redeems beleaguered followers from a desperate situation. Modern-day disciples, only too aware of their own fear and lack of faith, can take heart from such a story of rescue. The psalmist puts all this to music, but in such a way that God is thrust clearly into the social arena, into the conflict between warring ideologies, as a vindicator of those who have been victimized by the wicked.

The basis of Paul's appeal to the recalcitrant Corinthians warns, however, that God's redemptive work entails a corresponding human transformation; that reconciliation with God demands reconciliation with one another. The character of the community and its members (whether for good or ill) becomes an indicator whether the divine grace has taken root or has been in vain.

1 Samuel 17:(1a, 4-11, 19-23) 32-49

The story of David's renowned encounter with Goliath forms this lection, and, as the narrative is somewhat extended, the preacher is faced with a decision concerning how much of the text to include in the focus of his or her attention. The lectionary wisely lists only vs. 32-49 as the primary text, but the balance of the chapter will, of course, have to be taken into consideration as background.

The passage begins with David's resolve to engage the Philistine giant in battle (v. 32), and in doing so it brings to the forefront of the reader's/preacher's consideration the rightness of David's cause. Saul's protest that David cannot be a match for the giant (v. 33) is answered in words that, at first hearing, may seem to be a boastful accounting of David's own prowess. But on closer inspection, David's response (vs. 34-37a) moves into clearer perspective as a statement concerning the basic justice of Yahweh, Israel's God. David has been sustained in moments of great crisis not because, like Samson (Judg. 14:6), he is superior in strength to the wild beasts, but because Yahweh is unalterably opposed to all who prey on human happiness and well-being. In this moving speech, which, as much as any other text in the Old Testament, shapes our memory of David as the shepherd-king, the "flock" is paradigmatic of Israel and of humankind in general. The God of justice is committed to the preservation of faithful people and to the defense of those who cannot defend themselves. David, as the anointed agent of Yahweh, is thus designated to implement Yahweh's will in regard to the crucial matters of justice and equity. Saul's ultimate acquiescence (v. 37b) is often read as a submission by this tragic king to his own destiny. While that is true, Saul's blessing on David—"May Yahweh be with you"—is also the moment when (in this context, at least) Israel yields to Yahweh's just ways.

Verses 38-40 serve, in a literary sense, to heighten the reader's tension over the coming battle. But in a more important way these verses carry forward the themes already laid out in vs. 32-37. That David is uncomfortable in soldier's armor and, in the end, sloughs it off, emphasizes his vulnerability. This causes the partisan within us (it is impossible to be a neutral reader of this story) to move forward toward the edge of our seat, while it forces the theologian within us to acknowledge again that, more than a story about David, this is a story about Yahweh and about Yahweh's moral commitments. The giant will be defeated not because David is stronger or cleverer than the Philistine, but because Yahweh is both cleverer and stronger than either Goliath or David. (Notice that Goliath's name is never used in vs. 32–49, perhaps as a way of denying dignity to the oppressor.) The reference to the "shepherd's bag" (v. 40) is another signal concerning the paradigmatic quality of the narrative, while the skill of the writer in pulling us farther into the action is demonstrated by the final words of v. 40: "and [David] drew near to the Philistine."

The next section, vs. 41–47, inches us closer to the climactic event of the battlefield. In vs. 41–44 Goliath taunts David and, by implication, David's God, the human vulnerability of the young son of Jesse being mockingly scorned by the giant. First Samuel 16:12 is recalled in the description in v. 42 of David, whose boyish features only serve to infuriate the Philistine. In light of what David had done to the wild animals that threatened his flock, the taunt of v. 43 is ironic. The point of the whole narrative is that Goliath *is* a predator, and as God's agent of justice David will deal with him as such. The irony is carried one step farther by Goliath's hollow boast of v. 44, involving the "wild animals" to whom he alleges that he will feed David's carcass.

David's reply in vs. 45–47 goes to the heart of the matter, for it is not he, but Yahweh, who will decide the day. In these verses are brought together the various thematic threads that are woven into the fabric of the text. David, as Israel's new shepherd, will do the deed, but it is in reality the God who has chosen David and who loves justice who will strike down the Philistine champion. The "wild animal" motif is raised once more, this time as David returns Goliath's words (v. 46) and gives to them a meaning they never possessed when spoken by the Philistine. The worthless gods of the Philistine pantheon (v. 43) are properly understood to be the delusions they are when compared to the living presence of Yahweh—a reality that neither the Philistines nor anyone else will be able to deny (v. 46). Even the unconventional weapons of David— stones and a sling—are a witness to the unconventional power of Yahweh (v. 47).

All that is left now is for the narrator to describe the moment of combat, and this she or he does in the most economical of ways (vs. 48–49). If the language is spare, it is because the event needs little elaboration. There is no struggle, no question about the outcome. The battle has been decided even before it was joined. The death of Goliath signals that Israel's new king, this shepherd like no other, will defend his people against their oppressors. But more than that, it reaffirms that the God of Israel will never permit injustice to prevail.

Psalm 9:9–20

These verses of the larger psalm assume a triangle of social power and social reality. (Psalms 9 and 10 are commonly taken together as one larger unit.) One member of that triangle is the "enemy" or adversary, who is variously identified as "the wicked" or "the nations." The second member of the triangle is the speaker of Ps. 9, who is portrayed as oppressed (v. 9), afflicted (v. 12), suffering (v. 13), needy (v. 18), and poor (v. 18). The superscription of the psalm, as well as the lectionary connection to 1 Sam. 17, suggests that this speaker is the king in dire straits. That identification, however, is not necessary for the actual words of the text, and there is nothing that requires such an identification. More importantly, whoever the speaker is (and it may be any needy believer), is weak and helpless before the adversary. That is, the relations between the two are unequal. If these are the only two layers in the drama, then the adversary will surely prevail, and the speaker will be further disadvantaged.

The psalm, however, concerns the third member of the triangle, Yahweh, who is the powerful "equalizer." This equalizer adjusts the dynamics of social power so that the strong adversary cannot prevail and the weak petitioner can have a good outcome to life. In various voices of praise and petition, the psalm insists that social power is not a drama between two unequal parties, but always includes this Third Party, who thereby transforms all social reality. Everything depends on this Third Party, a character who decisively reshapes reality.

Psalm 9:9–12, verses of doxology, serve to identify and enhance Yahweh as a party to social reality. They have the practical, liturgical effect of "singing" Yahweh into a decisive role in the conflict about to be enacted. Yahweh is abruptly and tersely identified as the safe place for the oppressed who have no other safe place. Those who are otherwise without refuge or resource can count on and trust in this One whose name is known, because Yahweh is faithful and will stand by. The singing of the praises of v. 11 is not simply a liturgical experience, but in fact is a profoundly political act.

In the midst of this buoyant doxological affirmation, v. 13 voices a petition. The speaker asks God one more time, this time, right now, to be the God who "avenges blood" (v. 12), who will protect the honor and well-being of one who suffers and is victimized. The language might be taken to refer to those close to death in battle (see 1 Sam. 17), but more likely it is characteristic psalmic rhetoric, whereby any situation of distress is spoken of as the threat of death. In the context of doxology, the petition can be offered in great confidence.

After the brief petition of v. 13, the poem immediately returns to doxology in vs. 14–18. Indeed, a motivation for God to answer the petition of v. 13 is that if the petition is answered, the ones in trouble will promptly and eagerly return to the great choir that spends its energy "recounting," reciting, resaying all the praises, all the transformations, all the deliverances whereby God has reordered power, diminished threat (see the Gospel reading), and made new life possible.

Verses 15–18 seem to be an actual example of the "recounting" that is anticipated in v. 14. What is to be recounted as a celebration of God is that the very nations who dug a pit and hid a net for the speaker (perhaps the king) have fallen into their own pit and have been trapped in their own net. The speaker (the king or any poor believer) leads a charmed life, escaping the pit and the net. Though not explicitly stated, it is clear that it is Yahweh who has kept the speaker from these dangers and turned the traps against the trapper. Yahweh is indeed a "wild card" in the social process, so that outcomes do not follow the expected, prearranged sequence of the powerful. While Yahweh is absent in v. 15, and matters turned out in understated oddity, in vs. 16–17 it is explicitly Yahweh who inverts the social process.

The needy have a powerful defender and advocate, who keeps the social process open on their behalf, so that they are not the inevitable victims of the designs of the powerful. By the fidelity of God, public life is indeed kept open for the weak, poor, and oppressed.

On the basis of that bold, tireless affirmation, the rhetorical unit ends in a strident petition in vs. 19–20, escalating the request of v. 13. The speaker does not doubt the capacity of Yahweh. Yahweh only needs to be aroused and motivated to action. Yahweh is to "rise up" and get moving, in order to do Yahweh's characteristic thing. When Yahweh acts on behalf of the forgotten and marginated, it is clear that the pretentious and powerful are not as strong as they imagined, not gods and not godlike. The Philistine giant is a cipher for such pretentious human power. When faced by the inscrutable purposes of Yahweh, such pretentious power is "only human." The word used twice, 'ĕnôš (in v. 19 "mortals," in v. 20 "human"), means humanity in its futile weakness. The power of Yahweh yields a new perspective on human pretension. As with the Philistine, such human pretension is almost all hot air. And when the hot air evaporates before the real power of God, the weak are safe and have room for the living of their life. The very ones who are vulnerable and exposed now can be buoyant and celebrative. The difference in their situation is the powerful move of God, which staggers human history (see v. 10; 1 Sam. 17:45).

2 Corinthians 6:1–13

"Be reconciled to God—and to us!" Those are not Paul's exact words in 2 Cor. 6:1–13, but they nevertheless come close to capturing his appeal. This reading may pose significant problems for the preacher precisely because Paul so closely links the need for the Corinthians to be reconciled with God (5:20) to their need to be reconciled with Paul and with his fellow workers (6:11–13). Compounding the discomfort caused by this passage is the way Paul rehearses his own "credentials" in the form of the hardships he and his colleagues have endured and the virtues they have exercised in their ministry. Such apparent self-justification prompts the charge that Paul is arrogant; it also brings to mind those contemporary preachers who manipulate people for purposes that are blatantly self-serving. The evangelists who cultivate the flock for their own enrichment make preachers and teachers rightly nervous about passages such as this one.

Paul's time is not ours, however, and identifying contemporary pastors with Paul's apostolic office raises many problems. Some of those problems are historical. To take only the most obvious, the first decades of the church's life required a kind of charismatic and powerful leadership that has difficulty being translated into leadership appropriate to more institutionalized settings. In addition, taking Paul's letters and making of them a manual for contemporary church polity and practice confuses not only two very different historical periods but two different genres. Paul wrote letters, not rule books.

More important than these historical problems with attempting to identify Paul's ministry with that of others, however, is the underlying theological problem. To whom is this passage addressed? As part of the church's Bible, Paul's letters speak to the ordained and the laity alike—they do not speak two distinct words, one for congregations and another for pastors. "Open wide your hearts also" is not a word to be transferred so that twentieth-century pastors may use it to extract reconciliation from their churches (or manipulate them into feelings of guilt about a reconciliation they cannot achieve). Instead, the text addresses all believers alike, and reveals something about the way in which the gospel works in the world.

At the heart of that address in this particular text is a plea for reconciliation with God. The opening lines of the lection continue Paul's exhortation begun in 5:20: "Be reconciled to God." The familiarity of this line may itself obscure its novelty. Over against all those understandings of the human situation that perceive God to need propitiating or mollifying, here the situation is reversed! God has initiated reconciliation (vs. 18–19), God has sent ambassadors on behalf of that reconciliation, and it is human beings who need only to respond to God's reconciling act.

Chapter 6:1–2 continues this appeal by drawing attention to its urgency. The Corinthians should not allow God's grace to be "in vain," but should accept the reconciliation offered them. The "now" and the "day of salvation" of v. 2 place Paul's appeal in its eschatological context. Accepting God's reconciliation is crucial, not because God may withdraw the offer or change the terms, but because the Corinthians themselves need to understand the magnitude of God's gift.

This passage is not only about a relationship between God and the Corinthians, however. Already in 6:1, Paul refers to the "we" who work with God, and in 6:3 the subject becomes the nature of Paul's apostleship. In terms that recall the earlier extended discussion contrasting the way things seem to be with what they really are (see the discussion of 2 Cor. 5:6–17 for Proper 6), Paul itemizes first the difficulties the apostles have faced (vs. 4–5), then their exemplary behavior (vs. 6–7), and finally the anomalies created by the conflict between the way they are perceived by the world and the way they really are (vs. 8–10). He reminds the Corinthians of all this in order to demonstrate that he and his colleagues have indeed "commended" themselves, that is, they have behaved in a way that merited commendation.

With vs. 11–13 the appeal for reconciliation returns, this time an appeal for reconciliation to Paul rather than to God. Yet somehow the two forms of reconciliation are interrelated. As becomes clear throughout 2 Corinthians, Paul understands the relationship between the apostle and the church to be one from which there is and can be no exit. As Paul will boast of the Corinthians on the "day of the Lord," so will they boast of him (1:14); neither side can simply choose another partner.

The relationship between the apostle and the church is important for the gospel itself, not just as a means of securing divine approval. Elsewhere, Paul speaks about the faith of churches becoming a proclamation of the gospel. First Thessalonians eloquently describes the example of the Thessalonian church that has proved so powerful that Paul finds "no need" to preach. If that last statement partakes a bit of hyperbole, it nevertheless reveals the significance Paul attaches to the lives of believers. Their faith, their action, their manner of living the gospel reflects not only on the apostle through whom the gospel came to them, but on the gospel itself. In the relationship between Paul and the Corinthians, much is at stake.

Mark 4:35–41

The early part of Mark's Gospel relates in dramatic ways the in-breaking of God's reign in the life and actions of Jesus. The statement in Mark 1:14–15 of Jesus' preaching in Galilee ("The time is fulfilled, and the kingdom of God has come near") sets the agenda for the rehearsal of the incidents of his ministry that follow in the narrative. The section that begins at 4:35 and continues through 6:6 contains four extraordinary deeds (the calming of the storm, the healings of the Gerasene demoniac and the woman with a flow of blood, and the raising of Jairus's daughter), followed by a response to these deeds by the citizens in Jesus' hometown. In the unfolding of the story, the reader begins to get a sense of what it means that "the kingdom of God has come near."

The Gospel lection for this Sunday confronts us with the astounding event of the stilling of the winds and sea (4:35–41). The event is so remarkable that it is easy to get caught up in the interesting but not very fruitful question of whether, and how, Jesus did it. Historical probes are not totally unimportant, but going behind the text to question or verify the happening tends to divert the reader from the text itself and what it says. What has the preacher really accomplished if she or he convinces a congregation that the stilling really happened, or that there is a rational explanation for the phenomenon, or that the story is a pious fraud? Better to concentrate on the meaning of the story in its context.

The incident takes on added meaning in the recognition that the sea symbolizes throughout the Old Testament the abode of chaos. Repeatedly in the psalms God is praised as the One who "divided the sea by your might" and "broke the heads of the dragons in the waters" (Ps. 74:13; see Job 38:8–11). God's power at the time of the exodus from Egypt is described as a rebuke of the sea and a control of the waters (Pss. 106:9; 114). Thus, when Jesus calms the storm it is not merely a brute demonstration of power over nature, but a redemptive act in which the chaotic forces of the sea, like the demons, are "rebuked" (Mark 4:39). The miracle has a purpose in the rescue of disciples from fear and disorder.

With this recognition, a number of details of the narrative, including Jesus' dialogue with the disciples, make good sense. First, the trip at night across the sea was Jesus' plan (v. 35). This was not a diversion hatched up by the disciples to have a leisurely time with their leader away from the pressures of the crowd. Jesus took the initiative, and the disciples went along at his direction. They had every reason to blame him when the weather changed. After all, the journey was his idea.

Second, the narrator wants us to know that the squall was frightful. Verse 37 provides a picture of a boat in great distress, "already being swamped." The anguish of the disciples, then, was not ill-founded. They were not overreacting when they awakened Jesus with the frantic cry, "Do you not care that we are perishing?" Their situation was desperate, and they turned to the one who brought them on this trip in the first place.

Third, Jesus' sleep is revealing. His own trust in God brings remarkable peace, even in the face of the storm, and contrasts dramatically with the panic of the disciples at the chaos of the sea. His sleeping while the disciples fret is reminiscent of the scene, later, in Gethsemane when the situation is reversed—Jesus frets and the disciples sleep (14:32–41). There is a time for fretting and a time for sleep.

Fourth, it is difficult to type the disciples in light of their words and actions. Jesus' only words to them carry a gentle criticism (4:40). Their panic shows that they have not yet reached a point of profound trust. Though they have received special instructions from Jesus himself (v. 34), they are still asking, "Who is this?" At the same time, they are awe-struck by what Jesus has done. They tremble with the fear appropriate to those who have been in the presence of God's Son, and at least pose the critical question.

Investigating the details of the narrative leads one to the conclusion that the story recognizes those times in the life of the church when it is threatened by the forces of chaos and confusion, forces that turn out to be no match for the reign of God present in the person of Jesus. Certainly the account of the incident found in Matthew's narrative (Matt. 8:23–27) has moved clearly in such a direction—a story of fearful disciples ("you of little faith") and the calming and reassuring Jesus. But the stories present us not merely with the presence of Jesus, who shares our predicament amid the storms of life, but with the power of Jesus, who can do something about the storms. The text confronts us not so much with a strategy for coping, as with a promise of salvation.

PROPER 8

Ordinary Time 13

Sunday between June 26 and July 2 inclusive

On occasion the four passages designated by the lectionary for a given Sunday obviously evidence common themes or patterns that enable them to be neatly woven together into a single sermon. Sometimes common motifs emerge in two or three of the readings, or at least passages can be joined to one another to produce a unified thread. At other times, however, the texts move in different directions, with symbols and language that warrant their being considered on their own. Forcing them together for homiletical purposes either blunts the cutting edges of the passages or threatens to stretch the congregation's imagination beyond credulity.

The latter may be the situation for the readings for this Sunday. At least three of the four have their integrity as continuations from previous weeks. The first reading, for instance, continues a series from the books of Samuel depicting vignettes from the life of David. Today's lection focuses on the lament of David on hearing the news of the deaths of Jonathan and Saul. We hear the anguish of one who has lost in battle both a friend and an enemy, as well as the devastating sadness of war itself.

The epistolary selection is the fifth in a series of six readings from 2 Corinthians. The appeal made for the collection to be taken to Jerusalem is rooted in the grace manifest in Jesus' becoming "poor" and in the importance of the offering as an expression of the unity of Jews and Gentiles as one people of God.

Mark, of course, is the primary Gospel for the B cycle of the lectionary. The progression through the narrative reaches today the tightly interwoven stories of the raising of Jairus's daughter and the healing of the woman with a hemorrhage. The juxtaposing of the two characters and Jesus' interaction with both open interesting avenues for preaching.

Psalm 130 is the most likely selection to be used in conjunction with one or another of the passages. Operating from the vantage of one already forgiven, the psalmist anticipates from God the gift of what he does not yet have. Expectation is born of confidence and trust.

2 Samuel 1:1, 17-27

One of the remarkable things about David is the ability of his spirit to soar to great heights of creative expression at moments of profound meaning in his life or in that of the nation. Scoundrel that he could be, as witness the affair with Bathsheba and her husband, Uriah (2 Sam. 11-12), David was nonetheless capable of deep insights into the meaning of human life and into the implications for human life of the presence of the God of Israel. Even if it may not be completely correct in all its details, ancient Israel's memory of David as a tender and provocative poet/musician recognizes the extraordinary powers of the nation's second king.

According to the Deuteronomistic historians, those powers were deployed to their fullest extent in David's reaction to the deaths of Jonathan, his friend, and Saul, his enemy. David's lament seems to have found its way into an ancient anthology of texts entitled the Book of Jashar (the Upright One), which celebrated the exploits of some of Israel's earliest leaders (note Josh. 10:13). From that collection the lament was taken over in order to illuminate the character of David's heart at a pivotal occasion in the nation's life (2 Sam. 1:18).

The poetic power of the lament is unmistakable. Three times (vs. 19, 25, 27) a refrain is repeated: "How the mighty have fallen!" yet each occurrence is framed differently. In v. 19 the phrase appears alone, while in v. 25 it is followed by "in the midst of battle." Verse 27, which concludes the entire lament, appends to the refrain the added cry of anguish, "and the weapons of war perished!" Here the strength of the refrain moves beyond a recognition of the tragedy of the deaths of Israel's king and his son to a statement concerning the consummate sadness of war itself.

The opening line (v. 19a) sums up the mood of the entire poem, and in this regard it reminds the reader of other Old Testament laments (compare Ps. 22:1). The word translated by NRSV as "glory" may also mean "beauty" or "honor," so the poet seems intent on saying not only that Israel's "best and brightest" have fallen, but also felled are those human qualities of courage and loyalty which are quintessentially Israelite. The reader, of course, senses the irony in all of this: the "glory" is much more fully embodied in David, the singer of the song, than in either of its subjects. The very act of acknowledging the "glory" of Saul and Jonathan reveals the greater "glory" of David.

Much in this poetic tribute to Saul and Jonathan is somewhat predictable, even if expressed in literature of great beauty. The scorn felt for the enemies of one's people, which does not wish to permit them to rejoice at their victory (v. 20), and the aversion felt toward even the ground on which the lamented heroes died (v. 21) are sentiments that are understandable, if not especially remarkable. In a similar vein is the description of Saul and Jonathan as irresistible warriors (v. 22).

What is more noteworthy is the manner in which Saul and Jonathan are accorded equal, or at least similar, respect. They are both described (v. 23) as "beloved and lovely," "swifter than eagles, . . . stronger than lions." "In life and in death they were not divided [or separated]" may be a manner of reflecting positively on the character of Jonathan, in that he, unlike David who fled from Saul's presence and wound up in the Philistine army (1 Sam. 29), remained loyal to his father to the end.

The twofold nature of the tribute continues in that, while v. 26 is addressed to Jonathan's memory, v. 24 acknowledges the legacy of Saul. Saul's contribution to the nation's life takes the form of a metaphor in which a father clothes his daughters with fine clothing and jewelry (or is it a husband adorning his harem?). In a sense, this is a strange figure of speech, because the evidence suggests that the Israelite tribes were, on the whole, quite poor during Saul's lifetime. But the one thing that Saul did contribute to Israel's life was a sense of dignity, in that the Philistine threat and that of other hostile neighbors was met, if not dispelled. Because of Saul's leadership, Israel was able at least to begin the difficult journey from a tribal confederation to a genuine nation-state, an accomplishment much more to be treasured than rich garments and decorations.

Interestingly, Jonathan, the great warrior (1 Sam. 14), is celebrated most lavishly not for his great skills in battle, but for his personal loyalty to David (v. 26). The reader of today's lection will remember the narratives of Jonathan's commitment to David (1 Sam. 18–20), a devotion that flew right in the face of Jonathan's own self-interest, in that David's presence in Saul's court and his continued survival in the wilderness meant that David's claim to Israel's throne constituted a threat to Jonathan's own princely prerogatives. But because Jonathan's loyalty to David transcended his own personal concerns, it became in the memory of ancient Israel the epitome of what human friendship should be. Not even love between man and woman could surpass that of David and Jonathan.

And finally to the refrain once more (v. 27). The ultimate realization of the text is not just that Saul and Jonathan are dead, but that part of the legacy of war is overwhelming sadness.

Psalm 130

This well-known and beloved psalm has been read mostly through the Pauline-Lutheran notion of the wretchedness of "the human condition." And, indeed, "the human condition" of iniquity is present in Ps. 130:3, 8. The intention of the psalm, however, is not to comment on that wretchedness, but to speak about, and to enact, a transformation that liberates those in the depths into new freedom.

The psalm begins a passionate, pathos-filled petition. This is Israel's primal address to God, characteristically voiced from a situation of deep need and impotence. This petition is "out of the depths," from a deep valley where one can hardly muster a prayer. The noteworthy matter is that a faithful Israelite is not a mute Israelite. Even in such a situation of deep need, the Israelite still speaks, still names God, still voices a petition, still makes an insistence, still sounds needy, and in so doing, still hopes.

The petition is not specified, beyond wanting to be heard by God. Perhaps wanting to be heard at all is the first urging of any Israelite, for Israel knows that the conversation with God itself is a saving, liberating transaction. Israel wants to be heard, for being heard means being honored, taken seriously, and thereby empowered.

It is conventional to say that the core petition of this psalm is a prayer for forgiveness. I am inclined, however, to take vs. 3–4 not as the core petition, but as a quite subordinate clause which serves to support the petition of vs. 1–2. The speaker does not ask for forgiveness. The speaker acknowledges a large measure of iniquity, which on its own terms would preclude petition and disqualify the petitioner. The speaker knows and trusts, however, that God's forgiveness has long since overridden any disqualifying iniquity or guilt. Thus forgiveness is not sought, but is assumed as the basis of the conversation. This taken-as-certain forgiveness is not an outcome of devotion to Yahweh (fearing God = "revere"), but is the premise of revering God. Thus the speaker does not grovel in guilt, but accepts as a premise for petition that forgiveness has already been granted, even before the petition. The speaker is, then, revering

God, that is, taking God with utmost seriousness, but is doing so on the basis of a life long since pardoned. This is the prayer of a forgiven, untroubled speaker, not any longer looking back in guilt but willing to leave iniquity in the sure hands of God. The overriding tone of the psalm is one of glad liberation. The prayer is the voice of a genuinely free person.

The speaker thus looks forward in eager longing and expectation, watching for what God will do, confident that God's promises are reliable and that their newness will create great good and well-being. This is not a poem of groveling guilt, but of liberated expectation. In vs. 5–6, the sequence "wait/hope/wait" is the Hebrew triad *qûh, qûh, yḥl,* so that the initial term *qûh* is in the NRSV rendered both as "wait" and "hope," and is a synonym for *yḥl,* "wait." Thus "wait" and "hope" are complete synonyms. They both bespeak active, eager anticipation that God will bring a newness that is well beyond anything known in the present tense.

The triad of hope is reinforced by the double use of the verb "watch" *šmr,* which refers to the night watchman, vigil, or sentry who stands alertly on guard to anticipate any intrusion that will disrupt or disturb. The watching of a sentry can be defensive, but it can also be anticipatory, as in waiting for a messenger with an order or with a battle report, or the arrival of much-needed supplies. This petition waits for God's future, and welcomes it with eagerness.

Only now, in vs. 7–8, are the petition of vs. 1–2 and the watchful hope of vs. 5–6 given any substance. The verb "hope" (*yḥl*) in v. 7 picks up on the verbs of v. 5. But now we learn the reality of that hope. It is expected that God's *ḥesed,* God's steadfast, abiding loyalty will now act for Israel, for the depths have been the place where God's *ḥesed* has been absent. The psalm voices Erik Erikson's "basic trust," in which buoyant Israel hopes for that which it does not have in hand, because it trusts fully in God's faithfulness.

The content of that hope from God, the outcome of that *ḥesed,* is voiced in the double use of the verb "redeem." While the last phrase reduces "redeem" to the problem of sin (see vs. 3–4), in fact the term "redeem" in Israel carries all the liberating potential of God's acts related to every social condition that renders one powerless. Israel is redeemed from bondage, but individual persons are liberated as well from loneliness, sickness, and prison as well as from sin. Thus this psalm enacts, in anticipation, the entire drama of the gospel. The petitioner is in the depths, but the waiting and reliance upon God's *ḥesed* anticipate a whole new life of freedom, dignity, and well-being. The past acts of God wrought in *ḥesed* make present-tense confidence possible, even in a miserable circumstance.

2 Corinthians 8:7–15

Those who were reared with the tithe as a virtual rule of faith may find this passage strange. Paul does not hesitate to command certain behaviors, as in the case of the man living with his stepmother in 1 Cor. 5 or some portions of his discussion of marriage in 1 Cor. 7. Here, by contrast, no matter how strong his convictions about its importance, he *advises* the Corinthians to participate in the collection. He does not command.

In making the case for his advice, Paul appeals to the wealth and poverty of Jesus Christ. Jesus was rich and became poor for our sake "so that by his poverty you might become rich" (2 Cor. 8:9). Paul appeals to what the gospel has already accomplished, and implicitly urges the Corinthians to live out that accomplishment. To paraphrase, "Jesus has already made you rich, so you should act on the basis of that new reality."

Now what readers expect is the closing of the appeal in words something like the following: "Last year, you began not just to promise to make this gift but to make it. Now you need to finish the task." He does urge finishing the task, but notice the wording of v. 10: "You . . . began last year not only to do something but even to desire to do something." What sense does that ordering of statements make? You started not only to set money aside but even to desire to set money aside? Usually people speak of making a commitment to a project and then completing it, but Paul has reversed that order. The Corinthians have apparently made some start at the collection, but what is more important is that they *desired* to make that gift. What Paul implies is that the gift must be the result of a free decision rather than made from compulsion.

The final segment of the lesson makes that implicit point explicit: "*If the eagerness is there,* the gift is acceptable" (emphasis added). Admittedly, most people who ask for money would be all too happy to accept any check on which the signature is valid, whether given eagerly or with bitter reluctance. Paul works with a highly integrated sense of the whole person, and that wholeness certainly influences his understanding of giving. Particularly in the context of this collection for Jerusalem Christians, a gift that symbolizes the unity of Jew and Gentile in the church, the attitude toward the gift cannot be separated from the gift itself.

The final lines of this passage have to do with balance between these two parts of the community, Gentile Christians and the Jerusalem poor. In Rom. 15, Paul speaks of the spiritual debt Gentiles owe to Jews, a debt that is paid (in part, at least) by the collection. Here he argues in a more pragmatic vein, as did any number of moralists of his day. Balance is the ideal, so that those who have an abundance should assist others. He undergirds this principle with a quotation from Ex. 16:18, a quotation drawn from the story of God's gift of manna. Part of the miracle of the manna is that, no matter how much or how little individuals gathered, no one had too much or too little.

These closing lines of 8:7–15 are among the few times when Paul's discussion of the collection appeals to the Corinthians to consider the needs of others. That is not to say that he is indifferent to need, or that the Corinthians would not be swayed by a description of the need in Jerusalem, but need alone does not establish Paul's case. His case depends on the claim that God, in the gospel of Jesus Christ, has made available to Christians the gift of acting out among themselves the same love they see and experience in the obedience of Jesus Christ.

Some aspects of Paul's appeal for funds in 2 Cor. 8–9 seem blatantly manipulative and overstated. At the same time, this passage astonishes with its understatement. Paul sees this collection as a matter of immense significance in the life of the church, and its failure would be devastating. Nevertheless, he approaches it as a matter of grace rather than as a matter of obligation. Even his use of the generosity of Jesus points in this direction. He does not say, "Jesus gave himself for you, therefore you are obliged to give for others." Instead, the generosity of Jesus stands for the Corinthians to draw their own conclusions.

In another and shocking way this passage understates the matter of the collection: for whom is this fund being gathered? Its destination is "the poor among the saints at Jerusalem" (Rom. 15:26). These are poor Jewish Christians, almost certainly part of the Christian community under the leadership of Peter and James. While Peter and James and their wing of the church were not Paul's enemies, even the most naive reading of Acts and Galatians reveals some friction between them and Paul. Probably there was more than a little conflict. Paul, however, says nothing in 2 Corinthians about the fact that the collection will go to those whose understanding of the gospel differs substantially from his own. These are Christians who are in need. The offering does not celebrate their disunity; rather, he hopes that, by the grace of God, it will symbolize their unity.

Mark 5:21–43

The skillful manner in which the narrator has woven the two stories of the healing of the woman with a hemorrhage and the raising of Jairus's daughter in Mark 5:21–43 paves the way for a comparison of the two figures and the two incidents. In what has come to be characteristic Markan style, one story is interrupted by the intrusion of another story, which then is completed before the former story is resumed. The dramatic effect is remarkable and leads to all sorts of observations about how the two characters are similar and how they are different. Although either incident can be isolated as a text for preaching, something is gained by following the narrator in linking the two.

The similarities are obvious. Both characters take the initiative in dealing with Jesus, and both do so out of a desperate and hopeless situation. Jairus throws himself at Jesus' feet and repeatedly begs him to come and heal his daughter, who is near death. Any parent can identify with his pain and panic at the prospect of losing a child. The woman is in an equally desperate situation, having an apparently incurable hemorrhaging that has left her not only physically weak, but ritually unclean. For twelve years she has been treated as an outcast, isolated from the mainstream of Jewish religious and social life.

Both Jairus and the woman are confronted with pronouncements by the experts that their situations are beyond help. The interesting detail about the expenditure of all her money and the failure of the physicians to help the woman (5:26) not only testifies to the seriousness of her malady but also to the impotence of the professionals. Merely touching the hem of his garment, releasing power from Jesus, presents a startling contrast to the doctors' powerlessness. Likewise, Jairus is faced with the experts who seek to dissuade him from pursuing help from Jesus. There is no use: "Your daughter is dead" (5:35). One can imagine their side comments, lamenting Jairus's inability to accept the "truth" about his daughter. They "laugh" at Jesus' hopeful diagnosis (5:40). Had the woman accepted the results of the doctors' efforts or Jairus the announcement of the professionals, there apparently would have been no miracle.

In spite of their circumstances, both characters come to Jesus in faith. The text indicates no hesitancy in Jairus's plea, no "*If* you can help me, please do so." He has confidence that Jesus' touch will heal (5:23). Later, when friends come from the wake at Jairus's house to tell him of his daughter's death, Jesus' words probably should be translated, "Do not fear, only keep on believing" (5:36). It is rather astonishing that this esteemed religious leader of the synagogue would demonstrate such trust in another religious leader whom his fellow Jews were plotting to destroy (3:6). The woman also acts in faith. Like Jairus, she expects that physical contact with Jesus will bring her relief (5:27–28). She will not settle for the despairing results of the physicians. When she comes forward and identifies herself as the one who touched Jesus, he commends her faith. Verse 34 certainly refers to more than physical healing (literally, "your faith has saved you"). Since her illness has involved both religious and social isolation, what is confirmed is shalom, a wholeness, a restoration of enormous proportions.

But there are marked contrasts between these two characters who come to Jesus. Jairus is a leader of the synagogue, a respected religious official, who approaches Jesus in public, in the face of a large crowd. There is no reproach of Jairus hinted at in the text, except that he presents a sharply different picture from the nameless woman with the unmentionable problem that has kept her from attending Jairus's synagogue. Whether it was natural shyness or embarrassment about the nature of her illness or what, she decides to make her move in secret, anticipating that the pressing crowd will prevent her being exposed. Not meaning to, she gains Jesus' attention.

Here the "sandwiching" of the two stories is significant. The picture depicts Jesus hurrying to Jairus's house, when time is of the essence, yet stopping to search for and converse with the unclean woman without a name. She is of no less importance to Jesus than the child of this prominent religious leader. She becomes in the text a perpetual reminder that the socially and religiously marginal have a conspicuous place in the realization of God's reign.

A final word needs to be said on the miraculous character of the raising of Jairus's daughter. There is no question that the story describes a resuscitation of a corpse, confirmed by the girl's walking about and eating. But, like the raising of Lazarus in John 11, the girl is restored to an earthly existence from which she will still have to die. The attention of the narrative seems more focused on the persistent trust of Jairus, who believes in the power of Jesus and will not be dissuaded by the certitude of those voicing the claims of death. The report of the miracle serves to vindicate a faith that refuses to capitulate to such voices.

PROPER 9

Ordinary Time 14

*Sunday between
July 3 and 9 inclusive*

No issues demand so much careful thought in the church as those that cluster around the place of faith in the public arena. In what way can God's purposes be fulfilled in and through the actions of the state? How and to what end is power to be exercised? What is the role of church members in the political process?

The discussions of such issues in the Bible do not always provide clear-cut solutions to our modern problems, because the historical circumstances then and now are dramatically different. Israel as a state and Israel as a religious community are impossible to separate; the church in the first century is a marginal group totally outside the circles of power and hardly to be equated with the church in the West today.

Furthermore, the selections for this Sunday illustrate the highly dialectical relationship in which Old Testament and New Testament passages often stand with regard to such matters. Second Samuel 5 celebrates David's acceptance by the whole nation as the shepherd-king, the expression of the covenantal union between God and Israel. David as a political figure is to fulfill God's purposes, in spite of his many weaknesses. Psalm 48 sings of the wondrous city of Jerusalem, the national capital, at once the symbol of royal power and the symbol of divine promise.

Over against these affirmations of Israel's political structures come the texts from the New Testament. From 2 Cor. 12 we learn of Paul's thorn in the flesh and the clear word that God's true power comes to expression in weakness and not in the events that might otherwise seem to validate a mighty God—victories, successes, and the like. The criteria for discerning God's presence are radically redefined by the cross. The narrative for this is Mark 6, where Jesus is the prophet who is rejected in his own hometown and the Twelve are ordained for a mission that will also face rejection. Neither Jesus nor the Twelve can expect patronage from the political authorities, nor do they seek it.

The conclusion of the dialectical relationship of the text is not that the Old Testament deals with politics and the New Testament with spiritual matters. It is, rather, the acknowledgment that the state can sometimes be the agent of God's purposes and sometimes their enemy.

2 Samuel 5:1–5, 9–10

The Old Testament lections, which trace ancient Israel's transition from tribal confederation to monarchy, now reach an important point in this narrative of David's acceptance by all the tribes as Israel's king. The young son of Jesse had already been anointed by Samuel—at Yahweh's direction (1 Sam. 16, see Proper 6), and a somewhat older David had subsequently been accepted as ruler by the people of his native Judah (2 Sam. 2:1–4a). Now the leaders of the remaining tribes make the journey down to David's temporary capital at Hebron and profess that he is their king, as well. The interval between the two latter events has, of course, been punctuated by a "long war" (2 Sam. 3:1) involving those loyal to David, on the one hand, and, on the other, Saulite forces who support Ishbaal, or Ishbosheth, as he is also called. Only with the collapse of the Saulite cause is it now possible for David to claim the loyalty of a unified nation.

There is no completely satisfactory explanation for the deep north-south division which is later to result in the rupture of the kingdom, following the death of Solomon (1 Kings 12). But the present professions of loyalty by the Israelite (as contrasted with the Judahite) leaders are both a testimony to David's skill in bringing the nation together and, at the same time, a reminder that not even David's enormous personal charisma will be sufficient to heal this division permanently.

The manner in which our text describes this significant moment in David's career as Yahweh's anointed is noteworthy in several respects. Second Samuel 5:2 refers to David's personal rule over the nation as that of a "shepherd." This theme is sounded so often in the Old Testament that it is easy to allow its familiarity to dull its impact. The shepherd is the one who protects the flock and who, at the same time, leads them into that future which is appropriate and right. David's own vocation as a youth is certainly the foundation for this metaphor, and the manner in which it is reinforced at several points in the Old Testament text, such as 2 Sam. 7:8 and Ezek. 34:23–24, has led generations of both Jewish and Christian readers to stress the David-shepherd connection in their interpretation even of passages where the linkage is not tightly drawn by the text itself (for example, Ps. 23). Be that as it may, it is certainly an image that the Old Testament wishes the reader to retain, and, as is quite obvious, it is one that fundamentally shapes the New Testament understanding of the life and ministry of Jesus (as in John 10:11–18).

A second significant point in our lection is achieved in the use of the word "covenant" to denote the larger meaning of what is happening at this moment (v. 3). The text is intent on driving home a lesson which, like the shepherd image, is raised repeatedly, and that lesson is that David is no ordinary personality, nor is his rule an ordinary act of political suzerainty. Because David has been chosen by none other than Yahweh and has been anointed by Yahweh's agent, Samuel, there are important theological dimensions to this political relationship. In other words, the bond is not just between the people and David, but between the people and their God! David is, in one sense, the cement by which this bonding takes place. Second Samuel 7 is surely the most extensive expression within the Old Testament of the Davidic covenant, but it finds other literary formulations as well, as in 2 Kings 23:1–3, where the covenant ceremony of King Josiah is understood to be a renewal of that covenant embodied in the rule of King David (compare 2 Kings 22:2). Again, as in the matter of David as shepherd, the understanding of David as the incarnation of the covenantal union between God and the people is embraced in the Christian understanding of who Jesus is, so that the very name of the Christian scriptures, New Testament or New Covenant (a designation apparently made with Jer. 31:31–34 in mind), announces that in Jesus Christ, God's covenantal love has been reaffirmed in fresh and astounding ways.

A third important statement in the present lection is contained in 2 Sam. 5:10, which states, in effect, that Yahweh's choice of David is continually ratified as the anointed one pursues his kingly tasks. (Verse 9, which is included in the lectionary text, assumes information provided in vs. 6–8, which are not included. Because the omitted section is quite brief and may easily be accommodated in the liturgical reading of the text, the preacher may wish to treat all of vs. 1–10 as the lectionary unit. It is only fitting that this newly ordained and installed king should have a capital city that is emblematic of the nation's unity before God. And so the old citadel in Judean Hebron is left behind in favor of the newly conquered Jerusalem, which, with its Jebusite past, is linked to none of the Israelite tribes. Verse 9, therefore, not only provides a brief introduction to the theologically important v. 10 and to much that is yet to come in the nation's life, but it also concludes and summarizes an important phase in David's career.) Verse 10 affirms that the "mistake" made in the appointment of Saul, a "mistake" that Yahweh "regretted" (1 Sam. 15:11), has not been repeated. David will live up to the promises of the Lord and will, thereby, not only lead his people to greatness, but serve as personal confirmation that the purposes of the Lord are true. Not even David's enormous weaknesses (2 Sam. 11–12, see Propers 12 and 13) will be able to nullify the Lord's faithfulness to the people.

Psalm 48

Paired with the narrative account of King David's conquest of the ancient city of Jerusalem, Ps. 48 is a liturgical celebration of Jerusalem as the wondrous city of God's residence. The "city of God" (vs. 1, 8), with its Temple (v. 9), is "Mount Zion" (vs. 11, 12). It is commonly thought, however, that this poem celebrating Jerusalem as God's physical habitat is in fact an older hymn, which originally had nothing to do with the faith of Israel or with the city of Jerusalem but was appropriated for liturgical-political use there. The reference to the "far north" (v. 2) suggests that the psalm originally referred, in pre-Israelite mythology, to a mountain dwelling of the gods in the far north of the land bridge of the Fertile Crescent. All these old mythological legitimacies for the holy place as God's habitat have been preempted and reassigned in Davidic ideology in order to enhance Jerusalem, theologically and politically.

The psalm begins with magisterial praise for Yahweh, which is matched in v. 3 by a lyrical comment about God. Between v. 1a and v. 3, however, the opening lines are not about God, but about God's place in its loveliness. There runs through this psalm an inclination to merge together the wonder of God and the wonder of the city, so that the city itself takes on some of the theological significance that properly belongs only to God. Such a transposition serves the ideological purposes of the royal city and enhances the political claims and interests of the royal dynasty and apparatus that inhabit and control the city. Thus we are, in my judgment, required to hear this psalm with a good deal of suspicion about its ideological undercurrent.

The political spin-off of the theological legitimacy of the city is immediately evident in verses 4–8. The psalm imagines a scene in which kings hostile to Jerusalem gather to lay siege to and attack the city. When they arrive to begin the attack, however, they are awestruck by the city. They see not only its loveliness, but also its impenetrability. They realize in an instant that their mission is a foolish, impossible one. There is no way they can succeed against this citadel, so powerful and so lovely. In a quick turn, the bold attackers become aware of their own exposed, vulnerable situation. They are filled with fear and terror. Not only do they not attack the city, but in great fear they retreat, lucky to escape without being destroyed.

The attack on Jerusalem has turned out to be a complete reversal for those who attacked. The reversal has occurred without any gesture on the part of Jerusalem or its God. Jerusalem, in its formidable splendor, needed only to sit there immovable in order to have its own way. Thus defeat of the nations by Jerusalem may be read at three very different levels:

1. At a surface level, the city itself is triumphant and works the defeat.

2. At a theological level, it is the God who lives in the city who confounds the other, rival kings (on which see Ps. 2).

3. At a political level, it is the Davidic king (who is present here only by inference) who lives alongside of and in the service of Yahweh, who benefits from this scenario (see Ps. 2:7). Not only Jerusalem and its God, but also its political establishment, are thus enhanced and secured.

Verses 9–11 of Ps. 48 are still preoccupied with the place, with Mt. Zion and its Temple. There are, however, woven into the place-theme important affirmations about the God who inhabits this Temple, the God praised in vs. 1a, 3. In v. 9, a characteristic Israelite theme is announced, which we do not expect here, God's *ḥesed*, God's sure fidelity. This focus on God's own character is reinforced by reference to God's powerful name and God's triumphant right hand. Thus the psalm is not completely smitten by the place, but attends to the God who only restlessly stays in the city.

The same tension between place and person is evident in the concluding verses. The conclusion is again primarily impressed by the physical quality of the city. The poet invites the listener on a tour of the city, in order to inspect its impressive fortifications and to feel the safety and security that are palpable in the city. In the midst of that congratulatory eloquence, however, the psalm finally ends, not with the place, but with the person of God, the God who is utterly reliable and durable, who not only sits in the Temple, but who leads Israel's risky life.

There is no doubt that Jerusalem is a profoundly ambiguous symbol in the Old Testament. It is celebrated as the seat of royal power and as the residence of the God who orders the world well. It is critiqued and assaulted by the prophets as the locus of self-serving, self-deceiving royal ideology that must be overcome. It is the focus of Israel's most powerful promise from God.

In current theological practice, this ambiguity is clear in the function of the city in Jewish-Christian thought. On the one hand, in extreme forms of Zionist thinking the city that houses God has become a rallying point for intransigent political ideology. On the other hand, in much Christian urging Zion has been transposed into God's ultimate intention for reordering the world in new and faithful ways. And that same positive symbolization is embraced by many Jews as well. No doubt Jews and Christians, in their shared and separate traditions, must continue that vexing interpretive work of holding together the city as current locus of power and as anticipatory promise of ultimate well-being. In Mannheim's language, the city feeds both "ideology and utopia."

2 Corinthians 12:2–10

Exegetical imaginations occasionally run out of control with this passage. Attempts to coordinate Paul's comments about the "third heaven" with biographical details gleaned from elsewhere in his letters produce accounts that are interesting if not convincing. Speculation about Paul's "thorn in the flesh" ranges wildly from physical causes to psychological causes and even to marital distress. Along the way, unfortunately, the trees of such fanciful reconstructions obscure the forest of the letter's larger context.

Attention to context here is essential, or the passage will remain a collection of enigmas. In 2 Cor. 10–13, Paul constructs a sharp defense of his ministry by waging an equally sharp attack on some other Christian preachers who have made their way to Corinth. Portions of 1 Corinthians and preceding sections of 2 Corinthians already demonstrate that Paul's authority at Corinth is an unstable commodity, but here the situation is desperate. The so-called "super-apostles" (11:5) have attacked Paul on the ground that he does not sufficiently exhibit the powers appropriate to an apostle. He does not accomplish great deeds, he has not been the recipient of marvelous spiritual experiences, and he accomplishes no miracles. If he had such achievements, he would surely boast of them.

In response to these charges, Paul begins in 11:16 what is customarily referred to as his "fool's speech," a section of the letter in which he parodies his opponents. While he refuses to play their game of boasting about his real accomplishments, he does humor the Corinthians' need for apostolic boasting by boasting of things that are the mirror image of their expectations. Instead of boasting of things that show his strength and power, he boasts of those that demonstrate his weakness and vulnerability.

When Paul speaks of "a person in Christ," he almost certainly refers to himself (12:2). The remainder of the discussion of this vision makes little sense if Paul is not the recipient of it. Throughout this tiny narrative, Paul both tells of the vision and simultaneously distances himself from it, and referring to himself in the third person may serve to reinforce the attitude toward visions that he wishes to inculcate. Similarly, when Paul twice comments "whether in the body or out of the body I do not know; God knows," he attributes both the cause of this experience and its proper understanding to God alone.

Verses 5–7a reinforce Paul's reluctance about boasting. Although he could boast about himself, he insists that he will not do so (again with tongue in cheek). He will speak only of others or only of his weaknesses.

Verses 7b–9a move from "boasting" about visions to "boasting" about great deeds. Lest Paul become too elated with his own achievements, God gave him "a thorn," "a messenger of Satan." Whatever particular malady or difficulty this "thorn" might be is utterly insignificant, because the question is whether Paul can prevail over it or persuade God to do so on his behalf. Rather than boasting of his powerful ability to work wonders, Paul recalls three occasions on which he prayed for relief and three occasions on which his request was denied. If the scene depicted in vs. 1–4 is an inverted vision, this is an inverted miracle.

What response did the Corinthians make to Paul's dramatic, even outrageous, comments? Virtually no evidence exists that permits a historical answer to that question. As much as it is attractive to imagine that they saw the error of their judgment and adopted Paul's view of things, the arguments of Paul's detractors were strong ones. The arguments continue to be strong, even if not necessarily couched in terms of healings and visions. How are congregations and ministers assessed if not in terms of their powers, powers to attract quantities of people and quantities of money? That ongoing phenomenon may suggest that the question with which Paul and the Corinthians are struggling in this section of 2 Corinthians is not a question for only one moment in Christian history, but for every moment.

The closing lines of this passage sound themes that are familiar from 2 Cor. 1–9. Paul does not need a miraculous resolution of his difficulty, whatever its nature, because the Lord said, "My grace is sufficient for you, for power is made perfect in weakness" (12:9). This is not a glorification of weakness as such or for its own sake, but because in weakness "the power of Christ" dwells in Paul. Paul's very weakness is transformed into strength (v. 10).

An earlier lection from 2 Corinthians drew attention to the integral relationship Paul sees between the apostle and the congregation (see Proper 7 on 2 Cor. 6:1–13). Here the theological undergirding of that relationship becomes clear. Paul, like the Corinthians and all believers, experiences the life of Christ in his own person. The "body of Christ" imagery of 1 Cor. 12:12–31 draws on this same understanding. Because of the deep and abiding connection between the apostle and Christ, Paul is able to see his own weaknesses as instances in which the strength of the gospel can be manifested.

Mark 6:1–13

The choice of the parameters of the Gospel lesson for this Sunday seems unusual. The passage is composed of two fairly discrete sections. In most structural outlines Mark 6:1–6a serves as the conclusion to a section that has highlighted not only Jesus' mighty works but also the responses to him by particular individuals and groups. Mark 6:6b–13, in relating the call and sending out of the disciples, introduces a new section in which the ministry of Jesus moves out beyond Galilee and includes Gentiles as well as Jews. The preacher may want to select one or the other of the two sections as the text for the sermon.

The skeptical rejection of Jesus by the people of his hometown (vs. 1–6a) provides a fitting ending to the earlier section of the Gospel. On the one hand, the Pharisees, offended by Jesus' activities on the Sabbath, "conspired with the Herodians against him, how to destroy him" (3:6). Jesus' family, troubled by his behavior, "went out to restrain him" (3:21). The scribes from Jerusalem accused him of operating as an agent of Beelzebul (3:22). On the other hand, the woman with a twelve-year hemorrhage (5:34) and Jairus, the leader of the synagogue, demonstrate remarkable faith in Jesus, even in the face of detractors. Some seed fell along the path or on rocky ground or among the thorns, but some fell on good soil and bore fruit.

Two questions arise with this text. First, why do Jesus' fellow townspeople reject him? They are initially astonished at his teaching in the synagogue, but then begin to wonder how all this could come from the mouth of Mary's boy, the one with whom they had grown up. Then they reject him. The Greek verb translated "took offense" (6:3) is used elsewhere in Mark to depict those who begin but then fall away (4:17), those who start walking but then stumble (9:42–48), those who become deserters (14:27–29).

The defection of the Nazareth citizens is obviously linked to Jesus' roots. Their expectations preclude the possibility that he could be anything more than a hometown kid who is putting on airs. Their preconceived notions prevent their entertaining the thought that Jesus could be the embodiment of God's promised rule. And so another group who could, like Jesus' family, be called insiders turn out to be outsiders.

It is the same old story at the heart of many rejections of Jesus. When measured by the criteria set by the world as to what a religious leader worth his salt ought to be, he simply does not stand up well. He is not successful enough or influential enough or prestigious enough to merit a wholehearted commitment. His invasive presence is forestalled by the carefully constructed preconceptions that enable people to dismiss him.

The second question that arises is, does the story provide a clear statement about the necessity of faith as a precondition to Jesus' doing mighty works? Can God act only when we pray for it and expect it to happen? That appears to be the point of 6:5–6 and could be supported by the many miracle stories in which the faith of the recipient is mentioned *prior to* Jesus' action; for example, the leper (1:40–41), the paralytic (2:5), the woman with hemorrhaging (5:28, 34), and Jairus (5:22–23). The prominent exceptions, however, such as the exorcisms, prevent an unambiguous answer to the question, and perhaps suggest that the rejection at Nazareth is not primarily intended to provide a solution to the relation of faith and miracle. It seems more to serve as a dramatic contrast to the stories of other characters in need who simply trust Jesus' power and receive his help.

The second section of the lection (6:6b–13) describes the third call of the disciples (1:16–20; 3:13–19) and their mission in the surrounding villages. They are empowered and instructed by Jesus and apparently carry on a successful campaign, consisting of preaching, healing, and exorcism.

Three features of the commissioning are particularly instructive. (a) The disciples are authorized by Jesus (6:7). At the very heart of their mission lies a call of Jesus to be engaged in just this venture. This means that not only do they derive their direction from him, but he also gives them power to do the same mighty works that he has done. By his decision and not theirs, they become the extension of his ministry.

The point is worth repeating regularly in most congregations. Before the church is a voluntary organization it is a community constituted by the call and commission of Christ. Only then is it able to fulfill its mandate to preach and heal in the name of Jesus.

(b) Jesus' instructions call for lean, unencumbered disciples. The order to dispense with extra food and clothes and money is to be construed as a demand not for asceticism, but for simplicity. Traveling light has its dividends. The traveler is free from bearing unnecessary burdens and is not tempted to turn the journey into a venture for profit. Again, the point is worth reflection in these days when the church faces its own loss of status and power and struggles to know how to position itself for the future.

(c) The reality of rejection must be taken seriously. The shaking off the dust from the sandals may be a visible "testimony" to just how significant such a rejection is, done in the hope that a change of mind may yet take place. In any event, the disciples do not go with the promise that every listener of their sermons will repent. They should be neither surprised nor discouraged when doors are slammed in their faces. After all, Jesus has received just such a response from religious officials, from the citizens of his hometown, and even from his family.

PROPER 10

Ordinary Time 15

*Sunday between
July 10 and 16 inclusive*

"Ordinary time" in the church is indeed a time of joy. Three of these texts take up the theme of joy, and give varying expressions of the joy of faith. In the Old Testament reading, David dances a dance toward Yahweh, a dance of utter self-abandonment and of delight in the presence and blessing of God. It is disputed whether this is such an "innocent" Yahwistic dance as the narrator would have us believe, or if the king's ritual activity has traces of the sexually exotic. Either way, David dances the delight of creation.

The psalm is (as is 2 Sam. 6) perhaps worship before the ark. But now celebration in the presence of God has become more formidable, stylized, and self-conscious. The joy of this doxology is joy that the world safely belongs to God, and that this body of worshipers is admitted into the circle of those who have access to the blessings of the Creator. The lyrical, doxological affirmation of God's love for the world is given in grandest scope in the Epistle reading. The poet who crafted this doxology speaks in sweeping terms of the whole of reality caught up in God's great, generous intention.

The Gospel reading is not one of joy, but of violence, brutality, and death. (Three out of four texts for joy is not bad!) This text suggests that the joy of God's good news comes as threat against all pseudo-living (as embodied by Herod). It evokes violent resistance, which in turn eventuates in suffering, loss, death, and surely grief. The murder of John sets up the terrible dialectic of the gospel, "A time to mourn, and a time to dance" (Eccl. 3:4). While dance dominates this set of readings, the dance is so dangerous that we in our tenuous joy are always at risk of brutality inflicted for serious obedience. the world (like Herod) does not take active affirmation of God's rule readily. People lose their heads if they claim too much for the gospel—too much joy, too much demand.

2 Samuel 6:1–5, 12b–19

The presence of God in human life results in a joy that exceeds that generated b other relationships and by the usual day-to-day experiences of life. The present lection is sure of that fact, t the point of using a somewhat bizarre incident in David's life as the vehicle for transmitting its message.

The ark of the covenant has been ignored by the Deuteronomistic historians since they related the account of its return to the Israelites by the Philistines following the series of disasters that possession of the ark inflicted on these powerful enemies of Israel (1 Sam. 6:1–7:2). (The references to the ark in 1 Sam. 14:18 should be read as references to the priestly ephod. See NRSV marginal notes for that verse.) During the interim, the sacred chest has remained at the house of one Abinadab, who lived in the village of Kiriath-jearim, near Jerusalem (1 Sam. 7:1). But now David, directing the affairs of his kingdom from the city newly won from the Jebusites, intends to make of Jerusalem a spiritual as well as a political center. Therefore, he leads an enormous troop of warriors to the home of Abinadab to get possession of the ark and to bring it to its new home, where it will become a focal point for the nation's worship, much as when, during the days of Eli and Samuel, it rested at Shiloh.

As it stands, v. 5 seems to suggest that David and those who were with him were so overcome with emotion that they engaged in festive dancing as the ark made its way along toward Jerusalem (also note v. 14), while v. 16 appears to confirm this fact and to point out that the dancing was still in progress as the ark entered the city. Because the act of sacred dancing to the accompaniment of musical instruments was an activity associated with early Israelite prophecy (compare 1 Sam. 10:5, 10), it may simply be that David and his followers were seized by a spirit of prophetic ecstasy. That is, they gave way to a strong inner impulse to express their euphoria over all that Yahweh had so recently done in their lives and in the life of the nation. Those preachers on this text who wish to pursue this theme will be following a time-honored avenue of interpretation.

Yet there are certain nagging questions about David's dancing. The suggestion has been made by some that David is engaging himself in a ritual more associated with the worship of Baal than with the worship of Yahweh (compare 2 Sam. 6:20–22; it is curious that the issue of David's nakedness before Yahweh is not mentioned until near the end of the story—and outside the bounds of our lection). This certainly helps to explain why Michal, on witnessing the dancing procession, "despised [David] in her heart" (v. 16). Yet the text is not clear about all the reasons for Michal's emotion, and it may be that this daughter of Saul, who had once risked her life for David (1 Sam. 19:11–17), had subsequently fallen in love with her second husband, Paltiel, and that she was infuriated over David's treatment of this poor man (2 Sam. 3:12–16). We will never know the answer to these riddles, but the suggestion that David's dancing involved some type of irreverent ritual causes one to treat the significance of the dancing with some circumspection.

Omitted from the lectionary text are vs. 6–12a, the difficult story of the death of a good man who only wished to keep the ark from a nasty fall. The tale of Uzzah is similar to other narratives about the magical power of the ark, such as those found in 1 Sam. 5–6 (see especially 6:19). While these stories speak of a deep reverence for Yahweh on the part of the people of early Israel, they do so out of a literary and mythological framework to which people of our own time do not easily relate. Thus the preacher, like the lectionary, may wish to skirt vs. 6–12a, but at the same time she or he would do well to acknowledge what those verses are attempting to convey about the power of God as well as the quite limited manner in which they succeed in doing so.

The theme of joy reaches a climax in vs. 17–19, where the text describes a kind of eucharistic meal. First, the ark is placed in the special tent that David has pitched, a tent that will ultimately give way to Solomon's magnificent Temple on or near the same spot, but which for now stands as a memorial to the tabernacle that the tribes had carried with them during the days of their wilderness wanderings. Next David, who did not often fill a priestly role, but who has now dressed himself in the priestly ephod (v. 14), offers sacrifices to Yahweh. Finally, the people feast on bread, meat (see NRSV marginal note), and cakes of raisins in celebration of the goodness of God. We have no way of knowing what words were spoken on this occasion, but he may well have been something like:

> I will give thanks to Yahweh with my whole heart;
> I will tell of all your wonderful deeds.
> I will be gland and exult in you;
> I will sing praise to your name, O Most High.
> (Ps. 9:1–2)

David, who now presides over a newly united nation, who boasts a new capital city, and who takes pride in a new shrine of worship, looks boldly to the future, in joyful gratitude to the God who has ordained him to his high calling.

Yet the terrible reality of human sin, to which this text points in somewhat enigmatic ways, is close at hand. The moment of David's triumph is soon to be sullied by his lust and greed (see 2 Sam. 11–12, Propers 12 and 13).

Psalm 24

This psalm in three parts provides the script for a "liturgy of entrance," whereby in great procession the whole congregation of Israel makes festal entry into the Jerusalem Temple. The psalm is paired in the lectionary with the Samuel narrative that tells about David bringing the ark of God's presence into the royal city. It is plausible that what the narrative reports as a foundational historical event is in Ps. 24 scripted as a regularly repeated and reenacted liturgy long after David—the periodic reentry of God into the Temple.

The psalm begins with a great solemn declaration (vs. 1–2). Perhaps we can imagine this doxological assertion as announced by a priest, who stands at the head of the procession as it begins its way into the Temple.

The assertion is one of the most sweeping assertions of "creation theology" in all of the Bible. Such an assertion is peculiarly appropriate, both to the large scope of Davidic *political ambitions*, which are housed and legitimate in the Jerusalem Temple, and to the symbolism and *theological intent* of the theology of presence in Jerusalem. That theology is not especially focused on or limited to the historical traditions of Israel, but thinks large about God's ordering and governance of the whole of creation.

Specifically, the psalm begins with an inverted word order, not reflected in English translation. "To Yahweh belongs the earth," its inhabitants, its fullness. It is all Yahweh's property and possession, deriving its life from Yahweh's generosity and in return living its life for Yahweh in glad gratitude. This sweeping statement preempts any rival claims. Nothing of the world belongs to any other god or can rightly serve any other god. Nothing in the earth can rightly be held out as "private property," not even by ambitious and greedy kings. Thus, the theological affirmation of creation has the practical political effect of countering any political ambition to absolutism or ultimacy.

The reason the world belongs wholly to Yahweh is that it was

Yahweh who with enormous authority, and power to match, created a safe, dry place in the midst of the waters of chaos. Yahweh is the sole possessor of creation, because only Yahweh had the capacity and will to order chaos in ways that made worldly life possible. All of life belongs to Yahweh, because only Yahweh could permit, authorize, and evoke life.

The rhetoric of the psalm shifts abruptly in vs. 3–6. Now the question is, who is authorized and qualified to share in the liturgical procession into the Temple. These verses seem remote from the great declaration of vs. 1–2, except that the place to which access is granted is the great symbolic locus of the creator God. Entry here is access to the vision and reality of a Yahweh-ordered cosmos, which is rich in blessing. One is qualified to go there only by conforming to the rules of conduct that are not only commandments, but requirements of behavior ordained into the very fabric of creation. In violating them, one not only displeases God, but mocks the very created order we here acknowledge and celebrate. Thus, the condition of access to worship is glad respect for and practice of the ethical requirements that are intrinsic to the shape of creation. One cannot enter into the worship of the Creator if one has violated the rules of creation.

Thus, the question is posed: Who may enter into this happy liturgical procession (v. 3)? The answer, given in two guidelines, concerns the ones who in heart and hand are pure, and those who do not engage in falsehood or deceit. Stated positively, those admitted are those who conduct themselves in ways that respect neighbor, who enhance community, and who do not distort social relations for private benefit. Put more broadly, those admitted are those who live in ways that enhance the fragile ordering of creation. Note well that those elemental communal requirements do not derive from "the commandments," but may provide the elemental cultic materials out of which the more formal commandments were derived (so Mowinckel).

It is promised that those who so qualify as friends of creation may enter to where the creator God will be present (vs. 5–6). That place is known to be a place of blessing, vindication, and liberation (v. 5), a place worthy of glorification.

Now with the identity of the creator God asserted (vs. 1–2), and with the requirements of creation voiced and accepted (vs. 3–6), the procession begins toward the Temple (vs. 7–10). As the doors are approached, a litany ensues, ordering the gates of the Temple opened for entry. The one who enters first, who leads the procession, is not the priest or the people, but God, "King of glory." The visible enactment of this drama, it is widely assumed, concerns the entry of the ark upon which sits the invisible, triumphant God. The doors of the Temple are opened for the triumphal entry, made with singing and boisterous, celebrative applause. The one who comes is the God who is present in enormous power and brilliant splendor. This is the God who has defeated the powers of chaos and death, who has created a safe place in which the world may live.

As is always the case in such a sacramental enactment, this ritual dares to assert that those cosmic realities of victory, life, and wellbeing are visibly present, concrete, and available in this moment of worship drama. It is no wonder that the people entered the Temple with such exuberance. It is equally clear that to be disqualified from worship was to be given a sentence of excommunication, cut off from the life of glory, from the power of blessing, fated to death.

Ephesians 1:3–14

See the discussion of this passage under the Second Sunday After Christmas.

Mark 6:14–29

The story of the beheading of John the Baptist is hardly a text one would spontaneously choose for a sermon. Despite the fact that it is an intriguing tale that has been retold through the centuries in various media, its details of violence are too graphic, and its tragic ending leaves little room for good news. Furthermore, it is the only passage of this length in any of the Gospels not immediately focused on Jesus. Yet Matthew (14:1–12) and Mark (6:14–29) both include a detailed account of the incident, and Luke (9:9) at least alludes to it.

What function does the story, with its gory details, have in the broader narrative of Mark's Gospel? The most obvious thing concerns the parallelism between John and Jesus and between Herod and Pilate. John is initially introduced in Mark as the forerunner of Jesus, the messenger who prepares the way of the Lord and baptizes the beloved Son (1:2–11). The narrator dates the beginning of Jesus' public ministry from the arrest of John (1:14). While Luke establishes the connection between John and Jesus through parallel accounts of their conception, birth, naming, and childhood development (Luke 1–2), Mark ties the two together through their deaths.

Each innocently suffers at the hands of a vacillating political figure. Herod and Pilate both see good in the accused men brought before them, and left to themselves both would choose freedom over capital punishment. Yet, because of their own weaknesses, both let themselves be trapped by external circumstances and permit a violent death. In both stories disciples come, take the body, and place it in a tomb.

Readers of Mark's narrative already know that a conspiracy to destroy Jesus is underway (3:6). The brutal slaying of John alerts them to the fact that these things happen to righteous people and they have every reason to expect that it will happen to Jesus. Perhaps there is even a hint of Jesus' resurrection in the rumor voiced by Herod himself and spread among the people that Jesus was John-risen-from-the-dead.

The story serves yet another function. It is interjected between the sending out of the disciples on the journey through the surrounding villages (6:6b–13) and their report to Jesus of the successful mission (6:30), another example of Mark's "sandwiching" technique. In the midst of a positive account of the disciples' exorcisms, healings, and preaching comes this jolting description of the slaying of "a righteous and holy man" (6:20), who had provoked the political authorities by speaking the truth. Not only is the parallel drawn between John and Jesus; it is also drawn between John and the disciples. Just as the account prepares readers for Jesus' coming trials, it also prepares readers for the coming trials of disciples.

Mark's Gospel, much like the letters of Paul, is amazingly realistic about the fortunes of disciples. Even when there is reason for optimism, when exorcisms, healings, and effective preaching are taking place, the threat of political and even religious opposition is not far away. Believers should not be too surprised when the declaration of God;s judgment and mercy is met with hostility.

In a striking detail in the story, we are told that Herod has a fearful fascination with John. Though challenged by him for this marriage to his sister-in-law, Herod shields John from his wife's rage. Is he scared of John, or perhaps attracted to his fiery preaching? Who knows? But as is often the case in political contexts, personal respect is easily abandoned when circumstances ("regard for his oaths and for the guests," 6:26) warrant it. Although grieved, Herod orders John's death.

John's tragic end in a sense anticipates Jesus' words spoken to the disciples later at the Temple, when they are warned about being dragged before governors and kings and beaten in synagogues for the sake of the gospel (13:9–11). Truth-telling becomes a perilous venture in a world of Herods and Pilates. Even when one has friends in high places, there is little security.

PROPER 11

Ordinary Time 16

*Sunday between
July 17 and 23 inclusive*

Something new begins when God's powerful love and loving power are acted out. Both the Old Testament reading and the psalm concern the radical newness that is worked in Israel with the appearance of David. There is no doubt that David worked a political, sociological newness in ancient Israel. These two readings, however, focus on the *theological* impetus of David and his reign. What counts finally for Israel is that David embodies and institutionalizes God's *astonishing fidelity* to Israel, assuring that God will attend always to Israel's well-being.

This Davidic claim matches and prepares the way for the high christological claim made in the Epistle reading. Clearly Jesus, according to this text, runs well beyond David in envisioning and enacting a new, single community of humanity, which overrides our deepest divisions. Indeed our various divisions in church, race, and nation are shameless and frivolous, given God's intention. Clearly it is God's fidelity, nothing less, that makes an utter newness possible.

The Gospel reading, as we regularly notice, moves from grand, lyrical claim to the daily concreteness of Jesus. This Jesus of powerful, compassionate activity, nonetheless, is in continuity with the best of Davidic fidelity and the largeness of the Epistle vision. Where Jesus goes, newness is possible, humanity is restored, and creation functions fruitfully again. This "shepherd to the shepherdless" lets the "flock" of humanity live in its rightful, satisfied ways. Jesus is "greater than David" (according to Christian affirmation). But he does the same work as David in making new life possible. Around Jesus there erupts new life, the materials for which did not seem present until this inscrutable, faithful power does its work. In both David and Jesus, the community of this text is able to see that generous fidelity generates new life. Nothing else does!

2 Samuel 7:1–14a

A coat of many colors is one apt description of this passage. In historical terms, 2 Sam. 7 was a basic and constitutional literary formulation in the life of the Davidic kingdom, in that it enunciated the view that Yahweh had for all time selected the Davidic dynasty to be the representative of the God of Israel in the nation's life. This was understood to be a new covenant (although that word does not appear in our present text) or, more precisely, a new configuration of the ancient covenant that went back through Moses to Abraham. Although it is not entirely clear what shape this passage may have had before its incorporation into the great Deuteronomistic History during the time of King Josiah (c. 640–609 B.C.), the essential content of its message must have played an important political role during the time of the divided monarchy, when a different and competing royalist ideology, accompanied by a different and competing theology, prevailed in the Northern Kingdom. The political/theological message of 2 Sam. 7 is definitive: the Davidic dynasty is the means by which Yahweh governs Israel, and all who defy this dynasty are rebellious and apostate.

In addition to its central meaning, this text functions in other important ways. The question may well have been asked in antiquity as it could be asked today: Why did David, who in certain ways constructed the edifice of Israel's nationhood, not go on to construct the nation's most important building, the Jerusalem Temple? To discover just how vexing this problem was for certain thoughtful individuals in Israel-of-old, one need only read the Chronicler's account of the building of the Temple (1 Chron. 22–2 Chron. 5) and notice how much of the credit for the building is shifted from Solomon to David, as if to call attention to the fact that David was the real power behind the Temple construction. But 2 Sam. 7 had already supplied a solution to this problem, long before the Chronicler wrote: David *would* have built the Temple, but for the grace of God who built a "house" for David, instead (v. 11).

A third significant way in which this text functions is in terms of its location within the Deuteronomistic History, for it forms an important introduction to the dreadful story of David's sinful affair involving Bathsheba and Uriah the Hittite (2 Sam. 11–12, Propers 12 and 13). As will be discussed in connection with those texts, it is the prophet Nathan who steps forward to speak and act on behalf of Yahweh when the anointed human king fails. Second Samuel 7 serves as the moment when that respected prophet first comes to the reader's notice. We have no idea what series of events had brought this courageous man to play so important a role in David's court. David's favorite seer, Gad, had been at his side since David was a fugitive from Saul's anger (1 Sam. 22:5), but here we meet Nathan for the first time. It is his task now to correct David's vision of Yahweh's will by saying that Yahweh does not wish for David to build a house, because Yahweh wishes, first, to build a house for David. This is good news, of course, and we (to say nothing of David) now learn to trust Nathan as one who speaks the truth and who has at heart both Yahweh's and David's best interests. Thus we (and David!) will listen when Nathan soon excoriates David for his sinfulness (2 Sam. 12:7–12).

It must be admitted that some of these issues, especially those having to do with the political implications of the text, are of little moment to people in our own time. Of course, in light of the fact that the New Testament makes a great deal of the Davidic lineage of Jesus (Matt. 1:1–17 and elsewhere), there are certain messianic themes in this lection that are always pertinent for Christian worship and preaching. In this regard, notice may be taken of the shepherd imagery in v. 8 (compare 1 Sam. 16:1–13, Proper 6).

Perhaps one rich source of meaning for our or any time is to be found in the skillful manner in which the text plays upon the word *bêt*, "house." This term is variously used to refer to David's cedar palace (v. 2), the temple that neither David nor anyone else has built (v. 5–7), the Temple that Solomon will build (v. 13), and the family of David (v. 11; compare vs. 16, 18, 19, 29). The art of applying multiple meanings to a single word or phrase is, of course, a time-honored one, by which poets of many cultures have made their writings not only more interesting to the reader but also more expressive. (Compare the wordplay on *rûaḥ*, "breath," "wind," "spirit," or "Spirit" in Ezek. 37:1–14.) This device becomes one by which a writer communicates several ideas to his or her readers at the same time.

Thus, it will not stretch the meaning of our text to extend its central wordplay to the "house" in which modern worshipers gather for prayer and praise and to the "house" that they are. We constitute ourselves for worship in a church that is a building, but we are a church that exists independently of any particular building and which will continue to exist even if the particular church (building) with which the church (congregation or parish) is associated should tumble into ruins. Furthermore, our house is part of a larger, universal house, which cannot be contained in any house or combination of houses. Thus the pun of the ancient author(s) lives on in a fresh and specifically Christian context.

Psalm 89:20–37

Psalm 89 is the most extraordinary of the "royal psalms," because it contains the most remarkable assertions about David and David's dynasty. The part of the poem that constitutes our reading is a long oracle in the mouth of God (see v. 19). It is a loose, stylized, poetic rendering of the oracle uttered by Samuel in 2 Sam. 7, part of which is the Old Testament reading for this Sunday. The oracle is undifferentiated; it is the elaboration of a single motif, which seems not to have any discernible development. That single idea is that God has made a profound, unconditional promise to the line of David, and because of that promise the dynasty will endure as long as creation lasts. The psalm thus is a study in God's long-term, promissory, unconditional fidelity.

In the divine oracle, God recalls the initial identification of David and his anointment as a young boy (Ps. 89:20). With reference to the narrative of 1 Sam. 16:1–13, it is remembered that David had been unnoticed and unknown. In an inscrutable way, the boy David had surfaced as God's new candidate for leadership in Israel. The anointing carried with it for David and his descendants a guarantee to keep the "house of David" safe from all attacks. While God did indeed fight wars, it is God's hand and "arm," God's power, that is decisive for this family (Ps. 89:21). It is God's intervention that keeps God safe in every military conflict (see 2 Sam. 8:6, 14, wherein Yahweh is credited with David's victories).

In Ps. 89:24, Israel's most decisive words are used for Yahweh's commitment to David. It is God's *faithfulness* and *steadfast love* that are decisive for David's survival and well-being. In a remarkable linkage of theology and politics, our text asserts that God's fidelity reshapes the political, military process in Israel.

This commitment on God's part permits in Israel a high, sacral view of kingship, with enormous political benefits (vs. 26–27). In David's mouth, likely as a liturgical formulation, it is affirmed that God and king have a father-son relationship. That language is escalated to insist that the king is not only "son," but firstborn, that is, best loved and most valued. The language of father-son is conventional in royal rhetoric. The formula is a political methaphor, suggesting a peculiar role for the king, designation to exercise the authority of God and to enjoy the support of God for political ventures.

Verses 28–37 are for the most part a continued reiteration of the same statement of God's unconditional commitment to David. I distinguish this part of the oracle only because after v. 28 the divine oracle repeatedly uses the word we translate "forever," suggesting very long durability for this dynasty (vs. 28, 29, 36, 37). In v. 28, God's steadfast love, *ḥesed*, is again asserted, this time in parallel with the term "covenant."

In vs. 30–32, it is asserted that a disobedient act by a member of the dynasty will indeed evoke punishment from God. The promise does not make the royal family immune to divine command and divine sanction. However, the entire "if-then" formulation of vs. 30–32 is quite subordinate. The overarching, governing term is the adversative "but" in v. 33. There may be disobedience and punishment. That, however, is a subset to the ringing and decisive affirmation of v. 33: "I will not remove my *ḥesed*." Here the term *ḥesed* is in parallel to "faithfulness" (as in v. 24) and in parallel to "covenant" (as in v. 28). Here the three words converge, expressing God's unconditional, gracious commitment. In this moment, the Holy God has made an unconditional commitment to a particular historical power arrangement.

The last lines of our reading, vs. 35–37, reinforce this idea of limitless commitment by the phrase "once and for all" and the double use of "forever." The scope and density of the promise is breathtaking. We are, in my judgment, bound to conclude that the oracle is a remarkable piece of theological affirmation. On the one hand, I have no doubt that it is conventional royal hyperbole that serves the self-seeking ideological interests of the monarchy. On the other hand, and at the same time, this statement of ideological legitimacy, which is not innocent or disinterested, is an astonishing theological articulation of God's limitless graciousness.

Two compelling interpretative questions may be identified. First, we may ponder how it is that God's fidelity (see vs. 24, 28, 33) impinges on and makes a difference in David's world of *Realpolitik*. The oracle is not only a religious idea, but also a commitment with public force. Second, it is clear historically that the promise to the dynasty was not kept; the dynasty did not persist. Indeed, in this psalm, vs. 38–51 acknowledge that point. Political history is fraught with the surprises of power, and God's resolve was defeated in the historical process. How are we to adjudicate historical reality when it flies in the face of theological affirmation? One Christian interpretive maneuver, of course, is to see the continuation of the Davidic dynasty in the person of Jesus. Such a claim, however, is exceedingly problematic, and in itself provides no easy or convincing way out of the tension between theological resolve and *Realpolitik*. I do not believe the preacher can or must resolve this issue. But the issue must be aired, so as to protect us from both an easy transcendentalism and a jaded historicism, both of which escape too readily the tension that the psalm deliberately articulates.

Ephesians 2:11-22

The doxological motif in Ephesians makes a sharp turn in this familiar and important passage. Earlier portions of the letter offer praise to God for God's blessings to humankind; there the emphasis falls on God's actions in Jesus Christ and their consequences for the relationship between God and humankind. Believers receive "every spiritual blessing" (1:3) and the "riches of his grace" (1:7). In 2:11-22, by contrast, God is praised less for what is conventionally called the "vertical" result of God's action than for the "horizontal" result, its consequences for human beings. Three times in this passage the author employs the emphatic pronoun *hymeis* ("you Gentiles" in v. 11; "you" in v. 13; "you" in v. 22), which draws attention to the anthropological implications of the doxological motif.

The passage begins with a series of astonishing contrasts between the past of believers and their present. Those "Gentiles by birth" were formerly uncircumcised, "without Christ," "aliens from the commonwealth of Israel," "strangers to the covenants of promise," "having no hope," and "without God in the world." Each of these characterizations powerfully depicts a situation of alienation and estrangement. In the world of the first century, dominated as it was by the Roman state, being an outsider meant being rootless and isolated. The two references to "aliens" and "strangers" play on that need for belonging. Whether or not these Gentile Christians would have agreed with the description of themselves as "having no hope," the author's depiction of them summons up despair. That despair is only increased by the claim that they were "without God in the world," a claim that is at the same time objectively impossible (no human being can be without God) and yet subjectively true.

By contrast, "now in Christ" these believers have come near. No longer outsiders, they are part of one new group. They belong to "one new humanity," "citizens with the saints and also members of the household of God." This description reverses the earlier situation almost element for element. Believers no longer exist in alienation from God's people, but have been brought near. They no longer experience the powerlessness and alienation of strangers, but have become full citizens. Moreover, they are part of a household. Like all households, this one conveys on its members a certain status; because the household is God's, the status here is unimaginably high.

This dramatic reversal came about because of God's action in Jesus Christ. Ephesians 2:13–14 identifies that action specifically with Christ's death ("by the blood of Christ," "in his flesh"), complementing the author's earlier reference to the slavific character of Christ's resurrection (1:20). It is Jesus' death that brings down the "dividing wall, that is, the hostility between [Jew and Gentile]" and that enables the creation of "one new humanity."

One question in the ongoing debate regarding Pauline authorship of Ephesians concerns the likelihood of Paul's having thought of Jews and Gentiles becoming a single new humanity (by contrast with the language of grafting Gentiles onto the tree of Israel in Rom. 11:17–24). As important as that question is, it ought not to eclipse the fundamental point, namely, that the dramatic reversal of the Gentiles' situation comes about because, and solely because, of the death of Christ. They did not "earn" the disappearance of the "dividing wall," any more than Jews voluntarily opened the "commonwealth of Israel" to Gentiles. Both events occur as a result of God's initiative.

The final section of this passage abounds with imagery depicting the communal nature of this new humanity. Believers are members of God's household (v. 19), part of "a holy temple in the Lord" (v. 21), "a dwelling place for God" (v. 22). All of these images connect believers firmly both with one another as part of the "one new humanity" and with God. Christ, the "cornerstone" of this new edifice, provides the crucial link between believers and God.

Much in this passage dramatically insists on the ways in which the new life of believers differs from their old life. Their identity has radically changed. Their alignments and loyalties are new. The destruction of the dividing wall has created a new era. The death of Christ has brought about a new situation for humankind. Nevertheless, at least one lement in this passage points toward the continuity of this new situation with what has gone before, and that is the reference in v. 20 to the "apostles and prophets" as the foundation of God's household. Even the new humanity, in which the categories of Jew and Gentile no longer exist, builds nevertheless on the earlier teaching of the "apostles and prophets." The edifice of faith is not simply a new spiritual life, lacking any contact with the past. Those who have gone before form the very foundation of the household.

In the face of a contrast such as the author of Ephesians here depicts, many contemporary Christians would advise that the past be forgotten. "Put it behind you," "Let it go" would come the admonitions. Here, however, the admonition is one to remembrance. The passage itself begins with a call to remember the life of the past and its alienation (v. 11). This remembrance serves not simply as a kind of intellectual reminder of the past but as a means to thanksgiving, praise, and service. After all, those who are now part of God's household must inevitably reflect that status in this actions.

Mark 6:30–34, 53–56

Interruptions are always a problem. The preacher knows that. A carefully planned day can quickly dwindle away when on thing after another intrudes into the schedule. Our precious study time is wasted by repeated interruptions that break our train of thought and divert our attention. The same is true for all busy people. Handling interruptions gracefully becomes an art to which most of us aspire. It is instructive, then, to examine the narrative assigned for this Sunday and observe Jesus as he deals with the demands of the crowds that force a change of plans.

Actually the reading for this Sunday is composed of two distinct sections (Mark 6:30–34 and vs. 53–56), neither a "purple patch" and yet each with an important role in advancing the narrative. The first section (vs. 30–34) begins with the report of the disciples on their mission throughout the surrounding villages and then quickly becomes the setting for Jesus' spectacular feeding of the five thousand. Following the feeding and the unusual account of Jesus' walking on the water, the second section (vs. 53–56) provides a summary of Jesus' activities in and around Gennesaret, something of a transition to the ensuing debate with the scribes about the Jewish tradition.

In the first section, the disciples, who on their missionary journey traveled in separate pairs, need a debriefing. No doubt weary from their ventures, but with marvelous stories to tell of healings and teaching, they report to Jesus. He listens for a time and then, perceiving their exhaustion and sensing his own, proposes that they escape to a deserted place for a rest—a wonderful idea! The crowds are so constant that there has been no suitable time or place even to eat. Jesus and the disciples get into a boat and head down the shore to a favorite spot for a well-deserved moment of peace and quiet, a time for the renewal of the spirit as well as the body. Jesus is a sensitive shepherd to his flock.

But the crowds are not so easily diverted. They keep an eye on the boat and hurry ahead to the "favorite spot," arriving even before Jesus and the disciples. Their presence plays havoc with the plans to retreat, with the need for space away from their relentless demands. The crowds are constantly there interrupting.

Jesus and the disciples surely have reason for impatience, but the text says that when Jesus saw the crowd, "he had compassion for them, because they were like sheep without a shepherd" (v. 34). Rather than being an intrusion into the R and R, the crowd becomes the object of Jesus' deep concern. He observes their aimless wandering, their desperation as persons without direction and commitment, and he begins to teach them. He interprets, instructs, prods the people to get them to see a better way.

It is amazing how Jesus handles this interruption into his life and the life of the disciples, how his compassion for the intruders overrides his concern for order. In time, he will dismiss the crowds and find his own moment alone to pray (vs. 45–46), but not before being the shepherd to the shepherdless.

Few can handle interruptions with the grace and compassion that Jesus does. In fact, it may be better to read this story not from the perspective of Jesus but from the perspective of the crowd, one of those whose frantic and often unfocused life desperately seeks an answer. Jesus seems never put off by our interruptions, by our constant need of his compassion and teaching. This text affirms his extraordinary availability.

The other section of the Gospel reading for this Sunday contains one of Mark's famous summaries that serve to move along the early portion of the story (see 1:32–33; 3:7–12). No individuals are singled out, no specific miracles are elaborated, only the feverish activity of the throngs to get their sick family members and friends to Jesus for healing. The picture painted with broad strokes describes Jesus' enormous popularity and the pressing crowds wherever he goes.

The summary presents a striking contrast to the earlier scene at Nazareth, where Jesus "could do no deed of power" and where "he was amazed at their unbelief" (6:1–6a). At Gennesaret there are no obstacles in the way of his restoring health to afflicted people. These folks have no reluctance about who he is or what he is about that prevents their openness to his ministry. Their need and his touch are all that matter.

The old observation that the Christian faith is only for desperate people has a ring of truth to it. With them neither health nor affluence nor prior prejudices are impediments. Like the street people brought in to the banquet when the invited guests send their excuses, they don't plan to miss out on the good news offered by and embodied in Jesus.

Proper 12

Ordinary Time 17

*Sunday between
July 24 and 30 inclusive*

These texts scarcely form a coherent group. The two Old Testament texts fit well together. They suggest that autonomy (in the sense of not being accountable to anyone) is sheer stupidity, that it gets one in trouble and does damage to others. The psalm identifies the ultimate foolishness as the denial of God's reality and pertinence to our life. The Old Testament reading exhibits David as a genuinely foolish man. He had become so powerful that he imagined he as exempt from God's Torah and could act for his own desire. His self-indulgent misperception of his life as autonomous begins a terrible tale of destructiveness for his family. The psalm knows that such autonomy always leads to injury for the neighbor.

The Epistle reading is an exultant, doxological prayer, celebrating the wonder of God's glory, whereby the work of Christ's love gives access to the mystery of the Trinitarian God. To know the love of Christ in a way that "surpasses knowledge" is perhaps the evangelical antidote to the "foolishness" of David. The gospel does not given knowledge or information or "smarts" about everything. It does, however, give us the true measure of reality. It is in Jesus that we come to know a world bounded in every dimension by God's inscrutable but unfailing love. It is this inscrutable but trustworthy love that was absent from David's sense of himself. His misperception led to his destructiveness. The Gospel reading is of a very different kind. It focuses on two stunning deeds of Jesus that we can only receive as "miracle." The purpose of the narrative is to call attention to the extraordinary reality of Jesus' person and presence. It is this singular, unrivaled presence that transforms all reality. Our move into trust in the person of Jesus is the ultimate move from self-destructive foolishness to life-receiving sustenance.

While these New Testament texts are zealously christological, the Old Testament readings entertain the conviction that the same "wisdom" given in Christ was offered David in God's Torah, an offer he refused to his own terrible detriment. We, like David, need to pay attention to the ways our lives are bounded by the God of Torah and of love.

2 Samuel 11:1–15

Lies, adultery, and murder: such are the stuff of this sordid tale from the life of King David. It has often been remarked that the Bible, unlike much of other ancient literature, does not spare its greatest heroes, but subjects them to the same standards of morality and conduct that are applied to others. Impatient Moses (Num. 20:10–13), skeptical Sarah (Gen. 18:12), reluctant Jeremiah (Jer. 1:6), and cowardly Peter (Mark 14:66–72) are but a few of the other examples of this remarkable objectivity. But of all the graceless exploits of God's special men and women related in the Bible, none is more repulsive than David's dealings with Bathsheba and Uriah.

In fairness to David, it must be said that the author of this narrative allows the issue of original culpability to be shrouded in ambiguity. One manner of reading the story (and perhaps the one most often favored by readers) is to see David as the perpetrator who takes advantage of an innocent victim. Having been aroused by the sight of a naked Bathsheba, David then uses his political power to either seduce or rape her (another ambiguity in the tale). But it is also quite possible that Bathsheba entrapped David by exposing herself at a time and in a manner best calculated to produce a desired effect. This is the same Bathsheba who later colluded with Nathan to ensure that her son Solomon would become Israel's next king (1 Kings 1:13–31), so premeditation on her part cannot be ruled out in the present context. Such entrapment by Bathsheba would in no way exonerate David's shameful behavior, but, if true, it would mean that his guilt was to some extent shared. A remarkable feature about the manner in which this story is told is the facelessness of Bathsheba's personality. Nowhere does she speak (except v. 5). Nowhere does she act in any manner that would permit the reader to know the nature of her own emotions. The author of this story has often been faulted for this aspect of his or her literary style, and the charge has been made that it is a symptom of his (surely, in this case, his) debased view of women. But the countercharge may be made that, if he had sheltered a low opinion of women, he would not have taken so seriously the matter of David's sinful actions.

The dramatic manner in which David's treachery is contrasted with the fidelity of Uriah is another striking feature of this story.

When David learns that Bathsheba is pregnant, he recalls Uriah from the siege of Rabbah, the Ammonite capital (the ruins of Rabbah may still be seen today in the heart of Amman, the Jordanian capital city). David pretends to be seeking information about the conduct of the war, but his real purpose is to provide a reason for the world (and especially Uriah) to believe that, when the child is born some months hence, it is Uriah's son or daughter. The expression "wash your feet" in v. 8 should be understood as a euphemism for "have sex with your wife" (compare the similar euphemistic use of "feet," meaning "genitalia" or "nakedness," in Isa. 6:2). Had Uriah complied with the king's wishes, the adulterous affair would never have become public—or so David planned. But Uriah foils David's scheme by chastely sleeping in the servants' quarters, an act that he later explains to David is his way of keeping faith with his comrades in the field (v. 11).

Frustrated, David tries a different tactic by plying his subordinate with such strong drink that Uriah becomes intoxicated (v. 13). Still the faithful soldier refuses to go home to the hospitality of his wife, but again sleeps "on his couch with the servants of his lord." To see this fidelity for the remarkable thing that it is, one needs only to be reminded that Uriah is not even a native Israelite, but a Hittite mercenary, a descendant of that proud race which a few centuries before had ruled much of the land from the Mediterranean Sea to Mesopotamia. Yet his personal code of conduct is so above reproach that, quite unwittingly, he repeatedly stands in the way of David's treachery.

Finally, David resorts to his ultimate weapon. To have continued to permit Uriah's innocence to frustrate David's guilty intentions would have meant that eventually, when the child was born, it would be clear that Bathsheba had committed adultery. And so David orders Uriah's death. It may be argued that David's terrible deed was intended to protect Bathsheba more than himself, since—after the manner of despotic rulers—his part in the liaison could easily have been denied. But Bathsheba would certainly have been publicly stigmatized and, if the provisions of the Mosaic law were carried out, executed (Lev. 20:10). The murder of Uriah, as horrible as it is, is a kind of perverse commentary on David's concern for Bathsheba, another example of the convoluted motives of the principals of this drama. Verses 16–25 of 2 Sam. 11 are outside the limits of this present lection, but they cannot be ignored. The dreadful irony of innocent Uriah's unknowingly carrying back to his commander, Joab, his own death warrant is powerfully poignant, and causes the final verses of the lection (vs. 14–15) to be all the more significant. With the report (in v. 24) that David's orders have been carried out, the cycle of heartache and tragedy has, for the moment, been played out (but note 12:15b).

Israel's great king has become enmeshed in as repugnant a series of events as perhaps may be imagined, and the original author of this tale (presumably the writer of the so-called Succession Narrative) as well as the Deuteronomistic historians who have preserved it have remained centuries of readers that even the greatest men and women of God sometimes have feet of clay. (But compare 1 Chron. 20, which omits the story altogether.)

Psalm 14

This psalm (and its reiteration in Ps. 53) insists on behavioral foolishness as a practical manifestation of atheism. That is, serious atheism is not an intellectual idea, but it is a practical moral choice. In the phrasing of Dostoevsky, "Without God, everything is possible," for God's very reality sets limits to destructive possibilities. Psalm 14 is nicely linked to the David-Uriah-Bathsheba narrative, wherein David acts foolishly and destructively. Indeed, in his moment of careless, passionate aggression, David acts as if there were no moral accountability, so that everything is possible for him. Our reading of this psalm may suggest that in the Bible, theoretical intellectual atheism is of little interest and constitutes no serious threat to faith. The real threat is *practical* atheism, which is enacted as *moral autonomy*.

Verse 1 is one of the few times in the Bible in which there is a flat assertion denying the reality of God. Most often the issue in the Bible is not "no God" (atheism) but "wrong god" (idolatry). We may note three important matters about this assertion that there is no God: (*a*) the utterance is not out loud or explicit. It is "in their hearts," it is thought. It is an internal decision that shows up only in action, not in speech. (*b*) The action in which the thought of "no God" is manifest is not a "religious act." The act that exhibits the denial of God is an act of bad morality, marked by corruption. That is, the show of atheism is in destructive activity. (*c*) The thought and the deed are those of "fools," those who have no sense about the moral shape of their own existence. In their lack of discernment, such "fools" fail completely to understand their true situation in a morally constituted creation.

The antithesis of a fool is a wise person, one who rightly discerns the moral shape of reality (v. 2). Yahweh is presented as probing and searching to see if a wise person can be found (see Jer. 5:1–5). This is an imaginative device for asking the question whether one can indeed identify those whose lives are rightly inclined. The answer is given in v. 3. There are in the answer two positives, "all ... all" (in Hebrew the second "all" is "all alike") and two negatives, "no one ... not one." The second negative term picks up on the word in the second "all." The four terms together, two positive and two negative, have cumulative force, echoing the phrasing of v. 1, to assert that there are no wise who seek after God. Note that the language here is not an indictment of sinners. The rhetoric is of another kind. The indictment is not one of guilt, but of sheer, practical stupidity, of not knowing or having enough sense to avoid destructive action.

That generalization from v. 3 is now made much more specific, and the general indictment is turned toward the particular question of neighbor relations (v. 4). The particular form of "foolishness" cited here is the refusal to "call upon Yahweh," which is related to the social practice of consuming people, using them up, and devouring them with avaricious political and economic strategies. The foolish believe that in a autonomous world, one can abuse, oppress, and nullify other human beings if they are weak, because there is no larger reference and none to whom one is accountable.

But now the psalm can no longer maintain a posture of dispassionate analysis. The poem finally must "meddle," must make partisan assertions that are rooted in the very character of God (vs. 5–6). Those who imagine their actions can be unbridled and self-serving will have their lives filled with terrorizing anxiety. The reason that abuse of "the poor" becomes a risk for one's life is a theological reason. Finally, in the abuse of the poor the fool runs dead into the reality of God, who travels in the company of "the righteous," who in these lines are equated with the poor for whom God is refuge. That is, in abusing the poor, the foolish must confront the great Advocate of the poor, who always stands with and alongside the poor. The fool can never isolate the poor to deal with them alone, because the poor are always accompanied. In an acute moment of social analysis, the poem brings together astute social criticism and radical theological affirmation, echoing the proverbs:

> Those who oppress the poor insult their Maker,
> > but those who are kind to the needy honor him.
> > > (Prov. 14:31)

> Those who mock the poor insult their Maker;
> > those who are glad at calamity will not go unpunished.
> > > (Prov. 17:5)

Only the really stupid can imagine the poor to be alone and defenseless in the world. Apropos our Old Testament reading, only a very foolish David dares imagine that Uriah and Bathsheba are alone, without the watchful, guaranteeing attentiveness of Yahweh who calls even kings to responsibility.

As so often in these psalms, the last verse of Ps. 14 seems to be an addendum, linking a quite particular poem to more general concerns of Israel (v. 7). In this verse, the categories of "fool/poor" are transposed into general Israelite issues. The "fool," then, would seem to be the self-indulgent nations who imagine Israel to be a poor, defenseless, easy mark. The foolish nations stupidly abuse Israel without noticing the hovering, protective figure of Yahweh close at hand. In this prayer-wish, Israel invokes its refuge and protector, anticipating that Yahweh will intervene, correct abuse, and give Israel back its life. As David learned the cost of his aggressive stupidity, as the nations pay for their foolish abusiveness, so in our exploitative practices and polities we are always again learning that our foolishness does not eliminate the decisive actions of God from scenes of vulnerability.

Ephesians 3:14–21

The prayer that stands at the heart of this lection constitutes a significant challenge for the preacher. While the language of the prayer is powerful and moving, it begins with a depiction of God that many contemporary Christians will find problematic or even offensive, and it elsewhere employs language that is abstract and difficult to untangle. It may be important to acknowledge at the outset that this prayer, like much in human thought about God, seeks for far more than can be articulated in common speech.

The opening reference of Eph. 3:14–15 to "the Father, from whom every family in heaven and on earth takes its name" will provoke complaints that the Bible promotes a masculine God. That question is far too complex to be addressed here, apart from recalling that the Bible also employs maternal imagery with respect to God and everywhere insists that God is not merely a larger-than-life human being, either male or female. Here God the Father is connected with the naming of "every family." The note to the NRSV is slightly misleading, in that the word there translated "family" does not mean "fatherhood." The Greek word *patria* refers concretely to family, extended family, larger units of people who are somehow connected to one another, not to the abstract notion of "fatherhood."

Because *patria* is a cognate of *patēr*, the word for father, however, and English does not allow an adequate way to demonstrate that connection, the editors offer "fatherhood" as a substitute.

This tricky problem of moving from Greek to English is important here, since what the writer asserts is the connection between *patēr* and *patria*. That is, God who is called Father is the one through whom every family is named. The point is less concerned with "Father" than with the intimate and profound connection between God and the human family. Indeed, here "family" itself is no longer simply "human" family, as the writer invokes families both "in heaven" and "on earth." Whatever connectedness exists among human beings either here or elsewhere exists by virtue of their first and primary connection with God. To that connection the writer does obeisance, and dares to articulate a prayer on behalf of his correspondents.

In Greek, the prayer itself contains three main petitions of decreasing length, each of which is introduced in the same way (by a *hina*, or purpose, clause). The first petition consists of vs. 16–17, which primarily seek spiritual strength and growth for the author's addressees. Earlier parts of this letter celebrate the dramatic change God has brought about in the lives of these Gentile converts (for example, 2:1–3, 11–22), but the prayer recognizes that such change is never final or complete. Strength comes as God's gift through the Spirit, as God's gift through the indwelling of Christ, as God's gift through love. Attempts at describing each of these gifts analytically or parsing out various forms of growth will be futile, as the prayer piles up images of the growth invoked for believers. What is crucial, however, is to understand that the growth anticipated poems about because of God's ongoing and even intimate relationship with believers.

The second petition consists of v. 18 and the first half of v. 19 (through the words "that surpasses knowledge"). Here the prayer for growth takes on specificity in the request for understanding and for love. To comprehend "what is the breadth and length and height and depth" is surely to understand all that—and more than—human beings can indeed comprehend. Even beyond that knowledge, however, lies the love of Christ, beyond the very frontier of the human capacity for knowledge.

Because of its brevity, the final petition ("so that you may be filled with all the fullness of God") may appear to be an afterthought. On the contrary, the prayer for the "fullness of God" is the culmination of all prayer, in that it seeks the realization in fact of the connection posited in the introduction to the prayer, the connection between

God and the human family. The final lines of the passage adequately summarize this petition and the prayer itself as "far more than all we can ask or imagine."

The petitions of this prayer necessarily involve gifts to individual believers. There are, nevertheless, indications that these gifts are not private but have a deeply corporate significance. To begin with, the "you" in the passage is a plural "you," suggesting that all the addressees are connected here. More important, the phrase "with all the saints" (v. 18) places the addressees in the context of believers both local and distant. These gifts pertain to the whole people of God, not to a special few who are somehow spiritually talented. In addition, the phrase "glory in the church" (which sounds an odd tone to Protestant ears, but would be welcome in Orthodox Christian circles) identifies the addressees with the assembly of those who together bow before God. The gifts are individual in that they must be granted to and appropriated by individual Christians in their daily, individual, and sometimes achingly private lives. At the same time, however, the gifts are corporate in that those individual Christians do not exist apart from the larger community of faith.

John 6:1–21

This Sunday marks a change in the flow of the Gospel readings. For eight consecutive weeks the lectionary has followed the narrative of Mark (chs. 2 through 6) and will return later to pick up with Mark 7. Meanwhile, during the five-week hiatus in the Markan sequence, we are directed to the sixth chapter of John, a rather critical section that relates the feeding of the five thousand, Jesus' walking on the water to the disciples, the discourse on Jesus as the bread from heaven, and the mixed response of the disciples to Jesus' difficult teaching. shifting Gospels means shifting from one literary world to another, from one narrative with its assumptions, purposes, and strategies to another with a different set of assumptions, purposes, and strategies. Preachers following the lectionary need to be sensitive to the change in the literary and theological environment of the assigned passages.

The readings for this Sunday encompasses both the feeding of the multitude (6:1–15) and the strange event of Jesus' coming to the disciples on the sea (vs. 16–21). Both accounts merit preaching, and it may be that a choice is needed.

Two motifs run through John's story of the feeding, especially when it is compared with the stories in the other three Gospels. First, at the beginning of the story what seems critical is not Jesus' compassion for the hungry and "shepherdless" crowds (as in each of the other Gospels), but the lesson taught the disciples about not underestimating the power of Jesus. Jesus puts the question to Philip of how the crowds are to be fed, in order "to test him, for he himself knew what he was going to do" (6:6). Thinking logically, Philip responds with a plausible retort: "Six months' wages won't pay for the food needed to feed these people." Andrew jumps into the conversation by reporting the presence of one boy's lunch, but adds, "What is that among so many people?"

Interestingly, Jesus does not rebuke Philip and Andrew for their realistic assessments, but he takes charge of the situation, gives instructions to the disciples, distributes the loaves and fish himself, and then has the disciples gather the remains. The answer to their closed appraisals is a demonstration of divine power that blows realism into a cocked hat. The point is that cautious calculations that operate only on the basis of possibility, calculations otherwise revered in our world, ignore "the one who comes from above" (3:31), the One who redefines what is possible.

A second motif has to do with the superficial response of the crowds. They follow Jesus because of the marvelous "signs" he does, but we, the readers of the narrative, already know from other Passover incidents that Jesus is suspicious of those who are captivated only by the miracles he performs (2:23–25). On the one hand, the crowd declares that he is the promised prophet (6:14), but on the other hand, having been miraculously fed, they want to make him king (6:15).

The mind of the crowd is utilitarian. What can we get out of the miracle worker? A perpetual free lunch? Does it sound familiar? "What's in it for me?" It is the kind of thinking that skews the reality of grace and seeks to make of Jesus a genie or an errand boy to satisfy our human wants. It reverses the answer to the catechism question so that it would read: "Our chief end is to be glorified by God forever." From such thinking Jesus retreats—then and now.

The story of Jesus' walking on the water is a theophany, set over against the crowd's superficial response to Jesus. The setting is significant—rough seas, heavy winds, weary rowers, and the telling statement, "It was now dark, and Jesus had not yet come to them" (6:17). Jesus' withdrawal has left the disciples bereft of their leader, confused, and fearful. "Darkness" in John's Gospel is not only an indication of the time of day, but often also a vivid symbol for the circumstances of the actors.

In the moment of deep perplexity, Jesus appears on the water, creating even greater fear in the disciples. "It is I" (*egō eimi*)—a disclosure identifying Jesus as the one whom the disciples were expecting to join them, but at the same time associating him with the One whose name is "I am" (see 8:58). He is more than the promised prophet, and certainly not a wonder-worker who lets himself be captured by the crowd to supply their wishes. The text echoes Isa. 51:10–12, where the Lord is described as the one who dried up the waters at the time of the exodus from Egypt and who is identified as the "I am."

The theophany also becomes a redemptive event, in that Jesus speaks the powerful words, "Do not be afraid" (6:20), and immediately the boat arrives at the shore. The terrified disciples are calmed and rescued. The disclosure of who Jesus is turns out to be more than an intellectual matter for the philosophically curious; it is a saving matter that makes the difference between darkness and light, terror and peace, death and life.

Proper 13

Ordinary Time 18

Sunday between July 31 and August 6 inclusive

These texts may be understood around the injunction of the epistle, to "lead a life worthy of the calling." The call of God to a particular life is a deep conviction of the people of God. We confess that there is a purpose other than our own that is being worked through our life. Our growth is to become more responsive and attentive to, and congenial with, that larger purpose on which we do not get to vote.

In the Epistle reading, a "worthy" life consists in maximizing one's peculiar gifts for the sake of the community that is summoned to be a trusting, caring unity. An "unworthy" life is one that refuses to maximize one's gifts or, conversely, that refuses to offer those gifts for the sake of the community.

The Gospel reading uses the metaphor of bread (manna) to speak of utter trust in God, that is, to rely on God to give all that is needed for one's life. A worthy life is one that trusts completely and that relies only on God's good gifts. If this accent is a way of seeing coherence in these texts, then clearly David in the Old Testament lesson is not "worthy," because he did not yield his gifts to his community. He refused to live by God's gifts, trying to seize a peculiar destiny for himself.

In the psalm of confession, however, David does a complete about-face. He turns to God and entrusts his life to God's goodness. In this act of full (albeit belated) trust, David arrives belatedly at his "worthy calling." The worthy calling of the people of God concerns at the same time one's *reliance on God* and one's *concern for the community*. In his utter humanness, one can see David struggling with both these dimensions of his call. Our struggle is not very different from that of David. Our propensity to be self-indulgent is an enactment of our misgiving about God's fidelity. When we trust, we can care for community.

2 Samuel 11:26–12:13a

David's terrible sins of adultery and murder (2 Sam. 11:1–15, Proper 12) are now cast into the fierce light of Yahweh's justice, and Israel's greatest king is revealed to be little more than a common criminal. This lection is one of the greatest passages in the entire Bible, for it not only makes a devastating statement about the moral priorities of God, but it also abandons sentimentality and romanticism to portray the human condition as it actually is.

There is no hint in the text (11:26–27a) about the true feelings of Bathsheba. Just as her emotions are veiled in the narrative of David's lust, so we cannot determine from the sparse language of this passage whether her mourning was genuine or merely ceremonial. In any event, at its conclusion David brings her into his harem as another of his several wives, although his most favored one, to be sure.

But there is no ambiguity in the text's description of the reaction of Israel's God. Yahweh takes the initiative and virtually propels Nathan into David's presence (11:27b–12:1a; compare 2 Sam. 7: 1–17, Nathan's previous prophetic deliverance to David, and notice how it is David who there initiates the conversation with the Lord). It is a perilous moment in the prophet's life, for David's absolute power could easily cost Nathan his life (note Jer. 26:20–23, one of several instances in the Old Testament in which the words of a prophet resulted in danger or death for the bearer of Yahweh's word). But to his credit, Nathan is faithful to his calling; and the parable by which he draws David into an awareness of his own culpability is not just calculated by Nathan to ease his way into a sticky situation, but is designed to set a trap from which not even the most clever, self-justifying excuses will permit David to escape. When David, his moral indignation thoroughly aroused, denounces the greed of the villain in Nathan's tale, the snare is sprung. Nathan's "You are the man!" (v. 7a) is a truly decisive moment in human history, for, among other things, Nathan's statement affirms that there are certain moral norms for human life that not even the most powerful men and women may abrogate. Israel's God has brought forward even God's own anointed one to answer for his crimes.

In fact, the text makes it quite clear that David's guilt is all the greater precisely because he has been chosen by Yahweh (vs. 7b–12). If David had not been the recipient of the Lord's mercy, or if he had not been adopted by God into his special role in the life of the people, that would not excuse his adulterous act with Bathsheba or his murder of Uriah. But because David had been especially blessed, he could be expected to be especially responsible. David's terrible acts were nothing less than a rejection of God: "Why have you despised the word of the LORD?" (v. 9a).

The consequence of David's sin is to be tribulation and death (vs. 10–11). There can be no question that, in literary and theological terms, 2 Sam. 11–12 serves to introduce the dreadful events associated with the revolts of Absalom, Sheba, and Adonijah (2 Sam. 13–20; 1 Kings 1–2), material often identified as the so-called Succession Narrative or Court History. More specifically, Nathan's promise of 2 Sam. 12:11–12 anticipates the violation of David's harem by Absalom (2 Sam. 16:21–22) "in the sight of this very sun."

Chapter 12:12 carries strong echoes of 1 Sam. 16:7b (see Proper 6): "[Mortals] look on the outward appearance, but the LORD looks on the heart." This principle has now been affirmed, so that those evil deeds which humans (in this case, David) attempt to do in secret and which reflect the evil in their hearts are made public by the light of Yahweh's unremitting justice. It is precisely because the Lord knows David's heart that David's people, to say nothing of generations yet to be born, will "see" his great evil.

It is to David's enormous credit that he acknowledges his sin and, instead of venting his anger on Nathan, casts himself on the mercy of Yahweh. Tradition associates the moving lines of Ps. 51 with this occasion in David's life and, whether he actually penned them or not, they speak of the kind of catharsis that our present lection implies. "I have sinned against the LORD" is not only a statement of David's recognition of his sin, but the first enormous stride toward his restoration as a fallen, but redeemed, human being.

Not a few interpreters of this text have pointed out the apparent discrepancy between David's punishment and that of Saul. To be sure, David will suffer much hardship and pain in the years to come. But Saul lost his kingdom and ultimately his life, after what would seem to be less serious violations of God's will (1 Sam. 13; 15). The implication of our text is that the difference lay in David's acceptance of Yahweh's judgment, but Saul also confessed his sin and cast himself on the Lord's mercy (1 Sam. 15:24–25). Ultimately the reader of this text is thrown back upon a mystery concerning the will of God. Those who do God's work are not always the "best" people. Like Jacob, who prevailed over Esau, many who possess the greatest capacity for evil also own the largest potential for good. And so in response to the question, "Why did the Lord choose David over

Saul?" we can claim no logical answer. The only answer lies in the arena of God's grace. It is a mystery one cannot fathom until that far-off day when one can fathom completely the heart of God.

Psalm 51:1-12

The superscription of this psalm ties it directly to the narrative of 2 Sam. 11–12. Thus we are to read this psalm, in the first instance, as the voice of David as he recovers from his moment of destructive foolishness and reorients his life according to the moral shape of God's rule. Of course, the psalm does not belong exclusively to David, and we recite it along with David, as we also are recovering from our addiction to destructive foolishness. (See also Ps. 14, Proper 12, and the treatment of this psalm on Ash Wednesday.)

Psalm 51 begins with four insistent imperatives addressed to God (vs. 1–2), supported by the confession of v. 3. The four imperatives suggest that a covenanted Israelite, even in a moment of remorse and confession, is not reduced to chagrined silence, but still has the courage and freedom to address God with a strong insistence. David faces into his terrible failure, but he does not grovel. Rather, he proceeds in a direct way to take the actions that will permit a restored relationship with God. David is aware that restorative actions can come only from God, and he, David, will need to be a willing recipient of what God will do.

The first imperative is even more stark in Hebrew than in English. The psalm begins, "Grace me." David has complete confidence that Yahweh is able to do what is required in order to begin again. In the two clusters of terms in these verses are Israel's most distinctive theological vocabulary, and the two clusters make a powerful contrast. On the one hand, Yahweh's words in this prayer are "steadfast love" and "mercy" (*ḥesed, raḥămîm*), pointing to Yahweh's will to be compassionate. David's words, on the other hand, are "transgression," "iniquity," and "sin" (*pešaʻ, ʻāwōn, haṭṭāʼt*) Israel's comprehensive vocabulary for broken relations with God. David has no doubt that God's capacity for *steadfast love and mercy* is stronger than his own actions of *transgression, iniquity, and sin*, and that Yahweh will prevail. David acknowledges, without guile, his true situation, but submits his situation to the greater resolve of Yahweh.

Verses 4 and 5 serve to intensify the urgency of the initial petition. David makes three affirmations that intensify his imperatives. First, his struggle is with Yahweh, and his hope is from Yahweh (v. 4a).

This does not mean that he did not violate Uriah or Bathsheba, but the theological-moral crisis of his life is properly with Yahweh. It is with Yahweh that he must come to terms, and it is to Yahweh that he must look for rehabilitation. Second, David is in no position to bargain or negotiate (v. 4b). He has not a shred left of his usual self-confidence. David is willing, as he indicated to Nathan (2 Sam. 12:13), to submit and to take his chances with God, because he has no alternative. Third, David's life is permeated with failure toward God (v. 5). He is guilty "from the ground up." Without lessening the depth of the acknowledgment he makes, our interpretation, however, must resist any notion that this is an ontological statement, or that the psalm voices "original sin." It is, rather, the case that the crisis of David is massive and the need is total. There is no part of David's life or David's history that is withheld from this admission and this petition.

The psalm now presents the speaker as responsive, supple, and ready to be instructed, cleansed, and renovated by God (vs. 6–9). The verb "desire," which begins the unit, refers to what is pleasing to God and what qualified one for the cultic practice of communion. This section of the psalm concerns precisely cultic steps to restore communion. Thus "purging with hyssop" and "washing" are acts of ritual purification that may or may not here be metaphorical. In any case, David understands that restored communion does not happen simply by willing it, but that being acted on and being receptive to initiatives from "the other side" are decisive for rehabilitation.

In his moment of extreme need, David confesses that joy and gladness have vanished from his life, for a distorted relationship with God inevitably prevents life from being an innocent practice of joy. One cannot violate God and still know joy.

The final set of Davidic imperatives in our reading uses creation language (vs. 10–12). The verb "create" (*bārā'*) is the verb used at the beginning of the Bible. David's life has regressed to a shapeless chaos which he cannot manage or order, and so he awaits the powerful action of the ordering God to reshape his life. David waits, as chaos waited, for God to order. Moreover, David prays for a new *rûah*, a new energizing wind, not unlike the wind (spirit) of God in Gen. 1:2, which made new life possible. David's prayer for a clean heart, a new and right spirit—holy spirit, willing spirit—are all petitions that David should become God's new creation, which is possible only by God's magisterial activity (see 2 Cor. 5:17–18). This quite personal, intimate prayer uttered in deep need and helplessness is indeed the voice of chaos crying out to the Creator to make all things new.

This psalm has often been misread with an accent on guilt. There is no doubt that guilt is deeply present in this poem. The agenda of this psalm, however, is not guilt. David is not preoccupied with guilt, but with the new possibility for restored life and communion as a new gift from God. Because we live in a society deeply seduced into denial about our real disorder and needfulness, this psalm is a model of candor about failure, trouble, and need. What makes the candor possible in David's undaunted confidence in God, in God's willingness and God's capacity to make all things new.

Ephesians 4:1–16

Two problems that seem always to plague the church concern the nature of its leadership and the elusive character of Christian unity. In this lection, the author skillfully weaves together these two significant themes in terms of Christian vocation and the oneness of the body of Christ. The resulting statement acknowledges both the gifts granted to individuals and the importance of the context in which those gifts are employed and of the goals they are made to serve.

The opening appeal of Eph. 4:1–6 is framed in terms of Christian vocation: "Lead a life worthy of the calling to which you have been called." For those inclined to think that the category "calling" pertains only to those who are ordained, this statement may come as a surprise. The addressees as a whole are understood to be "called." Similar expressions that occur elsewhere (for example, in 1 Cor. 1:2 and 7:17–24) give evidence that this is not a passing remark. For the Pauline school, all believers are such because they have been "called" by God.

Ephesians 4:2–6 employs this notion of the common vocation of believers to urge behavior appropriate to that vocation. In v. 7 the author returns to the topic of vocation, here referring, however, to the specific gifts granted to each believer: "Each of us was given grace according to the measure of Christ's gift." The writer understands the quotation from Ps. 68:18 as supporting this point in the sense that Christ, as the one who ascends, makes gifts to the people. Interestingly, Ps. 68:18 actually refers to "receiving gifts from people" rather than giving them, raising the question whether the writer of Ephsians has remembered the psalm incorrectly or has deliberately misquoted it. (The digression in vs. 9–10 may reflect a need to insist on the reality of Jesus' earthly life over against an early docetic interpretation that would deny the reality of Jesus' bodily existence.)

That these "gifts" pertain to vocation becomes clear in v. 11, where they are interpreted as specific roles: apostles, prophets, evangelists, pastors, and teachers. This list differs somewhat from the list of gifts in 1 Cor. 12, which appears to order the roles in terms of their importance, as Paul argues there for the significance of all the gifts, whether minor or major. In both places the gifts serve the purpose of "building up the body of Christ," but here their immediate function is to "equip the saints for the work of ministry" (v. 12).

A first reading of the list of roles might appear to confirm the notion that only those Christians who serve as ordained ministers or other church "professionals" have a calling, and that the gifts given the church are confined to those individuals. From this observation a restricted and hierarchical understanding of leadership can emerge. But vs. 12–13 exactly counter that notion: the gifts of apostleship and pastoring and teaching and so forth exist in order to enable "the work of ministry." What emerges here is neither the highly democratized and often flabby notion that "everyone is a minister" nor the even more dangerous notion that ministry is limited to a few, but a clear understanding that all gifts exist to enhance the larger work of the church.

An integral part of "building up" the church, of course, is bringing about and maintaining its unity. Ephesians 4 eloquently describes the motivation behind Christian unity: "There is one body and one Spirit, just as you were called to the one hope of your calling, one Lord, one faith, one baptism, one God and Father of all, who is above all and through all and in all" (vs. 4–6). Because Christians share all these elements in common, "every effort" should be expended toward Christian unity.

The topic of unity returns in v. 13 as a goal of the church's ministry and as a barometer of Christian maturity. Those who are joined together by the church's ministry grow into "the unity of the faith." They "grow up in every way" (v. 15). Disunity, then, signals the spiritual immaturity of those who constitute the church.

The image of the church as a body, familiar from 1 Cor. 12, here returns with a couple of variations. First, the writer identifies Christ as the church's head, by contrast with 1 Corinthians, where the church *is* Christ's body (1 Cor. 12:27). Second, that head provides the coordination for the whole body. The striking imagery of the body being "knit together by every ligament" reinforces the role played by individual gifts in the maintenance of Christian unity.

This lection will be painful reading for contemporary Christians, for it recalls the scandal of Christian disunity. Even at the end of the century noted for significant developments in ecumenism, many parts of the church still cannot worship together or recognize a common ministry. In this context, the assertion that there is "one faith" and "one baptism" seems less a description of Christ's body than a statement of the hope toward which believers aim.

John 6:24-35

The assigned reading for this Sunday continues the focus on John 6, the chapter that relates the feeding of the multitude and the ensuing controversy stirred both in the crowd and among the disciples. The chapter reminds us that John contains narratives in which the dialogue functions at two levels, often leaving Jesus' dialogue partner confused but serving as effective communication to the reader. Rebirth, running (or living) water, blindness, and life carry double meanings. So in John 6, following the multiplication of the loaves, "bread" takes on a symbolic meaning, culminating in v. 35 with Jesus' statement, "I am the bread of life."

The narrative is carried along by three questions asked of Jesus by the crowd, questions that he answers but at a deeper level than they are asked. The questions provide a helpful entrée into the passage. First, "Rabbi, when did you come here?" (v. 25). The setting is carefully laid out by the narrator to confirm the miracle of Jesus' walking on the water (vs. 22-24) and to indicate just how persistent the crowds were in their pursuit of Jesus. When they had sought to make him king because he looked like a perpetual food supplier, he had retreated (v. 15). Now they track him to Capernaum.

Jesus addresses their persistence: "You are looking for me for all the wrong reasons. Don't become preoccupied with the food that still leaves you hungry, but with the food that endures for eternal life." Jesus can hardly be charged here with ignoring the physical needs of hungry people. After all, he has just fed five thousand all they could eat. At the same time, life is more than eating, and until the crowds understand that, they will not grasp who Jesus really is and what he is about.

We are getting close to the heart of the message of John's Gospel. Jesus' miracles are extraordinary deeds that rectify the situations of needy people—the sick, the hungry, the dying. But the results are not lasting unless the miracles are also perceived as signs pointing to the eternal gift of God in Jesus. The crowds' preoccupation with the benefits of the temporal has diverted them from seeing what really matters. Do they not mirror many modern people who endlessly pursue satisfactions (or even remedies) that have no ultimate significance, and yet overlook the life given by the Son of Man?

The second question of the crowds logically follows what Jesus has said: "What must we do to perform the works of God?" (v. 28). They have understood enough to want to push Jesus to find out what they can do to get beyond the continuous pursuit of unsatisfactory solutions. Jesus' reply is intriguing, reminiscent of the language of Paul. Instead of doing "works," the crowds are directed to "believe" in Jesus as the one sent by God.

The answer is simple, the one repeatedly advocated in John's narrative: Trust in God's special agent, have faith in what he says and in what he shows himself to be (for example, 3:14–18, 36; 4:39–42; 5:24, 38, 44–47). And yet the answer is not simple at all, for (as we shall later see) even the disciples find it difficult (6:60–69). Jesus speaks of it as "the work of God," meaning not only what God desires but also what God gives.

The miracle that really matters is the miracle of faith, when God breaks through the misconceptions we have held about life, our pursuit of unsatisfying answers, our self-centered worlds, to reveal the radically new age embodied in and taught by Jesus.

The third question of the crowds ask for a sign (6:30). It seems like a strange request in light of the miracle of feeding just performed, except that the crowds seem still to want Jesus to do it again, to be their source for physical food. They compare the feeding to the manna their ancestors ate in the wilderness, which came daily, and they (somewhat imprecisely) quote a text, "He gave them bread from heaven to eat" (Ex. 16:4, 15; Neh. 9:15; Ps. 78:24).

Jesus immediately offers a reinterpretation of the text. First, it was not Moses who gave the bread from heaven, as apparently the crowds think, but "my Father." Second, the verb should be present tense. God not only "gave" but "gives," freely and without limit. Third, the true bread from heaven is not manna, but Jesus himself.

The crowds, like the Samaritan woman at the well (John 4:15), remain confused, still asking for something they do not understand (6:34). Jesus' reinterpretation of the text has not sunk in. The symbolism escapes them, until v. 35 when Jesus removes the ambiguity. One might wish for a happy ending, as in the case of the Samaritan woman, but Jesus' dialogue partners now become "the Jews" who complain about his claim to be the bread from heaven (vs. 41, 52) and who later harden their opposition.

This passage and the next underscore the difficulties of faith, the intellectual, cultural, and even religious barriers that stand in the way of believing. The barriers are both ancient and modern. But the difficulties are overcome by grace, by the "work of God" that makes faith possible (6:29).

Proper 14

Ordinary Time 19

*Sunday between
August 7 and 13 inclusive*

David's deep distress over the death of his beloved son Absalom occupies the attention of both the Old Testament and Psalms lections. The passage from 2 Sam. 18 contains the narrative description of Absalom's death as well as David's pathetic reaction to it. On one level it is the story of the consequences of human sinfulness, but on another it is a profoundly moving portrait of natural human grief, in this instance that of an old man over the death of his son. The reader is both attracted to and repelled by the text, for it speaks volumes not only about what human life ought to be, but also about the manner in which we sinners actually shape the contours of our days and years.

The Psalm text is set as the penitential cry of one who is in David's anguished predicament. That there is some distance between Ps. 130 and the words David is actually recorded as speaking (2 Sam. 18:33) should be noted, but the two expressions are not contradictory, in that David's formless cry of pain is a "first step" toward a coherent prayer for God's merciful intervention. Thus the psalm gives voice to a hope that is only implied in the narrative of David's response to Absalom's tragic death.

The lection from Eph. 4 and 5 addresses the issue of what the Christian life is like and how it is to be lived. If, at first glance, the norms for Christian living seem somewhat legalistic, that initial impression is swept away by the reader's realization that for each "rule," there is supplied an accompanying reason. Truthful speech is important, for example, because "we are members of one another." An attitude of forgiveness toward others arises out of the realization that "God in Christ has forgiven you." The passage reaches a climax with the astonishing assertion that Christians are to be imitators not just of Paul or of Christ, but of none other than God.

John 6 contains Jesus' memorable words "I am the bread of life" (v. 35), and in the verses appointed from this chapter for this day that statement is both made and interpreted. Verses 41–51 may be understood as forming a type of exegesis of v. 35, in which it is made clear that the bread in question is not ordinary bread, but "bread . . . from heaven." Furthermore, emphasis is placed on the role of "the Father" in bringing persons into the mystery of who Jesus is, a mystery that is clarified and deepened by the affirmation that "the bread that I will give for the life of the world is my flesh" (v. 51).

2 Samuel 18:5–9, 15, 31–33

Such are the deadly fruits of David's sinfulness! That is the judgment of the Deuteronomistic historians who have transmitted to us the story (at least in its present form) of Absalom's rebellion and death and of David's sorrowful response. Nathan's ominous promise to David that "the sword shall never depart from your house" (2 Sam. 12:10; Proper 13) comes true in a number of important ways (Sheba's rebellion, 2 Sam. 20; Adonijah's rebellion, 1 Kings 1:5–2:25), but there are certain respects in which Absalom's attempt to wrest the kingdom from his father was for David the most bitter experience of all.

In all honesty it must be noted that the matter of culpability was far more complicated than a simple love triangle involving Bathsheba and Uriah the Hittite, even though that triangle produced the terrible crimes of adultery and murder. Amnon's rape of Tamar and Absalom's subsequent revenge on his brother (2 Sam. 13) are also factors in the equation, as is Absalom's overweening pride (2 Sam. 15:1–6). The text also leaves open the possibility that David's harem seethed with intrigue, as his various wives plotted to set their favorite sons in line to succeed their father. The rule of primogeniture was not yet established in Israel, for David himself had frustrated the efforts of Saul's heir Ishbaal (RSV: Ish-bosheth) to claim his father's kingdom (2 Sam. 3–4). And so the efforts of Bathsheba (successful, as it turned out) to place David's crown on her son's head (1 Kings 1:11–40) may have been duplicated by other of David's wives. In any event, the brief notice of 1 Kings 1:6, although entered into the record with Adonijah in mind, could just as well have been spoken of other of David's sons: "His father had never at any time displeased him by asking, 'Why have you done thus and so?' " One may compare David's treatment of Amnon after the rape of Tamar (2 Sam. 13:21) and his attitude toward Absalom following the murder of Amnon (13:37–39). The images of parental disarray—on the part of both father and mothers—are strongly suggested by the text.

When Absalom's revolt proves successful—at least to the extent of forcing David and his most loyal followers to flee from Jerusalem—David is torn between two conflicting emotions. On the one hand, he expects his army, led by his old friend Joab, to crush the rebels. But on the other, he openly yearns for the safety of his insurrectionist son (18:5). Just as it is easy to blame David for this whole sordid mess, so it is tempting to fault him for what may be perceived as a "soft" attitude toward Absalom. But it should be kept in mind that David had already lost one son to a violent death, and those same charismatic qualities that endeared Absalom to the population as a whole (15:6) also won him the love of David. Thus, David finds himself on the horns of a depressing dilemma: He is pulled to the one side by his devotion to his troops, and to the other by his deep affection for his defiant son. David's inability (or was it unwillingness?) to extricate himself from this trap ultimately earns for him a stinging rebuke from Joab and the certain disaffection of many of his followers (19:5–7).

While David is being paralyzed by his own emotional struggle, the larger battle—the one in the forest between the two armies—appears to move along according to its own rhythms. Actually, however, all these events are moving along according to the will of Yahweh, for it is Yahweh who, although rarely mentioned in the text, is nevertheless the guiding force behind all that unfolds. Second Samuel 17:14 has put the reader on notice that, although things seem to proceed on their own momentum, it is the Lord, not Joab or David, who will "bring ruin on Absalom." The lectionary text includes the description of how, during the fighting, Absalom is immobilized: "His head caught fast in the oak, and he was left hanging between heaven and earth" (18:9). It also includes the brief description of the attack on Absalom by David's troops (v. 15). But missing from the lectionary text is the information concerning Joab's participation in the young prince's death (v. 14), an important element in the future relations between David (and Solomon) and his faithful commander-in-chief (1 Kings 1:7; 2:28–35).

There are few more wrenching scenes in the Bible than that of David's grief when he learns that Absalom has been killed (2 Sam. 18:33). The repetitiveness of David's lament (notice the fivefold use of the word "son") is not only true to life, but it drives home to a reader who is three thousand years distant from the event itself the pathos and tragedy of the moment. It is almost as if we are reading in the newspaper of some death in one of the many wars that plague our own time. David has sinned, and both he and the nation have paid a terrible price—and the suffering is not yet at an end! Beyond the theology of the text, the reader empathizes with an old man's pain. We remember that the distress caused by a person's sinful deeds, as well as by the sinfulness of others, often continues to multiply itself long after the sin itself has been forgotten.

Psalm 130

For a full exposition of Ps. 130, see Proper 8. In this lection, the psalm is related to David's response to the death of Absalom, his feared rebel and treasured son. In his deep grief over his son, David is indeed "in the depths." It is instructive that David's sorrow is not at all marked by guilt, but only by impotence and helplessness in the face of his loss.

It would not be fair to say that David in the narrative expresses hope. Rather his words are unformed, pathos-filled grief, perhaps self-pity addressed to no one in particular, surely not to the God of hope. But then we may also judge that this "primal scream" of inchoate, unutterable grief is a first step in a more ordered act of petition and hope. And even if David does not address God in his grief, we dare affirm that this God hears undirected grief and takes it seriously, even if it is addressed only against the wind (compare the same undirected, but heard, grief in Ex. 2:23–25). When David's narrative of grief is encompassed in the psalm, we may imagine that the grief is received into the larger sphere of God's steadfast love, where it may be transformed into hope. In such an interpretation, our sense of David's grief in the psalm is carried well beyond what we are told in the narrative of Samuel. The lectionary juxtaposition of texts invites precisely this move from the poignant narrative to the more sure-handed psalm. In this interpretative maneuver, we pass from a raw presentation of human *hurt* to a God-received act of *hope*.

Ephesians 4:25–5:2

The words "So then" scarcely make for a catchy introduction, but those opening words are nevertheless a significant part of this lection. The preceding passage (Eph. 4:17–24) admonishes Christians to take up the new way of life, even the new self that has been granted them by God in Jesus Christ. That powerful and eloquent claim, however, may give rise to certain questions: What exactly does all of this mean? What does this new life look like? How will I know if I am living it?

Perhaps because of the inevitability of these questions, the author of Ephesians attempts to give flesh to the "new self" in the section that begins in 4:25 and extends through most of the remainder of the letter. Some of the content of this prolonged set of ethical admonitions offends contemporary readers (for example, the instructions for the submission of wives in 5:22–24 or the parallel word to slaves in 6:5–8), but the need to depict Christian life in concrete and understandable terms remains constant. The "So then" of v. 25, therefore, serves to identify the specific ethical commandments as aspects of the renewal depicted in 4:17–24.

Ephesians 4:25–5:2 contains a mixture of rules that do not readily lend themselves to categorization. Some of the rules parallel Old Testament passages (compare 4:25 with Zech. 8:16; and 4:26 with Ps. 4:4), while others have close parallels elsewhere in the New Testament (compare Eph. 4:28 with 1 Thess. 4:11) or in the philosophical instruction of the day. Several of these rules focus on speech and the harm done by thoughtless or malicious speech (Eph. 4:25, 29, 31–32), but others focus on wrongful action (vs. 26, 28). If some aspects of this instruction seem to pertain to life within the Christian community (v. 25), others clearly include life outside as well (v. 28).

On the whole, the content of these admonitions is not particularly innovative or striking. What does make the passage stand out is the way in which the writer interlaces ethical admonition and motivating assertion. For virtually every rule, a principle is adduced that underlies the rule and motivates its fulfillment. With the possible exception of the reference to the devil in v. 27, none of these assertions takes the form of a threat; rather, each appeals to the Christian identity that is regarded as a given.

Truthful speech becomes a requirement for the Christian community because "we are members of one another." "Membership" here is not the pallid latter-day notion of being enrolled on a list of participants in some organization; rather, being a "member" signifies belonging to the same body. In other words, Christians can no more tolerate lying to one another than the parts of one's body can deceive one another. It cannot be done.

The admonitions about anger and sin in v. 26 precede a general warning about making room for the devil. In several passages, New Testament writers refer to the devil's ability to take advantage of opportunity to deceive and mislead believers. By contrast with v. 25, then, the appeal here is to beware of forces outside the community that are capable of undermining the community's strength.

The third motivating assertion comes in v. 30: "And do not grieve the Holy Spirit of God, with which you were marked with a seal for the day of redemption." Christian behavior not only reflects on the community itself and can invite outside powers to destroy the community, but Christian behavior—or misbehavior—has the ability to *grieve* God's own Spirit. The severity of such grief is underscored by the reminder that it is the Spirit that provides the seal guaranteeing the redemption of believers.

Verse 32 provides the fourth assertion. Forgiveness must be practiced in the Christian community because "God in Christ has forgiven you." In common with many other biblical passages, this one invokes God's behavior as a motivational principle for Christian behavior. God's forgiveness of human beings enables them to learn what forgiveness is and obliges them to act that forgiveness out in their own lives.

All the individual ethical rules and motivating assertions come together in the final verses of the lection: "Therefore be imitators of God, as beloved children, and live in love, as Christ loved us and gave himself up for us, a fragrant offering and sacrifice to God." While Paul several times urges his congregations to imitate Christ or to imitate Paul himself as he imitates Christ (for example, 1 Cor. 4:16; 11:1), the admonition to imitate God comes as something of a surprise. Indeed, human beings fall into terrible peril when they wrongly imitate God, that is, God's knowledge or power or judgment. What Eph. 5:1–2 evokes, of course, is the particular character of God's love toward humankind, a love seen clearly in the sacrificial death of Jesus Christ.

Exegetes and ethicists have invested great energy in articulating the relationship between the indicative of the gospel and the imperative of human response. In this passage the two interweave in such a way as to make separating them virtually impossible. God's action in Jesus Christ demands certain behaviors of human beings, but along with the demand come the gifts that make the demand feasible: "membership," the seal of the Holy Spirit, the forgiveness of God, the love of Christ.

John 6:35, 41–51

One way to approach the Gospel reading is to think of John 6:35 ("I am the bread of life. Whoever comes to me will never be hungry, and whoever believes in me will never be thirsty") as the text and the remainder of the passage as the explanation of the text. The incident is clearly a teaching event, following on the heels of the feeding of the five thousand, and Jesus' conversation partners are no longer the crowds, as in the earlier portion of the chapter, but "the Jews." What are the implications of making such a claim as v. 35 asserts, regarding both Jesus' significance and the appropriate way of relating to him?

First, the clarification is important that as the bread of life Jesus is "the bread that came down from heaven" (vs. 38, 41, 50–51). Though described with an image from ordinary life, Jesus is unique. He even defies comparison with the miraculous manna that sustained the Israelites during their time in the wilderness. Those who ate the manna "died" (v. 49). They were nourished only for a day. But as the bread from heaven, Jesus gives the life of the age to come, the life that has about it the tang of eternity, "so that one may eat of it and not die" (v. 50). Even the reality of physical death is not ignored, since eternal life includes the promise that there will be a resurrection at the last day (vs. 39, 44, 54). The bread from heaven, then, satisfies the human hunger both now and for the future.

The religious authorities (designated "the Jews"), in line with their ancestors who "complained" at the exodus from Egypt (see Ex. 15:24; 16:2, 7–12; Num. 11:1), "complain" about the assertion that Jesus is the bread "from heaven" (John 6:41). How can a person whose name and address are well documented claim to be from God? The religious authorities know his mother and father, which precludes a heavenly origin. Their response to Jesus is blocked by a common-sense logic that takes on the character of certitude. Instead of being open to the divine claim, they judge it by human wisdom. What they know (or think they know) keeps them from the only knowledge that really matters.

Jesus answers the "complaint" of the authorities with a simple command not to complain (v. 43). He does not present a long argument, nor offer a demonstration or a proof. Apparently, there is no way to "argue" them into accepting that Jesus comes from above. The closed world of the authorities is impervious to the claims of Jesus. Only if they cease "complaining" can they be open to hear and be taught.

Jesus' interchange with the religious authorities is certainly informative about the task of evangelizing and being evangelized. People operating with closed systems, whether they be inside the church or out, cannot be argued into believing that Jesus is more than a guy from Nazareth. All the historical evidence in the world, and the most persuasive logic, will fall on deaf ears. The affirmations are made and the witness is borne, but it takes the action of God to evoke faith.

This leads to the second part of the explanation of John 6:35.

Coming to and believing in Jesus is an invitation made, but at the same time "No one can come to me unless drawn by the Father" (v. 44; compare vs. 37, 39). While the evangelist cannot ignore the self-centered, closed worlds of those to whom invitation is given, neither can the evangelist ignore the divine magnetic force that pulls humans out of those worlds to faith. The Greek verb translated as "drawn" in v. 44 appears again in 12:32: "And I, when I am lifted up . . . , will *draw* all people to myself (emphasis added)." Neither God nor Jesus as the agent of God is willing to let human resistance go unchallenged.

Another role of the Father in 6:45 supplements that of the magnetic force in v. 44. Citing a line from a song of praise to God's everlasting covenant of peace found in Isaiah, the text declares that "they shall all be taught by God" (see Isa. 54:13). God not only attracts but also instructs people in the divine intentions for the world, an instruction that leads to faith in Jesus.

Throughout this section the narrator recognizes the mysterious paradox of believing. On the one hand, invitations are given to which humans can respond. On the other hand, those who respond are drawn by the divine power, for nothing else can produce faith. As it is put earlier in dialogue, belief in Jesus is the work of God (John 6:29).

The third and final explanation of v. 35 provides a new and critical dimension to the symbol "bread." The bread from heaven is identified with the "flesh" of Jesus given for the life of the world (v. 51). The language is rather shockingly materialistic and anticipates the coming death of Jesus. The distinctiveness of the bread lies not only in its heavenly origin but in its very specific, historical expression in the crucified Jesus. In contrast to the misunderstanding of the crowds (vs. 14–15), the feeding proposed by Jesus is by no means a free lunch. It includes the costly giving up of life in order to procure life.

Proper 15

Ordinary Time 20

*Sunday between
August 14 and 20 inclusive*

The series of lections for this day begins with a focus on "wisdom." Solomon's prayer on his accession to the throne of David asking that God provide him with this quality forms the core of the Old Testament text. Yet that celebrated request, in spite of its obvious connection with the great flowering of Wisdom literature and thought during Solomon's reign, stands in stark contrast to the principles by which Solomon actually ruled—for the Solomon who seeks wisdom at the beginning of his reign is the same Solomon who so oppresses his people that many of them rebel immediately following his death. If it stands for nothing else, the passage from 1 Kings 3 is emblematic of the frequent distance between God's hopes for human life and the manner in which we, in fact, live.

Psalm 111 mirrors the ordered world and the somewhat predictable God envisioned by teachers of the wisdom schools. It also mirrors the controlled state of affairs that characterized the Solomonic politics and, no doubt, the Solomonic piety. The God who is the subject of Ps. 111 is both transcendent and trustworthy, a God of perfect wisdom. Almost forgotten in this majestic poem, however, is the realization that the God of Israel is also an unpredictable God of the most startling and merciful surprises.

Wisdom, in a somewhat different sense, is one of the characteristics of the Christian life that is identified in the lection from Eph. 5. The principles for this "new life" not only are identified in positive terms, but are also contrasted with their opposites. Christian people are to be "wise," not "unwise." They are to "understand . . . the will of the Lord," and are not to be "foolish" (lacking sense). They are to be sober, avoiding "debauchery." These features of the text, as well as others, remind the reader that the Christian life is always lived as an alternative to the dominant culture, whatever that culture may be.

John 6:51–59 shares much vocabulary with other parts of Jesus' discourse following the feeding of the five thousand, but the focus here is on the eucharistic meal. The startling phrases "eat my flesh" and "drink my blood," which seem cannibalistic on the surface, point to the mystery of the participation by believers in the death of Jesus. The text also points to the promise of eternal life extended to believers, by which is meant not only life beyond the grave, but a new quality of living in the present.

1 Kings 2:10–12; 3:3–14

First Kings 2:10–12, with which this lection begins, constitutes the "seam" that joins the story of David to that of his son and successor, Solomon. Yet this brief notice is more than a simple literary device by which the reader is carried from one generation to the next in the narrative of Israel's monarchy. It is also the goal toward which the Deuteronomistic History (and the Succession Narrative—also called the Court History—on which the Deuteronomistic historians drew for their information about the final years of David's reign) has been moving since the gripping tale of David's terrible sins involving Bathsheba and her husband, Uriah the Hittite (2 Sam. 11–12; Propers 12 and 13). The matter has now been settled: Bathsheba's son will be the next king of the line of David. Although he was not the son born out of their illicit embrace (2 Sam. 12:15–25), he was a son of Bathsheba, nonetheless. It is as if the text wishes to tell us that that sordid affair is now over. David's sin has been laid to rest, and out of a situation laced with evil God has crafted a gracious conclusion. Solomon's kingdom has been "firmly established" (1 Kings 2:12).

The narrative of Solomon's request for wisdom and of God's affirmation of that request (3:3–14) rests in a certain tension with other elements in the story of Solomon's reign. This passage begins with a statement that is clearly intended to prepare the reader for Solomon's great achievement in the building of the Jerusalem Temple (3:3–4). Solomon, like other Israelites, is in the habit of worshiping at one of the "high places," a term that in Samuel-Kings is often used in a pejorative sense. Solomon's generation, including the king himself, is not indicted here for performing a sinful act, but the reader is aware that, in time, that model Davidic king, Josiah, will perform an important act of cultic purification by purging the high places from the land and ordering that all worship take place at the Jerusalem Temple (2 Kings 23:4–20). Of course, there is no temple at the beginning of Solomon's reign, and the reliance of the people on high places at Gibeon and elsewhere underscores the need for

Solomon to fulfill Yahweh's promise to David recorded in 2 Sam. 7 (Proper 11).

However, the time is not quite ripe for Solomon's great building enterprise. Before that comes, the kind of king that Solomon is to be must be determined, and in that regard the operative term is wisdom. The reader is asked in 1 Kings 3:3–14 to suspend his or her knowledge of Solomon's real character: tyrannical to the point of grinding under the basic rights of Israel's people (5:13; 9:15). The reader is asked not to recall that so foolish was Solomon's rule that the first recorded political event after his death was the secession of the northern tribes (12:1–19). This text is a celebration of but one facet of Solomon's rule, yet a facet of extraordinary beauty and goodness: the flowering under Solomon of that cultural-intellectual movement which the ancient writers and modern scholars alike refer to as "wisdom."

It is impossible at this distance to reconstruct all the details of this great blossoming of the human spirit during the administration of Israel's second Davidic king, yet it surely involved a burgeoning role by the state in the administration of justice (3:16–28; notice also reference to a "Hall of Justice" in 7:7) and in the growth of those skills in law, statecraft, and education which a strengthened and centralized judiciary demands. We know that was a feature of wisdom among certain of Israel's neighbors, and it is only to be expected that these things should be characteristic of Israelite wisdom, as well. In addition, old literary forms associated with wisdom were rediscovered and revitalized, a fact reflected in the reference to Solomon in the books of Proverbs (Prov. 1:1) and Ecclesiastes (Eccl. 1:1; compare 1 Kings 4:32 for another kind of literary-artistic activity). And here and there we have brief glimpses in the biblical text of a wisdom feature we know most extensively from the literatures of ancient Egypt and Mesopotamia: an empirical science based on a keen observation of nature (1 Kings 4:33).

Only a writer very closely identified with the Solomonic court could describe these characteristics of the larger wisdom tradition as being examples of Solomon's personal wisdom. A more sober view, based on a reading of Solomon's record as a whole, would suggest that the king's wisdom in supporting the wisdom traditions in Israel was more than counterbalanced by Solomon's foolish policies of taxation and forced labor. (In this same vein, one may wish to compare the optimistic statement of 4:20 with the strong protests recorded in 12:4, protests that formed a prelude to the dissolution of the old Davidic monarchy.)

It may be, of course, that the Solomon of 1 Kings 3:3–14 is a young and godly Solomon (note 3:7), and that he is to be contrasted with an older Solomon best known for the harshness of his rule and for his disregard for the traditions of Israel and the well-being of the people. Undoubtedly the Deuteronomistic historians would wish us to read 3:14 in the light of 11:1–13. That is to say, Solomon earned the displeasure of the Lord precisely because he did *not* "walk in [God's] ways." The sad and ironic truth is that, when Solomon's life is measured by the words of his very own prayer to God, he must be deemed a miserable failure. That the Lord honored his prayer did not mean that he was absolved of all moral responsibility. And it would seem that his very blindness to that fact led to the tragic schism of the kingdom.

Psalm 111

This psalm is related by the lectionary to the beginning of the reign of Solomon. In his initial dream encounter, Solomon in his innocence accepts a world from God that is perfectly ordered, symmetrical, and reliable, guaranteed by a God who is faithful and "cool." That same world of ordered reliability and that same God of generous goodness are the subjects of this psalm. Two features of this psalm are to be noted at the outset. First, Psalm 111 is acrostic, which means that the first letter of each line (in Hebrew) goes through the alphabet in order. This suggests that the psalm is highly stylized, well ordered, and quite self-conscious in its rather didactic witness.

Second, the psalm is deliberately paired with Ps. 112, which is also acrostic and well ordered. The complementary themes of Pss. 111 and 112 are that Ps. 111 bears witness to an utterly reliable God, and Ps. 112 is a summons to one to live a human life of caring, responsible, neighborly concern in response to God. Our reading of Ps. 111 thus concerns only the first half of this double focus of witness and summons.

Verse 1 is a more or less liturgical introduction to a psalm that otherwise bears no obvious liturgical marks. Here there is an initial summons to praise (compare Ps. 112:1), a resolve to give thanks, and reference to the congregation. But that is all. The remainder of the psalm is a doxology, but it is cast as a highly intellectual and disciplined statement, which one senses is more instructional than it is liturgical (though the two are not completely mutually exclusive).

I am unable to detect any development or theme in the psalm. Indeed, the series of propositions that constitute the psalm could be arranged in almost any sequence, were it not for the acrostic method that dictates the present order.

The psalm begins its doxology in praise of God's "works" (v. 2). The same motif appears in v. 3 ("work," *pōʻal*), in v. 4 ("deeds," *niplāʼōt*), and in vs. 6 and 7 ("works," *maʻăśîm*). The God here praised has been busy and has accomplished much, which Israel remembers and values. Oddly, however, this psalm lacks all specificity and never gives any concrete context to all these mentions of "work." On the one hand, the term used in v. 4 might be rendered "miracles," and the references in v. 9 might suggest the exodus and Mt. Sinai; but we are not told. On the other hand, in v. 7 the "works" of Yahweh seem to be God's commands and precepts, which must be obeyed, but even this is not specified.

Thus, the notion of "works" seems almost to be an empty term with which the community seems familiar. We may learn a bit more if we notice that all these references to "works" support the recital of a number of descriptive adjectives. That is, this psalm seems to mention the works, not as concrete testimonies, but as a means of characterizing God's inclination toward the world. The terms concerning God include honor and majesty (v. 3), righteousness (v. 3), gracious and merciful (v. 4), faithful, just, and trustworthy (v. 7), faithfulness and uprightness (v. 8), holy and awesome (v. 9). To be sure, some of these terms are applied to God, some to God's commands and actions, and some to the quality of response that is expected. All of them, however, witness to the quality and shape of this God and the way God must be treated. This God is majestically remote, reliably and genuinely concerned, capable and willing to give life, ready to be obeyed in ways that match God's own character and purpose.

Thus it is telling that a psalm of praise places a great emphasis on covenant and command. Indeed, the generous, food-giving God gives food not to everyone, but to God's fearers (v. 5). God remembers the covenant, the commitments God has made, and the commandments God has issued. These commands are to be executed with faithfulness and uprightness (v. 8), and even the covenant is understood not as gracious self-giving, but as command (v. 9). Verse 10 sounds like a sapiential addendum, but its content is not different from the other parts of the psalm. Those who traffic with this God are those who meet God primarily in command and precept and who enact in the world a quality of life and ethic that mirrors God's own life.

This psalm contains little energy, imagination, or initiative. It is a rather flat exhortation in a doxological mode which assures that its listeners are on board and ready to consent in concrete ways. Such a bloodless, lifeless exposition might be expected in a Solomonic court, in which the freedom and spontaneity of God are largely submerged to the orderliness and propriety of a great, affluent enterprise. The high, symmetrical theology of this psalm is not to be taken lightly. But it is probably a piece of rhetoric that is congenial to an establishment community that highly (excessively?) prizes stability. The purpose of such praise as instruction is to invite "study" (v. 2), discipline, and respectability. The text resists any daring inventiveness, but does touch on the serious claims of faith for life. (See also the comments under Fourth Sunday After Epiphany.)

Ephesians 5:15–20

This lection continues the discussion begun in Eph. 4:25 about the specific characteristics of the "new self" given the Christian (see 4:24 and the introduction to the discussion of Eph. 4:25–5:2 under Proper 14). The framework of this passage consists of three sharp contrasts: "Live, not as unwise people but as wise" (v. 15); "do not be foolish, but understand" (v. 17); and "do not get drunk with wine, . . . but be filled with the Spirit" (v. 18). Supplementing these contrasts are the perplexing statement about time in v. 16 and the reminder of the need for thanksgiving in vs. 19–20.

The underlying contrasts in vs. 15–18 stand out more clearly in the Greek than they do in English translation. At the center of each contrast is the strong adversative conjunction *alla* ("but"). More important, if more difficult to see in English translation, each contrast focuses on a word with an alpha privative, that is, a word that begins with "a" or "an" and carries the idea of negating or neutralizing some positive concept. English has many such terms, such as "amoral" or "amorphous." This passage employs three such terms: *asophos* or "lacking wisdom" ("unwise" in the NRSV), *aphrōn* or "lacking sense" ("foolish" in the NRSV), and *asōtia* or "lacking sobriety" ("debauchery" in the NRSV). By contrasting these negative traits with their opposites, the author is able to emphasize the life-style desired for Christians.

The first contrast is between living wisely and unwisely, and this contrast lies beneath the others that follow. In this context, the admonition to be wise almost certainly refers to the kind of wisdom cultivated in the Jewish wisdom tradition. There, wisdom pertains not so much to the acquisition of intellectual knowledge as to the orientation of persons to the values approved by God. Living in keeping with God's commandments, pursuing those traits which make for peaceful and harmonious life, attending to God's wisdom—these are among the characteristics of wisdom in this usage.

The second contrast brings this understanding of wisdom to the surface: "So do not be foolish, but understand what the will of the Lord is" (v. 17). In the first-century philosophical tradition, the opposite of foolishness would be self-possession, discipline, independence of the spirit and the will. For the Christian, however, the wisdom that stands opposite foolishness is not one's own wisdom, but that which stems from understanding God's will.

The third contrast, that between being filled with wine ("debauchery") and being filled with the Spirit, offers a specific instance of human folly versus divine wisdom. Because some religious traditions did understand alcohol to be an aid to ecstatic experiences (as is reflected in Acts 2:13, 15), the contrast here is more substantive than might appear to be the case at first glance. For Christians, only the Spirit produces real ecstasy.

This passage employs language that has little currency in contemporary Western Christianity, and as a result it may seem remote and abstract. That would be an unfortunate conclusion, however, for the understanding of "wisdom" that pervades Western society has much in common with that against which early Christianity had to define itself. For example, it is said that "common sense" or "realism" dictate a certain kind of behavior, a set of priorities determined by money, by prestige, by autonomy. These are among the characteristics ascribed to "wisdom" in the modern world, whereas what the gospel counts as "wisdom" runs in quite a different direction.

Two sections of the lection remain to be addressed, that regarding time in v. 16 and that concerning thanksgiving in vs. 19–20. The first passage is difficult to translate; the verb the NRSV translates as "making the most of" literally means to "buy back" or "redeem." How one "buys" time and how that is related to the fact that "the days are evil" remains quite unclear. In a more eschatologically oriented writing, the conclusion might be that Christians are to make the most of the time available to them because only a few days remain prior to the Parousia. Ephesians, however, reflects more realized than future eschatology, making such an interpretation unlikely. Perhaps, in keeping with the passage as a whole, the intent is simply to encourage a careful use of time that is otherwise subject to the corruption that afflicts much of human life.

In the final lines of the passage, the writer encourages readers to "sing psalms and hymns and spiritual songs among yourselves, singing and making melody to the Lord in your hearts" (v. 19). This admonition seems out of place in the otherwise stern language of the reading, but it may be that such singing is understood as, after all, part of living in accordance with God's wisdom. Certainly the call to perpetual thanksgiving ("at all times and for everything," v. 20) understands thanksgiving within God's wisdom and probably as a powerful antidote to the world's foolishness.

Is it possible for any human being to be grateful "at all times and for everything"? Surely observation and experience make it very difficult to answer that question affirmatively, but the radical understanding of gratitude envisioned here nevertheless forms the very center of Christian response to the gospel.

John 6:51–58

The important terms and phrases that characterize Jesus' speech following the feeding of the five thousand appear and reappear throughout the discourse (John 6:22–59)—"bread of life," "bread that comes down from heaven," "manna that your ancestors ate," "the Father who sent me," "eternal life," "believe." At times their repetition lulls the reader into thinking that one verse sounds just like another and that there is no progression in the discourse. But the moves are subtle, and shifts occur without change of setting or great fanfare.

One such shift in the discourse occurs at 6:51, when the bread is described as something Jesus "will give for the life of the world" and is specifically identified as his "flesh." The allusion (for the reader at least) to the crucifixion is unmistakable. The bringing of eternal life is not without a death that has atoning significance.

The shift provokes an argument among the Jewish authorities. Some take Jesus' words literally, and apparently wonder if eating his flesh signifies cannibalism. Jesus' reply (heightened by the "Very truly" formula in v. 53) does not lessen the hardness of the symbolism, but in fact throws the disputing Jews into a worse dilemma by adding the even more offensive phrase "drink his blood."

Commentators at this point often debate whether John is a sacramental Gospel, in which this piece of Jesus' speech replaces the words of institution omitted at the Last Supper, or whether John is a nonsacramental Gospel and uses phrases like "eat my flesh" and "drink my blood" simply as vivid metaphors for abiding in Christ. The preacher has to pay attention to such an argument, because it will invariably determine when the text ought to be preached and how the sermon goes. Unfortunately the debate is often cast in terms of what the author of the Gospel did or did not intend by the words used. The problem is that modern readers cannot get back into the mind of an ancient author and figure out the intention behind the words. We are simply stuck with the words, and it is well-nigh impossible to escape their eucharistic flavor, particularly when they are drawn together with an allusion to Jesus' death. Keep in mind that the temporal setting for the whole chapter is the approaching Passover festival (v. 4). The symbolism of "eat my flesh" and "drink my blood" is simply too jolting without the traditional language of the Lord's Supper close by.

If this judgment is correct, then the shift at v. 51 has introduced new dimensions to the discourse. For one thing, the allusion to Jesus' death ties the gift of life to a concrete, historical figure, a "scandal of particularity." Eternal life is not a universal phenomenon that takes effect regardless of context or commitment. If readers (ancient or modern) are prone to a purely spiritual religion that somehow transcends the nitty-gritty aspects of life or avoids the realism of death, then the text brings them down to earth and refuses to tolerate either idealistic or docetic tendencies. At the heart of the Christian faith is the "flesh" of Jesus given for the life of the world, and believers are drawn into sharing that death: "Unless you eat the flesh of the Son of Man and drink his blood, you have no life in you" (v. 53).

The other new dimension to the discourse comes with the sacramental allusions. The passage invites preachers to reflect on its meaning when the congregation is gathered at the Table. Two motifs emerge more boldly than in the traditional eucharistic texts and warrant sermonic consideration. The first is that of participation (rather than, say, presence or sacrifice). The dominant verbs in the section are "eat" and "drink," rather than "believe" (as in vs. 35–47). Partaking of the sacrament draws one into the very life of Jesus. The characteristic Johannine verb "abide" appears in v. 56, with its connotations of mutuality and consistency. Ingesting the elements binds the participant in a unique way to the Son of Man, who "loses nothing" of what God has given him (v. 39).

The second motif connected to the eucharistic allusions is eternal life. Of course, life has been an urgent theme not only through the sixth chapter of John, but through the entire Gospel. Here its source is the living Father, who gives life to the Son, who in turn through the Lord's Supper gives life to participants (v. 57). "Eternal life" clearly implies more than an existence that continues without termination. Many would choose death over life if life were simply more of the same. Consistently in John, however, both "life" and "eternal life" signify life of the age to come, life with a distinctively new quality, authentic life fulfilling God's intentions.

Proper 16

Ordinary Time 21

*Sunday between
August 21 and 27 inclusive*

Worship is central to the life of the people of God. In various ways both Old and New Testaments affirm this reality, and in the case of the Old Testament that affirmation is often centered on the Jerusalem Temple.

The Old Testament lection for this day, as well as that from the Psalms, focuses on the splendid Temple of Solomon. The passage from 1 Kings 8, Solomon's prayer at the dedication of the sanctuary, places the presence of the living God squarely in the center of the nation's life. Yahweh is a God who cannot be framed by the human mind or contained by works of human hands. Yet there is no mistake that Yahweh is present in a specific place and on specific terms, and the life of the people is enriched and redirected as they incorporate this reality.

Psalm 84 is clearly a celebration of the life of worship carried on at the Temple. It is true that fascination with bricks and mortar, to say nothing of precious wood and metals, incorporates certain perils (compare Jer. 7:4). Yet the people's response to the beauty of the Solomonic edifice is prevented from lapsing into idolatry by the psalm's focus on the living Reality who is represented by all of this beauty. This is a hymn of praise not to a building, but to a Person. Furthermore, it is a hymn that understands that the God who is the object of sincere worship is not a means to some concocted end; God *is* the end of human worship and of human life.

In reading the passage from Eph. 6, one may be somewhat put off by all the military imagery. Yet if one moves beyond the culturally conditioned metaphors, larger realities emerge from the text, which are valid for the Christian life whatever the cultural context in which it is lived. One is the realization that the forces that would inhibit the Christian in her or his efforts at faithfulness are larger than the individual, larger even than the collected powers of the Christian community. Another is that against these cosmic powers the only protection lies in those qualities with which the faithful person has been endowed by the Spirit of God.

The passage from John 6 opens with the same startling words with which the Gospel lection for last Sunday concluded. Eating Jesus' flesh and drinking his blood proves just as troublesome for the disciples (v. 60) as it does for some modern readers. Yet, regardless of the metaphor one chooses, there is no mistaking the fact that the call of Christ includes difficult demands on the person who would be faithful. They are not impossible demands, however, for they are accompanied by reminders of the divine grace, of which the life, death, and resurrection of Jesus himself are the most visible and astonishing.

1 Kings 8:(1, 6, 10–11) 22–30, 41–43

The essential elements in Solomon's famed prayer at the dedication of the Temple constitute the lection for this day, together with a brief narrative introduction (vs. 1, 6, 10–11), which is provided in order to establish the context of Solomon's words. The reader of this passage has been prepared beforehand for this moment by Nathan's announcement to David that not only will Yahweh's house be built by David's son, but that Yahweh will build for David a "house," that is, a family (2 Sam. 7; Proper 11). This is nothing other than a declaration of a covenant relationship with David, a covenant that is both new, in the sense that it is focused on David and on the political dynasty that will come after him, and yet old, in the sense that it is a continuation of covenant arrangements with both Abraham (Gen. 15, 17) and Moses (Ex. 19–20). When Solomon, in this great prayer, refers to Yahweh's covenant with Israel (vs. 23, 24), it is clearly this old-new covenant that he has in mind.

There are many prayers recorded in the Old Testament, as anyone who is familiar with the book of psalms is well aware. But this is the most extended prayer quoted in the course of an Old Testament narrative (compare 2 Chron. 6) and, because of its priestly character, it bears certain similarities (as well as important dissimilarities) to Jesus' high-priestly prayer of John 17.

It will be recalled that David had fetched the ark of the covenant from Kiriath-jearim (1 Sam. 7:1), also known as Baale-judah (2 Sam. 6:1–5, Proper 10), and—after a harrowing journey—had settled the sacred talisman in a tent inside the newly captured Jebusite citadel, referred to in the text as the city of David, or Zion (1 Kings 8:1). Now upon the completion of the magnificent new Temple, Solomon directs one more journey for the ark, this one only a few hundred yards in length, in order that it may be installed in "the most holy place" of the Temple (8:6), "underneath the wings of the cherubim" (compare Isa. 6:1–8; Trinity Sunday). When the ark is placed in its new home, the importance of the moment is confirmed by a sign from God, a "cloud" which suffuses the Temple to such an extent that the priests are not able to carry out their duties. First Kings 8:11 equates this cloud with "the glory of the LORD," a phrase often used (in this or a similar form) in those parts of the Old Testament associated with ancient Israel's priests, where it is employed as a euphemism for the saving presence of Yahweh (compare Ex. 24:16; Ezek. 1:28). In other words, the bringing into the Temple of the ark of the covenant is taken to be that moment when, in a special manner, Yahweh's own presence comes to reside in the Temple dedicated to the worship of Israel's God. The Temple is not only beautiful aesthetically, it is the one place where—above all others—God is to be found!

The initial part of Solomon's prayer is a restatement of what Yahweh has promised in 2 Sam. 7: Yahweh will "never fail" (v.25) to provide a descendant of David to rule the nation and to represent Yahweh before the people. If the covenant with David should ever fall into decay, it will not be because Yahweh has been unfaithful, but because the people have not fulfilled their part of the covenantal agreement. That dreaded reality is recognized in the "if" clause of v. 25. (There are a number of signs that point to the fact that at least large portions of this prayer were written after the fall of Jerusalem in 587 B.C., vs. 46–53 being a particularly clear case in point. As did many of the prophets before them, the editors of this prayer—who shaped Solomon's words into the form in which we now have them—credited the destruction of the nation to the sinfulness of the people.)

The second part of the prayer (vs. 27–30), however, confronts the reality that the presence of Yahweh in the Temple, denoted by the "cloud" and "glory" of v. 11, is too anthropomorphic a concept to apply to the God of Israel. Neither the earth nor the heaven— including the highest heaven—(v. 27) is great enough to contain the transcendent majesty that is Yahweh. Certainly not this building of cedar and "costly stones" (1 Kings 5:17), splendid though it is! No, it is the *"name"* of Yahweh that dwells in the Jerusalem Temple (compare Deut. 12:5), and the presence of Yahweh's name provides a crucial interface between Israel and its God, without in any measure limiting the power and authority of this holy God. God's name has been especially sacred to the traditions of both Israel and the church, while the name of Jesus is recognized by Christians as possessing extraordinary significance (Phil. 2:10).

The larger text of Solomon's prayer contains a number of short sections, each beginning with "when" or "if," which address special circumstances (vs.31–32, 33–34, and the like). The lection for this day concludes with one of these "conditional" statements that is especially relevant for contemporary life. Verses 41–43, which plead for tolerance and inclusiveness in the worship of God, are an important reminder that the human race is, indeed, one family before God. An interesting aspect of this brief passage is that the inclusion of all seekers in the worshiping congregation is argued not just for its own sake, but for the purposes of evangelism as well. Hear the prayer of the foreigner, O Yahweh, "so that all the peoples of the earth may know your name and fear you" (v. 43).

Psalm 84

This psalm is a celebration of Zion. It was no doubt sung by the choirs of the Jerusalem Temple in celebration of the Temple. Thus it lives at the edge of self-congratulation. Every such exaltation of the church as building or institution runs the risk of falling in love with an idol. A close reading of the psalm, however, suggests that the celebration of the Temple regularly points beyond itself to the reality of God, who is the real source of life and the real focus of trust. Interpretation of this psalm which focuses on the Temple must carefully distinguish between the Temple as an end in itself (which it tended to become in the patronizing establishment religion of Solomon) and the Temple pointing beyond itself to the living God.

The opening, well-known lines concern the loveliness, beauty, and sense of hospitality that are embodied in the Temple (vs. 1–2). Solomon had gone to great effort and expense in order to assure its loveliness. This opening affirmation is apparently on the lips of a yearning pilgrim, who anticipates what it will be like to be present in this place which is one's true "home." This yearning desire, as in Ps. 122, regards the Temple as a place of "real presence," God's own "dwelling place." The term "dwelling place" (*škn*) means primarily the locus of God's sojourning; it does not mean permanent residence, as is the claim made in 1 Kings 8:12–13. In any case, these verses culminate in an affirmation about "the living God," the agent and source of vitality who can give life, power, and energy to all those who enter the presence.

In our own experience, temples are often infested with pigeons who live under the roof. Perhaps the Jerusalem Temple was a commodious place for such nesting. These lines (vs. 3–4), however, intend to take the nesting of birds as a metaphor for the "nesting" of worshipers who sing the happy songs of praise. The metaphor bespeaks serenity, innocence, and trusting delight. The object of such happy nesting, however, is not the commodious life of the worshiper, but it is "my King and my God," the one to whom assent is given with glad and intense loyalty. Thus the political metaphor of God as king coheres with "living God" in v. 2.

Verses 5–7 portray pilgrims en route to the Jerusalem Temple. Such pilgrims are indeed fortunate. Their very journey infuses them with well-being. The poet is aware that this journey of faith takes place in an arid climate. Nonetheless, the route of this pilgrimage is from water hole to water hole. On v. 6, the NRSV is curious, because the second line has "they make it a place of springs." An alternative reading may be, "from springs they drink." Most likely the line suggests that the pilgrims are recipients of water, not its generators. The lines suggest that pilgrimage to Jerusalem to worship is such a theologically freighted enterprise that providential care is exercised to assure well-being on the way. What interests us most is the evident hyperbolic theological formula of v. 7, "God of gods." While this formula may have become a formula for majesty, it originally referred to a polytheistic hierarchy, indicating that the God of Zion presides over, and is worshiped by, even the other gods.

The last unit (which might be subdivided) begins with "LORD God of hosts" (v. 8) and ends with "LORD of hosts" (v. 12; compare also the title addressed in vs. 1, 3). The God of Jerusalem is one of stupendous power, for the phrase means "Lord of the troops," with a capacity for decisive military action. Verses 8 and 9 issue a prayer of four imperatives, two for hearing, two for seeing. It is astonishing, however, that for all the urgency of the imperatives, this prayer in fact contains no concrete petition. That is, the pilgrim does not ask for anything from God, does not come to Jerusalem seeking a particular grant or gift. Rather, the prayer is a yearning for communion and presence, which are ends in themselves. The petition wants God to "look on the face." ("The anointed" here may refer to the king.) The petition echoes the familiar priestly blessing, "The LORD [causes] his face to shine upon you" (Num. 6:25). Being in the presence is itself a bestowal of life, blessing, and well-being, which is the goal of the pilgrimage. It is a crucial point that worship and communion are not instrumental means to anything else, but they are themselves "the real thing" for which the speaker yearns.

The remainder of the psalm waxes eloquent and enthusiastic about the sheer, unparalleled delight of Temple communion. The speaker prefers communion a thousand times to any other delight, and wants to dwell in the presence endlessly (v.10; see Ps. 23:6). The presence of God is as life-giving as the sun, as protective as a shield. God is a giver of all good (v.11). Complete trust (*bṭḥ*) in Yahweh is the culmination of well-being. This speaker has gathered all his desires and ripened them into a single desire, for communion with God.

Two accents become clear: First, what appears to be a poem about a *place* is a doxology about a *person*. The poem is saturated with names for God: Lord of hosts, living God, my King and my God, God of gods, God of Jacob who is sun, shield, water, nest—all in all. The Temple is only an access point to the reality of God. Second, in an inordinately utilitarian climate like ours, it is crucial to see that God is *end* and not *means*. Communion is the thing, the fulfillment of human life. This poem does not seek communion with God as a means toward anything else. In anticipation of and in the presence of this God, the life of the worshiper is completely reoriented, away from utility, toward communion. The one who utters this poem is prepared for the discipline and practice of communion, and knows that to be the ultimate delight of human life.

Ephesians 6:10–20

The martial imagery that dominates this reading clearly reflects the church's social setting at the end of the first century. The dominance of the Roman Empire and the pervasiveness of its military strength would have given descriptions of armor a ready currency with the audience of Ephesians. Tragically, the church's history of aligning itself with various empires makes it difficult to hear this passage afresh. Careful attention needs to be paid to the source and nature of the strength invoked if the passage is not to be seriously distorted.

Standing at the conclusion of the long section of ethical exhortations that begins in Eph. 4:17 (see the discussion under Proper 14), 6:10–20 opens with the general statement: "Finally, be strong in the Lord and in the strength of his power." The bare admonition "be strong" is subject to several misunderstandings. First, the strength that is sought here does not come all at once, for the verb is in present tense, suggesting ongoing action. Second, and more important, "be strong" might be heard as demanding that people become strong out of their own resources or by their own talents, but the admonition translates a passive imperative that has connotations of "being made strong" or "being empowered."

The closing words of v. 10 further clarify the nature of the strength envisioned here and how one acquires it. Strength "in the Lord and in the strength of his power" locates believers firmly in the sphere of God and understands them as persons who rely on God's action for their own strength. Language about "self-made" individuals seems increasingly inappropriate for any arena of human life, but it surely does not work in the arena of faith. Strength comes from God.

The remainder of the passage consists of a graphic description of the "armor" available to the Christian, and the threats that make that armor necessary. A verbal similarity makes the connection between vs. 10 and 11 closer than English translation can convey. The imperative at the beginning of v. 10, "be strong," is *endynamousthe* in Greek; and the imperative that begins v. 11, "put on," is *endysasthe* in Greek. That is to say, the two words look and sound similar, so that the act of putting on God's armor is connected with the strengthening admonished in v. 10.

Before describing God's armor in vs. 13–17, the writer depicts the need for it in vs. 11–12. The "wiles of the devil" demand that the faithful protect themselves. Here, as elsewhere, it is difficult to know whether the devil is to be understood as a personal force or as the personification of evil forces (for example, 4:27). The verse that follows may explain who the devil is or at least how the devil threatens believers.

The enemies against whom protection is needed are not "blood and flesh." This phrase does not mean that the enemies are somehow bodiless and invisible; rather, it regularly refers to human beings (for example, Matt. 16:17; 1 Cor. 15:50, but note that the usual order is reversed in Eph. 6:12). The powers that range themselves against the church are not human forces but metahuman: "the authorities," "the cosmic powers of this present darkness," "the spiritual forces of evil in the heavenly places." With these varying images the text conjures up a host of cosmic powers, powers that do battle not with human beings alone, but with God (see 1 Cor. 15:24–28 for the notion that God's final triumph involves the defeat of all competing powers).

Against these metahuman forces, believers must be prepared to defend themselves. Irony lurks just beneath the surface here, as believers prepare to defend themselves with an arsenal that consists of truth, righteousness, peace, faith, salvation, the Spirit, and the word of God. Against the cosmic powers, which appear to control the universe itself, human beings bring weapons whose effectiveness is less than obvious. How, for example, would faith protect against an opponent whose own arsenal presumably includes weapons human beings can scarcely imagine?

Two further observations will help to understand the importance of the armor of believers. First, with the exception of the "sword of the Spirit" (v. 17), these appear to be largely defensive weapons. Belt, breastplate, shoes, shield, and helmet are all items used to protect against the onslaught of an opponent; nothing is said here of offensive weapons. The second observation is closely related, namely, believers take up armor that permits them to "withstand" their opponents (v. 13), to "quench all the flaming arrows" (v. 16). This language suggests that the task of believers is to defend themselves and their faith against the enemies of God; the battle itself is left to God.

The passage closes with admonitions to prayer—prayer for oneself, for all the saints, and for the writer of the letter. The strength sought in this way takes the passage back to its opening admonition to find strength in the Lord. Only such strength, derived from God's own strength, can empower believers against the enemies of their faith.

John 6:56-69

How and why do some people believe and accept the gospel, while others with apparently the same intelligence and similar backgrounds want no part of it? If we knew the answer, would it make our own acceptance any easier or our own presentation of the gospel any more convincing? The questions are not irrelevant, nor are they ignored by the biblical writers. In fact, the Gospel reading for today, the last of five Sundays devoted to John 6, focuses on the response of the disciples to the hard teaching of Jesus, and makes no effort to hide the division between those who believe and those who refuse any longer to walk about with him. The fact that the split occurs among disciples themselves rather than between disciples and Jewish religious authorities brings the issues close to home. Though in narrative form, the questions raised are highly theological.

Four dimensions of the story are critical. First, the message of Jesus is difficult and tends to offend. Nothing in the text, including Peter's remarkable confession in 6:68-69, suggests that Jesus' words were in fact easy to accept, and that if the disciples who rejected them had not been so obstinate, they would have believed.

What made Jesus' words offensive? Was it the symbolism, which the disciples misconstrued, leaving them with the crude notion of literally eating Jesus' flesh and actually drinking his blood? Possibly. There is good reason, however, to think that the truly difficult issue was not understanding the metaphors, but accepting Jesus' demand for participation in his death as the way to ultimate life.

Even for readers more sophisticated than the disciples, who recognize that "eating" and "drinking" are verbal images for sharing in the destiny of Jesus, the words remain hard. Whether stated as "take up your cross and follow me" (as in the Synoptic Gospels) or the foolish preaching of the crucified Christ (as in Paul) or eating Jesus' flesh and drinking his blood (as in John), the Christian invitation at its heart contains a tough demand. The Jesus to be followed is no docetic figure whose arrest, trial, and crucifixion were rounds in a game of charades. "Believing" and "knowing" him involve participation in his death as a means to sharing his life.

Second, it is the Spirit that enables the disciples to embrace the difficulty and accept Jesus's words. The Spirit gives them the eyesight to perceive what Jesus is talking about: that the only way to life is through Jesus' death.

The statement that "the flesh is useless" in 6:63 is not meant to degrade the flesh. After all, the Word became flesh (1:14), and his flesh is the very life he has given for the world (6:51). One must eat of the flesh of the Son of Man to live (6:53). God's salvation is worked out precisely in the arena of the flesh and nowhere else. At the same time, a purely human perspective, a perspective of the "flesh," simply cannot make sense of Jesus' message. It employs categories that make these hard words even harder. The visible and measurable criteria that control a "fleshly" way of thinking only lead to complaints about Jesus' teaching (6:61). Only as the Spirit is active, teaching and testifying on behalf of Jesus and leading the disciples into all truth (14:17, 26; 15:26; 16:13), does real understanding take place.

Third, the reality of unbelief has to be taken seriously. It is not merely "out there" among the religious authorities who comprise the opposition to Jesus, but among the larger group of his disciples and even among the chosen Twelve. Since it is mentioned twice in this brief passage (6:64, 70–71), it is not a trivial detail.

Jesus is pictured as a seer, who perceives from the very beginning who would not believe and who would finally betray him. The narrator wants us to know that Jesus is not the victim of misguided hopes, who at the end dies disillusioned because good does not triumph over evil. All along, with eyes wide open to the presence of unbelief and destruction, he follows the plans given him by his Father.

While Judas and the disciples who turn away from following Jesus historically mirror members of the Johannine community who desert the faith, they also create an uneasiness among those of us who purport to be disciples. Who, reading the text, can help asking about his or her own place in the narrative?

Finally, while the passage has about it a somber note of unbelief, it also poignantly reminds us of divine grace. Verse 65 recalls earlier statements in the chapter (6:37, 39, 44) that no one comes to Jesus, unless by divine election, except as one is drawn and kept by the Father. The Twelve for whom Peter is the spokesperson are not smarter or more religious than the others who turn aside, nor are they necessarily the achievers. They are merely those "granted by the Father" (6:65). And yet election never becomes determinism. Jesus asks the Twelve whether they too will go away. They are free either to follow him or to abandon him.

The talk about how and why some people respond to the gospel and others do not in the final analysis can never degenerate into speculation. Joining with the church in Peter's confession that Jesus has the words of eternal life can only be thought of as a marvelous gift of the electing God.

PROPER 17

Ordinary Time 22

Sunday between August 28 and September 3 inclusive

The lections for this day are notable in that all (with the obvious exception of the Psalms lection) involve changes in the books from which the texts are drawn. The Old Testament passage shifts from Samuel-Kings to the Song of Solomon, the Epistle from Ephesians to James, the Gospel from John (back) to Mark.

The person who preaches from the Song of Solomon must first address the same question that vexed the ancient rabbis when they debated the canonicity of this anthology of love songs: What theology is implied here? Two possible answers emerge, the first being the traditional solution embraced in both synagogue and church. That is that these poems, often sensual, are allegories of the love between God/Christ and the community of faithful people. The other approach is to read the poems literally as the Bible's affirmation of the divinely endowed realities concerning creation and pro-/re-creation. Values may be found in either method of interpretation when employed in a careful and balanced way.

Psalm 45 is akin to the passage from the Song of Solomon, in that it, in a manner distinctive among the royal psalms, draws attention to certain aspects of human sexuality. Curiously, however, that part of the psalm (vs. 10–15) is not included in the lection. Rather, the text appointed to be read focuses on the majesty and beauty of the king, and could be read as an example of the kind of shallow flattery so often produced by sycophants at the court of a powerful monarch. But this text is saved from that interpretation by the emphasis on the role of the king as the bringer of justice (v. 7). As is clear from other parts of the Old Testament that affirm the value of Davidic kingship, Israel's monarchy was established in order that the king might do the good works of God (compare Ps. 72, Epiphany).

The text for James 1 is similar to recent lections from Ephesians in that it too is concerned with the manner in which the Christian life is to be lived. Of particular interest here is the issue of the means by which the Christian life may attain wholeness and integrity. How can faith and deeds cohere in some kind of unity? What is it that holds it all together? Those questions are answered in the end by affirming the mutual dependence of belief and action, and by pointing out that faith in God is made visible by deeds of compassion and honor.

The startling newness of Jesus' teaching is boldly illustrated by the text from Mark 7. In contrast to those who place great emphasis on liturgical requirements, Jesus insists that those qualities which impart purity or impurity to a person's life come from within. This is not to be understood as an argument for individualism in religious belief, but as a statement concerning the crucial matter of the orientation of the human heart. Persons spoil/redeem their lives and those of others not by whether they wash before eating (or some such ritual), but by their commitments. The subsequent healings of the possessed young girl and of the deaf man—neither of whom observed the "right" liturgy—serve as an exclamation point to Jesus' words.

Song of Solomon 2:8–13

The sequence of Old Testament lections that relates the rise of Israel's monarchy began with the story of God's call to Samuel (1 Sam. 3:1–20, Proper 4) and concluded with two narratives concerning King Solomon: his prayer for wisdom (1 Kings 2:10–12; 3:3–14; Proper 15) and his prayer at the dedication of the Temple (1 Kings 8:1, 6, 10–11, 22–30, 41–43; Proper 16). In order to retain a focus on Solomon, at the same time shifting away from the Deuteronomistic history, the lectionary now (Propers 17–20) introduces four texts that, in one fashion or another, invoke Solomon's name. With the exception of the passage for this day, all are from the book of Proverbs.

The Song of Solomon is among the more unusual books of the Bible, as those who are familiar with it are quite aware. Like Esther, it never uses the words God or Lord. But unlike Esther and its story of Jewish survival, the subject matter of the Song of Solomon transcends issues of ethnicity and nationhood and portrays the beauties of human sexuality. The several references to Solomon (1:1; 3:7, 9, 11; 8:11, 12) may or may not be clues to the origins of this literature, but they at least link these love poems with Israel's great king and, in the context of the lectionary cycle, provide a tie-in to this day's lection from Psalm 45.

According to rabbinic lore, the Song of Solomon was the subject of considerable debate among the Jewish sages associated with the *Bet Din* (House of Judgment) at Jamnia who, about A.D. 90, conferred their approval on what we now know as the canon of the Hebrew Bible. The book was ultimately deemed authoritative in matters of faith because it was judged to be an allegory on the love between God and Israel. In Christian circles a similar verdict was rendered, the lovers being understood to be Christ and the church, or Christ and the Christian individual. Whether one agrees that the allegorical method is validly applied in this case or not, it cannot be denied that these interpretations of the Song preserved for future generations a collection of poems of extraordinary beauty, literature that forever dispels the notion, sometimes voiced, that the concept of romantic love first emerged in the European Middle Ages and Renaissance.

Thus two primary hermeneutical avenues are open to those who wish to preach on this day's text (or any other from the Song of Solomon). One may wear the spectacles of allegory and view the lovers as God and the people of God. Ordinarily, allegory is a dangerous interpretative device, for it permits the exegete to read into the text almost anything he or she wishes. Any modern interpreter of this text must bridle his or her imagination, so that subjective meanings are not forced on the text. But because there are genuine examples of allegory in the Bible itself (for example, Ezek. 5:1–12; Mark 4:1–20) and—more to the point—because of the tradition in both synagogue and church that has read the Song of Solomon as allegory, the interpreter should feel free, within limits, to approach the Song in this manner.

The other principal avenue of interpretation is to read the text more literally and to listen to it speak of the God-given joy that derives from human sexuality. Some passages within the Song lend themselves quite easily to this straightforward interpretation (for example, S. of Sol. 3:1–5; 4:1–15), but the passage for this day would appear to be open to either approach.

Song of Solomon 2:8–13 is a text that speaks of the renewing power of love, either human or divine. The lover is portrayed in words that evoke images of strength and agility (vs. 8–9). He is "like a gazelle or a young stag," and his arrival, which may seem to modern readers as something of an intrusion (v. 9c), is in reality an invitation to the beloved to join him in his life in the larger world (vs. 10b, 13b). Having heard the lover's voice (v. 8a), the beloved now sees him and is enthralled. The beloved is also no longer satisfied with her former life behind "the lattice" (v. 9c), and knows that her future and that of the lover are one.

In this context, notice how the text first states the idea of the lover's call ("The voice of my beloved!" v. 8a) and twice reaffirms it by means of repeated words which function as something of a refrain: "Arise, my love, my fair one, and come away" (vs. 10b, 13b).

Then follow images of springtime and renewal. It is not without reason that—in the Jewish tradition—the Song of Solomon is traditionally read at Passover. In our text the metaphors now speak of new life: "winter is past," "flowers appear on the earth," the "vines are in blossom" and "give forth fragrance." Notice the subtle emphasis on fecundity, as in "the fig tree puts forth its figs" (v. 13a). That is to say: God has called Israel out of Egypt and into a productive new life. Christ has risen from the dead. The Spirit is alive and at work in the life of the church. Christ has come into the life of the individual man or woman and has transformed that life as can no other power or presence. Or (if one prefers a more literal—that is, sexual—interpretation), the devotion and commitment of one who is deeply loved have the power to infuse great purpose and meaning into a lover's life.

Psalm 45:1–2, 6–9

This psalm is a "royal psalm." That is, its subject is the king in Jerusalem, from the Davidic dynasty. Psalm 45 is a peculiar one among the royal psalms, because it exults in the person of the king, and unlike the other psalms of this type it does not push kingship toward the greater rule of Yahweh.

The opening verse identifies the subject of the psalm as a paean of praise for the king. Moreover, the last line suggests that the poem is a professional, highly stylized, self-conscious work of a court singer. Likely it is the work of someone on the court payroll who specializes in court dinners, programs, and celebrations, who engages in king-pleasing hyperbole and may indeed be ingratiating with winsome overstatement.

Verse 2 celebrates the overwhelming physical appearance of the king in characteristic court terminology. The king's lips are graced, which may mean the king is one of especially elegant speech. All the special and wondrous physical endowments of the king are taken as a blessing from God. The celebration of a human person is unusual in Israel's text (see 1 Sam. 16:7). We may suggest three possible interpretations:

1. It has long been conventional among Christians to read the royal psalms christologically, as referring to Jesus.

2. As indicated, this poem likely reflects regular court hyperbole. Thus there may be a tone of decadence about the poem—the wealthy leisure class endlessly enjoying, celebrating, and congratulating itself (see Amos 6:4–6). If this reading is pursued, one may suggest a "class" reading of such affluent self-celebration, for it is the leisure class that has the means and time for the celebration and enhancement of itself.

3. A third reading is suggested by the pairing of this psalm with a reading from Song of Solomon in the lectionary. If we take the Song of Solomon as a celebration of human loveliness in the context of innocent, passionate, erotic human love, then our poem is simply a wondrous affirmation of human loveliness, albeit here concerning the powerful. Bonhoeffer has suggested that the Song of Solomon is "creation theology," so that our poem is a celebration of humankind in the image of God. Whereas the poem affirms the king who can afford the effort to keep up a good appearance, the poem suggests a more genuine loveliness of all human creation and, derivatively, of all of creation. Concerning that loveliness, Galway Kinnell writes of the beauty even of a pig as one of God's splendid creatures:

> Saint Francis
> put his hand on the creased forehead
> of the sow, and told her in words and in touch
> blessings of the earth on the sow, and the sow
> began remembering all down her thick length,
> from the earthen snout all the way
> through the fodder and slops to the spiral curl of the tail,
> from the hard spininess spiked out from the spine
> down through the great broken heart
> to the milken dreaminess spurting and shuddering
> from the fourteen teats into the fourteen mouths sucking and
>   blowing beneath them;
> the long, perfect loveliness of sow.
>   ("Saint Francis and the Sow")

(On other "lovely" creatures, see Job 40:15–24; 41.) The psalm, paralleling the voice of the lover in the Song of Solomon, finds beauty in the one addressed, a beauty that may not be otherwise visible, but is visible and celebrated in the voice of this lover, who in creation theology is the Creator who finds the creature to be lovely—"very good".)

Verses 6–9 of Ps. 45 exposit the primal affirmation of v. 2. The initial phrase of v. 6 is interesting, if not problematic. The Hebrew addresses the king, who is said to sit on "God's throne" (see NRSV margin). This is the most exalted statement of the human king in all of the psalms, and comes close to recognizing in the king the very character of divinity. Even if this is court hyperbole (which I take it to be), it is in any case an exalted view of kingship, or by extrapolation (as I have suggested in the third alternative above), a high view of human creatureliness.

The lyrical celebration of the king recognizes the king as one who practices, guarantees, and insists on equity and righteousness, against all distorting unrighteousness (vs. 6–7a). This affirmation of the king relates to the conventional expectation that the king will execute justice for the realm (see Ps. 72:1–4).

The outcome of justice, it is affirmed, is extraordinary well-being and prosperity (45: 7b–9; see Ps. 72:5–7, 15–17). The decisive "therefore" of v. 7b establishes a cause-and-effect relation between justice (vs. 6–7a) and prosperity (vs. 7b–9). That is, prosperity is not arbitrary or autonomous, but is situated in the very fabric of creation, in a pattern of moral coherence. The moral shape of reality cannot be circumvented or thwarted.

The outcome of just rule is extravagance for the king (vs. 7b–9). The king (or by inference, any of God's beloved creatures) will enjoy what kings always enjoy—rich spices, scarce ivory, coveted gold, and much delight, all the things to enhance an existence of sheer and uninterrupted well-being. In Israel the route to such extravagance is not by way of rapacious power, but through neighbor practice (see Jer. 22:15–16). Creation in all its loveliness has a determined moral shape, which ties economic destiny closely to neighbor concern.

James 1:17–27

Typical of the letter of James, this lection presents several challenges to the preacher. Its primary interest lies less in articulating the theological implications of the gospel (in fact, Jesus is scarcely mentioned) than in clarifying what it means for Christians to live with the gospel. For that clarification, the writer draws on a number of traditional sources for ethical guidance and covers a disparate array of topics. The result resembles Jewish wisdom literature more than it does many other early Christian writings.

This particular lection touches on a bewildering variety of themes familiar from other literature. That Christians have received a new birth is familiar from John 3:1–10 and from 1 Peter 1:3; 2:2. The language of firstfruits is used by Paul in reference to Jesus' resurrection (1 Cor. 15:20). Similar advice about listening quickly and speaking only slowly appears in Sir. 5:11 (see Eccl. 5:2), and warnings about anger appear in Eccl. 7:9 and Prov. 15:1. The imperative of caring for orphans and widows both anticipates the lengthy discussion later in James and recalls prophetic imperatives regarding justice.

The verses that begin the passage (vs. 17–18) actually conclude the preceding discussion about temptation. By contrast with the notion that temptation comes from God (v. 13), the writer insists that good gifts (and not evil temptations) come from God. By contrast with the birth of sin and death described in 1:15, v. 18 describes the birth given believers; they come into being "by the word of truth" in order to be "first fruits of his creatures." God's plan is for goodness and for life, not for evil or for death. As the note in the NRSV suggests, the saying at the end of v. 17 ("there is no variation or shadow due to change") is somewhat unclear in the Greek manuscripts. What does seem clear, however, is the author's conviction that God may be relied on to continue to act in favor of God's creation.

With v. 19, the topic changes from God's actions to those expected of human beings. Despite the traditional, even folksy, character of the opening of this section, the movement within it is difficult. It begins with a statement about the importance of listening (by contrast with speaking or growing angry), suggesting that hearing is in itself an important act. However, v. 22 introduces the contrast between hearing and doing, in which hearing is subordinated to doing. Verse 26 returns to the dangers of speech, but only in order to move to the prophetic imperative of caring for those in need.

Any generalization about the twists and turns in this passage takes the risk of oversimplifying it, but it may nevertheless be helpful to see the author as struggling (here and throughout the letter) with the integrity of the Christian life. What gives Christian life some wholeness? What identifies the Christian life? How can belief and action be held together in a unity—or can they possibly be separated?

In vs. 19–27 that desire to articulate the integrity of the Christian life addresses two distinct issues: the character of speech and the character of action. The dangers of inappropriate speech reappear in the well-known discussion in 3:1–12 (see Proper 19). In this initial discussion, speech seems to be a metonymy for human thought. The author moves quickly from the admonition to be "slow to speak" to warnings about anger and wickedness (v. 21). More revealing still is v. 26, which equates the unbridled tongue with the heart that deceives itself. Writing centuries before the development of depth psychology, the author of James understands that even what purports to be casual speech reveals thoughts and feelings deep within the human heart.

Verse 22 moves from the integrity of thought and speech to the integrity of hearing and doing. The most characteristic theme of the letter, the demand to be "doers of the word," appears here for the first time and in its most theoretical form. Those who hear the gospel but do not act on it "are like those who look at themselves in a mirror" and "immediately forget what they were like." Given the prevalence of mirrors in contemporary Western society and the preoccupation with taking advantage of them, this analogy may seem inadequate. In common with other ancient writers, however, biblical writers refer to the ephemeral or insufficient nature of the mirror (for example, 1 Cor. 13:12). What is seen in a mirror must be viewed again and again, because the impression is gone as soon as one looks away. By contrast, the "perfect law, the law of liberty," enables people to live with what they see and to live out what they believe. The imperative of caring for orphans and widows (v. 27) provides a concrete example of this call to integrate hearing and doing.

The brief note at the end of v. 25 warrants close attention. Those who both hear and act on the gospel "will be blessed in their doing." In the never-ending quest to be sure that faith is "worth something" like any other commodity or acquisition, Christians often resort to calculating (privately if not publicly) the rewards they may receive because of their belief or because of their action. The writer of James does indeed identify a reward for those who act on the gospel, but the reward—the blessing—comes in the action itself.

Mark 7:1–8, 14–15, 21–23

After five Sundays in the Gospel of John, the lectionary today returns to the narrative of Mark, the primary Gospel of the B cycle. It takes up a passage that has undergone considerable misinterpretation through the years, in part because of a heavily jaundiced view of the Pharisees. They have most often been pictured as petty legalists out to feather their own caps and arrogant enough to think they can earn their way with God. The caricature has hardly left them with a positive press in most commentaries, and of course as such they can easily be dispensed with. But seeing them only in such a bad light is to miss the force of Jesus' challenge to an entire way of structuring life, as the old wineskins that cannot contain the dynamic of the new wine.

The broader context in which this interchange between Jesus and the Pharisees occurs presents an interesting backdrop. On the one hand, there are the two generous feedings of the hungry multitudes (6:30–44; 8:1–10), and an extravagant summary statement of Jesus' healings in and around Gennesaret (6:53–56). They pose a sharp contrast to the restrictive issue of washing hands before eating. On the other hand, the interchange with the Pharisees is followed by the stories of the persistent faith of the Gentile woman of Syrophoenician origin, who asks only for crumbs and whose daughter is healed, and the restoration of hearing and speech to the deaf man living in the Gentile area called the Decapolis (7:24–37). It is as if Jesus' critique of kosher laws ("Thus he declared all foods clean," 7:19) is then documented by the healings of these non-Jewish people.

The question raised by the Pharisees in 7:5 is apparently a sincere one, and the narrator tells us why in vs. 3–4. Ritual purity is an essential dimension of Pharisaic religion, an effort to claim Jewish identity in a world that was much happier with a polytheistic style. The Pharisees argued that the practice of eating with undefiled hands was an obligation imposed not on Temple priests only, but on all Jewish people who sought to be the holy nation they had been called to be. To heed a stipulation of the oral law ("the tradition of the elders") like this was not to escape into trivialities but to demonstrate how seriously the law of God is to be taken. Since Jesus is obviously a religious teacher, why do his disciples not take seriously the tradition of the elders, which is intended as a "fence" around the law to protect it? Why do they avoid this concern for holiness, which is so characteristically Jewish?

Jesus' first response to the Pharisees' query is an attack on the notion that the law of God needs to be protected by the tradition of the elders. Citing Isa. 29:13, Jesus charges the Pharisees with using the tradition to avoid the commandment of God. For example, the Pharisees can escape the obligations of the fifth commandment ("Honor your father and your mother") by a preoccupation with the regulation from the tradition about Corban—about property already dedicated to a special religious purpose. Put in other words, they are "making void the word of God through [the] tradition." The elevation of the oral law (or the tradition of the elders) to a place of parity alongside the Torah ultimately undercuts the Torah.

Jesus' second response, however, is even more substantive. "There is nothing outside a person that by going in can defile, but the things that come out are what defile" (Mark 7:15). The whole notion of ritual purity or of holiness based on food laws is undermined in one precise statement. What matters is the heart, the seat of the will, where decisions are made about one's neighbors. The condition of the heart, whether debased or pure, is far more critical than the food one eats or whether one attends to washing hands.

We cannot misconstrue Jesus' words here. They do not say that religion is a matter of inward piety rather than external behavior, that one's private spirituality is valued more highly than one's physical life in the world. Rather, Jesus warns that sin arises from within and leads to destructive deeds such as fornication, theft, murder, and the like (vs. 21–22). The lack of holiness is marked not by breaches in the cultic code, but in evil acts that spring from evil intentions.

This disagreement with the Pharisees is more than just a quibble about a legalistic interpretation, more than an attack on a corrupt religious sect. Jesus' words are aimed at the very structure of Pharisaic religion, how holiness and sin are defined, and how the word of God regulates the life of the people of God.

In contrast, the ensuing stories of healing for the daughter of a Syrophoenician woman and of restoring hearing and speech for a man of the Decapolis depict the gracious way God operates. Neither character knows much about ritual purity or the tradition of the elders, but both know about the divine grace that makes one whole. Jesus is not simply patching up the old in order to make it more serviceable. He inaugurates something entirely new.

Proper 18

Ordinary Time 23

*Sunday between
September 4 and 10 inclusive*

The lectionary often poses unplanned but interesting combinations of texts that stand in tension to one another. Rather than being mutually reinforcing, these passages view opposite poles of human experience, accurate perspectives that vary and are not easily harmonized. Such is the case with the four texts for this Sunday.

All four encourage the doing of good, but the differing arenas for action offer a rich counterpart. On the one hand, Ps. 125 envisions a morally reliable world, in which one cannot abuse one's neighbor and still expect good in one's environment. The petition is for God to do good to those who are good and to lead astray those who are wicked.

The "doing of good" in the other three passages, however, involves a movement beyond the standard quid pro quo. Justice has a particular direction to those who might not have experienced the world as such a coherent place, where good is rewarded and evil punished. Nothing is said about the moral condition of the marginalized. Proverbs 22, for example, reminds us that while the rich and the poor have the same origin, the Lord takes special note of the poor, pleads their case, and brings judgment on those who exploit them.

James 2 pays special attention to the poor by issuing a warning to those who ignore the poor in favor of the rich. Such acts of favoritism are incompatible with faith. Indifference to human need, whether evident in the good person or in the evil person, exposes faith as vain and useless.

Finally, Mark 7 includes two stories of Jesus' healing outsiders, those beyond the acceptable bounds of the Jews—the daughter of the Syrophoenician woman and the deaf man from the Decapolis. In the case of the former, it was not out of her high morality but from her desperate need that she pushed Jesus to cure her little daughter.

Sometimes life unfolds in a morally explainable fashion. The good succeed and the wicked are punished (so Ps. 125). But more often than not, moral categories cannot account for what happens to people. It is then that God takes up the cause of the victims, the poor and the outsiders, and the people of God are called to do likewise.

Proverbs 22:1-2, 8-9, 22-23

The wisdom of King Solomon is the theme that ties together the present section of the lectionary, from Solomon's accession to the throne and his prayer for wisdom (1 Kings 2:10–12; 3:4–14; Proper 15) to and including three texts from the book of Proverbs (Propers 18–20). It is clear from our knowledge of the literature of ancient Near Eastern peoples who were neighbors of the biblical Israelites that wisdom as a philosophical-theological-literary movement dates from a time much earlier than the reign of Solomon (c. 960–920 B.C.). Nevertheless, the book of Proverbs insists that, in some manner not specified, the second member of the Davidic dynasty was connected with the flourishing of wisdom in Israel (Prov. 1:1; 25:1), a view that is consistent with the Deuteronomistic history (1 Kings 4:29–34). Perhaps Solomon actually composed many of the axiomatic sayings preserved in this book. He may also have encouraged the collection and compilation of proverbial material already in the Israelite folk literature. In any event, the lectionary wishes to round out its focus on Solomon by casting attention on some of the literature associated with his name.

The passage for this day consists of three pairs of verses, the overall theme of which is wealth and poverty. (In the Hebrew each verse is a single line of poetry, so that the "pairs" of verses are actually poetic couplets.) The first pair (vs. 1–2) directs the attention of the reader to the nature of genuine wealth. True wealth does not consist in gold or silver or other tangible forms of treasure. It is rather to be found in the possession of a reputation for honor, integrity, and justice. The Hebrew word behind the English "favor" (*hēn*) has a verbal cognate that means something like "show compassion" or "deal generously," and is sometimes used with reference to the manner in which one treats persons who are poor and oppressed (as for example, Ps. 112:5). Thus that individual is truly wealthy whose life is shaped by a spirit of justice and mercy.

Proverbs 22:2 carries this thought one step farther. Rich people may appear to be different from the poor, but such difference is merely an illusion. Yahweh has made all men and women, both the rich and the poor, and all are equally under Yahweh's care and rule.

Such a vision of the common status of all human beings as creatures of God is one of the important elements within the Bible that laid strong foundations for the later development of democracy, not all of whose roots go back to ancient Greece.

The second pair of verses (vs. 8–9) contrasts the conduct of those who treat the poor unjustly with that of those who deal justly. Verse 8 seems to follow the thought of v. 7, which is not included in the lectionary passage but which nevertheless seems necessary for a proper understanding of vs. 8–9. Clearly the reference is to those persons who have authority over the weaker members of society, and who therefore have a special responsibility before God to care for their needs (note Ps. 72:1–4, 12–14). The Hebrew text supplies a pronoun in Prov. 22:8 that is missing from the NRSV (and from other English translations), and the phrase "the rod of *his* anger" (emphasis added) seems to suggest the action of the king or of some powerful official (compare Ps. 2:9 for another example of the "rod" as a symbol of sovereignty). Proverbs 22:8 affirms that those persons in authority who do not exercise justice and compassion toward the weak will see their authority fail. They are contrasted in v. 9 with the "generous," who "share their bread" (a symbol of power) and so are "blessed."

The final pair of verses (vs. 22–23) projects a meaning similar to that of vs. 7–9, except that the application appears to be somewhat more universal, in that all people, not just persons in authority, are addressed. Verse 22 reminds the reader that poor persons make easy targets for predators because their very weakness invites injustice. While the first line of v. 22 seems to refer to any kind of theft inflicted on the poor, the balance of the verse has to do with "legal robbery." The city gates were often the venue where cases of law were tried before the local elders, and the force of meaning here is that one should not despoil the weak even by manipulation of the law. The prophet Micah reserved a special measure of his scorn for such persons (Micah 2:1–5).

Those who attempt to savage poor and oppressed persons are in for a terrible realization: Yahweh is the champion of all who are too weak to champion themselves. The first line of Prov. 22:23, freely translated, runs something like: "The Lord will argue their lawsuit." In other words, no skillful misapplication of the law by those who are schooled in its nuances, in order to gain advantage over the poor, will be tolerated by the Lord. The Lord will confront all such persons in the ultimate tribunal of justice and will crush them.

Readers of the Old Testament often think of the summons to justice and the call to care for the needs of the poor as the stock-in-trade of the prophets. To be sure, the prophetic voices of ancient Israel often thundered just such a message, as the above reference to Micah attests. But the prophets had no monopoly on the insistence that God cares for the weak. Even here, in the coolly rational cadences of Proverbs, the reader is challenged with this same concern. It is further evidence of how near the heart of Israel's God lie the issues of justice and compassion.

Psalm 125

This psalm is one of a larger group, the "Songs of Ascents" (Pss. 120–134), which ostensibly concern a pilgrimage up to the Temple in Jerusalem. This psalm begins, then, with "Mount Zion" on its mind. It is immediately clear, however, that reference to Mt. Zion is only part of a rhetorical strategy in the psalm, and not a real concern of the poem. Rather, the psalm urges an equitable practice of justice in public affairs, an accent that resonates with the readings in Proverbs and James.

Psalm 125:1 and 2 are cast as sapiential sayings, which make an appeal to the stability and safety of the city of Jerusalem, which is, by common consent, impregnable and always safe from attack (see 2 Sam. 5:6). The psalm, however, refers to Mt. Zion only to make a comparison. The point of the comparison is the stability and safety of those who trust (*bṭḥ*). Trust in God generates stability and precludes any "tottering." Those who stay close to Yahweh are completely safe and immune to threat.

Verses 3–5b of Ps. 125 turn from assurances to moral affirmations. The introductory particle is elusive in its function. The NRSV renders "for," suggesting this is the cause of the assurance of vs. 1–2. Verse 3, however, sounds like a straightforward indicative assertion, not closely related to vs. 1–2. The assertion is that "the land allotted to the righteous" will not be ill-governed or ill-managed, in rapacious, covetous ways. The phrasing of this verse may be taken in two quite different ways. On the one hand, if the verse is related to Israel's tradition of land conquest, then its concern is general and public. The allotted land is the land of promise, and the "scepter" may refer to the rule of the king. On the other hand, the saying may be related to the wisdom tradition, as in our reading in Proverbs. In that reading, the "land allotted" refers not to a large theological promise, but simply to the land arrangements in a local, settled agricultural economy. Then the comment on governance may simply mean that the land is honored through just practices, and is not abused or exploited. On either reading, v. 3 suggests an interrelation between patterns of social power and the ways in which the land is cared for, honored, and kept productive. Both persons and land will be honored, or both together will be abused.

The indicative statement of v. 3 is followed in v. 4 by a prayer, the only petition of the psalm. "Those who are good" in this verse are the "righteous" who do no wrong in v. 3. The ones who do good are the pious, devout keepers of Torah who obey the commands and create a healthy environment of social stability. These upright are to receive "good" from God, that is, a blessing that will make the land fertile. This petition assumes a tight moral calculus without slippage, so that *doing good* is a precondition for *receiving good* (as in Ps. 1).

We expect a parallel statement in v. 5ab concerning the wicked. Such a parallel would be a petition that asked God to "do wicked" to "the wicked." The verse, however, is not a corresponding petition, but in fact is an indicative assertion that God will indeed do evil to evildoers and cause them to disappear. While the grammatical formulations of v. 4 (petition) and v. 5ab (assertion) are difficult, most likely they are intended to perform the same rhetorical function. They serve to guarantee that Israel does indeed live in a morally coherent, morally reliable world. This psalm, like Torah piety in general and Ps. 1 in particular, operates in a tight theory of "deeds-consequences." Good-neighbor practice makes for a secure position in the land.

The theory of moral coherence voiced in vs. 3–5b may sound to us like arrogant self-satisfaction, as those who prosper in the land congratulate themselves on their virtue. The same theory, however, can also be taken as a keen discernment that the capacity of the land to produce (as a gift from God) is indeed profoundly dependent on healthy, just social relations. That is, one cannot abuse neighbor and expect good to come in one's environment. If we take that reading of the verse, then we can detect that vs. 1 and 2, about *security*, are indeed dependent on vs. 3–5a, concerning *right living*.

We should also note, however, that this psalm has a narrow and conventional view of "good," in contrast to the readings in Proverbs and James. Here good is done for the "good-doers." In the other readings, it is urged and required that good must be done, especially to the true poor and needy, regardless of their moral qualification. The tension between those two urgings continues to be present among us and unresolved, even now.

The last phrase of the psalm (v. 5c) seems added on in order to claim the whole psalm for a specifically Jerusalem theology. That is, the links to "Israel" provide a clue for how the psalms are to be read canonically. But even if the line is an addendum, the line connects in two important ways with the preceding. On the one hand, the theme of *shalom* looks back to Jeru*shalom* in vs. 1–2. The city of Jerusalem is, in the Bible, the focal habitat of God's gift of well-being, where Israel will be secure in its identity. That is the whole point of pilgrimage to Jerusalem, to go to one's safe home. On the other hand, *shalom* is the outcome of the good-doing urged in vs. 3–5a. This last line of yearning for peace derives appropriately from what has gone before. It makes specific the hope, promise, and petition of the psalm. It knows the place where *God's good-doing* and *Israel's good-doing* converge.

James 2:1–10 (11–13) 14–17

Reacting against earlier excesses of moral and doctrinal rigidity, much Christianity in its North American setting has grown wary of any attempt to articulate the convictions or life-styles appropriate to faith. Congregations define themselves by their friendliness and accessibility rather than by their doctrines. In some quarters, to be "Christian" means little more than to be "nice."

To say the least, the Bible in all its variety sharply resists such flaccid understandings of what makes for Christian faith. An especially forceful example of such resistance comes to expression in the letter of James, in its insistence that faith cannot be made compatible with certain behaviors and attitudes. This particular lection takes up two related forms of "incompatibility"—the incompatibility between faith and favoritism (2:1–13), and the incompatibility between faith and indifference (vs. 14–26, although this lection ends at v. 17).

In the NRSV, the discussion on faith and favoritism begins with a question ("Do you with your acts of favoritism really believe in our glorious Lord Jesus Christ?"); the footnote rightly indicates, however, that this verse may be translated as an imperative statement ("hold the faith of our glorious Lord Jesus Christ without acts of favoritism"). Much exegetical labor has devoted itself to determining which translation better fits the context, but on either translation the implication is clear: belief in Jesus Christ cannot be made compatible with acts of favoritism.

Verses 2–4 bitingly illustrate what the writer understands by favoritism. The setting envisioned is a little unclear to the modern reader of James. Does the "assembly" refer to a gathering for worship or for settling disputes of some kind? And why, if the persons entering are Christian, as v. 4 seems to assume, do they need to be shown where to sit? Even the largest Christian gatherings at this time would not have required the use of ushers! These unclarities do not prevent the examples from making the point that any practice favoring the rich over the poor is abhorrent.

In vs. 5–7, the writer identifies both theological and practical reasons for this insistence. First, God has chosen the poor to be "rich in faith" and "heirs of the kingdom," notions that echo the Lukan form of the Beatitudes (Luke 6:20) as well as Paul's statement in 1 Cor. 1:26. Both the claim that God does not play favorites and the demand for corresponding human behavior have roots deep in Jewish tradition (see, for example, Lev. 19:15; Deut. 1:16–17; 16:18–20), as does much of the ethical exhortation in this letter. Second, partiality to the rich contradicts common sense, because "the rich . . . oppress you" and "drag you into court." In other words, currying favor with the rich and powerful does not produce the anticipated result, for they act to protect themselves. Christians likewise need to protect themselves by recalling who is their true benefactor.

Verses 8–13 take the author's analysis one step farther. Not only does favoritism contradict God's behavior and common sense; favoritism is sinful. To behave with partiality toward the rich is to violate the command to love the neighbor (v. 8) and to risk violating all of the law (vs. 9–10).

The second "incompatibility" addressed in this lection is that between faith and indifference. (This discussion begins in v. 14 and continues through v. 26, despite the conclusion of the lection with v. 17.) The word "indifference" may seem inappropriate, as the text does not speak about indifference but about the necessity of works as part of faith. Nevertheless, a closer reading will show that the neglect of works arises, in the author's view, because of indifference to human need.

Both vs. 14 and 17 state the principle that faith and works cannot be divorced from each other. "Can faith save you?" comes the question at the end of v. 14, a question that might introduce a soteriological discussion, except that "save" can refer to physical healing or safety, as it plainly does in vs. 15–16. The argument is that faith alone does not secure the well-being of those who are in need. Concrete acts are needed, rather than pious benedictions.

Verses 18–20 again assert the integral relationship between faith and works, and then two examples are offered. First comes Abraham, whose action of obedience with respect to the sacrifice of Isaac is said to complete his faith. Because of the frequently noted contrast between this discussion and that of Paul in Rom. 4, this example often eclipses the second and more intriguing one, that of Rahab (v.

25). The biblical story of Rahab says nothing about her faith (Josh. 2; 6:15–25), but both the New Testament and early Jewish writings reflect the tradition that she became a proselyte (see Matt. 1:5). Here her action is taken as in and of itself indicating her faith. By contrast with those who would send the hungry away to be filled with kind words, Rahab acted in a faithful manner.

Too much has been made of James's supposed emphasis on works as proving faith or assuring salvation. Reading this discussion in connection with the earlier part of the chapter demonstrates that what is at stake here is not some algorithm by which salvation is attained or faith is proved. Both parts of the chapter address behaviors that assume that faith can exist alongside indifference to human need. Observations derived from Jewish tradition, from Christian experience of God, and from common sense provide a forceful argument to the contrary: Faith always and everywhere reaches out to the neighbor, even as it responds to the prior "reach" of God.

Mark 7:24–37

It is difficult to appreciate the intensity of the struggles undergone by the early church as it opened its doors wide to non-Jews. Though Jesus and the original disciples were Jews and the church's roots were in the synagogues, modern readers of the New Testament (mostly Gentiles, of course) are amazed at what appears to be a Jewish resistance to becoming an ecumenical church. It is difficult, however, only until we take a good look at our own churches and begin to wrestle with the barriers, often invisible and unspoken, that continue to separate people of various races and nationalities. Suddenly the struggles of the early church no longer seem strange and remote.

Following Jesus' interchange with the Pharisees regarding ritual purity and the kosher food laws (Mark 7:1–23), two stories of Jesus' healing of non-Jewish figures serve to declare unequivocally that God's reign is not limited to historic Israel (vs. 24–37). The "mighty works" that document divine power happen to Gentiles as well as to Jews. Since each story has its own distinctive plot and dialogue, the preacher may want to select one or the other as a single text for the sermon.

While the encounter between the Syrophoenician woman and Jesus includes an act of healing, the stress falls not on the healing but on the circumstances of the woman and the exchange she has with Jesus. She is described as "a Gentile, of Syrophoenician origin" (v.

26), details we hardly need since we have already been told that the event occurred in "the region of Tyre," which lay in the province of Syria, well beyond the boundaries of Galilee. Her primary literary significance is bound up not so much with the fact that she is a woman or that she is the mother of a demon-possessed daughter, as with the fact that she is a non-Jew. Yet her gender and her intense pain at her daughter's condition cannot be ignored. Picture the scene: Jesus attempting an escape from the demands of the crowds (7:24; see 6:53–56), and finding a retreat in a house on an out-of-the-way street, only to meet this "pushy" woman who interrupts his privacy by pleading for help for her stricken child.

Jesus' initial response to the woman is sharp (7:27). The attempts of commentators to soften the saying miss the point. Even if the statement is a familiar Jewish maxim, or even if "dogs" really means "household pets," Jesus nevertheless is bluntly confronting the woman with the priority of the Jews in the divine economy, a point consistently affirmed throughout the New Testament. The opening of the door wide to non-Jews is not a rejection of the Jews. Despite their preoccupation with matters like ritual purity and clean and unclean foods, they retain their most-favored position.

The woman's reply to Jesus makes her a model of persistent faith. Her grave need and her apparent trust keep her from becoming discouraged at Jesus' remark. She does not argue the question of Jewish priority, but reminds Jesus of the inclusion of Gentiles and evokes from him the gift she desperately wants—the healing of her daughter.

On the one hand, the woman's acceptance of her status as a non-Jew presents a beautiful contrast to the Pharisees, who demand a tight adherence to the Jewish structure of religion (vs. 1–23). She begs only for what is due her as a needy being. On the other hand, her "pushiness" provides the church with a clear mandate for its mission beyond the bounds of Judaism, a mandate wrenched from the earthly Jesus himself and repeated time and again.

The story of the healing of the deaf man in the predominantly Gentile region of the Decapolis (vs. 31–37), while another example of the healing of an outsider, dwells on different details than the previous story. Given the description of the man's condition before and after the healing, and the elaborate steps taken by Jesus to restore hearing and speech, it becomes clear that the story, like many other miracle stories, affirms the divine power over human infirmities. The presence of God's dynamic reign is at work in Jesus. One who could not speak plainly because he could not hear now hears and speaks.

The nameless members of the crowd ("they") also play a prominent role in the narrative. They bring the deaf man to Jesus in the first place, and after the healing they refuse to observe the command to keep silent. Since the command is a bit inappropriate (no one can hide the man's changed condition), it serves to heighten the eagerness of the crowd to announce the event. "The more he ordered them, the more zealously they proclaimed it" (v. 36). They cannot keep silent about the marvelous good news of God's rule, and their verdict about Jesus is that "he has done everything well." In this second story, the crowds become the model for the church as those "astounded beyond measure," who fervently spread the word.

Proper 19

Ordinary Time 24

*Sunday between
September 11 and 17 inclusive*

The story of the human response to divine grace is the story of a lifelong venture. It has its moments of high drama, when the issues are clear and the demands costly. Fortunately, for most of us, those moments come not too often. At other times, the issues are filled with ambiguity, and decisive action is hard to come by. There are also lengthy periods when faithfulness seems more mundane. It consists of simply keeping at the task, struggling not to be overcome by our own weaknesses, sharing food with the hungry and seeking in small, usually unobserved ways to make the world a more humane place in which to live.

The texts for today depict four very different vignettes of response (or lack of it) to God's grace, all true to life and all instructive for the part we play in the story of human response. In Prov. 1, Wisdom takes to the streets to chide the people for their failure to discern God's will. The world is an orderly, coherent place where divine knowledge is readily available to those who seek it, to those who listen to Wisdom's voice. Decisions are not complex or fraught with ambiguity. Unfaithfulness consists simply of despising self-evident knowledge, of being deaf to Wisdom's voice, of waywardness and complacency.

The last half of Ps. 19 takes a much more upbeat stance toward human responsiveness. The secret is the Torah, God's gift that exhibits remarkable powers to enlighten the simpleminded and refresh the human soul. The psalmist is aware that he may not always be able to discern and obey the decrees of God, and he prays for forgiveness for hidden faults and protection from presumptuous sins. The conclusion is a simple commitment of words and thoughts to the care of God.

James 3 uncovers the incredible difficulty of taming the tongue. It may seem a trivial matter, but at the heart of faithful response to God is integrity, and undisciplined speech poses a constant threat. Even worship can be undermined by the tongue that degrades others while praising God.

Jesus, in talking to the disciples in Mark 8, speaks of responsiveness in terms of denying self, of taking up Christ's cross, and of following him. The faithful journey takes one along the very same path Jesus took—through (not around) Golgotha, but ultimately to Easter.

Proverbs 1:20–33

The second of three consecutive Old Testament lections from the book of Proverbs, ch. 1:20–33 personifies wisdom as a prophetess who unsuccessfully calls God's people from their "waywardness" and "complacency" (v. 32). This is not the only passage in canonical or deuterocanonical literature that adopts the persuasive device of personification to present the claims of Wisdom (one may wish to compare Job 28; Prov. 8:1–9:6; and Sir. 24:1–22). But only here are such striking parallels drawn between the role of Wisdom and that of ancient Israel's prophets.

The context for Wisdom's message is set in Prov. 1:20–21. One remembers the charge leveled against Amos, that he "conspired against [King Jeroboam] in the very center of the house of Israel" (Amos 7:10). Or Jeremiah, who was directed by the Lord to "stand in the gate . . . and proclaim there this word" (Jer. 7:2). Or the Servant of Yahweh described by Second Isaiah, whose uniqueness was portrayed, in part, by his uncharacteristic prophetic behavior:

> He will not cry or lift up his voice,
> or make it heard in the street.
> (Isa. 42:2)

Wisdom (who is always portrayed as a female figure) lives the calling of the prophetess in that she carries her message, that is, *Yahweh's* message, into the very heart of the city of the people of God, "in the squares" and "at the busiest corner."

The word that Wisdom delivers is one of distress. (Notice the double "How long?" in v. 22, part of the stylized language of lament, as in Ps. 13:1–2; Hab. 1:2). The cause of the prophetess's sorrow is human intransigence and willfulness, but the words used here are not typical of the prophetic vocabulary, "sin" or "injustice" or the like. Rather, they are offenses particularly heinous to the practitioners of wisdom: "being simple," "scoffing," and "hat[ing] knowledge." Behind this language is the deeply held conviction of Israel's wisdom teachers that a gracious God has placed at the disposal of men and women the ability to understand what God wants them both to be and to do. That is to say, God has created a world of order and coherence and, by studying that world (in terms both of what we might term "nature" and of "human nature") it is possible to understand God. Not all the mystery in life has been dispelled, to be sure, for there is still a need to "fear" the Lord (v. 29; compare 1:7). But the basic questions of life have been resolved and, if one is "wise" to God's ways, one is sure to flourish and be happy. Thus to fail to be "wise" is to violate one's own well-being and the purposes of God.

Verses 24–27 are, in the NRSV translation, a single sentence, but the passage contains several thoughts. Initially, there is the admonition to listen: "give heed" (v. 23a). The word literally means "to return" (*tāšûbû*), but it is reminiscent of Israel's great call to faithfulness: "*Hear*, O Israel: The LORD is our God, the LORD alone" (Deut. 6:4). The prophetess Wisdom has arisen to declare a word from God, and the people must pay close attention.

But the gist of that word is that the people are already closed to and ignorant of God's will for their lives. "I have called and you refused" (v. 24) is an indictment that resonates to Isa. 65:1–2; Jer. 7:13; Hos. 11:2, and other prophetic texts that emphasize Yahweh's overtures which have been repeatedly offered and just as repeatedly spurned. The prophetess Wisdom's paradoxical message of "Listen while I tell you how deaf you are" serves to underscore the callousness of the people and the frustration of Yahweh. Because of the people's hardened hearts, the prophetess Wisdom sees a certain tragic irony in the fact that when their vulnerability exposes them to danger, Yahweh will not respond to them (vs. 26–28). If her mockery (v. 26), which is also Yahweh's mockery, seems somehow out of place as being unsuited to a gracious God, it is simply a manner in which the passage underscores the reality that, having had no use for God in their more prosperous times, the people have no idea how to turn to God now that they are in great need (vs. 28–31). (Compare Ps. 2:4–6 for another example of Yahweh's mockery.)

The conclusion of the matter is contained in vs. 32–33, and in a manner characteristic of wisdom literature our passage balances a negative observation with one of a positive nature. Waywardness and complacency kill simpletons and fools—these latter terms serving as epithets for those who are too calloused to comprehend God's truths, which have been made understandable for all. By the same token, however, men and women who are alert to Wisdom's message (which is also Yahweh's message) will "be secure," "at ease," and will have no "dread of disaster" (v. 33).

Note should perhaps be taken here that, while this theology embraced by "orthodox" Israelite wisdom teachers possesses a certain compelling force, it was judged as being overly simplified by at least one "heterodox" wisdom practitioner. "When I applied my mind to know wisdom, . . . then I saw all the work of God, that no one can find out what is happening under the sun. . . . Even though those who are wise claim to know, they cannot find it out" (Eccl. 8:16–17). The dialogue between the books of Proverbs and Ecclesiastes reminds one that even the soundest theological understandings are incomplete and partial.

Psalm 19

The crucial question of Ps. 19 concerns the relation of its two parts to each other. It has often been judged that vs. 1–6 and vs. 7–14 are in fact unrelated poetic units, only inadvertently placed back to back. More recent readings suggest an integral relation between the two parts, affirming that the life-giving *power of Torah* (vs. 7–14) is definitional for the right *ordering of creation* (vs. 1–6).

The psalm begins with a wondrous (even if well-known) hymn to creation (vs. 1–6). To be sure, God is mentioned in v. 1. (Note, however, the reference is generic "El," and not the God of Israel.) After the initial reference, however, these lines focus on the wondrous, eloquent, majestic, doxological quality of creation (vs. 1–4a). Creation is not mute; creation is teeming with vigorous testimony that points beyond itself to the great God whose handiwork this world is. This poem is intentional, eloquent "creation theology." These initial verses are sweeping in time ("day to day . . . night to night" = *all the time*) and in space ("end of the world" = *everywhere*), so that in all its splendor the world is submitted back to God in delight.

In verses 4b–6 the generalized doxology of creation is made much more specific. Whereas the psalm begins with the largeness of the heavens, now the poem centers on the wondrous, reliable, daily round of the sun. God is here mentioned only in the initial premise, "he has set." From then on, it is all the sun. Sunrise is like the bustling energy and joy of a bridegroom on his wedding day, rising early and raring to go. Sunrise is like a vigorous track star, ready to do a thousand-meter day, completely confident and unintimidated. Then the sun sweeps its way from one end of the heavens to the other, warming and healing and giving life. It may be that this poem was originally praise for sun worship. In good Israelite creation faith, however, the sun is not worshiped, but along with all the creation is itself a worshiper.

The creation in which the sun rises reliably each day is an ordered world. It is not capricious, and it is not anxious about its shape for the coming day. One dimension of that reliable ordering is the Torah commandments of Israel (vs. 7–14). The Torah commandments are not simply moral insistences, but in fact are a discernment of the very shaping of the fabric of created reality. These commands specify the appropriate response to God's shaping of creation, which is required if life in the earth is to be safe and prosperous.

Thus after the doxology of creation in vs. 1–6, the psalm celebrates the goodness, generosity, and life-giving power of Yahweh's Torah. Note well, in v. 7 the reference is "the LORD," whereas the verses on creation referred to "El" (v. 1). As the poem draws closer to Israel's own moral discernment, the identity of God is drawn closer to Israel's own memory and confession.

The core of this unit consists of six parallel statements, all of which make roughly the same claim. In each, Yahweh is mentioned by name. In each, the commandments are designated by a different term, all of which are rough synonyms: torah ("law"), decrees, precepts, commandment, fear, ordinances. In each, an adjective is assigned to God's Torah, celebrating its inordinate value: perfect, sure, right, clear, pure, true. That is, the Torah is God's spectacular gift, as dazzling in its presence as is the sun in vs. 4b–6.

What interests us most, however, is that in each of the six statements, the Torah of God is said to be an active, effective, powerful agent, which can effect a change. That is, the Torah is a live force that can create a newness in the world. Thus the Torah "revives the soul," that is, restores selfhood, makes wise, gives joy, enlightens eyes, and lasts forever. The Torah is generative of new vitality and energy, as sure as the sun is a source of energy and life. Such a claim for Torah is not just Jewish hyperbole for obedience. It is, rather, the recognition that when life is liberated from competing loyalties, when one has a clear sense of priority and loyalty which coheres with one's true identity, without shame, guilt, or anxiety, then freedom, energy, and power are given. When one accepts one's role and identity as God's creature and lives in trustful response to the gift of God, one can enact all the glorious liberty of an unencumbered creature, beloved and empowered by the Creator.

This section of the psalm culminates with the characteristic sapiential affirmation that commands are precious, because they are the force and clue for a rightly ordered life. They are the heart's true desire, when the foolishness of greed (gold) and satiation (honey) are overcome.

The final prayer (vs. 11–14) offered in response to the command is a wise and self-knowing petition. The speaker knows that even in God's wondrously Torah-ordered creation, there are temptation, seduction, and fault. These verses anticipate the prayer, "Lead us not into temptation," that is, into a time of risk when we may be talked out of obedience. Finally it is not the rule of command, but the active work of God, that will keep us innocent.

The final, familiar petition of v. 14 is a wondrous statement of trustful submission. God is known to be utterly reliable, for this is the God of glorifying creation and life-giving Torah. The petitioner wants his life to conform completely and without reservation to the rule and expectation of God. This self-yielding act of piety withholds nothing from God; everything is exposed, nothing hidden. (See additional commentary under Third Sunday in Lent.)

James 3:1–12

> Sticks and stones may break my bones,
> but words can never harm me!

With these brave lines, countless youngsters ward off the taunts of their peers. The lines are learned from other children, and probably also from parents who hope to protect their children from the harm done by human speech. The lines carry within themselves their own contradiction, for if words did not in fact have the power to do harm, the lines would not be necessary. Depth psychology has demonstrated systematically and analytically what was already known from experience well before the writing of this lection: Words wound and even cripple—words spoken that cannot be retrieved, words withheld from others who ache to hear them, even words imputed to the minds of others in the imagination. Words can and do hurt.

The lection itself beings abruptly, without clear transition from the end of James 2, but the topic has been anticipated already in 1:19: "Be quick to listen, slow to speak, slow to anger." Here the author elaborates that admonition into a relentless warning about the power of human speech and the difficulties of controlling it. The tongue, like the bridle of a horse or the rudder of a ship, accomplishes far more than its size would seem to make possible. Despite the human ability to tame other species, "no one can tame the tongue."

If it seems that some lines from this lection might have been written by Ann Landers as easily as by an early Christian, that is because the passage contains much that is common knowledge. Like much else in James, parallels to some of this passage can be found in Jewish wisdom literature. Sirach, for example, laments that "the tongue of mortals may be their downfall" (5:13) and pronounces blessings on the one who "does not blunder with his lips" (14:1); Prov. 16:27 compares the speech of a scoundrel to a "scorching fire." The specific images of the bridle and the rudder occur frequently in Hellenistic literature. In other words, the passage draws heavily on conventional human experience.

At two points, the beginning and the end, the passage takes up issues of particular concern to the Christian community. The lection begins with a warning to those who would be teachers: "We who teach will be judged with greater strictness." Even lacking a clear transition from the preceding section, this reference to teachers surely has in view those who function as teachers within the Christian community, rather than teaching in a more general sense. As a task that almost always involves speech, teaching also risks the great evils that can be done by human speech.

The passage closes with two brief illustrations in James 3:11–12 that serve only to reinforce the point made in v. 9: "With [the tongue] we bless the Lord and Father, and with it we curse those who are made in the likeness of God." With these words, the writer powerfully epitomizes the problem he has been discussing, but now he does so from a theological perspective. The very same gift of speech that enables human beings to praise God also enables them to curse their fellow human beings. Such a contradiction ought not occur, but it does nevertheless.

If the common human experience reflected in this passage sounds at points more like Ann Landers than like sacred scripture, it departs from Ann Landers and other advice givers in one crucial respect: the author suggests no solution for the problem of human speech. No proposal about quenching the fire or its force tempers the analysis in any way. The result is a pessimistic interpretation of the human situation: no one can tame this force that simultaneously praises God and curses God's creation.

Perhaps that should be the preacher's approach to this passage as well. No three-point cure will solve this problem. Simply letting the wisdom of the text stand on its own terms may be an important element in allowing the entire community to hear and acknowledge the severity of the problem. It may also allow preachers to acknowledge that the text speaks to and for them as well (as it does to commentators also).

If the author of James does not offer a cure for the problem of the human tongue, the passage that follows might serve as something of an antidote. James 3:13–17 takes up the question of the true wisdom that has its origin in God, and 4:1–10 encourages friendship with God rather than with the world. Here, as earlier in the letter, what the author is after is what might be called integrity. Christian faith both permits and calls forth a relationship with God that has integrity; it operates out of God-given wisdom and out of a friendship, an allegiance, with God alone. That integrity then allows the writer to return, in 4:11–12, to questions of speech within the community and to urge Christians not to speak against one another. In other words, only the gifts of God can provide Christians with the means to overcome the problems inherent in human speech.

Mark 8:27–38

It is hard to overemphasize Mark 8:27–38, not only for the critical role it plays in the narrative structure of Mark, but for the questions it raises for believers about what it means to confess Jesus. In an almost strange way, the passage begins by focusing on something as harmless as public opinion, a recital of what people other than the disciples think about Jesus. Then the question is put to the disciples, "Who do *you* say that I am?" (emphasis added). The ensuing prediction of Jesus' suffering, rejection, death, and resurrection begins to bring the issue even closer to home by defining what type of Messiah Jesus is. Peter's objection is evidence that the point is getting across. Finally, the sayings on cross-bearing and losing one's life clarify the style of commitment to which those who confess Jesus are called. What starts out as an innocuous question ends up as a radical and challenging description of the Christian life.

The whole scene at Caesarea Philippi makes better sense when viewed in light of its context. Through most of the initial seven and a half chapters of the Gospel, the narrative focuses on the powerful activity of Jesus, evidenced in various sorts of mighty works that presage the inclusion of non-Jews and that provoke considerable opposition from the religious authorities.

All along, the disciples demonstrate little insight into what is happening, leading Jesus to ask in frustration, "Do you not yet understand?" (8:21). Then at Bethsaida Jesus cures a blind man in two stages: first partial sight and then full vision (vs. 22–26). From v. 27 the journey of Jesus and the disciples begins from Caesarea Philippi in the north to conclude at Jerusalem (11:1), a journey characterized not so much by mighty works as by intense instruction in the way of being disciples. Just prior to arriving at Jerusalem comes the restoration of sight to a second blind man, Bartimaeus, who "regained his sight and followed him on the way" (10:52). The section from 8:22 to 10:52, then, is an attempt to provide a vision for the disciples about the nature of who Jesus is and who the disciples are.

It is intriguing to consider 8:27–38 in terms of Peter's comments and actions. He is the one who gives the right answer to Jesus' question to the disciples (v. 29). But Peter is also the one who voices the objections to any notion that the Messiah must suffer, be rejected, and die (v. 32). Is Peter merely thickheaded? No—as a matter of fact, he is extremely perceptive. Better than anyone else, he realizes the contradiction in any notion of a suffering, dying Messiah. He expresses a universal complaint about the scandal at the heart of the Christian faith (see 1 Cor. 1:23). Could he typify the blind man who has arrived only at the stage of partial sight (Mark 8:24)?

What lies at the heart of Peter's rather high-handed objection? After all, Peter would know that opposition had been building, and that, though the crowds heard Jesus gladly, those in the power structure were plotting and scheming. It would be no surprise to hear that the future was fraught with danger. But Jesus talks openly about something else: "the Son of Man must (*dei*) undergo great suffering, and be rejected, . . . and be killed" (v. 31). The plotting and scheming is not happening outside the plan of God for the Messiah. Peter, in fact, catches a fleeting glimpse of the "divine necessity," of the kind of Messiah Jesus is to be, and he vehemently protests. Jesus takes it to be another temptation ("Satan") to divert him from his messianic vocation.

What Jesus says about Peter's protest aptly describes the situation: "You are setting your mind not on divine things but on human things" (v. 33, rendered much better in the NRSV than the RSV). Peter's objection to a crucified Messiah arises out of good common sense, a logical way of thinking, but it is a human perspective, and Jesus is offering God's point of view.

The notion that there is a way to Easter other than through the pain and rejection of Good Friday continues to be offered as good common sense. Religion should help to protect people from conflict and provide a solid set of values for successful living, so the logic goes. Positive thinkers see the cross, both Jesus' and ours, as obstacles to be overcome, not as a necessary piece of the divine plan which leads to resurrection.

The discipleship sayings that conclude the section (vs. 34–38) make plain that those who follow Jesus have to walk the same sort of journey that he walks. The item that needs clarification for many in our congregations is the phrase "take up their cross" in v. 34. The wording refers to a voluntary activity, to decisions made and strategies taken that may likely create opposition. The text is not referring to those unpredictable tragedies that occur to people regardless of their commitments ("This is my cross to bear"). Neither is it blessing the practice of being highly disagreeable, for whatever reason. Rather, at the heart of discipleship is a faithful following of the Messiah ("setting your mind . . . on divine things"), whose vocation carries him to Easter via Golgotha. (See additional commentary under Second Sunday in Lent.)

Proper 20

Ordinary Time 25

*Sunday between
September 18 and 24 inclusive*

Obedience takes many shapes. Since the contextual dynamics vary from circumstance to circumstance, from age to age, the precise contours of the loyal life vary accordingly, making it impossible even to contemplate a set of directives to cover every situation. New seasons demand new decisions. The four texts for this Sunday offer four scenarios of obedience, four occasions by which modern readers can be instructed in their struggles to be responsive to the gift of grace. Though one of the passages provides some valuable insights into God's intentions for all human beings, its use in preaching remains highly problematic because of its treatment of the "good wife" (Prov. 31:10–31).

The other three texts exhibit a common pattern—also disturbing, but in a different way. They confront the reader with sharp choices, with either-ors, allowing little or no space for the middle ground. Those of us trained in examining both sides of an issue, who are comfortable with "Yes, but . . ." answers, are tempted to argue that decisions are not so cut-and-dried. What about the murky ambiguity?

For instance, Ps. 1 (appearing for the second time in Year B) lays out two ways for the readers—either taking the path sinners walk or delighting in the law of God. One way has no staying power, the other prospers. The poem concludes with a statement of God's responses: "The LORD watches over the way of the righteous, but the way of the wicked will perish" (Ps. 1:6). No middle ground.

The reading from James does the same. Two kinds of wisdom are described. One is marked by envy, selfish ambition, and deceit; the other by peacefulness, gentleness, and mercy. The two are mutually exclusive. "Do you not know that friendship with the world is enmity with God? Therefore whoever wishes to be a friend of the world becomes an enemy of God" (James 4:4). An either-or. No middle ground.

In the form of a narrative, the Gospel reading presents a similar choice (Mark 9:30–37). The disciples argue about who will be the greatest, but Jesus responds by putting a little child, a symbol of the least, into their midst. The powerful or the powerless? No middle ground.

Could it be that ours is the time and place when such sharp choices need to be made? Could the uneasiness we feel with such clear-cut demands and the eagerness to explore the murky ambiguities in fact expose an unwillingness to heed the call of God?

Proverbs 31:10–31

There are a number of passages in ancient Israelite wisdom literature, both canonical and deuterocanonical, that project a view of the good wife (for example, Prov. 12:4; Sir. 26:1–4). The present text is noteworthy, however, in that it is the most elaborate such portrait, the twenty-two verses forming a perfect alphabetic acrostic. In addition, the figure of Wisdom herself seems to lie behind the text (notice v. 26a), and it may be that the passage is really an allegory on the nature of wisdom, not unlike the personification of Wisdom in Prov. 1:20–33 (Proper 19) and elsewhere. That possibility is strengthened by the first Hebrew word of v. 27 (in English: "She looks well to"), which is an almost exact homophone of the Greek word for wisdom, *sophia*. If that is an intentional wordplay, it goes a long way toward helping us establish a general date and setting for the composition of the passage.

Such considerations aside, however, this lection presents an enormous difficulty to the preacher for the simple reason that it embraces an understanding of the place of women in society that cannot be condoned today. To be sure, ancient Israel was not of one mind about the role of women, any more than is our contemporary Western world. Some texts seem to imply that a woman was little more than her husband's property, as in Ex. 20:17 where, in the catalog of the man's property, the wife is enrolled before the man's slaves and livestock, but after his house (compare Deut. 5:21). On the other hand, some Old Testament passages, including the present lection, concede a large measure of independence to a woman (v. 16). But in general terms it may be said that ancient Israel viewed an adult woman as a valued human being primarily in terms of her worth to her husband (important exceptions include Esther, Susanna, and Huldah—see 2 Kings 22:14–20, but notice how even Huldah is identified in terms of her husband). It must be stressed that ancient Israel was not alone in this attitude, for patriarchy was a social system that transcended national or ethnic boundaries. And while it may accurately be said that both Old and New Testaments sow the seeds for the ideal of the equality of all persons, regardless of gender (Deut. 21:10–14, progressive legislation for its day; and Gal. 3:28), it simply is not possible to transfer into our own setting the Old Testament understanding of a woman's role in society.

Therefore, the best that a preacher may do with this present lection is to avoid it. This is not to deny that the ancient poet intended to sketch the "good wife" in compassionate and sympathetic lines. It is also not to deny that there are certain valuable insights in this text into the nature of God's ideal for all human life, both male and female (note vs. 20, 26, 30). But the pervasive image is that of the wife as the member of the family who is responsible for those chores involving manual labor (vs. 15, 19, 22, 24), while her husband attends to matters that demand the intellect (v. 23, where the context is that of the husband's participation in the government of the community).

There are simply better texts in Proverbs on which one may preach, and one would be well advised to select one of these. It is astonishing that 31:10–31 should have been included in the Common Lectionary at all!

Psalm 1

For a full exposition of this psalm, see the Seventh Sunday of Easter. This group of lectionary readings provides several scenarios for a life lived in obedient faith. As such, each of these readings may be taken as an interpretive exposition of Ps. 1, which concerns a life aimed unreservedly at obedience to God's command. There is a great temptation to understand Ps. 1 in a narrow, legalistic way, as an exercise in punctilious overscrupulousness. These other readings will protect Ps. 1 from such a drastic misreading.

The woman characterized in Prov. 31 is one who knows her way around in the world. One can picture her as a tough operator in the world of economic power. But she is not simply shrewd and pragmatic. She is a woman who "fears the LORD" (Prov. 31:30) and who is preoccupied with doing God's will. We can imagine she is like a tree "planted by streams of water" (Ps. 1:3).

The Epistle reading offers a very different scenario of an obedient life. The catalog of the "fruits of the spirit" is not unlike the better-known inventory of Paul. The person envisioned here is one who is formed for habits (*habitus!*) of trust, obedience, and submission, which yield freedom and joy. In a different way, the Gospel reading portrays the truly obedient as the least and the innocent, as vulnerable as a child.

In all these portrayals, the Torah-shaped person is quite unlike models of personhood regnant in our culture. In this person there is no acquisitiveness, no anxiety, no self-sufficiency, no despair. The Torah provides another point of reference, another dynamic, and another destiny. These large promises and possibilities, however, pivot on concrete, elemental acts of praise, fear, and obedience.

James 3:13–4:3, 7–8a

How does wisdom manifest itself? What prompts people to identify some women and men as wise and to suspect that others are not so wise? To say that someone is wise, at least in contemporary English, suggests that the individual has maturity of insight, is unusually discerning, applies knowledge with careful judgment. Although wisdom is not associated with intellect alone, with mere intelligence, it is thought of in intellectual terms, as something that happens largely—although not entirely—in the head.

This lection has to do with wisdom, but it is wisdom understood in quite a different way. The question in James 3:13, at the very beginning of the lection, frames the entire discussion: "Who is wise and understanding among you?" In other words, how is wisdom perceived? The answer the text gives is surprising precisely for its nonintellectual character: "Show by your good life that your works are done with gentleness born of wisdom." To detect wisdom, then, what is to be examined is not primarily what a person thinks or says or writes, but how a person lives.

James 3:13–4:3 addresses the symptoms of wisdom, both godly wisdom and another kind of wisdom, which is "earthly, unspiritual, devilish" (3:15). With 4:4, the author articulates a sharp dichotomy between the wise and the unwise, characterizing the wise person as one who is an enemy of the world and the unwise as one who is "an enemy of God" (4:4). The passage culminates in the series of imperatives beginning with the primary instruction of v. 7: "Submit yourselves therefore to God."

As is the case elsewhere in James, this appeal for wisdom has much in common with what contemporary English would refer to as integrity (see the discussion earlier, on Proper 17 and Proper 19), the unity of thought and action. The assumption here is that action provides a symptom of the inner wisdom of a person; thus, the presence of envy, ambition, lying, boastfulness reveals a perverted wisdom, which comes from the devil. Real wisdom is "first pure, then peaceable, gentle, willing to yield, full of mercy and good fruits, without a trace of partiality or hypocrisy" (3:17). This assigning of various vices and virtues to differing wisdoms becomes more intense in 4:1–3, where the author introduces questions of internal conflict. When motives and behaviors are in conflict with one another, they provide another clue that wisdom is absent.

The sharp outburst that begins in v. 4 ("Adulterers!") recalls the prophetic charge of adultery against Israel (for example, Hos. 1–3; Isa. 57:3; Jer. 3:1–5). Just as the people of Israel could not be bound covenantally to Yahweh and yet serve other gods, the writer of James insists that Christians cannot be aligned both with God and with the world. Although vs. 4–6 fall outside the limits of the lectionary reading, they play an important role in the passage and, indeed, in the letter as a whole. Central to the Christian integrity for which this letter argues is the notion that Christians' lives must be aligned with God and only God.

Perhaps the lectionary omits these verses because of their negative assessment of "the world" ("friendship with the world is enmity with God," v. 4). That kind of language has sometimes given rise to a Christian indifference to human suffering, a withdrawal from engagement with the people of the world. The strident ethical tone of this letter should make it clear that the author is in no way advocating a retreat from engagement with humankind. Instead, the "friendship with the world" that must be avoided is a friendship with the values of the world—values that elevate the rich and powerful over the poor and marginalized, values that see only what is on the surface and do not look at the heart. That sort of "friendship with the world" is not friendship with the world's *people*.

How is true wisdom acquired? How is friendship with God achieved? Verses 7–10 begin to address those questions with a series of imperatives, starting with the most significant: "Submit yourselves therefore to God." Submission is defined both as resisting the devil so that he will withdraw and drawing near to God so that God will draw near to believers. The dualism of 4:4–6 continues here with the notion that nearness to God inevitably means distance from God's enemy, the devil.

Elsewhere in the New Testament, the language of submission sometimes appears in contexts that are painful for many modern readers. Women are admonished to submit to their husbands (Eph.

5:21–24; Col. 3:18; Titus 2:5), and slaves to their owners (Titus 2:9). Because submission has historically been urged on certain segments of the church and not on others, some readers will view this exhortation with suspicion.

In this context, however, submission to God has less to do with hierarchical structures of authority than it does with the possibility of trust. Human beings submit themselves to God as the one power in all the cosmos that can be trusted unequivocally. Trust in God drives away the devil. Trust in God draws God near. God may be relied on to provide wisdom and friendship, because God is inherently trustworthy.

Mark 9:30–37

An intriguing feature of Mark's narrative is the role played by the disciples. Called and commissioned by Jesus, given special instruction at various points in their association with Jesus, privileged to share intimate moments in his ministry, they nevertheless consistently get a bad press. They say inappropriate things. They keep children away from Jesus. They are anxious when they should be sleeping and sleep when they should be anxious. Continually they misunderstand what Jesus is teaching and doing.

The real problem with the disciples is that they all too easily become mirrors in which readers see themselves. Their failures and lack of understanding typify the patterns of successive generations, who are also slow to get the point and who persist in setting their minds on human things instead of divine things (Mark 8:33). If we become discouraged by seeing our own thoughts and actions reflected in the disciples, we can take heart that they were reclaimed following the resurrection and set by Jesus to a new task.

The Gospel reading for this Sunday is the second of the so-called Passion predictions of Jesus in Mark's Gospel and, like the others, is followed by a series of sayings on discipleship (9:30–37). In this brief exchange with Jesus, we discover three features of the disciples.

First, even after failure, the disciples are singled out for special instruction. The immediately preceding incident details the inability of the disciples to help the father and his son who was troubled with an unclean spirit (9:14–29). Jesus chides them harshly, since their failure has led to a squabble with the scribes: "How much longer must I put up with you?" (9:19). Yet on the ensuing trip he seeks to travel unnoticed so that he can have some private time with the disciples to continue to teach them about his own future and theirs. Their weakness has not diminished his zeal to prepare them for life in the reign of God.

If the disciples in some sense mirror the church, then we have to say that much of Jesus' instruction is not intended for the world, as general religious truths universally applicable to people regardless of their commitments. He is no Kahlil Gibran, whose spiritual insights are offered to the masses. Rather, what Jesus teaches is intended for followers who have been called and commissioned and who, while they often misunderstand, still are bound together in a special community. The one who teaches is not a spiritual guru, but the Lord, who singles out his disciples for special instruction.

Second, even the disciples find Jesus' message baffling. Though this is the second time Jesus pointedly predicts his destiny in Jerusalem, the disciples fail to understand and are so intimidated that they will not ask any questions (9:32). Their successive failures have totally deflated them. If that were not enough, we are told that on this very journey they got in an argument among themselves about who was the greatest. When Jesus queried them about the argument, they were so embarrassed they had nothing to say. They may not have understood much, but they knew enough to realize that their argument was completely out of line with what Jesus had been talking about. It has to be one of the lowest points in the history of their relationship with Jesus. They are baffled and humiliated. But Jesus is not through with them.

The third thing that happens to the disciples in the text is that they are taught a lesson in servanthood. The words on cross-bearing and losing one's life (8:34–38) are given more specificity when Jesus speaks of being last of all and servant of all (9:35). Strikingly, the disciples are not reprimanded for what seems like a ridiculous argument, but the whole notion of "greatness" is redefined. New categories are proposed for determining success and failure, winning and losing, achievement and unfulfillment. We begin to get an inkling of what setting our minds on divine thoughts really implies—not purely spiritual meditations, but attention to the least in such a radical way that we become the least.

Then comes the little child Jesus sets in their midst. It is not the child's naïveté or innocence or trustfulness that is highlighted here, but the child's lowly status, as one always under the authority of another and without rights. A chain of relationships is forged: welcome the little child in my name and you welcome me; welcome me and you are welcoming no less a one than God. A fellowship of hospitality is established between the little child, Jesus, and God.

Where the disciples have argued about greatness and with it, of course, power, they are directed by Jesus to open their arms to the powerless. What would happen if the church could begin to think and act this way? What if the notion of greatness could be conceived of in Jesus' terms?

Proper 21

Ordinary Time 26

Sunday between September 25 and October 1 inclusive

The Bible repeatedly pictures the people of God as a beleagured community, either having recently endured a time of vulnerability or anticipating one in the near future. Never is distress far away. It is clear, however, that in such moments of trouble special resources are always called on—the peculiar presence of God, and with it remarkable courage and hope on the part of the people. Our texts for this Sunday in varying ways take seriously human vulnerability and address the issue of divine aid and extraordinary courage.

Despite all the problems surrounding the book of Esther, it tells an astonishing story of one who acts boldly on behalf of God and God's apparently unsheltered people. She meets the challenge thrust upon her, and in her willingness to risk her own life shows herself to be a devout and pious woman. Though God's name does not appear in the narrative, it is clear that God's will is accomplished in the deliverance of the Jews.

Psalm 124 in a marvelously effective way celebrates God's help in the time of distress. The only explanation for protection from the angry enemy and rescue from the raging flood is Yahweh, the great sovereign of heaven and earth, who at the same time proves to be "our help." The playful rhetoric of the poem is not to be taken as a boastful claim that God is "on our side," but an expression of profound gratitude for divine deliverance.

The language about prayer as a resource for the healing of the sick in James 5 is a further reminder of the availability of God in times of difficulty and distress. Instead of being a gimmick to persuade God into doing something, prayer is depicted as a gift to the church, an invitation to invoke divine aid.

The Markan community is given sage words about its upcoming time of persecution ("Everyone will be salted with fire," Mark 9:49). Church members are called to a self-critical stance, to a quality of life free from offense to the weak and lowly, lest they turn out themselves to be "saltless" salt and good for nothing. Moreover, they are directed to embrace other pilgrims who minister in Jesus' name, lest they assume they alone are the chosen instruments of God.

A deep trust in God amid troubled times evidences an openness to divine aid, extraordinary courage, and a self-critical spirit.

Esther 7:1–6, 9–10; 9:20–22

The book of Esther has not been without its detractors over the years. For one thing, it has appeared to many to be devoid of theological purpose, in view of the complete absence of any direct mention of God (4:14 may be an oblique theological reference). The Greek-language additions made to Esther which are incorporated in the Septuagint, and which are notable for their expressions of piety, seem to have been a very early effort to compensate for this perceived lack of interest in the Almighty on the part of Esther's original author(s). For another thing, the book has struck many readers as being narrowly ethnocentric, its concern for Jewish survival seeming to loom in importance over any other issue. Still another focus of criticism has been the festival which, in the Jewish tradition, commemorates the events recounted in the book. Purim, whose establishment is cited in the closing verses of this day's lection (9:20–22), is an occasion of conspicuous consumption of food and drink, and—to many, at least—compares unfavorably with other significant occasions in the Jewish year. Finally, for many readers, there is the matter of the historicity of the story of Esther, in that modern scholars are virtually unanimous in regarding the book as fiction.

Given these objections, the question is an obvious one: Why read Esther at all?

The answer would seem to lie in the primary reason the book was accorded canonical status, and that almost certainly was the fact that it celebrated one Jewish person's loyalty to her people, even to the point of risking her life to save them. Esther is a story of tenacious courage and of a willingness to hope against all odds. And, although there are no recorded prayers or miracles, many devout Jews of the Hellenistic world (the period of the book's composition) who read this book—who understood all too well the vulnerability of their people in a hostile Gentile world—would have needed no coaching to comprehend that the deliverance of the Jews was nothing other than the will of God. In other words, Esther did not need to pray to be seen as a pious woman. Her willingness to sacrifice herself to save her people is the ultimate act of piety.

The author(s) of the present version of the story of Esther (many scholars are of the opinion that the story of Esther was told in one or more forms before being cast in the shape it retains in the Hebrew Bible, and there is—as noted above—another version of the story in the Septuagint) have set the stage for 7:1–6 in 5:9–14. There Haman, who does not yet know that Esther is a member of the group of people he has set out to destroy, anticipates with great relish the banquet with King Ahasuerus to which he has been invited by the queen. While he attempts to prevent his hatred of Mordecai from interfering with his obvious delight, he boasts to his wife and friends that no one else has been invited to share the royal table (5:12). What a fine fellow he thinks himself to be (note also 5:11)! When, like a dark shadow, the thought of insolent (so he seems to Haman) Mordecai casts itself across Haman's mind, the man is consoled by his wife Zeresh and friends and follows their advice to construct a tall gallows for the old Jew's execution.

Haman's hubris suffers a terrible wound the next day, however, when he is forced by the king to lavish enormous honors on Mordecai (6:1–13). The moment is made all the worse because it is Haman, mistakenly believing that the king is about to honor him, who has inflated the list of benefits which he is then forced to confer on the old Jew (6:7–9). The reader probably does not really need Zeresh's expression of prescience concerning the survivability of the Jews (6:13), but no one can now doubt what soon will happen.

The trap that Esther has set is dramatically sprung in 7:1–6, 9–10, the beginning of this day's lection. Haman, who thought his inclusion at the royal banquet was a badge of honor, is denounced by Esther, but only after the queen has cleverly kindled the king's anger against some unnamed person who would dare to plot against Esther's people. It is not until the king has been thoroughly aroused and demands to know the identity of the villain that Esther speaks his name: "this wicked Haman!" (v. 6). The irony of the scene is complete when one of the king's servants suggests that the gallows that Haman had built for Mordecai should be used for the execution of Haman instead (vs. 9–10).

The final verses of the lectionary passage (9:20–22) describe the inauguration of the Purim festival, which celebrates with great joy the deliverance of the Jews (Adar falls in February-March).

God's people have been saved (notice that in spite of its concern for the welfare of the Jews, the book of Esther is not anti-Gentile: see 9:3) and God's will has been done. Esther reminds all who would think otherwise that those who speak boldly about God and those who act boldly for God are not always one and the same persons.

Psalm 124

In this psalm, Israel voices its astonishment and gratitude for God's wondrous deliverance. The psalm knows that Israel, on its own, is characteristically exposed and vulnerable and cannot save itself. It understands that, reliant on its own power, Israel's course is hopeless. But it understands with equal clarity and honesty that Israel is not on its own, and therefore is not helpless. Israel's life is here discerned as an uneven conflict between Israel and its adversaries, in which the adversary is stronger. That much the psalm assumes; life is fundamentally agonistic, and Israel is characteristically at risk in an uneven competition.

The psalm moves, however, beyond such a social analysis to make a doxological assertion that alters the analysis. There is a third player in the drama of reality. Social reality is not only "us" and "them." In addition to these two uneven contestants, it is the "third force," Yahweh, who subverts all conventional realities of the social process and makes possible life in the world that is otherwise impossible. Thus Israel is clear that God is "for us." It answers the threat to its life in defiant certitude: "Therefore who can be against us?" The answer to that rhetorical question is, "Nobody of importance can be against us." The reality of God completely reshapes historical prospects and the communal destiny of this people, which relies on Yahweh.

The opening unit (vs. 1–5) of Ps. 124 seems to be in response to a quite concrete event of rescue, but that event is not specified for us. And since it is nonspecific, that event has become paradigmatic for Israel's lyric. That is, what happened here is what always happens to us, because of Yahweh. Thus the song generalizes from a specific event to a defining, persistent model of conflict, rescue, and assurance.

This unit is laid out in a clear pattern of protasis and apodosis, "If . . . then." The double conditional "if" entertains the negative possibility that Yahweh is *not* "on our side." The subjunctive is "contrary to fact," and, indeed, the entire protasis is contrary to fact, because Yahweh *is* "on our side." Thus the statement cast in a negative form intends to make a profoundly positive statement: "Yahweh is on our side!"

The negative statement entertains in playful rhetoric the negative alternative: What if Yahweh were not on our side? The formula of the last line of v. 1 suggests that this is a liturgical formula. The whole congregation is invited to speak and ponder this unhappy option.

The double "if" is followed by a triple "then," which hosts the unthinkable negative consequence of the unthinkable negative premise. It is no doubt telling that the double "if" is completed by the triple response, because the poem wants to state the negative option in as threatening a way as is possible. Thus vs. 3–5 portray Israel at the mercy of its enemies, as though Yahweh were not Israel's strong ally and advocate. What would happen is that Israel would be eaten alive (v. 3), and flooded over by the irresistible power of chaos and force of death (vs. 4–5). That is, Israel would be hopelessly lost.

This entire scenario in five elements (two plus three) is an act of liturgical playfulness. The words invite the congregation to play "What if . . .?" The intention, however, is to reach exactly the opposite conclusion—that of warm, reassuring, completely confident faith. In truth, Yahweh is on our side. And, therefore, in truth we are not swallowed up or swept away. While such a claim might in some contexts be arrogant and chauvinistic, here the affirmation is one of deep trust and relief. Because of God, only because of God, we are utterly safe.

Verses 6–7 now respond to the rejected scenario of vs. 1–5, by a full and direct affirmation of the truth of Yahweh. The formula of blessing is the classic Jewish one, "*Baruch adonai* . . ." It is an act of confident gratitude and praise, attributing great and good things to Yahweh and, conversely, ceding Israel's life over to God in awed gratitude. These lines acknowledge that the power for life, so generously given, is held, not in our hands, but in the sovereign hand of Yahweh.

Yahweh is "blessed" because Yahweh has not given this people over to the devouring enemy. Yahweh has acted decisively to prevent the scenario voiced in vs. 1–5. Because of Yahweh's action, Israel is completely safe, not "trapped" by the destructive enemy. This poem is then a voicing of trustful, grateful piety rooted in a quite concrete experience, when a negative alternative was quite possible. (The tale of Esther exhibits exactly such an improbable rescue as this psalm attests.)

Verse 8 adds a highly conventional and stylized doxology. It expresses two characteristic features of Israel's piety. On the one hand, Yahweh is the great sovereign of all reality. On the other hand, this great sovereign is specifically, concretely "our help." The "life power" of heaven and earth is mobilized in concrete rescue. Thus the quite conventional and likely free-floating formula fits well to conclude this psalm. It is the help of this God that has overridden Israel's threatening enemies and made Israel safe. The poem plays with and walks around the crucial conviction of evangelical faith: God is with us; . . . therefore, we are utterly, gladly, joyously, gratefully, safe. Israel, which cannot save, rescue, or defend itself, here names its great, unambiguous advocate. History is an arena inhabited by this decisive Protector, because of whom all the threats and options of life are radically redefined.

James 5:13–20

A first reading of this passage may send the preacher scurrying in some other direction. Discussions about prayer invariably raise a host of difficult pastoral questions, and this lection will certainly bring those questions to the foreground: If the "prayer of the righteous is powerful and effective," why is my loved one still ill? Does that mean that prayer is not powerful? Or does it mean that my prayer failed because I am not sufficiently righteous?

It will be important to recognize that the text does not constitute a systematic approach to the question of Christian prayer. Instead, the topic at hand, going back to James 5:12 and forward to the end of the letter, is that of appropriate speech. Throughout the letter, the author has been concerned to identify the problems of human speech (1:19; 3:1–12) and the way Christians can address those problems (for example, 4:11–12). Here that concern culminates with comments about swearing (5:12), prayer (vs. 13–18), and disciplining speech within the community (vs. 19–20).

Without understanding that perspective, even the opening half-verse appears ludicrous: "Are any among you suffering? They should pray." Taken out of context, one might conclude from this advice that the only approach to human suffering is prayer. Of course, earlier portions of the letter speak against such a simplistic approach (such as the call to responsibility for others in 2:14–16), as does the realization that all of this passage concerns itself with speech. One appropriate response to suffering is prayer. In the same way, one appropriate response to being cheerful is to "sing songs of praise." In both cases, the form of speech enjoined on the community addresses God.

The writer is able to comment briefly on these two introductory situations, but what follows in vs. 14–18 is a far more complicated problem. If those who suffer pray, and those who are in good spirits sing songs of praise, what of those who are ill? Despite the text's insistence that prayer is effective, the complex explanation indicates that prayer does not automatically and universally provide healing.

Verse 14 instructs the sick to call for the "elders of the church," who should pray and anoint them with oil in the Lord's name. Verse 15 explains that "the prayer of faith" saves the sick, but it remains unclear whether this "prayer of faith" refers only to the prayers of the elders or to any prayer that stems from faith. Instructions in v. 16 regarding prayer "for one another" further confuse matters by suggesting that not the elders alone, but all believers, ought to be engaged in prayer for the sick. The end of v. 15 adds that sins are forgiven through prayer, introducing what may be a separate topic, (prayer for the forgiveness of sins), although the reference to healing again in vs. 16 blurs the lines between the two issues.

Pointing out these apparent inconsistencies is important, because they suggest that the writer of the letter knows both the importance of prayer, the potential of prayer for healing, and the difficulties involved in asserting that prayer assures healing. The final statement of v. 16 is crucial: "The prayer of the righteous is powerful and effective." That statement introduces the example of Elijah, by whose prayer rain was withheld and by whose prayer rain again fell on the earth (vs. 17–18).

Several strands of early Christian literature attest to the ability of Christians to bring about healing. In addition to this passage in James, Paul refers to those who "work miracles" and those who have "gifts of healing" (1 Cor. 12:29–30). Luke provides several accounts in which Christian leaders perform healings in Jesus' name (for example, Acts 3:1–10). Christians continue to experience the power of prayer for healing. The distinction that becomes essential here is that between prayer as a gift and prayer as a tool. To assert, as various New Testament writers do, that God grants prayer as a gift, is to acknowledge that all healing comes from God. Through prayer individuals and communities approach God, seeking God's intervention, God's presence. Prayer does not, however, become a tool that Christians own and by which they manipulate God into doing their own will. As James 5:15 puts it, "The Lord will raise them up." It is God who grants the healing.

The final verses of this lection continue the larger topic of appropriate speech, although they move abruptly away from the immediate context and its discussion of prayer. Here the form of speech concerns that truth-telling that is necessary when believers stray from the truth: "Whoever brings back a sinner from wandering will save the sinner's soul from death and will cover a multitude of sins" (v. 20). This statement may seem a bit incomplete as an ending to the letter, but it nevertheless speaks both for the author and to the audience. The author surely hopes that this letter has performed the function here anticipated, that is, that the letter has served to move some believers back toward the truth and away from error. And the author hopes that those who receive the letter will do likewise, speaking the truth to one another and rescuing one another "from death."

Mark 9:38-50

One theologian has spoken of election as the sum of the gospel, the good news of divine grace that, despite our sinfulness, we are chosen and loved by God. But the awareness of being God's elect has often bred a form of elitism, a sense of self-importance that subtly builds barriers between groups and persons rather than bridges. For whatever reasons, the experience of being loved can lead to an unhealthy feeling of specialness, which questions others (as if God's love were somehow limited to a few) and at the same time fails to be self-critical. The problem is apparently not peculiar to the modern church, since the Gospel lesson designated for this Sunday is aimed at such a sense of self-importance among the original disciples.

The passage, Mark 9:38-50, is rather loosely put together and seems to reflect the problems of Mark's church. First, there is the interchange between John and Jesus about the alien exorcist (vs. 38-40), followed by a single saying that speaks of a reward for those who welcome Jesus' disciples (v. 41). A warning about the tragedy of leading "these little ones" astray (v. 42) in turn is followed by a patterned sequence of further warnings about causes for stumbling within oneself (vs. 43-48). The final two verses join disparate sayings about "salt," concluding with an injunction to be at peace with one another (vs. 49-50).

There is a certain irony about John's explanation of the disciples' action in trying to stop the alien exorcist. An earlier portion of the chapter records the failure of the disciples themselves to exorcise an unclean spirit from a young boy and Jesus' sharp rebuke (9:14-29), and now they want to restrain a successful exorcist simply because he is not one of their group. The issue is not whether the man is acting in the name and power of Jesus, but whether he is part of the chosen establishment. The outsider is forbidden—"we tried to stop him"—just as later the children were forbidden from coming to Jesus (10:13-16), exposing the exclusivism of the disciples. In light of their earlier failure, could his success have been a threat to their status?

Jesus answers with an inclusive word, and yet one that realistically recognizes the problem of unauthorized ministries (9:39). Space has to be made for mavericks and outsiders as long as they are not explicitly opponents of Jesus. The disciples need to nurture the gift of graciousness and generosity. They need to know that the people along the way who show them kindness will receive a reward for their graciousness and generosity (v. 41). In their welcome of the disciples, they provide a model the disciples would do well to emulate.

In the second half of the passage, the miscellaneous collection of sayings enjoins a stance of self-criticism. Instead of worrying about the ministries of outsiders, the disciples are directed to reflect on their own style of life and ministry. Is there anything they say or do that would serve as a stumbling block for the children of the church or new believers (taking "little ones" in both a narrow and a broad sense)? Having a huge millstone strung around one's neck and being thrown into the sea is a vivid image that underscores the seriousness of the issue.

Again, with arresting metaphors, disciples are urged to examine themselves and to determine if there are specific features of their lives that prevent a sincere and energetic service of God (vs. 43–48). Self-mutilation, hell, the ever-active worm, and the perpetual fire are symbols guaranteed to get the reader's attention. The preacher, however, faces the task of not letting them be a diversion from the main thrust of the injunctions, namely, a wholehearted commitment to the divine reign.

"Everyone will be salted with fire" probably intends to warn about the persecution and trials that the followers of Jesus will face. In the light of coming conflict, the disciples are urged not to lose their distinctiveness, not to succumb to the pressures to adopt the standards and ethos of the dominant social structure. If the saltiness is gone, then so is the salt's capacity to season. Only in maintaining their uniqueness as followers of the suffering Son of Man will the disciples be able to influence the surrounding culture. It is by no means an easy assignment, either for the original disciples or for later ones, but it is precisely what the elect are elected for—not privilege, but service.

The final charge is timely: "Be at peace with one another" (v. 50). If the future is to be "salted with fire," then the disciples no longer need to be quarreling among themselves about who is the greatest. "Salty" Christians cannot go it alone, but need one another in the community of memory and hope.

Despite its disjointedness, this passage provides a potent antidote to the ever-present temptation to overestimate one's own position as the chosen of God. Instead of questioning the validity of other active, and perhaps successful, groups, one is reminded in graphic fashion of the importance of self-criticism.

Proper 22

Ordinary Time 27

*Sunday between
October 2 and 8 inclusive*

These readings do not easily or obviously converge. There is, nonetheless, a richness of themes that occur in concert, bespeaking the power and depth of the gospel, themes of sovereign splendor, innocent trust, generous invitation, and hard demand. The preacher can choose to weave these together as they belong together in the faith, or focus on any particular combination among the themes.

The Epistle reading, by an appeal to a large inventory of theological-philosophical imagery, articulates all the fullness of God in the Person of Jesus. In this text as much as anywhere, the Christian claim that Jesus embodies and discloses God is grandly asserted. It is the God present in Jesus whom the church serves and trusts, and upon whom the world depends.

It is this God, known, served, and trusted in the Old Testament as well, who is the true subject of the Old Testament reading and the psalm. In the first verses of Job, the dramatic character called Job in full faithfulness enacts perfect response to the wonder of God. In spite of the distractions of his wife and of Satan, Job trusts this God fully. What Job embodies in his piety the psalm generalizes, so that all believers are invited to innocent communion with the God who is full of power, grace, and truth.

The Gospel teaching of Jesus begins in a hard demand about family and marriage. That hard demand belongs, so the text asserts, to the will of God. The text moves, however, to the trusting innocence of a child, an innocence that is not dependent on moral success. (In this regard the innocence of the child surpasses the faith of Job, which at this point is shaped by moral rectitude.) Indeed, it is the trusting innocence of a child (and that in the psalm) that is the proper response to the God of the epistle. Altogether the readings chronicle what it is like to be a person held firmly and gladly in trusting faith.

Job 1:1; 2:1-10

Four passages from Job constitute the Old Testament lections for this and succeeding weeks, with this day's text providing an introduction to the cycle. That the person Job is Everyman/Everywoman is evident enough even to the most casual reader, at least in the book's portrayal of the misfortunes of its chief character. What is remarkable about Job, however, and the quality that sets him apart from most other humans, is his faithfulness to his own moral and theological principles as well as his faithfulness to himself personally, to say nothing of his audacity in daring to confront God over the injustices of life. In the tersest possible manner, the text begins by sketching a portrait of a righteous and godly man who lives in some undetermined time and place (Job 1:1).

Outside the limits of the present lection, but essential to its meaning, is the tale of Satan's initial persecution of this good man (1:2–22). Both here and in the lection itself (2:1–10) we find the Old Testament struggling with the question of the origin of evil. No longer adequate is the old answer that Yahweh creates all things, both good and evil (compare 1 Sam. 16:14). And yet to be embraced is the concept of Satan as a transcendent being who acts independently of and contrary to God's will, as in later Judaism and Christianity. Rather, we are witnesses here to an intermediate position in which Satan (literally, "the Adversary" or "the Accuser"), while creating mischief for humans, does so in a manner that reveals his complete dependence on Yahweh. The Adversary, who has pointed out to Yahweh that Job is good only because he has lived a sheltered life (Job 1:10), initially proceeds by knocking away the supporting foundations of Job's happiness: his vast possessions and his close-knit family (1:13–19; compare vs. 3–5). Yet, although Job is deeply hurt by these losses, he does not rebel against God (v. 22).

Somewhat frustrated, Satan ratchets up the pressure on Job. The lectionary passage, in 2:1–8, describes how the Adversary inflicts a terrible skin condition on Job, a malady that is not only painfully uncomfortable (Job is forced to scratch himself with a piece of broken pottery, 2:8), but, as a form of leprosy, is an illness specified in the Torah as one that renders a person liturgically unclean as well as unfit to live among the other members of the community (Lev. 13, see especially vs. 45–46). Job's seat among the ashes is emblematic of his social isolation, as well as of his grief.

Note the play on words in v. 4. The significance of the phrase

"Skin for skin" is not totally clear, but it is probably borrowed from the world of the marketplace, where barter was the basis of the economy. In other words, Satan is saying to Yahweh, "Job's response to you will be measured according to the kind of suffering he is subjected to." But "skin" has a more ominous implication, for the phrase also tips off the reader as to what kind of torment Job is about to endure.

In theological terms, the most significant part of this day's lection is vs. 9–10, for here are contrasted two basic attitudes toward Job's misfortunes that (among several others) are identified by the book. On the one hand, Job's wife advises a kind of defiant resignation. (Incidentally, the canonical book of Job never tells us the name of Job's wife. But a Jewish document, the "Testament of Job," dating from about the first century B.C., refers to her as Sitis.) The unwillingness of generations of pious Jewish scribes to draft the words "Curse God" led them at this point to write instead "Bless God" (note 1:5), but it is clear, as NRSV has correctly noted, that Job's wife is urging her husband to deliver a malediction on Yahweh. Such an imprecation would involve, of course, more than a simple violation of the Third Commandment. It would be a rupture of Job's basic attitude of trust in God and, as well, a denial of all those qualities of goodness which had characterized Job's dealings with other people all his life (1:1). Job's moral behavior arose out of his commitment to Yahweh, and to deny one would have been to deny the other.

Job will have none of that, of course, and he simply reminds his wife that one must experience many things from the hand of Yahweh (v. 10), some positive, others negative. This attitude toward evil expressed by Job is in some tension with the views of the book's author(s), for Job does not admit to the reality of a satanic power, but (in a manner similar to the text from 1 Sam. 16 noted earlier in our discussion) vests all things in Yahweh's will. The theology expressed here is also at odds with some of Job's other statements, such as his later insistence that Yahweh does not permit evil to go unpunished (24:22–25). Be that as it may, this day's lection reaches a climax by affirming that, in spite of his terrible suffering, Job does not abandon his deep trust in God.

Thus an important note is struck about the character of this book's central figure. Job is one who fears and trusts God and who deals justly with his neighbors and, what is more, is one who will not depart from these basic commitments even under the harsh duress that has been visited on him. Such portraiture firmly establishes Job's theological and moral position in the debates that lie ahead.

Psalm 26

This psalm is the urgent petition of a genuinely pious person (Ps. 26:9–10). It is the prayer of one whose life is under threat, who prays to God, confident of a hearing, emboldened by fidelity that gives a right to pray. The parallel reading for today in Job 1–2 points to the assumption of faithful people, that they can indeed make claims on God. Our psalm is not yet required to face the severe theological problem of the book of Job, but still operates with innocent trust. In that context of innocent trust, it is evident that Israel's prayer is not all bogged down in guilt or in deference. This is a Joblike voice of faith, which is honest in need before God, and which counts heavily on God's honoring the prayer. This prayer exhibits a properly courageous posture before God, one of confident, trustful, honest need.

Verses 1–3 offer a twofold presentation of Israel's classic prayer of petition. That form of prayer is an urgent imperative addressed to God, followed by a reason introduced by "for" (or "because"), which gives God a motivation for answering the prayer. The first utterance of such a prayer is in v. 1. The simple imperative is "Vindicate me." The verb in Hebrew means to go to court and adjudicate the claim on my behalf. The verb suggests that in a social dispute the speaker is either at fault, and therefore rightly suffers, or is innocent and needs to be acquitted. The plea is for an acquittal from God. The motivation supporting this plea is twofold. First, the speaker has "walked in... integrity," that is, in an undivided loyalty (see Gen. 17:1). This is the same statement of responsible innocence insisted on by Job (see Job 27:5; 31:6). The claim is paralleled, secondly, by a statement of complete trust (confidence) in God. Anyone who is so faithful cannot be guilty, but deserves acquittal.

The same pattern of prayer is reiterated in vs. 2–3. Now there are three imperatives ("prove..., test,... try"), but the point is the same: "Find me innocent." The motivation in this unit is again twofold. The speaker responds to God's loyalty and faithfulness by living in loyalty and faithfulness, which takes the concrete form of obedience to Torah commands.

In vs. 1b and 3, the speaker has provided God with reasons for a verdict of acquittal. Now, in vs. 4–8, the statement of a motivation is greatly extended as an assertion of innocence and fidelity. This extended statement concerns two spheres of activity, social and cultic.

In the social sphere, the speaker asserts that he does not keep company with the worthless, hypocrites, evildoers, or wicked. These four terms may be given different nuances. Taken all together, they refer to the mockers who do not keep Torah and who thereby disrupt and jeopardize the order and health of the community. The "Torah piety" of the psalter is clear that "Torah keepers" refuse to associate with their detractors (see Pss. 1:1; 15:4). This psalmist, in contrast to those rejected persons, is a serious, disciplined, intentional Torah keeper.

In the cultic sphere, the speaker claims to be a full, regular, and enthusiastic participant in worship, thus giving visible evidence of loyalty to Yahweh. Such cultic devoutness includes regular ritual washing, which adequately overcomes the guilt that might evoke punishment (see Ps. 51:7; Isa. 1:16). The speaker participates in the pageantry and process of worship, sings songs of thanksgiving that testify to God's miraculous saving deeds. The psalmist is on record as having acknowledged God's decisive sovereignty in his life.

Affirmation of ritual participation culminates in the lyrical affirmation of delight in the Temple (v. 8). If this is taken metaphorically, the statement indicates delight in communion with God (compare Ps. 23:6). If, however, the statement is taken literally, this is one who spends inordinate amounts of time in the Temple. Either way, this is a person whose life is fully committed to and defined by attentiveness to Yahweh.

On the basis of this long reason given to God, the psalm now returns to an imperative petition, as in vs. 1a and 2. I suggest that v. 9 is the central point toward which the entire poem is aimed. The speaker is under threat from real enemies who are trying to destroy him. The enemies (sinners, the bloodthirsty) are perhaps the same as mentioned in vs. 4–5. Their mode of destructiveness is perhaps that they seek to bribe the court, so that the threat is that of a crooked, hired judge (v. 10; compare Deut. 16:18–20). The petition of Ps. 26:9 is an appeal to a "higher judge," God, who can intervene against bribed judges, and so secure the life of the speaker who is at risk from distorted justice.

Finally the speaker reiterates the theme of integrity with which the poem began. Verses 11 and 12 are again a petition ("redeem . . . be gracious") based on a plea of integrity (v. 11), anticipating an extravagant acknowledgment of Yahweh in the cult.

The psalm is a model of simple piety, which aims at communion with God and rescue by God. The psalm is a petition suggesting (*a*) that the speaker must turn to God, and (*b*) that the speaker has a right to expect something from God. Such a demanding petition, however, is not contextless. This petitionary voice is situated in a lifelong practice of devotion to Yahweh in every sphere of life. The speaker does not petition a stranger in court, but one to whom deep loyalty has been shown, and with whom deep communion has been shared.

Hebrews 1:1–4; 2:5–12

The four opening verses of Hebrews amply deserve their reputation as the most polished piece of rhetoric in the New Testament. Here the author combines alliteration and parallelism to produce an elegance that matches the importance of the subject matter. Various sources come into play here, including scriptural allusions (Ps. 110:1 in v. 3), Jewish reflection on the figure of Lady Wisdom, and early Christian traditions about the exaltation of Jesus. In other words, the writer pulls out all the stops to perform an overture that will capture the audience's attention.

As with other musical overtures, this one introduces important themes that will recur throughout the work. They include the following: Scripture as a vehicle by which God has spoken and continues to speak to God's people; the superiority of Jesus Christ to every being, both human and superhuman (that is, the angels); and the exaltation of Jesus over all things.

Thematically, what dominates these first verses is language about first and last things. That language appears initially in the formal contrast between God's former speech and God's present speech. Each element in the statement "Long ago God spoke to our ancestors ... by the prophets" finds its parallel in the one that follows. Instead of "long ago," God speaks "in these last days"; instead of speaking "to our ancestors," God speaks "to us"; instead of speaking "by the prophets," God speaks "by a Son." Nothing in this contrast questions the significance of God's earlier communication, but the identification of Jesus that follows makes the case for his superiority (important throughout Hebrews).

Following this introduction, the remaining lines of the prologue identify Jesus, again in terms of both first and last things, both Creation and eschaton. On the one hand, the early Christian notion that the Son was the instrument of creation ("through whom he also created the worlds," v. 2) is familiar to Christians and may arouse no particular curiosity. On the other hand, such an assertion contradicts the order of the physical universe as modern women and men understand it, and that should arouse a great deal of curiosity!

Here the author of Hebrews, like the author of the Fourth Gospel

(John 1:3), reflects ways of thinking familiar to the Judaism of his era. Jewish wisdom literature refers to Lady Wisdom as having been present at Creation, and later rabbinic literature describes the Torah as God's tool in creation. Probably in none of these cases is it supposed that Jesus, or Wisdom, or Torah was literally present and assisted God in creation, but the importance of each figure is such that believers cannot imagine a time in which they did not exist. As new parents are at first astonished by the presence of a baby but later wonder whether there was ever a time without that child, Christians come to ascribe to Jesus an existence even at Creation itself.

Not only is the Son present at the Creation, but the Son resembles God's own glory and being (see the similar statement about Lady Wisdom in Wisd. Sol. 7:25), "sustains" all things, and enables purification. These roles of sustenance and redemption characterize the work of the Son as God's heir. As a result, he is exalted to God's right hand and even beyond the angels on high. The Son's role at Creation has now a counterpart at the eschaton.

The passage that immediately follows this elegant overture consists of a series of biblical quotations loosely connected around the theme of the Son's superiority over the angels (1:5–14), followed by a warning about fidelity to the gospel (2:1–4). The lection proper concludes with another important christological theme of Hebrews, the reality and necessity and redemptive character of Jesus' suffering (2:5–12).

Like the figure of Ps. 8, Jesus became "lower than the angels." (The NRSV somewhat obscures this connection between Jesus and the figure of Ps. 8 by rendering the singular "man" or "son of man" as "human beings.") True, "all things" are to be subjected to Jesus, but he also endured "the suffering of death" (2:9). He names all God's children as his "brothers and sisters." In other words, he indeed became a human being like other human beings, and he suffered death as they do. Jesus' death, however, had consequences unlike the deaths of other human beings. Jesus' death was "for everyone" (v. 9) and brought about "salvation" and sanctification (vs. 10–11).

To the paradox of Jesus' presence at Creation and at the eschaton, the author of Hebrews here adds the paradox of Jesus' humanity. Only a Jesus who was in every respect human could become the appropriate sacrifice for human sin. But only a Jesus who bears "the exact imprint of God's very being" (1:3) would bear humankind the love necessary to make that sacrifice.

This lection will prove challenging because of its size as well as the enormity and significance of the themes it introduces. It will not easily lend itself to summary or epitome. Perhaps the sheer extravagance of the passage provides a starting point for reflection. Like all preachers, the preacher who composed Hebrews must resort to language that is extravagant because the gospel itself is extravagant.

(For additional comments on this passage, see the discussion of Hebrews 1:1–4 [5–12] under Christmas, Third Proper.)

Mark 10:2–16

The preacher may groan on discovering that the Gospel lesson for this Sunday includes the strict teaching of Jesus regarding divorce and remarriage in Mark 10:2–16. Dotted through the congregation are divorced persons and persons who have remarried following divorce, and for such people this passage will likely reopen old wounds and stir again feelings of failure. Therefore, sensitivity to pastoral needs must be a critical ingredient in the preacher's preparation of the sermon. It is clear that the purpose of the passage in its context is not to arouse guilt, and neither should the sermon. On the other hand, since the lection also contains the moving incident of Jesus' welcoming the children whom the disciples reject, and since it provides positive words about marriage, the passage should not be ignored.

The initial thing to observe about 10:2–9 is the way Jesus redirects the question of the Pharisees to make the conversation primarily a discussion about marriage, rather than divorce. The issue of divorce was not a debatable question among the Jews of Jesus' day, but the allowable grounds for divorce was a hot topic. The Pharisees no doubt hoped to get Jesus to commit himself one way or another on the interpretation of Deut. 24:1, either to side with the stringent position of the school of Shammai or with the permissive reading of the school of Hillel. Any response is bound to start a controversy.

The question "Is it lawful?" however, gets turned on its head. Jesus pushes behind Deut. 24 to Gen. 1–2, behind the stipulation of the law to the story of Creation, behind the legality of divorce to the intent of marriage. What emerges is the affirmation of marriage as the lifelong joining of two persons in a profound union ("one flesh"). Even fathers and mothers are to be left in the pursuit of this new relationship, attributed to no less than God (Mark 10:9).

Given the subversive words Jesus has already spoken about the family (3:31–35) and the prediction that the coming trials will split families apart (13:12), this statement of the indissoluble union of marriage presents a counteremphasis. Before debating the possible grounds for divorce, the Pharisees need to understand that marriage is a gift of God's good creation. Rather than resorting to a sweeping legal prohibition to exclude any and all divorce, Jesus recalls God's original intent for marriage. But since "hardness of heart" is not a problem peculiar to Moses' day, divorces must still take place—something implied in 10:11–12.

Immediately following the interchange with the Pharisees, the narrator appropriately tells the beautiful story of Jesus' blessing the little children (10:13–16). It says something about the importance of children and about the nature of God's reign, but it also says something about marriages, both those that succeed and those that fail.

Two parts of Jesus' angry retort to the disciples need highlighting.

1. "It is to such as these that the kingdom of God belongs" (10:14). The disciples have bought into ancient society's valuation of children—they are not important. Children have no status and no rights, and thus their presence is a nuisance. Jesus sees things differently. In fact, the rule of God belongs to persons like this—powerless, vulnerable, weak persons, who are often deemed a nuisance. In rejecting the children, the disciples have not just made a slight error of judgment—they have missed the whole point of Jesus' ministry.

2. "Whoever does not receive the kingdom of God as a little child will never enter it" (10:15). Not only do the children serve as poignant examples of those for whom the rule of God is intended, but also their manner of receiving it becomes the model for adults. The weight in 10:15 clearly falls on the verb "receive," which rules out the sentimental drivel about the innocence or naïveté of children, often offered as explanation of this verse. The text does not idealize any particular characteristic of children. Instead it talks about the receiving of the kingdom by powerless persons, who have no claims to stake out and no demands to make. The rule of God comes as pure, unadulterated grace, to hungry people at the crossroads and in the byways of life who are invited to attend a scrumptious banquet, and to children without status. They have no excuses to give, no dowries to offer, no bargaining chips. They are eager to be taken up into Jesus' arms and be blessed.

Now whether we are successful or unsuccessful at our marriages, whether we have managed to achieve the profound union God intends or from "hardness of heart" have wound up in a divorce court, the receiving of the kingdom like a little child still holds. We have no bargaining chips to trade in, nor does our history of failure disqualify us. It is just this incredible picture of otherwise rejected children welcomed and given a blessing that sustains both the happily married and the painfully separated.

PROPER 23

Ordinary Time 28

*Sunday between
October 9 and 15 inclusive*

There is a level at which the Bible understands the world in terms of moral order, moral responsibility, and moral symmetry. On most days, in stable contexts, that is enough. Unfortunately the church too often settles for such a "safe" reading of the Bible and such an "innocent" reading of the world. The texts in this grouping show the believing community driven beyond such conventions to extremity, in which the world can no longer be morally decoded. There is indeed something loose, wild, undomesticated, and inexplicable about the world that honest faith must take into account and must seek to relate to the reality of God.

The response of Job to the moral naïveté of Eliphaz is an honest acknowledgment of that inexplicable dimension of reality which the "friends" are unable to face. Job, however, does not lose heart or lose hope. Rather, he allows that God is well beyond him in a mystery that precludes easy decipherment. In the more familiar psalm, the poet has courage to speak about the reality of threat in a set of risky and venturesome metaphors. What is astonishing in the psalm is that this threat (as with Job) does not drive the speaker to unfaith, but to more insistent candor, which is addressed to the God who is expected to save. These biblical voices are models of courage in seeking God precisely where moral coherence breaks off. Clearly these texts invite the church well beyond our conventional moral certitude into the deeper mystery of God's enigmatic holiness.

In a different idiom, the Epistle reading moves toward the same daring profundity. The "word of God" is loosed in mercy and judgment; that judgment, however, is not contained in our usual acts of moral certitude. The Gospel reading does not easily join this discussion, except that even here, response to God moves drastically beyond any conventional morality to a complete surrender of all old securities and props. In his affirmation to the disciples, Jesus ends with a promise of God's "impossibility." This is talk about God that

Job and the psalmist would have understood. That God will not be contained in conventional morality pushes serious believers well beyond every conventional morality into daring, active, self-risking faith.

Job 23:1–9, 16–17

The second reading from the book of Job, out of a total sequence of four, constitutes part of Job's speech near the end of the major cycle of discourses in the book (Job 3–31). Three times each of Job's friends speaks (except Zophar, whose third speech appears to have been lost from the text), and each time Job replies. The passage at hand forms part of his reply to Eliphaz's final monologue (ch. 22) and states important aspects of Job's beliefs.

Eliphaz maintains what might be termed an "orthodox" view of the relation between the quality of one's life and the experiences one receives from the hand of God, and, although this speech is not a part of the lection for this day, it deserves attention because of the manner of Job's response to it. Eliphaz begins by arguing that, since our moral conduct can neither help nor hurt God, God has no self-interest in abrogating the processes of justice on behalf of any mortal (22:2–4). We receive from God exactly what we deserve and, since Job's conduct has been reprehensible (an allegation the reader knows to be false), Job's suffering is simply the logical expression of divine justice (vs. 5–11). One cannot escape from God's evenhanded ways, even though the events of life may sometimes seem to dictate differently (vs. 12–20). And so, Job, your peace lies in your acceptance of your fate and in your casting yourself on the justice of God (vs. 21–30).

Job's response is unequivocal. He agrees with Eliphaz that God is a just God and, what is more, that God is reasonable and merciful (note 23:6). The trouble is, Job cannot locate this God to lay his case before the divine tribunal. "Oh, that I knew where I might find him" (23:3) expresses the deep frustration of this righteous man and expresses, as well, the frustration of faithful men and women in every age who have experienced undeserved suffering. Job knows that he is innocent, that he is an "upright person" (v. 7). And since God is just, if Job could gain a hearing before the Almighty, the certain outcome would be his acquittal. But Job is simply unable to locate God. "If I go forward or backward or left or right, I cannot see him!" (see vs. 8–9).

The primary effect God has had on Job is to cause Job, not to love or honor God, but to be terrified of God's inexplicable ways (v. 16). Then Job succumbs to an all-too-human wish (at least in the view of the NRSV translators): to die and be forgotten forever. Verse 17 appears to be a counterpoint to Eliphaz's charge that Job mistakenly thinks that God is too distant to know or care what Job does. In 22:13–14, Eliphaz alleges that Job believes that God is hidden in the clouds (NRSV's "deep darkness" in v. 13 is a paraphrase of the Hebrew "heavy cloud"). And Job seems to reply, in the final verse of our lection, that perhaps such a dreadful thing is true, after all, since he has been unable to locate God. If it is, then he too wishes to be absorbed by the same obscurity that hides God!

At least that is the way the NRSV reads the verse. The Hebrew is quite different, for it expresses Job's continued and hopeful persistence. Not even an unreachable and awesome God can squelch Job and his affirmation of his own innocence. The REB translates vs. 16–17 as follows (compare NRSV marginal notes):

> It is God who makes me fainthearted,
> the Almighty who fills me with fear,
> yet I am not reduced to silence by the darkness
> or by the mystery which hides him.

Thus NRSV is probably off the mark in rendering v. 17 as a cry of resignation from Job. The verse is more likely an expression of Job's continued faithfulness to his belief in a gracious God and to his belief in his own innocence (as in vs. 10–12, not a part of the lection).

And here the matter is held in suspension. Job has confronted what is perhaps the most difficult question posed by Christian theology: How does one account for all the suffering that takes place in a world created and governed by a gracious God? When one replies, as Eliphaz does, that the answer lies in human sinfulness, there is ample evidence to affirm that Eliphaz is correct—but only partially so. Eliphaz's views do not take into account all the innumerable instances in which suffering is inflicted on men and women for no apparent reason whatsoever, from the ravages of nature to terrible diseases that cripple and kill. There simply are those terrible moments when no human sinfulness lies behind our pain. In those moments, where is God?

Job not only protests that Eliphaz's views are wrong, but he also, in his stated inability to locate God, confesses his own partial agnosticism in the face of his pain. It simply is not possible to know the mind of God in certain situations of life. It is not possible to dialogue with God over this matter and to come away with solutions that are completely satisfactory. Job finds God to be simply unreachable!

Job points to a dilemma whose solution he "cannot see" (v. 9b), but one for which Christian men and women find resolution in Jesus Christ (although Christians would also confess very imperfect knowledge in the matter). In Jesus Christ, God joined humankind in its suffering, both deserved and undeserved. The cross of Jesus Christ is that point in time and space where, more than any other, God identified with human suffering and experienced it to its fullest extent. Thus Job performs the enormous service of raising questions which he cannot answer and of pointing beyond himself to One who can.

Psalm 22:1–15

This psalm, familiar to us because of the quote of v. 1 in the Passion narrative (see Mark 15:34), recurs in the lectionary. The entire psalm is assigned for Good Friday. Verses 23–31 are used for the Second Sunday in Lent, and vs. 25–31 for the Fifth Sunday of Easter. Exposition is offered under these usages for those times in the lectionary.

Our verses make several standard maneuvers of a complaint prayer. The substantive issue is the absence of God, and the need for God, in a situation of enormous threat. The absence of God is the appropriate situation for the reading in Job as well. These texts are nicely complemented by the reading from Hebrews, which authorizes an "approach" to "the throne . . . with boldness." The psalm in its daring rhetoric is itself an exercise of bold approach to the throne of God, by a speaker who voices legitimate claims against God. It is important to notice that the assigned reading stops abruptly at Ps. 22:15, without any resolution of the voiced trouble. While we know of the resolution in the latter half of the psalm, there is something strategically compelling in a reading that for the moment refuses a resolution.

After the more familiar opening section of vs. 1–11, vs. 12–15 offer another series of complaints to communicate to God how desperate the situation is and how urgent an intervening action of God is. As is characteristic of complaint, the poet engages in hyperbolic speech in order to make the situation as grave as possible, in order to move God to presence and to decisive action. In vs. 12–13, the double metaphor of "bulls/lion" is used, likely referring to the socially powerful in the political community, who in their power devastate and exhaust conventionally pious and vulnerable people.

In vs. 14–15, the imagery is changed, though the voicing of needy complaint continues. In these verses, the image is of a physiological dismantling of the person of the speaker. Thus the dysfunction includes bones, heart, breast, mouth, jaws. The whole of the speaker's body has been completely broken. The imagery is graphic and culminates in the "dust of death." The descriptive language intends to motivate God to life-restoring action. There is here no doubt of God's capacity to save. All that is required is a motivation that will move the God of life against this sorry state of deathliness. God's power is certain; God's fidelity must be evoked afresh.

Hebrews 4:12–16

The strength of the imagery in the opening lines of this passage will initially attract readers, but many will find the implications of that imagery uncomfortable and unwelcome. Contemporary reflections on God as redeemer, as liberator, even as friend, leave little room for thinking of God or God's word as a "two-edged sword." Judgment language is out of fashion.

This particular depiction of "the word of God" is more than simply judgment language, however. It appears in the text as a response to Christian understanding of the gospel and the role scripture plays in that gospel. The preceding passage (Heb. 4:1–11) reflects on Ps. 95 and the notion of entering into God's "rest." The author sees in that concept a challenge to God's people to continue to be faithful; hence, the psalm *becomes* an instance of the discerning, judging, probing word of God. Verses 12–13, then, come as an afterthought, expressing warning but also thanksgiving and praise.

The personification of the word of God in this passage led some commentators in the early church to assume that the *logos* here refers to Christ. Although that identification is familiar from the prologue to John's Gospel, the context suggests that the word of God is understood as an aspect of God, as God's power of critical discernment, God's capacity for judgment. In addition, the personification of God's word in scripture (see, for example, Ps. 147:15, where the word "runs," and Wisd. Sol. 18:14–16, where the word "leaps" and touches heaven) and in other early Jewish writers suggests that here also the word refers to God rather than to Jesus.

Consistent with this personification of God's word is the vitality attributed to it. The word is "living and active"; it is "piercing until it divides." The first of these descriptions of the word's vitality refers to the way in which God's speech continues to play a role in the present life of the believing community. God spoke through the psalm discussed in Heb. 4:1–11, but God also continues to speak through that same psalm. This speech of God, past and present, plays an important role throughout Hebrews, beginning in 1:1–4.

The word of God also "pierces," with its characteristic discernment and judgment. Associations between judgment or the spirit and the sword are familiar from other New Testament writings (Eph. 6:17; Rev. 1:16; 2:12; 19:15). In this passage the imagery appears to fall apart when the word is said to divide "soul from spirit" and "joints from marrow." Since the places at which soul and spirit or joints and marrow are joined are nonexistent, such surgery is beyond the human imagination. That is just the point, of course: God's word accomplishes feats of discernment of which the human mind cannot even conceive.

This vivid portrait of the word of God and the inevitability of judgment concludes with the reminder that all are vulnerable to God "to whom we must render an account." That last word, "account," translates the Greek *logos*, as does "word" earlier in the passage. To the divine "word," then, a human "word" must be given in answer.

With v. 14, the writer takes up a different topic, that of the priesthood of Jesus, and vs. 14–16 have little literary or theological connection with vs. 12–13. (For more detailed comments on 4:14–16, see the discussion under Good Friday.) For readers who find the notion of God's discernment terrifying, however, as most surely do, the promise of the great high priest and his sacrifice comes as a word of comfort. God's judgment never stands without God's mercy.

Mark 10:17–31

Often the Bible acts as a mirror, throwing back to us reflections of ourselves or of our culture in the characters and conversations on the page. The questions asked, the attitudes exposed, the priorities held seem amazingly modern. Certainly this is the case with the figure traditionally called the rich young ruler (though Mark does not indicate that he was either young or a ruler). He could easily be dressed in contemporary garb and re-presented as a product of a mainline Protestant church. His religious heritage, his prosperity, and his sincerity are admirable qualities. It is interesting to observe the contrast between his noteworthy traits and the little children in the previous story, who come to Jesus as people without rights and recognition (compare Mark 10:13–16).

Actually the lection for the day is composed of three separate conversations, all three essential to an understanding of the passage. First is the interchange between Jesus and the rich man (10:17–22), followed by a dialogue between Jesus and the disciples (vs. 23–27), and concluding with a comment by Peter and a response by Jesus (vs. 28–31). All three conversations concern the critical topic of money.

The rich man has to be taken at face value and not made into a proud, self-righteous caricature. In coming, he kneels before Jesus and raises an existential question. When Jesus asks him about the commandments, his answer ("I have kept all these since my youth") is straightforward and need not be taken as an arrogant or presumptuous reply. In no way does Jesus' treatment of the man challenge or mock his integrity.

The key is 10:21: "Jesus, looking at him, loved him." Seeing him clear through, Jesus does not rebuke or discipline him, but loves him. It is more than admiration or respect or sentimentality. It is the gut-wrenching concern one has for a loved one about to take his own life. All that is important in a moment like that is to get the gun out of his hands and help him discover a reason to live. "You lack one thing; go, sell what you own, and give the money to the poor, and you will have treasure in heaven; then come, follow me." Wholehearted discipleship cannot take place until the ties to the man's possessions are broken, ties so intense and so enslaving that he can only hang his head and walk away grieving.

It is true that in a sermon the man's problem can be generalized and identified as anything that claims our highest loyalty, our ultimate concern, and prevents an uninhibited following of Jesus—not only wealth, but ambition, education, religion, and the like. But the conversations that follow with the disciples and Peter warn us about leaving the topic of money too quickly. Possessions have a peculiar and insidious way of becoming our masters. Precisely because they hold the potential for good as well as for evil, they easily seduce us and make us their slaves. Thus money remains the topic of conversation.

Jesus, in speaking to the disciples, is frank about the unusual difficulty facing a rich person who wants to live faithfully under the reign of God. The statement "It is easier for a camel to go through the eye of a needle than for someone who is rich to enter the kingdom of God" (10:25) in fact expresses a total (and rather ludicrous) impossibility. The disciples, no doubt thinking that riches are a material sign of God's blessing (a notion occasionally expressed in Jewish literature and certainly alive and well in Western Christianity), are thoroughly perplexed by what they hear, and ask in exasperation,

"Then who can be saved?" Jesus replies that it takes a miracle for a rich person to be saved—maybe one of God's hardest miracles!

While the later conversation with Peter rules out an ascetic reading of this story, one cannot escape the plain fact that having possessions and seriously wanting to be a Christian stand in great tension with each other. All our efforts to argue that this is someone else's story and not ours turn out to be mere rationalizations. The rich man remains a disturbing figure.

Jesus' response to Peter (10:29–31) rounds out the discussion about possessions. The requirement laid on the rich man is not a call to abandon the world and become wandering mendicants. Peter and the disciples have left all to follow Jesus, but they are promised recompense not only in the next world but also in this life—"houses, brothers and sisters, mothers and children, and fields." Their future is described as one not of deprivation and poverty, but as more than ample.

But there is a caveat: "with persecutions." Being a disciple never allows one to negotiate a permanent peace with the world, where of course wealth is a highly cherished and honored value. There always remains a critical tension with the world, which often results in hostility and violent opposition. Since the church cannot flee the arena in which it is called to live and serve, it needs the constant reminder that the first will be last and the last first.

PROPER 24

Ordinary Time 29

*Sunday between
October 16 and 22 inclusive*

It is characteristic of us that our God is too small, too predictable, too domesticated. These readings invite us to ponder the reality of God, who moves inscrutably and freely out beyond all our safe expectations and our conventional definitions. The sermon arising from these texts may make the church the most dangerous place in town, because it is the place where the awesome, hidden rule of God is spoken about unflinchingly.

The first three readings may create a context for the Gospel reading, which voices the largeness of God in a quite distinctive way. The psalm is a lyrical celebration of the wonder, order, and fruitfulness of creation. Notice of the productivity of creation, however, does not lead here to pride or to human ambition, but to glad, lyrical praise of the God who makes such a world possible. This large vision of the creator God is taken up in the Job reading, not simply to invite awe (which it does), but to silence human pretension and arrogance about the hidden things of God. It is this polemical doxology (on God's own lips) that overrides Job's self-serving insistence.

In a quite parallel fashion, the Epistle reading asserts the oddness of Jesus, as a priest who has no peer or parallel but stands well beyond all explanatory categories.

All these extravagant affirmations prepare us for the Gospel reading. The disciples (James and John) have fully embraced the wonder and power of Jesus. But they seek to turn his promise and power to their own advantage. In doing so, they show how badly they have misconstrued his intentions. In one of his most remarkable utterances, Jesus reverses field and redefines the largeness of the gospel. In truth, the powerful governance of the God who created the heavens and the earth is for the "lost," the needy, the enslaved. The gospel of God's greatness (voiced in the psalm, Job, and the epistle) is news intended especially for those who live outside the well-established order of social institutions. In the claim of the gospel, there is no ground for gloating or for preferential treatment, but only for solidarity in obedient ministry. The Gospel reading thus links the sweeping claims of creation to the day-to-day compassion of Jesus for the "least" of the creation.

Job 38:1-7 (34-41)

When all is said and done, it is God who has the final word. After Job has engaged his friends in a series of disputations about the nature of God, the meaning of human suffering, and a host of other issues (Job 3–31), and after Elihu has expressed his frustration with all the parties and delivers his own views (chs. 32–37), then and only then does Yahweh step forward to address Job. In the third of four consecutive lections from the book of Job, Yahweh begins to speak, and, in certain respects, the present text epitomizes the thrust of all that Yahweh has to say.

The Bible records few human beings for whom conversation with God was an easy task. Moses found himself talking to a burning bush (Ex. 3). Isaiah was engaged by a vision of God which, temporarily at least, sealed his lips (Isa. 6:1–8), and Jeremiah heard words from Yahweh that terrorized him (Jer. 1:6–8). Job's experience is similar, in that he is virtually silenced by a tour de force from Yahweh which, while it fails to answer the essential questions that Job has yearned to put to God, demonstrates the impossibility of challenging the Deity.

In its entirety (38:1–40:2) Yahweh's first reply to Job is an artfully crafted wisdom poem that concerns not only the power of Yahweh the creator, but Yahweh's wisdom, as well. In fact, it is Yahweh's special wisdom skills that are celebrated in this passage, and when these are compared to Job's own lack of wisdom, they are seen to be all the more remarkable. The characterization of Job as one who "darkens counsel by words without knowledge" (v. 2) quickly introduces the reader to the disparity between Job and the Deity he has dared to confront. "Stand up and answer the questions I will put to you" (see v. 3) is as deliberate a challenge as may be imagined and reminds the reader of other Old Testament passages, also written under wisdom influences, in which the asking of questions was calculated to be a test of character as well as of intelligence (Judg. 14:10–20; 1 Kings 10:1).

Apparently, instruction in the wisdom academies of ancient Israel often took the form of a series of questions, all of which had the same—or a similar—answer. By answering questions whose answer one did know and then applying that same answer to more problematic questions, the student advanced mentally along the stages of truth. (Notice the manner in which Amos, or someone writing in Amos's name, uses this method in Amos 3:3–8 in order to state the case for the validity of his own prophetic utterances.) The basic question that Yahweh puts to Job, although it is expressed in a number of variations, is: "Who possessed the wisdom to create the heavens and the earth?" And the obvious answer is: Only Yahweh! The answer is so obvious, in fact, that it is never directly stated. Yet no one could possibly be in any confusion over the matter. (Note especially vs. 35–36, with their play on the words "wisdom" and "understanding.") In fact, in a variation on the usual wisdom formulation, there is no apparent progression in this entire poem from questions whose answers are easily evident to those whose answers are uncertain. All Yahweh's questions are equally self-assertive: Yahweh and only Yahweh owns the craft ("wisdom," "understanding," "knowledge") to have created the heavens and the earth and to govern them day by day.

Job's sufferings are now seen as part of a vast scheme of things which is far too transcendent for any mere mortal to comprehend. Human wisdom is derivative of Yahweh's wisdom and, if there are areas that human wisdom cannot penetrate, it is not because Yahweh's wisdom is deficient. It is because human wisdom is too limited and puny. For all his persistence, Job cannot extricate himself from the limitations of his own creatureliness.

So, at last, Job has been granted his audience with Yahweh. The God who seemed so elusive before (23:1–9, Proper 23) is very much in evidence now. Yet Job is not prepared for this conversation, for the simple reason that Job has consistently underestimated God. This is a Deity of logic and order, as Job, like any good practitioner of wisdom, has maintained. Yet the logic and order are of a higher dimension than Job has ever imagined. The issue for Job is now seen to be, not "Why do I and other godly people suffer?" but "How may I find peace with God in the midst of my suffering?"

The text offers a straightforward answer, as remarkable for what it omits as for what it contains: You, Job, simply do not possess the wisdom to contest God. Therefore, trust God and you will be at peace.

Psalm 104:1–9, 24, 35c

This psalm, which celebrates the Creation, takes the marvels of creation as witnesses to the Creator and as occasions for praise of the

Creator. The psalm is matched to a reading from Job that also concerns creation. The Joban reading, however, concerns the *raw power* of Yahweh, who is beyond challenge, whereas Psalm 104 focuses on the *generosity* of God and the *splendor* of creation as the delicate work of Yahweh.

Only vs. 1 and 2a, matched by v. 35bc, directly concern the person of God. The opening two lines are familiar and stylized, voicing gratitude, awe, and wonder at the greatness of God.

The psalm immediately turns away from the person and appearance of God and concentrates on the work of God in creation. The psalm does a point-by-point inventory of creation, roughly paralleling the liturgic account of Gen. 1, and reflects the common view of ancient cosmology. That notion of the world imagines a "three-storied" universe, with the heavens above, the dry land, and the surging waters of chaos below the earth.

The heavens, that is, the expanse of the sky, receive the most attention in our section of the psalm (vs. 2b–4). Most decisive in this section of the psalm is the series of active verbs in which "you" (God) is the decisive subject. The largeness and the grandeur of the sky and all that majestic space are the object of God's powerful verbs: *You* "stretch out . . . set . . . make . . . ride . . . make." The heavens are founded on the waters as though God is a master engineer who builds a platform like those for offshore drilling, except that this construction is to provide a base for the entire universe. In that vault which anyone can see, clouds, wind, and lightning (fire and flames) are all achievements of God's staggering power. These elements in the sky are no mere objects, but are messengers and ministers in God's royal court. Thus the whole of the heavens is a great throne room designed to enhance the splendor of this sovereign, who rides in and out of court on the chariots of clouds.

The actual dry land receives only one verse of attention in the psalm (v. 5). The dry land is God's achievement, again with God as the subject of an active verb, "set." The most important claim made for the earth is that it will "never be shaken." That is, it is stable, utterly reliable land, and will not be jeopardized by the waters that surge below its foundation.

The third dimension of creation is "the deep" (*tĕhôm*, vs. 6–9; see Gen. 1:2). It is commonly thought that "the deep" is a Yahwistic rendering of "Tiamat," the active, evil sea monster who threatens all earthly order. It is noteworthy that, unlike the heavens (Ps. 104:2b–4) and the earth (v. 5), the deep is not formed (or stretched out, set, made) by God, but only "covered." It is already there in its surging, destructive power prior to and independent of Yahweh. Yahweh "covers" the deep, that is, throws a cloth over it which reduces its power and tames it, making it relatively safe and innocuous. The waters of the deep chaos are, however, not easily domesticated. They resist such containment, and they react with surging, violent power (vs. 7–8). They flee away, to escape God's sovereignty (see Ps. 114:3–6). They surge over the earth, over mountains and valleys (the psalm means to present a great storm). In the end, however, the waters of the deep must accept their assigned place in God's well-ordered world (vs. 8b–9; compare Jer. 5:22). God has set a limit, has erected a levee which guards the earth from the threat of chaos. The theological intent is to assert that Yahweh has indeed achieved dominance over chaos. As a consequence, the evil power of chaos must submit to this majestic governance; therefore, the earth is safe.

The lectionary selection has badly chopped up the lyrical power of the psalm by designating isolated verses for reading, now moving to v. 24. This verse occurs at the end of the long recital of vs. 1–23. (It is unfortunate that in the interest of brevity the recital has been truncated, for the recital offers a full, cumulative inventory of God's wonders in creation.) On the basis of that recital, the worshiping community surely will break out in unrestrained doxology. The mention of Yahweh in this verse is the only mention of the name since v. 1 (except for the inadvertent phrase in v. 16). The full recital makes us aware that God's works are multitudinous. God has done a lot! All of it is good! Moreover, it has all been done in God's wisdom. This is a wondrously defiant doxology when we know from experience about "the deep" (v. 6), the sea (v. 25), and Leviathan (v. 26). All of that notwithstanding, the world is safe!

Rather oddly, the lectionary committee ends the reading with a doxology, v. 35c, that reiterates v. 1. Clearly creation is not for analysis and explanation, but for lyrical, grateful celebration.

A theological reading of the world drives us not to knowledge and control, but to praise. As the world is referred back to God in adoration, we are aware that the world is not autonomous, not self-generated, not eternally preexisting, but exists because of the gracious power of Yahweh, who has made it all (. . . except "the deep," which is now well ordered). The upshot of this theological, doxological affirmation is that for us the world is a sure, safe, guarded, guaranteed home.

Hebrews 5:1-10

Central to this passage is the comparison between the human high priesthood and that of Jesus. Since that comparison has been addressed earlier (see the study of this passage for Good Friday), comments here are confined to three additional aspects of the text.

First, one problem of which teachers and preachers are increasingly aware is that of speaking about Judaism. The Holocaust finally made it impossible to ignore the results that follow when Christians define themselves and their beliefs by vilifying Jews. Much in the New Testament lends itself to such negative and hostile comparisons, of course. Early Christian writers, many of whom were Jews, engaged in debates with their own sisters and brothers, and resorted to depictions that would later fuel Christian anti-Judaism.

The author of Hebrews offers a different kind of comparison, one that merits attention. This passage depicts Jesus as a high priest who is like other high priests of Israel in his selection, his vulnerability, and his function. Even as the contrast emerges between Jesus and other priests, highlighting the superiority of Jesus, the high priests of Israel are not demeaned in any way.

A second feature of this text may be more important for preachers themselves than for preaching this particular passage, and that concerns the depiction of religious leaders. Hebrews 5:2 explains that the high priest is "able to deal gently with the ignorant and wayward, since he himself is subject to weakness." Jesus himself is said to have been vulnerable to the weakness of suffering. The wisdom of this insight deserves constant recall. The ability to deal with the needs of others emerges, not from one's own strength, but precisely from one's weakness. By even imagining that their adequacy depends on being "above" the foibles of others, priests misunderstand the basis on which they serve.

The third feature of this text is a simple reminder, also directed more to preachers than to preaching. According to v. 1, priests are "put in charge of things pertaining to God." The natural human weakness of priests does not in any way lessen their responsibility. Nothing said here implies that only priests have responsibility for "things pertaining to God," of course, but the peculiar responsibility of religious leaders is made clear. Terrifying as the prospect remains, the priest is in charge. What prevents the terror from overwhelming is the confidence that Christ himself has secured salvation for all.

Mark 10:35–45

The section in Mark's Gospel that includes Jesus' trip with the disciples from Caesarea Philippi in the north to Jerusalem in the south turns out to be a laboratory in discipleship, a crash course in what it means to follow Jesus (Mark 8:22–10:52). It is introduced by a story of a two-stage healing of a blind man, who finally "saw everything clearly" (8:25), and it is concluded by a story of the healing of a second blind man, who "regained his sight and followed him [Jesus] on the way" (10:52). Two outsiders are granted clear vision, while repeatedly the core of disciples demonstrate their blindness. Despite some moments here and there of apparent insight, the inner group of followers fail to get the point of what Jesus says and does.

The phenomenon creates both irritation and anxiety in readers of the story, who are led by the narrator to identify with the disciples. We are amazed at the obtuseness of the inner group, and yet we are disturbed by the realization that "they" are "us." Nowhere does this emerge more plainly than in these final incidents on the journey, just prior to the entry into Jerusalem.

The passage in today's lection is composed of two scenes: (1) The request of James and John for the prominent spots in the kingdom and Jesus' reply (10:35–40); (2) the anger of the other disciples at James and John, and Jesus' response (vs. 41–45).

The request of James and John seems incredibly audacious. Where have they been? Haven't they seen and heard what has been happening? Did they completely miss the point when Jesus put the little child in their midst, or blessed the group of children who otherwise seemed a nuisance, or confronted the rich man with the need to break with his possessions? Were they deaf to Jesus' words about his own future and the risks of what following him would mean? At least in Matthew's version of this story, it is the *mother* of James and John who makes the request in behalf of her sons (Matt. 20:20–21). That seems more plausible.

Even so, Jesus does not rebuke the brothers (as we might want to do), but tells them they do not know what they are asking, and confronts them with the symbols of Jesus' cup and baptism. The point is that the road to "glory" runs straight through the valley of suffering and death. Even to get to "glory," much less to occupy the seats of authority and prominence, one cannot bypass the events of Good Friday and their implications.

We might wish Jesus had chosen different symbols. Every time we come to the Lord's table to drink from the Communion cup and every time we witness a baptism or renew our own baptismal vows, we are reminded once again of the dangers and risks of being Jesus' followers. The cup has a bitter taste (Isa. 51:17), and the descent into the waters links us to the death of Jesus (Rom. 6:3–5). There is much to celebrate at the observance of the sacraments, but there are also the sobering symbols of Jesus' cup and baptism.

The anger of the other ten disciples at James and John surely reflects jealousy, and not righteous indignation. These two have jumped the gun on the others in jockeying for a place of power, and they are mad about it. Again, Jesus resists a rebuke, and instead poses the pagan authorities as models of how *not* to exercise leadership. The choice is between being tyrants or slaves, between domination and service. The criterion for leadership is not effectiveness (who gets the job done the quickest), but faithfulness (whether one has followed the model of Jesus). The text admits that such a style of leadership and life runs counter to the prevailing wisdom of the day, and thus may not make much sense to those whose eyes are stuck on the bottom line.

It is worth reflecting in a sermon on the paradoxes of being a servant-leader. On the one hand, the servant gives priority to the needs of persons and how service can be rendered to meet those needs. On the other hand, as a servant in the image of Jesus one is not bound to do whatever is asked, to be at the whims of others. Jesus is no less a servant in driving the money changers from the Temple than in healing the sick. His ministry and his self-giving death provide the term "servant" a new definition.

The final verse of the passage is important (10:45). Jesus turns out to be more than a model servant, more than a paradigm to be followed. It is a good thing, because we who claim to be disciples often don't do much better than the original Twelve. Like them, we miss the point, and suddenly stand in need of being served ourselves. The phrase "ransom for many" may not warrant an elaborate theory of the atonement, but it nevertheless expresses the saving character of Jesus' death, the act that redeems disciples who have a hard time being servants.

PROPER 25

Ordinary Time 30

*Sunday between
October 23 and 29 inclusive*

These texts are grouped arbitrarily and do not constitute any thematic unity. It is likely best to take each on its own terms. If, however, one insists on an identifying theme, it may be that such a coherence is found in *God's mercy*, that is, God's free, powerful capacity and readiness to bring distorted life to a good end.

This affirmation of God's overriding, rehabilitating mercy is most evident in the Psalm selection and the Gospel reading. The psalm is a voice of thanksgiving by a humble one who has no power to save himself or herself. The voice celebrates God's capacity and willingness to do what cannot be done by the speaker. In parallel fashion, Bartimaeus in the Gospel reading can be taken as the subject of the psalm, for he is a humble one, who asks for and receives transformative mercy from Jesus. Thus Jesus does the very miracles expected from the enactment of God's mercy.

The matter of mercy is not self-evident in the Job reading, for Job seems to respond in deference only to God's power. As our exegesis makes clear, however, in Job 42:10–17 God's mercy answers Job's deference with wondrous restorative generosity. The Joban theme is dense, and is not a simple offer of mercy, for the verses trade primarily on God's sovereignty. Such sovereignty, however, is crucial in making God's mercy reliable and effective.

The Epistle reading, with its high christological accent, asserts that Jesus is indeed the ontological guarantee and agent of God's capacity for reconciliation. God's mercy is not whimsical or capricious, but is fully and reliably given "once for all" in Jesus. All these texts invite confidence in God's good intention for God's creatures, who are greatly beloved.

Job 42:1-6, 10-17

The last of four readings from the book of Job describes the manner in which the issues with which Job has struggled are brought to a resolution. Those who read the biblical book in the hope of finding quick and easy answers to the most intractable questions theology can raise are bound to be disappointed. Yet the literature does propose certain solutions, but only the most patient of seekers after the truth will be completely set at ease by them.

In the initial section of the lection, Job 42:1-6, Job submits to the divine tour de force contained in chs. 38; 39; 40:6-41:34. Yahweh is simply too powerful and too wise for any mortal, and the realization has now dawned on Job that he cannot contest Yahweh's justice. His deeply held desire to bring Yahweh to account in a tribunal of law (23:1-9, Proper 23) has, in a sense, been fulfilled. Yet to his surprise Job has discovered that Yahweh's being so far transcends his own that normal categories of justice and equity are not applicable. Yahweh's ways are past finding out, and the only dialogue Job has been capable of maintaining with God has been essentially one-way. Job has been able only to listen as Yahweh reminded him of the gulf between them.

Job thus begins by consenting to Yahweh's irresistible logic. If he ever before doubted the power and wisdom of Yahweh, Job does so no longer. Chapter 42:2-6 might be paraphrased: "When I asked you to meet me in court, O Yahweh, I simply didn't know what I was talking about. But things are clearer to me now. I no longer wish to challenge you; I only wish to learn from your wisdom. I will be quiet while you answer my questions."

Verse 6 presents special difficulties, in that in NRSV it seems to describe a self-loathing on Job's part, something that is not only uncharacteristic of the subject of this biblical book, but that seems to contradict common understanding of a healthy person's attitude toward him- or herself. The problem may be more apparent than real, however, in that NRSV is following a long tradition in reading the verb *mā'as* as reflexive: "despise myself." Good critical commentaries on Job may be consulted for the technical details to this apparent problem, but it may be helpful here simply to follow the REB translation of v. 6a: "Therefore I yield."

As for v. 6b, while the NRSV's "repent" is a standard translation for the Hebrew verb *niḥam*, the word does not always bear the meaning "to be sorry for sin." Such a rendering would violate Job's insistence on his essential righteousness (note 23:7). The word actually has a wide range of meanings, which include "to have pity," "to have compassion," or even "to comfort oneself." And so the meaning here is probably something like: "[Job] admitted his mistake [in attempting to challenge Yahweh]." That interpretation at least has the virtue of agreeing with the rest of vs. 2–6, especially the second line of v. 3.

Verses 10–17 bring the affair of Job full circle. After Yahweh vindicated Job to his friends (vs. 7–9), Yahweh gave Job "twice as much as he had before" (v. 10) by heaping on him various kinds of treasures and by granting to him a new and abundant family (compare 42:13 with 1:2). Equally important, Job is reinstated to his former social position (42:11), while his happiness flows from the fact that "Yahweh blessed the latter days of Job more than his beginning" (v. 12).

It is tempting to read this passage as an effort by the author(s) of the book to connect divine rewards to human righteousness. After all, Job "repented" (v. 6) and Yahweh, after instructing Job's friends just how "right" Job is (v. 7), now lavishes on Job great benefits. The problem with that interpretation, of course, is that it flies in the face of what the book is all about. Job has insisted all along that he is righteous and that it is not an act of distrust to question Yahweh's ways. Not only that, but Job was "blameless and upright" (1:1) when Yahweh initially permitted Satan to torment him. Thus to connect the blessings of 42:10–17 with Job's expressions in vs. 2–6 would be to contradict a foundational aspect of the book.

Thus, the narrative of restoration should be read as an expression not of Yahweh's justice, but of Yahweh's mercy. Yahweh loves Job, and Yahweh has continued to love Job right through the time of his torment. One may presume that Yahweh's mercy would have expressed itself in time regardless of Job's attitudes. That Yahweh's mercy bears the kind of fruit it does and in the manner that it does is not a consequence of what Job says in vs. 2–6, but a happy accompaniment.

In other words, Yahweh loves Job as Yahweh loves all people. Yahweh has blessed Job as Yahweh intends to bless all people. To be sure, human willfulness and sin often distort our relations with God and with one another and frustrate God's mercy. But Job's new happiness is no more the result of some new righteousness on his part than his sufferings were the result of some terrible act of sin. God's ways are mysterious and past our understanding, but one thing is not in dispute: the God of Israel, the Father of Jesus Christ, is a God of compassion whose ultimate will for all persons is peace and joy.

Psalm 34:1-8 (19-22)

This song of thanksgiving is in the mouth of one who had been in a situation of threat, who had appealed to God, who as a result of the appeal had been rescued by God, and who now witnesses to the powerful rescue of God. The psalm is on the side of trouble resolved, only now looking back to the trouble through the lens of resolution. Thus the psalm nicely corresponds to the reading from Job, which is also about a generous restoration and rehabilitation wrought by God.

The beginning of Ps. 34 is one of praise to and celebration of Yahweh. The praise is unending. This is the voice of one who is so elated about rescue that he cannot stop speaking of the wonder and miracle of what has been given. A clue for the social location of this psalm is the summons to the "humble" (*ănāwîm* = poor, abused, v. 2) to hear the message and join in the act of exaltation. That is, the psalmist suggests that in his trouble, he was one of the powerless who had no hope of rescue. And then, belatedly, he found that Yahweh was attentive even to, and especially to, the abused who are without hope of rescue. Thus the inversion of circumstance wrought by God is even more astonishing.

Verses 4–7 are arranged in an antiphonal pattern, so that vs. 4 and 6 are personal testimony, answered in vs. 5 and 7 with statements of confidence and praise. As is characteristic in such a psalm, this one moves from quite concrete experience to large liturgical generalization.

In a standard formula of thanksgiving, the speaker remembers having prayed to Yahweh and being delivered by Yahweh (v. 4). In v. 6 the speaker refers to himself in the third person as "this poor [one]" (*'ānî*), who cried out and was saved. Thus vs. 4 and 6 are closely parallel. Both describe the transaction whereby God was mobilized into saving action. The two verses use different verbs for rescue, but the point is the same. In response to petition, God has answered and acted decisively. This "humble one" (*'ānî*) addressed other "humble ones," who may share confidence in the God who hears, answers, and acts.

The counterpoint to the personal testimony is given in vs. 5 and 7. In v. 5, the witness of v. 4 is turned into a summons to trust in God. The affirmation that "your faces shall never be ashamed" suggests that the poem is aimed exactly at those who are habitually ashamed, that is, those without power who are depreciated by society. The personal testimony becomes ground for hope for action by God, hope for all the others in a similar state.

Verse 7, by way of generalizing from personal experience, moves in a very different direction. Now a new character is introduced into the narrative plot. It is God's angel who bivouacs with the faithful, who is present and who intervenes to save (yet a third, different term for "deliver"). The effect of vs. 1–7 is to insist from personal experience that God is available and is prepared to act for those who need rescue.

Verse 8 constitutes a climactic statement for this rhetorical unit. This lyrical conclusion is a summons to the faithful and an affirmation that God is "good," that is, loyal, faithful, friendly, capable of bestowing blessing. The imperative "taste" is an odd one, which is thus far unanticipated in the text. It is most probable that "taste" here means to eat and enjoy the fruits of God's blessings. In Christian usage, this verse has been taken over as a eucharistic invitation, but in the Old Testament usage the verse does not suggest "tasting God," but rather enjoying God's good gifts.

The last line of v. 8 introduces something like a military image. The one who "takes refuge" is a *geber*, a bold, brave warrior. Thus the image is created of a man in battle who seeks protection from God; God is a protective fortress.

Verses 19–22 are a reprise on the main themes of the psalm. The context of the prayer is a recognition that righteous folk suffer "afflictions" that are indeed unwarranted. Thus the pairing of "afflictions" with "righteous" (v. 19) is an incongruity. The convergence happens. In the world of God's good ordering, however, that incongruity need not persist. Yahweh is a God who intervenes on behalf of the righteous to overcome undeserved abuse.

The themes of v. 19 are explicated in vs. 20–22, according to Yahweh's strict moral retribution. This God will protect the righteous whose lives (bodies) are under assault (v. 20), and death will come to the wicked who deserve it for their evil. Verses 21–22 are roughly symmetrical. The last verse picks up the positive assertion of v. 20, and affirms that God saves faithful subjects. In the final phrase, the term "refuge" is reiterated from v. 8.

These last verses, reiterating the themes begun in v. 11, are quite didactic, urging that God's governance rightly concerns the wicked and the righteous. That didactic note is a spin-off from the celebration of rescue in vs. 1–8. Whereas the humble person in vs. 1–8 is rescued, there the accent is not on just deserts, but on the wonder of deliverance. The didactic development of vs. 11–22 diminishes the exuberance of vs. 1–8 and reduces the wonder of deliverance to a sober moral principle. I suppose the diminishment and reduction are what invariably happen when a concrete experience of liberation is subordinated to an enduring general principle.

Hebrews 7:23–28

This lection provides a summary of the discussion of Jesus' priesthood that was introduced in Heb. 4:14 and preoccupied ch. 7. It also reintroduces the theme of Jesus' sacrifice, which will come to the fore in the section that follows. As a transitional passage, it aptly epitomizes Hebrews' treatment of Christ as the supreme and perfect high priest. Despite the importance thereby attached to the lection, by this point in Hebrews the comparison between the priesthood of Jesus and the earthly priesthood may have worn a bit thin. What began as a lively comparison and contrast between the role of the human priest and that of Jesus, by virtue of the detail given it grows somewhat tedious. Surely such a lengthy discussion might have been avoided.

Readers even minimally aware of Israel's traditions will, of course, recall the importance of the sacrificial system for many forms of Judaism in this period. If it was written in the aftermath of the destruction of the Temple in Jerusalem, as is often thought, Hebrews may reflect an early attempt at interpreting that event for a Jewish Christian audience; that is, because of the true sacrifice made by the priesthood of Jesus, the Jerusalem Temple is no longer needed. Jesus has replaced the Temple and its sacrificial system. Such an event would warrant the considerable detail lavished on it by the author of Hebrews.

Something else is at stake in this comparison between Jesus and the Temple priesthood that merits the attention given it, however, and that concerns the overcoming of routine. Few contemporary readers can appreciate the extent to which the sacrificial system is associated with the routinization of religious life. The use of that word, "routinization," is not intended to suggest in this instance that the Temple becomes less important or less meaningful, but that the system must ever be given attention. New priests must be found as the old die (7:23), and sacrifices must be offered "day after day" (v. 27), making the system part of the routine in human relationships with God. In this respect, the notion of Jesus as the perfect priest is similar to the Fourth Gospel's story of Jesus' encounter with the woman at the well. She comes routinely to draw water, and he offers her water that she will not need to draw again, shattering her routine and creating genuinely new possibilities for her life (John 4:7–

30). Like the water offered the Samaritan woman, then, the priesthood of Jesus is not simply a "new and improved priesthood," but a priesthood that brings to an end the need for human priests.

In three distinct but closely related ways this lection insists on that point. First, Jesus is superior to the "former priests" by virtue of the fact that he "holds his priesthood permanently" (Heb. 7:24). The way this point is made differs slightly from what might be anticipated. The passage begins with the observation that "the former priests were many in number, because they were prevented by death from continuing in office" (v. 23), prompting the expectation that Jesus would be said to continue because he does not die or because of his resurrection. What v. 24 actually says differs just slightly from that: "he holds his priesthood permanently, because he continues forever." Christ "continues," or, a bit more literally, "Christ remains," "Christ abides." The point is not merely that he lives longer than the "former priests," even as long as forever, but that he endures, persists, continues. The priesthood of Christ may be counted on because, like the God whose Son he is, Christ stands at the beginning and end of time (see 1:1–4).

Second, because of the fact that Christ continues forever, he offers the supreme intercession for humankind. The text scores this point in two ways, by asserting first that Christ is able to save "for all time" (or "completely"—the Greek is ambiguous), and then by recalling that Christ "always" lives to make intercession. The repetition involved in "all time" and "always," as in the Greek *panteles* and *pantote*, emphasizes the ultimacy of what is being said.

Third, Christ brings an end to human priests because, being perfect, he made the perfect sacrifice of himself. The description of Christ's perfection ("holy, blameless, undefiled, separated from sinners, and exalted above the heavens," v. 26) explains why he could become the perfect, the final sacrifice. Although Old Testament traditions serve constantly as a resource for the author of Hebrews, so do rhetoric and philosophical tradition. In this motif of perfection, the influence of Platonic thought can be detected, in which the physical world represents only shadows of the ideal world that lies beyond human grasp.

That preoccupation with the realm of the perfect, unattainable in human life, may seem remote from contemporary thought when cast in Platonic terms, but the pastoral force of the passage remains unchanged. What the notion of Jesus as the final, true, supreme high priest offers is the assurance that salvation continues as a possibility for human beings. No matter the ugliness of human life, the depravity of individual or corporate sin, the perfect sacrifice of Jesus brings forgiveness close by, an ever-present possibility.

Mark 10:46–52

The story of Jesus' restoration of sight to Bartimaeus, the blind beggar (Mark 10:46–52), holds an interest for the interpreter at two levels. At one level, it can be read as an isolated account of healing, a miracle story that becomes a call to discipleship. The dynamics at work between Bartimaeus, the crowds around him, and Jesus provide fertile grounds for reflecting on the nature of persistent faith.

At another level, however, the story invites comparison with other stories in Mark's Gospel—the woman healed of her hemorrhaging, the rich man who resists the call to follow Jesus, and the two disciples who seek places of authority and prominence in the coming kingdom. The other incidents help to highlight features of the Bartimaeus story that may not seem significant when read in isolation from the larger narrative. The preacher may have to choose one or the other level of interpretation as the narrative structure for a sermon, but not without a full investigation of the import of the story.

At the first level, it is clear that the incident is a healing narrative (which would have emphasized Jesus' power and included details of the healing itself) that is told as a story of discipleship. The ambiguity of the verb (*sōzō*) in Jesus' word to Bartimaeus (Mark 10:52) indicates the double-edged character of the event. The statement could be rendered, "Your faith has cured you" or "Your faith has made you whole" or even "Your faith has saved you." The physical cure is only part of a more complete restoration, a reality confirmed by the concluding observation that when Bartimaeus regained his sight he followed Jesus "on the way" (v. 52).

About the decision to become a disciple, two features stand out: Bartimaeus's persistence and Jesus' call. Bartimaeus has no companions to help him in getting Jesus' attention as he leaves Jericho. Seated by the road, his only option is to shout repeatedly, "Jesus, Son of David, have mercy on me!" The people around him are annoyed by his loud cries and sternly order him to be quiet, but he refuses to be silent. When Jesus hears his shouts and summons Bartimaeus, he thrusts aside his coat (perhaps used in begging) and eagerly jumps up to go to Jesus. His desperation, no doubt born of years of rejection and humiliation, overcomes the efforts of others to keep him blind and a beggar.

But Bartimaeus's persistence is paralleled by Jesus' call. Three times in v. 49 the verb appears (*phōneō*), not the usual Greek term used in other accounts (*kaleō*), but nonetheless conveying Jesus' part in seeking Bartimaeus. This story of becoming a disciple blends the insistence and tenacity of Bartimaeus with the summons of Jesus, a summons that even transforms the crowd from being naysayers to being conduits for the invitation.

However, it is at the second level that this story takes on its real significance. Bartimaeus is an outsider, who resembles the unnamed woman who touched the hem of Jesus' garment (5:25–34). Neither had friends to assist them; both are pushed to the edge of society; both take bold initiatives; and both are commended by Jesus with the same words ("Your faith has made you well"). They remind us of the many outsiders in the Markan narrative who are received or empowered by Jesus—the Gerasene demoniac, the Syrophoenician woman, the blind man at Bethsaida, the alien exorcist, and the little children. The powerless take a prominent place in the economy of God's new order.

The social and economic dimension of the Bartimaeus story is heightened further when it is compared with the story of the rich man (10:17–22). Though sincere, respectable, and religious, the rich man, when the chips are down, cannot break with his many possessions. He resists the invitation of Jesus and winds up a grieving nondisciple. In contrast, the beggar abandons the one possession mentioned (his coat) and gladly becomes a follower. The adage that the first will be last and the last first is already coming true.

Located where this story is in the structure of the Gospel, Bartimaeus also represents a dramatic contrast to the disciples. Through the journey to Jerusalem, they have misunderstood Jesus' words about his future destiny and his patient instruction about the nature of discipleship. While he talks about bearing crosses and serving, they argue about who will be the greatest in the kingdom. If anyone is blind, they are.

The contrast between the disciples and Bartimaeus becomes sharpest in the responses each gives to Jesus' question: "What do you want me to do for you?" James and John, the insiders, want guarantees of status in the coming kingdom, a privilege Jesus cannot give (10:36–37, 40). Bartimaeus, the outsider, wants vision, a gift Jesus immediately grants (10:51). The ones who think they see turn out to be blind, whereas the blind man gains real sight.

Jesus' question remains a revealing one to be answered by every would-be disciple: "What do you want me to do for you?" Our answer exposes our lust for power, our search for self-aggrandizement, or it uncovers our deep longing for sight.

Proper 26

Ordinary Time 31

Sunday between October 30 and November 5 inclusive

The juxtaposition of these four texts makes possible some important observations about the dynamic relationship between God's actions on behalf of human beings and the corresponding human obligation to the service of God and others. The readings begin with the familiar story of Ruth, an especially vivid example of vulnerability and loyalty. By virtue of circumstances beyond human control (famine, death), and by virtue of patriarchal values and practices, three women anticipate a terrifying future. Remaining with Naomi, Ruth lives out her love of neighbor, even though the cost could well be her own life.

The passage from Ruth says little of God's disposition toward the situation of Ruth and Naomi (apart from Naomi's despair in 1:13), but Ps. 146 does. Here the psalmist praises God as creator (vs. 5–6) but also, and more elaborately, as liberator. God "watches over the strangers"; God "upholds the orphan and the widow" (v. 9). Read alongside Ruth 1:1–18, this psalm interjects a strong element of hope and confidence into an otherwise bleak scenario.

Hebrews 9:11–14 continues the extended comparison between the Temple sacrifice and that of Jesus, in this instance emphasizing the accomplishments of the two sacrifices. That of Jesus achieves not just purification of the flesh but purification of the conscience "from dead works" (v. 14). This gift, however, demands a very specific response, consisting of the worship of the "living God" (v. 14). God's actions on behalf of human beings carry within them the demand that human beings acknowledge and serve God.

Elements of each of the preceding texts come together in the Gospel passage. The quotation of the Shema replays the doxological element in Ps. 146. The commandment to love God reinforces the conclusion to Heb. 9:11–14. And the commandment to love one's neighbor calls to mind Ruth's tenacious commitment to her mother-in-law. Precisely because God is "the Lord our God," God may be loved and God's creatures may be loved and treated with equity.

Ruth 1:1–18

In the Old Testament lections for this Sunday and the next, texts from the book of Ruth highlight a variety of themes of theological and human interest. The present passage prepares the reader and interpreter for the larger story that reaches its climax in next week's lection, in that it sets the conditions by which the drama unfolds: three women are widowed and, although custom might lead to the expectation that they would go their separate ways, Ruth refuses to abandon her mother-in-law, Naomi. Such is the kernel of this text, but the narrative is spun in a manner by which the essentials of the tale become a framework for a masterpiece of deep emotional satisfaction and artistic beauty.

The land of Moab was inhabited by a people who were Semitic kinfolk of the ancient Israelites, but relations between the two nations were rarely cordial (note, for example, 2 Sam. 8:2). Whether there is some special significance to the Moabite element in the story, or whether Moabites are viewed here as little more than sterotypical "foreigners," has been the subject of some discussion. In terms of interpreting the text in a contemporary setting the distinction makes little difference, the important dimension being that Naomi's two daughters-in-law, more importantly Ruth, were non-Israelites. Having made the point that the good Israelite family of Elimelech had expanded to include Orpah and Ruth, the initial section of the text (vs. 1–5) concludes with the notice that the two sons followed their father in death and that Naomi, already a widow, found herself childless as well.

The anguish of the moment elicits no elaboration from the text, for every ancient reader (hearer) of this story would have understood perfectly. In the patriarchal society of Israel-of-old any woman who was not attached to a male was at the mercy of economic and social forces that could very easily engulf her. For this reason the law of levirate marriage (Deut. 25:5–10) specified that a widow be claimed by the nearest male relative of the deceased. In this manner she and her children would be provided with a name, with a home, and with defenses against dangers that otherwise might have proved irresistible. The final sentence in Ruth 1:5 points to the painful reality that Naomi now had no such defenses.

Naomi's decision to return to Judah is motivated by no apparent fear of her Moabite neighbors, but by the fact that the famine, which had forced the migration of the family in the first place (v. 1), had now moderated (v. 6). Initially, Orpah and Ruth accompany Naomi, but at Naomi's urging Orpah returns to her own people (vs. 6–14). Naomi's logic is based on the fact that she is probably too old to find a new husband and, even if she did, she could never give birth to new sons. Thus the likelihood that some new male figure would enter the family to provide the protection specified in the law of levirate marriage is very slight indeed. The two younger women would therefore be much better off if they stayed among their own people and attempted to build new family arrangements there.

It is with great sadness that Orpah consents to the force of this reasoning and tells Naomi goodbye (v. 14). But not even the common sense of Naomi's appeal can persuade Ruth. Instead of leaving Naomi, Ruth, defying all prudence, "clung to her." Not even Naomi's citing of Orpah's example (v. 15) can change Ruth's mind.

Ruth's response to Naomi (vs. 16–17) has been cast as poetry in the NRSV because of cadences within the text. But the "old" RSV is nearer the style of the Hebrew text of Ruth, which, in the form in which it has been transmitted to us, represents these verses as prose. In any event, they are perhaps the most frequently quoted passage in the book, and not without reason. (Although the applications to which they have sometimes been put—at weddings, for example—seem to strain the context.) The statement is actually an oath, sworn before Yahweh (v. 17b), that Ruth intends to share Naomi's future. If there is no man to claim the elder woman and to give her the protection of family and home, Ruth will do all that she can to compensate for this deficiency. In the face of Ruth's determination, Naomi yields (v. 18).

Part of the power of this lection lies in its understated portrayal of the vulnerability of individuals in the face of forces over which they have no control. Like Abraham (Gen. 12:10) and Jacob (Gen. 42:1–2) before them, the family of Elimelech have been compelled to leave their home because of the threat of starvation. It was a drama familiar to ancient readers of this text, as it is to certain modern ones, as well.

More specifically, the text points to the vulnerability of the women. Without male protectors and breadwinners they possessed very limited resources, indeed. Naomi especially, since she was more elderly than her daughters-in-law, would be hard put to care for her own needs, and the good cheer with which she faces the bleak prospects of her future life (vs. 8–9) is based on few objective realities, other than the lifting of the famine in Judah. Realizing Naomi's unpromising future causes Ruth's devotion to be understood for the selfless commitment that it was.

But the present lection constitutes only the beginning of the narrative. The most important word is yet to be heard.

Psalm 146

Psalm 146 successfully combines doxology and sapiential instruction. The psalm is nicely enveloped in a familiar doxological formula in vs. 1 and 10. The sapiential instruction is equally evident in vs. 3–4. Verse 5 begins with a proverbial formula, but the proverbial form is immediately transformed into a doxology.

The introduction to the psalm is a standard, exuberant hymnic assertion. Verse 1 calls others to praise, v. 2 is a pledge and promise to praise "all my life long." In v. 2, praise seems not to be simply a concrete act, but a more general practice of ceding life over to God in glad self-abandonment.

Verses 3 and 4 are a negative piece of instruction which serves as a foil for the affirmation to follow in vs. 5–9. The double negative of v. 3 warns against looking to human agents, especially people in power, to give help. The reason human agents cannot give help in real crises is that they themselves are dependent, derivative creatures whose own life is a gift from God, and who therefore are not in fact self-starters. In characteristic sapiential fashion, the teaching affirms that things are not as they seem in the midst of human life. "Princes" may give the appearance of power and capacity to help, but they are themselves precarious and unreliable.

In v. 5, the psalm arrives at the positive counsel that is its main concern. Verse 5a begins as a standard wisdom saying, not unlike the familiar Beatitudes. The saying reiterates the term "help" from v. 3, this time positively. It is the God of Jacob, not any human agent, who is a source of real help and a ground for real hope. Thus God is contrasted with would-be human help.

At v. 6, what had been sapiential advice is transformed into a long doxological affirmation about Yahweh, detailing the kind of help Yahweh can give and the kind of hope Israel can rightly assign to Yahweh. In the Hebrew of vs. 6–7 there is a series of four participles with Yahweh as the subject.

The God of help and hope, on the one hand, is characteristically "making" heavens, the earth, and the sea. (On this triad, see Ps. 104, Proper 24.) This theme attests to God's magisterial power and to the right ordering of reality. The second participle, translated "keeps faith," likely belongs with the preceding, so that God's practice of fidelity is the maintenance of the creation in constancy. On the other hand, the doxology makes a large leap in v. 7 with two additional participles concerning justice for the oppressed and food for the hungry. The verb "execute" is the same as "made" in v. 6. Thus the hymn establishes that God's two great parallel works are creation and liberation for the poor, hungry, and oppressed. This latter theme of intervention for the oppressed is as central and as crucial for Israel's faith as is the theme of creation.

The second part of this doxology continues with a series of participles concerning God's ongoing actions. This series is different from the preceding, because in each phrase the name of Yahweh is asserted. Thus the phrasing makes an argument for the character of the God of Israel, in a very precise way. As we shall see in v. 10, the repeated liturgical mention of Yahweh has political force.

Yahweh's characteristic action takes place for the marginated who are without power, and takes the form of inversions in the power relations of public practice. In setting the prisoners free, Yahweh cancels debts and in fact implements the year of the jubilee (v. 7). Yahweh acts decisively for the blind, the bowed down, the righteous (presumably by inference, the powerless poor who have no rights). If "the righteous" are here understood, as they often are in Torah piety, as the pious but socially disadvantaged, then this entire list consists in those devalued by society (for example, by the very "princes" of v. 3), but who are nonetheless valued by Yahweh and offered new life. It takes no great imagination to see that this set of actions by Yahweh (verbs) and this list of constituents are echoed in the wonders of Jesus, which also characteristically concern the diminished and dysfunctional members of society (see Luke 7:22). Yahweh is portrayed as a powerfully partisan agent in the social process.

Verse 9c continues the list of constituents, but breaks the rhetorical pattern. Orphans and widows are included in Yahweh's primary constituency, but Yahweh's explicit name is absent from the formula. In any case, widows and orphans are those who have lost their male advocates and so stand with strangers and prisoners as socially defenseless and vulnerable in a patriarchal society. The last line of v. 9 adds a negative counterpoint concerning those for whom God does not intervene. In this negative assertion, Yahweh is not mentioned directly, but is the key actor in the ruin and abandonment of "the wicked."

The concluding formula of the psalm in v. 10 affirms the sovereign rule of Yahweh. This acclamation follows nicely from the repeated use of the name. It is as though Yahweh is urged as a candidate for the throne in vs. 7b–9, and now, finally, receives the domain that is rightly his. The entire psalm is an affirmation that God's decisive role in the power process gives hope to the otherwise powerless, and warns those who imagine they are autonomous agents who can order their own life as they please. The proclaimed sovereign is a deeply engaged transformative agent, giving the historical process a tilt toward the marginal in a way that is genuinely revolutionary.

Hebrews 9:11–14

Among the standard interpretative devices of the first century was the practice of arguing "from the lesser to the greater" (*qal wahomer*). If a characteristic could be attributed to something smaller or lesser, it was assumed a fortiori that the same or even greater characteristics could be attributed to something larger or greater. The New Testament provides many examples of such reasoning. When Jesus argues that, because God "clothes the grass of the field, which is alive today and tomorrow is thrown into the oven" (Matt. 6:30), God will also clothe human beings, he is using an argument "from the lesser to the greater." Another good example of such interpretative logic comes following Jesus' question, "Is there anyone among you who, if your child asks for bread, will give a stone?" (Matt. 7:9). The conclusion is clear that, if limited human parents care for their children, "how much more" will God, the supreme parent, care for God's children (Matt. 7:11). Paul employs the same technique when he contrasts the accomplishments of the finite trespass of Adam with Jesus Christ's gift of grace (Rom. 5:12–21).

Because these examples are familiar, it is easy to overlook the fact that this means of reasoning goes against modern notions of logic. After all, perhaps God provides clothing for plants because they are not able to fend for themselves! Recognizing the tremendous differences among human parents, can one reason the nature of God's parenting style by looking at that of human parents? Despite these problems, argument "from the lesser to the greater" needs to be understood in order to see how these various passages "work."

Much of Hebrews presupposes this kind of thinking by presenting Jesus as the high priest who is even greater than human high priests and who, therefore, accomplishes far more for humankind. This lection meticulously contrasts certain features of the atonement accomplished by human priests and that accomplished by Christ. As elsewhere, however, the author employs the contrast not only to embroider around a theme but also to encourage behavior that is appropriate to Christian faith.

The lection opens with what might appear to be an incidental reference: "But when Christ came." In Hebrews, however, references to the arrival of Christ often serve to recall his becoming Son or high priest. For example, 1:4 speaks of Christ as having "become [literally, arrived] as much superior to angels . . ." and 6:20 of his "having become [literally, arrived] a high priest forever." Here, an intensive form of the customary verb (*paraginomai*, rather than *ginomai*) makes the arrival even more dramatic.

The initial contrast implied in v. 11 is between the place of Christ's atonement and the place of the atonement accomplished by the customary sacrifices. He entered "through the greater and perfect tent." Lest the contrast with the Temple be missed, Hebrews further identifies the tent as "not made with hands" and "not of this creation." In other words, this place is made by God. Often interpreters allegorize this tent, seeing in it reference to the body of Christ. The context makes such conclusions unnecessary, for Christ is said to go "through" the tent to the "Holy Place." The discussion in vs. 6–9 clarifies the contrast, for there the author talks about the Yom Kippur sacrifice, in which annually the high priest enters into the "second" tent. Here Christ enters not annually into the "second" and more sacred place, but into the most sacred place imaginable, and only once.

Verse 12 introduces the second contrast, that having to do with the means of the sacrifice. What the human priests sacrifice are "the blood of goats and calves," but Christ sacrifices "his own blood." Verses 13–14 restate this part of the contrast; here it is the "blood of goat and bulls, with the sprinkling of the ashes of a heifer." The reference to the slaughter of the red heifer puzzles exegetes, for that ceremony is not connected with the Yom Kippur sacrifice. Possibly the association here arises because, by this time in Jewish tradition, the sacrifice of the red heifer has been associated with the high priest.

With v. 14, the "how much more" phrase identifies the point of this long series of contrasts; if the annual sacrifice of animals in a tent erected by human hands accomplished sanctification, what sanctification will be accomplished by the sacrifice of Christ in a place erected by God? The answer comes quickly. That earlier sacrifice covered things that defiled the flesh or things that caused ritual impurity; this new sacrifice cleanses "our conscience from dead works." The familiarity of language about "works" from the Pauline letters should not lead to the conclusion that these "dead works" are works of the Mosaic law. Elsewhere in Hebrews, the phrase "dead works" clearly refers to immoral actions (6:1), and that is its referent here as well.

The sacrifice of Christ, then, brings about cleansing from ritual impurity and forgiveness of sins. Something even greater is at stake, however, as the last words of the passage indicate: "to worship the living God!" This purification has a purpose beyond that of rectifying the individual's standing before God. It enables the worship of God. The verb "worship" translates the Greek *latreuein*, which connotes both cultic and ethical service (see, for example, *latreuein* as "serve" in Luke 1:74; Rom. 1:9; "worship" in Acts 24:14). Purification finally results in the sort of devotion to God that is as total as the sacrifice of Christ, who gave "his own blood."

Mark 12:28–34

The account of the giving of the two great commandments is listed each year in the lectionary cycle, as it occurs in the particular Gospel being highlighted for the year. Since the commands to love God totally and to love our neighbors as ourselves stand at the very heart of the faith, the account warrants regular consideration. And yet each of the Gospels offers a slightly different context and varying details, enough at least to provide the preacher with some variety in approaching the story.

Three distinctives of the Markan story are to be noted. For one thing, Mark 12:28–34 is substantially unlike the Matthean account in that the scribe who raises the question with Jesus appears to be very sincere, not out to entrap Jesus. He is emboldened to ask the question by the positive way Jesus has responded to other questions. He is in fact commended for the interpretation he offers on Jesus' answer and is told that he is "not far from the kingdom of God" (12:34). It is true that he apparently does not become a disciple, following Jesus, as Bartimaeus did, "on the way" (10:52). At the same time, there is no reason to take these final words as a condemnation of one who comes part way but not far enough. In preaching, there is certainly no warrant for making a scapegoat out of Mark's scribe.

A second distinctive is that Mark's story (unlike Matthew and Luke) reports the initial words of Jesus as including Deut. 6:4 as well as 6:5 ("Hear, O Israel: the Lord our God, the Lord is one"). The addition produces two effects. (*a*) It stresses *the peculiar audience* to which the commandment is addressed. To love God totally and to love neighbors are not injunctions expected of every Tom, Dick, and Harry. They are directed to a special community constituted by the redemptive acts of God. The church, as part of an extended "Israel," is then faced with a command that distinguishes it from surrounding communities and puts its life and relationships in a different light. (*b*) The presence of the Shema in Mark also stresses *the peculiar God* to be loved. The commandments are grounded in the character of a particular God, who refuses to be reckoned as one among a pantheon of deities and whose gracious history with the chosen people is well known. People are not being asked to love a God who is a ruthless tyrant or a genial Santa Claus, but a God whose identity has been revealed in the life of Israel and in the destiny of Jesus.

A third distinctive of the Markan story is the response of the scribe, who not only affirms Jesus' answer to his question but adds, "This is much more important than all whole burnt offerings and sacrifices" (Mark 12:33). The scribe's "wise" answer does not condemn cultic practices per se, but establishes a clear priority. Love of God and neighbor takes precedence over ritual performance. One might even argue that there is a relativizing of religion here, at least a relativizing of its trappings, ceremonies, and rites. At times they assume what seems like an inordinate amount of time and energy and money, but are set in a penultimate position by the great commandments.

How are we to handle the relationship of the two commandments? Jesus is asked, "Which commandment is the *first* of all?" (emphasis added). He answers with two commandments, identified as "first" and "second," and then adds, "There is no other commandment greater than these" (v. 31). The two commands clearly belong together, and together are set over against all other commandments.

In preaching, sometimes the stress needs to fall on the first commandment and at other times on the second commandment, but never one to the exclusion of the other. On occasion the point needs to be made that loving God is impossible without loving one's neighbors. Mysticism is no substitute for New Testament Christianity. The second command then becomes an explanation of how the first command can be put into practice. The context from which it comes in Leviticus specifically lists ways in which the poor are to be cared for and the weak are to be protected against exploitation (Lev. 19:9–18). In the words of 1 John 4:21, "Those who love God must love their brothers and sisters also."

On other occasions, however, an overemphasis on the second commandment to the neglect of the first results in a humanism that quickly loses its theological moorings. The second commandment cannot be absorbed into the first, as if when we love our neighbors we have thoroughly fulfilled the command to love God. The citation from Deut. 6:5 calls attention to a single-minded commitment (heart, soul), involving energetic activity (strength), and Mark adds the phrase "with all your mind." The total self is called to be engaged in the love of God, which I take to include such things as praise, thanksgiving, study, obedience, and faithfulness—as well as loving one's neighbor.

Finally, the combining of two Old Testament passages that use the verb "love" (instead of, say, "serve") cannot be ignored. Love, of course, is more than a feeling. It finds expression in concrete acts, and on a corporate level takes on the character of justice. And yet it ought not to be thought of as cold, emotionless charity. It connotes the elements of passion, of avid commitment, of zeal. We find them powerfully exhibited in Jesus himself, who models love in Mark's story and whose love for sinful people makes possible the hearing and obeying of the two great commandments.

PROPER 27

Ordinary Time 32

*Sunday between
November 6 and 12 inclusive*

Why bother with the past? The question that plagues every teacher of history has become critical in contemporary Western society. Those who regard the war in Vietnam as the remote past will be bewildered by discussions of anything removed from the rapidly changing present. In such an environment, the Bible seems particularly irrelevant, both because it comes out of centuries long dead and because it seems to stand facing the past, constantly preoccupied with persons and events in the history of Israel or the church.

Several of the readings for this Sunday demonstrate that the Bible's preoccupation with the past is simultaneously a preoccupation with the future. Christians live out of the past but into the future, and the relationship between the two is an important one. The story of Ruth seems a simple "once upon a time" kind of tale. Two women in dire circumstances remain loyal to each other and find happiness through the love and generosity of Boaz. But the conclusion to the story points forward rather than backward. Boaz and Ruth belong not only to Israel's past, but to the future God has in mind for Israel and, indeed, for all humankind (hence the reference to Ruth in Matt. 1:5).

Despite its patriarchal assumptions about the importance of having a "quiver full of" sons, the future orientation of Ps. 127 likewise contradicts any assumption that the Bible looks only backward. The psalmist wisely observes that a life that does not contribute to the future (whether through children or in some other manner) is a life "in vain." The psalmist also warns against assuming that the future can be provided for apart from the guardianship of the Lord.

With its elaborate treatment of the past action of Jesus, Hebrews might appear to be utterly wedged in the past or, at best, in some sense of timelessness. The conclusion to 9:24–28, however, anticipates the Parousia and depicts Christians as "eagerly waiting" for

Christ's return. The sacrifice Christ makes does not exist only in the past; it prepares for the future completion of salvation.

The story of the widow's penny in Mark 12 recalls another element in Ps. 127, that of the futility of labor that takes place apart from God. Those who work to secure their own positions but neglect to recognize God (as do the religious leaders and the wealthy in the story) live only in the present, acknowledging neither God's care in the past nor God's sovereignty over the future.

Ruth 3:1–5; 4:13–17

The lectionary, by providing the preacher with the introduction to the book of Ruth (1:1–18) in one week and the conclusion (4:13–17) in the next, has leaped over a number of texts that contain important dramatic and literary developments within this significant Old Testament story. In attempting to compensate for this deficiency, the lectionary suggests Ruth 3:1–5 (Naomi's instructions to Ruth concerning the manner of gaining Boaz's love) as a passage to accompany 4:13–17. The preacher, however, may wish to choose a more appropriate "bridge" between the introduction and conclusion, such as 2:1–13 (Ruth's first meeting with Boaz) or 4:7–12 (the manner in which Boaz ultimately claims Ruth as his bride). The suggestion of this commentary is that 4:7–12 be appended to the suggested lection in place of 3:1–5, thus allowing 4:7–17 to serve as the entire lection for this day.

To this point the story of Ruth has been a tale of tender love and of tough loyalty, a love and loyalty that have won for Ruth the notice of her husband's kinsman Boaz. It has not been, so far, a narrative devoid of theological interest, for Boaz declares that his own protection of Ruth is in fulfillment of Yahweh's will (2:12). Yet the story may easily have led the reader/interpreter to the wrong conclusion, namely, that Yahweh unfailingly rewards expressions of love and loyalty on the part of individuals by the return of these same qualities, an illusion that is contradicted by the common experiences of generations of readers of this story. And so it is not until the present passage is addressed that the true purpose of the story of Ruth becomes clear. Yahweh has a most remarkable surprise in store, a delightful turn of events for which the reader must wait until the very end of the tale.

The legal provisions that are assumed in this passage present certain difficulties to those who wish to harmonize them with other texts within the Old Testament, and the interested exegete may wish to refer to any of several critical commentaries that deal with this issue in an informed and helpful manner. To the person who reads the entire book of Ruth, the beginning of 4:7–17 is encountered with a certain relief. Verses 1–6 have described how an unnamed kinsman, who has a prior claim to the heritage of Elimelech, has refused (but barely!) to comply with the provisions in the laws of redemption (Lev. 25:25–38) which would have resulted in his claiming of Ruth as his wife. He has allowed this right/obligation to pass to Boaz, and Ruth 4:7–12 describes the scene by which this agreement is ratified before the necessary witnesses. The reader senses a narrow escape here!

The blessing of these witnesses may be understood as somewhat ritualistic, since they involve the customary wishes that the newlyweds should produce a large family (vs. 11–12). And yet these good wishes are a subtle hint of what is yet to be revealed, namely, that the significance of this entire narrative lies in the birth of a son, Obed (v. 17).

In vs. 13–17 we are given a reason for regarding this artfully crafted tale as more than just an engaging story of love and devotion. The good wishes of the witnesses to the contract by which Ruth became Boaz's wife are now realized: Obed is born (v. 13). The unidentified women who are present shower their congratulations on Naomi (v. 14), an echo of the opening of the story about Ruth (1:1–18), which highlighted the older woman's vulnerability. Now she too may claim the protection of a male who, although yet an infant, will be a "nourisher of your old age" (v. 15).

It is, of course, in the birth of Obed (v. 17) that the larger purpose of Ruth's loyalty and devotion and of Yahweh's goodness to her are now realized. The grandfather of none other than King David is the issue of the union between Ruth and Boaz. The reader is now in a position to understand that it was in order to bring about this happy consequence that Yahweh blessed and protected Ruth, and it is in celebration of this event that the narrative has been written and preserved. More than just a tale of perseverance and romance, the story of Ruth is a paradigm of the manner in which God works in the most unusual, unexpected, and benevolent ways!

It has been suggested that the book of Ruth is a product of the postexilic age and that it was issued as a subtle protest against the exclusivist attitudes that then prevailed (Ezra 9:1–4). Firm evidence for that argument is lacking, but one need not consider the book of Ruth as a late literary creation to appreciate its startling proclamation. Just when life seemed most hopeless for the widowed survivors of the family of Elimelech, Yahweh provided for their redemption.

But not out of the blue! There is no deus ex machina here. The love and faithfulness of Ruth become the vehicle by which Yahweh is enabled to do dramatic and wonderful things, not just for the women of Elimelech's family, but for all Israel—indeed, for all humankind. If Ruth had not been loyal to Naomi and thus willing to share her future, she would have gone the way of Orpah. Not only would we have heard no more of her, but the larger purposes of God would have been frustrated, purposes of which Ruth was completely ignorant at the time.

Out of the faithfulness of this woman—and a foreigner, at that!—God's redemptive intentions move one step forward. What has seemed to be merely another story of human love and kindness is now seen to be an important statement concerning the saving grace of God.

Psalm 127

This poem is sapiential in its casting. It consists of a series of wise observations based on recurrent human experience. The psalm is divided into a series of negative and then a series of positive statements.

The negative statements in Ps. 127:1 and 2 concern three human activities. The first two are stated conditionally. Both concern ambitious human activity that is the founding of a community or a society. The listener is warned against vanity—against the futility of establishing what cannot succeed. The teaching assumes that Yahweh can indeed build a house (which here means an extended family, not a building) and Yahweh can indeed found a city. In both cases, Yahweh's building and grounding determine the purpose, quality, and shape of social relations. The psalm envisions an extended family or city, that is, a concentration of human power, devoted to the purposes of Yahweh and committed to Yahweh's covenantal modes of power.

The possibility of a Yahweh-founded house or city is a live option. In the psalm, however, that positive option is only a foil for the warning the psalm wants to voice. The other option is to have a house or a city not directed toward Yahweh. Such an enterprise is "vain," an act of futility that cannot succeed or prosper. A house that is not covenanted to Yahweh is bound to flounder in self-destructiveness, and a city without reference to Yahweh is sure to end in acquisitiveness and injustice.

The third negative in v. 2 is even more direct and conclusive. This statement entertains no live Yahwistic alternative, unless the last line has that function. The main warning is that rising early and returning late, that is, long hours of strenuous work, is a futility. This warning seems to echo (or anticipate) the observations of Eccl. 2:18–20; 3:9–15, that excessive work is a vanity and cannot bring well-being or joy. The brief hint of an alternative is that God's beloved, those who are attuned to the purposes of Yahweh, do not destroy themselves in excessive work, but are able to have peaceful rest. As the NRSV note suggests, more than one reading of the Hebrew text is possible. Either way, the positive line anticipates Jesus' counsel against anxiety in Matt. 6:25–31.

The sayings of the psalm are more than prudential wisdom, but exhibit a faith affirmation that God's power for life is actively and concretely at work in the world. Even related to the mundane matters of human work, it is urged, we are justified (made safe) by faith rather than by feverish effort.

The positive counterpart of Ps. 127 may look back to v. 1a. If "house" means extended family, then in a patriarchal society the best thing that can happen is "sons." (In a more inclusive version of this sentiment, one may say that sons and daughters open a way to the future and permit a genuinely generative life. If, then, the accent is on generativity, we may imagine forms of it beyond the reproduction of heirs. This is, of course, beyond the actual horizon of the psalm, but seems a fair construct in our very different socioeconomic circumstance.)

If the high regard for sons and heirs is seen as the best thing that can happen to a "house" (which it is in the psalm), then perhaps the "vain" negative in v. 1 is a house that is able to have no heir because it is not congruent with God's blessing. Both the positive and the negative statements confess that God gives and withholds the gift that make a future possible. (See the narratives in Genesis concerning heirs.)

This latter part of the psalm contains the simple concern for the blessing of many sons. In v. 4, the sons are treated like arrows in a quiver. That is, they are the weapons and means of strength in a strategy for well-being and security. One must not approach the future "unarmed," that is, unblessed and without heirs.

The gift of sons gives a man in a patriarchal society standing in the community, indicating that he is prosperous, successful, blessed, virile, and approved by God. He can hold his head up in public. The down side is that a man without sons has reason in such a society to be ashamed, and is inevitably in a vulnerable position in the hard negotiations that constitute life in court or in the economy. Thus the success or failure of daily life derives from the giving or withholding of blessing by God.

I can think of no direct way to avoid the embarrassment of this patriarchal psalm in its preoccupation with sons. The whole argument of the psalm, back to v. 1, depends on this gift and this blessing.

This line of reasoning is in our context awkward on two counts. First, it is awkward because there is a valuing of sons as distinct from daughters, so that the psalm is blatantly exclusivist. Second, there is a valuing of children (heirs) in a society of many childless adults. In such a context as ours, two avenues of interpretation may be suggested. First, both the negative and positive parts of the psalm focus on Yahweh. The negative side is that variance from Yahweh's vision of the future is sure to fail. The positive side is that life with Yahweh yields gifts. In its urgency toward Yahweh, the psalm critiques every temptation to self-sufficiency. Second, most broadly construed, the accent on heirs insists that believers must be generative into the future. There are many ways to be generative, but all those ways resist absolutizing the status quo and valuing the present tense excessively.

Hebrews 9:24–28

While this lection recapitulates the contrast drawn in 9:11–14 between Christ's sacrifice and that of Yom Kippur, it focuses on a slightly different aspect of the sacrifice. The earlier passage emphasizes the differing victims of the sacrifice (animal blood versus that of Christ) and the result of the sacrifice (ritual purity versus purity of conscience). This passage emphasizes the high priest's action (entering into God's presence rather than into the sanctuary). It also interprets the sacrifice of Christ eschatologically, by contrast with the annual sacrifice of Yom Kippur.

Christ entered into heaven to "appear in the presence of God on our behalf" (Heb. 9:24). Perhaps as a result of thinking of God in terms of "friend" and "companion," Christians sometimes imagine that being in God's presence would be a comfortable and soothing experience. The troubles of the world would be left behind, and only the joy of contemplating God would remain. By contrast with this benign and wistful portrait of God's presence, the Bible reflects a very different understanding. Moses responds to the presence of God by turning away his face out of fear (Ex. 3:1–6). Even the messengers of God terrorize their audiences (for example, Luke 1:1; 2:9; 24:5). For Christ to enter the very presence of God (literally, "before the face of God") suggests a willingness to submit to unimaginable awe and fear. (Later christological reflection would suggest that Christ is already in God's presence, that Christ in fact *is* God's presence, but that reflection cannot be used to interpret this passage in Hebrews.)

Christ enters into this most holy of all places for salvific reasons, "on our behalf." This short phrase might be unnecessary, for the Yom Kippur sacrifice is also carried out on behalf of the people. Unlike the ordinary high priest, however, Christ has no need to sacrifice on his own behalf. In addition, this phrase guarantees that the entry into God's presence does not occur to satisfy some longing of Christ's, some personal need for self-glory. It occurs solely to meet the needs of the human community.

The notion that Christ's sacrifice occurs "once for all" appears already in Heb. 9:12, but here the author develops it further. Christ's sacrifice takes place once and only once because the one sacrifice is adequate to achieve salvation. Verses 25–26 point out the absurdity of Christ's sacrifice on any other terms. Had Christ sacrificed himself annually, as the high priest makes the annual sacrifice, he would have been crucified "again and again since the foundation of the world"! His one sacrifice, however, suffices to replace—and more than replace (see vs. 13–14)—the sacrifices made each year.

Here an eschatological element enters the discussion, for Christ's "once for all" sacrifice takes place at a particular time in history, "at the end of the age" (v. 26). The "in these last days" of the prologue to Hebrews returns here and will become more prominent in the final sections of the book (see, for example, 12:25–29). The phrase itself provides an important reminder that Christ's sacrifice signals more than the end of other things—the end of the Temple, the end of human priesthood, the end of sacrifices. Christ's sacrifice also signals the beginning of a new age.

The conclusion of the passage looks toward that new beginning by means of a perplexing analogy. Christ's death is like that of mortals who "die once, and after that the judgment." This curious phrase probably reflects a proverbial saying about the inevitability of death and judgment. The saying might be Christian in origin, but it might also reflect Hellenistic philosophical assumptions about the judgment of the soul following death. Whatever its history, the saying assumes that humans all meet the same fate of death and judgment.

Christ's death is said to be like this proverb in that Christ will "appear a second time." What the analogy assumes but does not explicitly state is that Christ's death, like that of mortals, takes place only once, and, again like mortals, Christ's death is followed by another stage. This new stage is not judgment but the Parousia, an event here closely associated with salvation ("to save those who are eagerly waiting for him") but, oddly enough, not with sin ("not to deal with sin").

That Christ's sacrifice deals with human sin in a salvific way is clear throughout Hebrews, but this passage amplifies that point. Salvation is more than removing the effects of sin, more even than purifying the conscience (9:14). Salvation also involves the association of believers with Christ himself. It is for this reason that the author adds that believers are "eagerly waiting for him" (see also Rom. 8:18–25; 1 Thess. 1:9–10; Rev. 22:20).

Some might interpret the "once for all" character of Christ's sacrifice, especially with the emphasis on entering into God's presence, to mean that Christ is no longer present with believers—by virtue of his unique position as the one High Priest and simultaneously the one perfect sacrifice, he is utterly removed from human beings. This promise about his coming "a second time" assures believers that he does not remain distant. They may eagerly await him, confident of his presence again.

Mark 12:38–44

Mark 12:38–44 regularly appears as the text for sermons during the time in the church's calendar called "stewardship season." The destitute widow becomes an ideal symbol for Christian generosity, since the two copper coins she gave represented all she had. On such an occasion the sermon often tends to overlook the rich people mentioned in the text and to downplay the behavior of the scribes, since stewardship season is not a time to offend the wealthier members whose quantitatively large gifts are needed to raise the budget. A treatment of the story at a different time in the church's life might yield a less sentimental and more prophetic reading.

Contextually, the location of the story is critical. The passage comes at the very end of the public ministry of Jesus, immediately preceding both the speech to the four disciples in which Jesus predicts the destruction of the Temple (ch. 13) and the Passion narrative itself (chs. 14–15). It represents the climactic event in the sequence that begins with the triumphal entry into Jerusalem and includes several incidents that point to the corruption of the Temple and the growing opposition of the religious authorities to Jesus; for example, the cursing of the fig tree (11:12–14, 20–25), the purifying of the Temple (11:15–19), the challenge of Jesus' authority in the Temple (11:27–33), the parable of the wicked tenants (12:1–12), the testing questions of the Pharisees and Sadducees (12:13–27), and the conversation about the Messiah while Jesus is in the Temple (12:35–37).

In a context like this, the attack on the scribes cannot be minimized. A single scribe, like the one who asked about the first commandment, might be commended (12:28–34), but the habitual behavior of the scribes as a group comes in for severe criticism. Their pretentious practices—strolling about in long robes, seeking public acclaim, taking the best seats at the synagogues and local banquets, lengthy prayers—mask their ruthless exploitation of poor people, in particular widows, who in a male-dominated society are left without defense. Jesus' denunciation of the scribes is reminiscent of the prophets who attack religious leaders for similar practices (for example, Isa. 10:1–2; Zech. 7:10). That the scribes were recognized religious leaders prods the readers of the text to ask questions about their own style of life, whether or not there is a contradiction between religious display and social practice.

Immediately following the condemnation of the scribes, the narrator establishes the powerful contrast between rich people putting large sums of money into the Temple treasury and the destitute widow giving her copper coins. At this point a decision has to be made by the interpreter exactly how to understand the symbol of the widow. A traditional reading lifts her up as an ideal figure, whose small gift is set over against the contributions of the rich and is honored because it comes out of her poverty—"all she had to live on." Jesus' comments in Mark 12:43–44 are taken as a commendation of the widow, making her a character, like the woman at Bethany who anoints Jesus' head (14:3–9), to be remembered for her extraordinary commitment.

Recently some commentators have argued that the traditional reading ignores the social and political dimensions of the text. Does 12:43–44 explicitly praise the widow's action? they ask. Why would she be commended for giving to a Temple whose destruction was at hand? Does she not rather serve as a concrete example of how innocent people are victimized by the Temple authorities? Jesus' comments about the widow are really a lament about her plight and continue the denunciation of the scribes, who instead of caring for this woman as the law directed them to do are robbing her of her last dime.

It may be that the two readings of the story need not be set so sharply against each other as some commentators propose. The scribes are pointedly condemned, no doubt about that (12:40). The widow in her destitution may concretely represent those many widows whose houses have been "devoured" by the scribes. Thus, in a direct way, the condemnation of the scribes is continued in the vignette about the widow. At the same time, it is hard to ignore the element of commendation in Jesus' words about the action of the widow. She is contrasted, not with the scribes who benefited from the offerings, but with "many rich people" who may or may not have earned their money unjustly.

In any case, the passage carries a strongly prophetic flavor and invites a sermon that probes the contradictions in our lives between the religious and the socioeconomic spheres. At the same time, it calls for a wholehearted self-giving that transcends dollars and cents.

PROPER 28

Ordinary Time 33

*Sunday between
November 13 and 19 inclusive*

At first glance, the only thing these readings appear to have in common is that each of them has some relationship to the priesthood (Hannah's confrontation with Eli, the priesthood of Jesus, the Temple setting of Mark 13:1–8). At a deeper level, however, each of the four passages becomes a reminder of the need for perseverance in matters of faith.

Beautiful, powerful, influential as it is, the story of Hannah will require sensitivity in retelling. Those who are themselves unable or unwilling to become parents may hear reproach in 1 Sam. 1–2 unless the preacher moves carefully. Others may wonder why their own prayers, either for children or for some other deep need or desire, are not answered as was Hannah's. Despite these tender spots, Hannah's story warrants recall, for it celebrates not only the gracious power of God (1 Sam. 2:2) but also the perseverance of an unlikely supplicant. Neither the passage of years nor the ridicule of Peninnah nor the pity of Elkanah nor the misunderstanding of Eli stops Hannah's appeal to God.

The author of Hebrews labors assiduously to contrast the priesthood of Jesus with that of human beings. When the passages from 1 Samuel are read alongside Hebrews, however, Eli becomes a succinct and dramatic embodiment of the contrast. While he acts carefully and responds generously to Hannah's petition, he nevertheless is unable to alter her situation. Only in the person and work of Jesus does the priesthood become that strong. Hannah, on the other hand, offers an excellent example of the "confidence" called for by the author of Hebrews (Heb. 10:19). She knows of God's ability to alter her situation, and she makes her "approach" (Heb. 10:22) with hope.

The Gospel lesson stands alone, not only because of the prophecy about the Temple's destruction, but also because it looks to be preoccupied with endings (the ending of the Temple and all that accompanies it) rather than with beginnings (the birth of a baby, the beginning of a new approach to God). The Markan "apocalypse" also concerns perseverance, however. It advocates the perseverance of believers in the face of trials, in the face of false prophets, in the face of impatience. Indeed expectation of an imminent Parousia calls for increased perseverance and enhanced powers of discernment.

1 Samuel 1:4–20

The Old Testament lection of this Sunday describes the circumstances surrounding the birth of Samuel, in clear anticipation of the narratives of the birth of Jesus soon to be read during Advent and Christmas. Those who preach from this text may wish to add the first three verses of 1 Sam. 1, since they set the context for the dramatic action involving Hannah and her family.

Readers of the Old Testament will be familiar with tales of other women who, by the grace of God, bore children under remarkable circumstances, Sarah perhaps being the most prominent example (Gen. 17:15–19; 18:9–15; 21:1–7). But the story of God's gift to Hannah is distinctive in that it has provided strong echoes in the New Testament narratives of Jesus' birth (especially Luke 1).

Theologically, the thrust of the story is unambiguous: Yahweh responded to the fervent prayer of a righteous and persecuted woman by graciously endowing her with a son. Furthermore, this act of love was not limited to Hannah only, for the gift was really intended for all Israel, in that Samuel becomes the one who leads the people through times of great difficulty in their transition from tribal confederation to monarchy. Although this latter theme is not emphasized in the present lection, it is unquestionably in the minds of the authors/editors of 1 Sam. 1–16, and is therefore implicit in this text.

Like so many other Old Testament narratives, this passage unfolds its theological agenda in a context rich in themes of human interest. The rivalry between the two wives (another reminder that polygamy was sometimes practiced in Israel-of-old), the cruelty of Peninnah, the indifference of Elkanah, the devotion of Hannah, the mental feebleness of Eli—all these facets of the story offer ample opportunities to study human beings as we really are. Our contradictions and our sinfulness, our limitations, and our possibilities, are all on display here.

Yet, as arresting as is the text's commentary on human nature, its focus is on the nature of God. It is not accidental that the drama is set against the background of the cult. The ordinary means that Yahweh has placed at the disposal of devout men and women by which they may enter into communion with the Almighty—prayer and sacrifice—are affirmed here as being especially valuable resources in times of anxiety and trouble. Shiloh was no run-of-the-mill sanctuary, although like other centers of worship in the Land of Promise it doubtless had a long history as a Canaanite shrine even before the coming of the Israelite tribes. Yet Shiloh at this time housed the Ark of Yahweh (1 Sam. 3:3), and so it was in a unique position to command the presence of pious Israelites. The text affirms the value of this shrine and of the worship practiced there, even as it admits the limitations of the officiating clergy (vs. 12–14).

Perhaps it is the weakness of Eli and his two sons (see 2:12) that leads to the story's account of how Hannah attempted to pray to Yahweh directly and without Eli's help. Eli is a bystander and onlooker (v. 9) as Hannah appeals to Yahweh out of the depths of her anguish. Subtle but unmistakable is the message of the passage that Yahweh has regard for every trusting and faithful person, be that person a priest like Eli, a head of household like Elkanah, or even an oppressed and childless woman like Hannah. Or *especially* an oppressed and childless woman like Hannah. One remembers here the words of Mary in a similar situation: "For he has looked with favor on the lowliness of his servant" (Luke 1:48). The God who answers Hannah's prayer is a God who has a profound and indissoluble bond with those who are relegated to the margins of life. Because of her faith, Hannah knows of this bond and lays claim to it.

But Eli is not *just* an onlooker to this forceful story of the faith of Hannah and of the grace of God. When he finally realizes the true nature of the events that are unfolding before him, Eli confers his blessing (v. 17). It is possible to understand Eli's words either as a promise ("The God of Israel will grant . . .") or as a prayer ("May the God of Israel grant . . ."), in that the Hebrew text will support either translation. Regardless of how she hears the priest's benediction, however, Hannah now finds a peaceful resolution to the fear that possessed her only moments before (v. 18, but see the marginal notations in NRSV).

The narrative is brought to a conclusion in a psychological as well as a theological sense by vs. 19–20. Yahweh grants Hannah's prayer, and Samuel is born. In her joy Hannah does not forget that Yahweh is responsible for this wonderful event, and confers on her son a name that recalls the circumstances of his conception and birth. Although the etymology of the name "Samuel" is not consistent with what is said in v. 20 (one may wish to consult a good critical commentary on 1 Samuel for the details of the problem involved), the point is clear: Yahweh has acted with great compassion toward a poor woman who had no other hope. Samuel is a gift of Yahweh's love.

The community of faith will soon celebrate the birth of another child who, in an even more important sense, was a gift to sinful humankind from a God of compassion and grace.

1 Sam. 2:1–10

This "Psalm selection" is obviously odd, because it settles on a "psalm" outside the book of Psalms. The poem is nonetheless psalmlike, having especially close connections to Ps. 113. The reading of 1 Sam. 1 presents a Hannah who is silent, hopeless, and ungifted. This poem marks a sharp contrast to ch. 1, because now Hannah is gifted with a son, buoyant with hope, and loud in her praise of God. The contrast between the two units may be a study of the way in which the muted are given voice by the generous gift of God.

Hannah speaks in a prayer. Her name is $ḥn$—"grace," or "graced." She is now graced by God with a son (see Ps. 127, Proper 27), which gives to her new voice, new power, new dignity, and new presence. Her initial lines are filled with herself, with first-person references: "my heart... my strength [horn, KJV]..., my God..., my mouth..., my enemies..., my victory." She is now able to claim all that is rightfully hers, no longer remaining mute and invisible. She speaks herself fully, but she speaks herself over to Yahweh in confidence and trust, in unguarded celebration.

Hannah's song of praise begins (after the gathering of herself in v. 1) with an acknowledgment of the incomparability of Yahweh in vs. 2 and 3. This large statement of God's distinctive holiness, without rival, is derived, in this narrative context, from the generous gift of a son in a context of barrenness. God's power for life against the barrenness of death changes everything for her. No other god has such power for life, none! It is this God, only this God, who knows and governs and decides and assesses. There is an enormous temptation in church interpretation, on the basis of Hannah's sweeping claim, to imagine that the church, on this basis, can make imperialistic theological claims. Note, however, that this incomparable God is holy, which means elusively refusing all our efforts to harness God for our purposes or to domesticate God for our agenda. This God is not only unrivaled in power, but unbridled in freedom.

This central portion of the poem (vs. 4–8) now proceeds to detail the characteristic actions of this incomparably holy God. What this God manifestly does is to invert social power, so that the first become last and the last become first. Read in Christian categories, the weakness of this God is stronger than human strength, the foolishness of this God is wiser than human wisdom (see 1 Cor. 1:25). As a consequence of God's inscrutable power to reverse social situations, the mighty and the feeble change lots, the full and the hungry change places, the barren and the fruitful trade destinies. Now, this rhetoric may seem like religious hyperbole—except that in the course of human experience, there are those inexplicable transfers of power and influence on which the weak and poor continue to base their outrageous hope. This text is the prayer of the marginal who continue to affirm that the holiness of Yahweh keeps the human process open for new possibility.

The rhetorical pattern is changed only slightly in vs. 6–7. Now the accent is not only on the inversion, but on the sovereign, singular, decisive authority of Yahweh who works those inversions. (Notice that in vs. 4–5, Yahweh is not mentioned, but only inferred.) It is clear that this is the God of Easter, who administers and embodies the power for life against the threat of death (v. 6). That power has concrete, economic-political manifestation. In v. 8, the nice symmetry of vs. 4–7 is given up. We are now able to see the real concern and agenda of the poem. The speaker is not nearly so interested in God's capacity to do the negative job of sending the full away. Rather the accent is on lifting the poor, raising the needy, and bringing them to well-being. We may suppose that such a raising to power entails displacing and dethroning other powers, but that is left unsaid in this exuberant affirmation.

The concluding verses anticipate harsh social conflict between the faithful and the wicked. It is God who will take sides, to be sure that the social conflict is settled rightly. The faithful may seem to be weaker and less competent, but God is the Great Equalizer, who makes it all come right. Verse 10 is a vigorous assertion that Yahweh is the decisive player in the historical process of power. In this one verse, Yahweh is twice named and once called "the Most High." Yahweh takes the whole of the earth as the arena of sovereignty, and so will dispose of friends and adversaries as God chooses. No wonder Hannah must sing!

In the last part of v. 10, the poem surprises us. Without any notice, Hannah sings of "his king, . . . his anointed." This is odd in context, because no king is even yet on the horizon of Israel in this narrative. The narrator, however, knows what is coming and anticipates. The true subject of the poem is David, who will be Yahweh's real king. The "real king" is this little nobody from Bethlehem, an unnoticed eighth son (1 Sam. 16:1–13)! David is the focus of the narrative to follow, and becomes the carrier of the hopes of all the weak, poor, and marginal.

This "psalm" effects a profound change of subject. In its context, it begins as praise for the birth of the baby in ch. 1. That quite domestic dimension of miracle and joy is transposed through the process of the poem. Eventually the poem becomes a vigorous comment about a public possibility still to come in Israel. The domestic and public aspects of Israel's faith are intertwined. It is the same wonder-working God who governs both and generates new possibilities in every aspect of life.

Hebrews 10:11–14 (15–18) 19–25

The first part of this lection (Heb. 10:11–18) brings to a conclusion the discussion of Christ's priesthood. Psalm 110 again provides an important basis for the author's reflection on Christ's role (v. 12). By contrast with the priests who must stand daily to offer sacrifices for sin, Christ's singular sacrifice enables him to sit at God's right hand, his work completed for all time. The quotation from Jer. 31:33–34 once again interprets Christ's act in light of the promise of a new covenant and the forgiveness of sin.

With the second part of the lection, Hebrews employs this theological treatment of Christ's priesthood and sacrifice as the grounds for exhortation. Verses 19–21 recall the outlines of the indicative, what has been accomplished by the "blood of Jesus." Verses 22–25 consist of three exhortations (hortatory subjunctives), each of which is taken up and developed in the section that begins with 11:1. Taken together, vs. 19–25 are one long sentence, suggesting the close connection between the actions of Jesus and the resulting consequences of those actions for Christian behavior.

In recalling the priesthood of Jesus, the writer appeals to the "confidence" believers have ("since we have confidence to enter the sanctuary," v. 19). The noun "confidence" (translating the Greek word *parrēsia*) refers to the boldness of Christians, a boldness that enables them to act in ways that will seem strange, even incomprehensible, to the outside world. In Acts, the "boldness" of Peter and John stuns the authorities, who know that they are not educated men (4:13; compare also 4:29, 31; 28:31). Paul speaks of proclaiming the gospel with "boldness," by contrast with the veiling of the law (2

Cor. 3:12). In this lection confidence or boldness enables Christians to "enter the sanctuary" of God and provides them with the strength to fulfill the three admonitions of Heb. 11:22–25 (compare 4:16).

The first admonition urges faith, "Let us approach with a true heart in full assurance of faith" (v. 22). This can occur since "our hearts [have been] sprinkled clean from an evil conscience and our bodies washed with pure water." The relationship between these two conditions is worth noting. Hebrews does not explicitly identify purification as a cause of faith, but neither is purification an end in itself. The purification brought about by Christ's sacrifice is a condition to which the response should be the "full assurance of faith." And faith enables believers to make their "approach." Exactly what approach this is remains unspecified, but the context suggests that it cannot be limited to cultic experience alone. Christ's priesthood makes possible an "approach" to God that involves all of life, inside and outside the sanctuary.

The second admonition is the shortest and reflects traditional Jewish and Christian convictions about the reliability of God's sovereign word: "Let us hold fast to the confession of our hope without wavering, for he who has promised is faithful." As elsewhere in the New Testament, for the author of Hebrews "hope" is not the equivalent of merely wishing for something; rather, hope suggests confident expectation about the future. Precisely because God has already fulfilled promises (6:13–15; 8:6–7; 11:11), God may be relied on to fulfill those promises that remain. For similar reasons, the long recitation of the faithful deeds of the "cloud of witnesses" results in the call to perseverance (12:1–2). The past serves as the basis for hopeful action in the future.

The most lengthy of the admonitions comes last (vs. 24–25). Initially, the notion of Christians "provoking" one another to "love and good deeds" may sound odd, as if Christians are being enjoined to manipulative behavior. Probably what the author intends is that believers should act in ways that become enticing for others, something like Paul's (presumably exaggerated) comment that the Thessalonians became such an example that Paul had no need to preach (1 Thess. 1:7–10). The sheer insight into human behavior here is impressive; both authors recognize the value of the living model through whom instruction comes indirectly.

The one "good deed" singled out in this exhortation may seem painfully contemporary: "not neglecting to meet together, as is the habit of some." Although it is notoriously difficult to reconstruct the situation of the community addressed in Hebrews, here surely a specific problem comes into view. "Some" are absenting themselves from the gatherings of the community for worship and instruction. The placement of this comment in a section that introduces general exhortations suggests that, for the author, the gathering of the community is a vital aspect of faithful existence and not to be taken lightly.

Finally, Christians are to encourage "one another, and all the more as you see the Day approaching." As often in the New Testament, exhortation and eschatology stand hand in hand. The section that follows reminds readers of the judgment that accompanies this "Day" and warns against moral laxity. The forgiveness acquired through Christ's sacrifice does not license believers to moral indifference but, on the contrary, enables them to act with confidence.

Mark 13:1-8

Commentators often note that Mark has two endings. One is found in chs. 14–16, including the story of Jesus' rejection, crucifixion, and resurrection. The other is ch. 13, which talks about a period beyond Jesus' resurrection—about the destruction of the Temple and the coming of the Son of Man. One selection from Mark 13 appears in the lectionary cycle as the Gospel reading for the First Sunday of Advent, while today's reading provides another opportunity to consider this chapter so pivotal to the interpretation of the Gospel.

One word about the chapter as a whole. The passage is replete with apocalyptic images and language, in concert with previous Jewish writings of the same genre. Yet it is helpful to read the chapter not so much as a predictive message about the future, but as a word addressing the issues pressing the Markan community at the time of writing. The events depicted in the chapter do not come out of the crystal ball of a divine soothsayer, but are the stuff of the community's everyday life. The violence of war, the impending (if not already completed) destruction of the Temple, the perilous existence of the church under persecution, the enticing voices of false prophets and false messiahs were urgent concerns for the Christian community, and Mark 13 speaks directly to them.

The initial words of Jesus announcing the demolition of the Temple and its surroundings take on a dramatic flavor in that they are prompted by the comment of one disciple about the grandeur of the buildings. Then the change of venue to the Mount of Olives "opposite the temple" and a narrowing of the audience to the inner four disciples precipitate a broadening of the discussion beyond the matter of the Temple to include "all these things," that is, the situation of the Markan community and its future.

In the first section of the chapter (13:1–8), three clear notes are sounded. First, the community will be forced to develop a spirit of discernment. In the midst of opposition from without, there is also the threat from within, from voices that speak "in my name" but seek to lead members of the community astray. The language of vs. 5–6 seems to reflect Deut. 13, where warnings are given to Israel regarding false prophets, who seductively and secretly tempt people to follow other gods. Those warnings take on an ominous quality by noting that the tempters may be members of one's own family, even "the wife you embrace, or your most intimate friend" (Deut. 13:6).

The modern church knows aplenty about voices that talk a good game, use many of the right formulas, but at heart worship at a different altar. There are those who offer a crossless religion, a Christianity without tears; other who wed the faith to the nation and demand a patriotic ideology; still others who are advocates of religion's utilitarian functions—arguing the importance of prayer as an effective means of self-enhancement.

The text provides no criteria for distinguishing the false voices from the true voices, no litmus test to determine authenticity. Rather, the mention of the false prophets alerts the church not to be gullible, not to be taken in by every pious voice that has a new idea. The church is to listen carefully and to think clearly, and in so doing to nurture a spirit of discernment.

Second, the church's precarious situation demands of it incredible patience. Believers are not to get excited about this or that event, this or that voice, and assume that it portends the final coming of the kingdom. Instead of becoming frantically alarmist, the church is to take the long look, to be patient.

It has often been the temptation of an active church to assume that the eradication of the most pressing evil or the achievement of the most immediate goal will somehow usher in the reign of God. Success then brings with it a certain disillusionment, because there remain so many more evils to eradicate, so many more goals to achieve. The text indicates, however, that the calendar is in God's hands, and that neither omens nor accomplishments guarantee the ultimate fulfillment of God's purposes. What is called for is patience.

Third, in spite of all that transpires, the church is invited to be hopeful. Wars, threats of wars, earthquakes, famines represent the worldly chaos in which the Markan community finds itself. The woes may be changed, but any church that remains faithful is bound to find itself beleaguered and vulnerable. There will be little objective data to warrant optimism about the future.

And yet all this chaos is understood to be "the beginning of the birthpangs" (13:8). The image is striking. It takes seriously the reality of the present sufferings. There is no Pollyanna denial of pain. But in the economy of God the sufferings have a purpose. They signal the end of a long time of waiting and the coming birth of new life. The sufferings do not lead to despair, but to hope, to the anticipated dawn of God's new day.

CHRIST THE KING OR REIGN OF CHRIST

Proper 29
Ordinary Time 34

*Sunday between
November 20 and 26 inclusive*

Power. The word itself conjures up an almost endless array of images: military armaments, personal charisma, political might, physical force, social influence, thermonuclear energy, freakish events of nature. For those outside the circles of power, moving inside seems the key to success and happiness, but gaining power almost always means learning the limits of that power. Politicians discover the powers teamed up against even (or perhaps especially) their best plans. Parents find that their control over their children is not what they had anticipated. Even the power to bring about good is subject to corruption.

Few weeks in the lectionary can offer the opportunity this one does for reflection on the nature of power *and* of powerlessness. Second Samuel 23:1–7 celebrates the "everlasting covenant" with David's house, and the season of Advent will celebrate God's fulfillment of that covenant with all people. The passage also clearly identifies David's power as derived power. David has power as the one whom "God exalted," the "anointed of the God of Jacob, the favorite of the Strong One of Israel" (23:1). David's power comes to him as sheer gift, and his power depends entirely on God's sustaining that gift.

Psalm 132 makes explicit the derivative and contingent character of David's power. "If your sons keep my covenant" (v. 12), they will occupy the Davidic throne forever. Despite the achievements of David and the blessings bestowed on him, "his" power does not belong to him, but to the God who establishes him on the throne.

The titles ascribed to God and to Jesus in Rev. 1:4b–8 strongly reinforce the nature of God's power. If David and his colleagues are kings, Jesus is "the ruler of the kings of the earth" (v. 5). Even those who put Jesus to death, those who acted with power, will eventually learn that their power has been utterly overturned (v. 7). Only the one who stands at the beginning and the end holds real power (v. 8).

Although the scene from Jesus' trial before Pilate may seem strangely out of place just before Advent, the confrontation there between the world's understanding of Pilate and that of Jesus admirably completes this series of texts. Pilate, who thinks he has power, in fact has little, and the power he does have (to put Jesus to death) will be overturned. Jesus, who appears utterly powerless, is the only one who knows where power comes from and what it means.

2 Samuel 23:1–7

The Old Testament lesson for the last Sunday of the liturgical year anticipates the celebration of Advent and Christmas in that it commemorates God's covenant with the house of David and looks forward to the final and eternal reign of God. The text, which represents itself as "the last words of David" (2 Sam. 23:1), is a psalm that echoes certain themes found in the canonical Psalter (compare Pss. 72; 132), as well as in other parts of the Hebrew Bible (2 Sam. 7:1–17).

Clearly, one of the realities that the author of this poem wished to emphasize is the person of David and the perpetual legitimacy of the Davidic dynasty. (Critical commentaries on 2 Samuel may be consulted for the reasons why some scholars feel that the author of this passage is not to be identified as David himself.) The introduction (v. 1) contains four epithets that mark David as being distinctive:

> son of Jesse,
> the man whom God exalted,
> the anointed of the God of Jacob,
> the favorite of the Strong One of Israel.

Furthermore, David is the one through whom the spirit of Yahweh speaks (v. 2; compare Isa. 61:1–2). He is "like the light of morning," like "the sun rising . . . gleaming" (v. 4). In these latter phrases the combination of images relating to truth and light are especially appropriate for the coming celebration of Advent and Christmastide. The ultimate Davidic king, Jesus Christ, to an even greater extent than the original Davidic king, is the one who dispels darkness by the illumination of God's word (John 1:5).

Yet truth does not stand as an abstraction here, for it is closely linked to Yahweh's justice. At the heart of the theology of the Davidic covenant was the understanding that the individual who sat on Jerusalem's throne would ensure the well-being of all individuals within the kingdom. It was the role of the Davidic monarch to

> judge your [Yahweh's] people with righteousness,
>> and your poor with justice.
>>> (Ps. 72:2)

"The weak and the needy" come in for special consideration (Ps. 72:13) and the Davidic ruler has not lived up to the calling of his office until he has secured their safety.

It is not surprising, then, that in the midst of the language that elevates the figure of David and portrays him as the bringer of truth and light, our poem remembers David as

> one who rules over people justly,
>> ruling in the fear of God.
>>> (2 Sam. 23:3)

The human instrument by which the just rule of God is made evident in the lives of men and women is the Davidic king.

The justice of the Davidic king may be immediate and temporal, and it is certainly in this manner that many Old Testament passages conceive of the issue. Solomon's role as judge, for example, is remembered not only with respect to his wisdom in individual cases (1 Kings 3:16–28), but also in the construction of a special Hall of Justice (1 Kings 7:7). But the end of the church's year and the anticipation of Advent is also an occasion to think beyond the moment and to remember God's promise of an eternal kingdom inaugurated by a second advent of the Davidic king Jesus Christ. In this context our poem speaks of the "everlasting covenant" with David, "ordered . . . and secure" (v. 5) for all time. The passage goes on to describe, in metaphoric language, the ultimate overthrow of evil in all its forms (vs. 6–7).

The end of the church's year may, on one level, remind one of the cyclical nature of the seasons and of much of human life. Qoheleth ("the Teacher"), like many others, was impressed with the fact that all that goes around comes around.

> Round and round goes the wind,
>> and on its circuits the wind returns.
>> . . . .
> What has been is what will be,
>> and what has been done is what will be done;
>> there is nothing new under the sun.
>>> (Eccl. 1:6, 9)

In a sense the end of the Pentecost/Trinity season is confirmation of the circular quality of much within human experience. Like the path of the sun, whose course determines the tides of life, that which rose some weeks ago is now declining to its end, only to be revived again some weeks hence.

However, Advent looms ahead to contradict the notion that human existence is endlessly cyclical. Although embedded within a framework that is little more than a revolving wheel, Advent and its annual recurrences boldly announce that God has broken humankind's slavery to the wheel of sin and that, finally and in God's own time, the second advent of the Son of David will usher in an eternal kingdom of justice, truth, and light. Like fish in a stream, who know little of what lies beyond the water's edge, we who are confined to the world of injustice and sin can little imagine the nature of the reign of God's anointed one. And because of our limitations we are forced to use the elements of our transient life to symbolize the realities that lie beyond. Thus the seasons of the church year, which come and go and come again, are but poor emblems for the realities of God, which neither come nor go, but simply are. Justice, truth, and light. These qualities characterized the first advent and will determine the character of the second advent, whenever it may occur. We may be assured concerning that, because he who will come has already come. We have met him and we know the nature of his kingdom, a kingdom that is and that is yet to be.

Psalm 132:1-12 (13-18)

This psalm, one of the "royal psalms," concerns the role of David in moving the ark of Yahweh into the city of Jerusalem. The narrative of 2 Sam. 6 suggests that this was an historical event, wrought by David with much pious pageantry. It is equally plausible, however, that the movement of the ark was a regular, repeated event in Israel's liturgical calendar. The retrieval of the ark is a dramatic way of establishing and asserting the "real presence" of God in the shrine of Jerusalem. A second derivative reality also operates in the movement of the ark. Because the king is caretaker, custodian, and champion of the ark in the shrine, the ark is inevitably linked to the dynasty of David, and serves willy-nilly to help legitimate that dynasty.

Psalm 132:1-5 asserts the remarkable piety of David. According to this text, David pledged his utter devotion to Yahweh, such devotion that David made it a primary pledge of his monarchy that he would remain unsatisfied until Yahweh's ark was adequately housed. It may be that this sentiment refers to David's statement in 2 Sam. 7:2, but that resolve on David's part is much less than is reported here. Thus the statement of David is not to be assessed historically, but as a liturgical enactment of the resolve of the dynasty. The statement helps to show that the dynasty was passionately concerned for Yahweh. Whether authentic or not, such piety is no doubt politically useful.

Verses 6 and 7 of Ps. 132 purport to add a historical note, but the locus of the ark here may be only liturgical (see 1 Sam. 7:1–2; 2 Sam. 6:1–15). The ark as "dwelling place" and "footstool" is taken to be the throne on which the invisible God sits. The ark is indeed a vehicle for "real presence."

Now the God who sits on the ark is addressed directly (Ps. 132:8–10). (See Num. 10:35–36 for a like pointed address to the ark.) The God of the ark is addressed, seeking authorization for the recognition of priests who will be legitimated to supervise the shrine. Thus the reiteration of the oath of David serves to legitimate the priesthood, which is in fact a tool of the king. (See the Epistle reading concerning another priestly authorization.) The address to the ark and the request for a priest, however, are for "David's sake" (Ps. 132:10). Thus it is recognized that priestly authorization was a gesture useful for the king.

The Davidic agenda in Psalm 132, hinted at in vs. 1–5 and vs. 8–10, now becomes explicit in vs. 11 and 12. In v. 2, David has made an oath to Yahweh; now Yahweh makes a corresponding oath to David. This oath appears to be an alternative rendering of the great promise of 2 Sam. 7:11–16, also reiterated in Ps. 89:28–37. Only here, the promise is made conditional, as it is not in 2 Sam. 7: "If your sons keep my covenant . . . . " One can see by comparing this version of the promise to the other renditions that there are powerful political interests at work in establishing a right version of the promise. By making the monarchy conditional on Torah obedience, this version completely undermines the monarchic claim of a guaranteed (ontological?) future, and subordinates the king to the Torah. In the end then, the king has no special, privileged promise from God, but is like every other Israelite, subject to the Torah requirements and vulnerable to Torah sanctions of blessing and curse. Thus monarchy is thereby emptied of its theological pretension and seen to be only a provisional political arrangement.

Having considerably minimized the claims of the monarchy,

Psalm 132 now proceeds to make its primary positive point in vs. 13–18, that Yahweh has indeed chosen Zion as a normative habitat. It is conventional to lump together the Temple claim and the royal claim; in practice they no doubt reinforce each other. Here, however, at least in theory, monarchy is diminished in theological significance, and Temple (= ark) is elevated in importance.

Beginning at v. 14, the remainder of the psalm is a decree in the mouth of God, who sits on the ark. Yahweh affirms that Zion is a chosen, enduring place of presence. Zion, where the ark and Yahweh dwell, will be a place of special blessing and prosperity. Note well, precise reference is made to bread for the poor (v. 15). Zion will be a place of faithful, effective, joyous priests (v. 16). Thus a full liturgical apparatus is founded and authorized. In the end, the Davidic claim cannot be nullified, and it is here reasserted (vs. 17–18).

This is an odd text, and one is left unsure of its intention. Paired as is with other readings, we may note some pertinent accent points: (1) Full, real presence in worship is affirmed. (2) That full, real presence requires an authorized priesthood, on which see the Epistle reading. (3) The Temple presence is oddly in tension with political interests and ambitions. Those political ambitions are acknowledged, toned down, and then finally affirmed. One can see the Gospel reading as an overlay of this tension, for the kingship is always "of this world/not of this world." (4) Whereas the presence is assured, the political apparatus attached to it is more precarious. Even in such a self-conscious text, it is recognized that religious reality does not easily match up with political legitimacy. Finally, after *presence*, it is *Torah* obedience that makes political authority viable.

Revelation 1:4b–8

By the end of the first century of the Christian era, the letter had established itself as an authoritative vehicle for instruction within the Christian church. Not only the heirs of Paul, but Ignatius and Polycarp, among others, chose the letter form through which to communicate their interpretations of the faith. The influence of that form appears even in Revelation, a writing that largely consists of visions. Both in the letters to the seven churches (chs. 2–3) and in its overall framework, the writer of Revelation adopts the letter structure.

This particular passage comes from the formal introduction to the letter and announces some of the key issues of the text as a whole (for the closing of the letter, see 22:21). Chapter 1:4a, which falls outside the limits of the lection, contains a brief identification of writer and addressee. The lection proper consists of the greeting (vs. 4b–5) and the doxology (vs. 5b–6), followed by two separate prophetic statements (vs. 7 and 8).

One notable feature of the passage is its lengthy descriptions of God and of Jesus. Verse 4 describes God as the one "who is and who was and who is to come." The passage concludes with an even more extended description of God as "the Alpha and the Omega," "who is and who was and who is to come, the Almighty." Although Jesus is also described extensively, there the language tends to be more functional in nature, depicting Jesus' work: "the faithful witness, the firstborn of the dead, and the ruler of the kings of the earth." Jesus is also "him who loves us and freed us from our sins by his blood, and made us to be a kingdom." In both cases, but especially in the compilation of titles for God, what these descriptions reflect is the tendency in the ancient world to heap up titles for deities or for significant individuals.

The writer of Revelation makes use of titles for God that would have been familiar from a variety of sources. The God "who is and who was and who is to come," of course, recalls Ex. 3:14. For ancient readers, it could also have recalled the oracle at Dodona addressed to Zeus: "Zeus was, Zeus is, Zeus shall be; O mighty Zeus." Both statements depict the existence of the deity in past, present, and future, and both claim prophetic powers for the deity. Identifying God as "the Alpha and the Omega" probably reflects Hellenistic magical convictions about the properties of the Greek vowels. "Says the Lord God," by contrast, is a prophetic formula reflective of the Hebrew Bible (see, for example, Ezek. 6:3; 7:2). In other words, the author of Revelation not only heaps up titles for God but draws them from a wide range of sources in an effort to ground the narrative that follows in concepts of God that had currency for his audience, thereby increasing its authority.

These lengthy descriptions of God and of Jesus also serve to introduce some themes that are important for the work as a whole. One of these is the necessity of the church's faithful witness. Here, as in Rev. 3:14, Jesus Christ provides the premier model because he is "the faithful witness." Later in Revelation, that faithfulness is praised in the figure of Antipas (2:13), and reward is promised for all those who remain faithful (17:14). The book ends with promises that its own words may be regarded as faithful ("trustworthy" in the NRSV, 21:5; 22:6).

Another of the themes introduced here is the crucial apocalyptic notion of the return of Jesus. The prophetic utterance of v. 7 combines elements of Dan. 7:13 ("coming with the clouds of heaven") and Zech. 12:10 ("when they look on the one whom they have pierced"). Although Matt. 24:30 likewise combines elements of those two passages, the present passage startles with its graphic depiction of what it means that "every eye" will see Jesus' return. "Even those who pierced him," like much in this book, reminds readers that "every eye" includes some for whom the Parousia must mean the terrible unveiling of their own twisted judgment.

That "all the tribes of the earth will wail" reinforces the motif of judgment, but it also introduces a powerful ambiguity. Does the "wailing" of all people "on his account" come about because they recognize their guilty involvement in Jesus' death, or does it result from their own loss of life and of power? Zechariah 12:10 clearly refers to mourning over the one "whom they have pierced," for the passage continues: "they shall mourn for him, as one mourns for an only child, and weep bitterly over him, as one weeps over a firstborn." On the other hand, Revelation later on narrates in some detail the inappropriate grief of those whose lives were intertwined with Babylon (for example, ch. 18). Perhaps the wailing anticipated in 1:7 includes both of these forms of grief, the grief of those who recognize their own culpability and of those who persist in misunderstanding who truly possesses power and might.

For the Christian community, of course, the author of Revelation offers a message of hope, and this too appears already in the opening lines of the work. The brief statement, "So it is to be. Amen" at the end of the first prophetic utterance (1:7) quietly but firmly asserts that the church's hope derives from its utter confidence that Jesus will indeed return. The God "who is and who was and who is to come" may be relied on, whatever the fears and shortcomings of the human community.

John 18:33-37

There are few stories in the whole of the Bible told with such finesse and power as John's narration of Jesus before Pilate. The drama begins at John 18:28 and continues through 19:16, with an epilogue at 19:19-22. The passage for this Sunday (18:33-37) occurs as one scene in this intriguing interchange, which includes not only Jesus and Pilate but also the religious authorities. The broader narrative is often cited in literary studies as an example of the effective use of dramatic irony.

The narrative is structured by the physical movement of Pilate back and forth from inside his headquarters of Jerusalem, where Jesus is held, to the religious authorities standing outside the building (18:28–29, 33, 38b; 19:4, 9, 13). The reader is let in on the irony of this structure in 18:28, when the narrator explains that the religious authorities did not want to enter Pilate's headquarters so as to avoid ritual defilement, since the Passover was near. So religious and pious are these leaders who are scheming to do away with God's agent in creation, the Messiah, the King of Israel! The scene reported in 18:33–38a occurs inside the headquarters and thus relates a conversation between Jesus and Pilate, but the religious leaders bringing charges against Jesus are only a step away.

There are at least three directions in which the preacher could move in a sermon on this passage. First, ignoring the limits imposed by the lectionary, one could focus on the broader drama, and particularly the role of Pilate. Pilate typifies that person or institution confronted with a critical decision who has instincts in one direction but is pressured by the circumstances to move reluctantly in the opposite direction. This emerges in the assigned passage when Pilate responds to Jesus with the unusual question: "I am not a Jew, am I?" (18:35). At one level, the obvious answer is "Of course not." But at another level, Pilate is beginning to implicate himself in the cause of the Jews, and before the trial is over will have ended up on their side.

Pilate begins the trial as the judge, the figure with authority, and even late in the drama still thinks he retains such power ("Do you not know that I have power to release you, and power to crucify you?" 19:10). But increasingly the religious leaders rob him of his power and box him into a corner, so that he yields to their power (19:16). All the while, the reader is aware that the real judge, the one with ultimate power, is the prisoner, Jesus. Pilate, like most power brokers, lives in a world of illusion of power and is mocked by his ultimate lack of power.

The second direction in which the preacher could move with this passage is to focus on Jesus as the King of the Jews. The title looms as the primary category for Jesus in John's Passion narrative. "Are you the King of Jews?" Pilate asks (18:33). Jesus' reply is actually a question, intended not so much to seek information from Pilate as to confront him with his own commitments ("Who do others say that I am?" "Who do you say that I am?"; see 18:34; compare Matt. 16:13–15). The chief priests are later faced with the same choice and reply, "We have no king but the emperor" (19:15).

The soldiers carry out an actual ceremony of coronation for King Jesus (no mention in John of mocking or pretense) in 19:2–5. And following the crucifixion, Pilate insists that the inscription put on the cross cannot be removed or changed (19:19-22).

The category of king may seem remote to most contemporary congregations, and yet as a political term it retains amazing relevance. So often the issues that demand decisions of people and communities are political in nature, and in the final analysis boil down to the choice between Jesus and Caesar.

The third direction in which the preacher could move is to concentrate on Jesus' words about the nature of his rule (18:36-37). The claim that "my kingdom is not from this world" is not to imply that Jesus and his followers have no role to play in human affairs, in the struggle for justice and peace. Instead the claim distinguishes Jesus' rule from the various forms of power that mark most earthly institutions. Domination, violence, and economic exploitation are common (and some would say even necessary) weapons of maintaining power. Jesus' power obviously derives from a different source.

Jesus wants to talk about "truth," an utterly strange topic to Pilate (and to most imperial figures). He operates in a carefully maintained world of illusion, and the presence of one whose mission is to strip away the illusions and point to what is really real poses an enormous threat. "Dis-illusionment" is precisely what Pilate needs if he is to be set on the road to truth, but it is what he fears the most.

Truth is always threatening, and particularly so when the one in our midst is the way, the truth, and the life (14:6). His very presence calls into question the many erroneous perceptions on which our worlds are constructed. At the same time, he is the Life-giver, and he gives it abundantly.

All Saints

*November 1 or the
first Sunday in November*

With the celebration of All Saints, the church looks backward to recall with gratitude the lives of its predecessors in the faith. Both distant forebears and those whose lives remain painfully close come to mind as believers reflect on the past. The lectionary readings for this Sunday interpret this remembrance squarely in the context of God's future, however, converting recollection into hope.

These texts anticipate God's future in terms that are cosmic at the same time that they are intensely concrete and personal. Isaiah 25:6–9 imagines a scene out of *Babette's Feast*, with the God of creation spreading a table for all people. Very real requirements of food and drink provide a way of assuring people that God's future includes care for even their most basic needs. Both Isaiah and the writer of Revelation look forward to the end of human grief, and envision God as the comforter who will bring an end to tears, even an end to death itself. For all who experience the pain of grief and loss, this promise looms unbearably large.

As magnificent as they are, these concrete and personal aspects of God's future are only symptoms of that true future, a salvation that is characterized by the dwelling of God with God's own people and in God's new city (Rev. 21:1–4). It is because God will live among humankind that God will feed and comfort. Read in this context, the psalm assigned for this Sunday interprets that final victory in light of God's role as creator. The one who established the earth over against the chaos of the seas (Ps. 24:1–2) can be counted on to redeem that earth.

As marvelous as it is to contemplate, even solid confidence in God's future does not diminish the sense that these promises remain distant. When will come an end to the pain of hunger and the grief of loneliness? Biblical writers wisely refrain from answering such questions, aware that the answers can come only from the One who holds that future. Jesus' raising of Lazarus, however, like Jesus' own resurrection, reminds Christians that the future breaks through even in the present. This specific act of healing not only turns the grief of Mary and Martha into joy; it also signals God's power even over death itself. God's future is close at hand.

Isaiah 25:6–9

That God has a gracious and happy future in store for the people of faith is an axiom explored by various biblical writers, each of whom provides his or her own special nuances to this near-universal theme. The present text, contained in the so-called Isaiah apocalypse (Isa. 24–27), is prodigious in its joy, abandoning any cause for caution or doubt on the part of the Lord's people concerning the shape of their ultimate tomorrow. Indeed, this text goes beyond many of the same genre in that it makes no distinction between those in Israel who have been faithful to Yahweh and all of humankind. *All* peoples will participate in the banquet of the kingdom of God, a time when all sorrow and death will be decisively overruled.

Mount Zion, the site of Solomon's Temple and, subsequently, the Temple of Zerubbabel, earned a place in the thought of the Old Testament as the special venue of the divine-human encounter. To be sure, the Deuteronomistic historians record Solomon's prayer that not even "this house that I have built" (1 Kings 8:27) can contain the living God, and Ezekiel declared the liberating message to the Jewish exiles in Babylon that Yahweh was not confined in the far-off Jerusalem Temple (Ezek. 10:18–22). Nevertheless, Zion was *the place* above all others where Yahweh graciously met the people (note Pss. 15; 24), and thus it is not surprising that in much postexilic literature Zion is that spot on which is focused the Jews' deepest eschatological hopes (compare Joel 3:17). Isaiah 25:6–9 affirms those hopes and agrees on the role of Zion in the coming rule of God.

Verse 6 "sets the table," as it were, for this eschatological banquet, this "feast" that is to usher in the reign of Yahweh. Notice that each of the three phrases that describe the delectable food is repeated, as if to emphasize the extravagant and sumptuous nature of the festival: "feast," "rich food," "well-aged wines."

The only hint of judgment in the passage appears in v. 7, in which it is affirmed that "the shroud" (literally, "the wrapping") and "the sheet" (literally, "that which is woven") that cover "all peoples/all nations" will be destroyed by Yahweh. The symbolism here is not entirely clear, but the textiles appear to be emblematic of mourning, perhaps over the reality of human sin or over the previous absence—

or apparent absence—of Yahweh from the life of the people. But the cause for mourning has now been banished, for Yahweh is present and Yahweh has "swallowed up death [and sin] forever." Incidentally, the phrase "all peoples," which appears in vs. 6 and 7 (compare "his people" in v. 8), may, when standing alone, mean either "all Israel" or "all humankind." But the parallel "all nations" in v. 7 clearly signals that the focus of this passage is not just on Israel, but on all men and women everywhere. Thus that which is judged and abolished is sin and death, and that which is affirmed and given new life is the entire human race.

Sorrow is exiled, according to v. 8, and the affirmation is here repeated that the sinfulness ("disgrace") of men and women has been destroyed. "For the Lord has spoken" is a favorite phrase among the prophets to remind the reader (or hearer) of the text that it is, indeed, a word from the living God.

Isaiah 25:9 recalls other prophets who, at least as early as the time of Amos (Amos 5:18–20), ominously warned of an impending "day of Yahweh" when the earth would be laid waste and human sinfulness punished. "That day" is indeed coming, declares our prophet, but it is not a time to fear. Contrary to what some have said, "that day" will be an occasion when the long-awaited appearance of God will take place and, since it is the nature of this God to save, "that day" will be a time of gladness and great joy. (Compare Jer. 31:31–34 for a similar portrayal of the day [or days] of Yahweh.) The entire Isaiah passage is rounded out by 25:10a, which reaches back to v. 6 and reaffirms that it is "on this mountain" that these joyful events will transpire. (Verse 10a is not a part of the lectionary text. However, NRSV reflects the text of the Hebrew Bible by grouping this line with vs. 6–9; thus anyone preaching from this text may wish to do the same.)

As stated above, many texts within both Old and New Testaments declare the ultimate redemption of faithful persons and the joyful inauguration of the reign of God. But Isa. 25:6–9 carries the proclamation of salvation one daring step farther. Not just a faithful remnant will be saved. Not just Israel will be saved. "All peoples," "all nations" will be delivered. God will banish sorrow from "all faces." Sin and death will be exiled from "all the earth." (This persistent use of "all" is a drumbeat which the reader simply cannot ignore.)

How is it that all humankind will be ultimately reclaimed by a just and compassionate God? The text does not answer that question. In fact, it does not even bother to raise it. Perhaps implicit in the prophet's thought is the realization that the God who made creation good in the first place has the power and desire to restore it to goodness in the end.

Psalm 24

For a full exposition of this psalm, see Proper 10. In relation to the other readings in this day's lections, Ps. 24 is understood to be a great hymn celebrating the victory and full established sovereignty of Yahweh. This is indeed "the king of glory" before whom all other powers must yield.

The readings in Isa. 25 and Rev. 21 bespeak God's ultimate triumph over all powers of evil and death, when there will be no more pain or tears. The alternate reading in the Wisdom of Solomon turns the matter especially to consolation for the dead, and the Gospel reading links God's triumph concretely to the death and raising of Lazarus.

On All Saints' Day, it is proper that God's victory over evil and death should be related to the death of our loved ones. It is equally important, however, that God's great victory should not be too tightly linked to our sense of grief and loss. For on this day we remember not only our loved ones. We also treasure the saints of the church who have suffered and died in their resistance to the power of evil, and who were destroyed by the power of evil. Thus much more largely, the texts of this day, Ps. 24 among them, celebrate God's cosmic victory over all deathliness. This victory offers to us not only comfort in loss, but freedom and courage in the face of the continued, blatant threat of evil that takes daily, concrete form in our midst. The psalm offers not only consolation in death, but courage for faithful living in the face of deathly powers.

Revelation 21:1–6a

Many who know well the landscape of scripture still experience Revelation as a foreign territory, even a wilderness, of wild events, unfamiliar imagery, and bewildering characters. Particularly the visions, which constitute the bulk of the narrative, offer travelers little rest or comfort. Novices who seek guidance from more experienced travelers find little help between the extreme positions of those who interpret each and every line in terms of some latter-day event and those who would simply ignore the text altogether. Finally, the vision of ch. 21 appears, and with it comes familiar language that is welcome to the weary navigator: the new Jerusalem, the dwelling of God with God's people, the end of death and grief. The sense of the familiar is ironic, of course; while the language and the promises are familiar, this new creation is no less a promise yet to be fulfilled than it was when written in the late first century.

The landscape of the vision is cosmic in scope. It requires first the passing away of all things. Other New Testament texts anticipate the end of heaven and earth (Matt. 5:18; 2 Peter 3:10–13), but nowhere as graphically as here. Already in Rev. 20:11 the presence of one on "a great white throne" prompts the report that "the earth and the heaven fled from his presence, and no place was found for them." This picture of heaven and earth running away from the divine presence dramatically conveys both the manifest power of God and the helpless state to which other "powers" have been reduced. The importance of this new situation requires its repetition in 21:1 and 4. Heaven and earth not only search for a new resting place; they have simply "passed away."

Chapter 21:1 adds the comment that "the sea was no more," a comment that seems strangely superfluous. If "the first heaven and the first earth" passed away, would that disappearance not involve the sea also? Specific inclusion of the sea signals the triumph of God over chaos. As in ancient literature generally, in the New Testament also the sea represents the chaos over which human beings have no control (13:1–2; see also Matt. 8:23–27; Acts 27:13–41).

After the demise of "the first heaven and the first earth," and even of chaos itself, God makes "all things new." Using the language of Isaiah (65:17; 66:22), the author introduces God's action of renewal, which includes three aspects: location (the new Jerusalem), the presence of God, and the demise of death itself. The new Jerusalem has been promised already in 3:12, and is portrayed in all its amazing splendor in the remainder of the chapter (see also Ezek. 48:30–35). It contrasts in every way with the depiction of Babylon, and the certainty of this new place offers believers hope that they will come to have a place as well.

Despite the vision's celebration of this new location, it only provides a backdrop for the central promise of the vision: "See, the home of God is among mortals." The oracle of v. 3 powerfully replays the ancient promise that God will dwell alongside God's people (Lev. 26:12; Ezek. 37:27; John 1:14; 2 Cor. 6:16). Literally, the verse may be translated as follows: "Behold, the tabernacle of God with the people, and God tabernacles with them." Over against massive evidence that the world has strayed so far from God that nothing can redeem it, and even over against the author's own convictions about the disasters that inevitably lie ahead, he emphatically asserts the validity of the promise that God will "dwell with them as their God."

One result of God's making a "home" with humankind is the promise that God "will wipe every tear from their eyes. Death will be no more; mourning and crying and pain will be no more" (Rev. 21:4; see also 7:17; Isa. 25:8; 35:10; 51:11; 65:19; Jer. 31:16). The verse ends by reiterating the opening of the lection ("for the first things have passed away"), suggesting that this part of the vision also is to be understood cosmically. That is, among the "first things" that are to disappear are "mourning and crying and pain." Like Paul's apocalyptic vision in 1 Corinthians, this one involves the death of death itself (1 Cor. 15:54–57).

Does this cosmic context suggest that a pastoral interpretation of these words, such as is implicit when they are read in memorial services, is inappropriate? Certainly not. If much of the narrative of Revelation lies far beyond the experience, even beyond the imaginations, of many Christians, these lines are painfully accessible. The promise that God's future will include an end to grief is a promise Christians can understand and by which they can be sustained. Here the vision comes to the doorstep. That, of course, is one of the primary goals of this mystifying text: to offer comfort and strength to those in desperate need.

The passage concludes with words that reiterate the central thrust of all of Revelation. God stands at the beginning and at the end, not simply of human lives, but of history, of creation itself (21:6a). As creator of that life, God holds all of it responsible and will demand an accounting (vs. 6b–8).

John 11:32–44

One of the problems the preacher faces when preaching from the wonderful narratives of John's Gospel is that they tend to be long. They stretch to the very limit the congregation's ability to stick with the reading of the lesson. Yet the narratives have an integrity about them that makes it difficult to slice them into smaller pieces for a shorter reading. The pieces apart from the larger story do not make good sense. Some device, such as a quick retelling of the whole story, is almost always necessary to provide continuity and context.

This is certainly true with the narrative of the raising of Lazarus. Jesus' love for the three who lived at Bethany, his refusal to come when Lazarus was sick, his waiting until Lazarus dies, his statement ahead of time that he intends to raise Lazarus, the initial encounter with Martha (which in many regards is reproduced in the second encounter with Mary), the statement that Jesus is the resurrection and the life, Martha's confession of faith, the presence of the mourners—all these are important features of the story leading to the actual raising of Lazarus, which is the focal point of today's lesson (John 11:32-44). The preacher cannot assume the congregation is abreast of all these details without relating them.

The story occupies a strategic place in the structure of John's Gospel. It is the last of the signs Jesus performs during his public ministry, and is the event that triggers the plot to crucify him (11:55-57; 12:9-11). Furthermore, the incident brings to a climax one of the major motifs of the Gospel, namely, that Jesus is the bringer of life.

In looking at 11:32-44 in light of the larger narrative, three features of the story stand out. First, there is no muting the stark reality of death. Martha's horror at Jesus' command to roll back the stone from the tomb reminds us that the spiced but unembalmed body was beginning to decay (v. 39). Mary weeps; the mourners weep. The naturalness of grief is everywhere evident.

We are also twice told that Jesus "was greatly disturbed in spirit and deeply moved" (vs. 33, 38), and that when he saw the tomb he too "began to weep" (v. 35). What are we to make of this rather unusual (for John at least) emotional Jesus? The references have intrigued the commentators, who offer a wide variety of explanations. Are they expressions of Jesus' humanity? his identification with the grief of Martha and Mary? his anger at the weeping and wailing of the mourners? his indignation at the yet unbridled power of death? When the interpreter thinks in terms of the effect of the references in the story, then any or all of these explanations are possible. At the very least, Jesus does not remain calm and serene as one unmoved and detached from the human scene. He is deeply disturbed at death's devastating force—something he finally overcomes only through his own death.

The second critical feature of the story is Jesus himself as the bringer of resurrection and life. When Jesus comes with Martha to the tomb, the readers have been prepared ahead of time for what will happen, and yet the scene is still dramatic and startling. Like Martha, we have no capacity to imagine what takes place, no prior experience with which to identify the event—Jesus' prayer, the loud voice, and the emergence of the dead man still wrapped in the burial cloths. It is such a shock, something utterly new and strange. Resurrection is like that, always like that—an unexplained, unparalleled happening. It is the emergence of the smelly, decaying corpse, coming, at the voice of Jesus, to life.

And then the words, "Unbind him, and let him go" (v. 44). Loosed from the bonds of death, freed from the shackles of the past, let go into a new future—resurrection is a liberation.

The third critical feature of the story is the repeated word that the event reveals the glory of God (vs. 4, 40). There is more here than the resuscitation of a corpse. Lazarus apparently would have to die sometime later and not be revived like this again. Always for John, miracles are "signs," events that point beyond themselves to something else (better, to some*one* else). As the narrator comments about the first of Jesus' miracles, the changing of water into wine at the marriage feast at Cana, Jesus "revealed his glory" (2:11). Whether stated as the glory of Jesus or the glory of God, glory signifies a revelation (see 1:14).

Put another way, the raising of Lazarus foreshadows Jesus' own resurrection, that moment in Jesus' departure (together with his death) that is called his hour of glorification (see 12:27–28; 13:31–32; 17:1–5, 24). As extraordinary as the raising of Lazarus is, we miss the point of the miracle if we miss the ultimate reality to which it points, namely, the revelation of a death-destroying, life-giving God. A marvelous word for All Saints' Day.

A sign confronts travelers with a decision, to go or not to go. The Jews who accompanied Mary either believed Jesus or joined the plot to do away with him (11:45–46). This miracle then precipitates a crisis. It becomes the point at which decisions have to be made—whether to believe in Jesus and catch a glimpse of the divine glory or to reject him and be overcome by death.

INDEX OF LECTIONARY READINGS

Old Testament		6:1–5, 12b–19	422–24	20	386–88
		7:1–11, 16	32–34	22	261–63
Genesis		7:1–14a	429–31	22:1–15	544–45
1:1–5	97–99	11:1–15	439–41	22:23–31	204–06
9:8–17	192–94	11:26–12:13a	449–51	22:25–31	310–12
17:1–7, 15–16	202–4	18:5–9, 15,		23	300–302
		31–33	458–60	24	424–26
Exodus		23:1–7	597–99	25:1–10	194–96
12:1–14	251–52			26	535–37
20:1–17	212–13	1 Kings		29	99–101, 358
		2:10–12; 3:3–14	466–68	30	146–47
Numbers		8:1, 6, 10–11,		34:1–8, 19–22	560–62
21:4–9	221–23	22–30, 41–43	475–77	41	155–57
				45:1–2, 6–9	487–89
Deuteronomy		2 Kings		47	330–31
18:15–20	125–27	2:1–12	173–75	48	414–16
		5:1–14	143–45	50:1–6	175–77
Ruth				51:1–17	185–86
1:1–18	567–69	Esther		51:1–12	451–53
3:1–5; 4:13–17	577–79	7:1–6, 9–10;		62:5–12	118–20
		9:20–22	512–24	72:1–7, 10–14	89–91
1 Samuel				80:1–7, 17–19	4–6
1:4–20	587–89	Job		84	477–79
2:1–10	589–91	1:1; 2:1–10	533–34	85:1–2, 8–13	14–16
3:1–20	105–7, 364–66	23:1–9, 16–17	542–44	89:20–37	431–33
8:4–20;		38:1–7, 34–41	550–51	96	43–45
11:14–15	374–86	42:1–6, 10–17	558–60	97	53–54
15:34–16:13	384–86			98	61–63, 320–22
17:1a, 4–11,		Psalms		103:1–13, 22	165–67
19–23, 32–49	393–94	1	339–41	104:1–9, 24, 45c	551–53
		4	290–92	104:24–34, 35b	349–50
2 Samuel		9:9–20	395–97	107:1–3, 17–22	223–25
1:1, 17–27	403–5	14	441–43	111	127–29, 468–70
5:1–5, 9–10	412–14	19	213–16, 507–9	116:1–2, 12–19	252–54

614

INDEX OF LECTIONARY READINGS

118:1–2, 19–29	243–45	Hosea		12:28–34	573–75
118:14–24	271–72	2:14–20	163–65	12:38–44	583–85
119:9–16	233–35			13:1–8	593–95
124	525–27	Joel		13:24–37	8–10
125	497–99	2:1–2, 12–17a	183–85		
126	24–26			Luke	
127	579–81	Jonah		1:26–38	38–40
130	405–6, 460	3:1–5, 10	115–17	1:47–55	34–36
132:1–18	599–601			2:1–20	47–49, 56–58
133	280–81	**New Testament**		2:22–40	75–77
138	376–78			24:36–48	294–96
139:1–6,	108–10,	Matthew		24:44–53	333–35
13–18	366–68	2:1–12	93–95		
146	569–71	6:1–6, 16–21	188–90	John	
147:1–11, 20c	136–38			1:1–14	65–67
147:12–20	80–82	Mark		1:1–18	84–86
148	71–73	1:1–8	18–20	1:6–8, 19–28	28–30
		1:4–11	103–4	1:43–51	112–14
Proverbs		1:9–15	198–200	2:13–22	218–19
1:20–33	505–7	1:14–20	122–24	3:1–17	360–62
22:1–2, 8–9,		1:21–28	131–33	3:14–21	227–29
22–23	495–97	1:29–39	140–42	6:1–21	445–47
31:10–31	515–17	1:40–45	149–51	6:24–35	455–56
		2:1–12	159–61	6:35, 41–51	462–64
Song of Solomon		2:13–22	169–71	6:51–58	472–73
2:8–13	485–87	2:23–3:6	370–72	6:56–69	481–83
		3:20–35	380–82	10:11–18	304–6
Isaiah		4:26–34	390–91	11:32–44	611–13
6:1–8	356–58	4:35–41	399–401	12:20–33	237–39
9:2–7	42–43	5:21–43	408–10	13:1–17, 31b–35	257–58
25:6–9	607–9	6:1–13	397–99	15:1–8	314–16
40:1–11	12–14	6:14–29	426–27	15:9–17	324–26
40:21–31	134–36	6:30–34, 53–56	435–37	15:26–27;	
43:18–25	153–55	7:1–8, 14–15,		16:4b–15	353–54
50:4–9a	241–43	21–23	491–93	17:6–19	343–45
52:7–10	60–61	7:24–37	501–3	18:1–19:42	266–67
52:13–53:12	260–61	8:27–38	511–13	18:33–37	603–5
60:1–6	87–89	8:31–38	208–10	20:1–18	274–76
61:1–4, 8–11	22–24	9:2–9	179–81	20:19–31	284–86
61:10–62:3	69–71	9:30–37	519–21		
62:6–12	51–52	9:38–50	529–31	Acts	
64:1–9	2–4	10:2–16	539–40	1:1–11	328–30
		10:17–31	546–48	1:15–17, 21–26	337–39
Jeremiah		10:35–45	555–56	2:1–21	347–49
31:7–14	79–80	10:46–52	564–65	3:12–19	288–89
31:31–34	231–33	11:1–11	247–49	4:5–12	298–300

4:32–35	278–80	8:7–15	407–08	4:14–16; 5:7–9	264–65
8:26–40	308–10	12:2–10	416–18	5:1–10	554
10:34–43	269–71			5:5–10	235–37
10:44–48	318–20	Galatians		7:23–28	562–64
19:1–7	101–2	4:4–7	73–75	9:11–14	571–73
				9:24–28	581–83
Romans		Ephesians		10:11–25	591–93
4:13–25	206–8	1:3–14	82–84		
8:12–17	358–60	1:15–23	331–33	James	
8:22–27	351–53	2:1–10	225–27	1:17–27	489–91
16:25–27	36–38	2:11–22	433–35	2:1–17	499–501
		3:1–12	91–93	3:1–12	509–11
1 Corinthians		3:14–21	443–45	3:13–4:3; 7–8a	517–19
1:3–9	6–8	4:1–16	453–55	5:13–20	527–29
1:18–25	216–18	4:25–5:2	460–62		
6:12–20	110–12	5:15–20	470–72	1 Peter	
7:29–31	120–22	6:10–20	479–81	3:18–22	196–98
8:1–13	130–31				
9:16–23	138–40	Philippians		2 Peter	
9:24–27	147–49	2:5–11	245–47	3:8–15a	16–18
11:23–26	255–56				
15:1–11	272–74	1 Thessalonians		1 John	
		5:16–24	26–28	1:1–2:2	282–84
2 Corinthians				3:1–7	292–94
1:18–22	157–59	Titus		3:16–24	302–4
3:1–6	167–69	2:11–14	45–47	4:7–21	312–14
4:3–6	177–79	3:4–7	54–56	5:1–6	322–24
4:5–12	368–70			5:9–13	341–43
4:13–5:1	378–80	Hebrews			
5:6–17	388–89	1:1–12	63–65	Revelation	
5:20b–6:10	187–88	1:1–4; 2:5–12	537–39	1:4b–8	601–3
6:1–13	418–20	4:12–16	545–46	21:1–6a	609–11

www.ingramcontent.com/pod-product-compliance
Lightning Source LLC
Chambersburg PA
CBHW051931290426
44110CB00015B/1944